S0-AJD-134

PRICES

PRICES

BY

GEORGE F. WARREN, Ph.D.
Professor of Agricultural Economics and Farm Management, at Cornell University

AND

FRANK A. PEARSON, Ph.D.
Professor of Prices and Statistics, at Cornell University

SIXTH PRINTING

NEW YORK
JOHN WILEY & SONS, Inc.
London: CHAPMAN & HALL, Limited
1933

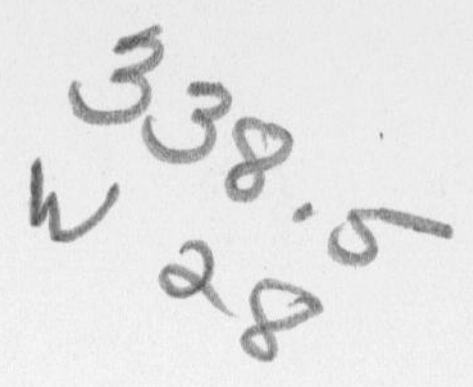

First Printing, February, 1933
Second Printing, May, 1933
Third Printing, July, 1933
Fourth Printing, October, 1933
Fifth Printing, November, 1933
Sixth Printing, January, 1934

Printed in U. S. A.

THE HADDON CRAFTSMEN, INC.
CAMDEN, N. J.

PREFACE

The problems of production are being solved so that we can go forward rapidly in well-being if only the exchange system will work. One reason why progress in production is more rapid than monetary progress is that production is subject to individual experimentation. The individual who has a new idea tries it out, even though he is ridiculed by the public. If the idea works, the successful demonstration hastens general adoption. Monetary progress can come only by legislation. It can proceed only as fast as popular education and vested interests that would be temporarily inconvenienced allow it to go.

Popular education cannot outrun science. We have spent millions on chemical and engineering research but are only just beginning to spend money on economic science. Civilization progresses very irregularly, first in one field and then in another. It advances much like an amoeba. Medicine made little progress until the recent development of knowledge of bacteria. Knowledge of heredity made little progress until Mendel's law was discovered. The progress of civilization is now being held up by lack of economic knowledge. What little is known—not merely theorized about—has not become common knowledge as has the information about bacteria. The progress of such knowledge is dependent on statistical research. In the words of Lord Kelvin, "When you can measure what you are speaking about and express it in numbers, you know something about it, but when you cannot measure it, when you cannot express it in numbers, your knowledge is of a meagre and unsatisfactory kind."

It is the aim of this work to add something to the science of economics, something to the dissemination of knowledge, and to help individuals with their immediate problems, so that they may adjust their affairs to the probable economic weather.

A knowledge of the laws of prices is essential for personal business success because every business transaction involves a guess as to the future of prices. Such knowledge not only is essential for the individual but also is vital for national stability. Many persons blame Congress, or the democratic form of government, or the organization of society based on private enterprise for the business collapse.

These things are no more to blame for this collapse than they are to blame for the stalling of an automobile when the battery fails. If the battery fails, the thing to correct is the battery—not the gasoline, or the engine, or the grade of the road. If the exchange cog in our business machinery breaks, the thing to correct is that cog.

The individual has two tasks. One is to forecast the future of prices and conduct his affairs accordingly. The other is to inform himself and help in guiding public opinion so that national progress may be made. It is hoped that this book may help him in both respects.

G. F. Warren
F. A. Pearson

Ithaca, New York,
January 10, 1933

THIRD PRINTING

Data in some of the tables have been brought up to date. A new chapter on prices following the suspension of the gold standard has been added.

G. F. W.
F. A. P.

Ithaca, New York,
June 10, 1933

CONTENTS

PRICES

CHAPTER I

MEASURES OF VALUE

The world is passing through the greatest economic catastrophe that has ever occurred. This is primarily a price problem. Public and private debts and all business affairs were adjusted to the price levels that had prevailed for many years. The decline in commodity prices has made it impossible to pay international debts. Individual indebtedness incurred at the previous price level is equally difficult to pay. Business practices based on experiences of the past generation have ceased to be a reliable guide. Sound public and private procedure depends on a correct diagnosis of causes and probable future tendencies.

Importance of price analysis.—Many factors combine to make prices what they are. These causes may be analyzed just as a substance may be analyzed chemically, and the proportion due to each cause ultimately may be determined. The science of price analysis is still new but has progressed far enough to be of help.

The more highly civilized society becomes, the greater the tendency for violent price fluctuations. The better each producer is prepared to meet the needs of the future, the better he will serve public welfare and the greater will be his reward. The better the consumer understands prices, the better he will be able to guide his purchases and invest his savings.

As civilization progresses there is greater and greater division of labor and increasing dependence on purchased rather than home-made articles. New things are also added to our requirements, so that a constantly increasing proportion of the things that are necessary for human happiness is purchased. At the same time, because of improved means of communication and the concentration of population in large cities, great masses of people come to act in unison. This accentuates price cycles. The multiplication of injustices brought about by price changes are important not only as they affect individuals, but as they affect the stability of nations. The constant increase in the injury caused by price changes is an inevitable result of the advance in civilization.

Price changes can be reduced by adopting a more stable measure of value and by having producers and consumers understand the scientific principles involved, so that an increasing number of individuals will act by reason rather than by mob suggestion. But stabilization of the purchasing power of the monetary unit is necessary to solve the most serious of the price problems.

Division of labor made civilization possible.—For many centuries the division of labor was within the family or community. Problems of exchange were simple. With the great progress in manufacturing and transportation, which began about a century ago, the problems of exchange became more prominent. But it is within the last twenty-five to fifty years that transportation and large-scale production have made problems of exchange of supreme importance.

Agriculture was one of the last industries to become commercialized. In 1820 in the United States, 83 per cent of all persons gainfully employed were engaged in agriculture. Farmers produced practically all their necessities and most of their luxuries. A hundred years later, in 1920, only 26 per cent of the persons gainfully employed were in agriculture. At the latter date about one-half of the food used by farmers was produced at home. Half of the food, all the clothing, and nearly all the other necessities for living and for the farm business were purchased. The farmer was formerly concerned with the weeds and weather. He is still concerned with these but is now even more interested in the price received for his products, and prices which he must pay for his purchases.

By specialization, each of us produces so much of something that each of us can have more of everything. The battery that keeps this modern machine running is the medium of exchange—money. When money is stable in value, the machine works well. When inflation occurs, it runs too fast. When deflation occurs, it stalls, sales stop, unemployment is common, and there is starvation in the midst of plenty.

Effects of changing prices.—Prices are ever changing. They change from hour to hour, from day to day, season to season, and year to year. Every change affects the relationships of individuals, of groups of people, and of nations. Prices are both a cause and an effect. Many factors combine to make prices what they are. But changes in prices in turn are the causes of all manner of readjustments. Changes in prices cause the most far-reaching changes in human relationships.

The proportion of the good things of life that goes to thrifty old persons who have saved money, to farmers, to railroad workers, to teachers, is changed whenever the general price level rises or falls.

Price changes are even more important in their effect on the total production and national welfare. When prices are rising, industry is stimulated. Those who borrow to produce, or buy for sale on a later market, prosper. The government that is in debt finds payment easy because taxes that are high in dollars are low in goods and are easily paid. Taxes are so easy of payment that governments are likely to take on new needed services and contract further debts. Buying in advance of needs is stimulated. A spirit of optimism and good will prevails.

When prices fall, most of these things are reversed. Buying is checked; unemployment occurs; borrowers suffer; and creditors lose because they are unable to collect. Farmers have hard times and are discontented. Agricultural legislation is demanded. Unemployed persons have to be fed at public expense.

If price changes are gradual, adjustment is made with less friction. Violent changes cause so many injustices that man is arrayed against man, class against class, and nation against nation.

Prices a guide to production and consumption.—Prices are the major criterion by which the producer can know what society wants. The only way the farmer can tell whether to produce cabbages or wheat is on the basis of price. The only way that his son can determine whether society wants him to be a farmer or a coal miner or doctor is on the basis of price. The woman with the market basket, the retailer who must sell to live, the farmer who must have fence wire to keep his cattle in, the steel producer who must sell in order to operate his mill—all combine to make prices. The algebraic sum of all the millions of transactions between all the buyers and sellers of the world makes prices. The system does not always work perfectly, but no committee could guide the millions of producers to meet human needs so well as prices guide them—provided the medium of exchange functions properly. When it functions badly, the people turn to dictators and social control.

Only through prices can consumption be wisely guided. We would all like porterhouse steak and Packard cars, but these require so much human effort to produce that it is not possible to produce enough for all. Hens do not lay many eggs in winter. Consumers would like them in winter as well as or better than in summer. By raising prices in winter, the supply is made to last. By making prices very low in the spring, consumption is stimulated. Any committee that sets out to regulate prices must also regulate consumption, and in the end will find it necessary to regulate nearly every human action.

If the quantity of money is suddenly increased or decreased it disorganizes production, as prices are then not a true measure of demand or supply. Since money has usually been very unstable, the adjustment of production to demand has been seriously interfered with. When money falls in value, governments set up innumerable food administrators and committees to prevent prices of the thousands of things from rising rather than correct the one thing that is causing the trouble. Since the price guide for consumption is lost, these committees have to regulate almost every human act, even to deciding whether eggs may be served on toast or whether the two must be served separately, as was ordered by the United States Food Administration.

When prices rise, the government's activities are primarily for the protection of the consumer. When money rises in value, strenuous efforts are put forth to protect producers and creditors. Efforts are made to prevent each commodity from falling in price, at a time when the whole price level must fall. Every country builds its tariff walls higher and puts on import restrictions and restrictions under the guise of sanitary regulations in order to prevent others from selling in "our market." States devise schemes to handicap non-resident corporations.

The government is called on to give bounties for exports, to buy products to be held off the market or to be dumped in the sea, as Brazil did with coffee.

Groups of producers of this and that commodity organize to hold the price of "our" product up by allotting production or sales territory, price-fixing agreements, dumping of products abroad, and the like. Occasionally these measures help for a short time, but usually they break down with a violent crash as was the case with wheat, rubber, sugar, and copper.

Corporations make agreements to hold prices up. They discover that they cannot hold up both prices and sales. The government is also called on to organize farmers and other unorganized producers so that they may attempt the same futile procedure.

Public service agencies are able to show reduced income and consequent necessity of rate increases, but the public decides the volume of business at these rates. Next, these agencies attempt to have the government place handicaps on their competitors. The propaganda against trucks in 1932 falls in this class. The railroads asked for rate increases, reduced wages, and limitation of competition.

Since debts cannot be paid, the government is called on to take over private debts of banks, railroads, farmers, and home owners.

Since trade and industry are prostrate, millions are unemployed and must be fed by the various units of government in order to prevent riots.

Since taxes are burdensome, the public demands that the government cease carrying on its regular functions, hoping thereby to reduce taxes. Loans to business agencies and funds to feed the poor may more than offset the savings. Since taxes do not yield the usual income, new and heavier taxes have to be levied on prostrate industry. The net result is new taxes and less service.

Inability of unemployed persons to buy, allows stocks of goods to accumulate and results in the illusion of over-production. Exaggerated statements of capacity to produce are made and efforts are put forth to find means to permanently curtail production, under the childish assumption that if each of us produces less, each of us can have more.

Since the exchange system breaks down, the form of government and the organization of society based on private enterprise are challenged.

Since society as a whole does not know what to do, it is sometimes proposed that some individual seize power, assuming that he would thereby become all wise. When there is no knowledge, the people turn to some one who promises everything and accept him on faith. A political faith becomes religion to be accepted without question. When there is no knowledge the people perish, but dictators flourish.

The proposal is made that persons in cities should return to farms and reestablish the self-sufficient farms of our forefathers.

All these and other changes are proposed or attempted on every occasion when money rises decidedly in value. Rather than allow Mohammed to go to the mountain, the attempt is made not only to bring the mountain, but the universe, to Mohammed.

INDEX NUMBERS

Measure of value.—The perfection of refined measures of value has lagged behind other inventions. Innumerable things have been used as money, and important improvements have been made from time to time. A scientific measure of value should be of unchanging value, just as a foot is of unchanging length.

For many years men used stones as measures of weight and the human foot as a measure of length. These crude measures have been replaced by scientific measures, but no unchanging measure of value has yet come into use. Gold is now the most generally accepted measure of value, but gold changes violently in value. Sometimes it will buy large quantities of other things and at other times it will buy but little, just as a horse will at times buy large quantities of other things and at other times will buy but little.

It has taken centuries for the establishment of accurate methods for weighing and measuring. Many controversies have been waged over these questions, and much injustice has resulted from the lack of accurate measures. In the early history of the United States, many controversies between states arose because of differences in weights and measures. The making of measures of value has been even more difficult, and the problem is not yet solved. When great changes in the value of money occur, human relationships are disorganized and great injustices result. The confusion that follows is more serious than the confusion that would arise if a yardstick of variable length were used, because value is less tangible than length and less easily understood. Employer and laborer, seller and customer, should have measures of value as unchangeable as the yard and the pound. In the absence of such a fixed measure of value, index numbers furnish the most accurate method of measurement yet devised.

Definition of index numbers.—It is difficult to compare prices of different commodities directly. If wheat is $1.00 a bushel and coffee 10 cents a pound, one must make comparison with previous prices before he can judge which of these is relatively high or low. The price of wheat may be compared with wheat prices for a previous period on a percentage basis, and similarly coffee prices may be compared with previous prices. If the wheat price is 90 per cent of the previous price and coffee 110 per cent of the previous price, the 90 may be compared with 110. These figures represent index numbers for prices of these two products.

If index numbers are obtained for many commodities, and averaged, it is possible to judge the general price level. For example, the United States Bureau of Labor Statistics publishes an index number of wholesale prices of 784 commodities. Wholesale prices in 1920 more than doubled when compared with the five-year average before the war, but by 1932 were below the pre-war level. Usually the best way of judging the price of a particular commodity is to make comparison with the general price level as represented by some such index number as the one given above. For example, in June 1932, the index number for all commodities was 93. The index of the farm price of wheat was 41; of cotton, 36. Compared with other things, wheat and cotton were very cheap.

Two price problems.—Two great price problems are variations in prices of individual commodities and variations in the general price level of all commodities. The general price level is always changing, and the prices of individual commodities are always fluctuating about the general price level.

The movements of the general price level in the Civil War period and the fluctuations in the price of hogs about the general level of

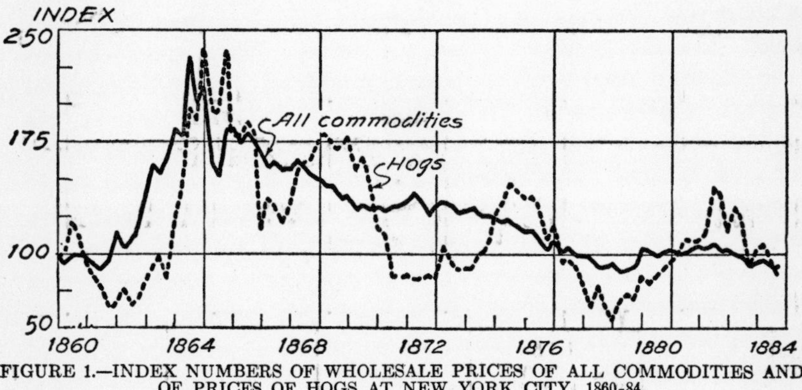

FIGURE 1.—INDEX NUMBERS OF WHOLESALE PRICES OF ALL COMMODITIES AND OF PRICES OF HOGS AT NEW YORK CITY, 1860-84.
1856-60 = 100.
The usual hog cycle continued but fluctuated about a declining base.

commodity prices are shown in figure 1. The hog cycle was important, but the serious thing was the decline in the general level of commodity prices which dragged the hog cycle down. The same comparisons for the World War period are shown in figure 2. The whole price structure declined from 244 in May 1920 to 93 in June 1932. The major part of the decline in the price of hogs was not due to the hog cycle, but to a general collapse in all prices.

Similar comparisons for wheat during the Civil War period are shown in figure 3. Wheat prices fluctuated violently, primarily because of variations in weather. After the Civil War, these fluctuations were about a steadily declining base. Wheat prices and all commodity prices for the World War period are shown in figure 4. Wheat prices again fluctuated around a declining base. It is to be expected that wheat prices will continue to follow the general price level and fluctuate about it. There seems to be no fundamental reason for anticipating a change in these relationships at the present time.

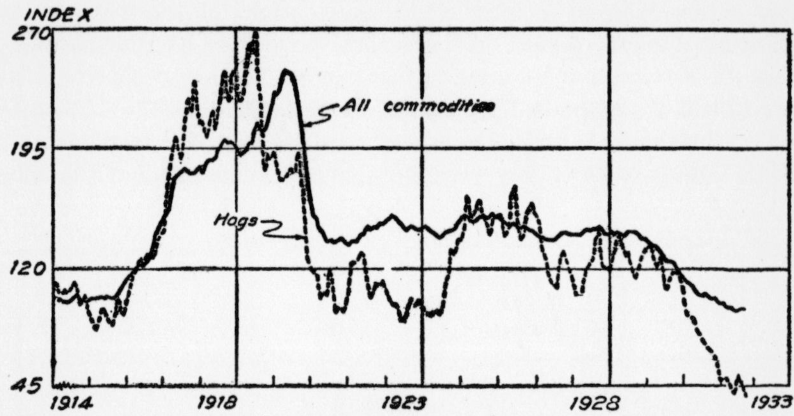

FIGURE 2.—INDEX NUMBERS OF WHOLESALE PRICES OF ALL COMMODITIES AND PRICES OF HEAVY HOGS AT CHICAGO, 1914-32.
1910-14 = 100.
As in the Civil War period, the hog cycle continues but is dragged downward by the decline of the whole price structure. It is to be expected that hog prices will continue to fluctuate about the general price level.

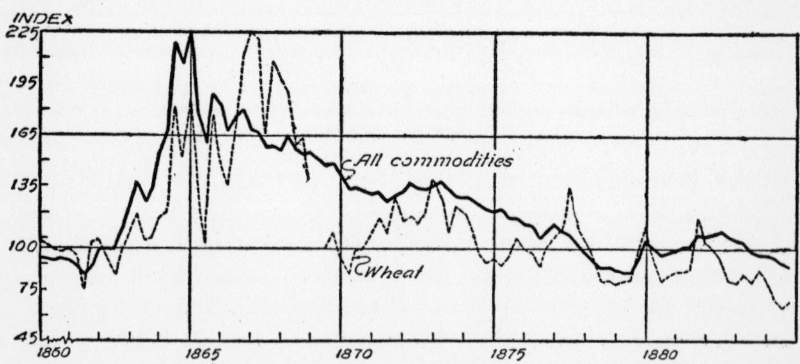

FIGURE 3.—INDEX NUMBERS OF WHOLESALE PRICES OF ALL COMMODITIES AND PRICES OF WINTER WHEAT AT NEW YORK CITY, 1860-84.
1856-60 = 100.
Wheat prices fluctuated about the general price level, which steadily declined.

It is extremely difficult to imagine a fluctuating price fluctuating about a fluctuating base. The inability to imagine the conditions shown in figures 1 to 4 leads to erroneous actions. It also makes it difficult to appreciate the underlying principles governing prices.

Many persons imagine that a stable general average of commodity prices would mean stability in each commodity. It would mean that the hog cycle would fluctuate about a stable base. Price changes would therefore be due to changes in the supply of or demand for hogs rather than to a crash in the foundations of the whole price structure. Violent changes in the general price level also increase the violence of price changes due to other causes. The hog cycle would be less violent if the general price level were stable.

Occasionally a change in methods of production or in demand permanently lowers or raises the price of a given commodity, but the fluc-

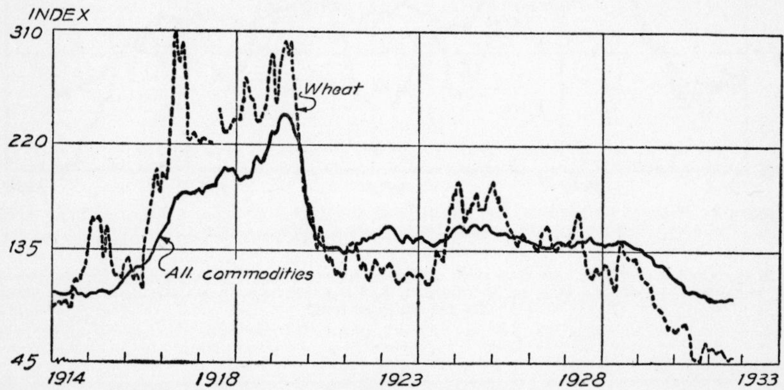

FIGURE 4.—INDEX NUMBERS OF WHOLESALE PRICES OF ALL COMMODITIES AND PRICE OF NO. 2 HARD WINTER WHEAT AT KANSAS CITY, 1914-32.
1910-14 = 100.

Wheat prices again fluctuated about the general price level. It is to be expected that this relationship will continue.

tuations continue, and if a new base is taken the prices again fluctuate about the general price level.

Index numbers are useful in measuring the fluctuations in the price of particular commodities and are even more important in measuring the change in the price level of all commodities. The change in the general price level shows the relative value of money. When the general price level is rising, money is becoming cheap. When prices are falling, money is growing dear. Most of the interest in index numbers comes at times when there are unusual changes in the purchasing power of money and hence in the general price level.

It is always necessary to compare the price of an individual commodity with the general price level if one is to form an accurate judgment. For the rough and ready practices of ordinary human relations this comparison is often ignored. This works fairly well when the general price level is fairly stable. When the general price level changes unusually rapidly it confuses the minds of men. It then becomes absolutely necessary to correct one's ideas of prices by comparison with the general price level.

Bureau of Labor index of wholesale prices.—In 1902, the United States Bureau of Labor Statistics began the publication of a monthly

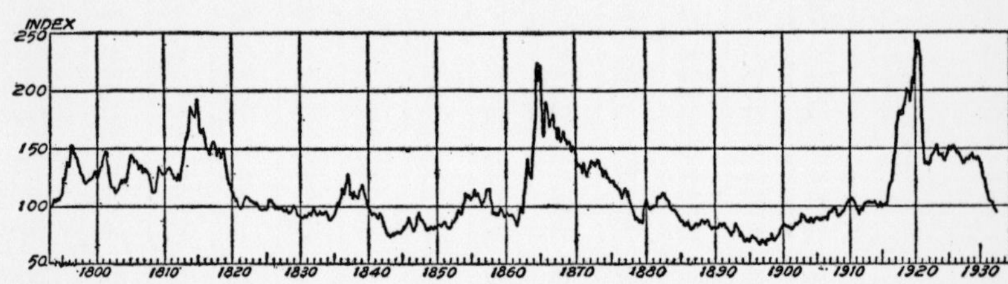

FIGURE 5.—WHOLESALE PRICES IN THE UNITED STATES FOR 140 YEARS, 1793-1932. 1910-14 = 100.

During most of the last 140 years, instability of the general price level has been the most important problem of agriculture and industry. The periods of rising prices have been periods of prosperity, and periods of falling prices have been periods of distress.

index number. In earlier years, the number of commodities varied from 250 to 260. In 1932, the index number included 784 commodities, and weekly publication was begun. This index number represents very accurately the general trend of wholesale prices in the United States.

TABLE 1.—INDEX NUMBERS OF THE WHOLESALE PRICES OF ALL COMMODITIES, 1720 TO 1933*

(1910–14 = 100)

Year	Jan.	Feb.	Mar.	Apr.	May	June	July	Aug.	Sept.	Oct.	Nov.	Dec.	Average
1720	58	58	56	53	52	54	54	54	58	58	....	....	....
1721	....	....	54	52	....	....	....	....	52	....	....	52	....
1722	....	....	....	....	....	....	....	....	....	....	....	....	....
1723	....	....	....	....	....	....	....	....	....	....	....	....	....
1724	....	....	....	....	....	....	....	....	....	....	....	....	....
1725	....	....	....	....	....	....	....	....	....	....	....	....	....
1726	....	....	....	....	54	....	57	....	60	60	....	....	....
1727	....	60	59	....	....	....	....	....	....	....	....	....	....
1728	....	....	54	....	51	....	....	....	....	....	....	....	....
1729	....	50	46	46	....	....	49	50	51	....	....	....	....
1730	....	....	....	....	....	63	....	....	....	....	....	....	....
1731	53	....	....	....	50	....	....	....	....	....	....	....	....
1732	....	....	....	....	....	45	....	....	....	47	....	....	....
1733	....	....	....	....	....	....	....	....	....	....	....	....	....
1734	....	....	....	....	....	....	....	....	....	....	....	....	....
1735	....	....	....	....	....	....	....	....	....	....	....	....	....
1736	....	....	45	44	44	....	....	49	....	....	....	....	....
1737	....	....	....	....	....	....	....	....	....	....	....	....	....
1738	....	....	....	....	....	....	....	....	....	....	....	....	....
1739	....	....	....	....	....	....	....	....	53	50	50	....	....
1740	....	....	53	....	....	....	....	....	....	....	....	....	....
1741	....	....	....	....	....	....	....	....	....	....	....	....	....

TABLE 1 (*Continued*)

Year	Jan.	Feb.	Mar.	Apr.	May	June	July	Aug.	Sept.	Oct.	Nov.	Dec.	Average
1742	....	....	....	....	....	....	....	....	....	....	....	....	....
1743	....	....	....	....	....	....	....	....	....	....	....	....	....
1744	....	....	....	....	....	....	....	....	....	....	....	43	....
1745	42	....	....	....	....	....	....	44	....	....	....	50	....
1746	....	....	....	....	....	....	....	....	....	....	....	....	....
1747	....	....	....	....	....	....	....	....	....	....	....	....	....
1748	....	....	....	....	....	....	75	75	75	75	76	78	....
1749	77	75	74	73	71	67	66	61	59	62	66	64	68
1750	62	58	56	56	56	57	61	61	63	64	66	64	60
1751	64	63	66	62	62	63	66	68	68	65	67	67	65
1752	67	67	64	63	64	67	67	68	68	67	69	65	66
1753	68	67	65	65	65	65	65	65	65	64	65	65	65
1754	65	63	62	62	63	63	66	67	66	71	67	65	65
1755	66	64	62	66	64	65	66	68	69	69	70	66	66
1756	66	66	64	67	68	67	67	67	69	69	64	63	66
1757	62	60	60	61	64	66	68	69	69	70	68	68	65
1758	67	66	66	67	68	68	68	71	72	74	76	77	70
1759	78	79	79	78	77	78	77	81	84	79	80	79	79
1760	86	79	77	77	77	76	78	78	80	80	85	83	79
1761	83	84	78	77	75	78	73	71	72	77	78	78	77
1762	83	82	83	79	85	84	84	92	93	96	96	86	87
1763	93	92	83	80	76	80	76	75	75	75	75	73	79
1764	79	79	74	71	73	72	71	73	74	74	75	71	74
1765	72	76	68	68	72	71	73	73	73	74	74	77	72
1766	75	76	74	73	72	71	71	70	72	73	75	76	73
1767	72	74	75	75	78	81	81	76	78	78	76	76	77
1768	74	74	73	74	70	72	72	72	74	77	77	76	74
1769	76	77	76	75	77	76	75	76	76	80	78	78	77
1770	78	78	77	75	74	77	77	76	79	79	79	77	77
1771	72	72	73	75	76	80	83	84	83	85	81	83	79
1772	84	89	85	87	90	90	92	92	89	95	87	92	89
1773	89	89	89	87	85	82	81	85	80	80	80	78	84
1774	78	78	78	77	76	77	77	75	73	76	77	76	76
1775	75	74	72	72	72	71	74	75	78	79	79	76	75
1776	75	74	78	82	84	91	92	92	93	93	93	93	86
1777	109	124	124	124	124	124	124	124	124	124	124	124	123
1778	121	127	127	127	127	127	127	127	167	166	166	166	140
1779	165	232	232	232	232	232	232	232	232	232	232	232	226
1780	232	232	232	232	232	232	232	216	216	216	216	216	225
1781	216	216	216	216	216	216	216	216	216	216	216	216	216
1782	216	216	....	....	....	....	....	....	....	....	....	....	....
1783	....	....	....	....	....	....	....	....	....	....	....	....	....
1784	....	....	....	....	....	....	....	....	....	....	....	....	....
1785	97	97	95	93	93	94	91	89	90	90	90	89	92
1786	89	89	89	87	87	87	85	85	90	94	96	97	90
1787	97	96	95	93	92	92	88	88	87	85	85	84	90
1788	....	....	82	....	....	....	....	....	....	....	....	85	....
1789	86	87	85	85	85	89	88	86	86	88	86	85	86
1790	86	87	91	92	92	92	91	91	92	90	89	86	90
1791	86	84	83	84	84	84	83	85	85	86	86	85	85
1792	....	....	....	....	....	....	....	....	....	....	....	....	....
1793	....	....	....	98	100	101	102	105	106	103	103	100	102
1794	106	106	108	103	105	106	108	108	110	111	111	115	108
1795	124	123	123	126	131	136	139	137	135	136	134	134	131
1796	141	143	152	151	152	151	148	144	144	148	143	142	146
1797	140	142	136	132	132	131	129	128	126	124	127	126	131
1798	127	125	123	123	121	119	120	120	120	121	122	123	122
1799	124	123	123	122	123	124	126	126	127	129	130	130	126
1800	127	125	125	123	125	127	129	131	133	134	135	134	129
1801	140	142	144	145	146	147	148	146	145	139	136	129	142
1802	126	121	119	117	116	117	117	116	116	115	113	111	117
1803	113	113	114	114	115	116	118	122	123	123	119	122	118
1804	123	123	124	122	120	121	122	124	128	130	134	139	126
1805	140	141	145	144	142	143	140	138	139	139	140	139	141
1806	137	137	134	132	133	132	136	135	135	133	129	130	134
1807	131	133	132	130	131	131	130	129	129	128	127	126	130
1808	124	119	115	112	112	112	112	113	113	113	117	121	115
1809	124	126	135	133	132	132	129	129	130	127	129	128	130

TABLE 1 (*Continued*)

Year	Jan.	Feb.	Mar.	Apr.	May	June	July	Aug.	Sept.	Oct.	Nov.	Dec.	Average
1810	128	130	128	129	131	130	133	132	134	133	133	131	131
1811	132	128	127	127	128	124	124	126	124	125	124	122	126
1812	127	129	128	126	122	125	128	133	135	137	142	144	131
1813	150	152	153	157	160	158	159	161	164	171	178	186	162
1814	186	184	182	182	179	179	178	177	177	183	187	193	182
1815	193	185	176	166	164	165	163	165	166	166	168	163	170
1816	160	160	158	151	150	150	150	149	148	144	145	149	151
1817	152	155	156	156	157	154	149	153	147	145	144	146	151
1818	149	151	149	144	142	144	142	147	146	151	149	145	147
1819	141	137	134	130	125	124	121	119	119	120	117	114	125
1820	114	113	109	106	108	106	104	107	106	103	100	100	106
1821	100	99	98	98	100	99	100	103	105	107	108	109	102
1822	109	108	108	108	107	107	106	104	104	104	106	104	106
1823	104	104	103	103	102	103	104	104	103	102	99	100	103
1824	98	97	97	96	97	98	98	98	98	99	99	98	98
1825	97	98	98	102	106	107	106	105	106	105	104	103	103
1826	103	102	100	100	98	99	101	98	98	98	98	98	99
1827	99	99	99	99	98	97	96	96	96	96	96	99	98
1828	98	97	95	94	94	95	95	95	96	99	99	101	97
1829	102	100	99	99	97	97	93	92	92	92	92	91	96
1830	91	91	91	89	90	91	91	92	93	92	91	90	91
1831	91	92	93	95	95	94	93	92	94	95	96	96	94
1832	100	98	97	93	93	92	92	92	93	94	95	96	95
1833	96	94	93	94	94	93	93	95	96	96	96	95	95
1834	92	92	90	88	88	88	88	89	90	90	90	91	90
1835	92	93	94	97	100	102	104	104	102	101	102	106	100
1836	107	108	112	116	115	111	110	112	115	120	122	123	114
1837	123	129	127	120	110	110	113	111	107	107	110	114	115
1838	112	109	108	108	109	107	107	107	110	115	115	116	110
1839	117	119	118	119	116	114	111	109	108	106	104	102	112
1840	99	99	97	97	95	93	92	93	94	94	94	94	95
1841	93	93	91	90	91	89	90	92	95	93	92	91	92
1842	90	88	86	84	83	82	81	79	77	77	75	76	82
1843	76	74	73	74	75	75	76	76	77	75	77	77	75
1844	76	77	77	78	78	77	77	77	77	77	78	78	77
1845	79	79	81	83	83	82	82	83	85	85	88	91	83
1846	89	87	86	85	83	81	79	78	78	82	83	83	83
1847	84	90	92	93	93	95	91	88	89	88	89	87	90
1848	85	85	84	84	83	80	79	79	81	82	80	80	82
1849	83	83	83	82	81	80	81	81	83	82	81	82	82
1850	83	84	85	84	84	84	84	83	83	84	85	85	84
1851	87	87	86	85	84	82	81	81	81	81	81	81	83
1852	83	85	87	86	86	86	88	90	91	91	93	95	88
1853	96	97	97	95	94	93	93	95	97	101	102	103	97
1854	105	112	109	109	109	110	106	108	110	105	108	107	108
1855	107	107	109	111	114	115	109	109	109	109	111	112	110
1856	108	107	106	105	102	99	102	104	103	105	107	108	105
1857	111	113	115	114	115	114	114	115	114	106	101	98	111
1858	93	93	95	95	94	92	92	94	94	94	92	93	93
1859	95	99	99	98	97	97	95	92	91	90	92	93	95
1860	94	94	94	93	93	91	92	92	92	93	93	91	93
1861	92	90	90	89	88	85	83	85	86	89	92	94	89
1862	98	99	98	98	95	94	98	105	107	111	120	123	104
1863	126	137	141	137	130	126	127	127	123	134	142	148	133
1864	153	156	161	168	174	189	219	225	225	207	216	222	193
1865	223	217	206	179	169	159	161	168	179	190	189	184	185
1866	181	176	173	166	171	172	174	175	174	179	175	169	174
1867	168	167	166	167	168	159	158	168	158	159	156	155	162
1868	157	158	163	165	163	158	157	158	157	154	153	153	158
1869	155	157	154	151	149	147	148	153	152	149	149	147	151
1870	142	138	135	134	136	135	135	134	134	133	131	128	135
1871	131	135	137	132	129	127	127	125	128	130	130	133	130
1872	133	133	135	138	138	137	135	136	137	134	138	136	136
1873	136	139	139	139	136	132	132	132	132	129	125	128	133
1874	130	130	130	128	127	124	125	124	124	122	121	121	126
1875	121	121	121	122	119	117	117	118	117	117	116	115	118
1876	114	114	114	113	109	106	106	107	108	110	111	113	110
1877	115	112	107	110	112	106	107	103	102	102	100	100	106

TABLE 1 (*Concluded*)

Year	Jan.	Feb.	Mar.	Apr.	May	June	July	Aug.	Sept.	Oct.	Nov.	Dec.	Average
1878	97	96	94	93	90	88	89	90	90	89	88	86	91
1879	87	88	87	86	86	85	86	86	89	94	99	102	90
1880	105	105	106	102	99	97	97	97	98	98	99	100	100
1881	99	100	100	101	100	100	101	103	107	108	107	107	103
1882	107	108	108	109	110	111	110	111	108	107	106	105	108
1883	105	106	105	104	103	100	98	98	97	97	96	97	101
1884	97	97	97	95	93	93	92	92	91	90	88	87	93
1885	87	88	86	87	85	83	84	84	83	83	84	86	85
1886	84	84	83	82	80	79	80	81	81	81	81	82	82
1887	84	85	85	85	85	84	83	84	83	84	85	87	85
1888	88	87	87	86	85	84	85	85	85	86	87	87	86
1889	84	83	82	82	80	80	80	80	81	81	81	82	81
1890	80	80	80	80	81	81	81	84	85	85	83	83	82
1891	82	83	84	85	84	82	81	81	80	80	79	79	82
1892	77	77	75	74	74	74	76	77	77	77	79	80	76
1893	83	84	82	81	80	78	76	73	76	77	75	74	78
1894	72	71	69	69	69	69	69	71	72	70	70	69	70
1895	69	69	69	72	73	74	73	72	72	72	72	71	71
1896	70	69	69	68	67	66	66	66	66	68	70	70	68
1897	68	68	68	67	66	66	66	69	71	70	70	70	68
1898	70	71	71	71	76	71	70	70	70	70	70	71	71
1899	71	73	73	74	74	75	76	77	80	81	82	83	77
1900	83	84	84	84	82	81	82	81	82	81	81	80	82
1901	81	80	80	79	79	79	80	81	82	82	83	84	81
1902	83	83	83	84	85	86	86	85	86	92	89	90	86
1903	91	91	88	88	86	86	86	86	87	86	85	85	87
1904	87	89	88	87	85	85	85	86	87	87	89	89	87
1905	89	89	88	88	87	87	87	88	87	87	88	89	88
1906	89	89	89	89	90	90	87	89	90	92	93	94	90
1907	93	95	94	94	96	97	97	97	97	98	94	92	95
1908	91	90	90	91	91	91	92	92	92	93	94	95	92
1909	94	95	95	97	98	99	99	100	101	103	104	105	99
1910	104	104	106	107	105	104	104	103	102	99	97	97	103
1911	97	94	95	92	92	92	93	96	97	97	96	95	95
1912	96	97	99	102	102	101	101	102	103	103	103	102	101
1913	103	102	102	102	101	101	102	102	103	103	102	101	102
1914	100	100	99	99	98	98	99	101	103	99	99	98	99
1915	99	100	100	100	101	100	101	100	100	103	105	108	101
1916	112	115	117	119	121	121	122	124	127	133	142	145	125
1917	149	153	157	167	176	178	180	182	180	178	179	180	172
1918	183	179	185	187	187	188	193	196	201	199	199	199	191
1919	196	190	192	194	198	198	206	211	206	207	211	220	202
1920	230	229	232	242	244	243	242	236	227	211	195	176	226
1921	167	153	150	144	141	136	136	137	136	137	138	136	143
1922	134	136	136	136	140	141	145	144	145	145	147	147	141
1923	149	151	153	152	149	147	144	143	146	145	144	143	147
1924	145	146	144	142	140	139	140	142	142	143	145	148	143
1925	150	152	152	149	148	150	152	152	151	151	153	151	151
1926†	151	149	147	147	147	147	145	145	146	145	144	143	146
1927	141	140	138	137	138	137	138	139	141	141	141	141	139
1928	141	140	139	141	142	141	142	143	144	141	140	140	141
1929	140	139	140	139	138	139	141	141	140	139	137	136	139
1930	135	134	132	131	130	127	123	123	123	121	119	116	126
1931	114	112	111	109	107	105	105	105	104	103	103	100	107
1932	98	97	96	96	94	93	94	95	95	94	93	91	95
1933	89	87	88	88	92	95	101	102	103	104			

* On the 1926 base the average for all commodities of the Bureau of Labor Statistics for the five years 1910 to 1914 is 68.46. The index numbers for 1890 and later years are converted to the 1910–14 base by multiplying by 1.460707. The all-commodity index with variable group weights before 1890 is computed from the 11 groups with the following weights: farm products varied from 35 in 1799 to 25 in 1889; foods, from 27 to 25; hides and leather, from 5 to 4; textiles, from 8 to 10; fuel and lighting, from 4 to 10; metals and metal products, from 4 to 10; building materials, 10; chemicals and drugs, from 0.5 to 1.0; house furnishings, 1.0; spirits, from 5 to 3; and miscellaneous, from 1.5 to 1.0. In each case, when the weights were changed, one-ninetieth of the change was made each year.

† Based on 784 commodities for 1926 and later years. United States Department of Labor, Bureau of Labor Statistics mimeograph release No. 4313, January 1932.

An index number of wholesale prices for 213 years.—In order to have a continuous series of index numbers, the writers have calculated prices for 113 to 146 commodities from 1797 to 1890. The index numbers based on these commodities are connected with the United States Bureau of Labor Statistics index numbers to complete the series for 135 years,[1] (table 1, figure 5). This series was extended back to 1720 by Dr. Herman Stoker (figure 6).

From 1720 to the outbreak of the Revolutionary War, prices were as usual very irregular but there was a gradual rise. After the chaos of the Revolutionary War, prices fell below the pre-war level. Creditors then attempted to collect a dear dollar for each cheap dollar they had loaned during the war period, and were therefore in many cases not able to collect anything.

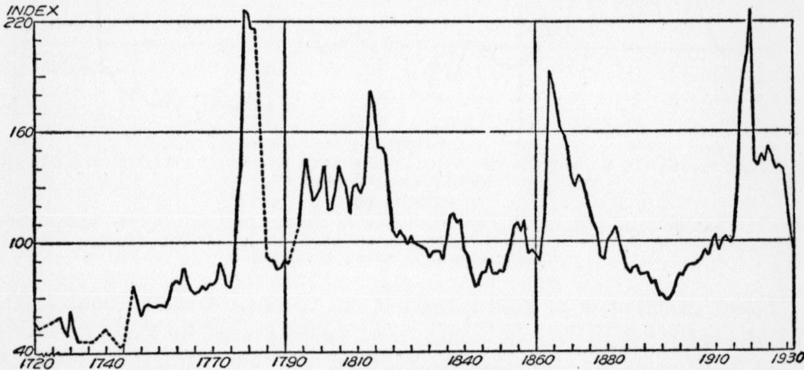

FIGURE 6.—INDEX NUMBERS OF WHOLESALE PRICES IN THE UNITED STATES FOR 213 YEARS, 1720-1932.
1910-14 = 100.
Commodity prices were high during the Revolutionary War, the War of 1812, and the Civil and World Wars. After each war, prices declined.

The French Revolution broke out in 1789 and gold and silver were abandoned, and the reduced demand made them cheap. From 1789 to 1796, prices in the United States rose 70 per cent on a metal basis. The resulting prosperity had much to do with the success of Washington's administration and the firm establishment of the Union. When attempts were made to reestablish metal currencies, prices fell (figures 6 and 7).

During the War of 1812, prices rose still higher because of large

[1] Warren, G. F., Pearson, F. A., and Stoker, H. M., Wholesale Prices for 213 Years, 1720 to 1932, Cornell University Agricultural Experiment Station, Memoir 142, p. 6, November 1932. Warren, G. F., and Pearson, F. A., Wholesale Prices in the United States for 135 Years, Farm Economics No. 72, pp. 1586-87, September 1931.

issues of paper money. After this war, three factors combined to cause a terrible price collapse. The paper money was reduced, world demand for silver and gold increased, and the production of these did not keep pace with the growth of world business.

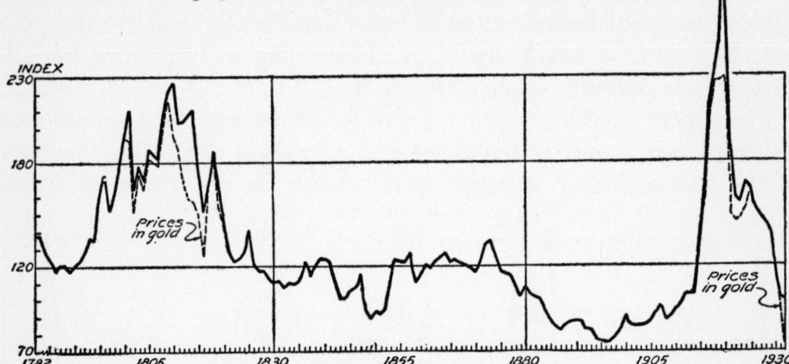

FIGURE 7.—INDEX NUMBERS OF WHOLESALE PRICES OF ALL COMMODITIES IN ENGLAND, 1782-1932.
1910-14 = 100.

For the Napoleonic and World War periods, prices in currency and in gold are both shown. Prices in gold, as well as in currency, have been so erratic as to interfere seriously with the development of a modern civilization.

Great discoveries of gold caused prices to begin to rise about 1850. Gold continued to fall in value until 1873. Prices in England on a gold basis rose 51 per cent from 1849 to 1873. Since the United States was not on a gold basis in the Civil War period, prices in this

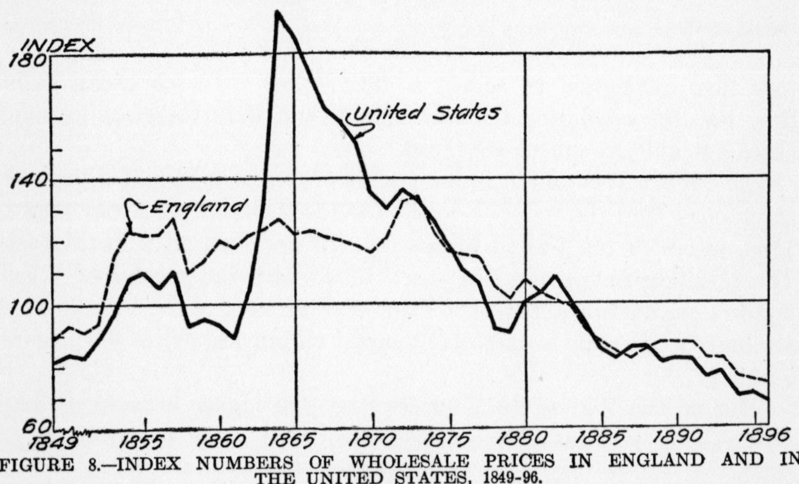

FIGURE 8.—INDEX NUMBERS OF WHOLESALE PRICES IN ENGLAND AND IN THE UNITED STATES, 1849-96.
1910-14 = 100.

The price chaos in England was due to the value of gold. Most of that in the United States was due to the same cause, but this was accentuated by changes in the amount of paper money.

country rose even higher. The popular assumption is that the rise in prices was all due to paper money and that the long decline that began in 1864 was also due to paper money. Prices in England, which throughout this period were on a gold basis, fell 45 per cent from 1873 to 1896. Prices in the United States in the same period fell 49 per cent.

After the long period of gold shortage, gold was found in large quantities, and prices in the United States rose 51 per cent from 1896 to 1910 (table 1).

The low demand for gold during the World War period caused prices in the United States to more than double. High demand coupled with some shortage in production brought prices back to pre-war by means of two price crashes.

Index numbers in other countries.—Index numbers of wholesale prices in England are given in table 8, page 75, and figure 7. Prices rose very high during the Napoleonic War period because

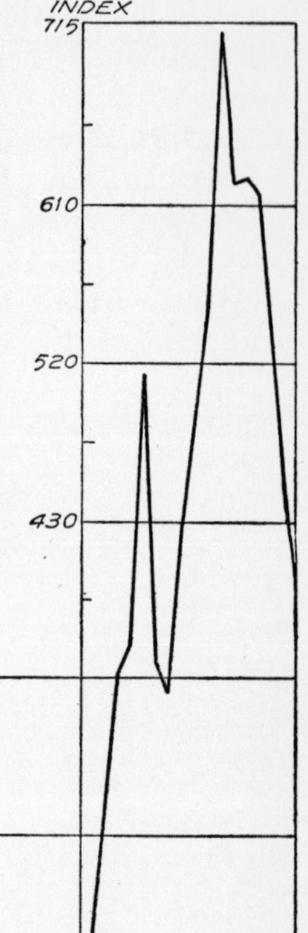

FIGURE 9.—INDEX NUMBERS OF WHOLESALE PRICES IN FRANCE, 1857-1932. 1910-14 = 100.

In 1932, prices in France were four times as high as before the war.

of large supplies of gold and because gold payments were suspended. They were high from 1853 to 1873 because of large new supplies of gold. They fell with the steadily growing deficiency of gold until 1896. The new discoveries of gold then caused prices to rise until the outbreak of the war. During the World War period, prices rose very rapidly. Nominal prices in gold also rose rapidly because of the decline in the value of gold. With the attempt to restore the gold standard, prices fell below pre-war. Prices for other countries are shown in table 2.

Prices in England and in the United States are shown in figure 8. Prices followed the same course except when the gold standard was suspended in the United States during the Civil War and in England during the World War.

Prices in France are shown in figure 9. Prices rose very high in the World War period and were four times the pre-war level in 1932 because the weight of gold in the franc was reduced. Since all business is done in francs, the price level of four times pre-war is the only price level that concerns the French citizen in his business affairs.

TABLE 2.—INDEX NUMBERS OF WHOLESALE PRICES IN VARIOUS COUNTRIES, 1913–1933*

Country.....	Canada	Australia	South Africa	Germany	Netherlands	France	Italy	Denmark	Japan	India	North China
Commodities†	502	92	188	400	48	45	140	118	56	72	106
Base‡.......	1913	July 1914	1913	1913	1913	1913	1913	1913	1913	July 1914	1913
1913	100	....	100	100	100	100	100	100	100	....	100
1914........	102	100	97	105	109	102	95	105	95	100	100
1915........	110	141	107	142	146	140	133	145	97	....	102
1916........	132	132	123	152	226	188	202	172	117	....	110
1917........	179	146	141	179	276	262	299	239	147	....	119
1918........	199	170	153	217	373	339	409	308	193	236	122
1919........	209	180	165	415	304	356	364	309	236	222	121
1920........	244	218	223	1,486	292	509	631	401	259	216	132
1921........	172	167	161	1,911	182	345	577	263	200	199	132
1922........	152	154	129	34,182	160	327	562	188	196	187	129
1923........	153	170	127	16,620§	151	419	575	211	199	181	134
1924........	155	165	129	137	156	488	585	237	206	182	139
1925........	160	162	128	142	155	551	690	210	202	159	145
1926........	156	161	123	134	145	703	602	163	179	148	149
1927........	152	159	124	138	148	617	495	153	170	148	153
1928........	151	157	121	140	149	620	462	153	171	145	161
1929........	149	158	116	137	142	611	445	150	166	141	165
1930........	135	140	103	125	117	532	383	130	137	116	173
1931........	113	125	100	111	97	452	328	114	116	96	182
1932........	105	125	92	97	79	344	304	117	122	91	169
July 1933....	111	128	95	94	73	397	279		137	91	152

* Monthly Labor Review, Bureau of Labor Statistics, United States Department of Labor, Vol. 23, No. 6, pp. 213–14, December 1926, and Vol. 33, No. 6, pp. 238–9, December 1931; Wholesale Prices, Bureau of Labor Statistics, United States Department of Labor, pp. 23–25, April 1933; Federal Reserve Bulletin, Federal Reserve Board at Washington, Vol. 18, No. 8, p. 516, August 1932; Statistisches Jahrbuch für das Deutsche Reich 1923, p. 284, 1923, and 1924/25. Int. Wirt. 1, Deutsches Reich 1925; The Statist, July 16, 1932; and Nankai Weekly Statistical Service, Nankai University, Tientsin, China, Vol. III, No. 22, p. 109, June 2, 1930, and Vol. V, No. 29, p. 129, July 18, 1932.

† Changes in the number of commodities are as follows: Canada, 238 commodities prior to 1926; Italy, 36 commodities prior to 1920, 76 commodities in 1920 and 1921, 100 commodities in 1922, and 107 commodities prior to 1926; Denmark, 33 commodities prior to 1925; and India, 42 commodities prior to 1926.

‡ Index numbers were converted to the 1913 base as follows: Canada, from the base 1926, by multiplying by 1.562; Australia, from the base 1911, by multiplying by 0.08767; South Africa, from the base 1910, by multiplying by 0.089; France, from the base July 1914, by multiplying by 0.9794; Denmark, from the base July 1, 1912–June 30, 1914, by multiplying by 1.05; Japan, from the base October 1900, by multiplying by 0.7553; and North China from the base 1926, by multiplying by 1.489.

§ 000,000,000 omitted.

This price level is just as real to the Frenchman as our price level is to us.

HISTORY OF INDEX NUMBERS

Early index numbers.—Interest in index numbers has always been greatest when prices were changing radically. Soon after the discovery of America, the large amounts of silver and gold brought to Europe from the new world resulted in a great rise in prices.

In 1738, Dutot made price comparisons showing that a group of representative commodities cost 12 times as much in 1735 as they did in 1508.[2] Another early index number was prepared by an Italian who made studies to determine the effect of the discovery of America on the purchasing power of precious metals. He compared the percentage change in prices of grain, wine, and oil from 1500 to 1750.[3]

The instability of money in Massachusetts led to attempts to correct the injustices to soldiers. A law was passed in 1778 that provided for determining the rate of depreciation of money. Index numbers based on the prices of corn, beef, wool, and sole leather were prepared. Soldiers were paid in notes. The amount of cash to be received when the notes were paid was to vary with the prices of these commodities. Soldiers then had stabilized money. The following is a quotation from one of these notes:

"Both Principal and Interest to be paid in the then current money of said State, in a greater or less Sum, according as Five Bushels of CORN, Sixty-eight Pounds and four-sevenths Parts of a Pound of BEEF, Ten Pounds of SHEEP'S WOOL, and Sixteen Pounds of SOLE LEATHER shall then cost, more or less than One Hundred and Thirty Pounds current Money, at the then current Prices of said Articles.—This Sum being Thirty-two Times and an Half what the same Quantities of the same Articles would cost at Prices affixed to them in a Law of this State made in the Year of our Lord One Thousand Seven Hundred and Seventy-seven ——"[4].

This made these notes far more stable in real value than any notes written in gold or silver.

At the close of the eighteenth century, Sir George Shuckburgh-Evelyn made a detailed study of weights and measures and inci-

[2] Dutot, Réflexions politiques sur les finances et le commerce, 1738.

[3] Carli, G. R., Del valore e della proporzione de' metalli monetati con i generi in Italia prima delle Scöperte dell'Indie col confronto del valore e della proporzione de' tempi nostri, 1764.

[4] Fisher, W. C., The Tabular Standard in Massachusetts History, Quarterly Journal of Economics, Vol. XXVII, p. 437, May 1913.

dentally studied appreciation in prices. He estimated that prices in England increased 20 times from 1050 to 1800.[5]

The instability of prices in the early days of the United States led Samuel Blodget[6] to study prices with a view to obtaining, "a common measure, for all estimates of real, instead of mere nominal expenditure; the variations in prices have often been so sudden that an average for any three months must sometimes appear doubtful to those who have not full time for enquiry."

During the Napoleonic Wars, prices rose very high. Price fluctuations and inconvertible paper currency became political issues and were given much study. In England, David Ricardo, Arthur Young, and Thomas Tooke wrote many articles on prices, currency, and rents, but they made little use of index numbers.

After the Napoleonic Wars, prices fell very rapidly. Agriculture and industry were greatly depressed. An agricultural inquiry was made in England in 1822 to determine the causes of the great decline in prices. This phenomenal decline resulted in all manner of injustices to many classes in the population. It was particularly serious for debtors.

In times when copper, hides, wampum, and the like were used as money, if the supply became scarce or over-abundant, new kinds of money were sought. So whenever our present money becomes unstable in buying power, various devices for stabilization are suggested. The use of index numbers is a modern proposal to cure the old disease, for which society has thus far provided no remedy.

The first suggestions for the use of index numbers in Europe for this purpose that the writers have noted were made following the Napoleonic Wars. Lowe attempted to measure the "power of money in purchase" in order that debts may be paid in the same relative values.[7] In 1833, Scrope suggested that "the mean of prices would be a sufficient measure of value" and added that the "tabular standard will measure this value." He pointed out that a contract should be stabilized "by changing its numerical amount in proportion to the change in its power to purchase."[8]

After prices became somewhat stabilized, interest in prices and index numbers declined. The next period of interest came after the

[5] Shuckburgh-Evelyn, Sir George, An account of some Endeavors to ascertain a standard of weight and measure, Philosophical Transactions of the Royal Society of London, Vol. LXXXVIII, Part I, Article VIII, p. 175-6, 1798.

[6] Blodget, Samuel, Economica, p. 141, 1806.

[7] Lowe, Joseph, The Present State of England in Regard to Agriculture, Trade and Finance, London, p. 302, and App. p. 85, 1824.

[8] Scrope, G. P., Principles of Political Economy, p. 408, 1833.

discovery of gold in California and in Australia. After this period of rising prices, Jevons in England and Soetbeer in Germany made intensive studies.[9]

The rapid rise in prices in the United States that accompanied the Civil War led Hunt's Merchants' Magazine[10] to publish a statement of the advance in prices that followed the suspension of specie payment in December 1861. In this period, prices doubled.

Index numbers stimulated by the decline in prices.—The last three decades of the nineteenth century were characterized by a persistent decline in prices in the gold-using countries, and prices and the money question became political issues. One of the best discussions of index numbers and price problems of that time was made in England. The British Association for the Advancement of Science appointed a committee of notable scholars for the purpose of investigating the best methods of ascertaining and measuring variations in the value of the monetary standard.[11]

In the United States, Congress conducted several governmental inquiries concerning currency and prices. The report prepared by the Senate Committee on Finance is the most important of these.[12]

Index numbers of the Aldrich Report.—The first serious effort to construct index numbers showing the trend of commodity prices was made in 1886 by the United States Treasury.[13]

[9] Jevons, W. S., Investigations in Currency and Finance, London, 1884. Soetbeer, Adolph, Materialien zur Erlauterung und Beurteilung der wirtschaftlichen Edelmetallverhältnisse und der Wahrungsfrage, Berlin, 1885.

[10] Hunt's Merchants' Magazine, Vol. 50, p. 132. The aggregate value of 55 commodities were:

January 1862	$ 804
April 1862	844
January 1863	1812
March 1863	1524
July 1863	1324
October 1863	1455
January 1864	1693

This compilation is of interest, as it was one of the first index numbers prepared in this country, and because of the nature of the compilations. In January 1862, coal oil was entered as 30 cents per gallon, pig iron $24 per ton, oats 38 cents per bushel, and corn $59.25 per hundred bushels. These sums and similar ones were added together. A small change in the price of corn, therefore, would have more effect on the aggregate value than a large change in the price of oats.

[11] Report of committee, Reports of British Association for the Advancement of Science, 1887, 1888, 1889, 1890.

[12] Wholesale Prices, Wages, and Transportation, Report by Mr. Aldrich from the Committee on Finance, 52nd Congress, 2nd Session, Report 1394, March 1893.

[13] Tables showing the prices of commodities, United States Treasury, State-

The long period of declining prices finally resulted in an investigation by Congress. The Aldrich Report[14] was published in 1893. It included an extensive report of prices from 1840 to 1891. Three index numbers were prepared. Each omitted farm products except those that were ready for food. One index assumed 31 per cent of the prices to be constant. Another index was unweighted and therefore resulted in such peculiarities as giving pocket knives a weight of 11 and brick a weight of 0.5.[15]

The best index was a weighted index, but gave food a high weight and omitted farm products. In spite of these facts, the index gave a good idea of the movement of prices from 1840 to 1890.

Index numbers stimulated by the high cost of living.—After 1896, prices began to rise all over the world. The high cost of living became the cry of the day, and the study of prices by means of index numbers received a new impetus. In 1897, Bradstreet's index number was begun. In 1901, Dun's Review started an index number designed to show changes, in dollars, of the cost of given quantities of certain commodities. The United States Bureau of Labor Statistics started an index number of prices in 1902, which was a continuation of the index numbers of the Aldrich Report. Gibson's index number was started in 1910, and the Annalist's in 1913.

Index numbers of the World War period.—The spectacular rise in prices that followed the outbreak of the World War resulted in more interest in index numbers than had ever before been shown. The decline of prices after the war and the even more drastic decline in the price of farm products further increased the interest in index numbers and in measures of value.

The War Industries Board published 57 bulletins on prices during the war.[16] This agency constructed an index number comprising 1474 commodities, and made an extensive study of prices in controlled and uncontrolled industries.

In February 1918, G. F. Warren presented index numbers of farm

ments Nos. 17 to 25 inclusive of the Quarterly Report, No. 3, Series 1885-86, of the Chief of the Bureau of Statistics, p. 565, 1886.

[14] Wholesale Prices, Wages, and Transportation, Report by Mr. Aldrich from the Committee on Finance of the United States Congress, 52nd Congress, 2nd Session, Report 1394, Part I, pp. 61-93, March 1893.

[15] Warren, G. F., Pearson, F. A., and Stoker, H. M., Wholesale Prices for 213 Years, 1720 to 1932, Cornell University Agricultural Experiment Station Memoir 142, November 1932.

[16] Mitchell, W. C., and others, History of Prices During the War, Price Section of War Industries Board, 1919.

prices at farmers' meetings. This material was published in various places.[17]

The Joint Commission of Agricultural Inquiry was created by Congress in the late spring of 1921 and instructed to inquire into the agricultural crisis and its causes. An exhaustive study of agricultural prices is contained in its report which was submitted by Sidney Anderson and printed October 15, 1921.[18]

In 1921, the Harvard Committee on Economic Research began the publication of a price index of business cycles.[19]

These are but a few of the great mass of studies of index numbers begun as a result of the enormous price changes brought about by the World War. From no index numbers of any consequence in the Civil War period and the deflation of the nineties, index numbers have come to be matters of every-day conversation and daily news. If this rate of progress continues, it is only a matter of time until the public is sufficiently informed concerning prices, so that a more stable measure of value will be adopted.

Dates of first publication of 157 index numbers.—The dates of first publication of 157 index numbers of wholesale prices in various countries were tabulated with the following results. Four appeared before 1800. Seven were first published in the period from 1812 to 1838. These were doubtless stimulated by the striking rise and later decline in prices that occurred during and after the Napoleonic Wars. Index numbers are not usually published at the exact period of price disturbance but after the disturbance has continued for some time. From 1838 to 1864 very little interest was taken in index numbers. From 1864 to 1880, 14 new index numbers were published, and 38 more appeared before 1897. This interest was aroused by the world-wide decline in prices in all gold-using countries. The gradual increases in prices and cost of living resulted in the publi-

[17] Warren, G. F., Some Purposes of Price Fixing and Its Results, American Economic Review Supp., Vol. IX, No. 1, p. 233, March 1919; Prices of Farm Products, Journal of Farm Economics, Vol. II, No. 2, p. 61, April 1920; Prices of Farm Products in the United States, United States Department of Agriculture, Bul. 999, August 1921; Prices of Farm Products in New York, Cornell University Agricultural Experiment Station Bul. 416, January 1923. Warren, G. F., and Pearson, F. A., The Agricultural Situation, 1924. Warren, G. F., Farm Economics.

[18] The Agricultural Crisis and Its Causes, Report of the Joint Commission of Agricultural Inquiry, Submitted by Sidney Anderson, 67th Congress, 1st Session, Report 408, Part I, 1921.

[19] Persons, W. M., and Coyle, E. S., A Commodity Price Index of Business Cycles, The Review of Economic Statistics, Preliminary Vol. 3, No. 11, pp. 353 ff., 1921.

cation of 18 new index numbers in the two years 1911 and 1912, more than had been started in the preceding decade. Many old index numbers were rejuvenated and new ones compiled as a result of the World War. Many hundreds of index numbers have been prepared since 1914. The greatest number were prepared in Germany, where many towns had statistical offices to compute index numbers to be used as a basis for paying wages.

BIBLIOGRAPHY

Fisher, Irving, The Making of Index Numbers. 1922.

King, W. I., Index Numbers Elucidated. 1930.

Mitchell, W. C., Index Number of Wholesale Prices in the United States and Foreign Countries. United States Bureau of Labor Statistics, Bulletin 284. 1921.

Persons, W. M., Fisher's Formula for Index Numbers. Review of Economic Statistics, Preliminary Vol. 3, pp. 103-113. May 1921.

Persons, W. M., The Construction of Index Numbers. 1928.

Warren, G. F., Pearson, F. A., and Stoker, H. M., Wholesale Prices for 213 Years, 1720 to 1932. Cornell University Agricultural Experiment Station Memoir 142, November 1932.

Report on Best Methods of Ascertaining and Measuring Variations in the Value of the Monetary Standard. Report of the British Association for the Advancement of Science. Report of 57th meeting, p. 247, 1887; Report of 58th meeting, p. 181, 1888; Report of 59th meeting, p. 133, 1889; Report of 60th meeting, p. 485, 1890.

Wholesale Prices, Wages, and Transportation. Report of Committee on Finance of the United States Senate. 52nd Congress, Second Session, Report No. 1394. 1893.

CHAPTER II

INDEX NUMBERS FOR IMPORTANT GROUPS OF COMMODITIES

The index numbers for all commodities showing the general level of prices are composed of 11 different groups (table 3). Over the century, some of these groups have risen in price because of increasing scarcity, or increasing cost of production. Other groups have

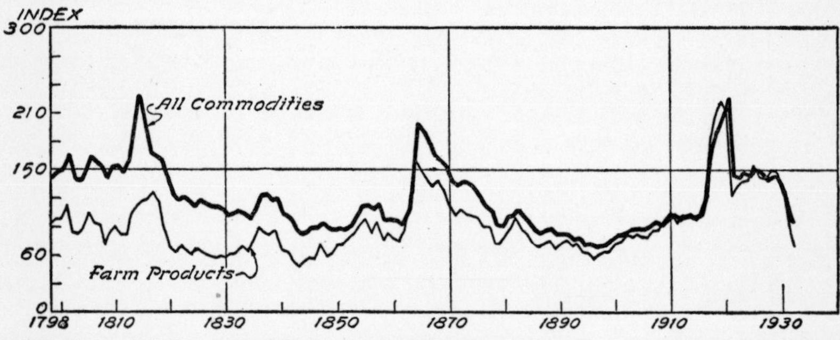

FIGURE 10.—INDEX NUMBERS OF WHOLESALE PRICES OF FARM PRODUCTS AND ALL COMMODITIES, 1798-1932.
1910-14 = 100.
During the past century, prices of farm products have risen relative to all commodities.

fallen in price because of new inventions, or ease in production or transportation. In general, industrial products have fallen, and biological products, except textiles, have risen. When all these are combined into the general price level, the trend for 137 years has been slightly downward except for the World War period. The chief characteristics of the prices of all commodities are extreme fluctuations and long periods of rise or decline.

Farm products.—The farm products group is a mixture of many things. The combined result is a gradual rise (figure 10, table 3). As in all the other groups, the great irregularities are due to fluctuations in the prices of all commodities, or the value of money, rather than to any peculiarities of the farm products group. The declining prices following 1864 and 1920 were in each case popularly attributed to

TABLE 3.—INDEX NUMBERS OF WHOLESALE PRICES IN THE UNITED STATES, 1786–1933

Year	Farm products	Foods	Hides and leather products	Textile products	Fuel and lighting	Metals and metal products	Building materials	Chemicals and drugs	Spirits	House furnishing goods	Miscellaneous	All commodities
1786	75	....	....	....	....	....	....	....	....	....	....	90
1787	78	103	....	....	127	236	36	....	15	....	148	90
1788	....	....	....	....	....	....	....	....	....	....	....	....
1789	68	94	....	....	99	250	35	....	16	....	152	86
1790	68	104	....	....	95	247	35	....	17	....	141	90
1791	57	99	....	....	100	240	34	....	19	....	148	85
1792	....	....	....	....	....	....	....	....	....	....	....	....
1793	75	125	....	....	122	240	39	....	22	....	163	102
1794	76	135	....	....	125	258	40	....	23	....	158	108
1795	102	163	....	....	155	259	56	....	25	....	220	131
1796	116	186	....	....	150	284	58	....	31	....	204	146
1797	98	163	....	....	144	299	54	....	26	....	177	131
1798	93	145	65	226	131	304	51	442	26	....	177	122
1799	98	147	62	227	150	310	51	523	24	....	206	126
1800	99	157	62	225	159	322	51	427	25	....	194	129
1801	113	177	71	236	167	348	55	445	27	....	173	142
1802	84	132	80	230	153	301	55	377	24	....	145	117
1803	83	135	83	232	152	290	53	431	25	....	138	118
1804	89	142	84	252	182	300	56	493	23	....	149	126
1805	106	162	85	270	196	309	58	511	24	....	165	141
1806	95	150	85	280	153	328	58	519	23	....	179	134
1807	92	142	82	274	161	327	59	440	22	....	173	130
1808	71	113	79	279	148	336	57	455	23	....	164	115
1809	83	129	73	323	147	350	60	538	27	....	197	130
1810	90	139	75	278	167	332	59	483	29	....	208	131
1811	82	140	73	243	166	325	57	570	31	....	204	126
1812	81	141	72	257	185	356	58	735	34	....	234	131
1813	104	172	77	291	334	419	63	848	37	....	251	162
1814	112	181	96	300	525	464	69	814	48	....	246	182
1815	117	187	85	300	318	399	76	538	41	....	202	170
1816	119	172	86	274	190	310	68	376	34	....	177	151
1817	126	184	95	268	141	277	60	327	31	....	156	151
1818	117	172	113	275	149	279	56	318	29	....	149	147
1819	87	140	101	233	162	285	55	306	24	....	144	125
1820	68	109	83	211	157	270	53	300	22	....	124	106
1821	64	102	89	215	142	261	50	306	21	....	129	102
1822	70	109	93	218	138	257	50	342	21	....	118	106
1823	64	108	97	209	131	247	49	320	20	....	119	103
1824	61	99	97	191	133	242	48	304	19	....	119	98
1825	67	100	99	198	131	279	50	313	22	....	114	103
1826	62	98	91	188	138	269	52	298	21	....	110	99
1827	59	100	87	186	137	243	51	287	21	....	112	98
1828	58	99	90	190	138	234	51	251	19	....	113	97
1829	59	100	85	182	133	227	49	222	19	....	117	96
1830	58	94	85	181	116	209	47	207	19	....	111	91
1831	61	98	91	179	112	209	49	211	23	....	111	94
1832	63	99	85	161	137	212	49	226	22	....	110	95
1833	69	100	76	162	111	205	51	220	22	....	105	95
1834	64	93	70	161	101	201	52	212	19	....	109	90
1835	75	107	74	170	111	206	52	225	23	....	126	100
1836	89	128	78	177	130	241	53	251	25	....	130	114
1837	84	132	80	167	130	243	70	264	25	....	119	115
1838	82	128	80	157	121	219	70	257	25	....	120	110
1839	86	126	90	159	122	220	70	250	25	....	122	112
1840	65	102	80	146	105	204	65	238	21	128	108	95
1841	64	90	86	140	111	204	67	220	19	121	113	92
1842	53	80	72	132	94	183	62	203	17	113	111	82
1843	48	77	69	114	87	172	58	188	19	99	109	75
1844	52	72	66	125	90	179	59	187	20	108	96	77
1845	58	84	63	125	96	189	64	178	21	107	85	83
1846	58	84	57	122	88	191	64	164	20	110	86	83
1847	72	96	66	117	90	186	61	156	24	117	99	90
1848	59	87	56	113	93	170	61	153	22	111	99	82
1849	62	88	64	111	93	155	58	152	21	110	92	82

TABLE 3 (*Continued*)

Year	Farm products	Foods	Hides and leather products	Textile products	Fuel and lighting	Metals and metal products	Building materials	Chemicals and drugs	Spirits	House furnishing goods	Miscellaneous	All commodities
1850.......	71	84	67	116	95	147	61	154	21	114	88	84
1851.......	71	84	65	115	87	141	61	153	20	117	86	83
1852.......	77	95	70	113	93	144	64	156	19	118	89	89
1853.......	83	98	84	119	102	186	67	169	22	128	96	97
1854.......	93	117	100	124	121	191	70	174	27	129	103	108
1855.......	98	126	104	125	102	176	71	178	31	129	103	110
1856.......	84	116	121	129	97	174	73	176	30	128	114	105
1857.......	95	123	139	138	97	173	73	171	27	130	107	111
1858.......	76	97	110	123	90	154	67	168	23	121	102	93
1859.......	82	99	115	120	93	150	64	168	24	118	98	95
1860.......	77	96	102	119	98	149	65	175	23	117	98	93
1861.......	75	89	90	120	80	152	63	174	21	110	98	89
1862.......	86	107	108	147	87	180	69	206	28	124	122	104
1863.......	113	123	133	206	125	236	88	234	45	165	146	133
1864.......	162	189	164	264	197	354	114	297	106	222	189	193
1865.......	148	180	152	266	214	306	118	300	150	214	175	185
1866.......	140	173	146	245	160	278	128	283	154	220	170	174
1867.......	133	167	132	220	144	248	120	229	146	196	162	162
1868.......	138	171	126	197	149	225	116	204	117	178	153	158
1869.......	128	154	134	194	166	227	110	227	86	178	136	151
1870.......	112	139	128	179	134	200	101	199	78	164	128	135
1871.......	102	130	126	170	152	203	102	177	74	154	120	130
1872.......	108	121	130	177	153	257	107	175	73	159	125	136
1873.......	103	122	132	175	148	243	106	181	75	160	115	133
1874.......	102	126	128	151	135	194	101	176	78	149	111	126
1875.......	99	120	123	141	128	175	90	149	88	134	98	118
1876.......	89	113	104	138	127	157	84	140	86	123	98	110
1877.......	89	115	109	125	108	141	80	136	86	118	95	106
1878.......	72	93	95	115	93	126	72	127	82	109	88	91
1879.......	72	90	100	114	80	134	74	120	82	105	90	90
1880.......	80	96	113	128	92	166	81	120	83	117	91	100
1881.......	89	106	109	119	91	150	83	120	81	109	90	103
1882.......	99	114	108	119	92	157	88	114	80	109	93	108
1883.......	87	103	107	116	89	144	85	110	83	110	93	101
1884.......	82	93	111	109	77	124	84	105	81	105	78	93
1885.......	72	84	105	105	72	109	81	100	79	99	78	85
1886.......	68	78	101	100	70	110	82	99	79	94	74	82
1887.......	71	86	92	98	70	119	81	97	77	92	75	85
1888.......	75	86	86	98	72	121	80	103	80	94	73	86
1889.......	67	79	80	99	71	116	81	101	74	94	80	81
1890.......	71	86	74	103	72	123	84	90	....	91	89	82
1891.......	76	85	74	97	70	108	80	91	....	92	86	82
1892.......	69	79	73	98	66	98	76	92	....	88	79	76
1893.......	72	85	70	96	67	90	75	90	....	88	81	78
1894.......	63	75	67	82	65	77	72	81	....	83	78	70
1895.......	62	73	77	79	76	83	70	80	....	80	81	71
1896.......	56	68	70	77	75	83	70	80	....	80	82	68
1897.......	60	71	71	76	64	76	68	87	....	78	84	68
1898.......	63	74	75	80	65	77	72	95	....	81	85	71
1899.......	64	74	77	85	78	117	79	100	....	82	88	77
1900.......	71	79	77	95	88	115	84	101	....	90	93	82
1901.......	74	78	76	85	85	109	80	104	....	90	85	81
1902.......	82	83	79	88	98	107	82	107	....	90	80	86
1903.......	78	81	77	94	114	106	85	104	....	93	90	87
1904.......	82	84	77	94	101	94	82	104	....	92	99	87
1905.......	79	85	84	96	94	104	87	101	....	91	107	88
1906.......	80	83	89	104	99	120	98	95	....	94	105	90
1907.......	87	88	90	113	103	129	103	97	....	101	98	95
1908.......	87	91	86	97	102	101	94	98	....	95	89	92
1909.......	98	97	95	100	98	99	97	98	....	95	118	99
1910.......	104	101	93	104	90	100	100	101	....	99	139	103
1911.......	94	96	91	99	89	95	100	101	....	97	99	95
1912.......	102	104	100	99	97	105	101	99	....	97	97	101
1913.......	100	100	106	102	116	106	103	99	....	103	85	102
1914.......	100	100	110	97	107	94	96	100	....	104	82	99

TABLE 3 (*Concluded*)

Year	Farm products	Foods	Hides and leather products	Textile products	Fuel and lighting	Metals and metal products	Building materials	Chemicals and drugs	Spirits	House furnishing goods	Miscellaneous	All commodities
1915	100	101	117	96	98	101	97	138	....	103	79	101
1916	118	117	145	125	141	137	123	198	....	113	91	125
1917	181	162	192	175	200	177	160	203	....	136	111	172
1918	208	185	195	244	207	160	179	225	....	171	122	191
1919	221	201	270	240	198	153	209	193	....	194	126	202
1920	211	213	266	293	311	175	272	203	....	260	152	226
1921	124	140	169	168	184	138	177	142	....	207	99	143
1922	132	136	162	178	204	121	176	124	....	190	84	147
1923	138	144	162	198	185	128	197	125	....	200	91	147
1924	140	141	157	190	175	125	185	122	....	192	85	143
1925	154	155	163	192	183	121	184	125	....	189	99	151
1926	141	155	155	178	190	117	181	124	....	184	91	146
1927	139	150	167	170	168	113	172	119	....	179	83	139
1928	149	156	188	170	160	114	171	118	....	174	78	141
1929	147	155	169	161	158	118	173	116	....	173	75	139
1930	124	141	155	143	149	108	163	110	....	170	71	126
1931	91	116	134	118	128	99	144	98	....	156	63	107
1932	68	95	113	99	133	94	130	91	....	138	59	95
1933	*72*	*94*	*125*	*114*	*127*	*94*	*139*	*90*	....	*139*	*56*	*96*

Figures in italics are preliminary.

over-production. In each case, the decline was primarily the result of a rise in the value of money.

Farm food products.—An index number for American farm food products was prepared. This group does not include hay, grass seeds, cotton, wool, flax, etc., that were included in the farm product group. It was not used in making the general index because all the items in the farm food group are included in the farm product group.

The long-time trend of this group is upward in comparison with all commodities, a tendency that will probably continue (table 4, figure 11). The short-time fluctuations of this group are popularly attributed to supply and demand. It will be observed, however, that most of them are coincident with the movements of the whole price structure, so that they cannot be explained by any peculiarities of the farm product group.

Wheat.—Throughout the centuries, wheat has been very stable in value compared with all commodities, except for short-time fluctuations, which are primarily due to weather. This stable value is continuing in recent times, as shown in figure 12. Many persons attributed the decline of prices in the nineties to the invention of the grain binder and the threshing machine. They attribute the decline since 1920 to the tractor and combine. There seems to be no reason for supposing that wheat will either decline or rise permanently in comparison with all commodities. The striking disparity between wheat and all commodities in 1932 is undoubtedly temporary.

Corn.—The price of corn follows all commodities fairly closely (figure 13). The major fluctuations are the same as the fluctuations

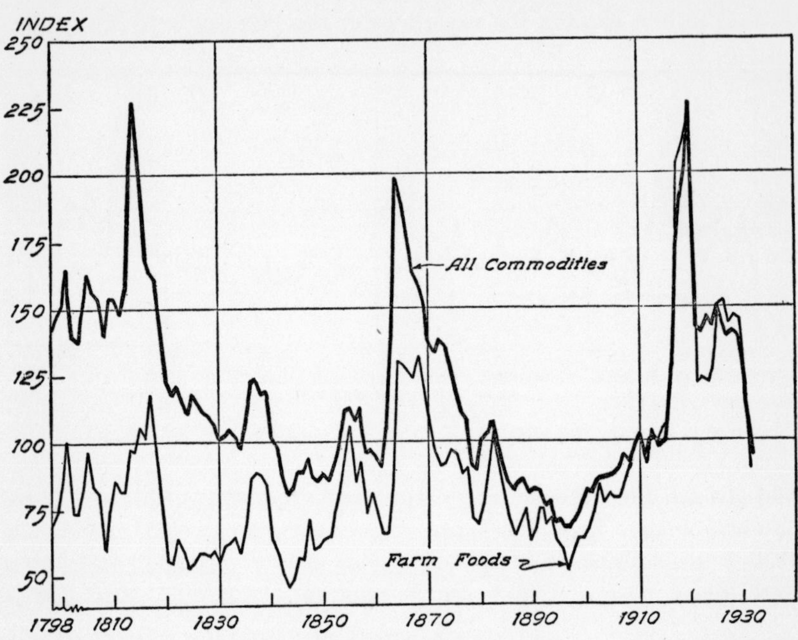

FIGURE 11.—INDEX NUMBERS OF WHOLESALE PRICES OF FARM FOODS AND ALL COMMODITIES, 1798-1932.
1910-14 = 100.
The wholesale prices of American-grown farm foods have risen relative to all commodities.

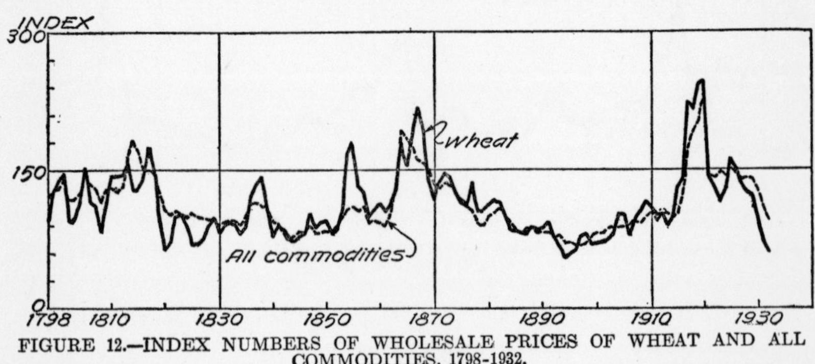

FIGURE 12.—INDEX NUMBERS OF WHOLESALE PRICES OF WHEAT AND ALL COMMODITIES, 1798-1932.
1910-14 = 100.
The price of wheat has followed with great regularity the general level of all commodities.

in the average of all commodities and are, therefore, due to some factor not peculiar to corn. Fluctuations in the amount of paper currency and the amount of the yellow metal rather than the amount of yellow corn explain most of the changes in corn prices. Those who attribute recent declines in the price of corn to over-production would do well to first explain the variations of the last century. Minor fluctuations are due to the effects of the weather on corn yields and to the number of hogs kept. The corn crops harvested in 1881, 1901, and 1930 were striking cases of low yields due to drought, and prices were above normal. There are no striking changes in price due to sudden changes in acreage planted. The acreage of corn harvested in the drought years is low because much of the crop fails.

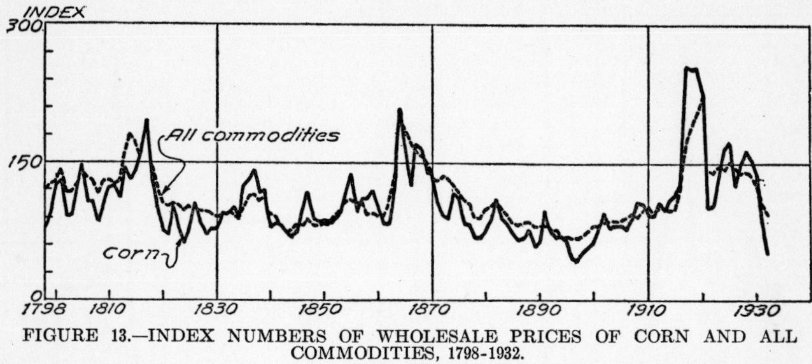

FIGURE 13.—INDEX NUMBERS OF WHOLESALE PRICES OF CORN AND ALL COMMODITIES, 1798-1932.
1910-14 = 100.
The price of corn has followed very closely the general level of all commodities.

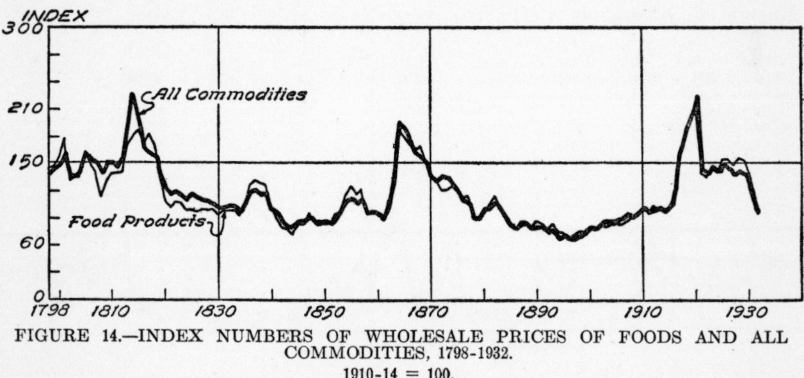

FIGURE 14.—INDEX NUMBERS OF WHOLESALE PRICES OF FOODS AND ALL COMMODITIES, 1798-1932.
1910-14 = 100.
Food products have changed approximately the same as the average for all commodities.

Foods.—Foods show about the same trend as prices of all commodities (table 3, figure 14). This index includes American-grown

TABLE 4.—INDEX NUMBERS OF WHOLESALE PRICES OF GROUPS OF COMMODITIES IN THE UNITED STATES, 1798–1932

1910–14 = 100

Year	Farm foods	Lumber	30 Basic commodities	Year	Farm foods	Lumber	30 Basic commodities	Year	Farm foods	Lumber	30 Basic commodities
1798	70	24	128	1848	60	41	82	1898	64	58	67
1799	75	23	132	1849	61	40	84	1899	64	64	76
1800	86	24	133	1850	64	43	88	1900	67	69	86
1801	101	27	146	1851	65	43	87	1901	74	66	82
1802	74	27	123	1852	75	46	91	1902	84	71	89
1803	74	24	129	1853	82	47	103	1903	77	76	88
1804	82	26	139	1854	97	48	113	1904	81	78	85
1805	97	27	149	1855	106	51	114	1905	79	82	89
1806	84	27	143	1856	85	52	115	1906	79	92	92
1807	81	27	139	1857	93	53	123	1907	85	98	99
1808	60	26	130	1858	74	48	104	1908	91	94	91
1809	75	26	142	1859	81	46	104	1909	100	98	97
1810	86	26	145	1860	74	46	102	1910	99	98	102
1811	82	25	137	1861	66	45	101	1911	91	98	95
1812	82	24	143	1862	66	48	135	1912	104	102	100
1813	98	25	180	1863	84	58	182	1913	99	103	102
1814	97	27	221	1864	130	74	253	1914	105	98	98
1815	106	37	189	1865	129	79	211	1915	107	95	103
1816	102	35	153	1866	126	87	185	1916	131	108	131
1817	118	31	146	1867	125	83	169	1917	203	141	201
1818	99	28	145	1868	132	80	167	1918	209	163	214
1819	77	28	132	1869	118	75	162	1919	217	221	217
1820	56	27	114	1870	109	71	143	1920	217	323	231
1821	55	26	111	1871	96	72	135	1921	121	174	126
1822	64	25	115	1872	91	74	145	1922	123	193	146
1823	60	26	109	1873	92	75	140	1923	122	219	158
1824	54	26	107	1874	97	72	131	1924	127	194	151
1825	56	27	125	1875	95	66	124	1925	150	197	157
1826	59	28	114	1876	88	62	112	1926	152	196	146
1827	59	29	109	1877	90	59	108	1927	143	183	139
1828	58	29	107	1878	71	54	92	1928	146	177	143
1829	60	28	102	1879	69	55	93	1929	145	184	141
1830	56	27	98	1880	76	59	104	1930	124	167	118
1831	62	29	102	1881	90	63	106	1931	89	136	90
1832	63	29	104	1882	102	66	112	1932	67	115	74
1833	65	30	106	1883	89	64	102				
1834	59	31	101	1884	81	64	94				
1835	69	31	114	1885	71	61	86				
1836	87	32	130	1886	65	62	82				
1837	89	45	123	1887	69	63	85				
1838	88	45	116	1888	75	62	87				
1839	84	45	118	1889	63	62	83				
1840	64	42	97	1890	68	62	83				
1841	59	43	94	1891	78	61	82				
1842	51	40	82	1892	69	59	75				
1843	46	37	79	1893	72	60	77				
1844	49	39	82	1894	63	59	67				
1845	57	43	86	1895	60	57	69				
1846	56	42	86	1896	52	57	65				
1847	71	41	92	1897	59	55	64				

foods, which have risen in price, and sugar, salt, pepper, coffee, tea, spices, and other imported foods, the prices of which have fallen.

Hides and leather.—When the country was sparsely populated, the number of cattle per capita was high and hides were relatively cheap. The long-time trend in the price of hides is steadily upward (table

3, figure 15). There is no indication that the use of leather substitutes has changed this long-time tendency.

Cotton.—Compared with the average of all commodities, cotton declined until about 1820 (figure 16). This was doubtless due to improvements in methods of ginning and possibly in part to a rapid increase in the amount of slave labor. Cotton was extremely high-priced during the Civil War because of low production and the blockade. The fluctuations in the price of cotton are violent because of business conditions and the boll-weevil, but there is no reason for expecting cotton prices to be long out of line with the average of all commodities.

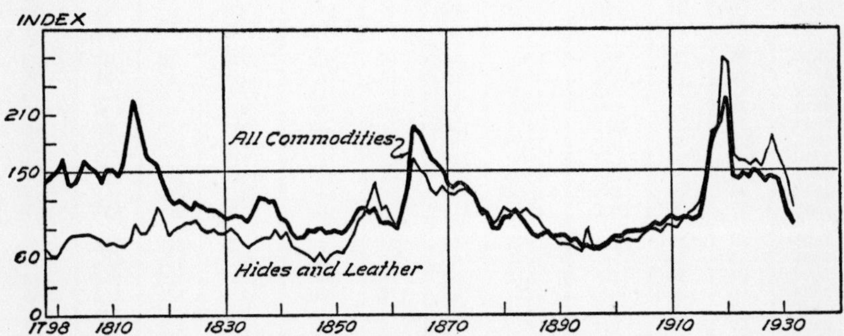

FIGURE 15.—INDEX NUMBERS OF WHOLESALE PRICES OF HIDES AND LEATHER AND ALL COMMODITIES, 1798-1932.
1910-14 = 100.
Hides and leather have risen compared with all commodities.

It will be noted that cotton, corn, and wheat prices have followed the average of all commodities very closely. The direct products of the soil average very stable in value. Livestock and their products tend to rise in price as the country becomes more densely settled. Although cotton is very stable in value, textiles have declined.

Textiles.—The course of prices of textiles has been downward (table 3, figure 17). This is primarily due to lower costs of their manufacture.

Fuel and lighting.—The general tendency of prices of fuel and lighting is downward (table 3, figure 18). Fuel rose very high in each war period, because of transportation difficulties. The long-time downward tendency is due to cheaper methods of production and cheaper transportation of coal, oil, and electricity.

Metals and metal products.—In the earlier years, a large part of the metals was imported. The discovery of better mines, cheaper transportation, and better methods of production have reduced prices of metals in comparison with all commodities (table 3, figure 19).

Pig iron.—Prices of pig iron have shown a striking tendency to decline. During times of war, prices rise very high (figure 20).

Copper.—Copper has fallen somewhat in price, but much less than pig iron (figure 21).

Building materials.—Building materials have risen in price in comparison with the average of all commodities (table 3, figure 22). This index includes lumber, which has risen, and metals, cement, brick, and other industrial products which have fallen in price.

Lumber. — Owing to growing scarcity of supplies and long-distance shipment, lumber has risen strikingly in value, a trend which promises to continue indefinitely into the future (table 4, figure 23).

For the five years before the World War, lumber was worth about four times the prices of 130 years ago, although the price of all commodities had declined. Much is said about the substitution of other materials for lumber. Such substitution has to be made, but prices of lumber show no inclination to discontinue their steady rise as compared with all commodities. Prices rose very high in the reconstruction period following each war, and fell during the panics

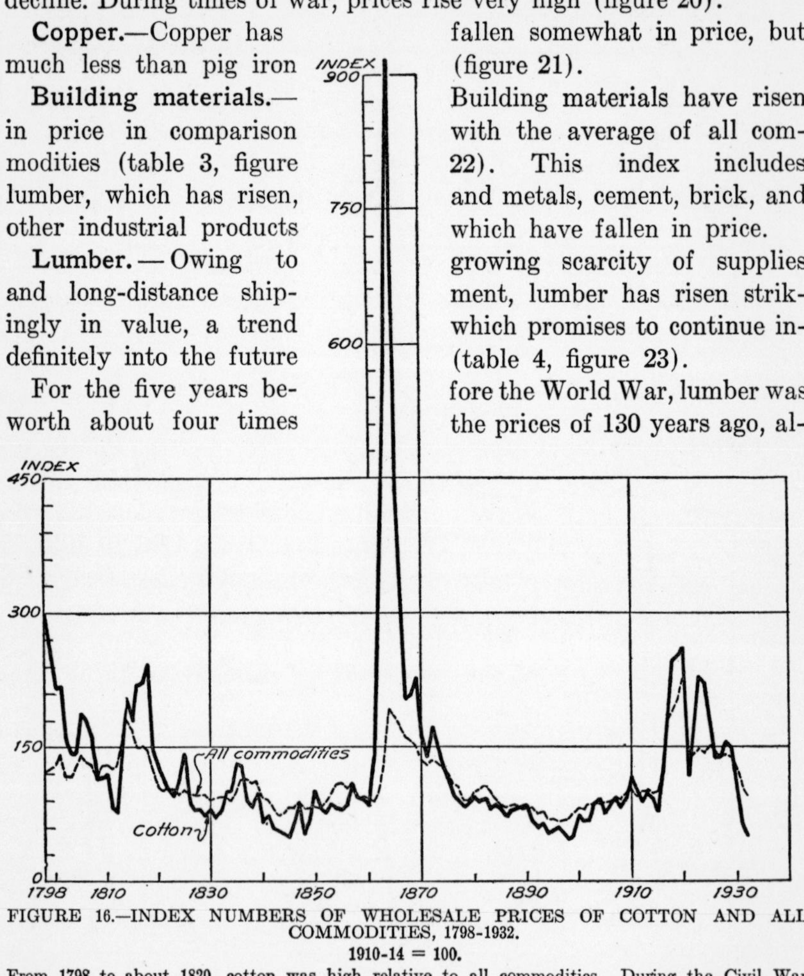

FIGURE 16.—INDEX NUMBERS OF WHOLESALE PRICES OF COTTON AND ALL COMMODITIES, 1798-1932.
1910-14 = 100.

From 1798 to about 1820, cotton was high relative to all commodities. During the Civil War period, prices of cotton rose to enormous heights. With these exceptions, cotton has followed very closely the average of all commodities.

of 1873 and 1929. Such temporary changes should not be confused with the long-time trend.

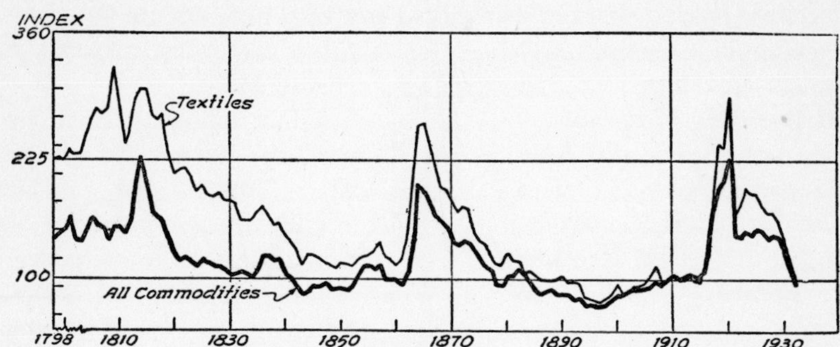

FIGURE 17.—INDEX NUMBERS OF WHOLESALE PRICES OF TEXTILE PRODUCTS AND ALL COMMODITIES, 1798-1932.

1910-14 = 100.

There is a decided tendency for textiles to decline relative to the average of all commodities.

Owing to the rapid expansion of the country and the limited supplies of timber, there has been a steady increase in the purchasing power of the wholesale prices of lumber (figure 24). From 1798 to 1914, the purchasing power of lumber increased at the compound rate of 1.54 per cent per year.[1]

Chemicals and drugs.—Lumber presents one of the most striking examples of rising prices,

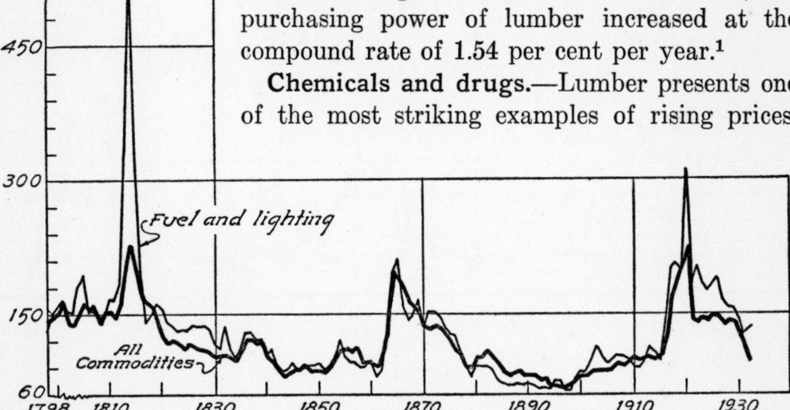

FIGURE 18.—INDEX NUMBERS OF WHOLESALE PRICES OF FUEL AND LIGHTING AND ALL COMMODITIES, 1798-1932.

1910-14 = 100.

Fuel and lighting have declined in price relative to all commodities.

whereas drugs and chemicals are striking examples of declining prices (table 3, figure 25).

[1] $y = 34.439\ (1.0154)^x$. Origin at 1839.

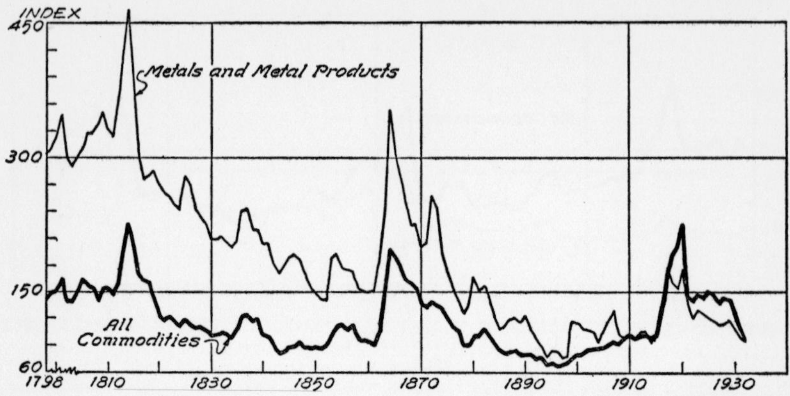

FIGURE 19.—INDEX NUMBERS OF WHOLESALE PRICES OF METALS AND METAL PRODUCTS AND ALL COMMODITIES, 1798-1932.
1910-14 = 100.
During the past century, metals have declined in price compared with all commodities.

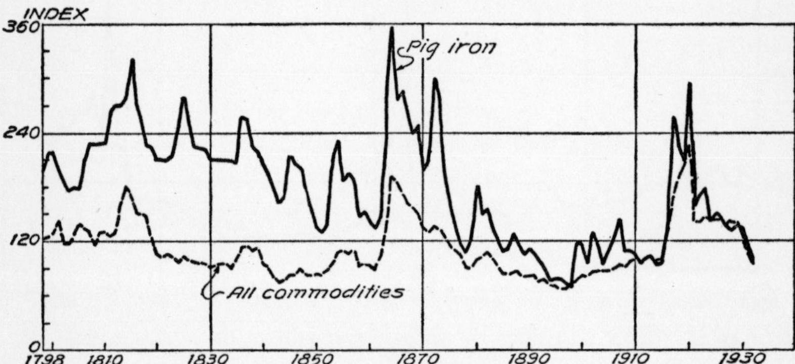

FIGURE 20.—INDEX NUMBERS OF WHOLESALE PRICES OF PIG IRON AND ALL COMMODITIES, 1798-1932.
1910-14 = 100.
Pig iron fluctuates violently with prosperity and depression. Pig iron prices have declined strikingly compared with the general level of all commodities.

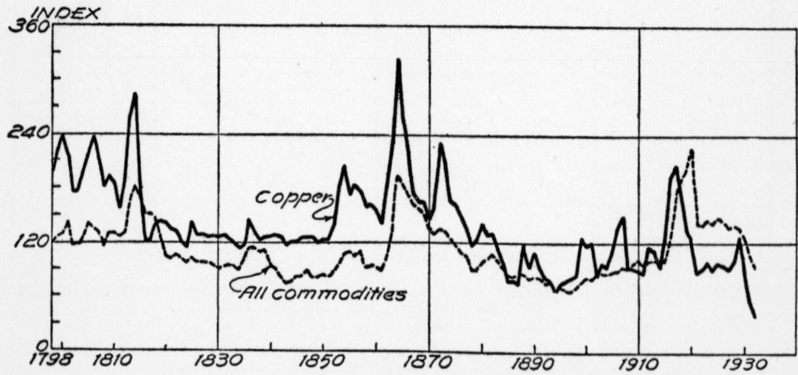

FIGURE 21.—INDEX NUMBERS OF WHOLESALE PRICES OF COPPER AND ALL COMMODITIES, 1798-1932.
1910-14 = 100.
Copper has declined relative to the average of all commodities

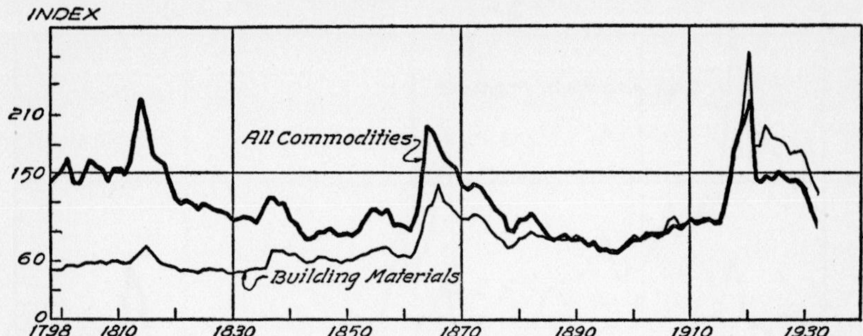

FIGURE 22.—INDEX NUMBERS OF WHOLESALE PRICES OF BUILDING MATERIALS AND ALL COMMODITIES, 1798-1932.

1910-14 = 100.

Building materials rose in price compared with the average of all commodities.

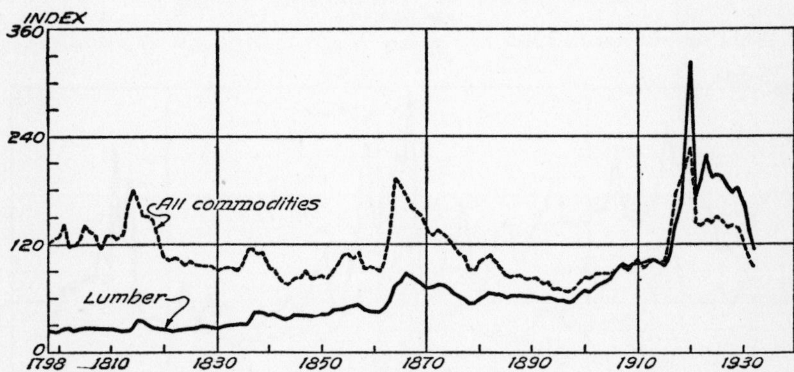

FIGURE 23.—INDEX NUMBERS OF WHOLESALE PRICES OF LUMBER AND ALL COMMODITIES, 1798-1932.

1910-14 = 100.

Lumber has steadily risen in price compared with the general level of all commodities.

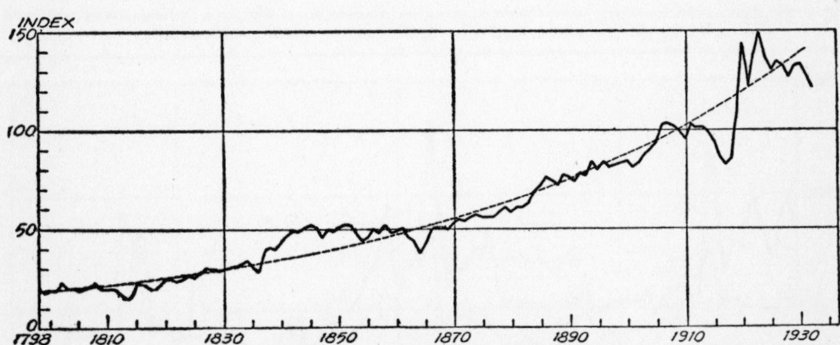

FIGURE 24.—INDEX NUMBERS OF THE PURCHASING POWER OF WHOLESALE PRICES OF LUMBER, 1798-1932.

1910-14 = 100.

There has been a steady increase in the purchasing power of the price of lumber from 1798 to the present time. From 1798 to 1914, the purchasing power of lumber increased at the compound rate of 1.54 per cent per year.

Spirits.—In the early part of the century, alcoholic drinks were largely imported. The substitution of drinks made from American grain reduced prices at first. Heavy taxes, which raised prices in the Civil War period, were maintained thereafter (table 3, figure 26).

Miscellaneous and house-furnishing groups.—Miscellaneous and house-furnishing products declined in price compared with all commodities (table 3).

Basic commodities.—An index number of 30 basic commodities has been constructed. This index includes prices of farm products, minerals, textiles, and the like, that are relatively flexible (table 4). The general trend in prices of these 30 basic commodities is approximately the same as the general price level (figure 27). It fluctuates more violently than the general price level. In July 1932, the index of the general price level was 94, and of 30 basic commodities, 71.

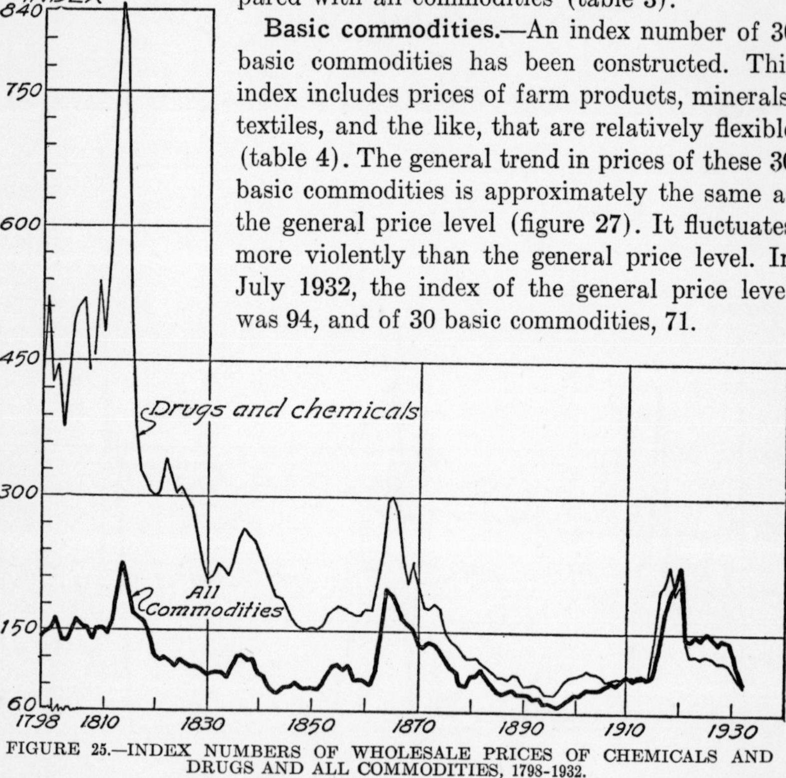

FIGURE 25.—INDEX NUMBERS OF WHOLESALE PRICES OF CHEMICALS AND DRUGS AND ALL COMMODITIES, 1798-1932.
1910-14 = 100.
Chemicals and drugs declined strikingly compared with all commodities.

Gold.—Since the price of gold is fixed by law, it does not change except when the law is changed. It changes in exactly the same way as the price of a postage stamp changes, but the value of gold changes with the supply of and demand for it. The value of gold compared with prices of all commodities is shown in figure 28.

Over long periods of time, there are differences in the trends of commodity prices for different groups. These differences lead to great

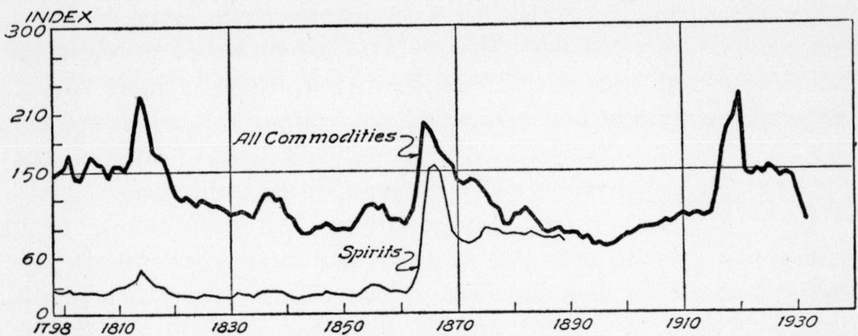

FIGURE 26.—INDEX NUMBERS OF WHOLESALE PRICES OF SPIRITS AND ALL COMMODITIES, 1798-1932.

1910-14 = 100.

Spirits have steadily risen compared with the general level of all commodities.

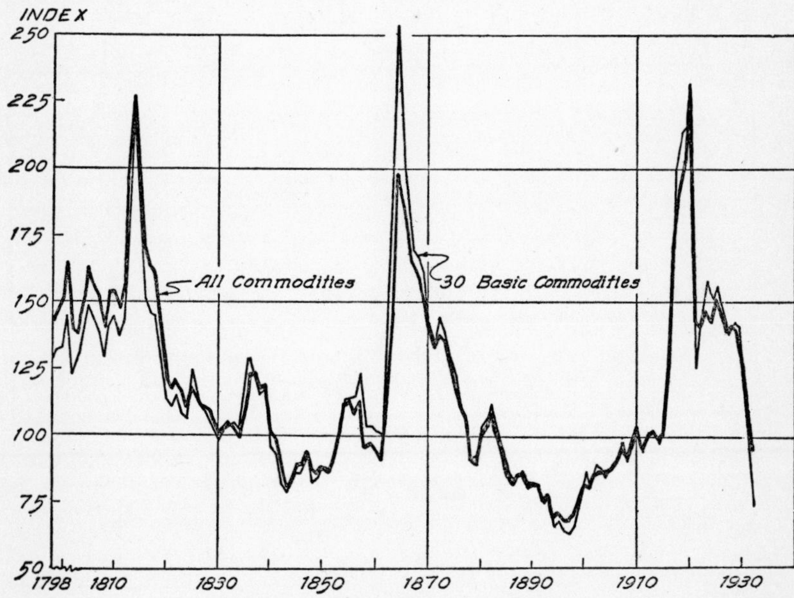

FIGURE 27.—INDEX NUMBERS OF WHOLESALE PRICES OF 30 BASIC COMMODITIES AND ALL COMMODITIES, 1798-1932.

1910-14 = 100.

Over a century, the movement of basic commodities has been very similar to the movement of all commodities. When prices were stable, the two index numbers moved together. When prices changed violently, the basic commodity index moved more violently than the all-commodity index.

confusion. The differences are even greater when a single commodity rather than a group is used. Many persons who are unable to understand relative price movements conclude that a single commodity can be a more stable measure of value than all commodities. They arrive at this conclusion by accepting the illusion that the commodity which they choose as a measure of value ceases to fluctuate in value. This is similar to the simplification of astronomy that comes by assuming

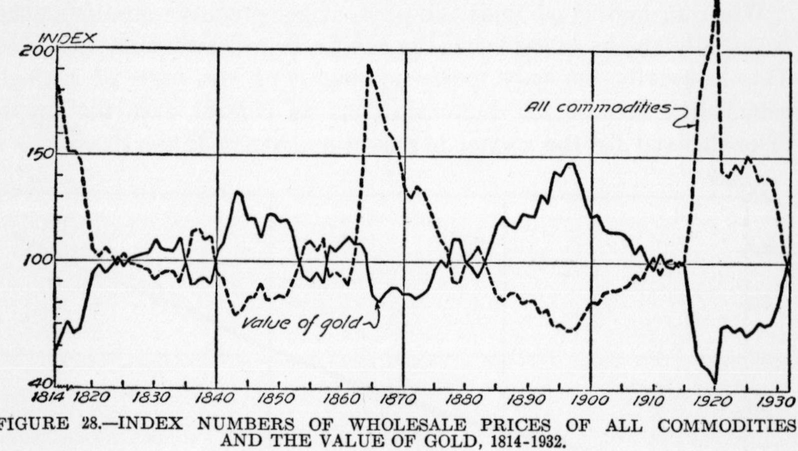

FIGURE 28.—INDEX NUMBERS OF WHOLESALE PRICES OF ALL COMMODITIES AND THE VALUE OF GOLD, 1814-1932.
1910-14 = 100.
Although the price of gold is fixed by law, the value of gold fluctuates violently.

the earth to be stationary. Unfortunately, the assumption that the earth is stationary, or that gold, silver, or copper can be made stationary in value after any one of them is chosen as money, has no effect on the facts.

BIBLIOGRAPHY

Warren, G. F., Pearson, F. A., and Stoker, H. M., Wholesale Prices for 213 Years, 1720-1932. Cornell University Agricultural Experiment Station Memoir 142. 1932.

Wholesale Prices, 1931. United States Bureau of Labor Statistics Bulletin 572. 1932.

CHAPTER III

PHYSICAL VOLUME OF PRODUCTION

When an individual finds the price of his product unsatisfactory, he usually thinks of reducing the supply in order to raise the price. This is usually the only means of improving the price of a single commodity because the individual has no control over the supply of or demand for the commodity used as money. If the product is a

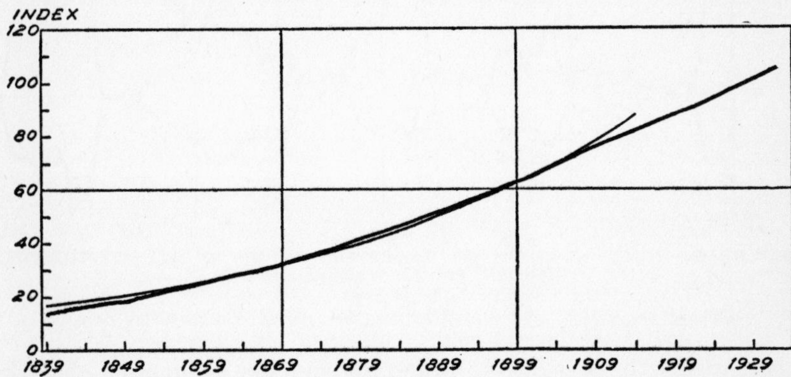

FIGURE 29.—INDEX NUMBERS OF THE POPULATION OF CONTINENTAL UNITED STATES, 1839-1932.
1926-30 = 100.
From 1839 to 1914, the population of continental United States increased 2.28 per cent per year. From 1915 to 1929, the rate was 1.46 per cent per year.

specialty, he may try advertising. This same reasoning is erroneously carried over from the individual's commodity to all commodities. If there is too much wheat, the price is relatively low. If there is too little, the price is relatively high. If the whole price level rises, the popular opinion is that there is a shortage of everything. Every time in history when prices have declined, the usual explanation has been that there was a general over-production of everything. An intelligent consideration of the price problem must consider population and production.

Population.—From 1839 to 1914, the population of continental United States increased at the rate of 2.28 per cent per year (figure

29). During the 15-year period, 1915 to 1929, the rate fell to 1.46 per cent per year. Prior to the World War, there was some slowing down in the rate of increase.

From 1840 to 1914, the population of Europe, North and South America, and Australia,[1] increased at the compound rate of 1.11 per cent per year.

Production of food and feed crops.—To be significant, production must be measured in physical quantities—bushels, tons, pounds, and the like.

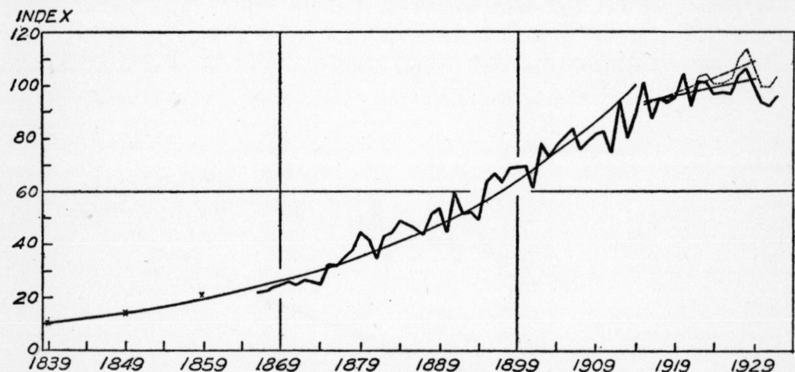

FIGURE 30.—INDEX NUMBERS OF THE VOLUME OF FOOD AND FEED CROPS PRODUCED IN THE UNITED STATES, 1839-1932.

1926-30 = 100.

From 1839 to 1914, production increased at the rate of 3.02 per cent per year. From 1915 to 1929, it increased only 0.60 per cent per year. The upper curve shows production corrected for the reduced number of horses and mules.

Since a bushel of wheat is more important than a bushel of corn, it is given a correspondingly greater weight in the index of production. The index numbers for food and feed crops were made by adding together bushels of wheat, bushels of potatoes, bushels of corn, quarts of strawberries, and 27 other crops all combined according to their importance. The purpose of the index was to include only basic commodities. Livestock is not included. This is all produced from crops except the portion which is grown on pasture. All these crops combined in accordance with their importance are shown in figure 30 and table 5. The index of production increased from 10 in 1839 to 90 in 1914. The annual compound rate of increase during this period was 3.02 per cent.

In popular opinion, the rapid increase was the cause of the agri-

[1] Willcox, W. F., International Migrations, Publications of the National Bureau of Economic Research, Inc., Report 18, Vol. 2, Appendix 1, pp. 641-4, 1931.

cultural depression. As a matter of fact, the increase from 1915 to 1929 was only 0.6 per cent per year.

From 1839 to 1914, the production of food and feed crops per capita increased at the rate of 0.74 per cent per year (figure 31). This rate of increase was declining slightly before the war.

From 1915 to 1929, the production per capita decreased 0.85 per cent per year, which was even faster than the former rate of increase. A part of this decrease was called for by the reduction in the number of horses and mules. After making allowance for this, the decrease was 0.29 per cent per year.

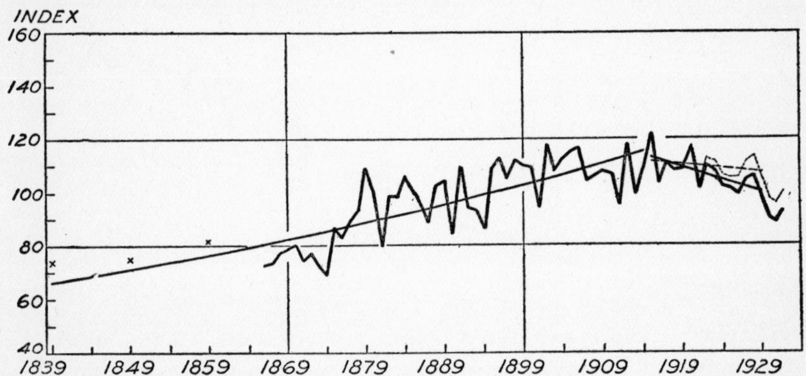

FIGURE 31.—INDEX NUMBERS OF THE PRODUCTION OF FOOD AND FEED CROPS PER CAPITA IN THE UNITED STATES, 1839-1932.

1926-30 = 100.

From 1839 to 1900, the production of food and feed crops increased 0.86 per cent per year; from 1901 to 1914, decreased 0.2 per cent per year; and from 1915 to 1929, decreased 0.29 per cent per year, when adjusted for the changes in the number of horses and mules.

Lumber.—From 1839 to 1907, the board feet of lumber cut in the United States increased nearly 30 times. Since then, lumber production has declined. The production of forest products in 1932 was the lowest since 1867 (figure 32).

From 1839 to 1907, the production of forest products normally increased at the compound rate of 4.14 per cent per year (table 5). This was a more rapid increase than that for crop production. From 1915 to 1929, the annual rate of increase was only 0.60 per cent per year.

From 1839 to 1907, lumber production per capita increased at a decreasing rate (figure 33). Since 1907, there has been a decline in the production per capita, except for a slight increase during the expansion in building construction, 1922 to 1929.

The production of forest products per capita in 1932 was approximately the same as in 1839.

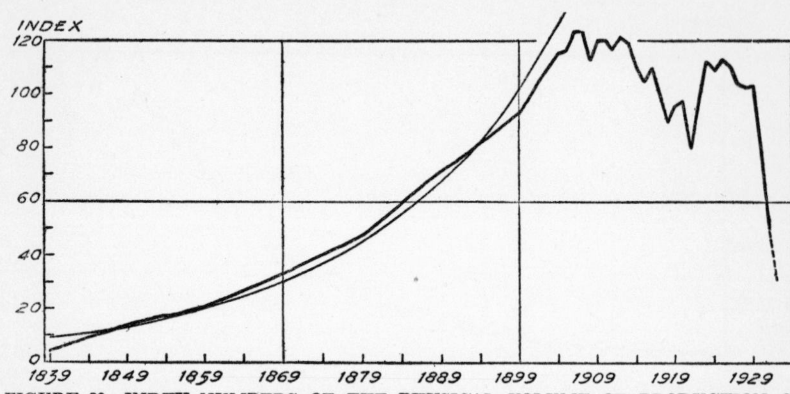

FIGURE 32.—INDEX NUMBERS OF THE PHYSICAL VOLUME OF PRODUCTION OF FOREST PRODUCTS IN THE UNITED STATES, 1839-1932.

1926-30 = 100.

The production of lumber and pulpwood increased rapidly until 1907, and since then has declined. From 1839 to 1907, production of lumber and pulpwood increased at the rate of 4.14 per cent per year. Production in 1932 was lower than that sixty-five years ago.

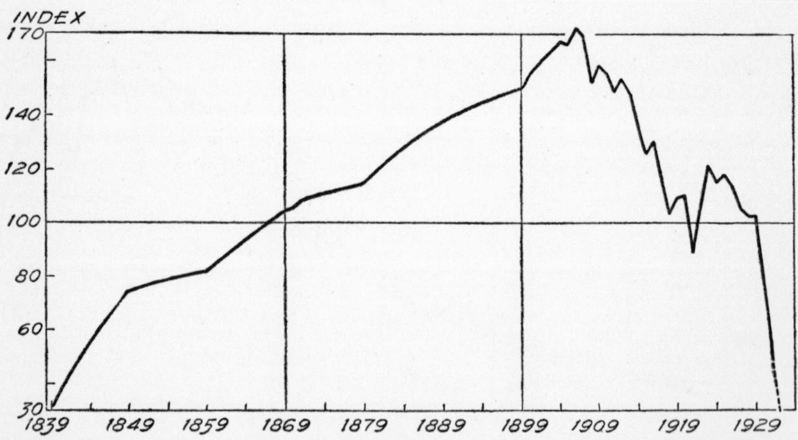

FIGURE 33.—INDEX NUMBERS OF THE PHYSICAL VOLUME OF PRODUCTION OF FOREST PRODUCTS PER CAPITA IN THE UNITED STATES, 1839-1932.

1926-30 = 100.

The production of forest products per capita reached a peak in 1906. Since that time, it has declined very rapidly. From 1915 to 1929, production per capita has declined at the rate of 0.85 per cent per year.

Coal.—The production of bituminous and anthracite coal reached a peak in 1918, and since that time has declined (figure 34).

From 1839 to 1914, the production of coal increased 6.22 per cent per year, and from 1915 to 1929, declined 0.25 per cent per year. This has caused great distress in coal mining areas.

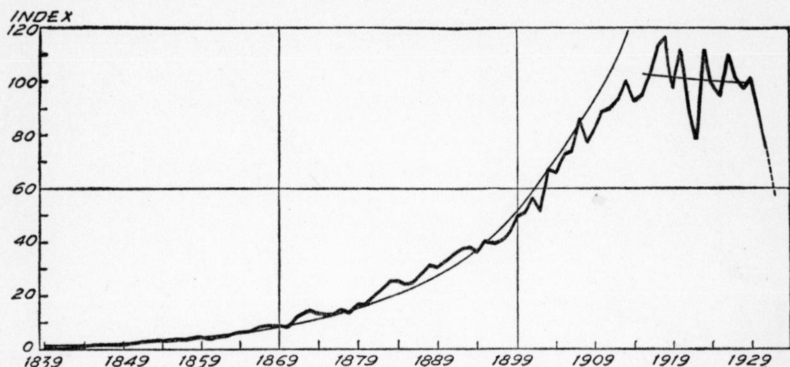

FIGURE 34.—INDEX NUMBERS OF THE PHYSICAL VOLUME OF COAL PRODUCED IN THE UNITED STATES, 1839-1932.

1926-30 = 100.

From 1839 to 1914, the production of coal increased at the rate of 6.22 per cent per year. From 1915 to 1929, the production declined at the rate of 0.25 per cent per year. Production in 1932 was approximately the same as that thirty years ago. Other sources of power have displaced coal.

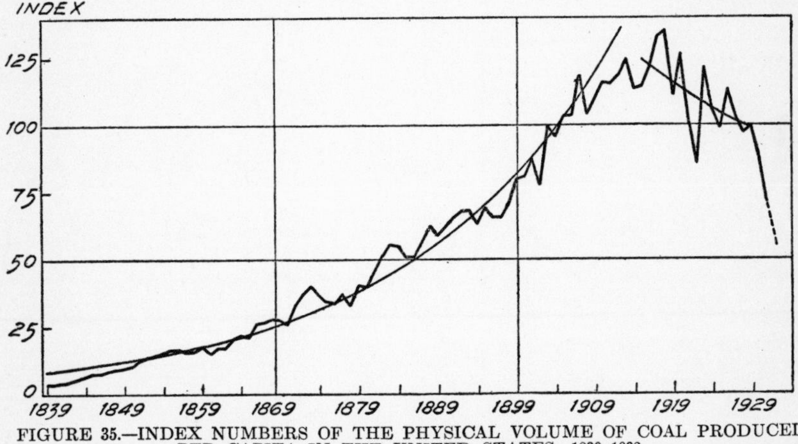

FIGURE 35.—INDEX NUMBERS OF THE PHYSICAL VOLUME OF COAL PRODUCED PER CAPITA IN THE UNITED STATES, 1839-1932.

1926-30 = 100.

From 1839 to 1914, the production of coal per capita increased at the rate of 3.86 per cent per year. From 1915 to 1929, production per capita declined 1.69 per cent per year. The maelstrom of 1929-32 reduced the production of coal per capita in 1932 to that of fifty years ago.

From 1839 to 1914, the production per capita increased 3.86 per cent per year, and from 1915 to 1929, decreased 1.69 per cent. The production per capita in 1932 was approximately the same as that

TABLE 5.—INDEX NUMBERS OF PHYSICAL VOLUME OF PRODUCTION IN THE UNITED STATES, 1839–1932*

1926–30 = 100

Year	Population	Food and feed crops	Total crop production	Forest products	Electricity from water power	All fuel and water power	All minerals and water power	Total basic production†	Food and feed crops per capita	All minerals, and water power per capita	Total basic production per capita‡
1839	13.94	10.33	10.61	4.18	....	0.51	0.45	4.29	74.10	3.23	30.77
1840	14.27	....	....	5.16	....	0.53	0.46	....	....	3.22	....
1841	14.77	....	....	6.15	....	0.58	0.49	....	....	3.32	....
1842	15.28	....	....	7.13	....	0.64	0.52	....	....	3.40	....
1843	15.86	....	....	8.12	....	0.70	0.60	....	....	3.78	....
1844	16.36	....	....	9.11	....	0.80	0.71	....	....	4.34	....
1845	16.86	....	....	10.09	....	0.91	0.83	....	....	4.92	....
1846	17.36	....	....	11.08	....	0.96	0.91	....	....	5.24	....
1847	17.86	....	....	12.06	....	1.06	0.98	....	....	5.49	....
1848	18.36	....	....	13.05	....	1.12	1.02	....	....	5.56	....
1849	18.86	14.09	14.07	14.04	....	1.19	1.01	6.73	74.71	5.36	35.68
1850	19.45	....	....	14.72	....	1.25	1.02	....	....	5.24	....
1851	20.12	....	....	15.41	....	1.47	1.14	....	....	5.67	....
1852	20.78	....	....	16.09	....	1.60	1.21	....	....	5.82	....
1853	21.45	....	....	16.78	....	1.68	1.29	....	....	6.01	....
1854	22.20	....	....	17.47	....	1.86	1.42	....	....	6.40	....
1855	22.87	....	....	18.15	....	1.99	1.52	....	....	6.65	....
1856	23.54	....	....	18.84	....	2.07	1.61	....	....	6.84	....
1857	24.21	....	....	19.53	....	2.05	1.57	....	....	6.48	....
1858	24.96	....	....	20.21	....	2.12	1.60	....	....	6.41	....
1859	25.63	20.84	22.92	20.90	....	2.33	1.77	11.30	81.31	6.91	44.09
1860	26.29	....	....	22.13	....	2.19	1.71	....	....	6.50	....
1861	26.88	....	....	23.36	....	2.50	1.87	....	....	6.96	....
1862	27.46	....	....	24.59	....	2.60	1.98	....	....	7.21	....
1863	28.05	....	....	25.82	....	2.98	2.28	....	....	8.13	....
1864	28.63	....	....	27.05	....	3.15	2.46	....	....	8.59	....
1865	29.30	....	....	28.28	....	3.15	2.40	....	....	8.19	....
1866	29.88	21.71	20.55	29.51	....	3.80	2.91	10.81	72.66	9.74	36.18
1867	30.47	22.38	21.48	30.74	....	3.92	3.05	11.38	73.45	10.01	37.35
1868	31.05	23.95	22.84	31.97	....	4.14	3.23	12.02	77.13	10.40	38.71
1869	31.64	24.81	23.63	33.21	....	4.19	3.36	12.49	78.41	10.62	39.48
1870	32.30	25.90	25.65	34.18	....	4.13	3.34	13.40	80.37	10.34	41.49
1871	33.22	24.66	23.46	35.99	....	5.12	4.02	12.82	74.23	12.10	38.59
1872	34.22	26.47	26.40	37.39	....	5.82	4.77	14.57	77.35	13.94	42.58
1873	35.14	25.52	25.46	38.78	....	6.44	5.25	14.37	72.62	14.94	40.89
1874	36.14	25.07	24.87	40.18	....	6.12	5.05	13.97	69.37	13.97	38.66
1875	37.15	32.27	32.40	41.57	....	5.84	4.75	17.08	86.86	12.79	45.98
1876	38.06	31.76	31.36	42.97	....	5.93	4.84	16.83	83.45	12.72	44.22
1877	39.07	34.99	34.16	44.36	....	6.70	5.43	18.41	89.56	13.90	47.12
1878	39.98	37.44	36.85	45.75	....	6.30	5.33	19.68	93.65	13.33	49.22
1879	40.98	44.69	43.24	47.15	....	7.71	6.31	23.03	109.05	15.40	56.20
1880	41.99	42.02	41.79	49.55	....	7.97	6.85	22.70	100.07	16.31	54.06
1881	42.99	34.56	34.77	51.95	....	9.02	7.71	20.25	80.39	17.93	47.10
1882	44.07	43.41	43.66	54.35	....	10.28	8.77	24.96	98.50	19.90	56.64
1883	45.16	44.48	43.26	56.75	0.04	10.96	9.29	25.07	98.49	20.57	55.51
1884	46.24	49.09	47.29	59.16	0.09	11.12	9.31	27.26	106.16	20.13	58.95
1885	47.33	47.94	47.19	61.56	0.13	10.76	9.15	27.21	101.29	19.33	57.49
1886	48.33	46.15	45.52	63.96	0.17	11.26	9.99	26.96	95.49	20.67	55.78
1887	49.42	43.90	43.83	66.36	0.21	12.48	11.16	27.18	88.83	22.58	55.00
1888	50.50	51.87	50.80	68.77	0.24	13.84	12.19	30.69	102.71	24.14	60.77
1889	51.59	53.86	52.45	71.17	0.28	13.64	12.53	31.69	104.40	24.29	61.43
1890	52.67	44.49	46.14	73.40	0.31	14.90	13.96	30.09	84.47	26.50	57.13
1891	53.76	59.41	58.94	75.63	0.34	16.08	14.61	36.18	110.51	27.18	67.30
1892	54.84	51.85	50.37	77.87	0.37	16.65	15.51	32.85	94.55	28.28	59.90
1893	55.93	52.23	51.42	80.10	0.49	16.89	14.86	32.84	93.38	26.57	58.72
1894	57.01	49.20	50.54	82.34	0.61	16.21	14.28	32.90	86.30	25.05	57.71
1895	58.10	63.39	60.42	84.57	0.73	17.99	16.51	38.78	109.10	28.42	66.75
1896	59.18	66.99	64.47	86.80	0.86	17.94	16.50	40.82	113.20	27.88	68.98
1897	60.27	63.43	64.15	89.03	0.98	18.26	17.27	41.27	105.24	28.65	68.48

TABLE 5 (*Concluded*)

Year	Population	Food and feed crops	Total crop production	Forest products	Electricity from water power	All fuel and water power	All minerals and water power	Total basic production†	Food and feed crops per capita	All minerals, and water power per capita	Total basic production per capita‡
1898	61.35	69.15	69.37	91.27	1.29	19.25	18.82	44.20	112.71	30.68	72.05
1899	62.44	69.20	69.05	93.50	1.59	21.80	21.30	46.20	110.83	34.11	73.99
1900	63.52	69.61	69.04	97.88	2.02	22.82	22.33	47.03	109.59	35.15	74.04
1901	64.86	61.38	61.65	102.21	2.45	25.35	24.71	44.57	94.63	38.10	68.72
1902	66.28	78.19	76.66	106.56	3.07	24.49	25.31	52.55	117.97	38.19	79.28
1903	67.61	73.15	71.74	110.91	3.61	30.92	29.55	53.29	108.19	43.71	78.82
1904	68.95	77.68	78.43	115.26	4.35	31.48	30.03	57.20	112.66	43.55	82.96
1905	70.28	81.07	78.57	116.66	5.02	34.87	35.12	60.47	115.35	49.97	86.04
1906	71.62	83.78	83.41	123.67	6.06	35.68	37.14	63.87	116.98	51.86	89.18
1907	73.04	76.03	75.01	123.83	7.18	41.88	41.22	61.90	104.09	56.43	84.75
1908	74.37	79.14	79.60	112.90	8.33	39.19	36.17	60.91	106.41	48.64	81.90
1909	75.71	81.85	81.45	120.18	9.68	42.08	42.69	65.86	108.11	56.39	86.99
1910	77.05	82.58	81.85	120.07	11.02	45.68	46.10	67.45	107.18	59.83	87.54
1911	78.21	74.76	78.63	116.49	12.43	46.64	45.94	65.07	95.59	58.74	83.20
1912	79.38	93.67	92.68	121.81	14.17	48.66	50.60	75.80	118.00	63.74	95.49
1913	80.55	80.14	81.81	119.32	16.41	52.43	53.63	71.30	99.49	66.58	88.52
1914	81.72	89.71	91.77	110.32	19.23	50.87	50.05	74.36	109.78	61.25	90.99
1915	82.89	101.11	96.79	104.36	22.66	53.02	55.66	79.49	121.98	67.14	95.90
1916	84.14	87.18	85.65	110.10	26.94	58.00	66.61	78.78	103.61	79.17	93.63
1917	85.31	94.92	92.17	100.04	31.15	64.46	70.59	83.42	111.26	82.75	97.78
1918	86.48	93.86	92.41	89.36	35.27	66.85	70.81	83.21	108.53	81.88	96.22
1919	87.65	95.30	93.38	95.79	39.80	61.76	62.98	80.81	108.73	71.85	92.20
1920	88.90	103.26	101.84	97.85	48.40	71.22	71.51	88.72	116.15	80.44	99.80
1921	90.32	91.77	86.09	80.52	45.28	63.73	56.09	73.00	101.61	62.10	80.82
1922	91.74	101.36	96.11	97.81	53.35	64.30	64.95	83.11	110.49	70.80	90.59
1923	93.07	101.06	96.83	112.96	62.62	86.31	86.97	93.41	108.58	93.45	100.37
1924	94.49	96.82	95.43	109.17	66.64	82.75	82.63	91.28	102.47	87.45	96.60
1925	95.83	97.12	98.69	113.25	74.90	84.86	87.61	95.01	101.35	91.42	99.14
1926	97.25	96.72	99.89	110.62	84.70	93.78	95.81	99.35	99.46	98.52	102.16
1927	98.58	103.69	100.90	104.00	91.47	97.56	97.65	99.65	105.18	99.06	101.09
1928	100.00	106.31	104.85	102.79	101.56	99.02	100.68	103.09	106.31	100.68	103.09
1929	101.42	99.85	100.14	103.89	111.96	108.85	110.10	103.66	98.45	108.56	102.21
1930	102.75	93.41	94.21	78.78	110.31	100.81	95.78	93.14	90.91	93.22	90.65
1931	*103.59*	*92.30*	*95.96*	*50.01*	*106.13*	*90.50*	*79.52*	*85.27*	*89.10*	*76.76*	*82.31*
1932	*104.17*	*96.31*	*92.90*	*30.94*	*96.26*	*78.69*	*62.36*	*73.56*	*92.45*	*59.86*	*70.62*
Rate of change§											
1839–1914	2.28	3.02	3.03	....	....	5.96	6.43	4.03	0.74	4.08	1.73
1839–1900	....	....	....	....	....	....	....	....	0.86	....	....
1839–1907	....	....	....	4.14	....	....	....	....	....	....	....
1901–1914	....	....	....	....	....	....	....	....	−0.20	....	....
1915–1919	....	....	....	....	....	....	....	....	−1.82	....	....
1920–1929	....	....	....	....	....	....	....	....	−1.05	....	....
1915–1929	1.46	0.60	0.85	0.60	....	4.84	4.31	2.11	−0.85	2.80	0.64
1915–1929¶	....	1.17	1.33	....	....	....	....	....	−0.29	....	....

Figures in italics are preliminary.

* Warren, G. F., and Pearson, F. A., The Physical Volume of Production in the United States, Cornell University Agricultural Experiment Station Memoir 144, 1932.

† In the index numbers with variable group weights, each group is weighted in accordance with comparative values in different periods.

‡ Based on total basic production, variable group weights.

§ The rates of change are based on the equation $y = ar^x$.

¶ Rate of change when adjustment is made for horses and mules, 1915–29.

50 years ago (figure 35). Other sources of power have replaced coal, and coal is used more efficiently than formerly.

Mineral production.—Minerals include coal, petroleum, natural gas, iron, scrap iron and other secondary metals, lead, copper, and practically all the important minerals. Water power is included in this group. From 1839 to 1914, the production of minerals, fuel, and power increased at the rate of 6.43 per cent per year (figure 36). From 1915 to 1929, it increased at the rate of 4.31 per cent per year.

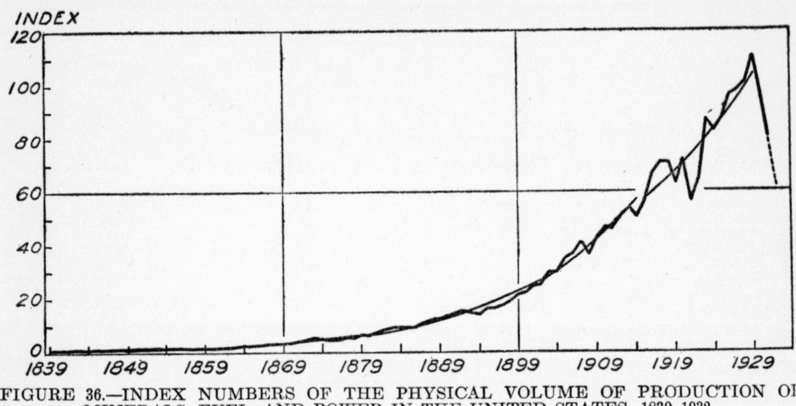

FIGURE 36.—INDEX NUMBERS OF THE PHYSICAL VOLUME OF PRODUCTION OF MINERALS, FUEL, AND POWER IN THE UNITED STATES, 1839-1932.

1926-30 = 100.

From 1839 to 1914, the production of minerals, fuel, and power increased at the rate of 6.43 per cent per year. From 1915 to 1929, the average rate of increase was 4.31 per cent.

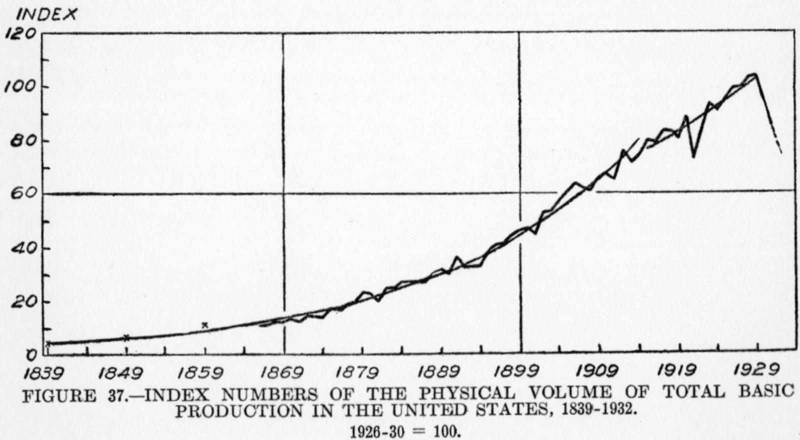

FIGURE 37.—INDEX NUMBERS OF THE PHYSICAL VOLUME OF TOTAL BASIC PRODUCTION IN THE UNITED STATES, 1839-1932.

1926-30 = 100.

From 1839 to 1914, the total volume of basic production increased at the rate of 4.03 per cent per year; and from 1915 to 1929, production increased only 2.11 per cent per year.

Total production.—When all crops, forest products, and mineral production are combined, an index of total basic production is obtained. From 1839 to 1914, this index increased at the rate of 4.03 per cent per year. From 1915 to 1929, it increased 2.11 per cent per year.

Before the war, the total basic production per capita increased 1.73 per cent per year. From 1915 to 1929, it increased only 0.64 per cent per year (figures 37 and 38).

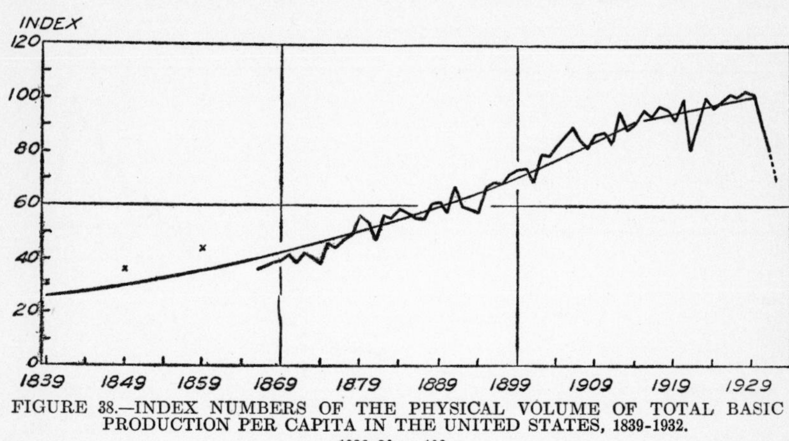

FIGURE 38.—INDEX NUMBERS OF THE PHYSICAL VOLUME OF TOTAL BASIC PRODUCTION PER CAPITA IN THE UNITED STATES, 1839-1932.

1926-30 = 100.

From 1839 to 1914, the total basic production per capita increased at the rate of 1.73 per cent, and from 1915 to 1929, only 0.64 per cent.

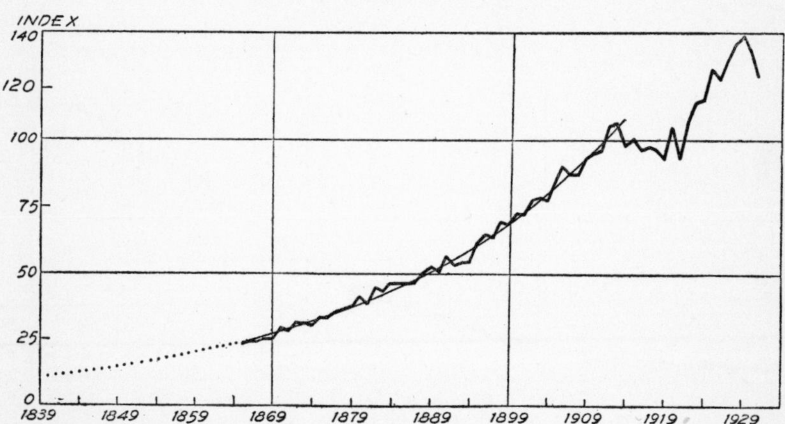

FIGURE 39.—SNYDER'S INDEX NUMBERS OF WORLD PHYSICAL VOLUME OF PRODUCTION, 1840-1931.

1910-14 = 100.

From 1865 to 1914, the world's physical volume of production normally increased 3.15 per cent per year. Production was materially reduced by the World War and by the Panics of 1920 and 1929, but is gradually increasing.

World production.—Snyder's physical volume of world production increased at the rate of 3.15 per cent per year (table 6 and figure 39). This rate of increase was much reduced by the war.

From 1865 to 1914, world production per capita increased 1.91 per cent per year (figure 40). From 1914 to 1921, production was very low. The war checked the normal rate of increase.

TABLE 6.—INDEX NUMBERS OF WORLD PRODUCTION, 1840–1932*

1910–14 = 100

Year	World physical volume of production	Physical volume of production per capita	Year	World physical volume of production	Physical volume of production per capita	Year	World physical volume of production	Physical volume of production per capita	Year	World physical volume of production	Physical volume of production per capita
1840	11	24	1870	29	48	1900	72	85	1930	133	105
1841	11	23	1871	28	46	1901	72	84	1931	124	95
1842	12	22	1872	31	50	1902	77	89	1932	118	89
1843	12	26	1873	31	50	1903	78	90			
1844	12	26	1874	30	48	1904	77	88			
1845	13	28	1875	33	53	1905	84	94			
1846	13	28	1876	33	53	1906	90	98			
1847	14	29	1877	35	55	1907	87	94			
1848	14	29	1878	36	56	1908	87	92			
1849	15	31	1879	37	57	1909	93	97			
1850	15	30	1880	41	63	1910	95	98			
1851	15	29	1881	38	58	1911	96	97			
1852	16	31	1882	44	66	1912	105	105			
1853	16	31	1883	43	62	1913	106	105			
1854	17	33	1884	46	66	1914	98	95			
1855	17	33	1885	46	64	1915	100	96			
1856	18	34	1886	46	63	1916	96	92			
1857	19	35	1887	46	63	1917	97	92			
1858	19	35	1888	50	67	1918	96	91			
1859	20	36	1889	52	69	1919	93	87			
1860	20	36	1890	50	65	1920	105	97			
1861	21	38	1891	56	72	1921	93	87			
1862	22	39	1892	53	68	1922	107	101			
1863	22	39	1893	54	69	1923	114	108			
1864	23	40	1894	54	68	1924	115	110			
1865	23	40	1895	61	76	1925	126	119			
1866	24	42	1896	64	78	1926	123	112			
1867	24	42	1897	63	76	1927	130	115			
1868	25	42	1898	69	82	1928	137	116			
1869	25	41	1899	68	81	1929	140	113			

* The index numbers of world physical volume of production from 1865 to 1932 were prepared by Carl Snyder and furnished through the courtesy of the Federal Reserve Bank of New York.

The index was originally calculated on a 1923–25 base. To convert to the 1910–14 base, multiply by 0.002979.

The equation of total production from 1865 to 1914 was $y = 23.830\ (1.0315)^x$; from 1880 to 1896, $y = 26.931\ (1.0265)^x$; and from 1897 to 1913, $y = 24.663\ (1.0307)^x$.

The equation of production per capita, from 1865 to 1914, was $y = 25.983\ (1.0191)^x$; from 1880 to 1896, $y = 36.853\ (1.0122)^x$; and from 1897 to 1913, $y = 29.462\ (1.0173)^x$.

An index number of world physical volume of production of cotton, coal, and pig iron was calculated for 1840, 1850, and 1860. These index numbers were 12, 14, and 24. For the same years the Snyder curve projected backwards gave index numbers of 11, 15, and 20. An index number for the same years was calculated including steam and sailing vessels, miles of railroad, cotton, coal, and pig iron. The index numbers of ten-year periods from 1840 to 1890 were as follows: 11, 15, 23, 28, 39, and 53, and the Snyder index for the same years was 11, 15, 20, 29, 41, and 50. These index numbers agreed very closely with the projected Snyder index.

These index numbers from 1840 to 1865 are the Snyder curve, $y = 23.830\ (1.0315)^x$, projected. These are, of course, only approximations and do not show variations from year to year.

Production per capita is based on the population for Europe, America, and Australia, as reported by Willcox, W. F., International Migrations, Publications of the National Bureau of Economic Research, Inc., Report 18, Vol. 2, Appendix 1, pp. 641–4, 1931.

Causes of low production per capita.—The low production per capita during the World War is easily explained by the fact that such a large percentage of the able-bodied men were in the army. After the war, financial deflation caused so much unemployment as to keep production low. The attempts of the various countries to prevent imports also interfered with production.

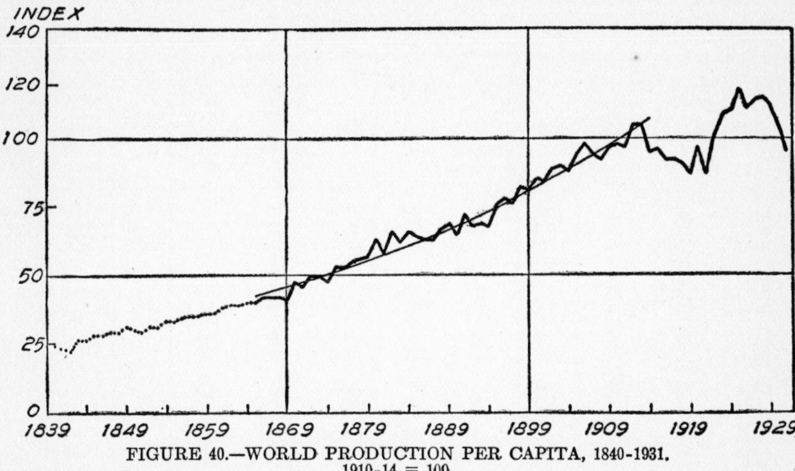

FIGURE 40.—WORLD PRODUCTION PER CAPITA, 1840-1931.
1910-14 = 100.

From 1865 to 1914, the world's physical volume of production per capita increased 1.91 per cent per year. For many years before the war, production per capita proceeded with great regularity. During the World War period, it was strikingly decreased. This is contrary to the popular opinion, but shows that man cannot fight and produce at the same time.

All these figures indicate that there is no basis for the belief that high production is the cause of the depression.

ORDERLY PRODUCTION

Wheat.—Whenever inflation or deflation occurs, attention is turned to the individual commodities in an effort to explain the situation. In the nineties and again in the present agricultural depression, the popular explanation was that wheat production had been unduly expanded and that farmers should shift to other crops.

Most of the variations in production from year to year are due to the weather (figure 41). There were three periods of rather high wheat production: 1878-1884, 1898-1903, and 1915-1920.

It should be remembered that it is acres planted that indicates the efforts in production. The acreage figures ordinarily quoted are acres harvested, which show considerable variation, a large part of which is due to the weather because many acres are sometimes left unharvested.

The acres of wheat harvested per capita are shown in figure 42. The very low acreage in 1917 was due to a large abandonment of winter wheat. There were three periods of high acreage per capita about 20

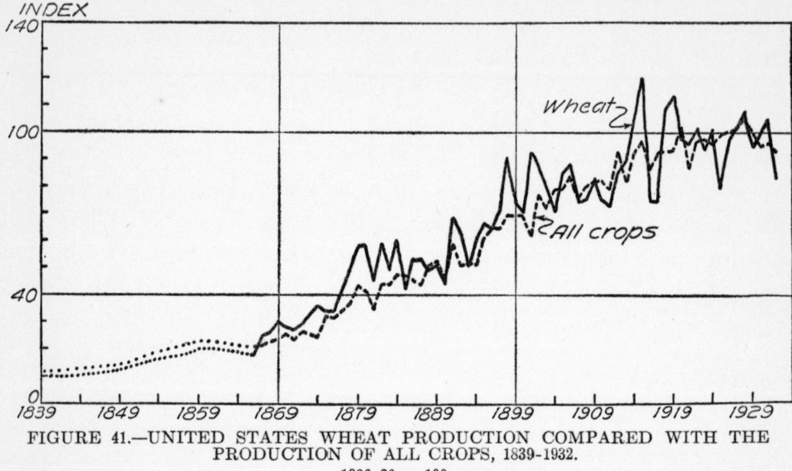

FIGURE 41.—UNITED STATES WHEAT PRODUCTION COMPARED WITH THE PRODUCTION OF ALL CROPS, 1839-1932.

1926-30 = 100.

Wheat production has followed all crops very closely, except for three periods of high production and variations due to weather.[2]

FIGURE 42.—INDEX NUMBERS OF THE ACREAGE OF WHEAT HARVESTED PER CAPITA IN THE UNITED STATES, 1866-1932.

1926-30 = 100.

There were three periods of high acreage per capita about 20 years apart. The low acreage in 1917 was due to abandonment of winter wheat because of winter injury.

years apart. The acreage per capita for 1931 was the lowest in two generations.

[2] It would be slightly better to compare wheat production with the production of all other crops, but the two curves follow each other so closely that it leads to no error in conclusion to include wheat, with the weight that it receives, in all crops. Previous to 1866, data for the census years only are included.

Most of the wheat planted in New York State is harvested. The acreage reported is therefore a fair indication of the acreage that was planted.[3] There have been three distinct cycles since 1865 with high acreages about 20 years apart (figure 43). The same cycle is shown for England (figure 159, page 313).

Apparently we are moving into a period of low production. Probably about the time the public clamor for reduced acreage reaches a peak, wheat production will be too low.

The movement in wheat production is associated with a slight cyclical tendency for all agriculture, indicated in figure 44. There is a slight tendency for a period of high production every 20 years: about

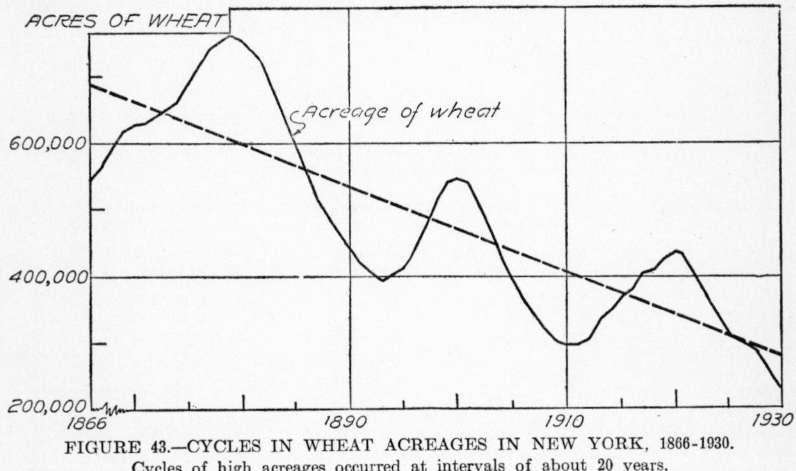

FIGURE 43.—CYCLES IN WHEAT ACREAGES IN NEW YORK, 1866-1930.
Cycles of high acreages occurred at intervals of about 20 years.

1839, 1859, 1879, 1899, and 1919. More persons are born on farms than are needed. This results in a permanent movement out of agriculture. Apparently this movement is slightly too rapid in one generation and slightly too slow in the succeeding generation. This does not explain the price collapses after the World War.

In the nineties when farm products were so low, production was also low.

Wheat production per capita follows fairly closely the production of all crops (figure 44). The production per capita has been declining since the World War.

World wheat production and the production of all crops are shown

[3] Mereness, E. H., Effect of Changes in the Price on the Acreage and Production of Wheat in New York, Farm Economics, No. 75, p. 1738, May 1932.

in figure 45. Since 1900, wheat production has kept pace with the production of other farm products, but has been a little lower relative to other crops than it was before that time.

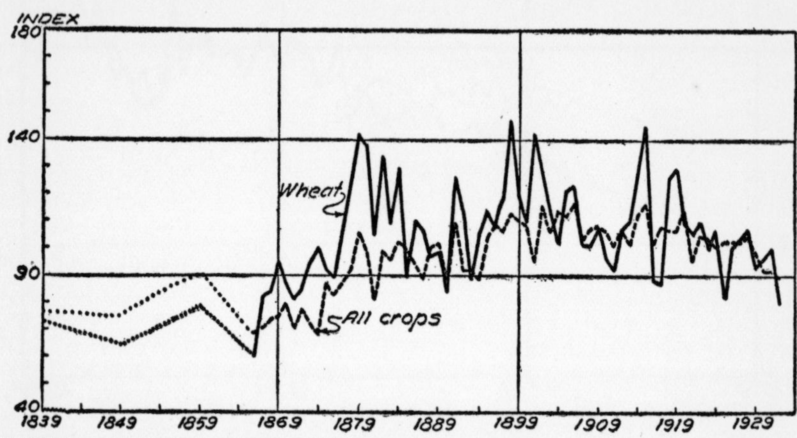

FIGURE 44.—UNITED STATES PRODUCTION OF WHEAT PER CAPITA COMPARED WITH THE PRODUCTION OF ALL CROPS PER CAPITA, 1839-1932.
1926-30 = 100.
The production of wheat per capita follows very closely the production of all crops per capita. Since 1900, there has been a slow and gradual decline in the production per capita.

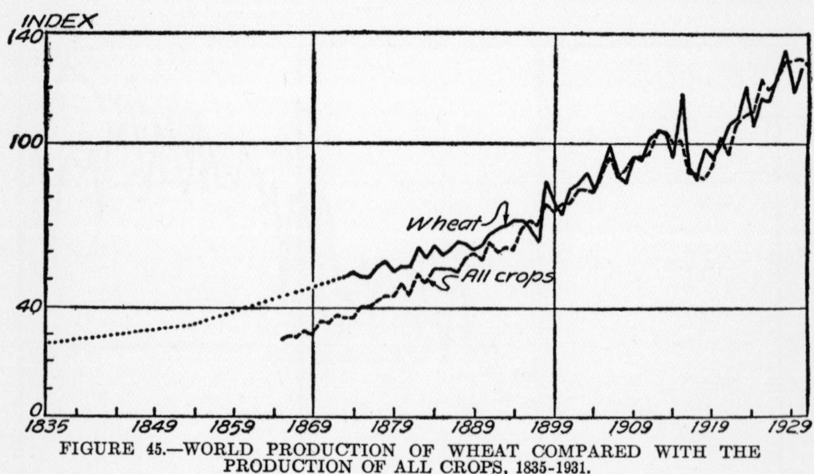

FIGURE 45.—WORLD PRODUCTION OF WHEAT COMPARED WITH THE PRODUCTION OF ALL CROPS, 1835-1931.
1910-14 = 100.
Since 1900, wheat production and the production of all crops followed the same general course.

World crop production per capita and world wheat production per capita were low during the war period, and have declined in recent years (figure 46).

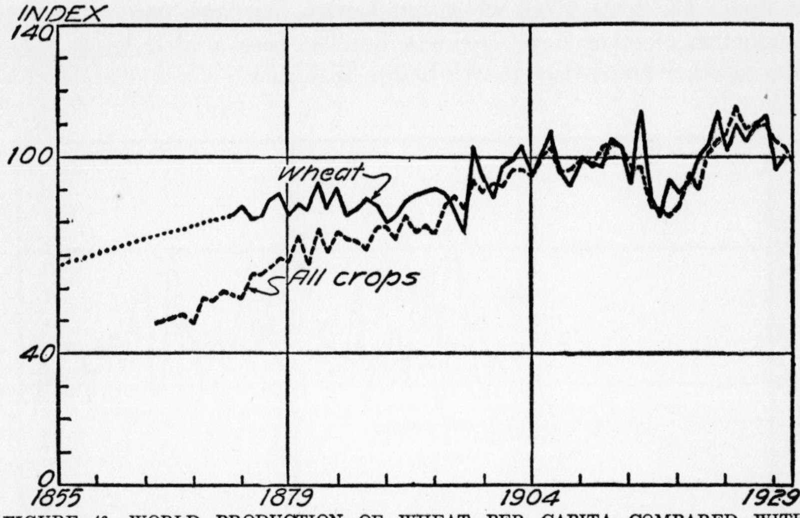

FIGURE 46.—WORLD PRODUCTION OF WHEAT PER CAPITA COMPARED WITH THE PRODUCTION OF ALL CROPS PER CAPITA, 1855-1931.

1910-14 = 100.

There is a very striking agreement between the production of wheat and the production of all crops. The world production of wheat in recent years has not been excessive compared with the production of other products or compared with the long-time trend.

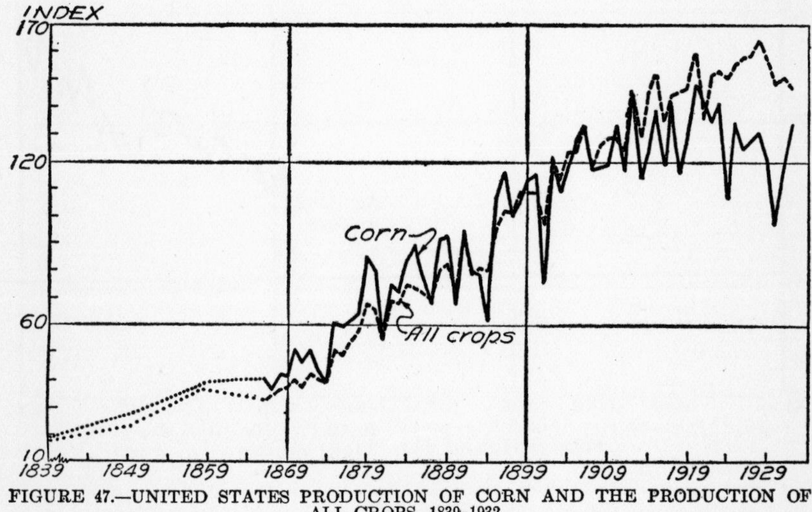

FIGURE 47.—UNITED STATES PRODUCTION OF CORN AND THE PRODUCTION OF ALL CROPS, 1839-1932.

1880-1914 = 100.

Up to about 1910, the production of corn expanded in about the same proportion as the production of all crops. Since then, corn production has declined in spite of the increase in the production of all crops.

The data do not indicate that the world wheat acreage should be reduced.

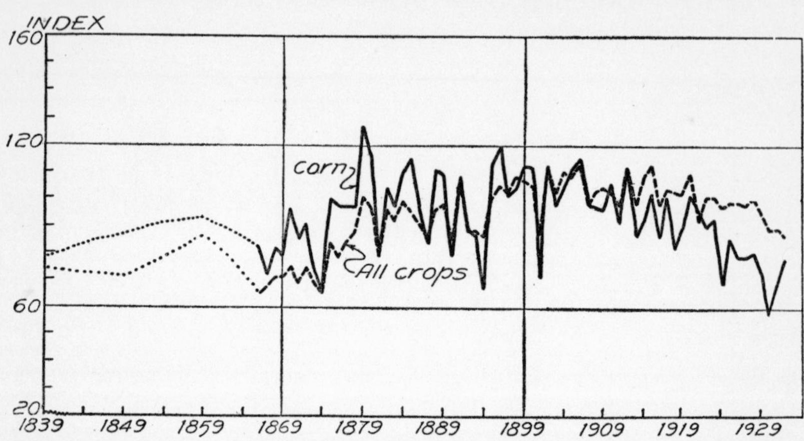

FIGURE 48.—UNITED STATES PRODUCTION OF CORN PER CAPITA COMPARED WITH THE PRODUCTION OF ALL CROPS PER CAPITA, 1839-1932.
1880-1914 = 100.

From 1869 to 1910, the production of corn per capita followed very closely the production of all crops. In recent years, there has been a striking decline in the production of corn per capita.

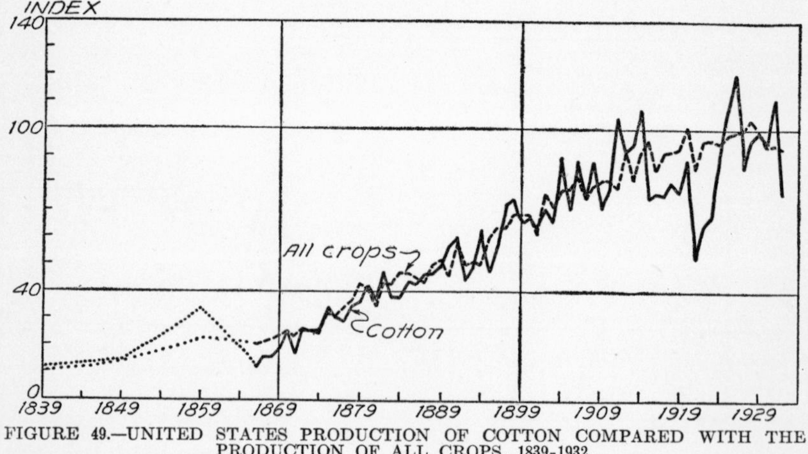

FIGURE 49.—UNITED STATES PRODUCTION OF COTTON COMPARED WITH THE PRODUCTION OF ALL CROPS, 1839-1932.
1926-30 = 100.

The production of cotton has followed very closely the production of all crops. From 1915 to 1923, there was a succession of comparatively short crops.

Corn.—Until recent years, the production of corn in the United States kept fairly close to that of all crops. Since 1910, it has not kept pace with the production of other crops. The production was particularly low in 1930, owing to a severe drought (figures 47 and 48).

World production of corn kept fairly close to the production of other crops for many years, but has been low since 1924.

Cotton.—The United States production of cotton has in general followed the production of other crops very closely, but in recent years

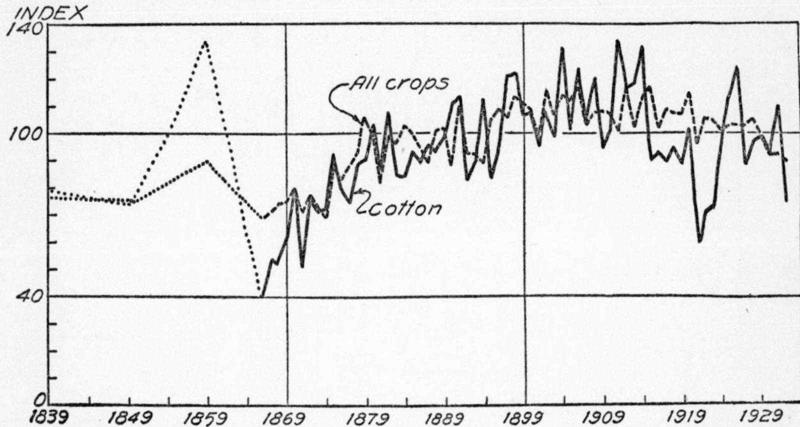

FIGURE 50.—UNITED STATES PRODUCTION OF COTTON PER CAPITA COMPARED WITH THE PRODUCTION OF ALL CROPS PER CAPITA, 1839-1932.
1926-30 = 100.
The production of cotton per capita follows very closely the production of all crops per capita.

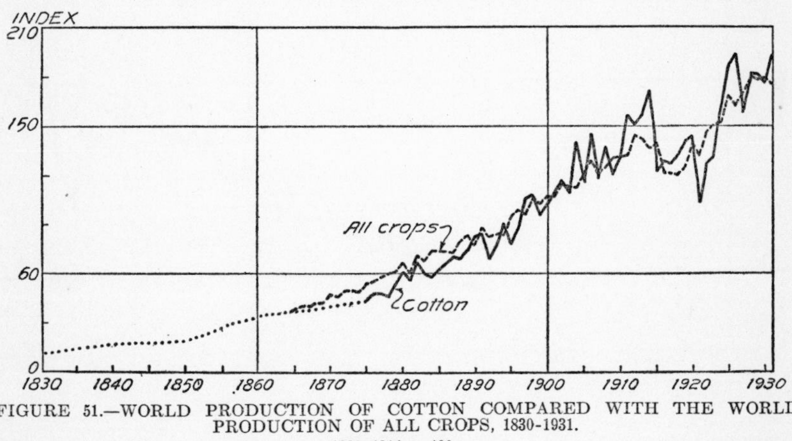

FIGURE 51.—WORLD PRODUCTION OF COTTON COMPARED WITH THE WORLD PRODUCTION OF ALL CROPS, 1830-1931.
1880-1914 = 100.
The world production of cotton has followed with remarkable similarity the production of all crops.

the fluctuations have been extremely violent (figures 49 and 50). This has been due in no small measure to the boll-weevil. In some years the boll-weevil damage is so slight that the production is very high.

The production in 1927-30 was not high. Production in 1931 was high and the demand was very low. The cotton situation was therefore bad because the low consumption resulted in the piling up of stocks.

World production of cotton and of other crops is shown in figures 51 and 52. Cotton has kept reasonably close to all other crops.

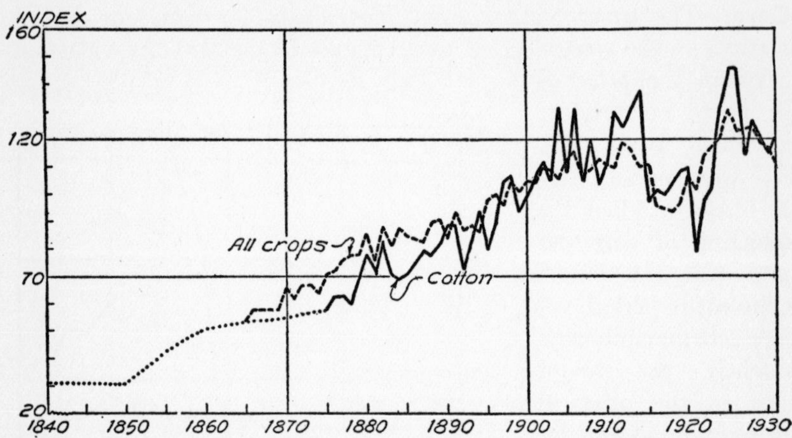

FIGURE 52.—WORLD PRODUCTION OF COTTON PER CAPITA COMPARED WITH THE PRODUCTION OF ALL CROPS PER CAPITA, 1840-1931.
1880-1914 = 100.
The production of cotton per capita follows the general course of the production of all crops per capita.

No indication has been found for a striking change in the need for any one major crop or for all crops.

PRODUCTION AND PRICE

All commodities.—The total basic production of all commodities per capita in percentage of the preceding five years is shown in figure 53. Only a little of the changes in prices would be suspected from this curve. There was a long period of rising prices from 1896 to 1914; a violent rise in prices from 1914 to 1920, followed by two violent declines. Certainly no one would have forecasted the price changes by looking at the changes in production.

For an explanation of the price changes, we must look outside the commodities themselves. The logical place to look is at the other side of the price equation—the supply of and demand for money.

Wheat.—The production of wheat per capita and the December prices of wheat at New York City are shown in figure 54. As in the case of all commodities, it is evident that prices cannot be explained by looking at production.

The production of wheat per capita compared with the purchasing power of the December price of wheat in terms of all commodities is shown in figure 55. The production of wheat does have considerable relationship to the purchasing power of wheat, i.e., to the amount of all goods that a bushel of wheat would exchange for (page 58).

Corn.—The overwhelming price movements for corn are due to variations in the general price level (figures 13 and 48). Any attempt to explain the price of corn based on production alone would fail. This was particularly true in 1930, when the production of corn per capita was the lowest for the entire period, yet prices fell precipitously. Evidently the major factor in the price of corn must be looked for outside the production of corn.

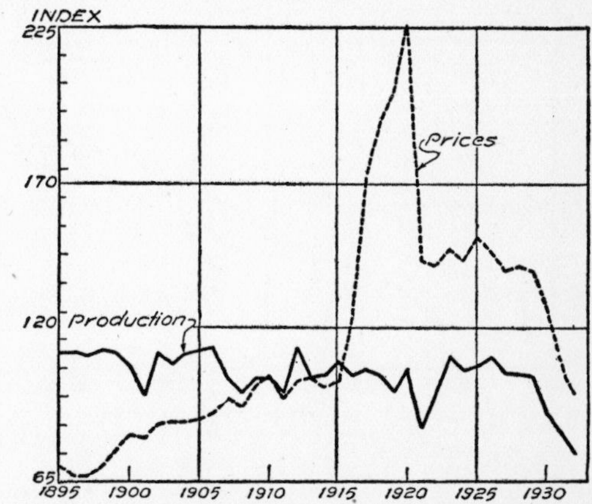

FIGURE 53.—PRODUCTION OF BASIC COMMODITIES PER CAPITA IN PER CENT OF THE PREVIOUS FIVE YEARS AND WHOLESALE PRICES OF ALL COMMODITIES, 1895-1932.

1910-14 = 100.

Prices cannot be explained by variations in production. They can be explained by variations in the supply of and demand for gold.

Cotton.—These major price movements for cotton are not explained by the production curve (figures 16 and 52). There is some short-time relationship of production to prices. Evidently one must look beyond cotton to explain the movement of cotton prices.

Prices as an indication of over-production.—Relative prices furnish some indication of the relative abundance of different commodities provided wholesale prices are compared with wholesale prices and retail prices with retail prices. Prices paid to farmers for food and wholesale prices of all commodities are shown in figure 56 and tables 29 and 1. From 1917 to 1919, prices for food were slightly higher than other wholesale prices. From 1920 to 1924, they were slightly lower than all commodities. From 1925 to 1929, food was higher than all commodities. The same conclusions hold if city wholesale prices of food are used (table 4).

From these data, one would infer that there was probably a slight shortage of food for three years followed by a surplus which in turn was followed by a period in which the food supply was normal.

Retail prices of American-grown food and the cost of living are shown in figure 57 and tables 30 and 36. From 1917 to 1919, food was higher in price than the cost of living. In the period 1920-25, the situation was reversed. From 1926 to 1930, food at retail averaged nearly as high as the cost of living.

Some of these relationships are due to different amounts of lag, when inflation and deflation occur, but they seem to suggest that

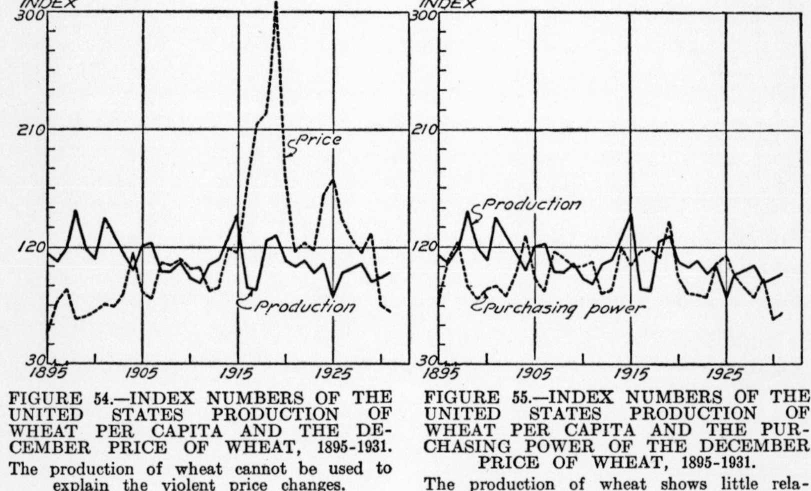

FIGURE 54.—INDEX NUMBERS OF THE UNITED STATES PRODUCTION OF WHEAT PER CAPITA AND THE DECEMBER PRICE OF WHEAT, 1895-1931.
The production of wheat cannot be used to explain the violent price changes.

FIGURE 55.—INDEX NUMBERS OF THE UNITED STATES PRODUCTION OF WHEAT PER CAPITA AND THE PURCHASING POWER OF THE DECEMBER PRICE OF WHEAT, 1895-1931.
The production of wheat shows little relationship to prices, but it shows considerable relationship to the purchasing power.

there was a surplus of food for about five years, followed by a five-year period when there was no surplus. When the food production per capita is low and when the food sells for a price as high as prices of other commodities taken at the same point in the channels of trade, there is no evidence of a surplus.

Neither the production of any one commodity nor the production of all commodities can be relied on to show the most important price movements. Attempts to control the general price level through production are evidently doomed to failure. If the price of one commodity is out of line with all commodities, it may be brought into line by changing its production; but when the whole price level falls, this method cannot be followed.

Geographical changes in production.—It has been contended that striking geographic changes in production will take place which will

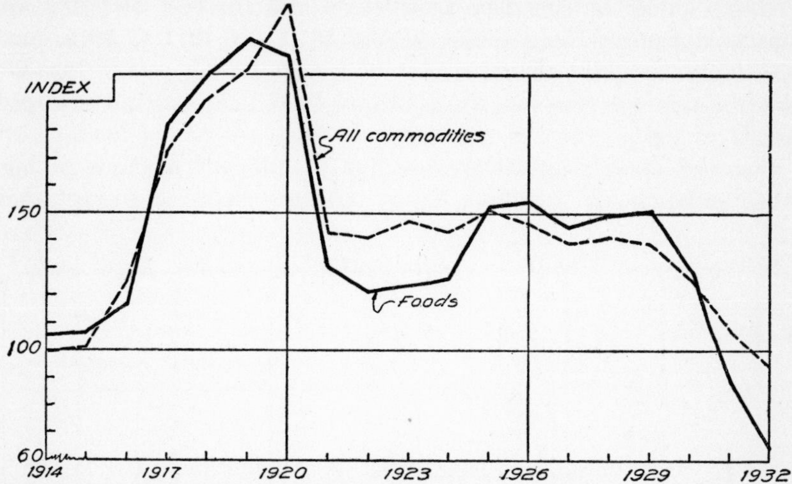

FIGURE 56.—INDEX NUMBERS OF PRICES PAID TO FARMERS FOR FOOD AND PRICES OF ALL COMMODITIES, 1914-32.

1910-14 = 100.

From 1920 to 1924, food was low in relation to all commodities. From 1925 to 1929, food was high compared with all commodities.

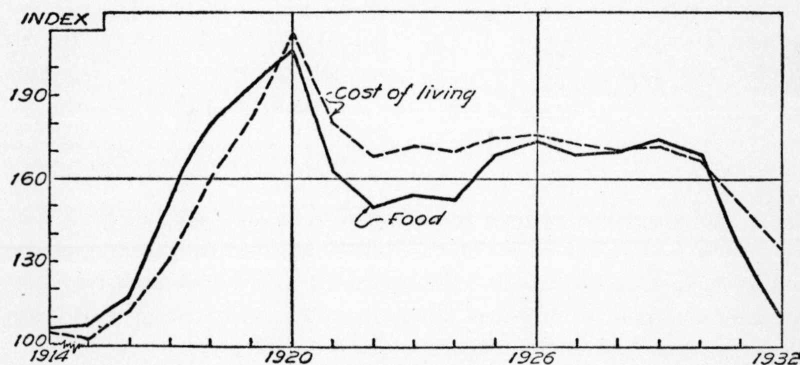

FIGURE 57.—INDEX NUMBERS OF RETAIL PRICES OF FOOD AND THE COST OF LIVING, 1914-32.

1910-14 = 100.

From 1920 to 1925, the cost of living was higher than food at retail. From 1926 to 1930, they were about alike.

disturb the normal course of events and will increase crop production more than has been the case in the past. It is doubtful that the expected increased production in Russia, Siberia, or the Tropics will result in greater changes in the physical volume of crop production than did the great geographical changes in production that occurred in the United States from 1840 to 1900, when the agricultural products of the middle west were made available to the world.

Technological changes in transportation.—It is also contended that future changes in transportation will change the rates of increase in physical volume of production. Certainly we cannot now foresee what will happen in the field of aviation, transportation of power, and the like. Men living in the days of sailing vessels did not foresee the revolution in water transportation that came with steam. The substitution of the railroad for the turnpike, the auto for the buggy, and the truck for the wagon were quite as striking changes as our grandchildren are likely to see, yet these innovations produced no striking changes in the physical volume of production.

Technological changes in production.—Whenever deflation occurs, it is attributed to the introduction of new machinery, and spectacular instances are cited of great increases in efficiency. These increases are far less than they appear. A common fallacy is to compare the amount of wheat that a farmer can raise with a tractor and combine with the amount he can raise with horses and the threshing machine. Superficial observation counts all this as increase in efficiency, but many invisible men are working back of the tractor. The farmer raised the horses and raised the feed for them. These horses did the work of producing wheat and hauling it to town and raising their own feed. With the new methods, only the farm worker is visible, but work that he formerly did is now done by a large number of other workers who mine the iron, roll the steel, and make and transport the tractor. Still other workers are producing, transporting, and refining oil. Others are producing combines and trucks. Still others print catalogues, and sell and finance the machines. The total time of the farmer and all these invisible workers must be combined to determine the real increase in efficiency in wheat production. The saving of human time is greatly exaggerated when superficial comparisons are made.

A new machine in a factory causes the discharge of many men; the employment of many other men to make and transport the machine and the power to run it are less obvious but just as real.

The introduction of machinery does not take place in all operations at once. For any given factory it may be sudden. For all industry it is very gradual—first here and then there a new machine is introduced.

The cream separator, power churn, reaper, grain binder, truck, tractor, corn husker, combine, milk refrigeration, power loom, Bessemer process, McKay sewing machine, rayon, cracking process, motorization of industry, stamping machines, internal-combustion engine, carbon dioxide ice, paper towels and napkins, pneumatic tire, radio, arc welding, and the like, all instituted great technological changes in production. So far as can be observed, these technological changes produced no perceptible change in the rate of increase in physical volume of production, because they did not all occur at once, and most of them set numbers of invisible men at work back of the new machine so that the increase in efficiency was not so great as it appears from superficial observation.

Many wild statements are made about the capacity of the nation to double or treble production. It is impossible for the nation suddenly to increase its production above the normal trend. It is possible for production to be suddenly decreased by severe unemployment, such as occurred in 1921 and 1932. After such periods, production can quickly return to the normal level. It is very unfortunate that, in periods when money rises in value, unwise efforts are put forth to reduce the nation's output. There is some danger that some of these proposals may reduce output and so prevent the steady progress in the physical well-being which is so much desired.

Surplus plants.—When deflation occurs, multitudes of plants are idle and unemployed persons begin to estimate the production that would occur if all plants worked full time. They reach two fallacious conclusions: that the nation's output could be increased many times and that the number of plants is far too great.

They assume that unlimited labor supply and raw materials are available for each plant, and arrive at the illusion of enormous capacity for multiplying output. They forget that if every plant worked every hour in the day, it would require more labor and raw materials than exist. It would be very easy for a single plant to multiply its output in accordance with the fantastic estimates.

This is a common error in economic thinking. It assumes that what all can do is the sum of what each could do, without giving attention to the effect that this would have on basic conditions.

This type of estimation also fails to take into consideration the normal status of a progressive society. More chairs and beds are needed than there are people. We cannot expect all the hotels to be filled every night of the year.

In an active society, there are new factories and obsolescent factories. The new ones may work most of the time. There are old ones in all degrees of decadence. The demand must be supplied when it comes. If the demand is high, the old factories work for a time.

Much of the demand is seasonal. It is often cheaper to have a surplus plant capacity that is idle part of the year than to run a plant making products that will not be wanted for many months and that must be financed and stored.

Demand is often regional. It may be cheaper to have a regional plant to supply the needs of that region even though a plant at some distant point may be idle.

In periods of extreme fluctuations, too many plants of a particular type may be built. Of other types of plants, there may be too few; just as the country may have too many cattle and too few hogs.

There are also movements of industry from one section of the country to another. This requires that plants in one area go out of use. This is usually done by operating only in periods of special prosperity for a time before they permanently close.

Variations in plant capacity are influenced by business cycles and have some influence on cycles. They may be a cause of a severe depression in one industry but are never the cause of a major depression in all industries.

BIBLIOGRAPHY

Day, E. E., An Index of the Physical Volume of Production, The Review of Economic Statistics, Vol. II, pp. 246-259, September 1920; Vol. II, pp. 287-299, October 1920; Vol. II, pp. 361-67, December 1920; Vol. III, pp. 19-22, January 1921; Vol. VI, No. 3, pp. 193-204, July 1924.

Day, E. E., and Persons, W. M., An Index of the Physical Volume of Production, The Review of Economic Statistics, Vol. II, pp. 309-337. November 1920.

Day, E. E., and Thomas, W., The Growth of Manufactures, 1899 to 1923, United States Department of Commerce, Bureau of Census Monograph VIII, 1928.

Hamlin, S., and others, The Menace of Overproduction. 1930.

Persons, W. M., Forecasting Business Cycles, pp. 86, 170, 180, 182, and 188. 1931.

Snyder, C., Overproduction and Business Cycles, Proceedings of the Academy of Political Science, Vol. XIV, No. 3, pp. 5-31. June 1931.

Snyder, C., New Measures of the Relations of Credit and Trade, Proceedings of the Academy of Political Science, Vol. XIII, No. 4, pp. 16-34. January 1930.

Stewart, W. W., An Index Number of Production, The American Economic Review, Vol. XI, No. 1, pp. 57-69. March 1921.

Studensky, G. A., The Agricultural Depression and the Technical Revolution in Farming, Journal of Farm Economics, Vol. XII, No. 4, pp. 552-572. October 1930.

Warren, G. F., and Pearson, F. A., Physical Volume of Production in the United States, Farm Economics No. 74, pp. 1678-1685. February 1932.

Warren, G. F., and Pearson, F. A., Physical Volume of Production in the

United States, Cornell University Agricultural Experiment Station, Memoir 144. 1932.

Memorandum on Production and Trade, 1923 to 1928/29. League of Nations II. Economic and Financial 1930. II. 8. June 1930.

Review of World Production, 1925-1931. League of Nations II. Economic and Financial 1932. II. A. 13. July 1932.

CHAPTER IV

MONEY

What is money?—"Money is the medium of exchange. Whatever performs this function, does this work, is money, no matter what it is made of, and no matter how it came to be a medium at first, or why it continues to be such. So long as, in any community, there is an article which all producers take freely and as a matter of course, in exchange for whatever they have to sell . . . that article is money, be it white, yellow, or black, hard or soft, animal, vegetable, or mineral. There is no other test of money than this."[1]

The most primitive way of exchanging goods is by barter. This has serious limitations. If one has a horse that he does not want and desires a cow, he must find another person who has a cow but prefers to exchange it for a horse. Since the horse and cow may not be considered to be equally valuable, much trouble is likely to occur in finding something to throw in, to balance the trade. The difficulties of transferring property by barter are so great that even in primitive society some kind of money is commonly used for many transactions. Aristotle said, "To effect their exchanges, men contrived something to give and take among themselves, which, being valuable in itself, had the advantage of being easily passed from hand to hand for the needs of life—such as iron or silver, or something else of that kind of which they first determined merely the size and weight, but eventually put a stamp on it in order to save the trouble of weighing, for the stamp was placed there as a sign of value."[2]

In the most primitive society, goods were exchanged by barter, but this method was so inconvenient that the idea developed of using one commodity as a medium of exchange. This was the first step in developing a measure of value. Whenever a group of men move into a region where there is no money, they soon begin to use one commodity or a few commodities as money. In pioneer days, hunters and

[1] Walker, Francis A., Political Economy, Advanced course, 3rd edition, p. 123, 1887. Henry Holt and Co., Publishers.

[2] Aristotle, Politics, I, 9.

trappers commonly chose some fur as the medium of exchange. Beaver skins were commonly used.

The early settlers in Virginia used tobacco.

In 1642, Virginia passed an act making it illegal to make contracts based on silver, and tobacco became the legal medium of exchange.[3] In order to prevent inflation, the tobacco acreage was restricted by requiring the settlers to raise a certain proportion of corn and wheat.

In Maryland also, tobacco was the chief medium of exchange. Salaries of members of the Assembly, private obligations, lawyers' fees, and donations to clergymen were fixed in pounds of tobacco. Because of its bulk, uncertain quality, absence of inspection, and increasing production, protests arose.[4] The increased production caused a depreciation of the tobacco currency, and prices of other things rose, just as prices rise when any other kind of money is increased. To meet the situation, plants were destroyed and attempts made to control acreage, and demands were made for some other kind of money.

In Massachusetts, cattle were used as money. Apparently taxes were no more popular than when paid in gold, for it is recorded that the farmers paid their taxes with inferior cattle. In 1719, South Carolina made rice legal tender for payment of taxes.[5]

The Romans used cattle as money. When they adopted copper and silver, they stamped the figure of an ox on the coins.

Our vocabulary gives other indications of cattle money. The word "pecuniary" comes from a Latin word meaning cattle; "fee" from

[3] Holmes, A., American Annals, Vol. 1, pp. 204-5, 1805, reports that the price of passage from England was in terms of tobacco. "Sir Edward Sandys, the treasurer, proposed to the Virginia company to send over a freight of young women, to become wives for the planters. The proposal was applauded; and ninety girls, 'young and uncorrupt,' were sent over in the ships, that arrived this year (1620); and, the year following, sixty more, handsome, and well recommended to the company for their virtuous education and demeanor. The price of a wife, at the first, was one hundred pounds of tobacco: but, as the number became scarce, the price was increased to one hundred and fifty pounds, the value of which, in money, was three shillings per pound. This debt for wives, it was ordered, should have the precedency of all other debts, and be first recoverable."

According to Gouge, W. M., A Short History of Paper Money and Banking in the United States, Part II, p. 4, 1833, "The Rev. Mr. Weems, a Virginia writer, intimates that it would have done a man's heart good, to see the gallant, young Virginians, hastening to the water side, when a ship arrived from London, each carrying a bundle of the best tobacco under his arm, and each taking back with him a beautiful and virtuous young wife."

[4] Behrens, K. L., Paper Money in Maryland, 1727-1789, Johns Hopkins University Studies in Historical and Political Science Series XLI, No. 1, pp. 10-11, 1923.

[5] Angell, N., The Story of Money, pp. 84, 85, 1930.

a Germanic word for cattle; "rupee" from a Sanscrit word meaning cattle.

The second great step in advance was made when the metal was weighed and stamped, that is, when coinage began.

A third important step was taken when individuals and governments became so reliable that paper certificates for a given amount of the commodity passed instead of the commodity itself.

Some of the characteristics that make a commodity good for use as money are high value for its volume and weight, divisibility, durability, uniformity, and stability in value. Gold and silver have generally satisfied these requirements better than other commodities. They have all the characteristics except the important one of stability in value.

No single commodity has a stable value.—The world has generally used some single commodity as money. The particular commodity chosen has been extremely variable. Silver has been used for a considerable time and is still used by the majority of mankind. The single gold standard has been used for a relatively short time. Innumerable commodities have been tried; salt, ivory, hides, horses, wampum, copper, iron, tin, lead, silver, gold, platinum, have all been used as money, and no one of them has been found satisfactory because no single commodity is stable when compared with the average of all other commodities. Whenever the one that happened to be used as money either increased or decreased in value compared to the average of all commodities, unsatisfactory conditions developed. Monetary history is one of chaotic change from one commodity to another, in the search for something that has a stable value. This search has ever failed and is doomed to eternal failure, because there is no such thing as a single commodity which is stable in value. The law of supply and demand cannot thus easily be repealed.

The value of any commodity varies with the supply of it and the demand for it. Selecting a commodity as money does not prevent the law of supply and demand from operating on it. It does increase the demand. When a commodity is selected as money, it has its price fixed for payment of debts and for other purposes. Its ratio to other commodities is not fixed. For example, when copper was used as money and large quantities of it were found, its price was fixed for debts and other payments, but its value relative to cattle was not fixed and cattle rose in price. The "money illusion" is so universal that in such a circumstance practically everyone believed that it was the high demand for cattle or short supply of them rather than the large supply of money which made cattle high in price, or believed that the owners of cattle were profiteering.

When various countries began to change to the gold standard, the lessened demand for silver reduced its value and raised prices in China, which was on a silver basis. During the World War period, when most of the countries of the world stopped using gold as money, the lessened demand for gold reduced its value as compared with other commodities. In both cases the popular explanation was that the increase in prices was due to scarcity of all commodities or to profiteering.

The very high demand for gold after the Panic of 1929 greatly increased its value. The money illusion still held almost as fully as in the days of the Egyptians, and the common explanation was overproduction of everything else rather than the high demand for gold.

Subsidiary coins.—No single commodity can be divided into convenient small units and at the same time make convenient large units. For paying large sums, silver is too bulky. For small units, gold is so valuable as to make the coins too small. Silver also is too valuable to make a convenient-sized coin of the lowest denomination. Hence the use of nickel and copper for the smaller subdivisions of the currency. Originally the smaller coins were intended to be worth their face value, but this resulted in having them melted whenever values of the particular metals rose, therefore they are now made small enough so that they are worth less as metal than as coin.

Paper money.—In the most primitive society the medium of exchange has to be of intrinsic value in itself, but as civilization progresses a part or all of the currency can be made up of promises to pay. The precious metals are left in the care of the government or some commercial agent where they will not wear out.

For very small units, metal is more convenient; but for large amounts, paper is lighter and less likely to be lost. As confidence develops, practically all gold comes to be held in vaults and the actual currency is paper. The amount of paper money may be greater than the amount of metal on which it is based, hence the use of paper money may increase the amount of the medium of exchange and affect prices. The simplest form of paper money is a certificate stating that the equivalent quantity of precious metal is deposited and is available on demand. This is really a warehouse receipt for gold. But some currencies have passed this stage and more paper is in circulation than there is precious metal on deposit. The paper then has back of it some metal, and some government or private credit. Paper money bears somewhat the same relationship to gold that a meal ticket bears to a meal. The amount of paper that can be circulated without falling below par depends on the economic and political stability of the country. In a general way, the limits are fairly well known. If paper is issued far beyond these limits, the confidence of the public is shaken, and so many persons call for the redemption of the paper in gold that the government cannot meet the demands. More gold must be obtained, the paper reduced, or specie payment must be suspended. During the World War, most of the countries of the world suspended specie payment. Many of them also suspended gold payments in 1931.

Bank credit.—A more recent development is the use of bank checks as a medium of exchange. It is estimated that checks are used in about 90 per cent of all business transactions in the United States. With our present system, the gold is largely held by the government and in the Federal Reserve Banks. The commercial banks depend largely on paper currency. Actual business is done largely with checks. There may be more paper currency than gold, and there is more bank credit than paper money. Just as paper money is more easily transferred than gold, so bank checks are more easily transferred than paper money. In the United States, the amount of currency per dollar of gold has declined for many years, but the amount of bank credit has risen.

A bank check passing from man to man replaces money. This makes it possible for a greater number of transactions to be made at a given price level with a given quantity of currency. If checks were not used, prices would be lower.

Clearing-houses.—Another means of increasing the amount of business that one dollar can do in a year is the clearing-house system. If there are three banks in a town, each one will cash checks drawn on the others. At the close of business each day, the balances could be settled by each bank collecting for all the checks it cashed for the other banks, but a simpler method is to settle the combined net balances. Settlement for a large district may be made in the same way.

The first clearing-house was opened in New York City in 1853. A bank facilitates exchange between individuals or groups. Individuals settle their claims against each other by the transfer of bank credit. Banks settle their claims against each other by transfer of credits in the clearing-house. In each case, only the net balance of all claims is paid. The use of the clearing-house reduces the amount of money that must be transferred from one part of the country to another. This again increases the number of transactions which a dollar can make.

With the progress of civilization, many devices have been employed to reduce the bulkiness and to hasten the transfer of money and at the same time to throw adequate safeguards around the institutions that have made this possible. Gold and silver are the basis of nearly all monetary standards, but paper money, credit, and checks have supplemented them or often replaced them so that a proper interpretation of the price question involves an appreciation of all the instruments that facilitate exchange, whether they be gold, silver, paper, checks, or credit. But if the country is on a metal basis, the basic fact that is always of primary importance is the supply of the money metal and the demand for it.

A managed paper currency may be used as money, but this has usually occurred when the metal currency has broken down so that it is a means of procedure when the metal standard has failed. It could be maintained permanently in a stable country.

What is a price?—Price is a ratio of the value of a given amount of some commodity or service to the value of a given amount of the commodity used as money. It is a ratio of two values. Each value is determined by the supply of and demand for that thing.

The given amount of the money commodity is given a money name so that confusion arises. For example, 23.22 grains of gold is named a dollar. But this is merely a duplicate name for 23.22 grains of gold. Naming it a dollar does not change the fact any more than naming 2000 pounds a ton changes it.

There are four variables in price, not two. A high price may be due to a short supply of the commodity or a high demand for it, or may be due to a large supply of the commodity used as money or a low demand for it, or it may be due to some combination of these variables.

Most of the popular errors about prices are due to the assumption that price is dependent on two factors only, that is, the supply of and demand for the particular commodity or service.

Payment may be made by note, check, or paper currency, but these are only convenient go-betweens. They represent the standard money (gold), just as the value of an order for a bushel of wheat is determined by the value of wheat.

The value of gold is determined by its supply and by the demand for it as money and for use in the arts. The use of checks to replace gold currency does not affect the value of gold except that by substitution they reduce the world demand for gold. A more rapid use of gold enables an ounce of it to perform more services and so reduces world demand. But price remains the ratio of two values—the value of the commodity to the value of gold.

The price of wheat may be expressed as follows:

Ratio of supply of and demand for gold to supply of and demand for wheat = price of wheat, or

$$\frac{\text{Supply of gold and demand for wheat}}{\text{Demand for gold and supply of wheat}} = \text{Price of wheat}$$

If the expression is to be in dollars per bushel, then the units of measure are 60 pounds for wheat and 23.22 grains for gold.[6]

If there is a large amount of wheat, it reduces the price. If there is a large demand, it increases the price. If the supply of gold is high, it increases the price of wheat. If there is a large demand for gold, it reduces the price of wheat.

If the supply of gold were doubled, the price of wheat would be doubled. If the supply of wheat were doubled, it would halve the price of wheat. There are no examples for wheat as extreme as this, but there are examples that show the shape of the curve (page 89).

If 100 bushels of wheat are required to buy a horse and if at a later date 200 bushels are necessary, the value of horses in terms of wheat has doubled, and the value of wheat in terms of horses has decreased by one-half. If wheat were used for money, we would say that horses had doubled in price. If horses were used for money, we would say that wheat had fallen in price. Whether the change is due to a rise in the value of horses or to a drop in the value of wheat cannot be determined until horses and wheat are compared with other things. If when buying many different things it is found that wheat generally will exchange for half as much as formerly, it is evident that wheat is cheap. If it is found that horses generally exchange for twice the usual amount of other things, the conclusion is that horses are high. The relation of gold to prices is little understood, but it is no different from the illustration given above.

Value of gold and price of gold.—From April 2, 1792, to June 27, 1834, the price of gold in the United States was fixed at $19.39 per ounce. Since 1834, except during the Civil War when its price was not fixed, it has been fixed at $20.67 per ounce regardless of the supply of it or demand for it. Although a legislative act may fix the price of gold, that is, may name a given weight of it as one dollar, it cannot fix the value.

[6] The gold dollar is a gold piece weighing 25.8 grains, nine-tenths fine. This makes it contain 23.22 grains of pure gold.

Value is comparative.—There is no such thing as absolute value any more than there is absolute length. All measurement is comparative. There is, of course, no way of determining the value of gold or the length of anything except by comparing it with something other than itself. Therefore, gold must be compared with something other than a dollar, which is merely another name for 23.22 grains of fine gold. Of course, 23 grains of gold are always worth 23 grains of gold. A pound of silver is also always worth a pound of silver.

The prices of ten important basic commodities are given in table 7. In June 1929, a bushel of corn at Chicago was worth 92 cents. Two years later it was worth 57 cents. This merely means that in 1929 an ounce of gold exchanged for 1260 pounds of corn. Two years later, it exchanged for 2033 pounds of corn, although the corn crop was 26 per cent smaller, in fact, the smallest crop in 29 years. In spite of this extremely short crop, it took 61 per cent more corn to buy a given weight of gold than was required in 1929.

In 1929, an ounce of gold would exchange for 194 pounds of hogs

TABLE 7.—POUNDS OF COMMODITIES REQUIRED TO BUY AN OUNCE OF GOLD IN JUNE 1929 AND JUNE 1931*

Commodity	Prices		Pounds required to buy an ounce of gold		Per cent increase
	June 1929	June 1931	June 1929	June 1931	
Corn, contract grade, Chicago, per bushel	$ 0.92	$ 0.57	1260	2033	61
Wheat, No. 2 red, Chicago, per bushel	1.22	0.75	1016	1656	63
Hogs, fair to choice heavy butchers, Chicago, per 100 pounds	10.66	6.50	194	318	64
Cotton, middling, New York, pound	0.188	0.084	110	246	124
Pig iron, basic valley furnace, per ton	18.50	15.50	2235	2667	19
Copper ingot electrolytic, refinery, per pound	0.178	0.0825	116	251	116
Lead, pig, New York, per pound	0.070	0.0375	295	551	87
Tin, pig, New York, per pound	0.443	0.225	47	92	96
Zinc, slab, New York, per pound	0.070	0.0355	295	582	97
Sulfate of ammonia, New York, per 100 pounds	2.22	1.85	931	1117	20
Average increase	....	....	....	....	75

* Warren, G. F., and Pearson, F. A., Value of Gold, Farm Economics No. 71, p. 1552, June 1931.

at Chicago. In 1931, it would exchange for 318 pounds. The supply of hogs had decreased 10 per cent, but it required 64 per cent more hogs to get an ounce of gold.

The cotton crop was almost as large in the second case as in the first, and it required 124 per cent more cotton to get an ounce of gold than was required in 1929.

On the average, the exchange value of gold for the ten commodities increased 75 per cent (table 7). This change was not due to the change in the supply of the commodities, because it applied to commodities, the supply of which was very short. When compared with the average of 784 commodities, gold increased 32 per cent in value. Since it was not the supply of other commodities that caused the change, there must have been a general decline in the demand for goods, or else the change was due to gold.

It should never be forgotten that so long as the United States is on a gold basis every dollar is 23.22 grains of gold, whether the certificate entitling the bearer to get it is a silver dollar, a paper dollar, or a check; just as a bushel of wheat is 60 pounds whether it be in one's hands as wheat, or a warehouse receipt, a bill of lading, or a future purchase on a grain market. These evidences of possession cannot permanently affect the value of wheat.

Purchasing power.—In order to tell whether a commodity is high or low in value, it may be compared with the level of prices of all commodities. For example, in 1929, the average farm price of wheat was 17 per cent above pre-war and the average of all commodities was 39 per cent above pre-war. Wheat was therefore relatively low in price. Its purchasing power was 84 ($1.17 \div 1.39 = 0.84$). This means that a bushel of wheat would buy 16 per cent less than the usual quantity of all commodities. Purchasing power is usually calculated by dividing the index number of prices by the average prices of all commodities at wholesale (table 1, page 10). The power to purchase other things is sometimes calculated.

Index numbers of prices of beef cattle and the purchasing power of beef cattle are shown in figure 58. This shows that cattle were high in price in 1919, but since everything else was high, the purchasing power was low. The price was high in spite of a surplus of cattle, because gold had a very low value. The true situation of the cattle industry is shown by the purchasing power. There was a surplus of cattle and the purchasing power was low.

If gold were stable in value, the two curves would be identical.

Fluctuations in the purchasing power of cattle are due to the supply of and demand for them, but fluctuations in price of cattle away from the purchasing power are due to the supply of gold and demand for it.

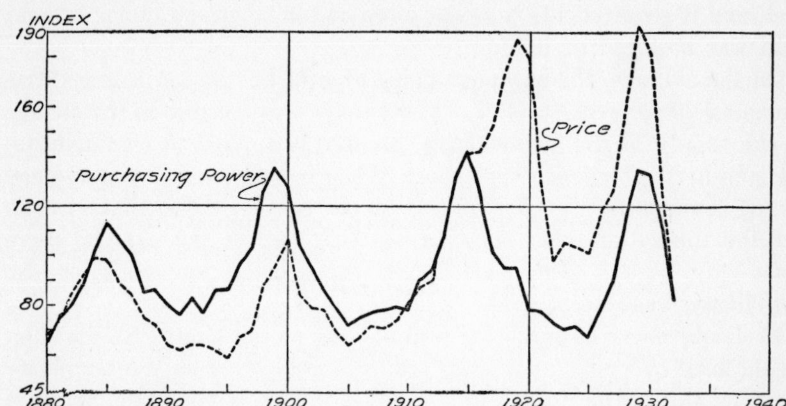

FIGURE 58.—INDEX NUMBERS OF THE JANUARY 1 FARM PRICE OF BEEF CATTLE AND THE PURCHASING POWER OF BEEF CATTLE IN THE UNITED STATES, 1880-1932. 1910-14 = 100.

The cycles in purchasing power of cattle are due to variations in supply of and demand for cattle. Fluctuations of prices from the purchasing power are due to the supply of or demand for gold. In 1919, prices were high in spite of a high supply.

BIBLIOGRAPHY

Angell, N., The Story of Money. 1930.

Cannan, E., Modern Currency and the Regulation of Its Value. 1931.

Cannan, E., Money: Its Connexion with Rising and Falling Prices. 1926.

Cassel, G., The World's Monetary Problems. 1921.

Cassel, G., The Theory of Social Economy. 1924.

Edie, L. D., Money, Bank Credit, and Prices. 1928.

Foster, W. T., and Catchings, W., Money, Pollak Foundation for Economic Research, No. 2, 1923.

Hawtrey, R. G., Currency and Credit. 1923.

Hayek, F. A., Prices and Production. 1931.

Helfferich, K., Money. 1927.

Keynes, J. M., Monetary Reform. 1924.

Marshall, A., Money, Credit, and Commerce. 1923.

Menger, K., On the Origin of Money. Economic Journal, Vol. II, pp. 239-255. June 1892.

Price, L. L., Money and Its Relation to Prices. 1913.

Robertson, D. H., Money. 1922.

Walker, F. A., Money. 1878.

Walker, F. A., Money in its Relations to Trade and Industry. 1889.

CHAPTER V

GOLD AND PRICES

VALUE OF GOLD

Value of gold in England.—The value of gold in England for 151 years shows the comparative amounts of other commodities that could be bought with an ounce of gold (figure 59 and table 8). Gold reached the highest value it has ever attained in 1932. Its value was even higher than in 1896. From 1914 to 1932, the fluctuations were more violent than at any previous time in 150 years. The value of gold has never been even approximately stable for more than a few years.

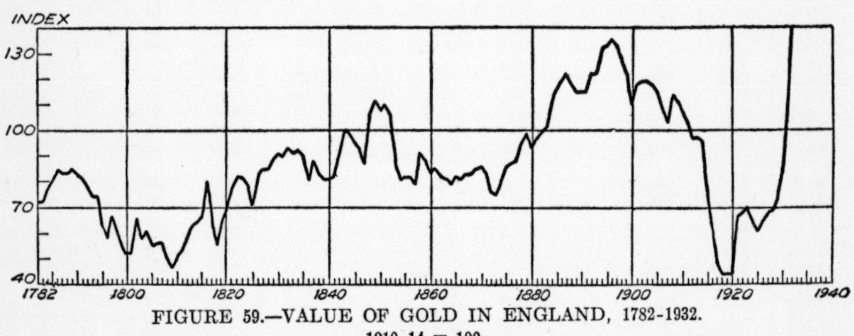

FIGURE 59.—VALUE OF GOLD IN ENGLAND, 1782-1932.
1910-14 = 100.

The amount of goods at wholesale prices that a given quantity of gold would exchange for in England has fluctuated violently during the past 150 years. Gold was rapidly rising in value in 1932.

Value of gold in the United States.—The changes in the amount of goods that could be purchased with an ounce of gold in the United States have been much the same as in England (figure 28). Gold reached the highest value ever known in the United States in 1896. There was another period of very high values in 1843. The lowest value ever known was in 1920. After 1920, the value of gold rose with great rapidity.

Previous to 1885, prices in England are a better measure of the value of gold than are prices in the United States. When a country is not on a gold basis, prices in currency, even though converted to gold, are somewhat theoretical.

TABLE 8.—WHOLESALE PRICES AND VALUE OF GOLD IN ENGLAND, 1782–1932*

1910–14 = 100

Year	Prices in currency	Prices in gold	Value of gold	Year	Prices in currency	Prices in gold	Value of gold	Year	Prices in currency	Prices in gold	Value of gold
....	....	....	....	1830	110	110	91	1880	107	107	93
....	....	....	....	1831	111	111	90	1881	103	103	97
1782	138	138	72	1832	107	107	93	1882	101	101	99
1783	138	138	72	1833	110	110	91	1883	99	99	101
1784	128	128	78	1834	109	109	92	1884	92	92	109
1785	124	124	81	1835	111	111	90	1885	87	87	115
1786	117	117	85	1836	123	123	81	1886	84	84	119
1787	121	121	83	1837	114	114	88	1887	82	82	122
1788	121	121	83	1838	120	120	83	1888	85	85	118
1789	117	117	85	1839	124	124	81	1889	87	87	115
1790	121	121	83	1840	124	124	81	1890	87	87	115
1791	123	123	81	1841	122	122	82	1891	87	87	115
1792	128	128	78	1842	110	110	91	1892	82	82	122
1793	136	136	74	1843	100	100	100	1893	82	82	122
1794	135	135	74	1844	101	101	99	1894	76	76	132
1795	162	162	62	1845	105	105	95	1895	75	75	133
1796	173	173	58	1846	107	107	93	1896	74	74	135
1797	152	152	66	1847	115	115	87	1897	75	75	133
1798	163	163	61	1848	94	94	106	1898	78	78	128
1799	180	180	56	1849	89	89	112	1899	82	82	122
1800	194	194	52	1850	93	93	108	1900	91	91	110
1801	211	193	52	1851	91	91	110	1901	85	85	118
1802	164	152	66	1852	94	94	106	1902	84	84	119
1803	178	173	58	1853	115	115	87	1903	84	84	119
1804	169	164	61	1854	123	123	81	1904	85	85	118
1805	188	182	55	1855	122	122	82	1905	87	87	115
1806	184	180	56	1856	122	122	82	1906	93	93	108
1807	182	178	56	1857	127	127	79	1907	97	97	103
1808	207	200	50	1858	110	110	91	1908	88	88	114
1809	222	216	46	1859	114	114	88	1909	90	90	111
1810	227	196	51	1860	120	120	83	1910	94	94	106
1811	203	188	53	1861	118	118	85	1911	97	97	103
1812	204	167	60	1862	122	122	82	1912	103	103	97
1813	207	159	63	1863	124	124	81	1913	103	103	97
1814	211	157	64	1864	127	127	79	1914	103	104	96
1815	182	150	67	1865	122	122	82	1915	131	128	78
1816	151	125	80	1866	123	123	81	1916	165	161	62
1817	165	162	62	1867	121	121	83	1917	212	207	48
1818	187	182	55	1868	120	120	83	1918	232	227	44
1819	162	154	65	1869	118	118	85	1919	249	227	44
1820	146	142	70	1870	116	116	86	1920	304	229	44
1821	128	128	78	1871	121	121	83	1921	188	149	67
1822	122	122	82	1872	132	132	76	1922	159	145	68
1823	124	124	81	1873	134	134	75	1923	156	147	70
1824	128	128	78	1874	123	123	81	1924	168	153	65
1825	141	141	71	1875	116	116	86	1925	165	164	61
1826	121	121	83	1876	115	115	87	1926	153	153	65
1827	117	117	85	1877	114	114	88	1927	148	148	68
1828	117	117	85	1878	105	105	95	1928	145	145	69
1829	112	112	89	1879	101	101	99	1929	139	139	72
								1930	117	117	85
								1931	100	93	108
								1932	97	70	143

* Prices from 1782 to 1820, Jevons, W. S., On the Variation of Prices of the Currency since 1782, Journal of Royal Statistical Society, Vol. 28, pp. 314–15, June 1865.

1821–1845, Sauerbeck, Augustus, Prices of Commodities and the Precious Metals, Journal of Royal Statistical Society, Vol. 49, p. 634, September 1886.

1846–1885, Sauerbeck, Augustus, Prices of Commodities and the Precious Metals, Journal of Royal Statistical Society, Vol. 49, p. 648, September 1886.

1886–1920, Editor of the Statist, Wholesale Prices of Commodities in 1920, Journal of Royal Statistical Society, Vol. 84, part 2, p. 260, March 1921.

1921–1929, Editor of the Statist, Wholesale Prices of Commodities in 1929, Journal of Royal Statistical Society, Vol. 93, Part II, p. 279, March 1930.

The data on the 1867–77 base were converted to 1910–14 = 100 by multiplying by 1.2107.

The yearly figures were obtained by multiplying the yearly Statist figures (an average of 52 quotations) by 1.2107.

Similar material was presented in: Warren, G. F., and Pearson, F. A., The Agricultural Situation, p. 263, August 1924, John Wiley & Sons, New York; Warren, G. F., Pearson, F. A., and Stoker, H. M., Wholesale Prices for 213 Years, 1720 to 1932, Cornell University Agricultural Experiment Station Memoir 142, November 1932.

Index numbers of wholesale prices in the United States divided by the currency value of gold are given in table 9.

TABLE 9.—INDEX NUMBERS OF WHOLESALE PRICES IN THE UNITED STATES FROM TABLE 1 MULTIPLIED BY THE GOLD VALUE OF CURRENCY* (TABLE 69)

1910–14 = 100

Year	Jan.	Feb.	Mar.	Apr.	May	June	July	Aug.	Sept.	Oct.	Nov.	Dec.	Average
1814	186	184	182	182	179	179	178	177	159	165	166	172	176
1815	164	181	167	157	156	146	140	144	144	139	147	143	152
1816	140	146	138	136	131	131	141	142	144	141	143	146	140
1817	148	151	156	156	157	154	149	153	147	145	144	146	151
1837	123	129	127	120	105	100	104	102	99	102	104	109	110
1838	108	106	106	107	108	107	107	107	110	115	115	116	109
1862	96	96	96	97	92	88	85	92	90	86	92	93	92
1863	87	85	91	90	87	87	97	101	92	91	96	98	92
1864	98	98	99	97	99	90	85	89	101	100	92	98	96
1865	103	106	118	120	125	114	113	117	124	131	129	126	119
1866	129	127	133	130	130	116	115	118	120	121	122	124	124
1867	125	122	123	123	123	116	113	119	110	111	112	115	118
1868	113	112	117	119	117	113	110	109	109	112	114	113	113
1869	114	117	117	114	107	106	109	114	111	114	118	121	114
1870	117	116	120	118	119	120	116	114	117	118	118	116	117
1871	118	121	123	119	116	113	113	111	112	115	117	122	117
1872	122	121	123	124	121	120	118	119	121	118	122	121	121
1873	121	122	120	118	116	113	114	114	117	118	115	116	117
1874	117	116	116	113	113	112	114	113	113	111	109	108	113
1875	108	106	105	106	103	100	102	104	101	101	101	101	103
1876	101	101	100	100	97	94	95	96	98	100	102	105	99
1877	108	106	102	104	105	101	102	98	99	99	97	97	102
1878	95	94	93	92	89	87	89	90	90	89	88	86	90

* These are often called prices in gold. Very few transactions were made in gold. Prices would have been different had gold been used.

GOLD STOCKS AND PRICES

World gold stocks and prices in England.—World monetary stocks of gold are always rising (tables 10 and 11). This fact often leads to the erroneous belief that there is an adequate supply of gold. For instance, monetary stocks of gold increased from 138 million ounces in 1873 to 169 million ounces in 1890. This was used as an argument to show that the low prices of the nineties were not due to gold.

The world's monetary stocks of gold in 1914 were 388 million ounces. In 1931, they were 577 million ounces. This fact was used to prove that there must be enough gold.

The true measure of the adequacy of the monetary supply is whether there is enough to maintain the price level to which society is most nearly adjusted.

TABLE 10.—RELATION BETWEEN WORLD MONETARY STOCKS OF GOLD AND WORLD PHYSICAL VOLUME OF PRODUCTION AND WHOLESALE PRICES IN ENGLAND*

1880–1914 = 100

Year	Stocks of gold	Physical volume of production	Ratio	Prices in England
1850	23	22	105	105
1870	57	42	136	131
1890	73	74	99	98
1910	147	140	105	106

* From table 11.

World monetary stocks of gold are given in tables 10 and 11. From 1850 to 1910, monetary stocks of gold increased from 54 to 340 million ounces. The index numbers of gold stocks increased from 23 to 147 when the stocks of 1880-1914 are called 100.

In the same period, the physical volume of world production of all commodities increased from 22 to 140.

If the gold stock of 23 is divided by a production of 22, the result expressed as a percentage is 105. If the gold stocks of 147, sixty years later, are divided by 140, the same ratio, 105, is obtained.

Prices in England in 1850 were 105 and in 1910 were 106. The ratio of the stocks of gold to the production of other things remained the same, and prices were stable.

From 1850 to 1870, gold increased faster than the production of other things, so that the ratio of gold to other production increased from 105 to 136 and prices rose from 105 to 131.

From 1870 to 1890, gold increased from an index of 131 to 169, or 29 per cent. The production of other things increased 76 per cent. The gold stocks did not keep pace with other things. The ratio of gold to other things fell from 136 to 99, and prices fell from 131 to 98.

From 1890 to 1910, the ratio increased from 99 to 105 and prices rose from 98 to 106.

These relationships for the entire period are given in table 11 and figure 60. Although there are considerable variations in short periods of time, prices for 75 years before the war were generally very close to the quantity of monetary gold divided by the quantity of other things.

The five-year averages show how closely the relationship holds in

TABLE 11.—RELATION BETWEEN MONETARY STOCKS OF GOLD AND THE PHYSICAL VOLUME OF PRODUCTION AND WHOLESALE PRICES IN ENGLAND, 1839–1932*

Year	Estimated world's stock of monetary gold at the end of year, millions of fine ounces†	Index numbers of world's stock of monetary gold. 1880–1914 = 100†	Index numbers of world's physical volume of production. 1880–1914 = 100‡	Ratio, gold divided by production.	Index numbers of wholesale prices in gold in England. 1880–1914 = 100§
1880–1914...	231	100	100	100	100
1840–44.....	47	20	*17*	*118*	125
1845–49.....	49	21	*20*	*105*	115
1850–54.....	63	27	*24*	*113*	116
1855–59.....	89	38	*28*	*136*	134
1860–64.....	107	46	*32*	*144*	137
1865–69.....	122	53	36	147	136
1870–74.....	136	59	44	134	141
1875–79.....	146	63	52	121	124
1880–84.....	154	67	63	106	113
1885–89.....	162	70	71	99	96
1890–94.....	178	77	79	97	93
1895–99.....	209	90	96	94	87
1900–04.....	249	108	111	97	97
1905–09.....	304	131	131	100	102
1910–14.....	362	157	148	106	113
1915–19.....	433	187	143	131	214
1920–24.....	481	208	159	131	186
1925–29.....	525	227	194	117	169
1839........	46	20	*16*	*125*	140
1840........	46	20	*16*	*125*	140
1841........	47	20	*17*	*118*	137
1842........	47	20	*17*	*118*	124
1843........	47	20	*18*	*111*	113
1844........	47	20	*18*	*111*	114
1845........	48	21	*19*	*111*	118
1846........	48	21	*20*	*105*	120
1847........	49	21	*20*	*105*	129
1848........	49	21	*21*	*100*	106
1849........	52	22	*22*	*100*	100
1850........	54	23	*22*	*105*	105
1851........	57	25	*23*	*109*	102
1852........	63	27	*24*	*113*	106
1853........	69	30	*24*	*125*	129
1854........	74	32	*25*	*128*	138
1855........	80	35	*26*	*135*	137
1856........	85	37	*27*	*137*	137
1857........	90	39	*28*	*139*	143
1858........	94	41	*28*	*146*	124
1859........	98	42	*29*	*145*	128
1860........	102	44	*30*	*147*	135
1861........	105	45	*31*	*145*	133
1862........	108	47	*32*	*147*	137
1863........	110	48	*33*	*145*	140
1864........	112	48	*34*	*141*	143
1865........	115	50	34	147	137
1866........	119	51	35	146	138
1867........	122	53	36	147	136
1868........	125	54	38	142	135
1869........	128	55	37	149	133
1870........	131	57	42	136	131
1871........	134	58	42	138	136
1872........	136	59	45	131	149
1873........	138	60	45	133	151
1874........	140	61	45	136	138
1875........	141	61	49	124	131
1876........	144	62	49	127	129
1877........	146	63	52	121	128
1878........	149	64	54	119	118
1879........	150	65	55	118	114

TABLE 11 (*Concluded*)

Year	Estimated world's stock of monetary gold at the end of year, millions of fine ounces†	Index numbers of world's stock of monetary gold. 1880–1914 = 100†	Index numbers of world's physical volume of production. 1880–1914 = 100‡	Ratio, gold divided by production.	Index numbers of wholesale prices in gold in England. 1880–1914 = 100§
1880	151	65	60	108	120
1881	153	66	56	118	116
1882	154	67	65	103	114
1883	155	67	63	106	111
1884	156	67	68	99	104
1885	158	68	68	100	98
1886	160	69	68	101	95
1887	162	70	68	103	92
1888	165	71	75	95	96
1889	167	72	77	94	98
1890	169	73	74	99	98
1891	173	75	83	90	98
1892	177	77	78	99	92
1893	182	79	80	99	92
1894	189	82	80	103	86
1895	195	84	90	93	84
1896	201	87	94	93	83
1897	208	90	94	96	84
1898	217	94	102	92	88
1899	226	98	101	97	92
1900	233	101	106	95	102
1901	241	104	107	97	96
1902	249	108	114	95	95
1903	257	111	115	97	95
1904	266	115	115	100	96
1905	280	121	125	97	98
1906	290	125	134	93	105
1907	301	130	129	101	109
1908	317	137	129	106	99
1909	330	143	138	104	101
1910	340	147	140	105	106
1911	351	152	143	106	109
1912	360	156	156	100	116
1913	372	161	157	103	116
1914	388	168	146	115	117
1915	407	176	148	119	144
1916	423	183	142	129	181
1917	434	188	144	131	233
1918	449	194	142	137	255
1919	452	195	138	141	255
1920	463	200	156	128	258
1921	476	206	138	149	168
1922	481	208	159	131	163
1923	490	212	169	125	165
1924	493	213	171	125	172
1925	501	217	187	116	185
1926	513	222	183	121	172
1927	525	227	192	118	167
1928	537	232	202	115	163
1929	550	238	208	114	156
1930	*563*	*243*	197	*123*	132
1931	*577*	*250*	184	*136*	106
1932			175		

The figures in italics are estimates.

* Warren, G. F., and Pearson, F. A., Money and Prices, Farm Economics No. 74, pp. 1686–7, February 1932.

† Warren, G. F., and Pearson, F. A., Relation of Gold to Prices, Farm Economics No. 69, pp. 1461–2, February 1931. Kitchin, J., The Supply of Gold Compared with the Prices of Commodities, Interim Report of the Gold Delegation of the Financial Committee of the League of Nations, Document C.375. M. 161, Annex XI, pp. 79–85, September 1930. The index numbers of the world's stock of monetary gold were converted to the 35-year base, 1880–1914, by multiplying by 0.43247. The fine ounces of gold may be converted to dollars by multiplying by $20.67.

‡ The index numbers of the world's physical volume of production are from table 6, p. 48, converted to an 1880–1914 base.

§ Table 8, p. 75. These index numbers were converted to the 35-year base, 1880–1914, from the 1910–14 base by multiplying by 1.1254. They may also be converted to the 35-year base from the eleven-year base, 1867–77, by multiplying by 1.3625.

each period. The widest divergence is shown for the five years 1865-1869 when gold divided by production averaged 147, while prices in England were 136, or a 7 per cent difference in the relationship. About the same percentage difference occurred for the five years 1895-99 and for 1910-14. For a number of years in the nineties, prices were low. This was a period of severe depression, and doubtless considerable gold was hoarded. During most of this period, the Bank of England paid a premium for gold.[1]

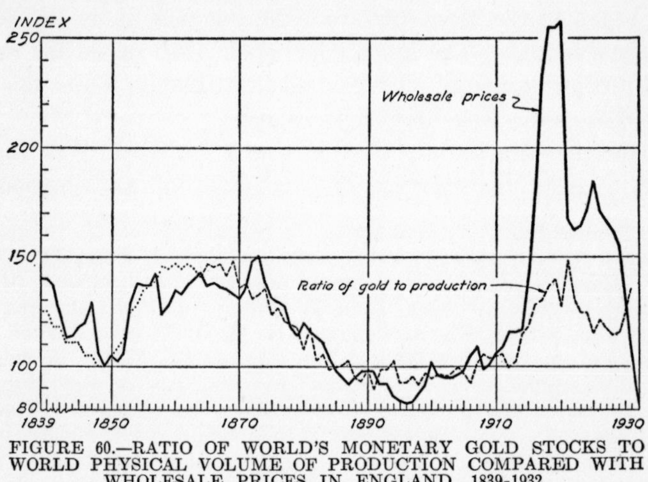

FIGURE 60.—RATIO OF WORLD'S MONETARY GOLD STOCKS TO WORLD PHYSICAL VOLUME OF PRODUCTION COMPARED WITH WHOLESALE PRICES IN ENGLAND, 1839-1932.
1880-1914 = 100.

For the 75 years before the World War, prices rose if the world's monetary stocks of gold increased faster than the production of other things and fell if gold increased less rapidly. An exception occurred during and after the World War when most of the countries of the world discontinued the gold standard. However, the relationship has been restored.

Short-time fluctuations are affected by other factors. The final fluctuations in the price level from the gold relationships are the algebraic sum of short-time variations in crops, due to weather, livestock cycles, business cycles, and to some other causes. In the 75 years before the war these variations were always temporary.

This 75-year relationship may be expressed as follows:

$$\frac{\text{Gold}}{\text{Physical volume of production}} = \text{Prices.}$$

For 75 years before the World War, world monetary stocks of gold had to increase at the same rate as the world physical volume of production in order to maintain stable commodity prices in England. If

[1] Report of the Director of the Mint, 1900, p. 206. 1900.

gold stocks increased more rapidly than other things, prices rose; if they increased less rapidly, prices fell.[2]

The abnormally high prices from 1915 to 1930 were explained, in part, by the reduced demand for gold (page 112) and, in part, by the low production of other things. The world physical volume of production was low from 1914 to 1925. The abnormally low production raised the ratio of gold stocks to production in that period, and accounted for the rise in the gold-to-production ratio line. World production of goods began to rise from 1923 to 1929, but was at no time equal to the normal increase. The low production in 1930 raised the ratio line. A still further decrease in 1931 raised it strikingly. These fluctuations do not change the long-time relationships.

Apparently wars, like the Civil War and the World War (figures 37 and 39), check the increase in production of all commodities or

[2] This formula has no relationship to the formula $MV = PT$. It expresses the relationship between monetary gold, production of basic commodities and commodity prices. No one of these factors corresponds to any factor in $MV = PT$.

By another method, Kitchin, J., in The Supply of Gold Compared with the Prices of Commodities, Interim Report of the Gold Delegation of the Financial Committee of the League of Nations, Document C. 375. M. 161, September 1930, arrived at substantially the same results. He found that for more than 75 years before the war, if the world stocks of monetary gold increased more rapidly than 3.1 per cent per year, prices rose. If they increased less rapidly, prices fell.

Stated as a law, he found that the ratio of actual stocks of gold to what the stocks would be if increased 3.1 per cent per year equaled prices.

Warren, G. F., and Pearson, F. A.: Relation of Gold to Prices, Farm Economics No. 69, pp. 1460-66, February 1931, and The Future of the General Price Level, Journal of Farm Economics, Vol. XIV, No. 1, pp. 23-46, January 1932, found the same principles to apply to world monetary stocks of gold and prices in the United States, France, Denmark, and Germany.

Regardless of the differences in the commodities included in the index numbers for the different countries and regardless of the banking systems, a definite and uniform compound rate of increase in monetary gold stocks was necessary for many years before the war in order to maintain stable commodity prices. If gold stocks increased faster than this normal rate, prices rose. If gold stocks increased less rapidly, prices fell.

It should be noted that it is the monetary stocks of gold and not gold production that had to increase 3.1 per cent per year to maintain stable prices. It is, of course, the total stocks and not the production of a single year that determines value.

Cassel, G., The Theory of Social Economy, p. 447, 1924, has shown that for the period 1850 to 1910, "*The main cause of the secular variations of the general price-level lies in the changes of the relative gold-supply.*" He indicates that the gold supply must increase about 3 per cent per year to maintain stable prices.

Woytinsky, W., Das Ratsel der langen Wellen, Schmollers Jahrbuch, 55.Jahrgang, Viertes Heft, p. 30, 1931, maintains that world gold stocks must increase 3.142 per cent per year to maintain stable prices.

actually lower it. Apparently, after recovery occurs, the increase again proceeds at a normal rate. If this is the case, the world's gold supply would need to have increased a little less than 3.15 per cent per year since 1914 to sustain pre-war prices with what would now be normal production, but from the lower base it would probably need to increase about 3.15 per cent per year for the future.

In recent years, the world stocks of monetary gold have not been increasing as much as 3.15 per cent per year. Gold production is increasing, but it would have to increase strikingly to allow world

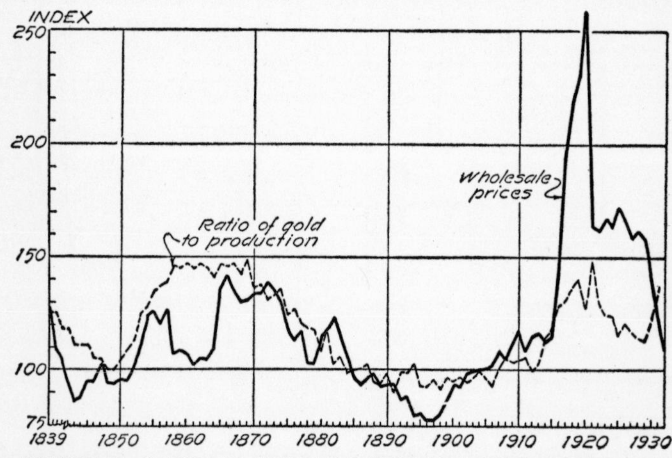

FIGURE 61.—RATIO OF WORLD'S MONETARY GOLD STOCKS TO WORLD PHYSICAL VOLUME OF PRODUCTION COMPARED WITH WHOLESALE PRICES IN THE UNITED STATES, 1839-1932. 1880-1914 = 100.

Except for the Civil War and World War periods, when the world's monetary stocks of gold increased faster than the production of other things, prices rose. Conversely, when the monetary stocks increased less rapidly than the production of other things, prices fell. The normal relationship was reestablished in 1931.

monetary stocks to increase 3 per cent per year. Some economists have been misled by making calculations on the rate of increase in gold production since 1922. This is doubly fallacious. It begins measurement from an abnormally low point, and would be incorrect in any event, for it is world monetary stocks of gold and not gold production that must increase at the same rate as other things in order to maintain stable prices.

World gold stocks and prices in the United States.—In the five-year period 1885-89, the world monetary stocks of gold were 70 when the average for 1880-1914 = 100 (table 12). The world physical volume of production was 71. The ratio of gold to production was 99, and wholesale prices in the United States were 96. Fifteen years later, the world gold stocks had increased 54 per cent, and the world physical volume of production, 56 per cent. The ratio of gold to production was 97, and prices were 97.

In 1929, many persons contended that the world gold stocks were higher than ever before and so they must be ample. The stocks had increased 42 per cent in the 15 years from 1914 to 1929. In the equal

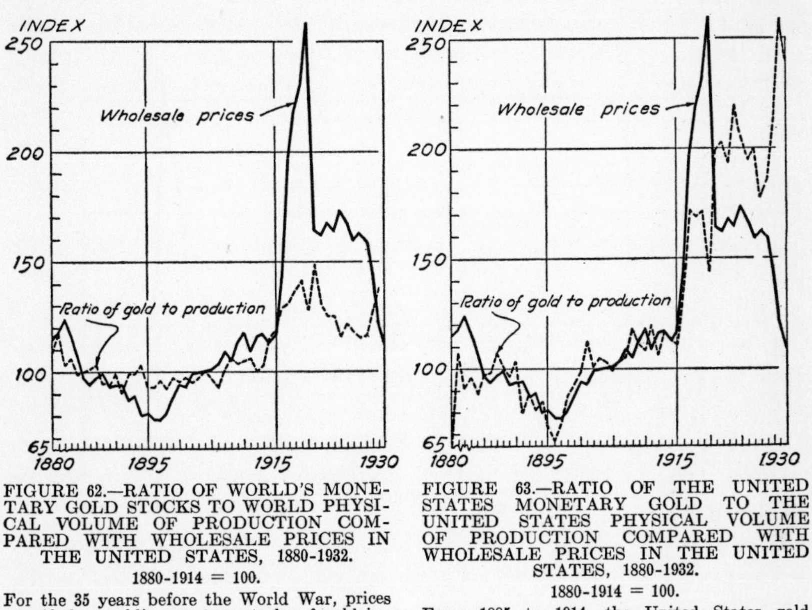

FIGURE 62.—RATIO OF WORLD'S MONETARY GOLD STOCKS TO WORLD PHYSICAL VOLUME OF PRODUCTION COMPARED WITH WHOLESALE PRICES IN THE UNITED STATES, 1880-1932.

1880-1914 = 100.

For the 35 years before the World War, prices rose if the world's monetary stocks of gold increased faster than the production of other things and fell if gold increased less rapidly. An exception occurred when most of the countries of the world discontinued the gold standard. However, the relationship has been restored.

FIGURE 63.—RATIO OF THE UNITED STATES MONETARY GOLD TO THE UNITED STATES PHYSICAL VOLUME OF PRODUCTION COMPARED WITH WHOLESALE PRICES IN THE UNITED STATES, 1880-1932.

1880-1914 = 100.

From 1885 to 1914, the United States gold divided by the United States production of other commodities equaled prices.

period previously given, the 54 per cent increase in gold was only sufficient to maintain prices. There was therefore no reason for assuming that the 42 per cent increase in gold was more than sufficient to maintain pre-war prices with normal production of other things, and all the gold-world back on a gold basis. The error of any such assumption was shown by the events of 1932.

Figure 62 and table 12 show the relationships of the gold-to-production ratio to prices since 1880. Prices in the United States were more erratic than those in England primarily because of financial difficulties during the 20 years following the return to the gold basis in 1879.

In general, prices rose when gold stocks increased more rapidly than production and fell when they increased less rapidly.

From 1839 to 1880, wholesale prices in the United States were lower than the gold supply would suggest. The discrepancy was very great from 1858 to 1865. This was due to the Panic of 1857 and the inflation during the war. When inflation occurs, the value of money declines faster than prices rise so that a theoretical price in gold is low.

United States gold stocks and prices.—In 1885, the United States had $589,000,000 of monetary gold, and in 1897, $696,000,000. In 1897, some persons contended that there must be enough gold as the supply had increased 18 per cent. In the same period, the United States physical volume of production increased at the normal rate, or 52 per cent.

In 1885, the ratio of gold to production was 97, and wholesale prices were 97, when the 35 years, 1880-1914, is 100.

In 1897, the ratio of gold to production was 75, and wholesale prices were 78.

During the period when the country was off the gold standard, wholesale prices were higher than the small amount of gold would be expected to support. Specie payment was resumed in 1879 and prices continued high relative to gold for the following six years. All the data since 1880 are shown in figure 63 and table 12.

From 1885 to 1914, the highest discrepancy between prices and the gold-to-production ratio was for 1900 to 1904, when the ratio was 104, but prices averaged only 97. The discrepancy was 7 per cent. No other five-year period showed a discrepancy of more than 4 per cent.

For the 30-year period 1885 to 1914, monetary stocks of gold in the United States had to increase at the same rate as the physical volume of production in the United States in order to maintain stable commodity prices. If gold stocks increased more rapidly than the production of other things, prices rose; if gold increased less rapidly, prices fell.

From 1892 to 1899, prices in the United States were below the normal relationships to world stocks of gold, but were not below their normal relationships to stocks of gold in the United States. The United States returned to the gold standard in 1879, but the long years of falling prices, resulting bankruptcy, unemployment, and political controversies were such that it shook the faith of Europe in the ability of the United States to maintain the gold standard. Securities were returned and sold on the New York market and other means were taken

TABLE 12.—RELATION BETWEEN MONETARY STOCKS OF GOLD AND THE PHYSICAL VOLUME OF PRODUCTION AND WHOLESALE PRICES IN THE UNITED STATES, 1839–1932*

Year	Estimated world's stock of monetary gold at the end of the year, millions of fine ounces†	Index numbers of world's stock of monetary gold. 1880–1914 = 100†	Index numbers of the world's physical volume of production. 1880–1914 = 100†	Ratio, gold divided by production	Index numbers of United States wholesale prices in gold. 1880–1914 = 100‡	United States gold stocks, millions of dollars§	Index numbers of United States gold stocks. 1880–1914 = 100§	Index of United States physical volume of production. 1880–1914 = 100¶	Ratio, U. S. gold divided by U. S. production	Per cent of world's stock of gold held in the United States
1880–1914	231	100	100	100	100	1003	100	100	100	20
1840–44	47	20	*17*	*118*	96	....	....	....	....	....
1845–49	49	21	*20*	*105*	96	....	....	....	....	....
1850–54	63	27	*24*	*113*	105	....	....	....	....	....
1855–59	89	38	*28*	*136*	118	....	....	....	....	....
1860–64	107	46	*32*	*144*	105	246	25	....	....	11
1865–69	122	53	36	147	135	175	17	....	....	7
1870–74	136	59	44	134	134	157	16	31	52	6
1875–79	146	63	52	121	111	176	18	43	42	6
1880–84	154	67	63	106	116	485	48	54	89	15
1885–89	162	70	71	99	96	644	64	64	100	19
1890–94	178	77	79	97	89	646	64	74	86	18
1895–99	209	90	96	94	81	751	75	95	79	17
1900–04	249	108	111	97	97	1186	118	114	104	23
1905–09	304	131	131	100	107	1512	151	140	108	24
1910–14	362	157	148	106	115	1794	179	159	113	24
1915–19	433	187	143	131	181	2785	278	182	153	31
1920–24	481	208	159	131	183	3693	368	193	191	37
1925–29	525	227	194	117	165	4366	435	224	194	40
1839	46	20	*16*	*125*	128	....	....	....	....	....
1840	46	20	*16*	*125*	109	....	....	....	....	....
1841	47	20	*17*	*118*	105	....	....	....	....	....
1842	47	20	*17*	*118*	94	....	....	....	....	....
1843	47	20	*18*	*111*	86	....	....	....	....	....
1844	47	20	*18*	*111*	88	....	....	....	....	....
1845	48	21	*19*	*111*	95	....	....	....	....	....
1846	48	21	*20*	*105*	95	....	....	....	....	....
1847	49	21	*20*	*105*	103	....	....	....	....	....
1848	49	21	*21*	*100*	94	....	....	....	....	....
1849	52	22	*22*	*100*	94	....	....	....	....	....
1850	54	23	*22*	*105*	96	....	....	....	....	....
1851	57	25	*23*	*109*	95	....	....	....	....	....
1852	63	27	*24*	*113*	102	....	....	....	....	....
1853	69	30	*24*	*125*	111	....	....	....	....	....
1854	74	32	*25*	*128*	124	....	....	....	....	....
1855	80	35	*26*	*135*	126	....	....	....	....	....
1856	85	37	*27*	*137*	120	....	....	....	....	....
1857	90	39	*28*	*139*	127	....	....	....	....	....
1858	94	41	*28*	*146*	107	....	....	....	....	....
1859	98	42	*29*	*145*	109	....	....	....	....	....
1860	102	44	*30*	*147*	107	214	21	....	....	10
1861	105	45	*31*	*145*	102	270	27	....	....	12
1862	108	47	*32*	*147*	105	283	28	....	....	13
1863	110	48	*33*	*145*	105	260	26	....	....	11
1864	112	48	*34*	*141*	110	203	20	....	....	9
1865	115	50	34	147	136	189	19	....	....	8
1866	119	51	35	146	141	167	17	24	71	7
1867	122	53	36	147	135	186	19	26	73	7
1868	125	54	38	142	130	160	16	27	59	6
1869	128	55	37	149	131	173	17	28	61	7
1870	131	57	42	136	134	190	19	30	63	7
1871	134	58	42	138	134	164	16	29	55	6
1872	136	59	45	131	139	148	15	33	45	5
1873	138	60	45	133	134	135	13	32	41	5
1874	140	61	45	136	130	147	15	31	48	5
1875	141	61	49	124	118	121	12	38	32	4
1876	144	62	49	127	113	130	13	38	34	4
1877	146	63	52	121	117	168	17	41	41	6
1878	149	64	54	119	103	213	21	44	48	7
1879	150	65	55	118	103	246	25	52	48	8

TABLE 12 (*Concluded*)

Year	Estimated world's stock of monetary gold at the end of the year, millions of fine ounces†	Index numbers of world's stock of monetary gold. 1880–1914 = 100†	Index numbers of the world's physical volume of production. 1880–1914 = 100†	Ratio, gold divided by production	Index numbers of United States wholesale prices in gold. 1880–1914 = 100‡	United States gold stocks, millions of dollars§	Index numbers of United States gold stocks. 1880–1914 = 100§	Index of United States physical volume of production. 1880–1914 = 100¶	Ratio, U. S. gold divided by U. S. production	Per cent of world's stock of gold held in the United States
1880..........	151	65	60	108	115	352	35	51	69	11
1881..........	153	66	56	118	118	478	48	45	107	15
1882..........	154	67	65	103	124	507	51	56	91	16
1883..........	155	67	63	106	116	543	54	56	96	17
1884..........	156	67	68	99	107	546	54	61	89	17
1885..........	158	68	68	100	97	589	59	61	97	18
1886..........	160	69	68	101	94	591	59	60	98	18
1887..........	162	70	68	103	97	655	65	61	107	20
1888..........	165	71	75	95	99	706	70	69	101	21
1889..........	167	72	77	94	93	680	68	71	96	20
1890..........	169	73	74	99	94	696	69	67	103	20
1891..........	173	75	83	90	94	647	65	81	80	18
1892..........	177	77	78	99	87	664	66	74	89	18
1893..........	182	79	80	99	89	598	60	74	81	16
1894..........	189	82	80	103	80	627	63	74	85	16
1895..........	195	84	90	93	81	636	63	87	72	16
1896..........	201	87	94	93	78	600	60	91	66	14
1897..........	208	90	94	96	78	696	69	92	75	16
1898..........	217	94	102	92	81	862	86	99	87	19
1899..........	226	98	101	97	88	963	96	104	92	21
1900..........	233	101	106	95	94	1034	103	105	98	21
1901..........	241	104	107	97	93	1125	112	100	112	23
1902..........	249	108	114	95	99	1193	119	118	101	23
1903..........	257	111	115	97	100	1249	125	119	105	24
1904..........	266	115	115	100	100	1328	132	128	103	24
1905..........	280	121	125	97	101	1358	135	136	99	23
1906..........	290	125	134	93	103	1476	147	143	103	25
1907..........	301	130	129	101	109	1466	146	139	105	24
1908..........	317	137	129	106	105	1618	161	137	118	25
1909..........	330	143	138	104	113	1642	164	148	111	24
1910..........	340	147	140	105	118	1636	163	151	108	23
1911..........	351	152	143	106	109	1753	175	146	120	24
1912..........	360	156	156	100	116	1818	181	170	106	24
1913..........	372	161	157	103	117	1871	187	160	117	24
1914..........	388	168	146	115	113	1891	189	167	113	24
1915..........	407	176	148	119	116	1986	198	178	111	24
1916..........	423	183	142	129	143	2445	244	177	138	28
1917..........	434	188	144	131	197	3220	321	187	172	36
1918..........	449	194	142	137	219	3163	315	186	169	34
1919..........	452	195	138	141	231	3113	310	181	171	33
1920..........	463	200	156	128	259	2865	286	199	144	30
1921..........	476	206	138	149	164	3275	327	164	199	33
1922..........	481	208	159	131	162	3785	377	186	203	38
1923..........	490	212	169	125	168	4050	404	209	193	40
1924..........	493	213	171	125	164	4488	448	205	219	44
1925..........	501	217	187	116	173	4365	435	213	204	42
1926..........	513	222	183	121	167	4447	444	223	199	42
1927..........	525	227	192	118	159	4587	457	223	205	42
1928..........	537	232	202	115	162	4109	410	231	177	37
1929..........	550	238	208	114	159	4324	431	232	186	38
1930..........	*563*	*243*	197	*123*	144	4535	452	209	216	*39*
1931..........	*577*	*250*	184	*136*	123	4956	494	*191*	259	*42*
1932..........	....	....	175	....	*109*	3919	391	*165*	*237*	*31*

The figures in italics are estimates.

* Warren, G. F., and Pearson, F. A., Money and Prices, Farm Economics No. 74, pp. 1689–90, February 1932.

† Table 11.

‡ Tables 1 and 9. To convert from the 1910–14 base to the 1880–1914 base, multiply by 1.14604.

§ Statistical Abstract of the United States, United States Department of Commerce, 1922. Forty-fifth Number, p. 512, 1923, and the Fifty-second Number, pp. 246–7, 1930. The index numbers were converted to the 35-year base, 1880–1914, by multiplying by 0.09973.

¶ Table 5, p. 44. The index numbers were converted from the five-year base, 1926–30, to the 35-year base, 1880–1914, by multiplying by 2.2411.

to withdraw gold from the United States. This resulted in a price level lower than the world stocks would call for. Low as prices were, they were high compared to the United States gold stocks.

A similar situation existed in England. Gold payments were resumed in 1925, but six years of effort resulted in so much unemployment and political agitation, that the world doubted the ability of England to maintain the gold standard. The same devices were used to withdraw gold, and it became impossible for England to maintain the gold standard. Index numbers of wholesale prices in England were low relative to world stocks of gold, but were high relative to English gold stocks. For two years, prices in England had been declining in advance

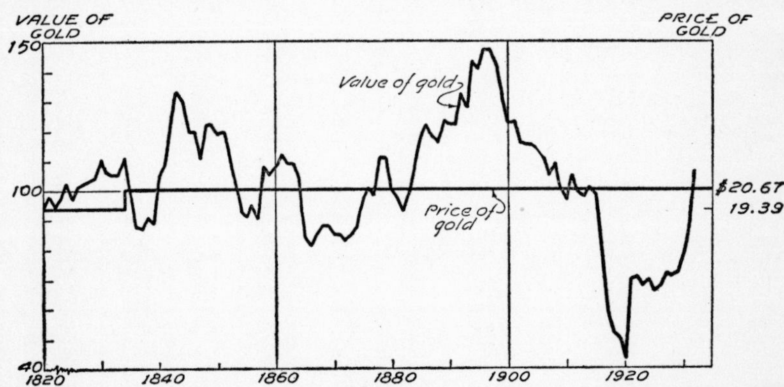

FIGURE 64.—VALUE OF GOLD AND PRICE OF GOLD IN THE UNITED STATES, 1820-1932.

Since 1834, the price of gold has been $20.67 per ounce, but the value fluctuates violently.

of the decline of prices in the United States. The major factor controlling prices was world gold supply, but the location of the supply had some influence.

Supply of gold and price of gold.—On April 2, 1792, Congress fixed the price of gold at $19.39 per ounce. This fixed price was maintained for 33 years regardless of the supply of it or demand for it except from August 1814 to February 20, 1817 (figure 64).

On June 28, 1834, Congress raised the price of gold to $20.67 per ounce (figure 64). This fixed price has again been maintained continuously regardless of the supply of gold or demand for it, except during the Panics of 1837 and 1857 and for the period February 25, 1862, to January 1, 1879.

England suspended the legal fixed price of gold from August 16, 1914, to May 13, 1925, and on September 21, 1931.

Supply of gold and value of gold.—The relationships of supply to the purchasing power of many products has been calculated. The

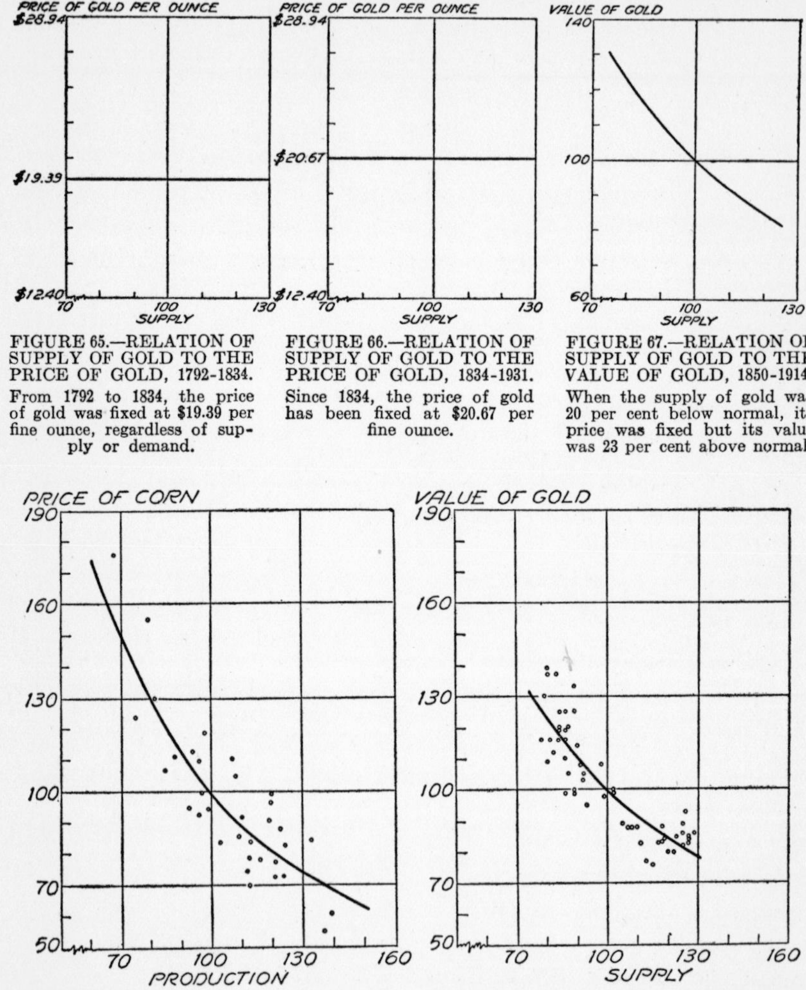

FIGURE 65.—RELATION OF SUPPLY OF GOLD TO THE PRICE OF GOLD, 1792-1834.

From 1792 to 1834, the price of gold was fixed at $19.39 per fine ounce, regardless of supply or demand.

FIGURE 66.—RELATION OF SUPPLY OF GOLD TO THE PRICE OF GOLD, 1834-1931.

Since 1834, the price of gold has been fixed at $20.67 per fine ounce.

FIGURE 67.—RELATION OF SUPPLY OF GOLD TO THE VALUE OF GOLD, 1850-1914.

When the supply of gold was 20 per cent below normal, its price was fixed but its value was 23 per cent above normal.

FIGURE 68.—RELATION OF THE UNITED STATES PRODUCTION OF CORN TO THE PURCHASING POWER OF THE UNITED STATES FARM PRICE, 1875-1913.

When the United States production of corn was 20 per cent below normal, the purchasing power of the United States farm price was 28 per cent above normal.

FIGURE 69.—RELATION OF THE WORLD SUPPLY OF GOLD TO ITS PURCHASING POWER IN ENGLAND, 1850-1914.

When the supply of gold was 20 per cent below normal, the value of gold was 23 per cent above normal.

supply of each year is compared with the normal supply for that year. The purchasing power for the year is the amount of all commodities

TABLE 13.—RELATIVE SUPPLY OF GOLD, LIVESTOCK, AND GRAIN RELATED TO PURCHASING POWER

	Supply 20 per cent below normal	Supply 20 per cent above normal
	Per cent that purchasing power was above normal	Per cent that purchasing power was below normal
United States production of		
Hay related to purchasing power of the New York farm price, 1875–1913	23	16
Oats related to purchasing power of the United States farm price, 1875–1913	23	16
Corn related to purchasing power of the United States farm price, 1875–1913	28	18
Wheat related to purchasing power of the May future price in December, Chicago, 1890–1913	24	16
Hogs related to purchasing power of the Chicago price of heavy hogs, 1877–1913*	22	15
Cattle related to purchasing power of the Chicago price of steers, 1891–1915*	17	12
World production of		
Wheat related to Liverpool price of red wheat, 1899–1913	24	16
World stocks of		
Gold related to price of gold†	00	00
Gold related to purchasing power of gold in England, 1850–1914	23	15

* The production of hogs was measured by the total weight packed in the West, November to February, 1877–78 to 1913–14. The purchasing power of hogs was the Chicago price of heavy hogs for the same period divided by the index of wholesale prices of all commodities.

The production of cattle was measured by the receipts at Chicago 1890–1914. The purchasing power was the Chicago price of 1200–1500 pound steers divided by the index of wholesale prices of all commodities, January 1891 to 1915.

The material included in this table was taken from Warren, G. F., and Pearson, F. A., Interrelationships of Supply and Price, Cornell University Agricultural Experiment Station Bulletin 466, pp. 106–113, March 1928.

† The relative stocks of gold are based on the ratio of the monetary stocks of gold to the world physical volume of production, table 11.

Warren, G. F., and Pearson, F. A., Supply-Price Relationships, paper read before the Econometric Society, June 23, 1932, at Syracuse University.

at wholesale prices for which the product would exchange. The purchasing power might be defined as "real price" just as the "real wages" are distinguished from money wages.

The relationships of supply to purchasing power for a number of products are given in table 13. When the United States corn crop was 20 per cent below normal, a bushel of corn would buy 28 per cent more than the normal amount of all commodities. If the crop was 20 per cent above normal, a bushel of corn would exchange for 18 per cent less than the normal amount (figure 68).

The price of gold is fixed, but its value can be measured in the same way as the value of corn is measured—by the relative quantities of all commodities for which it would exchange (table 13 and figure 69).

The supply of gold is measured by comparing the world monetary stock of gold with its normal relationship to the total production of all other commodities.

When the world monetary supply of gold was 20 per cent below normal, its purchasing power was 23 per cent above normal. When the supply was 20 per cent above normal, its purchasing power was 15 per cent below normal.

For nearly all the products listed in table 13, the relationship is practically that of a half supply being worth double the usual value. That is, a 50-per-cent-of-normal supply, which is a 50 per cent decrease, gives a 200 value, which is a 100 per cent increase. If this relationship held exactly, a 20 per cent decrease in supply would be accompanied by a 25 per cent increase in value. This is practically the relationship of the supply of corn, wheat, or gold to its value.

The relative supply of gold affects the purchasing power of gold in exactly the same way and by practically the same amount that the supplies of wheat, hay, oats, corn, hogs, and cattle affect their purchasing powers. There is one difference. Gold is so easily moved that location has little effect on value. A high supply of corn affects prices far from market more adversely than it affects prices at trade centers.

Since 1915, world gold production has not increased fast enough to maintain a stable price level with a normal increase in business and normal demand for gold (page 103).

The great rise in prices in the United States was due to the fact that most of the gold-using world ceased to use gold and ceased to bid for it. This reduced the demand and the value of gold, and commodity prices rose. When the whole world began to bid frantically for gold, its value rose and commodity prices collapsed.

The frantic demand for gold carried prices lower than the level that probably would have existed had there been no war. Even without a war, there would doubtless have been some price decline, but since price relationships would not have been adjusted to a price level above pre-war, the result would probably have been no more serious than in previous periods of gold shortage.

The major source of the difficulty was low demand for gold for many years, which resulted in having price relationships, debts, and taxes approximately adjusted to a commodity price level about 50 per cent above pre-war; followed by world-wide frantic effort to return to gold, which caused price chaos and made it impossible to pay debts.

MONEY, CREDIT, AND PRICES

Monetary circulation.—The monetary circulation per capita has been extremely erratic, but for 75 years before the war the compound rate of increase was 1.59 per cent[3] per year (figure 70, table 14). Apparently the rate of increase was the same from 1784 to 1914. This rate of increase was a little less than the rate of increase in physical volume of production (page 47).

During the War of 1812, the circulation per capita nearly doubled. Circulation was also high in 1837. From 1860 to 1864, circulation

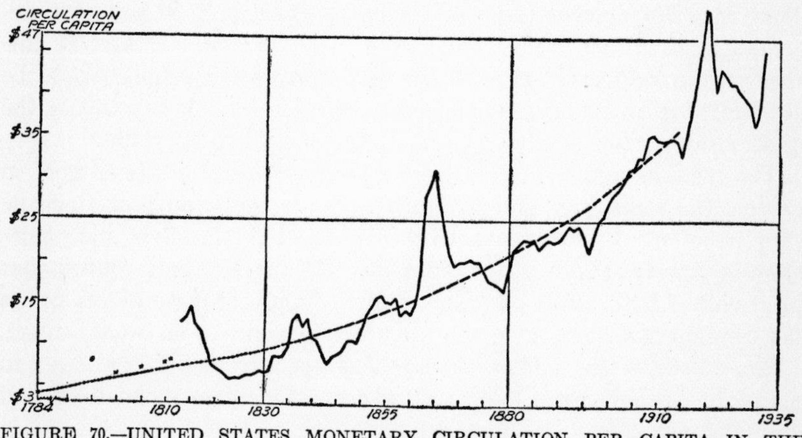

FIGURE 70.—UNITED STATES MONETARY CIRCULATION PER CAPITA IN THE UNITED STATES, 1784-1932.

From 1839 to 1914, the circulation per capita was very erratic, but increased at the compound rate of 1.59 per cent per year; it increased at about this rate from 1784 to 1914.

doubled and prices doubled. Prices and monetary circulation were not so closely related in the World War period.

The total monetary circulation divided by physical volume of production is compared with prices in figure 71. Previous to 1885, prices were more closely related to monetary circulation than to the gold supply. The gold standard was adopted in 1873, and specie payment resumed in 1879. From 1885 to 1914, prices were more closely associated with United States gold supply than with monetary circulation.

Bank credit.—The amount of loans and discounts and United States government and other securities held by all reporting banks in the United States is a measure of the nation's bank credit (table 14). For 75 years before the war, bank credit increased at the compound

[3] From 1839 to 1914, $y = 11.00\ (1.0159)^x$, origin at 1839.

TABLE 14.—MONETARY CIRCULATION AND BANK CREDIT IN THE UNITED STATES, 1784–1933

Year	Total monetary circulation* 000,000	Loans, discounts, and securities of all reporting banks† 000,000	Circulation per capita	Loans, discounts, and securities per capita	Year	Total monetary circulation* 000,000	Loans, discounts, and securities of all reporting banks† 000,000	Circulation per capita	Loans, discounts, and securities per capita
....	....	....	....	....	1865	$1084	$ 930	$31.18	$26.50
....	....	....	....	....	1866	940	1165	26.49	32.54
1784	$ 12.0	....	$ 4.00	....	1867	859	1245	23.73	34.11
1790	11.5	....	3.03	....	1868	772	1285	20.88	34.54
1795	35.0	....	7.78	....	1869	741	1281	19.62	33.80
1800	27	....	4.99	....	1870	775	1334	20.10	34.47
1805	43.5	....	7.02	....	1871	794	1469	20.08	36.91
1811	58.1	....	7.96	....	1872	829	1603	20.43	39.10
1813	101	....	12.78	....	1873	838	2161	20.11	51.33
1814	109	....	13.29	....	1874	864	2296	20.18	53.03
1815	124	....	14.59	....	1875	834	2550	18.97	57.30
1816	109	....	12.53	....	1876	807	2545	17.88	55.81
1817	104	....	11.69	....	1877	814	2573	17.56	54.98
1818	89	....	9.78	....	1878	820	2435	17.23	50.84
1819	72	....	7.74	....	1879	819	2646	16.75	53.89
1820	67	....	6.96	....	1880	973	2566	19.41	51.01
1821	68	....	6.87	....	1881	1114	2887	21.71	56.06
1822	64	....	6.27	....	1882	1174	3105	22.37	58.81
1823	62	....	5.90	....	1883	1230	3262	22.91	60.30
1824	66	....	6.06	....	1884	1244	3302	22.65	59.60
1825	67	....	5.98	....	1885	1293	3314	23.02	58.45
1826	74	....	6.43	....	1886	1253	3486	21.82	60.21
1827	76	....	6.44	....	1887	1318	3954	22.45	66.79
1828	80	....	6.55	....	1888	1372	4292	22.88	70.94
1829	86	....	6.88	....	1889	1380	4607	22.52	74.55
1830	87	....	6.69	....	1890	1429	5027	22.82	79.67
1831	93	....	7.04	....	1891	1497	5210	23.45	80.90
1832	117	....	8.64	....	1892	1601	5621	24.60	85.56
1833	120	....	8.60	....	1893	1597	5735	24.07	85.60
1834	124	$330	8.64	....	1894	1661	5530	24.56	80.97
1835	146	374	9.86	....	1895	1602	5834	23.24	83.82
1836	200	470	13.17	....	1896	1506	5926	21.44	83.58
1837	217	537	13.87	....	1897	1641	5948	22.92	82.38
1838	199	520	12.33	....	1898	1838	6512	25.19	88.60
1839	220	528	13.26	$31.62	1899	1904	7357	25.62	98.36
1840	186	505	10.91	29.53	1900	2081	8156	27.28	107.17
1841	186	451	10.59	25.48	1901	2203	9246	28.34	119.00
1842	164	349	9.02	19.07	1902	2279	10,228	28.81	128.82
1843	147	283	7.87	14.89	1903	2400	11,099	29.82	137.02
1844	167	288	8.68	14.69	1904	2553	11,601	31.18	140.45
1845	178	309	8.95	15.30	1905	2623	12,980	31.51	154.16
1846	193	333	9.43	16.01	1906	2775	13,925	32.77	162.30
1847	224	330	10.59	15.42	1907	2814	15,058	32.69	172.09
1848	232	370	10.66	16.82	1908	3079	14,831	35.19	166.45
1849	233	356	10.34	15.75	1909	3149	16,069	35.41	177.17
1850	279	385	12.02	16.52	1910	3149	17,210	34.84	186.46
1851	330	436	13.76	18.09	1911	3263	18,061	34.72	192.75
1852	361	453	14.63	18.19	1912	3335	19,275	34.87	202.68
1853	402	431	15.80	16.77	1913	3419	19,991	35.12	207.16
1854	426	601	16.10	22.59	1914	3459	20,880	34.93	213.28
1855	418	629	15.34	22.96	1915	3320	21,599	32.96	217.51
1856	426	683	15.16	24.22	1916	3649	24,698	35.63	245.02
1857	457	743	15.81	25.62	1917	4066	28,619	39.05	280.03
1858	409	643	13.78	21.51	1918	4482	32,213	42.33	310.94
1859	439	721	14.35	23.49	1919	4877	37,078	45.95	353.12
1860	435	762	13.85	24.19	1920	5468	42,153	51.38	395.80
1861	484	771	15.11	23.94	1921	4911	40,055	45.29	370.19
1862	606	746	18.52	22.67	1922	4463	40,261	40.61	366.34
1863	931	840	27.78	25.00	1923	4823	43,922	43.18	393.92
1864	1008	705	29.60	20.55	1924	4849	45,542	42.64	402.31

TABLE 14 (*Concluded*)

Year	Total monetary circulation* 000,000	Loans, discounts, and securities of all reporting banks† 000,000	Circulation per capita	Loans, discounts, and securities per capita	Year	Total monetary circulation* 000,000	Loans, discounts, and securities of all reporting banks† 000,000	Circulation per capita	Loans, discounts, and securities per capita
1925	$4815	$49,132	$41.73	$427.98	1930	$4522	$58,455	$36.71	$474.86
1926	4885	51,866	41.71	445.20	1931	4822	55,271	38.86	442.88
1927	4851	54,569	40.90	462.06	1932	5695	46,313	45.63	371.10
1928	4797	58,364	39.97	487.18	1933	5721		45.51	
1929	4746	58,782	39.08	483.80					

* 1784–1829, Hepburn, A. B., History of Coinage and Currency in the United States and the Perennial Contest for Sound Money, pp. 75, 120, 1903.
1830–1859, Annual Report of the Comptroller of the Currency to the Second Session of the Sixty-Sixth Congress, December 1919, Vol. 2, p. 34, 1920.
1860–1931, Annual Report of the Secretary of the Treasury on the State of Finances for the Fiscal Year ended June 30, 1928, pp. 550–1, 1928, and for fiscal year ended June 30, 1931, p. 547, 1932.
† Annual Report of the Comptroller of the Currency, 1931, pp. 1023–5, 1932.

rate of 6.05 per cent[4] per year. During the last 13 years of the period, the rate was slightly higher. In this same period, the physical volume

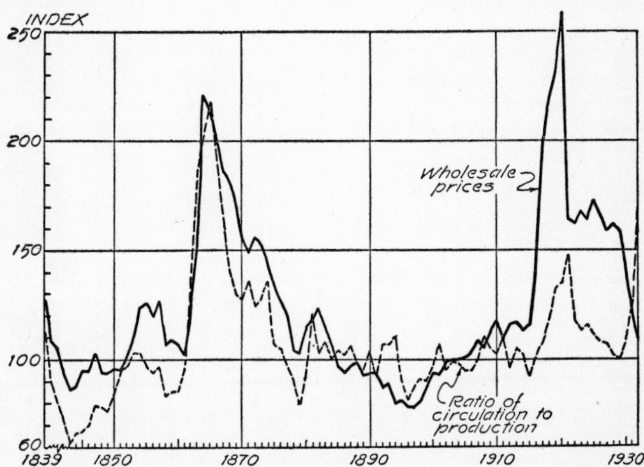

FIGURE 71.—RATIO OF THE UNITED STATES MONETARY CIRCULATION TO THE UNITED STATES PHYSICAL VOLUME OF PRODUCTION COMPARED WITH WHOLESALE PRICES, 1839-1932. 1880-1914 = 100.

For 75 years before the war, the relative amounts of monetary circulation showed considerable relation to prices.

of production increased at only 4.03 per cent per year (table 5, page 44). From 1885 to 1914, the monetary stocks of gold had to increase as

[4] From 1839 to 1914, $y = 2.7035\ (1.0605)^x$, origin 1839.

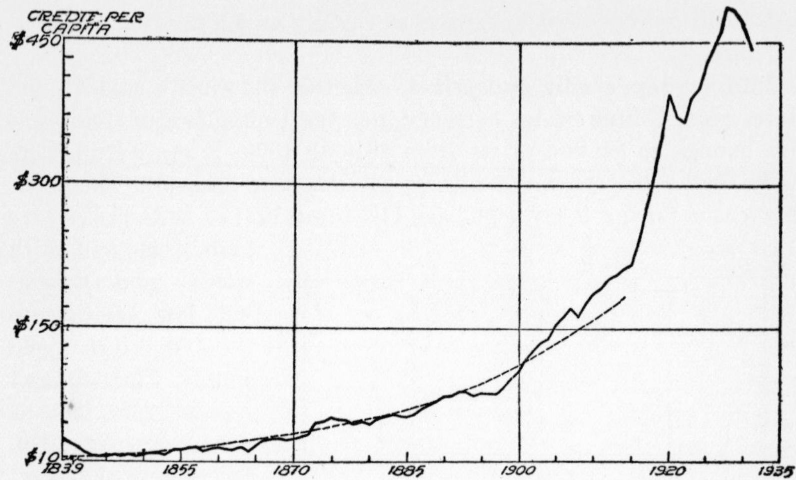

FIGURE 72.—BANK CREDIT PER CAPITA IN THE UNITED STATES, 1839-1931. For 75 years before the war, bank credit per capita increased 3.58 per cent per year. This was about twice the rate of increase in the physical volume of basic production per capita (1.73 per cent).

fast as production of basic commodities in order to maintain stable prices. Credit had to increase much more rapidly.

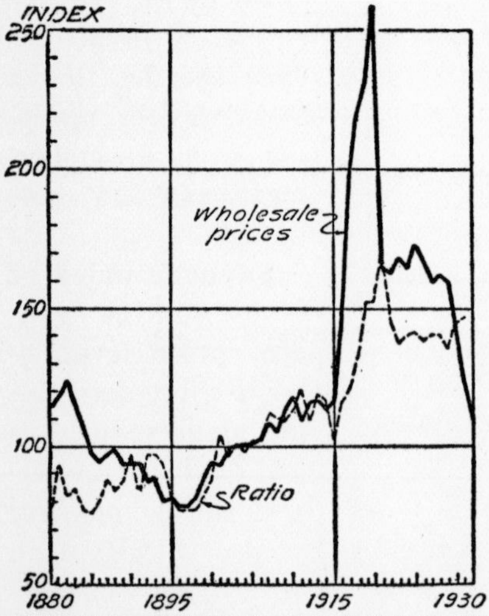

For 75 years before the war, the bank credit per capita increased at the compound rate of 3.58 per cent[5] per year (figure 72). The production of basic commodities per capita increased at the rate of 1.73 per cent per year (table 5, page 44).

Actual bank credit related to credit increased 5.5 per cent per year, and compared with the physical volume of production is shown in figure 73. From 1890 to 1914, if credit increased 5.5 per cent and production 4 per cent, prices were stable.

After 1914, production increased less than 4 per cent, so

FIGURE 73.—RELATION OF ACTUAL BANK CREDIT TO CREDIT INCREASED 5.5 PER CENT RELATED TO PHYSICAL VOLUME OF PRODUCTION, COMPARED WITH PRICES, 1880-1932.
1880-1914 = 100.
Before the war, if credit increased 5.5 per cent per year, it was about sufficient to maintain stable prices when production increased 4 per cent per year.

[5] From 1839 to 1914, $y = 13.170 (1.0358)^x$, origin 1839.

that credit did not need to expand as rapidly as 5.5 per cent to maintain prices.

Gold, money, credit, and prices.—Neither the world's gold, United States gold, United States currency, nor the United States credit was high enough to explain prices from 1916 to 1920. Prices were abnormally high when compared with every monetary measure. The probable reason for this is given on page 112. From 1921 to 1929, prices were high compared with world gold supply, but low relative to the American gold supply. The apparent reason for this is given on page 114. Prices were high compared with monetary circulation, but low compared with bank credit.

In all cases, the erratic results for 1931 are due to the small divisor resulting from unemployment and low production.

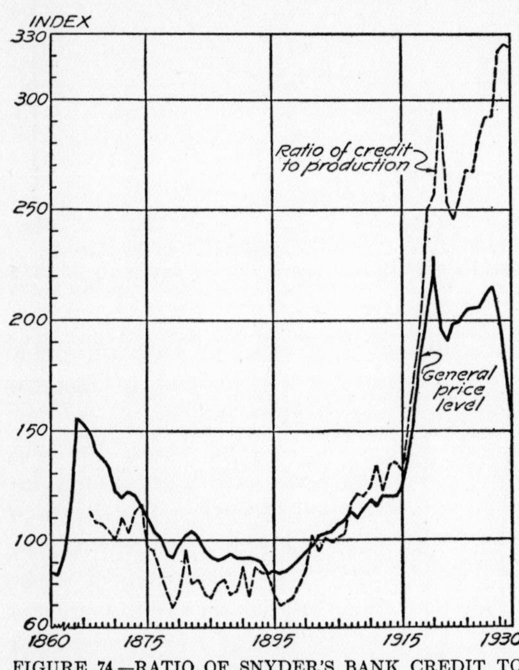

FIGURE 74.—RATIO OF SNYDER'S BANK CREDIT TO PRODUCTION COMPARED WITH SNYDER'S "GENERAL PRICE LEVEL," 1860-1932. 1880-1914 = 100.

Credit must rise faster than production in order to maintain stable prices.

Snyder's index of credit and the "general price level."—Snyder prepared index numbers of loans and discounts and investments of national banks. The ratio of these to the physical volume of production is shown in figure 74. He also calculated an index to measure all monetary transactions. This included wholesale prices, retail prices, wages, and the cost of living. It is evident that credit had to expand more rapidly than production in order to keep this price level stable.

Comparison of estimated and actual prices.—From all the studies here enumerated, it is evident that bank credit must increase considerably more rapidly than production to maintain stable prices. It also appears that monetary circulation does not have to increase quite so rapidly as production in order to maintain stable prices. Apparently, both the world and United States gold supply must increase as rapidly as the production of other commodities if prices are to be stable.

GOLD PRODUCTION

Gold production.—Since the supply of and demand for gold determine the level of prices, the most important price consideration is gold. World gold production is shown in table 15 and figure 75. This is an important consideration for any one who invests in city real estate, agriculture, life insurance, or other long-time investments. Since the business of the world grows rapidly, any period when gold does not increase at an equally rapid rate is a period of gold shortage. From 1520 to 1680, gold production rose very little. This did not seriously interfere with business because silver was the common medium of exchange. From 1680 to 1800, production increased and gold became somewhat cheaper in terms of silver. After the discoveries in

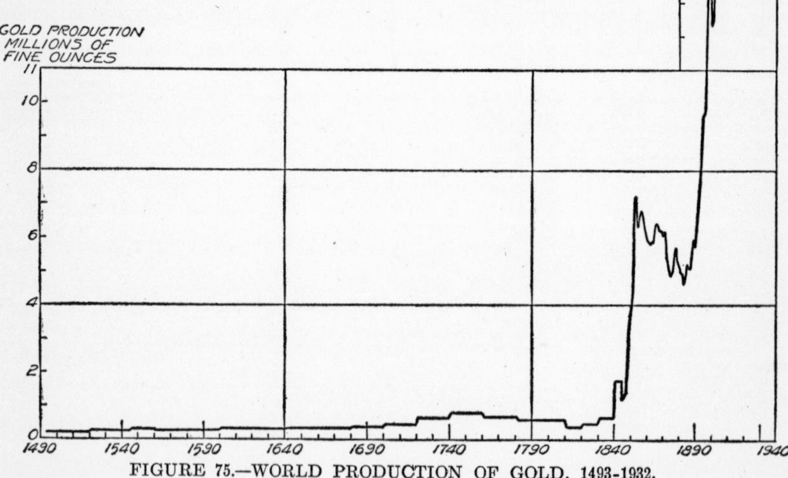

FIGURE 75.—WORLD PRODUCTION OF GOLD, 1493-1932.

From 1840 to 1860, gold production rose rapidly. Another large increase occurred from 1890 to 1914. Both these periods were characterized by rising prices and general prosperity.

California and Australia, production mounted rapidly from 1840 to 1860. A decline in production then began and the production was less in 1890 than that 38 years previous. A rapid increase then began, and

TABLE 15.—WORLD GOLD PRODUCTION, 1493–1932*

Period	Average annual production, thousands of fine ounces	Index 1880–1914 = 100	Year	Annual production, thousands of fine ounces	Index 1880–1914 = 100	Year	Annual production, thousands of fine ounces	Index 1880–1914 = 100
1493–1520	186	2	1860	5,932	48	1900	12,315	100
1521–1544	230	2	1861	5,885	48	1901	12,626	103
1545–1560	274	2	1862	5,815	47	1902	14,355	117
Twenty-year			1863	5,932	48	1903	15,853	129
average			1864	5,862	48	1904	16,804	137
1561–1580	220	2	1865	6,380	52	1905	18,396	150
1581–1600	237	2	1866	6,450	52	1906	19,471	158
1601–1620	274	2	1867	6,262	51	1907	19,977	163
1621–1640	267	2	1868	6,238	51	1908	21,422	174
1641–1660	282	2	1869	6,215	51	1909	21,965	179
1661–1680	298	2						
			1870	6,050	49	1910	22,022	179
1681–1700	346	3	1871	6,238	51	1911	22,397	182
1701–1720	412	3	1872	5,650	46	1912	22,605	184
1721–1740	613	5	1873	5,297	43	1913	22,255	181
1741–1760	791	6	1874	4,967	40	1914	21,302	173
1761–1780	665	5	1875	4,873	40	1915	22,738	185
1781–1800	572	5	1876	5,016	41	1916	22,031	179
Ten-year			1877	5,512	45	1917	20,346	166
average			1878	5,761	47	1918	18,614	151
1801–1810	572	5	1879	5,262	43	1919	17,698	144
1811–1820	368	3						
1821–1830	457	4	1880	5,149	42	1920	16,130	131
1831–1840	652	5	1881	4,984	41	1921	15,975	130
1841–1850	1,761	14	1882	4,934	40	1922	15,452	126
			1883	4,615	38	1923	17,791	145
Annual			1884	4,921	40	1924	19,031	155
1845	1,177	10	1885	5,246	43	1925	19,026	155
1846	1,342	11	1886	5,136	42	1926	19,349	157
1847	1,412	11	1887	5,117	42	1927	19,431	158
1848	1,813	15	1888	5,331	43	1928	19,700	160
1849	3,154	26	1889	5,974	49	1929	19,500	159
1850	3,555	29	1890	5,749	47	1930	20,160	164
1851	4,049	33	1891	6,320	51	1931	22,819	186
1852	6,709	55	1892	7,094	58	1932	*23,718*	*193*
1853	7,227	59	1893	7,619	62			
1854	6,309	51	1894	8,764	71			
1855	6,639	54	1895	9,615	78			
1856	6,827	56	1896	9,784	80			
1857	6,662	54	1897	11,420	93			
1858	6,309	51	1898	13,878	113			
1859	6,074	49	1899	14,838	121			

Figures in italics are estimates.

* The data for world's gold production were taken from the following sources: 1493–1844 and 1876–1930, Annual Report of the Director of the Mint, for the Fiscal Year Ended June 30, 1931, p. 242, 1931.

The estimates from 1493 to 1840 are those compiled by Dr. Adolph Soetbeer.

The annual estimates from 1845 to 1875 are those reported by Joseph Kitchin, Union Corporation Limited, London.

From 1880 to 1914, the average annual production was 12,293 thousand fine ounces. The index numbers were therefore obtained by multiplying by 0.0081347.

From 1831 to 1930, the world's total gold production was 931,645,000 fine ounces.

a new peak was reached in 1912-15. Production then declined very rapidly until 1922, and then increased.

Effect of prices on gold production.—When gold is scarce compared with other commodities, it has a high value, that is, the prices of other commodities become low in countries that use gold for money. The search for gold is then very vigorous.

The long period of declining prices from 1814 to 1843 resulted in a world-wide search for gold, and it was found in Australia and California (table 1). This caused a considerable rise in prices from 1850 to 1870. The gold mines ran out and prices began a long decline which culminated in 1896. This long decline in prices was a great handicap to agriculture and other industries, but stimulated the search for gold. The long and feverish search was finally rewarded by discoveries in South Africa, Colorado, and Alaska.

During the World War period, gold ceased to be used for monetary purposes in most of the world. This increased the supplies in countries

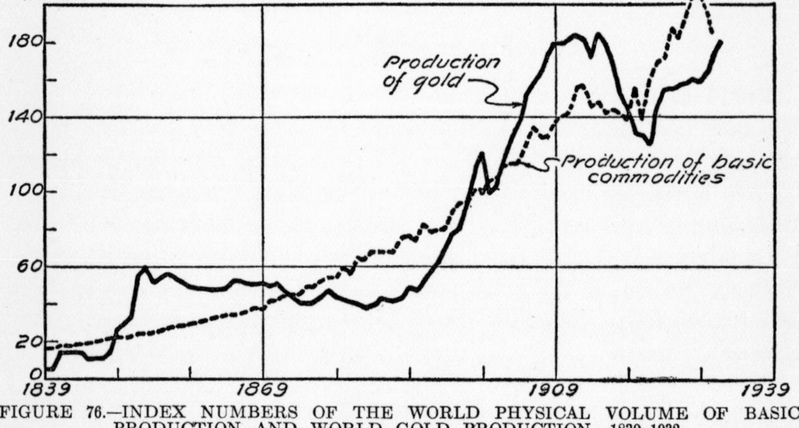

FIGURE 76.—INDEX NUMBERS OF THE WORLD PHYSICAL VOLUME OF BASIC PRODUCTION AND WORLD GOLD PRODUCTION, 1839-1932.
1880-1914 = 100.
The world gold production fluctuates more violently than world physical volume of production of all other commodities.

that continued to use gold and lowered the value of gold. Gold would buy less than half the pre-war amount of other things. The known gold mines had already reached their peak of production; this combined with the low value of gold reduced production by more than one-fourth. With the decline in commodity prices, or the rise in the value of gold, production of gold increased, but the production in 1931 was still below that 23 years previous.

The discovery of gold is largely fortuitous, but it is more likely to be discovered when it is vigorously searched for. Unfortunately, there is no assurance that vigorous search will bring it in any particular generation or in any particular amount.

Production of gold and of other basic commodities.—From 1865 to 1914, the world production of other commodities increased, decade after decade, at a very uniform rate of about 3.15 per cent per year (table 6, page 48). The only serious interruption in 90 years was the low production caused by the World War.

Gold production is very irregular because it depends on accidental discoveries. Considerable amounts were found from 1849 to 1860. No other large discovery occurred until the nineties. The production of the five-year period 1855-59 was higher than for any other five-year period up to 1890 (figure 76).

Since it is the stock of gold and not the production that determines prices, a period of high gold production does not at once have its full effect on prices. A period of low gold production has a cumulative effect in reducing prices.

USE OF GOLD IN INDUSTRY

World consumption of gold.—Gold and silver have many uses. This fact, and the fact that small quantities were very valuable, making them easy to transport, led to their use as money. Use as money did not lessen the desirability of use for other purposes. Whenever either one is used as money, the additional use increases its value. When silver was demonetized, the reduced demand reduced its value. Precisely the same thing happened to gold during the World War period when many countries ceased to use gold and to bid for it. This reduced its value.

The consumption of gold as a commodity used in industry is affected by value the same as the use of other commodities is affected by value.

World consumption of gold per capita in industry increased whenever the value of gold was low, and decreased when the value was high. In periods of depression, as during the World War, considerable jewelry is turned into the monetary stock. But in no year has there been added to the monetary stock as much gold as the world's total gold production in that year. In the year 1918, only 17 million ounces of gold were produced but 15 million were added to the monetary stocks. This was very unusual. In that year, the additions from jewelry and other sources were almost equal to the amount used in industry.

In the five-year period 1925-29, gold production amounted to 97 million ounces, of which 57 million were added to monetary stocks and 40 million were used in industry. The addition to monetary stocks was 11.4 million ounces per year, and the amount used in industry was 8 million.

There is a long-time tendency to increase the amount of gold used in industry about as rapidly as the use of other commodities increases. From 1845-49 to 1910-14, the consumption of gold in industry increased at the compound rate of 3.01 per cent per year.[6] The production of all other commodities increased at a compound rate of 3.15 per cent per year (page 47).

If gold were not used as money, the production necessary to keep its value stable compared with other commodities would apparently need to increase at the same rate as the production of other basic commodities, because normal consumption increased at about this rate.

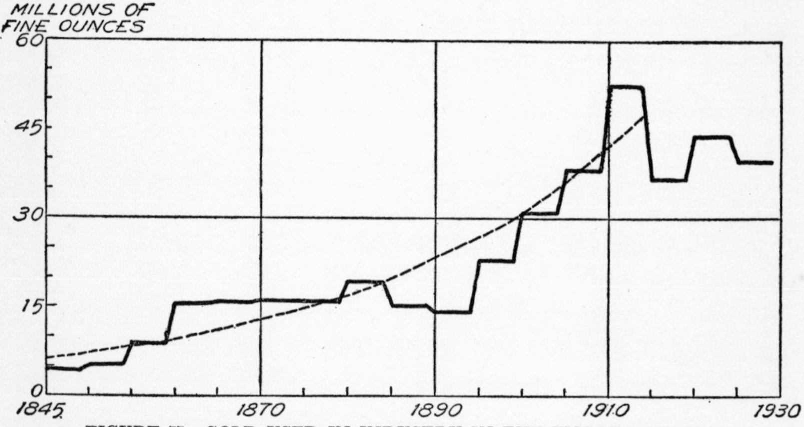

FIGURE 77.—GOLD USED IN INDUSTRY IN THE WORLD, 1845-1929.
The gold used in industry increases when gold has a low value and decreases when it has a high value. The long-time tendency of consumption increases at the same rate as the consumption of basic commodities, about 3 per cent per year.

When monetary stocks also increase at this same rate, the value of gold is stable.

Whenever any commodity is chosen as money, an additional use for it is provided by law which does not in any way detract from its desirability for other uses. If such a commodity is to maintain a stable value after being designated as money, the production of it must increase fast enough to maintain a stable value for industrial uses and in addition it must be produced in sufficient quantity to maintain a stable value for monetary uses. No such commodity can ever be found outside of "Alice in Wonderland."

Use of gold in industry in the United States.—The normal increase in the consumption of gold in industry in the United States is at the rate of 2.3 per cent per year (figure 78). During the eighties,

[6] $y = 6115.0\ (1.0301)^x$.

TABLE 16.—GOLD USED PER CAPITA IN INDUSTRY IN THE WORLD, 1845–1929

Five-year period	Total gold production, thousands of fine ounces*	Gold added to monetary stocks, thousands of fine ounces†	Per cent of production added to monetary stocks	Gold used in industry, thousands of fine ounces‡	World population, millions§	Gold used in industry per thousand of population, fine ounces
1845–49	8,898	4,473	50	4,425	1009	4.4
1850–54	27,849	22,599	81	5,250	1021	5.1
1855–59	32,511	23,776	73	8,735	1046	8.4
1860–64	29,426	13,889	47	15,537	1114	13.9
1865–69	31,545	15,772	50	15,773	1177	13.4
1870–74	28,202	12,006	43	16,196	1322	12.3
1875–79	26,424	10,593	40	15,831	1386	11.4
1880–84	24,603	5,414	22	19,189	1423	13.5
1885–89	26,804	11,535	43	15,269	1492	10.2
1890–94	35,546	21,422	60	14,124	1520	9.3
1895–99	59,535	36,724	62	22,811	1529	14.9
1900–04	71,953	40,961	57	30,992	1544	20.1
1905–09	101,231	63,090	62	38,141	1545	24.7
1910–14	110,581	58,146	53	52,435	1651	31.8
1915–19	101,427	64,738	64	36,689	1683	21.8
1920–24	84,379	40,255	48	44,124	1751	25.2
1925–29	97,059	57,205	59	39,854	1840	21.7
1850–1929	889,075	498,125	56	390,950	....	....

* Table 15.
† Table 11.
‡ The total world gold production less the amount used for monetary stocks is assumed to be used in industry. Small quantities are lost. Small quantities of other basic commodities are also lost.
§ Willcox, W. F., International Migration, National Bureau of Economic Research, No. 18, Vol. 2. Appendix I, p. 643. 1931.

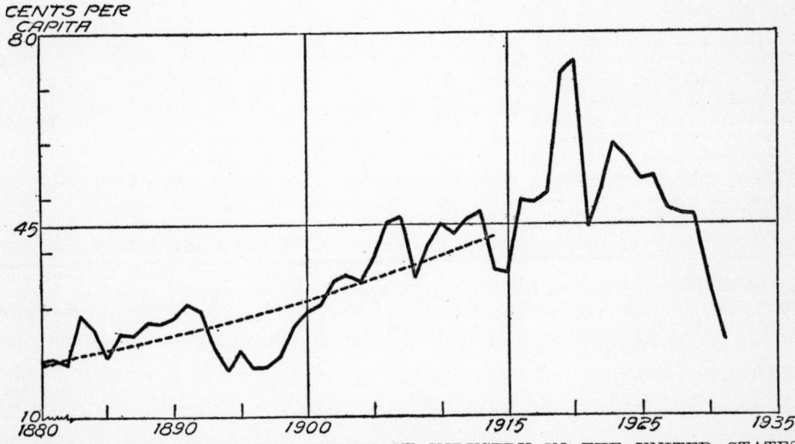

FIGURE 78.—GOLD USED PER CAPITA IN INDUSTRY IN THE UNITED STATES, 1880-1931.

From 1893 to 1899, the consumption of gold per capita in industry was low. With increasing production and declining value of gold, consumption increased rapidly from 1900 to 1920. Since then, consumption has declined. From 1880 to 1914, consumption normally increased 2.3 per cent per year.[7]

[7] The equation of trend from 1880 to 1914 is $y = 19.863\ (1.02313)^x$.

the gold used **annually in** industry amounted to 20 to 25 cents per capita. In 1896 and 1897, when gold was very valuable, the consumption amounted to only 19 cents. From 1897 to 1913, when prices were rising, there was a rapid increase in consumption per capita. During 1920, when wages were high and money was cheap, 75 cents worth of gold was used per capita. The next year there was a severe depression and only 45 cents worth was used (table 17). The consumption per capita in 1931, $0.235, was the lowest reported since 1898.

World gold production and additions to monetary stocks.—In the 80 years from 1850 to 1929, total world gold production amounted

TABLE 17.—GOLD USED IN MANUFACTURES AND THE ARTS IN THE UNITED STATES, 1880–1931*

Year	Total	Per capita	Year	Total	Per capita
1880	$10,105,432	$0.201	1910	$41,787,152	$0.453
1881	10,566,742	0.205	1911	40,834,292	0.436
1882	10,514,707	0.199	1912	43,977,257	0.462
1883	15,435,462	0.285	1913	45,864,066	0.475
1884	14,500,000	0.262	1914	36,137,075	0.369
1885	11,824,742	0.209	1915	36,126,353	0.364
1886	14,526,690	0.251	1916	50,042,175	0.497
1887	14,810,346	0.250	1917	50,415,641	0.493
1888	16,514,842	0.273	1918	53,014,385	0.512
1889	16,697,056	0.270	1919	76,132,251	0.725
1890	17,655,960	0.280	1920	79,715,087	0.748
1891	19,686,916	0.306	1921	48,455,477	0.448
1892	19,329,074	0.294	1922	56,613,658	0.515
1893	15,435,901	0.230	1923	66,892,245	0.600
1894	12,658,604	0.185	1924	64,791,440	0.573
1895	15,429,085	0.222	1925	61,225,870	0.533
1896	13,395,934	0.189	1926	62,990,839	0.541
1897	13,870,231	0.192	1927	56,819,728	0.481
1898	15,565,879	0.212	1928	56,581,659	0.472
1899	19,847,178	0.265	1929	56,903,667	0.469
1900	22,148,142	0.291	1930	42,689,379	0.347
1901	23,868,956	0.307	1931	29,157,865	0.235
1902	27,682,847	0.349			
1903	29,063,551	0.359			
1904	28,655,963	0.347			
1905	33,208,615	0.394			
1906	39,126,763	0.456			
1907	40,727,070	0.466			
1908	31,476,091	0.353			
1909	37,628,769	0.415			

* The figures for gold used in manufactures and the arts were obtained from the Annual Report of the Director of the Mint for the Fiscal Year Ended June 30, 1921, p. 62, 1921, and the report for 1931, p. 40, 1931.

The annual value of gold used in the arts was divided by the population of continental United States as reported in the Statistical Abstract of the United States, 1930, Fifty-second Number, p. 3, 1930.

to 889,000,000 ounces (table 16). In this same period, the world's monetary stocks of gold increased by 498,000,000 ounces, or 56 per cent of the production was added to monetary stocks. The remaining portion of the production was used for industrial purposes. From 1920 to 1929, 54 per cent of production was added to monetary stocks.

When production is low, a smaller amount is used in industry, but a higher percentage of the production is so used.

Gold production, gold stocks, and prices.—Some economists have made the misleading statement that since 1922 gold production has been increasing as rapidly as the production of other things, and they therefore assume that production is rapid enough. The unscientific

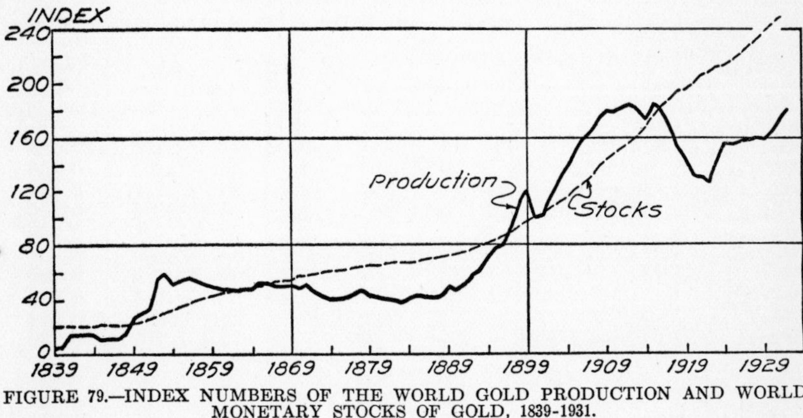

FIGURE 79.—INDEX NUMBERS OF THE WORLD GOLD PRODUCTION AND WORLD MONETARY STOCKS OF GOLD, 1839-1931.
1880-1914 = 100.
World gold production is very erratic. It has a slow but cumulative effect on monetary stocks.

nature of this statement is shown by figures 76 and 77. They chose a low point in production for a starting point. The same statement could have been made in 1884 but would not have forecasted the decline in prices that lasted for 12 years. World stocks of gold compared with the production of other things did correctly indicate prices, as they have done for recent years except during the period 1915-30, when much of the world was not using gold.

If a five-year-old-size suit is purchased for a ten-year-old boy, and if each year a suit one year larger is purchased, it does not follow that the suits will fit, just because the size increases at the same rate as the boy grows. If the start had been with a suit for a fifteen-year-old, the steady increase would have been equally ridiculous the other way. It is very surprising that such a manifest error has been accepted by many economists. It completely ignores the most elementary principles of economics. It is the supply of a commodity on hand and not the year's production that affects its value. A bale of cotton that was carried over from the 1931 crop will affect prices exactly as much as a bale that was grown in 1932. In the case of gold, this fallacy is far worse because world stocks of gold should be nearly 18 times one year's production.

For a stable and equitable price level, world monetary stocks of gold must first be large enough to sustain the price level to which society is adjusted and must thereafter increase at the same rate as the production of other commodities, or about 3.15 per cent per year.

In order to have the monetary stocks increased 3.15 per cent per year when only 56 per cent of the production is added to monetary stocks, world production must be 5.6 per cent of world monetary stocks of gold ($3.15 \div 0.56 = 5.6$).

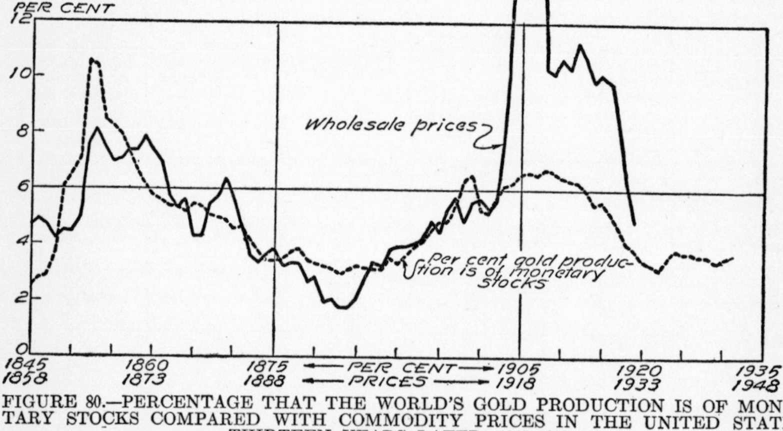

FIGURE 80.—PERCENTAGE THAT THE WORLD'S GOLD PRODUCTION IS OF MONETARY STOCKS COMPARED WITH COMMODITY PRICES IN THE UNITED STATES THIRTEEN YEARS LATER, 1845-1932.

1880-1914 = 100.

When gold production is high relative to monetary stocks, prices rise. Conversely, when production is low relative to monetary stocks, prices fall. The price changes lag compared with production because it is gold stocks that control prices.

From 1850 to 1854, production of gold was 8.8 per cent of stocks. This high production resulted in a rapid rise in prices.

For over 30 years ending with 1897, gold production was too low to maintain a stable price level and prices steadily declined. Prices in England dropped 45 per cent from 1873 to 1896.

For 85 years, there was only one five-year period in which gold production was less than 5.6 per cent of monetary stocks, that was not followed by a decline in prices in England. In every five-year period in which production was more than 5.6 per cent of stocks, a rise in prices followed.

The percentage that the world's annual gold production is of monetary stocks as compared with the rate required for the maintenance of stable prices is shown in figure 80.

The relation of gold production to monetary stocks and prices in the United States 13 years later is shown in figure 80. Since excessive production piles up stocks, it has a cumulative effect on prices. Since deficient production results in a cumulative deficiency in monetary stocks, the decline in commodity prices lags behind the change in production.

Beginning with prices and world stocks in adjustment, world gold stocks should increase 3.15 per cent per year to maintain stable prices.

TABLE 18.—WORLD GOLD PRODUCTION AND WORLD MONETARY STOCKS OF GOLD, 1845–1929*

Five-year periods	Average annual world's production of gold, 000 fine ounces†	Estimated world's stock of monetary gold at end of the year, 000,000 fine ounces‡	Per cent gold production is of monetary stocks	Per cent change in index numbers of wholesale prices in England.‡ 1800–1914 =100	Per cent change in index numbers of wholesale prices in the United States.§ 1880–1914 =100
1880–1914........	12,293	231	5.3		
1845–49..........	1,780	49	3.6	− 8	0
1850–54..........	5,570	63	8.8	+ 1	+ 9
1855–59..........	6,502	89	7.3	+16	+12
1860–64..........	5,885	107	5.5	+ 2	Civil
1865–69..........	6,309	122	5.2	− 1	War
1870–74..........	5,640	136	4.1	+ 4	− 1
1875–79..........	5,285	146	3.6	−12	−17
1880–84..........	4,921	154	3.2	− 9	+ 5
1885–89..........	5,361	162	3.3	−15	−17
1890–94..........	7,109	178	4.0	− 3	− 7
1895–99..........	11,907	209	5.7	− 6	− 9
1900–04..........	14,391	249	5.8	+11	+20
1905–09..........	20,246	304	6.7	+ 5	+10
1910–14..........	22,116	362	6.1	+11	+ 7
1915–19..........	20,285	433	4.7	World War	World War
1920–24..........	16,876	481	3.5	−13	+ 1
1925–29..........	19,401	525	3.7	− 9	−10

* Based on averages for periods.
† Table 15.
‡ Table 11.
§ Table 12.

This requires that the world's gold production should be equal to 5.6 per cent of the world monetary stock of gold.[8] The actual production

[8] Since the growth of the use of gold in industry is almost the same as the normal growth of business, an increase in production of 3.15 per cent per year would maintain stable prices if at the starting point world stocks and prices were in adjustment, and if production for the starting year were 5.6 per cent of world stocks.

in 1929 was considerably less than 4 per cent of monetary stocks. In 1929, we therefore had a combined situation of the business world adjusted to a price level about 40 to 50 per cent higher than the world gold supply could be expected to support, a rate of gold production too low to support even pre-war prices, and a frantic demand for gold.

It is impossible to state how much of the decline in gold production was due to the decline in its value during the war period. Apparently prices would soon have begun to decline had there been no war.

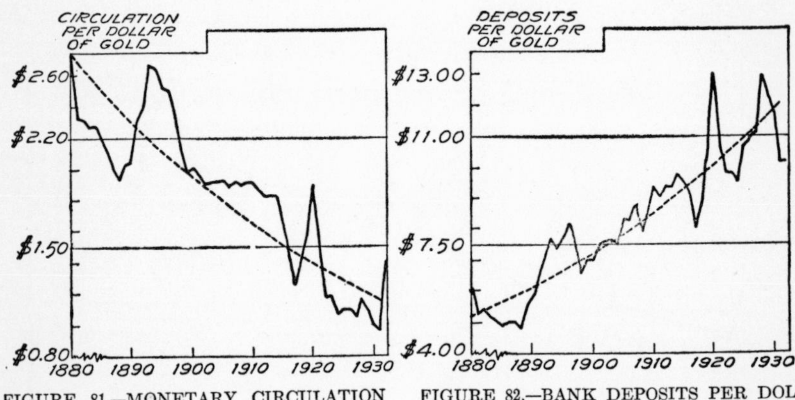

FIGURE 81.—MONETARY CIRCULATION PER DOLLAR OF GOLD IN THE UNITED STATES, 1880-1932.

Monetary circulation per dollar of gold has decreased at the rate of 1.66 per cent per year.

FIGURE 82.—BANK DEPOSITS PER DOLLAR OF GOLD IN THE UNITED STATES, 1880-1932.

Bank deposits per dollar of gold have increased at the rate of 1.68 per cent per year.

To increase the gold stocks of about 577 million ounces in 1931 by 3.15 per cent and provide for normal industrial use, would call for a gold production of about 32 million ounces in 1932. The actual production was less than three-fourths of this amount. With industry proceeding in a normal way and all the world established on a gold basis and prices adjusted to the gold supply, the rate of production would call for a price decline of about 1 per cent per year.

Efficiency in the use of gold.—The high prices before 1930 were often erroneously attributed to a sudden and violent permanent increase in the efficiency with which gold was used. This error led to expectation that high prices would continue. For several years after prices fell, the same error led to the expectation that the price level would be automatically restored.

In the 50-year period, the monetary circulation of the United States steadily declined in proportion to gold (table 19). Bank deposits (or credit) steadily rose in proportion to gold.

For 52 years, 1880-1931, the average rate of decrease of monetary circulation per dollar of gold was 1.66 per cent per year[9] (figure 81).

In this same period, bank deposits per dollar of gold increased at the rate of 1.68 per cent per year[10] (figure 82).

In these 52 years, the sum of monetary circulation plus bank deposits per dollar of gold increased 1.06 per cent per year.[11] There is no indication that the Federal Reserve system has stimulated this increase (figure 83).

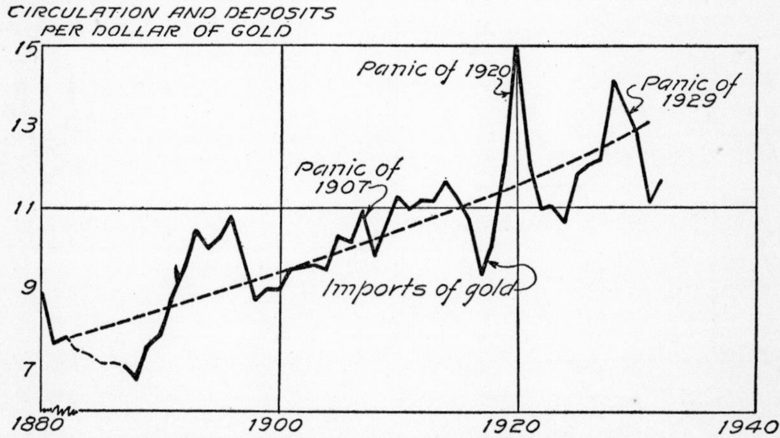

FIGURE 83.—MONETARY CIRCULATION PLUS DEPOSITS PER DOLLAR OF GOLD IN THE UNITED STATES, 1880-1932.

For 52 years, monetary circulation plus deposits per dollar of gold increased about 1 per cent per year. If any change has occurred in recent years, it appears that the rate of increase in the efficiency in the use of gold is less rapid than formerly.

For five years before the war, the average amount of monetary circulation plus bank deposits per dollar of gold in the United States was $11.23. From 1923 to 1927, the average was $11.56. This shows less than the normal increase. This sum reached $14.92 in 1920, and a severe panic occurred. In 1928, this sum reached $14.13. Apparently there is a limit to the amount of currency and credit that can be built up on an ounce of gold (figure 83). Fiat credit seems to be more treacherous than an equal amount of fiat money.

The fact that world gold production has had to increase with the production of other things in order to maintain stable commodity

[9] $y = 2.7283\ (0.98342)^x$.
[10] $y = 5.2186\ (1.0168)^x$.
[11] $y = 7.5857\ (1.0106)^x$.

TABLE 19.—MONETARY GOLD, MONEY IN CIRCULATION, AND BANK DEPOSITS IN THE UNITED STATES ON JUNE 30, 1880–1933

Period or year	Monetary gold coin and bullion* 000,000 omitted	Total monetary circulation† 000,000 omitted	Total individual deposits‡ 000,000 omitted	Monetary circulation per dollar of gold	Deposits per dollar of gold	Monetary circulation plus deposits per dollar of gold
1880–89	$ 565	$1,235	$ 2,943	$2.23	$ 5.25	$ 7.48
1890–99	699	1,628	4,962	2.33	7.10	9.43
1900–09	1,349	2,596	10,792	1.92	8.00	9.92
1910–19	2,290	3,702	21,210	1.62	9.26	10.88
1920–29	4,029	4,861	44,510	1.21	11.05	12.26
1880	352	973	2,134	2.76	6.06	8.82
1881	478	1,114	2,539	2.33	5.31	7.64
1882	507	1,174	2,756	2.32	5.44	7.76
1883	543	1,230	2,824¶	2.27	5.20¶	7.47¶
1884	546	1,244	2,782¶	2.28	5.10¶	7.38¶
1885	589	1,293	2,910¶	2.20	4.94¶	7.14¶
1886	591	1,253	2,981¶	2.12	5.04¶	7.16¶
1887	655	1,318	3,304	2.01	5.05	7.06
1888	706	1,372	3,419	1.94	4.84	6.78
1889	680	1,380	3,776	2.03	5.55	7.58
1890	696	1,429	4,061	2.05	5.83	7.88
1891	647	1,497	4,197	2.31	6.49	8.80
1892	664	1,601	4,665	2.41	7.03	9.44
1893	598	1,597	4,627	2.67	7.74	10.41
1894	627	1,661	4,651	2.65	7.42	10.07
1895	636	1,602	4,921	2.52	7.74	10.26
1896	600	1,506	4,945	2.51	8.24	10.75
1897	696	1,641	5,095	2.36	7.32	9.68
1898	862	1,838	5,688	2.13	6.60	8.73
1899	963	1,904	6,769	1.98	7.03	9.01
1900	1,034	2,081	7,239	2.01	7.00	9.01
1901	1,125	2,203	8,461	1.96	7.52	9.48
1902	1,193	2,279	9,105	1.91	7.63	9.54
1903	1,249	2,400	9,554	1.92	7.65	9.57
1904	1,328	2,553	10,001	1.92	7.53	9.45
1905	1,358	2,623	11,351	1.93	8.36	10.29
1906	1,476	2,775	12,216	1.88	8.28	10.16
1907	1,466	2,814	13,100	1.92	8.94	10.86
1908	1,618	3,079	12,785	1.90	7.90	9.80
1909	1,642	3,149	14,108	1.92	8.59	10.51
1910	1,636	3,149	15,283	1.92	9.34	11.26
1911	1,753	3,263	15,906	1.86	9.07	10.93
1912	1,818	3,335	17,024	1.83	9.36	11.19
1913	1,871	3,419	17,476	1.83	9.34	11.17
1914	1,891	3,459	18,518	1.83	9.79	11.62
1915	1,986	3,320	18,966	1.67	9.55	11.22
1916	2,445	3,649	22,526	1.49	9.21	10.70
1917	3,220	4,066	26,058	1.26	8.09	9.35
1918	3,163	4,482	27,716	1.42	8.76	10.18
1919	3,113	4,877	32,629	1.57	10.48	12.05
1920	2,865	5,468	37,268	1.91	13.01	14.92
1921	3,274	4,911	34,791	1.50	10.62	12.12
1922	3,785	4,463	37,144	1.18	9.81	10.99
1923	4,050	4,823	39,984	1.19	9.87	11.06
1924	4,488	4,849	42,904	1.08	9.56	10.64
1925	4,365	4,815	46,715	1.10	10.70	11.80
1926	4,447	4,885	48,827	1.10	10.98	12.08
1927	4,587	4,851	51,062	1.06	11.13	12.19
1928	4,109	4,797	53,245	1.17	12.96	14.13
1929	4,324	4,746	53,158	1.10	12.29	13.39
1930§	4,535	4,522	53,564	1.00	11.81	12.81
1931§	4,956	4,822	50,485	0.97	10.19	11.16
1932	3,919	5,695	41,180	1.45	10.51	11.96
1933	4,318	5,721		1.32		

* Statistical Abstract of the United States 1930, United States Department of Commerce, 52nd Number, pp. 246–7. 1930.

† From 1880 to 1899 inclusive, Statistical Abstract of the United States 1923, No. 46, p. 605, 1924; and from 1900 to 1929, Statistical Abstract of the United States 1930, No. 52, p. 247, 1930.

‡ From 1880 to 1914, Statistical Abstract 1923, No. 46, p. 798, 1924, and from 1915 to 1929 from Statistical Abstract of the United States 1930, No. 52, p. 262, 1930.

§ Annual Report of the Comptroller of the Currency, December 1, 1930, pp. 57 and 138, 1931; and Text of the Annual Report of the Comptroller of the Currency, pp. 128 and 146, December 1931.

¶ The deposits for private banks are not available for 1883–86. These deposits in 1882 represented 10.7 per cent of the total deposits and in 1887 they represented 2.9 per cent of the total. The deposits for the private banks were estimated for the 4 years, 1883–86, by linear interpolation. Those estimates were added to the deposits for all banks except private banks to get the estimated totals.

prices is challenged because there is increased efficiency in the use of gold due to the use of checks, more rapid transmission of money, and numerous other factors. It makes no difference how many of these things may be demonstrated, the fact remains that gold had to increase with the production of other things to maintain stable prices (page 80). The question to explain is why this is true.

The small increase in the efficiency in the use of gold is easily offset by other factors. Some of these may be that there is a steady decrease in self-sufficiency, not only of individuals but of communities. The number of transactions to handle a given volume of physical production has increased. When bread was made in the home, fewer transactions were involved than when bread is purchased. Increased fabrication may have occurred. There is a steadily increasing number of non-commodity transactions. Newspaper, radio, hospital, and moving picture employees and laborers are relatively more numerous than formerly. When commodity prices are stable, wages rise and require more money. All these things have been occurring gradually throughout the 75-year period. The efficiency in the use of gold has also been increasing gradually. Whatever the explanation, the simple fact that the general course of prices has been determined by the ratio of gold stocks to production of other things is established.

It was often said that the United States had more gold in 1929 than it needed and that the gold was sterilized. The total credit outstanding was high in proportion to total gold supply, indicating that the gold was fully used (table 19). It was so fully used as to cause a reaction.

It is also contended that whereas an increase of gold stocks formerly may have been necessary, it is not now, because the period from 1839 to 1914 was a time when a shift was being made from silver to gold. This shift is still continuing. There is also a steady shift from silver to gold paper in the gold-using countries. England recently attempted to put India on a gold basis. Mexico oscillates between silver and gold. Many countries in South America have never securely established the gold basis. If gold continues its progress as money, the rising demand will go on for years.

These various contentions are further answered by the fact that in the United States, which was on a gold basis from 1880 to 1914 and which made numerous changes in the banking system, it was necessary for our gold stocks to increase as fast as the production of other things in order to maintain stable prices.

Can a country make gold cheap?—Suppose one country should expand its currency or credit in proportion to gold as long as it could remain on a gold basis; how much could it raise commodity prices? So far as world demand for gold was reduced by that country's getting along with less than its normal share of world gold, world prices would be raised, but this would be a very limited amount.

A tariff can raise prices of some commodities, but it does not seem to raise the whole price level much. Index numbers of prices in the United States and England are surprisingly alike. Considering prices for 1910-14 as 100, prices in both England and the United States in 1929 were 139. Prices in England in 1829 were 112; American prices were then 96 for all commodities and 102 for basic commodities. In this century, ocean transportation costs declined so that our prices should have been lower at the earlier date. The index numbers may not be equally representative of their respective countries, but the similarity is very striking. When either country left the gold basis, its prices were different. Apparently a country can either control its price level or remain on a gold basis, but trying to do both is attempting to regulate the value of gold, which is probably more difficult than regulating the value of cotton.

Apparently the possibility of any country's making gold cheap compared with other commodities is very limited so long as both gold and other commodities move in international trade. Tariffs and manipulation may make one product high, but raising a price level is a difficult matter. If one country expands its credit per ounce of gold, instead of raising commodity prices much, it is likely to raise prices of securities and finally result in transferring gold to other countries, so that any little rise that comes in commodity prices is lost.

If all countries suddenly decided to get along with a much higher amount of credit and currency per ounce of gold, some results might be obtained, but this does not come except by slow growth. It is not to be expected after the greatest period of monetary chaos in modern times, if not in all history. The act neither of one country nor of all countries can easily reduce the value of gold except by demonetizing it. Nor can an international agreement cause the citizens of the world to change their ideas of how small they will allow reserves to go without desiring to hold the gold. If they are prohibited from getting gold, the gold basis is abandoned.

Apparently we should not expect a given gold supply with a given volume of business to support as high a price level as it would have supported before the war. A report of the Gold Delegation of the

League of Nations[12] states that gold stocks are ample, and that prices should rise. It implies that they are ample to support the pre-deflation price level. This, like innumerable reports and opinions, is based on an imagined pyramid of credit that has never occurred. It is in the realm of hope and imagination rather than science or probability. No man and no nation should base business procedure on such a wish.

Gold is a commodity—not a myth.—Its value cannot be controlled by any country. No other commodity is so completely dominated by

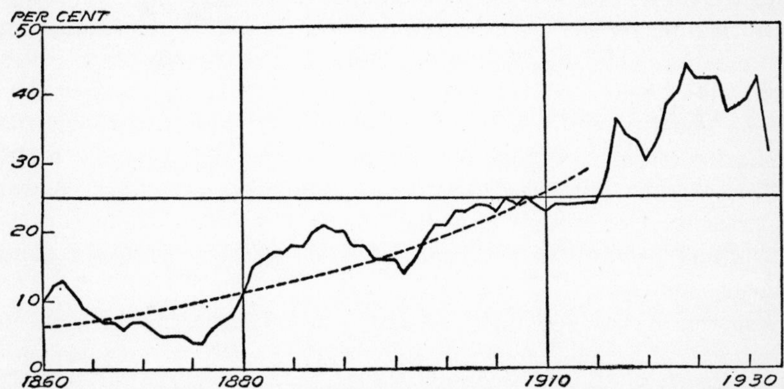

FIGURE 84.—PERCENTAGE OF THE WORLD'S GOLD STOCKS HELD IN THE UNITED STATES, 1860-1932.

The percentage of the world gold stocks held in the United States has tended to increase but at a very irregular rate.[13] The proportion was abnormally high for 1915-31.

world supply and world demand. Other commodities of high value per pound, such as platinum and diamonds, would be as completely dominated by world supply and demand, but they are subject to tariffs and other trade restrictions.

Gold stocks in the United States.—From 1839 to 1914, and probably since the settlement of the country, the physical volume of production in the United States increased more rapidly than the physical volume of production of the world. Since the war the differences in rate have declined. From the five-year pre-war average to 1929, the physical volume of production in the United States increased 46 per cent and world physical volume 40 per cent.

The percentage of the world stocks of gold in the United States has

[12] New York Times, June 11, 1932.

[13] From 1860 to 1914, the proportion of the world's gold stocks held in the United States increased at the same rate of 2.86 per cent per year. $y = 6.3029 (1.02859)^x$.

been extremely irregular, but was gradually rising (figure 84 and table 12).

It fell to only 4 per cent in the Civil War period during the suspension of specie payment, rose rapidly in the eighties, but declined in the nineties. For the five years before the war the United States had an average of 24 per cent of the world's gold supply. If the supply had been distributed in 1929 in accordance with the relative increases in physical volume of production the United States would have had 25 per cent of the total. It actually had 38 per cent.

During the early part of the panic most of the nations continued to pay their debts to the United States and in 1931 its gold stocks rose to 42 per cent of the total monetary supply of gold. Many countries discontinued paying interest on their bonds, and foreign balances were withdrawn so that in 1932 the United States had about a third of the world's monetary stock of gold. This resulted in fear that the gold standard could not be maintained. This is quite out of keeping with the idea that gold is being used efficiently.

From the five-year pre-war average to 1929, monetary stocks of gold in the United States increased 141 per cent although the total world gold increased only 52 per cent. Had this amount of gold been as effective on commodity prices as the gold supply previous to the war, prices in the United States would have been materially higher than they were in 1929.

WHY WERE PRICES HIGH?

Why were prices high from 1915 to 1920?—The real problem that requires explanation is not why prices fell when the world went back to a gold basis, but why prices in the gold-using countries were so high from 1915 to 1929. With the outbreak of the war, most of the countries of the world discontinued the use of gold and gave little attention to gold supplies. Gold moved to the few places where there was a market for it. The reduced demand for gold made it cheap, or made prices rise in the few countries that remained on the gold basis.

The popular explanation is that shortage of food made high prices, but the price of silver rose slightly more than prices of other things. In 1920, commodity prices in gold rose to an index of 226. The ounces of silver that an ounce of gold would buy fell from the 5-year pre-war average of 36.35 to 15.31, or the index of the price of silver was 237 (table 25).

Gold was worth only 44 per cent of its pre-war value in buying commodities and was worth only 42 per cent of its pre-war value in buying silver.

The values of commodities in terms of gold and of silver are shown in figure 85. In 1918, commodities rose to 191 in terms of gold, when pre-war is 100. When compared with silver, commodities were 104 compared with the pre-war average. Attempts to explain high prices in terms of war demand for food do not explain why commodities were worth only a little more than pre-war in terms of silver or in terms of practically anything else except gold. Certainly there must have been some commodities not used for food or war supplies. It was

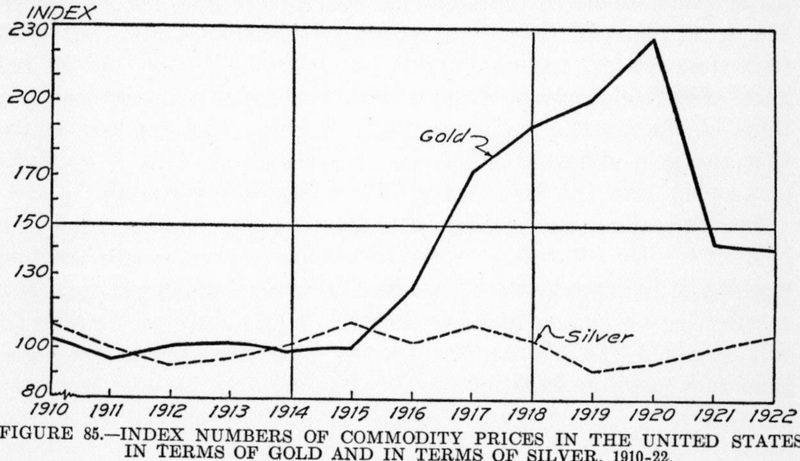

FIGURE 85.—INDEX NUMBERS OF COMMODITY PRICES IN THE UNITED STATES IN TERMS OF GOLD AND IN TERMS OF SILVER, 1910-22.
1910-14 = 100.

Prices in gold more than doubled, but the value of commodities in terms of silver was fairly stable, during the war period. The primary factor in the rise of commodity prices was the low demand for gold.

gold rather than commodities that changed in value. The value of gold was determined primarily by world supply and world demand, not by location. After 1923, silver fell in value when compared with all commodities. This is easily explained by the melting down of subsidiary coins in gold-using countries and by the attempts of India and other silver-using countries to shift to gold.

From 1915 to 1920, the government bought large amounts of commodities in the early stages of their passage through the channels of trade and completed the passage through industry to soldiers, and to Europe, without the use of money. This must have greatly reduced the monetary transactions for a given physical volume of production.

Government and private hoarding of goods also contributed to high prices by stopping the number of transactions that would have occurred if the goods had gone through the channels of trade. England did not sell the last of her war supplies of pork until 1921. Italy was rationing her hoard of sugar in 1921, not to hold prices down (world prices were very low), but to get rid of the sugar at a high price.

Why were prices high from 1921 to 1929?—From 1921 to 1929, prices were at all times high for the world gold supply, but were low for the United States gold supply. It seems probable that the growing interest of the world in accumulating gold so as to go back to the gold standard was steadily influencing the value of gold. The return to gold is a slow process. The demand for gold grows gradually both before and after the first attempt to establish a limited gold exchange standard. This is only one step in a slow process. Countries that are on a paper basis find it easy to sell in gold countries and difficult to buy from them. Gold balances were gradually accumulated. In many cases, the countries were willing to allow the gold to remain in the United States after they had acquired control of it in the form of commercial or bank credits in this country. Gold held in this way would not be expected to have its usual efficiency in supporting commodity prices.

This gold was available, however, on short-time credits for stock-market speculation and caused credit expansion. Gold is a commodity the exchange value of which for other commodities seems to be controlled in the same way as the value of other commodities, by world supply and world demand. Mere credit expansion is not sufficient fully to control this, but may cause speculation in securities (page 110).

This explanation of prices is based on world demand for gold. Demand is not so easily measurable as the supply of gold and the production of commodities. Therefore, there cannot be as undebatable a conclusion as one would wish. A sound explanation of an event should have made the forecasting of that event possible if the facts on which it is explained were known in advance. The writers have at all times forecasted the return of gold to its pre-war value or higher, but the basis has not been so secure as a forecast based on supply (page 117).

Why prices fell.—The world's gold production in 1930 was less than the production 22 years before that date. Prices below pre-war levels would have been expected had it not been for the check in the production of other things which the war caused.

World monetary stocks of gold in 1929 were 52 per cent above the five-year pre-war average. If the world physical volume of production of commodities had continued to increase at the pre-war rate, it would have been 69 per cent above the pre-war average. Fortunately for the price level, the world physical volume of production of all commodities was only 40 per cent above pre-war. The normal expectation was, therefore, that prices in 1929 would have been 9 per cent above pre-war ($1.52 \div 1.40 = 1.09$).

The years of low demand for gold resulted in business in the United States becoming adjusted to a price level about 40 to 50 per cent above pre-war. Prices in 1929 averaged 139. The amount of gold necessary to sustain that price level, with all the world back on a gold basis and the volume of production of 1929, was about double pre-war ($1.39 \times 1.40 = 1.95$). To sustain this price level would have required about 28 per cent more gold stocks than existed in 1929 ($1.95 \div 1.52 = 1.28$). This would have required 704 million ounces of world monetary stocks of gold instead of the 550 million ounces which had been accumulated in all history.

The attempt of all the gold-using world to return to a gold basis brought prices back to their normal relationship to gold.

Before the other countries began to desire to have the gold back again, wholesale prices in the United States were about 40 to 50 per cent above pre-war.

England and other countries made the mistake of thinking that they could go back on the gold basis by deflating to the level of prices in the United States. They did not realize that this increased demand for gold would lower prices in both countries.

One after another, the various countries began to move toward the reestablishment of the gold standard. Sweden returned to the gold basis on April 1, 1924; Germany, in the fall of 1924; England and the Netherlands, on April 28, 1925; Belgium, October 25, 1926; Italy, December 22, 1927; and France, June 25, 1928.

These countries did not return to a free gold coinage but to a gold exchange basis so that one could get gold bars if he had money enough, and could give a good reason for desiring gold. In February 1932, in France, it required about $8000 to buy a gold bar. The only way that most Europeans could get gold was to buy American coins. Our $20 gold pieces were sold at $21.50 in France. This demand was so keen that New York banks tried to prevent the movement.[14] The demand was accentuated by the attempt of India to shift to a gold basis.

[14] New York Times, p. 26, February 3, 1932.

The vigorous bidding for gold made it very valuable, regardless of its location. The United States held large stocks of gold, but the world demand determined its value. The demand for gold gradually grew until there was a world-wide panic to get it. This panic grew worse and worse until the fall of 1931, when England and a large number of other countries discontinued the gold standard.

Price level to which business is adapted.—Many economists have been misled by attempting to explain the price level on the basis of gold supply alone without considering the price level to which business was adjusted. The low value of gold and resulting high prices from 1916 to 1928 were due to low demand for gold for monetary uses. The gold panic of 1929 and the collapse in the price structure were due to a sudden world-wide return of the demand for gold. On the pre-war relationships of gold to production of commodities there was about enough gold to sustain pre-war prices. The demand was greater than if there had been no war because every country desired high reserves to reestablish confidence. There were large international public and private debts. Trade conditions were erratic, making it difficult to settle international balances by trade. Each country, therefore, needed more gold reserves than normal to be safe. Since there was only gold enough for about pre-war prices with normal demand, prices below pre-war were and are to be expected. But all the gold-using countries that had not reduced the weight of gold in their coins had become adjusted to a commodity price level of about 40 to 50 per cent above pre-war.

There is nothing mysterious about the rise and fall in the value of gold. It follows the same laws that govern the value of any other commodity. When there was little demand for it, its value fell. When the frantic demand developed, its value rose.

It is often said that our present situation is a result of the war. It is a result of the war in that the war caused the low demand for gold. The price level and all human relationships became adjusted to this low value of gold. The price collapse resulting from the return of demand for gold brought on the same consequences that would at any time follow such a rise in the value of currency. The price collapse could have been avoided by monetary legislation.

Demand for gold and silver during the Napoleonic War Period.—The French Revolution broke out in 1789. Metal was abandoned as a basis of money in France. From 1789 to 1796, prices in England on a metal basis rose 48 per cent. England suspended metal payments on February 26, 1797. Prices in the United States on a metal basis rose

70 per cent from 1789 to 1796. The United States continued on the metal basis until the War of 1812. High prices continued until the various countries began to reestablish metal currencies. England spent several years in attempting to reestablish a metal basis. She finally returned to the metal basis on May 1, 1821. Prices in England expressed in metal fell 30 per cent from 1818 to 1821. Prices in the United States, which was on a metal basis, fell 31 per cent. The experiences were similar to the recent occurrences, but were less severe (figures 6 and 8, pages 14 and 15).

PRICE FORECASTS BASED ON THE SUPPLY OF AND DEMAND FOR GOLD

In all science, the ability to forecast results of a given force is one of the important tests to determine whether or not it is science. During the past eighteen years, forecasts have often been based on "a new economic era," anticipated efficiency in the use of gold, the idea that gold is merely a tradition, and that central bank policy and credit can control prices. These same bases are still being used by many persons. The following are a few of the many forecasts based on the supply of and demand for gold:

Oct. 31, 1918. "We may expect a slump in prices such as occurred following the Civil War, with a recovery and then a gradual lowering of prices. When the slump comes will be a time when general encouragement will need to be given." Warren, G. F.: Unpublished manuscript read at meeting of New York State Farm Bureau Federation, Oct. 31, 1918. Also presented at 24 meetings of farmers in various states.

February 1919. "Figure 2 shows the wholesale prices of all commodities during this war and during the Civil War. In each case the five-year average before the war is 100. It will be seen that prices rose at about the same rate as during the Civil War. In each case nearly all of the rise in prices took place in three years, and in each case prices doubled. After the Civil War, it was twelve years before the general price level reached the pre-war basis.

"It does not necessarily follow that prices will drop at the same rate following this war. The rate of drop in the general price level depends primarily on the financial policy that is followed. Ordinarily the period when currency of all kinds will be at its maximum would be expected to come a few months after the floating of the last government loan. . . .

"As the volume of currency is contracted prices will fall. A rather rapid drop in prices such as occurred after the Civil War is to be expected, followed by a gradual lowering of prices." Warren, G. F.: Why Are Prices High? Extension Service News, Volume II, No. 2, February 1919.

(*Note:* The campaign for the sale of the Victory Loan was April 21 to May 10, 1919.)

April 10, 1920. "EXPECT PANIC BEFORE PRICES ARE NORMAL." "WILL COME DOWN AS THEY WENT UP, ROCKETLIKE." Headline of a reprint in the Rochester Democrat and Chronicle, April 10, 1920.

January 1923. After discussing the movement of gold to the United States, its probable return, gold mining, credit, and the use of gold in industry, the following conclusion was reached:

"The latter combination of circumstances seems more probable than the former, and the chances seem to be that a generally declining price level is to be expected, of course with the usual short-time periods of rise and fall, but with a general tendency downward, as shown in figures 1, 2, and 3. It should be remembered, however, that other persons who have studied the same facts believe otherwise. So much depends on the production and movements of gold, and on financial policies, that long-time forecasts are uncertain."

"Judging by past experiences and by present tendencies, the following seem the most probable future trends of prices:

"1. Prices will be more erratic than formerly, and more unforeseen changes will occur.

"2. The up-and-down swings will be much more violent than before the war, but will, in general, decrease in violence as the years go by.

"3. The long-time tendency of prices will probably be downward, and is likely to approach or reach the pre-war level in from ten to fifteen years. This conclusion is not accepted as probable by all students of prices.

"4. If the general tendency is downward, the cycles of high and low will swing about a declining base. Each major rise will probably fall short of the previous high point. Each important decline will probably go lower than the previous low point.

"5. Prices of each individual commodity will continue to swing about the general price level. Unless some permanent change has taken place, those things that are below the general price level may be expected to rise and those that are above the general price level may be expected to fall.

"6. Wages may be expected to lag behind prices. Serious periods of unemployment may be expected at times." Warren, G. F.: Cornell University Agr. Exp. Sta. Bul. 416, January 1923, pp. 10, 37.

May 24, 1923. "Two or three times in the next ten years we may expect periods of severe business depression. It would not be surprising if one of these would be a very trying time.

"In order to be prepared to meet these situations, farmers should be cautious about having large sums of money due at any one time. If farm prices rise enough to make it possible, debts should be paid. Those who have large mortgages coming due in the next ten years would do well to consider converting them to the Land Bank form before interest rates rise. The ten-year tendency of interest rates may be downward but the tendency for the next year or two promises to be upward.

"Those who are working for wages will probably never again have a better time for saving money. Some are using this opportunity to go heavily in debt. The wiser course is to save the money now and buy the desired thing in the future when all or most of the purchase price has been saved. " Warren, G. F.: Farm Economics No. 3, May 24, 1923, p. 17.

Oct. 24, 1923. "While the present outlook is good, there are so many unstable elements in the present price structure and in world affairs that the conservative course is for debt payment whenever possible rather than expansion of the farm business. For those who are working for wages, this is the time to save money." Warren, G. F.: Farm Economics No. 8, Oct. 24, 1923, p. 64.

Nov. 20, 1923. After discussing the building and business situation, the following conclusion was reached:

"Why should all the above be presented when times are so good in cities? Because the more fully such possibilities are appreciated, the more cautious men become when there is too much optimism and the more optimistic they are when bad times come. Many of those who are too optimistic in good times are the very ones who are too pessimistic in bad times. A full appreciation of all the facts might also prevent too large a movement from farms to cities." Warren, G. F.: Farm Economics No. 9, Nov. 20, 1923, p. 81.

January 1924. "Summarizing all the probabilities, my guess is that the general tendency of prices for the next ten to fifteen years will be downward and that prices will closely approach or possibly go below the pre-war basis." . . .

"Fluctuations will be greater than normal. Unusually bad periods of unemployment will occur. The first bad one will probably come when city real estate prices are adjusted." Warren, G. F.: An Attempt to Forecast the Future Trend of Farm Prices, Journal of Farm Economics, January 1924, pp. 33-35.

February 11, 1924. "For reasons, a very few of which are given in Bulletin 416, my guess is that the general tendency of prices for the next ten to fifteen years will be downward and that prices will closely approach or possibly go below the pre-war basis. If prices do not decline the procedure recommended will be too conservative. But since there is certainly considerable danger that prices will fall the conservative procedure is safest. If the guess is correct, the status of agriculture can be forecast with considerable accuracy. Agriculture is now injured by a period of falling prices even more than it was after the Civil War because it is more commercial than formerly." Warren, G. F.: Farm Economics No. 11, February 8, 1924, p. 92.

Then follow 28 recommendations that result as corollaries.

February 1924. "The writer's guess is that the tendency of the general price level will be downward for some years, and that the prewar level will be approximately reached in about a decade." Warren, G. F.: The Agricultural Depression, Quarterly Journal of Economics, Vol. XXXVIII, February 1924, p. 213.

August 1924. "Apparently the only things that can make gold continue to be so cheap are increased supply or decreased demand."

"Following the World War, prices did not fall so soon as after the Civil War, but they fell more precipitously and fell farther. There is considerable similarity between the price movements of the Civil War and World War periods. The writers expect this similarity to continue."

"The demand for house room is very elastic. Before many years a reaction is likely to come. When it comes and there is unemployment in cities the population will suddenly find that much less room is necessary. Thrifty persons who have bought homes with a small payment down are likely to find their equities wiped out just as thrifty young farmers found their savings gone when farm values were readjusted. In any violent period of downward readjustment there is a time when prices go far too low. City houses have a very real and permanent value, but there may be periods when these values cannot be converted into cash at anywhere near their true worth, just as it is now impossible to convert farm houses, barns, and tile drains into cash at their true worth. Banks are more involved in the financing of city real estate than they are in financing farms.

The severest test of banks is likely to come when city real estate values are readjusted." Warren, G. F., and Pearson, F. A.: The Agricultural Situation, August 1924, pp. 260, 264, and 272.

Jan. 31, 1925. "Figure 1 shows the price of many commodities at wholesale during the Civil War and World War periods. The curve of prices following the World War is very similar to the curves of prices following the Civil War, the War of 1812, and the Napoleonic Wars in Europe. The curves represent changes in prices due to the reestablishment of an equilibrium of gold supplies in various countries and the establishment of an equilibrium between other commodities and gold. Just now, prices are rising and promise to rise more than they did in 1923, but regardless of how high they rise this year or whether they remain high for a year or two, there is a strong presumption that the tendency over a series of years will be downward. For this reason the safe procedure is:

"1. To exercise care in buying anything that is much above its pre-war price unless it will pay for itself quickly." Warren, G. F., and Pearson, F. A.: Farm Economics, No. 21, Jan. 31, 1925, p. 229. This is followed by six other conclusions:

Nov. 5, 1925. "Nothing makes prices rise so rapidly as rising prices. Industrial stocks in October were selling at 143 per cent above pre-war. Real estate in the large cities is more than double pre-war, and Florida building lots are selling at fabulous prices, because the buyer hopes to sell at still higher prices.

"Whatever the reaction in the next few months or few years may be, it seems probable that some of the present gold supply will ultimately go back to the place from which it came. If this occurs, an ultimate decline in prices is to be expected. The safe procedure for farmers is to use every opportunity to pay debts, especially if this can be done with farm products that are temporarily high in price. If prices are low, reasonable expansion may be safe, but, under the present circumstances, expansion on borrowed money is usually dangerous if prices are high. It is a good year to pay debts with potatoes rather than expand the potato acreage. The farmer who is out of debt may safely continue to farm in the usual way.

"Care in expenditures is also the safe policy for those city persons who are purchasing everything on the installment plan, in the expectation that cheap food, high wages, and full employment will continue forever." Warren, G. F., and Pearson, F. A.: Farm Economics No. 29, Nov. 5, 1925, pp. 346, 347.

February 1927. "Prices of white pine and brick for the Civil

War period and of yellow pine and brick for the World War period, are shown in Figure 1. The period of inflation during the Civil War resulted in such a low buying power of wages that building was discontinued. When deflation occurred, wages had a high buying power because food was very cheap, and because of the shortage of buildings due to the discontinuance of building during inflation. A building boom resulted. Building was overdone. Building materials were cheap for six years, after which recovery occurred. Thus far the Civil War description has been repeated." Warren, G. F., and Pearson, F. A.: Farm Economics No. 42, February 1927, p. 611.

June 1927. "Severe financial crises have occurred in Japan and in Germany.

"The multitude of city residences built in the United States in the last few years are becoming less readily salable."

"Prices of industrial stocks are still booming. If a man had invested $100 in average industrial stocks before the war, he would now be able to sell for $273. If he had invested in farm land, he would have great difficulty in selling. If he were able to sell at prices as quoted by the United States Department of Agriculture, he would get one-third above pre-war prices. In most parts of the country it is impossible to sell at any such figure. As is usually the case with prices on farm land, the quotations lag far behind the facts.

"The statement is often made that an unwarranted boom in farm land occurred in 1920. It will be noted that the peak of land prices was twice pre-war prices, whereas industrial stocks in May 1927 are two and two-thirds times pre-war prices. City real estate is also very high. If there were an unwarranted rise in farm land in 1920, what can be said of the present situation in cities?" Warren, G. F., and Pearson, F. A.: Farm Economics No. 45, June 1927, p. 682.

February 1929. "The most striking feature of the year 1928 was the phenomenal boom in the prices of stocks. The first part of the rise was a reaction from depressed prices. High earnings later justified a further rise in prices. After the rapid rise had continued for a time, much of the buying was not due to anticipated earnings, but to an anticipated advance in prices. When a market reaches this situation, it rises because it rises, and goes on indefinitely until a reaction comes. . . .

"In the similar period following the Civil War, there was a time when city houses were as difficult to sell as farms are now. After the Civil War, there was a short period of reaction followed by a building boom and a rise in the stock market which resulted in a decided reaction 9 years after deflation began. Thus far, the changes have been very similar, but more violent. This is the ninth year since deflation began, and while it is not certain that a reaction will come this year, caution in business affairs, particularly in debts, seems advisable." Warren, G. F., and Pearson, F. A.: Farm Economics No. 57, February 1929, p. 1026.

Aug. 22, 1930. "My guess is that wholesale prices will fall below pre-war, that is, gold will become more valuable than it was before the war, just as occurred after the Napoleonic Wars and after the Civil War. When it becomes valuable enough, it will be hunted for with vigor, and, in time, possibly enough will be found to raise prices. . . .

"If my diagnosis is correct, the individual American farmer should anticipate a still lower price level, except for commodities that are already below pre-war prices. . . . He should be careful about long-time debts, except for things that are below pre-war prices. . . .

"The Farm Board began by lending to cooperatives to enable them to hold cotton and wheat. In a period of financial deflation, holding is unusually hazardous and is not likely to be successful except when prices are distinctly below the general price level. . . .

"When the public finds that tariffs, export bounties, credit, and so forth, will not cure the depression, probably it will turn to money, as it did in 1896. There is then danger that the movement will be to a currency less stable than gold. What is needed is a currency more stable than gold. If this diagnosis is correct, it is time now to educate the public on money. When the question becomes political, it will be too late for real study." Warren, G. F.: Causes and Probable Duration of the Agricultural Depression, Proceedings of the International Conference of Agricultural Economists, Vol. 2, 1930, pp. 110-113.

Jan. 10, 1933. It will be observed that these price forecasts have not been based on how many men were killed in the war, on new economic eras, psychology, confidence, technological unemployment, over-production, bank policy, speculation, installment buying, fear of starvation because of efficiency, or any other of the innumerable mystical or hazy ideas in which the price level is shrouded. They are based on the very simple fact of the supply of and demand for the commodity which controls the price level—gold. One of the chief criticisms of this work is that it is so simple that it cannot be true. Truth is always simple. Ignorance is mystical.

Whatever the temporary price level, the future outlook is that for some years gold will have more than its pre-war value, or that prices will average below pre-war in any country that keeps its pre-war currency, and that extremely violent fluctuations will continue. It is, of course, conceivable, although highly improbable, that gold will be definitely and permanently abandoned as money by a large part of the world and thus its value will be reduced. It is also possible that the terrible years of bankruptcy and unemployment will result in finding gold in sufficient quantities to cause inflation in a later generation. It is safer for any farmer, laborer, or business man to make his plans on the basis of low prices than to think that we can wish the price level up or borrow it up. We can legislate it up, but it is unsafe to base business plans on this hope. The bases for price forecasts are given in chapter XXIII.

The debts to which reference has been so frequently made are here, and they will be here until disposed of by endless bankruptcies or by a return of the price level to the level that prevailed when the money was borrowed. They are not disposed of by borrowing to pay the interest or by shifting them to the government, unless the government fails to collect. Probably some time in the next few years, enough of the properties will be disposed of to new owners at panic prices so that business can begin again. Prosperity is not yet "just around the corner." It may be comforting to think that it is, but fiscal plans should not be made on a comforting wish.

When the bankruptcies are over, the nation can again be prosperous. If the deflation plan is followed to the bitter end, it will mean the life-time economic ruin of millions of individuals but will not hurt the next generation unless the foolish laws which are being passed remain to plague them.

The individual who has a good farm or home should ordinarily hold it as long as possible in the hope that some temporary rise in prices, by legislation or some other means, may be found to save the property, because giving up means the loss of everything.

The chief explanation of any human ill whose cause is unknown has always been personal sin or error. The suffering is a merited punishment and useful education for the sufferer. It would be sacrilegious to interfere with such a benign provision for purification of his soul and edification of his mind. The sufferer is not always agreed on the matter. He often attributes the results to witchcraft of someone with an "evil eye," or to Congress.

Most of the discussions in every period of deflation fall in this class. The man who has failed in business or who is out of work is blamed for it, and he often blames himself. In times like the present, this is adding insult to injury. Most of the failures are not because of "unsound business" but because of "unstable money," for which no individual is to blame. The business man who has failed should not be despondent or commit suicide. He should feel like a man who has just gone through a tornado, stripped of his property but escaped with his life. His family and friends should treat him accordingly.

The present depression is not an act of God for the purification of men's souls. It is not a business cycle.

It is not due to extravagant living. It is not due to unsound business practices. It is not due to over-production. It is not due to too great efficiency. It is not due to lack of confidence, but is the cause of lack of confidence.

It is due to high demand for gold following a period of low demand for gold.

It teaches the devastating effects of deflation, but teaches no other lesson that is good for society. The one lesson to be learned from it is that, if we are to have deflation, the miser is the wise man. The modern version of the miser who sells short is even wiser. The man who actively engages in business, producing things that the world needs, is foolish.

Studies of cost accounts on farms have shown that the best farmers have lost the most. When products are practically unsalable, the man who used good seed, sprayed or otherwise cared for his crops, loses more than the man who spent little and did little.

BIBLIOGRAPHY

Aftalion, A., The Causes and Effects of Movements of Gold into France, Selected Documents on the Distribution of Gold Submitted to the Gold Delegation of the Financial Committee, League of Nations II. Economic and Financial. 1931. II. A. 7. C. 102. M. 38. 1931. II. A, p. 7. February 1931.

Cassel, G., The Theory of Social Economy, pp. 434-467. 1924.

Cassel, G., The Supply of Gold, Interim Report of the Gold Delegation of the Financial Committee, League of Nations II. Economic and Financial. 1930. II. 26. C. 375. M. 161. 1930. II. Annex X, p. 71. September 1930.

Delmar, A., History of the Precious Metals from the Earliest Times to the Present. 1880.

Edie, L. D., Gold Production and Prices before and after the World War, Indiana University Studies, Vol. XV, No. 78. March 1928.

Edie, L. D., Money, Bank Credit, and Prices. 1928.

Edie, L. D., Rate of Increase of the Monetary Gold Stock in the United States, Journal of Political Economy, Vol. XXXVI, No. 5, pp. 560-68. October 1928.

Haberler, G., Die Kaufkraft des Geldes und die Stabilisierung der Wirtschaft. Schmollers Jahrbuch, 55. Jahrgang, Sechstes Heft, pp. 33-63. 1931.

Hawtrey, R. G., The Gold Standard in Theory and Practice. 1931.

Hawtrey, R. G., Trade Depression and the Way Out. 1931.

Jevons, W. S., Investigations in Currency and Finance. 1884.

Kemmerer, E. W., Money and Credit Instruments in their Relation to General Prices, Second Edition. 1909.

Kemmerer, E. W., The Gold Standard and the Present Economic Situation. Proceedings of American Philosophical Society, Vol. LXXI, No. 3, pp. 85-104. April 1932.

Kitchin, J., The Position of Gold. The Review of Economic Statistics, Preliminary Vol. III, pp. 257-263, August 25, 1921; Vol. VI, No. 2, pp. 73-76, April 1924; Vol. VIII, No. 3, pp. 114-119, July 1926; Vol. XI, No. 2, pp. 64-67, May 1929; and Vol. XIV, No. 3, pp. 126-131, August 15, 1932.

Kitchin, J., The Supply of Gold Compared with Prices of Commodities, Interim Report of the Gold Delegation of the Financial Committee, League of Nations II. Economic and Financial. 1930. II. 26. C. 375. M. 161. 1930. II. Annex XI, p. 79. September 1930.

Lehfeldt, R. A., Gold, Prices, and the Witwatersrand. 1919.

Lehfeldt, R. A., Controlling the Output of Gold. 1926.

Mlynarski, F., The Functioning of the Gold Standard, A Memorandum Submitted to the Gold Delegation of the Financial Committee of the League of Nations II. Economic and Financial, II. A. 25. F. 979 (F. Gold/67 [1]). September 1931.

Robertson, D. H., Money. 1922.

Rogers, J. H., America Weighs Her Gold. 1931.

Shibata, K., An Examination of Professor Cassel's Quantity Theory of Money. Kyoto University Economic Review, Vol. VII, No. 1, pp. 52-84. July 1932.

Stamp, J., Gold and the Price Level.

Strakosch, H., Monetary Stability and the Gold Standard, Selected Documents Submitted to the Gold Delegation of the Financial Committee, League of Nations II. Economic and Financial. 1930. II. 34. C. 374. M. 160. 1930. II, p. 8. 1930.

Strakosch, H., The Economic Consequences of Changes in the Value of Gold, Selected Documents Submitted to the Gold Delegation of the Financial Committee, League of Nations II. Economic and Financial 1930. II. 34. C. 374. M. 160. 1930. II, p. 20, 1930.

Wilcoxen, L. C., World Prices and the Precious Metals, Journal of the American Statistical Association, Vol. XXVII, No. 178, pp. 129-140. June 1932.

Woytinsky, W., Internationale Hebung der Preise als Ausweg aus der Krise, Veröffentlichungen der Frankfurter Gesellschaft für Konjunkturforschung. 1931.

Wright, P. Q., Gold and Monetary Stabilization, The University of Chicago Press. 1932.

Discussion on the paper presented by the Industrial Institute on An Experiment in the Application of Mathematical Methods of Statistical Analysis to Series of Economic Data, Journal of the Royal Statistical Society, Vol. XCV, Part II, pp. 187-278, January 1932.

The Purchasing Power of Gold. Report of the Gold Delegation of the Financial Committee. League of Nations II. Economic and Financial, 1932. II. A. 12. C. 502. M. 243. 1932. II. A. June 1932.

CHAPTER VI

SHORT-TIME VARIATIONS IN THE PRICE LEVEL

It has been shown that, for 75 years before the war, the monetary stocks of gold divided by the production of other commodities equalled prices and that there was no tendency for a given weight of gold to support either a higher or lower price level than the average for 75 years before the war. There are short-time fluctuations of prices away from the normal relationship (figure 60, page 80). To what are these variations due?

Price momentum.—Whenever any force causes a sudden price change, prices tend to be carried too far because of the law of price momentum. If some force should call for a reduction of 10 per cent in the price level, the adjustment would not come by a drop of 10 per cent. A drop of more than 10 per cent would occur, which would be followed by too much recovery, which in turn would be followed by a drop. By a succession of smaller and smaller overshootings, adjustment would finally occur. The initial cause of the price movement may be any one of many forces such as changes in the gold supply, business cycles, etc.

Low production resulting from low prices.—Whenever a sudden decline in price occurs, industrial production is quickly curtailed (page 46). This enters into total production, and the index of total production is somewhat reduced. In extreme cases, as in 1921 and 1931-32, a large decline in production occurs. The reduced production divided into the gold supply gives a high answer, which would call for high prices. In this case, the reduced production was a result of low prices. This results in a number of short price movements in the opposite direction from that which the ratio would indicate. For example, in 1921, production was so curtailed that gold divided by production was higher than for the preceding or following year. Such an increased ratio is the opposite of the regular relationship. It is also a cause of recovery in prices. There are a considerable number of short-time movements of this nature (figure 60). They are usually followed by prices a little higher than would be anticipated. To make these short-time deviations fit prices, they should be compared with prices at a later date.

Business cycles.—There is no such thing as a definite business cycle. There are a large number of cycles of different length for wheat, hogs, sheep, poultry, cattle, cotton, and automobile production, for building construction, and for prices of pig iron, stocks, bonds, etc. The algebraic sum of all these cycles properly weighted makes the business cycle. Therefore no two cycles are alike. The way to forecast future business cycles is to estimate each of the elements of the business cycle and to combine them according to their relative importance. Business cycles are somewhat like heredity; there is no such thing as the reproduction of a given plant or animal. By studying the individual factors of inheritance each working independently or sometimes linked, definite forecasts can be made of the character of the offspring.

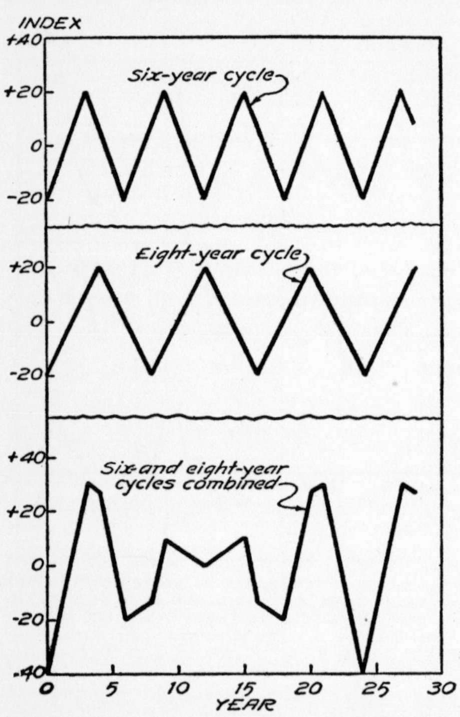

FIGURE 86.—A SIX-YEAR AND AN EIGHT-YEAR CYCLE, AND THE TWO COMBINED.

The 6- and 8-year cycles are regular. The resultant of the two appears irregular but is regular and repeats itself every 24 years. From an inspection of the lower curve, one would not suspect that it was the addition of two regular curves.

Before Mendel's Law was discovered, knowledge of inheritance was a matter of confusion. Crosses seemed to give an infinite variety of forms without much reason. When it was learned that there were a large number of unit characters, each inherited independently or occasionally linked with another, the apparent chaos was found to be orderly procedure by law. For example, if white-faced, horned Hereford cattle are crossed with black, hornless Angus cattle, the black bodies, white faces, and hornless characters are dominant. All the calves are hornless and white-faced with black bodies. When these calves are crossed with a Hereford, all of the next generation have white faces. About one-fourth are hornless with red bodies and look like hornless Herefords. About one-fourth are hornless with white faces and black bodies. About one-fourth are horned with black bodies and white faces. About one-fourth are horned with red bodies and white faces, and look like purebred Herefords.

An even more confusing example is the roan Shorthorn, which is a case of incomplete dominance when red and white animals are crossed, the color of which cannot be established as a fixed color. All this apparent confusion is a result of law.

Combination of cycles of different lengths.—A perfect cycle of mathematical regularity three years in length, and another of perfect regularity four years in length, are added in figure 86.[1] Although each of the independent curves rises to the same height, the sum of the two gives successive highs that are not alike.

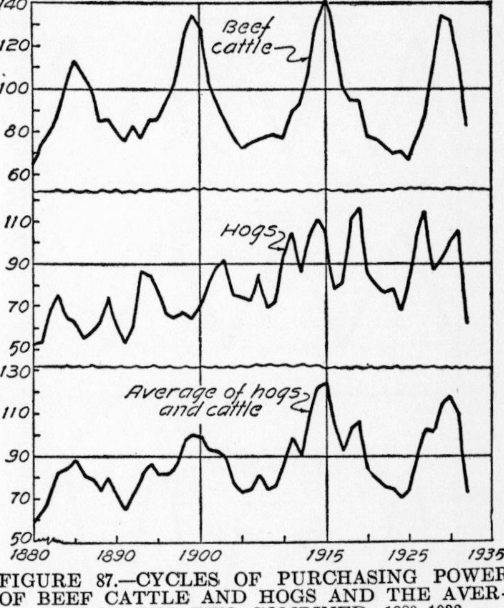

FIGURE 87.—CYCLES OF PURCHASING POWER OF BEEF CATTLE AND HOGS AND THE AVERAGE OF THE TWO COMBINED, 1880-1932. 1910-14 = 100.

The beef cycle is about 14 years long, and the hog cycle about 4 years. If a farmer normally sold equal average values of cattle and hogs, the combined curve would indicate the purchasing power of his income.

It can readily be seen that when not two but many independent curves are put together, the resultant may appear disorderly when in fact it is orderly.

The above is a theoretical case. An actual example is shown by the beef and hog cycles which should be watched by the banker and cattle feeder. The hog cycle is usually about four years in length and the beef cattle cycle about 14 years. The purchasing power of a farmer who produces a steady supply of hogs is shown by the hog cycle (figure 87), and the purchasing power of a farmer who pro-

[1] McNiece, T. M., The Formation of Economic Cycles, paper presented at the annual meeting of the American Statistical Association at Washington, D. C., December 29, 1931.

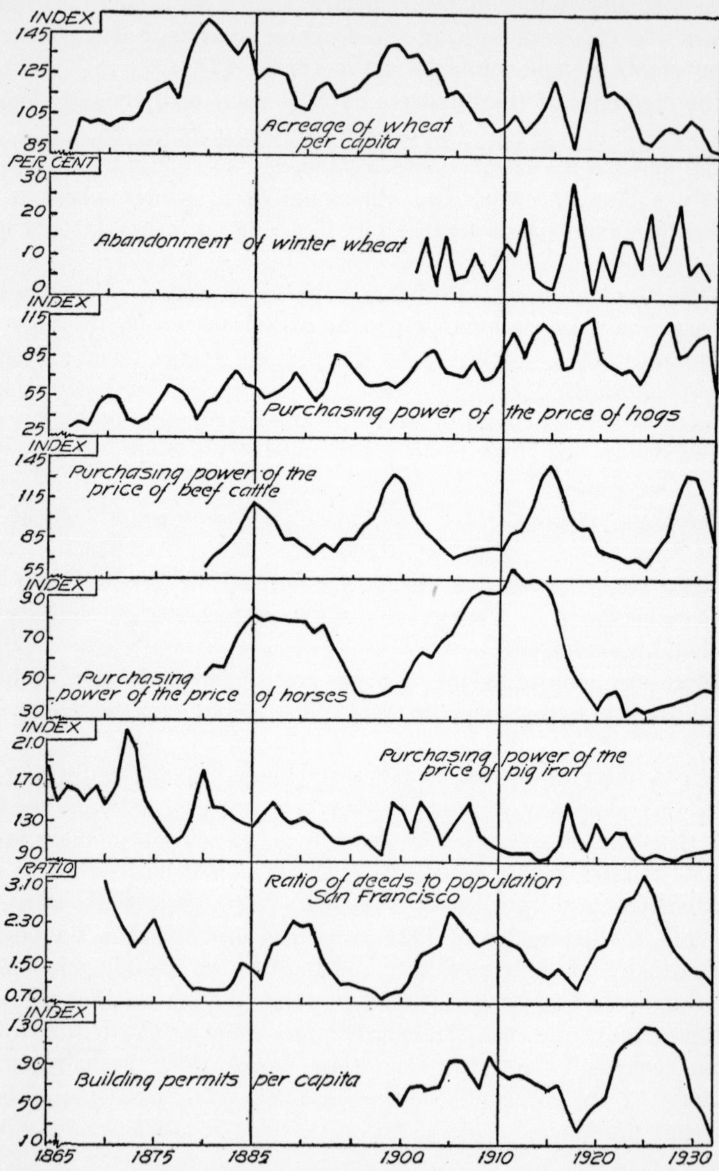

FIGURE 88.—A FEW OF THE MANY CYCLES WHICH ARE COMPONENTS OF THE BUSINESS CYCLE IN THE UNITED STATES.

The algebraic sum of all these and many other factors properly weighted makes the business cycle. Therefore no two business cycles are alike, although the components may be more or less regular.

duces a steady supply of beef cattle is shown by the cattle cycle. A farmer who produces both, in equal average values, has a purchasing power shown by the combined curve (figure 87).

The elements of the business cycle.—Some of the many elements which result in a given condition are shown in figure 88.

The acreage of wheat shows a tendency to fluctuate in approximately a 20-year cycle. The abandonment of winter wheat is due to weather and is non-cyclical but like other weather factors influences business.

When new railroads were being built, construction of new railway mileage was more or less cyclical in periods of about 15 years.

The quantity of building in the United States seems to follow a cyclical course.

There is a very definite cycle in the production of beef cattle. The peaks are about 14 to 16 years apart. This results in a cycle of purchasing power.

The hog cycle is slightly more irregular but is usually about four years long.

There seems to be a cycle in the purchasing power of pig iron.

There seems to be a very definite cycle in real estate activity and the building industry.

There are definite cycles of over- and under-production of horses about 25 years from peak to peak. The recent depression has been prolonged by the introduction of trucks and tractors, and the recovery is likely to be violent, but the cycle will undoubtedly continue.

All these and a multitude of other factors go to make up the business situation. When sufficient study is given to each of these factors and its relative importance is determined, it will be possible to forecast business conditions with a considerable degree of accuracy. For example, the depression of 1921 came in a low period in the building cycle whereas the depression of 1929 came at a high point in the building cycle. Both these depressions came in a period when there was a high supply of cattle. The former one came at the bottom of the horse cycle and the latter one when horses were becoming scarce. Because of the difference in the various cycles, particularly building, and differences in debt, the depression of 1929 was inevitably more severe and will be much longer than the depression of 1920.

Forecasting on the basis of the idea that there is a definite "business cycle" is very treacherous. When forecasts are made based on the components of the business cycle, much greater accuracy will be obtained.

CHAPTER VII

COMPARISON OF PANICS

All the great panics have come, not as business cycles, but as a result of a drop to a new and lower price level. These declines were accompanied by violent business cycles, but the change to the new price level was the major trouble. The cyclical reaction restored only a small percentage of previous prices.

Price collapse vs. business cycles.—Seven major panics have occurred in the United States: The Panics of 1818, 1837, 1864, 1873, 1893, 1920, and 1929.

After the Panic of 1864, there was a continuous readjustment of prices to a lower level until 1896. The peak of every cycle was lower than the previous peak. This resulted in several severe panics, the worst of which was the Panic of 1873.

From 1896 to 1910, prices were steadily rising, so that the peak in every business cycle was higher than the previous peak. No severe panic occurred. In fact, no serious panic has ever occurred in a period when the general trend of prices was up. It is probably impossible to have a serious panic in such a period. The bankers had a bad panic in 1907 but this was not a severe business panic.

Even if commodity prices were stable, there would be business cycles. Either rising or falling prices increase the violence of these cycles. Falling prices cause greater violence than an equal rise in prices. From 1880 to 1896, commodity prices declined at the rate of 3.6 per cent per year. Business cycles were more violent than from 1897 to 1914. The reason for the greater violence is that severe debt liquidation is necessary when prices fall to permanently lower levels.

Business cycles when prices are rising.—The generation of farmers and business men who gained their experience from 1864 to 1896 found that what they learned was wrong in the next generation. Those who gained their experiences from 1896 to 1920 did not know how to act with falling prices because all their experiences were gained in a period of rising prices.

When prices are rising, large increases are followed by short declines. From 1896 to 1907, commodity prices rose 24 points. They then fell 5 points and rose 12 (table 20). When prices are falling, violent declines are followed by minor rises.

TABLE 20.—WHOLESALE COMMODITY PRICE CHANGES IN BUSINESS CYCLES THAT OCCURRED IN PERIODS OF RISING PRICES

Year	Wholesale prices*	Points rise	Points fall
Lowest 3 months of 1896	66	..	..
Highest 3 months of 1902	90	24	..
Lowest 3 months of 1904	85	..	5
Highest 3 months of 1907	97	12	..
Lowest 3 months of 1908	90	..	7
Highest 3 months of 1910	106	16	..
Lowest 3 months of 1911	92	..	14
Highest 3 months of 1913	103	11	..

* Table 1, p. 10.

Business cycles combined with price collapse.—The price collapse that began in 1864 reduced commodity prices by 61 points (table 21). This was followed by a recovery of 16 points, a decline of 33, a recovery of 7, and a decline of 27. After the Panic of 1873 was over, there was a recovery of 25 points and a decline of 31.

After the Panic of 1921, there was a decline of 107, a recovery of 16, a decline of 48.

TABLE 21.—BUSINESS CYCLES DURING PERIODS OF PRECIPITOUS DECLINES IN PRICES

	Civil War				World War			
	Year	Wholesale prices*	Points fall	Points rise	Year	Wholesale prices*	Points fall	Points rise
First major drop								
Highest 3 months	1864	224	....	....	1920	243	....	....
Lowest 3 months	1865	163	61	....	1921	136	107	....
Highest 3 months	1866	179	....	16	1923	152	....	16
Second major drop								
Highest 3 months	1873	139	....	....	1929	141	....	....
Lowest 3 months	1876	106	33	....	1932	93†	48	....
Highest 3 months	1877	113	....	7				
Lowest 3 months	1879	86	27	....				
Highest 3 months	1882	111	....	25				
Lowest 3 months	1886	80	31	....				
Highest 3 months	1888	87	....	7				
Lowest 3 months	1894	69	18	....				

* Table 1, p. 10.
† June.

The Panics of 1864 and 1920.—Major declines in prices in the United States occurred in 1864, and 1920. In each case, the decline came after a period of reduced building, so that there was a general shortage of permanent equipment. These declines came after relatively short periods of high prices before debts had become adjusted to the price level. In each of these periods, prices paid to farmers declined much more than retail prices—as they always do. After the price decline, there was in each case a period of major construction. The writers have frequently called attention to the combination of cheap food and shortage of building that, in each case, resulted in the unusual prosperity of cities and industries.[1]

At the time of the Panic of 1920, there was a shortage of building and railroad equipment. Debts had not risen greatly, except the national debt and farm mortgages. As soon as the stocks of goods on the shelves were exhausted, the country was ready to begin business. Prices paid to farmers declined much more than retail prices, as they always do. This decreased the buying power of farmers and increased the buying power of city workers. Only a small percentage of the income was required to pay for the food supply. The cities assumed that this was a permanent change and expanded the demand for housing and other items in the cost of living. A reconstruction boom developed. This made unusual profits in industry and caused the stock market to rise too high. The city prosperity and opportunity for savings led many persons to build or buy their own homes. Of course, they built these homes in proportion to their incomes, incurring debts which could have been paid at the price level at which they were incurred but could not be paid when the price structure collapsed.

Duration of three major panics.—Three major panics have occurred after a period of active building construction. In each of these cases, the public and private indebtedness had become adjusted to the price level and was somewhat high even at the price level. These were the Panics of 1837, 1873, and 1929. A panic in which indebtedness on real estate is high must be a long panic if the commodity price level drops sufficiently to disturb mortgages. A stock market crash can be liquidated quickly, but the process of mortgage

[1] Warren, G. F., Relation of Cheap Food to the Building Boom, Farm Economics, No. 9, p. 81, November 1923. Warren, G. F., and Pearson, F. A., Business Conditions, Farm Economics, No. 31, p. 371, Feb. 6, 1926; Purchasing Power of City Wages for Products Other than Food, Farm Economics, No. 42, p. 612, February 1927; Business Conditions, Farm Economics, No. 57, p. 1026, February 1929; Rents and Prices of Building Materials, Farm Economics, No. 62, p. 1179, November 1929; High Production or Deflation, Farm Economics, No. 68, p. 1429, November 1930; Adjustment to Lower Costs, Farm Economics, No. 69, p. 1466, February 1931.

liquidation is very slow. For several years, borrowers and lenders both hold on, expecting that prosperity is "just around the corner." There are no market quotations for homes so that neither party realizes the situation. When foreclosures do occur, properties are commonly taken over by the creditors, partly because of the dearth of buyers and partly because the creditors do not realize the situation. Before it is cleared up, the creditors must be willing to sell at market prices and the properties must pass back into the hands of persons who want them. Many creditors still held farms in 1932 that were taken over in 1921. These were held because of unwillingness to accept the loss, expectation of profit, or fear of breaking the market. Before such a situation is cleared up, these properties must pass into the hands of persons who want them. This is entirely different from the process of liquidating prices of stocks and bonds which are usually sold on the market of the day and not taken over by the creditors.

In the Panic of 1837, the decline in prices lasted six years. In the Panic of 1873, prices also declined for six years. There is no reason for supposing that the process of taking over of a large share of the homes and other real estate in America will be accomplished more quickly this time. Of course, if the commodity price level is raised so as to restore equities, liquidation will not be necessary.

So long as the liquidation of mortgaged real estate is occurring, little building is to be expected; and so long as little building is done, unemployment is to be expected. Attempts to stimulate building by reducing wages result in further bankruptcy. A house is worth no more than the cost to build it. Reducing costs of new buildings reduces values of all the property.

Every reduction in costs destroys a new set of equities and causes additional properties to be thrown on the market.

When enough properties are thrown on the market, prices may be so reduced as to be below tax payments so that properties that are free from debt may be drawn into the maelstrom.

It is debts, not wages, that stand in the way of recovery. Little building and limited prosperity can be expected until debts are adjusted to the price level, or the price level reflated to the level at which the debts were contracted.

Apparently it takes about six or seven years to go through the process of deciding that it is necessary to foreclose, foreclosing, deciding to sell at the market, and actually making the sale. Such liquidation has nothing to do with whether there are enough houses. It is a process of writing debts down. It causes unemployment and the appearance of a surplus of houses.

After the Panics of 1837 and 1873, very serious conditions continued until new gold mines were found.

Price declines during three major panics.—In the Panic of 1929 the decline in wholesale prices of all commodities was 30 per cent in three years. In the first three years of the Panic of 1873, the decline in prices was only 18 per cent. In 1837, it was 23 per cent (table 22). Not only was the decline in prices far greater in the Panic of 1929 than the declines in 1837 or 1873, but also the credit structure was far more complicated. In 1873, farms were much more nearly self-sufficient than they are today. No large debts were incurred for the purchase of machinery. A much higher proportion of the city population was self-employed. There were relatively few public services and taxes were therefore less important. The United States has had no previous experience with a panic of this severity and no one can foresee what social and political disturbances may occur if the policy of deflation continues.

Prices of 30 basic commodities[2] indicate the severity of the three panics (table 23). They declined 29 per cent in the first three years of the Panic of 1837, 20 per cent in the first three years of the Panic of 1873, and 46 per cent in the first three years of the Panic of 1929. During the Panic of 1929, the prices of basic commodities declined as much in three years as they did in six years after the other panics.

After the six years of declining prices, in the Panics of 1837 and 1873, there were in each case about four years of rising prices.

TABLE 22.—CHANGES IN WHOLESALE COMMODITY PRICES* DURING THREE MAJOR PANICS

Panic of 1837		Panic of 1873		Panic of 1929	
February 1837	129	February 1873	139	February 1929	139
February 1840	99	February 1876	114	February 1932	97
February 1843	74	February 1879	88	February 1935	?
Per cent decline		Per cent decline		Per cent decline	
in 3 years	23	in 3 years	18	in 3 years	30
in 6 years	43	in 6 years	37	in 6 years	?

* Table 1, p. 10.

[2] Warren, G. F., and Pearson, F. A., Index Numbers of Prices of 30 Basic Commodities in the United States, Farm Economics No. 24, p. 1704, February 1932.

The prices of these basic commodities reached 69 per cent of prewar in June 1932. They were so low that some recovery had to occur.

TABLE 23.—CHANGES IN PRICES OF 30 BASIC COMMODITIES DURING THREE MAJOR PANICS

Panic of 1837		Panic of 1873		Panic of 1929	
February 1837	140	February 1873	148	February 1929	145
February 1840	100	February 1876	118	February 1932	78
February 1843	75	February 1879	88	February 1935	?
Per cent decline		Per cent decline		Per cent decline	
in 3 years	29	in 3 years	20	in 3 years	46
in 6 years	46	in 6 years	41	in 6 years	?

Price recoveries in three major panics.—For the period after 1920, the experiences following the Napoleonic Wars, and the Civil War have proved to be a better guide than the knowledge gained by the business experiences of the present generation.

Nine years after deflation began there was in each case a violent drop, but this was far more violent after the Panic of 1929. All the adjustments since 1920 have been similar to those following 1864 and of about the same duration, but more violent.

After three years of declining prices following the Panic of 1837, prices of some short-time goods such as hides and leather recovered for a time. There was a period of price stability for the average of all commodities.

After three years of declining prices following the Panic of 1873, there was some recovery in the prices of short-time goods. Food products at wholesale rose 19 per cent; hides and leather, 29 per cent. Metals, building materials, and house furnishings declined or rose very little. All commodities at wholesale prices rose 8 per cent. Prices were fairly stable for about a year. The explanation is that a shortage of shoes and some other short-time goods developed, so that a suppressed business cycle occurred.

Real estate debts were not liquidated, houses were for sale at bankrupt prices, and the construction industry could not proceed. In such a panic period, a business cycle that causes a rise in prices and some stability may be called a suppressed business cycle—just as there are submerged mountains in the bottom of the ocean.

By the middle of 1879, debts and real estate were sufficiently liquidated to cause prices of houses to rise. The six years of depression had resulted in a shortage of building. Four years of improved prices followed. All commodities at wholesale prices rose from an index of 85 in June 1879 to 111 in June 1882 (table 1, page 10).

Apparently the same set of circumstances occurred after the depression of 1929. A recovery due to shortage of short-time goods came in 1932. Many persons assumed that this was the end of the depression, but the debts were not liquidated. During the Panic of 1873, the maximum number of bank and business failures came in the last three years. If the present policy of deflation is pursued to the bitter end, there may be a similar experience.

The real end of depression that began in 1864 came in 1896.

In the Panic of 1929, variations in the demand for gold were dominating (page 112).

CHAPTER VIII

SILVER

Production of silver.—In the last 100 years **(1831-1930)**, the world's silver production was 10,658,588,000 ounces (table 24 and figure 89). In the same period, the production of gold amounted to

TABLE 24.—WORLD SILVER PRODUCTION, 1493–1932*

Period	Annual production, thousands of fine ounces	Index 1880–1914 = 100	Year	Annual production, thousands of fine ounces	Index 1880–1914 = 100	Year	Annual production, thousands of fine ounces	Index 1880–1914 = 100
1493–1520...	1,511	1	1877........	74,175	48	1906........	165,998	108
1521–44.....	2,900	2	1878........	78,291	51	1907........	184,784	120
1545–60.....	10,018	7	1879........	78,876	51	1908........	204,104	133
Twenty-year						1909........	213,392	139
average			1880........	77,903	51			
1561–80...	9,629	6	1881........	84,488	55	1910........	221,428	144
1581–1600.	13,469	9	1882........	88,274	57	1911........	227,129	148
1601–20...	13,597	9	1883........	89,956	58	1912........	225,899	147
1621–40...	12,655	8	1884........	82,308	53	1913........	227,520	148
1641–60...	11,777	8	1885........	91,998	60	1914........	177,247	115
1661–80...	10,835	7	1886........	95,485	62	1915........	189,454	123
1681–1700.	10,993	7	1887........	97,149	63	1916........	174,632	113
1701–20...	11,433	7	1888........	110,031	71	1917........	179,890	117
1721–40...	13,863	9	1889........	126,564	82	1918........	203,428	132
1741–60...	17,141	11				1919........	179,932	117
1761–80...	20,986	14	1890........	134,429	87			
1781–1800.	28,263	18	1891........	138,283	90	1920........	173,345	113
Ten-year			1892........	154,377	100	1921........	171,581	111
average			1893........	166,594	108	1922........	209,829	136
1801–10...	28,661	19	1894........	164,829	107	1923........	246,276	160
1811–20...	17,338	11	1895........	167,745	109	1924........	239,680	156
1821–30...	15,355	10	1896........	157,321	102	1925........	245,280	159
1831–40...	19,735	13	1897........	160,765	104	1926........	253,806	165
1841–50...	25,337	16	1898........	169,537	110	1927........	251,397	163
Five-year			1899........	168,806	110	1928........	257,925	168
average						1929........	260,970	170
1851–55...	30,998	20	1900........	173,689	113			
1856–60...	29,117	19	1901........	173,101	112	1930........	248,139	161
1861–65...	35,773	23	1902........	162,936	106	1931........	192,710	125
1866–70...	44,357	29	1903........	167,814	109	1932........	*155,000*†	*101*†
1871–75...	66,853	43	1904........	164,274	107			
1876......	66,932	43	1905........	172,393	112			

* 1493–1800, Laughlin, J. L., Money, Credit, and Prices, Vol. I, p. 510. The University of Chicago Press, 1931.

1801–1927, Merrill, C. W., Summarized Data of Silver Production, Bureau of Mines, United States Department of Commerce, Economic Paper 8, pp. 4, 5, 6, 1930.

1928–30, Annual Report of the Director of the Mint for the Fiscal Year Ended June 30, 1931, p. 242, 1931.

The average annual production from 1880 to 1914 was 153, 959,000 fine ounces. The index numbers were obtained by multiplying by 0.0006495.

From 1831 to 1930 the world's total silver was 10,658,588,000 fine ounces.

† Estimated.

931,645,000 ounces (table 15). The production of silver was 11.4 times that of gold.

The production of silver and gold shows the same general tendency to rise, but they have been quite different for considerable periods of time. A phenomenal increase in gold production began in 1849. The resulting low value of gold was probably the cause of the countries of Continental Europe changing to the gold standard (page 143). The production of gold then declined and great distress resulted.

Production of silver compared with production of basic commodities.—The world's production of silver and of basic commodities is shown in figure 90. Production of silver has kept approximately in line with that of basic commodities. Probably the reason for this is that much of the silver production is connected with the production of lead, copper, and other metals, whereas most of the gold comes

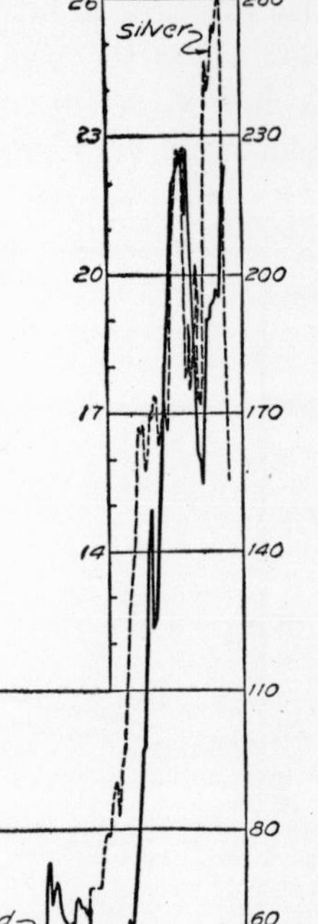

FIGURE 89.—WORLD'S PRODUCTION OF GOLD AND SILVER, 1493-1932. The production of both gold and silver has been very erratic.

from gold mines, the discovery of which is fortuitous. The production might have been somewhat different if silver had been used as money in all countries.

The world production of gold has been very erratic as compared with the world's physical volume of production of other things (figure 76). During the past century, there have been two periods of high production. The low production for many years after the Civil War resulted in declining prices, heavy burdens to debtors, severe unemployment, and great suffering, particularly in the areas far from market.

The high production which followed resulted in rising prices and a period of general good will. In the latter part of the period, the rise in prices in advance of wage increases caused considerable agitation about the high cost of living. Since 1916, production has again been low. A commodity whose production is as erratic as that of gold must vary greatly in value.

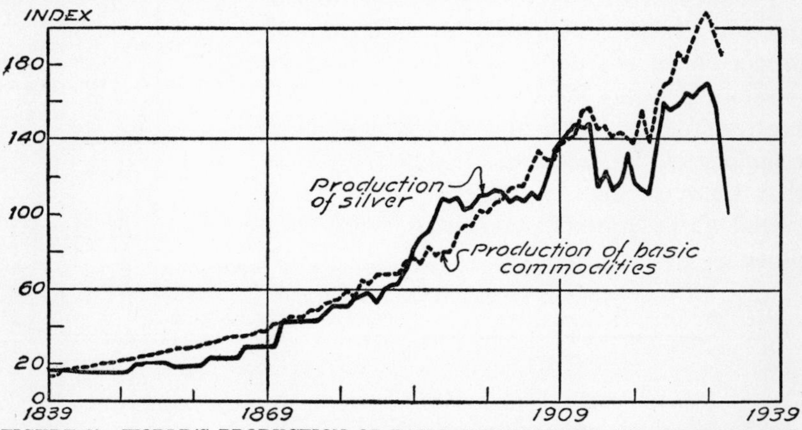

FIGURE 90.—WORLD'S PRODUCTION OF BASIC COMMODITIES AND WORLD'S PRODUCTION OF SILVER, 1839-1932.
1880-1914 = 100.
The world's production of silver follows the production of other basic commodities fairly closely but the relationship is not sufficiently close to make it a stable measure of value.

The production of silver has come much nearer the production of other things than has the production of gold.

Neither gold nor silver nor any other precious metal can be expected to increase at such a rate as to have a stable value. A combination of gold and silver would be much more stable than gold.

About the time that the world began to demonetize silver, the production of silver increased somewhat more rapidly than the production of other commodities. The decline in the price of silver was commonly attributed to over-production of silver. The major factor was demonetization. The world production of silver has responded to falling silver prices. From 1915 to 1932, world silver production has been low relative to the production of other basic commodities (figure 90). The supply of silver has not been so low as the production would indicate, as the amount available for consumption is the sum of the demonetized silver thrown on the market plus production.

Since the supply of demonetized silver coming on the market will be less in the future, silver will probably rise in price compared with other commodities.

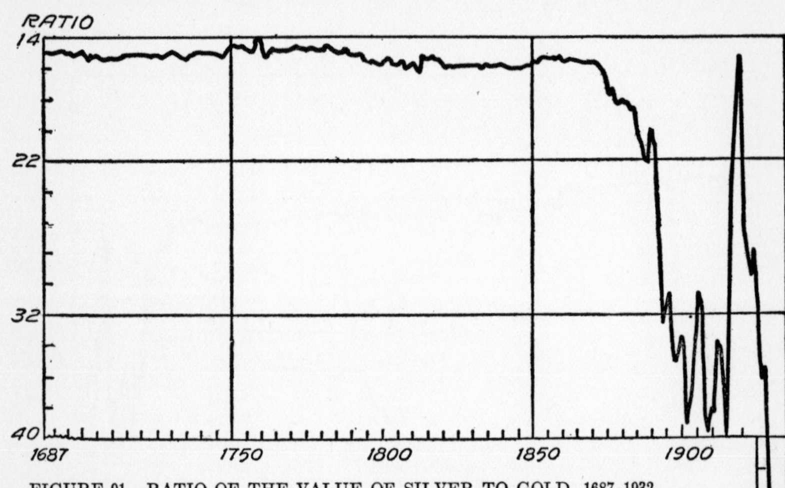

FIGURE 91.—RATIO OF THE VALUE OF SILVER TO GOLD, 1687-1932.
The relative values of silver and gold were comparatively stable until silver was demonetized in the United States and western Europe. The rise in the ratio during the World War and the drop thereafter were due to changes in the value of gold because of demand.

Relative values of gold and silver.—Most of the time previous to 1600, the relative values of gold to silver ranged between 10:1 and 15:1 (table 25). The ratios varied in different years and in different countries but were usually between these two limits. From 1620 to 1870, the ratio varied from 14:1 to 16:1.

For centuries both gold and silver were used as money in Europe. Usually there was an attempt to keep them at some fixed price ratio.

From 1687 to about 1870, the value of silver in terms of gold was remarkably stable at a ratio of about 15½ to 1. Beginning about 1870, as the various countries turned to the gold basis, this historic ratio declined precipitously, and in 1902, it took 39.15 ounces of silver to buy one ounce of gold (figure 91). During the World War, silver rose to the approximate level (15 to 1) that had prevailed for over 300 years. This rise in the price of silver was not due to a scarcity of silver or to remonetization of silver. It was due to a depreciation in the value of gold. The high prices for silver encouraged many gold-standard countries to sell their stocks of silver, and the low value of gold encouraged other countries to shift to a gold standard. When most of the countries returned to the gold standard, the price of silver began to decline,

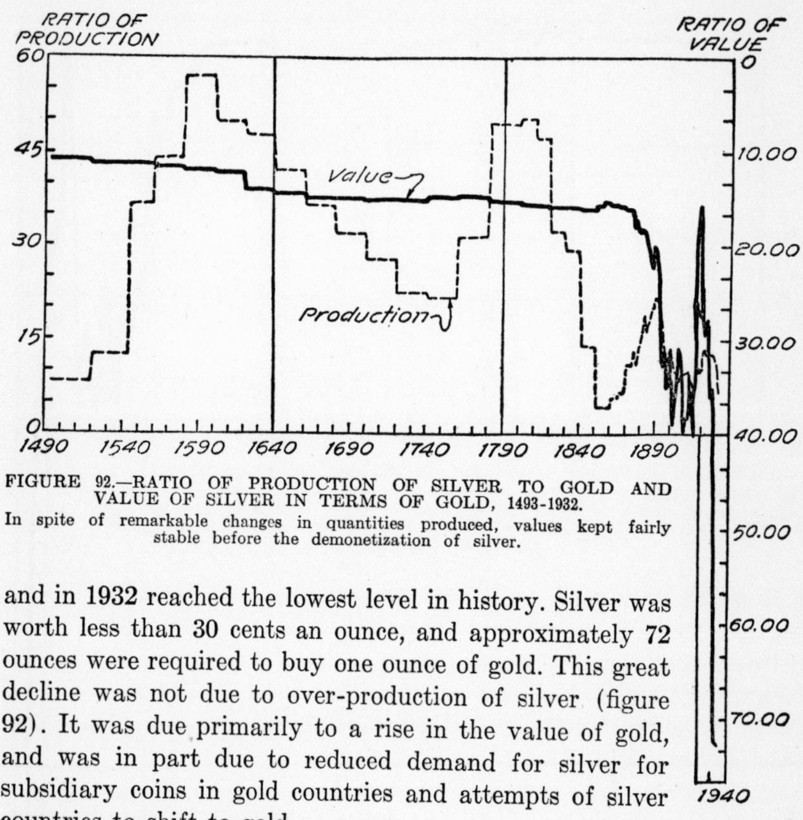

FIGURE 92.—RATIO OF PRODUCTION OF SILVER TO GOLD AND VALUE OF SILVER IN TERMS OF GOLD, 1493-1932.
In spite of remarkable changes in quantities produced, values kept fairly stable before the demonetization of silver.

and in 1932 reached the lowest level in history. Silver was worth less than 30 cents an ounce, and approximately 72 ounces were required to buy one ounce of gold. This great decline was not due to over-production of silver (figure 92). It was due primarily to a rise in the value of gold, and was in part due to reduced demand for silver for subsidiary coins in gold countries and attempts of silver countries to shift to gold.

Production and value of silver and gold.—The ratio of production of silver to the production of gold illustrates strikingly the high production of gold compared to silver just before most of the world adopted the gold standard (figure 92 and tables 25 and 26).

In spite of great variations in relative production, the relative values were kept fairly stable for the two centuries preceding the adoption of the gold standard.

Adoption of the gold standard.—Previous to 1377, Great Britain was on a silver basis. From that time until 1816, it usually attempted

TABLE 25.—OUNCES OF SILVER REQUIRED TO BUY ONE OUNCE OF GOLD, 1670 B.C.–A.D. 1932*

Period	Ratio	Year	Ratio	Year	Ratio	Year	Ratio	Year	Ratio	Year	Ratio
B.C.		1700	14.81	1750	14.55	1800	15.68	1850	15.70	1900	33.33
1670–1269	13.33	1701	15.07	1751	14.39	1801	15.46	1851	15.46	1901	34.68
731	13.33	1702	15.52	1752	14.50	1802	15.26	1852	15.59	1902	39.15
660	15.00	1703	15.17	1753	14.54	1803	15.41	1853	15.33	1903	38.10
465–429	14.50	1704	15.22	1754	14.48	1804	15.41	1854	15.33	1904	35.70
440	14.00	1705	15.11	1755	14.68	1805	15.79	1855	15.38	1905	33.87
359	12.50	1706	15.27	1756	14.94	1806	15.52	1856	15.38	1906	30.54
338	11.50	1707	15.44	1757	14.87	1807	15.43	1857	15.27	1907	31.24
336	10.00	1708	15.41	1758	14.85	1808	16.08	1858	15.38	1908	38.64
300	12.00	1709	15.31	1759	14.15	1809	15.96	1859	15.19	1909	39.74
217	11.91	1710	15.22	1760	14.14	1810	15.77	1860	15.29	1910	38.22
189	12.50	1711	15.29	1761	14.54	1811	15.53	1861	15.50	1911	38.33
87–78	11.91	1712	15.31	1762	15.27	1812	16.11	1862	15.35	1912	33.62
59–44	8.93	1713	15.24	1763	14.99	1813	16.25	1863	15.37	1913	34.19
31–14	11.91	1714	15.13	1764	14.70	1814	15.04	1864	15.37	1914	37.37
		1715	15.11	1765	14.83	1815	15.26	1865	15.44	1915	39.84
A.D.		1716	15.09	1766	14.80	1816	15.28	1866	15.43	1916	30.11
54–68	10.31	1717	15.13	1767	14.85	1817	15.11	1867	15.57	1917	23.09
98–117	9.38	1718	15.11	1768	14.80	1818	15.35	1868	15.59	1918	19.84
284–305	13.89	1719	15.09	1769	14.72	1819	15.33	1869	15.60	1919	16.53
323–337	13.89	1720	15.04	1770	14.62	1820	15.62	1870	15.57	1920	15.31
361–363	14.40	1721	15.05	1771	14.66	1821	15.95	1871	15.57	1921	25.60
422	18.00	1722	15.17	1772	14.52	1822	15.80	1872	15.63	1922	27.41
527–1453	15.00	1723	15.20	1773	14.62	1823	15.84	1873	15.93	1923	29.52
1501–1520	10.75	1724	15.11	1774	14.62	1824	15.82	1874	16.16	1924	27.76
1521–1540	11.25	1725	15.11	1775	14.72	1825	15.70	1875	16.64	1925	29.38
1541–1560	11.30	1726	15.15	1776	14.55	1826	15.76	1876	17.75	1926	32.88
1561–1580	11.50	1727	15.24	1777	14.54	1827	15.74	1877	17.20	1927	36.22
1581–1600	11.80	1728	15.11	1778	14.68	1828	15.78	1878	17.92	1928	35.26
1601–1620	12.25	1729	14.92	1779	14.80	1829	15.78	1879	18.39	1929	38.54
1621–1640	14.00	1730	14.81	1780	14.72	1830	15.82	1880	18.05	1930	53.38
1641–1660	14.50	1731	14.94	1781	14.78	1831	15.72	1881	18.25	1931	*72.02*†
1661–1680	15.00	1732	15.09	1782	14.42	1832	15.73	1882	18.20	1932	*72.27*†
1681–1700	15.00	1733	15.18	1783	14.48	1833	15.93	1883	18.64		
		1734	15.39	1784	14.70	1834	15.73	1884	18.61		
Year		1735	15.41	1785	14.92	1835	15.80	1885	19.41		
1687	14.94	1736	15.18	1786	14.96	1836	15.72	1886	20.78		
1688	14.94	1737	15.02	1787	14.92	1837	15.83	1887	21.10		
1689	15.02	1738	14.91	1788	14.65	1838	15.85	1888	22.00		
		1739	14.91	1789	14.75	1839	15.62	1889	22.10		
1690	15.02	1740	14.94	1790	15.04	1840	15.62	1890	19.75		
1691	14.98	1741	14.92	1791	15.05	1841	15.70	1891	20.92		
1692	14.92	1742	14.85	1792	15.17	1842	15.87	1892	23.72		
1693	14.83	1743	14.85	1793	15.00	1843	15.93	1893	26.49		
1694	14.87	1744	14.87	1794	15.37	1844	15.85	1894	32.56		
1695	15.02	1745	14.98	1795	15.55	1845	15.92	1895	31.60		
1696	15.00	1746	15.13	1796	15.65	1846	15.90	1896	30.59		
1697	15.20	1747	15.26	1797	15.41	1847	15.80	1897	34.20		
1698	15.07	1748	15.11	1798	15.59	1848	15.85	1898	35.03		
1699	14.94	1749	14.80	1799	15.74	1849	15.78	1899	34.36		

* Laughlin, J. L., Money, Credit, and Prices, Vol. I, pp. 95–96, The University of Chicago Press, 1931. Annual Report of the Secretary of the Treasury on the State of the Finance for the Fiscal Year Ended June 30, 1931, p. 703, 1932.

† Estimated.

to maintain both silver and gold coins at some fixed ratio. England had a ratio of 16 to 1; other countries had a ratio of 15½ to 1. This accident resulted in shifting England from bimetallism to gold (page 159).

In 1797, gold payments were suspended because of financial problems resulting from wars. England was on an inconvertible paper basis

TABLE 26.—RATIO OF PRODUCTION OF SILVER TO PRODUCTION OF GOLD, 1493–1932

Period	Production of silver, thousands of fine ounces*	Production of gold, thousands of fine ounces†	Ratio of production of silver to production of gold
1493–1520..	1,511	186	8.1
1521–44....	2,900	230	12.6
1545–60....	10,018	274	36.6
20-yr. ave.:			
1561–80....	9,629	220	43.8
1581–1600..	13,469	237	56.8
1601–20....	13,597	274	49.6
1621–40....	12,655	267	47.4
1641–60....	11,777	282	41.8
1661–80....	10,835	298	36.4
1681–1700..	10,993	346	31.8
1701–20....	11,433	412	27.8
1721–40....	13,863	613	22.6
1741–60....	17,141	791	21.7
1761–80....	20,986	666	31.5
1781–1800..	28,263	572	49.4
10-yr. ave.:			
1801–10....	28,661	572	50.1
1811–20....	17,338	368	47.1
1821–30....	15,355	457	33.6
1831–40....	19,735	652	30.3
1841–50....	25,337	1,761	14.4
5-yr. ave.:			
1851–55....	30,998	6,187	5.0
1856–60....	29,117	6,361	4.6
1861–65....	35,773	5,975	6.0
1866–70....	44,357	6,243	7.1
1871–75....	66,853	5,405	12.4
Year:			
1876.......	66,932	5,016	13.3
1877.......	74,175	5,512	13.5
1878.......	78,291	5,761	13.6
1879.......	78,876	5,262	15.0
1880.......	77,903	5,149	15.1
1881.......	84,488	4,984	17.0
1882.......	88,274	4,934	17.9
1883.......	89,956	4,615	19.5
1884.......	82,308	4,921	16.7
1885.......	91,998	5,246	17.5
1886.......	95,485	5,136	18.6
1887.......	97,149	5,117	19.0
1888.......	110,031	5,331	20.6
1889.......	126,564	5,974	21.2

Year	Production of silver, thousands of fine ounces*	Production of gold, thousands of fine ounces†	Ratio of production of silver to production of gold
1890.......	134,429	5,749	23.4
1891.......	138,283	6,320	21.9
1892.......	154,377	7,094	21.8
1893.......	166,594	7,619	21.9
1894.......	164,829	8,764	18.8
1895.......	167,745	9,615	17.4
1896.......	157,321	9,784	16.1
1897.......	160,765	11,420	14.1
1898.......	169,537	13,878	12.2
1899.......	168,806	14,838	11.4
1900.......	173,689	12,315	14.1
1901.......	173,101	12,626	13.7
1902.......	162,936	14,355	11.4
1903.......	167,814	15,853	10.6
1904.......	164,274	16,804	9.8
1905.......	172,393	18,396	9.4
1906.......	165,998	19,471	8.5
1907.......	184,784	19,977	9.2
1908.......	204,104	21,422	9.5
1909.......	213,392	21,965	9.7
1910.......	221,428	22,022	10.1
1911.......	227,129	22,397	10.1
1912.......	225,899	22,605	10.0
1913.......	227,520	22,255	10.2
1914.......	177,247	21,302	8.3
1915.......	189,454	22,738	8.3
1916.......	174,632	22,031	7.9
1917.......	179,890	20,346	8.8
1918.......	203,428	18,614	10.9
1919.......	179,932	17,698	10.2
1920.......	173,345	16,130	10.7
1921.......	171,581	15,975	10.7
1922.......	209,829	15,452	13.6
1923.......	246,276	17,791	13.8
1924.......	239,680	19,031	12.6
1925.......	245,280	19,026	12.9
1926.......	253,806	19,349	13.1
1927.......	251,397	19,431	12.9
1928.......	257,925	19,700	13.1
1929.......	260,970	19,500	13.4
1930.......	248,139	20,160	12.3
1931.......	192,710	22,819	8.4
1932.......	*155,000*	*23,718*	*6.5*

The figures in italics are estimates. * Table 24, p. 139. † Table 15, p. 97.

for 20 years. In 1816, a single gold standard was provided for. The currency reached par in 1821 and was maintained until August 6, 1914.[1] The gold standard was again established April 28, 1925, and abandoned September 21, 1931.

The first coinage law of the United States in 1792 established the gold dollar containing 24.75 grains of pure gold and the silver dollar at 15 times this weight.

[1] Laughlin, J. L., Money, Credit, and Prices, Vol. 2, p. 529, 1931. Young, J. P., European Currency and Finance, Commission of Gold and Silver Inquiry, United States Senate Resolution 469, 67th Congress, Serial 9, Vol. 1, p. 276, 1925.

In 1834, an act was passed changing the ratio to 16:1 by reducing the amount of gold in the dollar. This reduced the weight of gold in the dollar by 6.26 per cent; but silver was worth more than this ratio in Europe, and silver dollars rapidly disappeared from circulation. The shift from silver to gold was an unintentional result of establishing this ratio of 16:1 at a time when France[2] had a ratio of 15½ to 1. Gold tended to disappear from circulation in France, and silver disappeared in the United States. Probably, if all countries had had the same ratio, both gold and silver would have continued to circulate in all countries. But in France cheap silver drove out gold, and in the United States cheap gold drove out silver and put the country on the gold standard. The small coins, as well as the dollars, disappeared. To remedy this an act was passed in the United States in 1853 reducing the weights of the fractional coins so that it would be unprofitable to melt them.

By the Act of 1873, the bimetallic standard was abandoned and the gold dollar containing 23.22 grains of gold was adopted.[3]

In the Civil War period, paper money was issued in such amounts that it depreciated below the value of the silver in the fractional currency; silver again disappeared from circulation, and fractional paper currency was substituted.

Most of the countries of Western Europe continued on the gold and silver basis until the seventies. Nearly all the countries of Northwestern Europe began to shift to the gold standard, but this required many years for completion. Russia gradually changed to a gold basis. The change was practically completed by 1896. India was in the process of shifting to a gold basis previous to the Panic of 1929.

The gradual demonetization of silver threw large amounts of it on the market as metal and decreased its value. In exactly the same manner, the substitution of paper for gold in the World War period threw large amounts of gold onto the few markets that were open to it and resulted in a tremendous decline in its value. In this period, gold declined to such an extent that, in 1920, 15.31 ounces of silver were worth an ounce of gold. This is often referred to as a rise in the value of silver. It was in fact a decline in the value of gold. The silver-using countries continued to use silver as money and silver continued its normal relation to other commodities. In the United States, in 1920, an ounce of gold would buy less than half as much as it would have

[2] Laughlin, J. L., Money, Credit, and Prices, Vol. 1, p. 178, 1931.

[3] Annual Report of the Director of the Mint for the Fiscal Year Ended June 30, 1931, p. 88, 1931.

purchased in the five years before the war, but silver would buy the same amount that it would have purchased before the war (figures 91 and 92).

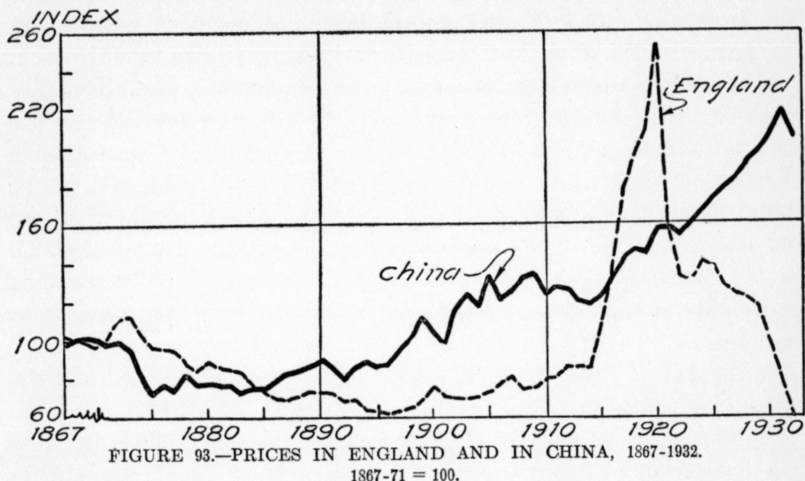

FIGURE 93.—PRICES IN ENGLAND AND IN CHINA, 1867-1932.
1867-71 = 100.

Since 1875, there has been a gradual rise in prices in China. English prices have had two long periods of price decline and one period of rising prices.

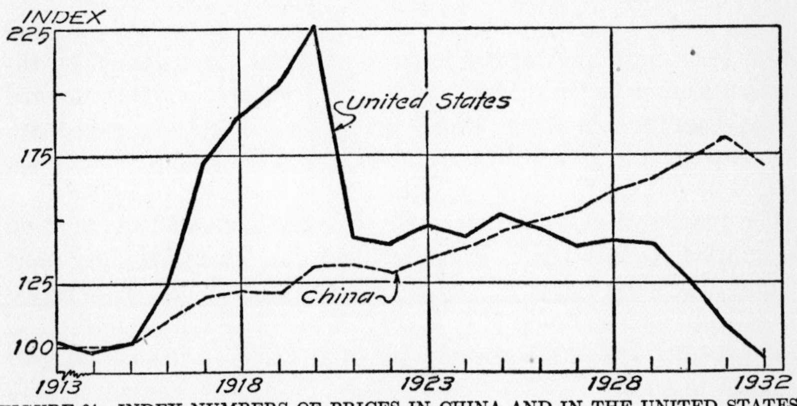

FIGURE 94.—INDEX NUMBERS OF PRICES IN CHINA AND IN THE UNITED STATES, 1913-32.
Pre-war = 100.

Prices are on a gold basis in the United States and on a silver basis in China. Prices have been more erratic in the United States than in China.

Prices in China.—From 1873 to 1896, production of gold was very low and prices in England declined 45 per cent (table 8 and figure 7). Silver production was low in the latter part of the period, and prices in China declined slightly. In this period, silver was more stable than gold. From 1896 to 1914, there was a great increase in the amount of gold mined and prices in England rose 39 per cent. In China, prices increased 38 per cent. In this period, neither silver nor gold had a stable value, but silver was as stable as gold (figure 93).

From 1929 to 1932, prices in China rose, and financial and business conditions were similar to those in the United States from 1896 to 1914. Debts were easy to pay, there was no unusual agricultural depression or unusual unemployment, and it was easy to make money in China (figure 94).

TABLE 27.—WHOLESALE PRICES IN THE UNITED STATES AND ENGLAND ON A GOLD BASIS AND IN CHINA ON A SILVER BASIS, 1867–1932
1867–1871 = 100

Year	United States*	England†	China‡
1867	102	101	98
1868	98	100	101
1869	98	99	102
1870	101	97	101
1871	101	101	98
1872	104	111	100
1873	101	113	96
1874	98	103	81
1875	89	97	72
1876	85	96	77
1877	88	95	74
1878	78	88	83
1879	78	84	77
1880	86	89	78
1881	89	86	77
1882	93	85	77
1883	87	83	73
1884	80	77	75
1885	73	73	75
1886	71	70	79
1887	73	69	83
1888	74	71	84
1889	70	73	86

Year	United States*	England†	China‡
1890	71	73	90
1891	71	73	85
1892	66	69	79
1893	67	69	86
1894	60	64	89
1895	61	63	86
1896	59	62	87
1897	59	63	95
1898	61	65	101
1899	66	69	112
1900	71	76	104
1901	70	71	97
1902	74	70	116
1903	75	70	124
1904	75	71	118
1905	76	73	133
1906	78	78	120
1907	82	81	125
1908	79	74	133
1909	85	75	134
1910	89	79	123
1911	82	81	128
1912	87	86	127

Year	United States*	England†	China‡	North China§
1913	88	86	120	120
1914	85	86	121	119
1915	87	110	139	123
1916	108	138	145	133
1917	149	177	136	143
1918	165	195	156	147
1919	174	209	150	145
1920	195	255	176	159
1921	123	157	167	159
1922	122	133	163	154
1923	127	131	....	161
1924	123	141	....	167
1925	130	138	....	174
1926	126	128	....	179
1927	120	124	....	184
1928	122	122	....	193
1929	120	117	....	198
1930	109	98	....	207
1931	92	79	....	219
1932	82	59	....	203

* The index numbers of wholesale prices in gold in the United States averaged 115.8 from 1867–71, when 1910–14 = 100. They were converted to the five-year base, 1867–71, by multiplying by 0.86356.

† Table 8, page 75. The index numbers of wholesale prices in gold in England averaged 98.6 from 1867 to 1871, if 1867–77 = 100. They were converted to the five-year base, 1867–71, by multiplying by 1.01420.

‡ Tang, C. Y., An Economic Study of Chinese Agriculture, unpublished manuscript, Cornell University, pp. 488–89, 1924. The index numbers of prices in China in terms of silver averaged 83.22 from 1867 to 1871, if 1913 = 100. They were converted to the five-year base, 1867–71, by multiplying by 1.20163.

§ Nankai Weekly Statistical Service, Nankai University, Tientsin, China, Vol. III, No. 22, p. 109, June 2, 1930; Vol. V, No. 5, p. 19, Feb. 1, 1932. The index numbers were converted to the five-year base, 1867–71, by multiplying by 1.786.

BIBLIOGRAPHY

Barbour, D., The Theory of Bimetallism and the Effects of the Partial Demonetisation of Silver on England and India.

Chang, L. L., Farm Prices in Wuchin, Kiangsu, China. Chinese Economics Journal, Vol. X, No. 6, pp. 449-512. June 1932.

Gregory, T. E., The Silver Situation: Problems and Possibilities. 1932.

Harvey, W. H., Coin's Financial School. 1894.

Horton, S. D., Silver in Europe. 1890.

Jevons, W. S., Investigations in Currency and Finance. 1884.

Kann, E., The Currencies of China. An Investigation of Silver and Gold Transactions Affecting China. 1927.

Kemmerer, E. W., The Recent Rise in the Price of Silver, and Some of its Monetary Consequences. Quarterly Economic Journal, Vol. XXVI, No. 2, pp. 215-74. February 1912.

Kemmerer, E. W., and others, Project of Law for the Gradual Introduction of a Gold-Standard Currency System in China, together with a report in support thereof. Submitted to the Minister of Finance by the Commission of Financial Experts on November 11, 1929.

Laughlin, J. L., The History of Bimetallism in the United States. 1895.

Magee, J. D., The World's Production of Gold and Silver from 1493 to 1905. Journal of Political Economy, Vol. XVIII, No. 1, pp. 50-58. January 1910.

Pinnick, A. W., Silver and China. An Investigation of the Monetary Problems Governing China's Trade and Prosperity. 1930.

Salter, A., The Silver Problem. Political Science Quarterly, Vol. XLVI, No. 3, pp. 321-334. September 1931.

Taussig, F. W., The Silver Situation in the United States. 1893.

Walker, F. A., International Bimetallism. 1896.

White, B., Silver, Its History and Romance. 1917.

Wilcoxen, L. C., World Prices and the Precious Metals, Journal of the American Statistical Association, Vol. XXVII, No. 178, pp. 129-140. June, 1932.

Final Report of the Royal Commission appointed to inquire into the recent changes in the relative values of the precious metals; with minutes of evidence and appendixes. 1888.

Report from the Select Committee on the Depreciation of silver, together with the Proceedings of the Committee, minutes of evidence, and appendix. 1876.

CHAPTER IX

STABILIZING THE PRICE LEVEL

One of the most important problems in all human relationships is the establishment of reliable measures. After many years of effort, weights and measures of length have been established so that a yard is always the same length and a pound is always the same weight.

Units of measure.—Some of the efforts in establishing weights and measures are indicated by the following:

Koebel's work on surveying in Germany stated that the length of a foot should be determined in the following way:

"To find the length of a rood in the right and lawful way and according to scientific usage you shall do as follows: Stand at the door of a church on Sunday and bid sixteen men to stop, tall ones and small ones, as they happen to pass out when the service is finished; then make them put their left feet one behind another and the length thus obtained shall be a right and lawful rood to measure and survey land with, and the sixteenth part of it shall be a right and lawful foot."

Note that he calls this "scientific usage." It was far more scientific than any measure of value that has yet been adopted.

Ultimately the length of a foot was standardized, but each country arrived at a different standard so that in different provinces and countries there were many different lengths called a foot.

In England, Henry I established a yard as the distance from the point of his nose to the end of his thumb.

Among the Greeks and Romans the pace was the unit of measure corresponding to the yard.

In Asia Minor and in Egypt, the cubit was the common unit of measurement. It was the length of the forearm from the elbow to the end of the middle finger.

In England in 1224, three barley corns were established as one inch; 12 inches, one foot; 3 feet, one ell. The grains of barley were to be dry, taken from the middle of the head, and laid end to end.

In 1266, an act declared that the English penny, "called a sterling, shall weigh thirty-two wheat corns in the midst of the ear; and twenty pence do make an ounce; and twelve ounces a pound."[1]

It took much longer to learn to measure such a thing as temperature. Our thermometer was in the process of development from about 1654 to 1736.[2] Our common measures of length and weight and the calendar are still very crude affairs.

Measures of value.—Only a few centuries ago, the best measure of length in England was three grains of barley taken from the center of the head. A standard abstract measure of length such as the present yard was beyond the imagination of the times.

Today, we are using a given weight of a commodity as a measure of value. An abstract measure of value such as an index number of the average prices of 784 commodities is just beginning to be comprehended. We had no American index numbers of any consequence before 1890. The common use of these by newspapers is a very recent development.

How well a measure of weight serves as a measure of value is described by a committee on monetary policy appointed by the British Association for the Advancement of Science.

"The price history of the century before the war affords abundant evidence that the gold standard has neither kept the price level stable, nor—except temporarily and by accident—forced it to follow any other reasonable course. Nor are there grounds for greater optimism with regard to the future."[3]

It must be remembered, however, that gold is better than a less stable measure. Uncontrolled paper is often, but not always, worse than gold.

Accurate measures of weight have been established so that it is not necessary to use grains of barley, which vary according to the weather, soil, and other factors. But measures of value are still dependent on success in discovering and mining a single commodity—gold. The

[1] Barnett, R. W., "Pound," Palgrave Dictionary of Political Economy, Vol. III, p. 178, 1908.

[2] The type of thermometer familiar at the present time containing a liquid hermetically sealed in a glass tube with a bulb was brought into general use by Grand Duke Ferdinand II. He was said to have possessed such an instrument as early as 1654. As a result of the work of G. D. Fahrenheit, about 1736, the freezing and boiling points were recognized as convenient fixed points from which to work.

[3] Clapham, J. H., and others, Monetary Policy, Report of Sub-Committee on Currency and Gold Standard, appointed by the British Association for the Advancement of Science, p. 62, P. S. King & Son, 1921.

solution of the problem of a stable measure of value will go far in establishing peaceful relations among men.

A number of proposals have been made toward the establishment of reliable measures of value that will not take property from the debtor and give it to the creditor, nor take property from the creditor and give it to the debtor, and that will not stop industry and throw millions out of work, and array man against man. Unchangeable measures of weight are trivial in importance as compared with a stable measure of value.

It does not matter what the price level is, after society is adjusted to it. Stability is the essential. If a country has become adjusted to any price level, that is the basis at which stabilization should occur. If the price level has been strikingly changing, some things adjust themselves quickly and some slowly. There is then no possible way to overcome all injustice, but commodity prices should be stabilized at the level which would cause the least total sum of injustice and injury to business.

When we see how recently our present measures of weight, length, and temperature were developed, it is not surprising that measures of value have not been perfected. One commodity after another has been chosen as a measure of value. But no commodity is free from changes in value due to the supply of it or demand for it. If the supply of it increases or if the demand decreases, its value is reduced. If the supply decreases or if the demand increases, its value increases. The value of gold is no more stable than is the value of many other commodities, but no commodities have been found that are better than gold and silver. By defining our dollar as so many grains of gold, we have fixed the weight of the dollar but have not fixed its value.

The world-wide misfortunes that have resulted from rising and falling commodity prices since the outbreak of the World War have increased interest in various proposals for stabilizing prices.

What stability means.—An ounce of gold is, of course, always worth an ounce of gold, and an ounce of silver is worth an ounce of silver. Value is comparative. Primitive attempts to measure value compare everything with some one thing. Since everything changes in value, including the commodity taken as a standard itself, such a primitive measure is wholly unadapted to modern civilization, and next to war is probably its most serious menace. The only reliable way of determining the value of one thing is to compare it with many things. If John is 10 per cent taller than James, we know practically nothing about the height of either of them. If we compare John with hundreds of other people and find that he is 5 per cent taller than the average, we do know something about his height.

In June 1929, an ounce of gold would exchange for 2235 pounds of pig iron (table 7, page 71). Two years later, it would exchange for 2667 pounds. Since we have fixed the price of gold, the price of pig iron has declined. If by law pig iron were used as money, and therefore had its price fixed, the price of gold would have risen. In neither case would we know whether the change was due to a rise in the value of gold or to a fall in the value of pig iron, or to a rise or a decline in the value of both commodities, with a disproportionate rise in gold or

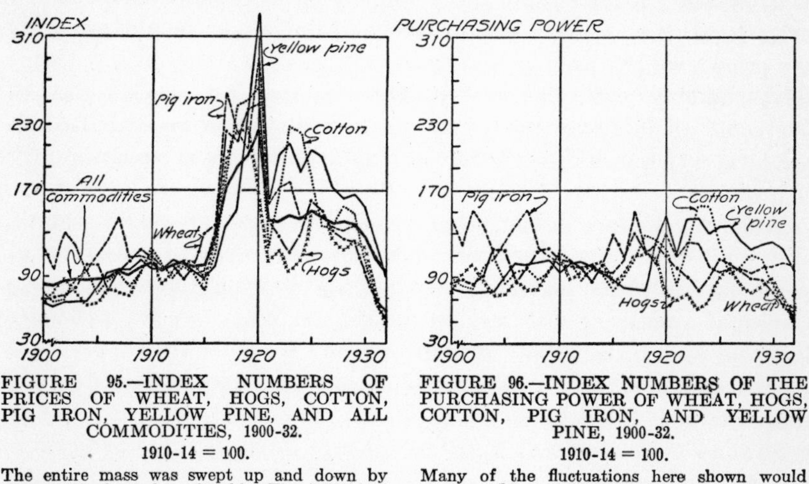

FIGURE 95.—INDEX NUMBERS OF PRICES OF WHEAT, HOGS, COTTON, PIG IRON, YELLOW PINE, AND ALL COMMODITIES, 1900-32.
1910-14 = 100.
The entire mass was swept up and down by changes in the value of gold. The individual commodities fluctuated within the mass owing to their own peculiarities.

FIGURE 96.—INDEX NUMBERS OF THE PURCHASING POWER OF WHEAT, HOGS, COTTON, PIG IRON, AND YELLOW PINE, 1900-32.
1910-14 = 100.
Many of the fluctuations here shown would continue if a stable measure of value were used.

a disproportionate decline in pig iron. By comparing with many commodities, it was found that both had risen in value but that gold had risen more (table 7, page 71).

Stabilizing the price level does not mean that any single commodity would be free from fluctuation in price due to the supply of it and demand for it. It does mean that commodity prices would be free from being swept up or down as a mass, because of changes in the supply of or demand for gold. The prices of wheat, hogs, cotton, pig iron, yellow pine, and the average of all commodities from 1900 to 1932, are shown in figure 95. These five products and the average of all commodities were swept upward and downward as a mass. Within the mass, each product had its own peculiar fluctuations.

The purchasing power of these same commodities is shown in figure 96, that is, the changes in value when compared with the average of hundreds of commodities rather than with the single commodity, gold. This gives some idea of how prices of these things would have fluctuated had there been a stable measure of value. Prices would have been more stable than this figure indicates because changes due to the value of money decidedly increase the fluctuations that are due to supply of the commodity and demand for it. Whenever prices start to move violently regardless of the cause, they overshoot the mark. Changes in the general level of prices also cause changes in demand. For example, the rise in the value of gold resulted in unemployment, reduced the demand for cotton and pine, and caused much of the decline in 1929 to 1932. A stable general price level would reduce these price fluctuations.

Changes in demand, or exhaustion of supplies, will cause some commodities to rise in price with a stable average price level. Other commodities would decline. Seasonal fluctuations would continue. The fluctuating mass would be stable, but no one thing in the mass would be stable. Because of exhaustion of the forests, lumber would rise in price as it has been doing for a century. Because of new processes, iron would become cheaper. Many of the products that result from biological action would rise in price, and many that result from mechanical action would decline.

Stable wage level undesirable.—Some persons have thought that an ideal money would be a wage money so that wages would always be stable, and that increases in the efficiency of labor should result in a decline in commodity prices and stable wages rather than a stable average of commodity prices and rising wages. This would be extremely unfortunate for laborers, farmers, and all other business men and a serious damage to society as a whole.

There is a steady increase in the work accomplished by an hour of labor. The increase in efficiency in production of basic commodities per capita is about 1.7 per cent per year (page 47). When one hires labor, it is not hours of social contact that he desires. It is output. If one should borrow a wage money which would buy him ten days of labor and agree to repay it at a later date, he would be returning to the creditor a greater product than that which he borrowed. Since it is product and not hours of society that the debtor and creditor are interested in, such a money would be unjust.

Such a money would require that the price of commodities fall as the efficiency of labor increases.

From the laborer's standpoint, it is also much better to have stable commodity prices and rising wages than vice versa.

Fixed commodity prices with rising wages not only make it possible for an efficient employer to succeed but they also enable an efficient workman to receive promotion. If total wages are stable, the only way to promote the highly efficient worker is by lowering the inefficient worker. This is difficult to do. Therefore, the efficient worker is likely to fail to be promoted and incentive is lost. But if total wages rise as labor efficiency increases, the inefficient worker may continue to draw his old wage while the highly efficient one is promoted. This opens the door of opportunity for efficiency and results in much more human happiness than would otherwise be attained. Since the door of opportunity is opened for the efficient worker, this method of procedure in turn becomes a stimulus to efficiency.

Anyone who has ever dealt with a group of employees knows the vast difference between attempting to discriminate in payment by a process of lowering the poor rather than by one of raising the good.

The purchasing power of wages rises as efficiency increases. Human beings will be happier if the result is accomplished by fixed commodity prices and rising wages rather than by fixed wages and falling commodity prices, even though the actual status is the same. But the actual status will not be the same, because, if commodity prices decline, enterprise is penalized, the goods on the shelves shrink in value before they are paid for, business failures are increased, and the total unemployment in a decade will be greater.

Another objection to a wage money is that it is not possible to describe the amount and quality of a day's work.

The wage level in the United States was practically stationary from 1887 to 1898, but prices were declining. The effect on labor was so serious that Bryan's "Cross of Gold and Crown of Thorns" speech dealt with the devastating effect of declining commodity prices on the brow of labor.

If wages rise gradually with increase in efficiency, the shift from inefficient to efficient plants is accomplished by raising wages in the efficient plant and leaving them stationary in the inefficient plant. This can be accomplished without serious difficulty. Such a shift takes place gradually, allowing operators and workers to make the change with least difficulty. It gives the inefficient plant time to make debt adjustments before closing rather than go bankrupt. It gives workers a chance to shift gradually to other work or other plants. If the average of wages remained constant the inefficient plant would have to reduce wages in proportion to the increase in efficient plants. Such a process is so difficult that strikes and unemployment would occur. Rather than risk these, the inefficient plant would be likely to go on until a sudden and violent adjustment was necessary, which injures the owners, the creditors, and the laborers.

If the average of all money payments including wages and commodity prices were kept constant, the same objection would hold so far as wages affected the average.

Commodity prices should be stable.—The credit structure of the world is based primarily on commodities. Farmers borrow money through the Land Bank system for a period of 35 years to lay tile drains, irrigate land, construct buildings, and raise wheat and hogs. Railroads borrow money for an indefinite number of years to buy steel rails. Factories buy raw materials on credit, which they must own during the manufacturing processes. The storekeeper's credit is based on the goods on the shelves. The value of buildings and factories and the laborer's home is dependent on the value of the commodities used in constructing them.

The equities of the building and loan associations and the bond holders are reduced if commodities decline in price. If wholesale commodity prices are kept stable and wages rise as efficiency increases, the portion of the house value based on wages also tends to be stabilized. The day's work costs more, but more work is done in a day. The only depreciation is then due to obsolescence and wear.

If the average price level of basic commodities is to fall as rapidly as efficiency increases, all fixed investments based on previous purchases of commodities must depreciate in value. This would interfere with the entire credit structure. For example, if all the materials included in a house are to decline in price at the average rate of increase in efficiency of labor, there would have to be a special depreciation on houses of about 1.7 per cent per year. Therefore, any laborer who bought a house through a building and loan association would have a dead weight against his success. Not only would he have to maintain the house in the condition in which he purchased it and pay interest on his investment, but also he would have a hidden burden which would affect the security of the loan and steadily eat into his savings. He does not want a money that will enable him to hire a day's work five years from now. He wants a money that will enable him to pay his contracted debt five years from now. His future obligations are secured by property, not by contracts for future labor. Similarly, the farmer who spends money to drain land, fix buildings, raise orchards, put up fences, and so forth, does not want a constant depreciation in the average of all these items. He can proceed successfully when some depreciate and others rise. For example, wooden fence posts grow more costly; the barbed wire on the fence grows less costly. But with a stable basic commodity price level, the farmer who goes in debt for a fence may hope that he can sell the fence, together with his farm, at a later date with no more loss than ordinary depreciation and obsolescence.

Every handler of goods is concerned with stability of basic commodity prices. There is a long time between the initial production and final sale to the consumer. If prices steadily decline, there is a perpetual hidden loss on inventories. Such a situation puts a premium on ultra-conservatism. The wise man invests all his money in government bonds or hoards it, and allows someone else to take the risk of falling prices.

There was a time when debts were payable in labor. If the debtor could not pay, he became the lender's slave until he had worked out the debt. This was at a time when there was little increase in efficiency (page 315). That time has passed. The lender now takes the debtor's commodities, if he is not paid. He cannot take the man.

What commodity prices should be stabilized?—The centuries of effort to find a commodity that would be stable in value as compared with other commodities have been in the right direction but can never be successful, because no commodity is free from fluctuations in supply and demand. The only possible solution of the problem is to give attention to many commodities rather than to just one.

In practically all monetary history, the attempt has been to get a basic commodity. Gold, not jewelry, has been used as money; silver, not silverware; beaver skins, not beaver coats; and iron rather than tools—have generally been used. This is sound in principle, and if we are to learn by these centuries of experience we will attempt to find a measure of value that will keep wholesale prices rather than retail prices at a stable level. It is preferable that these wholesale prices be as basic as possible, but there is also an advantage in having a large number of commodities.

Since basic commodities change in price more promptly than manufactured commodities, they give warning for the necessary action before changes have gone too far.

If only a very few commodities were used, it would be better to use those that are readily transported, thus avoiding the question of location.

If any one of the many index numbers of wholesale prices of a large number of commodities could be kept at a reasonably stable level for a series of years, the great calamities that come with financial inflation and deflation would be avoided. The fluctuations in the value of gold or any other single commodity are so great that any kind of a wholesale commodity price index would be such a phenomenal improvement as to make the details relatively unimportant. Most of the time, society is suffering from inflation or deflation.

Undoubtedly, the best measure of commodity prices to use as a basis for stabilization is the United States Bureau of Labor Statistics index numbers of wholesale prices of all commodities, but an index of 30 to 50 important basic commodities would do very well. The course of the two is practically identical in long periods of time (figure 27, page 37).

Although the index numbers of wholesale prices would undoubtedly be the best ones to stabilize, those of retail prices could be used. It is much more difficult to obtain comparable figures, however, because retail prices vary with the class of store, delivery, credit, and refinement of the article.

Comparison of a period of falling prices with a period of rising prices.—For the 17 years 1880-96, prices declined 3.6 per cent per year.[4] For the 17 years, 1897 to 1913, prices rose 2.3 per cent per year. The former period was characterized by a large number of failures of farmers, business concerns, and banks, by unemployment, tramps, strikes, riots, Coxey's army, and populism.

The second period was characterized by disappearance of tramps,[5] full employment, agricultural prosperity, rapid development of agricultural education and other public services, and improvement in housing facilities. In the latter part of the period, the rising costs of living became a problem.

The stimulating effect of a century of rising prices after gold and silver came from America is described on pages 322 and 324. During this century, prices rose 1.6 per cent per year.

So far as can be judged by history, the best periods for humanity

[4] 1880-96: $y = 113.85\ (0.96355)^x$. 1897-1913: $y = 73.187\ (1.0231)^x$.

[5] As a result of the long period of declining prices, the state of New York decided to purchase a farm to which tramps could be sent. G. F. Warren was on the commission to choose this farm. The purchase was made a few years after prices began to rise. The farm was not needed. During the war, it was used for a military camp. With declining prices, specimens of the tramp species have reappeared.

have been periods when commodity prices were rising slightly. Any effort to stabilize prices should make sure that no decline will occur, even at the risk of having a slight rise.

Bimetallism.—For centuries, gold and silver were jointly used as money. Sometimes coins of both kinds circulated at any value ratio that the public saw fit to place on them. More generally in modern times fixed legal ratios were established. These ratios were often changed. For about three centuries, the ratios varied from 15:1 to 16:1 (table 25, page 144).

In 1696, John Locke, Sir Isaac Newton, and Lord Somers were appointed to deal with the reformation of the currency of England. They fixed the ratio at 16 to 1. France and most of the other countries had a ratio of 15½ to 1. Silver therefore drifted to France and gold to England—not because of any intrinsic differences between gold and silver, but because of the differences in the laws. Newton subsequently recommended that the ratio be made the same as in other countries, but the change was not made. "In 1816, Lord Liverpool, seeing that the Mint was little employed in coining silver, came to the conclusion that England was 'naturally a gold country,' and that 'gold was the natural currency of England,' and closed the mints to the free coinage of silver, and adopted the Gold Standard."[6]

The initial shift in the United States to the gold standard was also the result of an accident. The failure of gold and silver to circulate concurrently led to the Coinage Act of June 28, 1834. "There was a tendency to select a single standard and that of silver. But politics intervened, not only because of a sectional interest derived from the discovery of gold in North Carolina, but also from the taking-up of a gold currency as a battle-cry in the war against the United States Bank."[7]

After the Franco-Prussian War, Germany compelled France to pay a large indemnity in gold and decided to follow the example of England and adopt the gold standard.

If the recommendation of Sir Isaac Newton had been adopted, the monetary history of the world might have been very different.

In 1873, the United States demonetized silver. At about this time, the countries of Continental Europe also demonetized it. After these acts, silver began to decline in value as compared with gold. Most of

[6] Lord Desborough, On Money, p. 19, 1932.

[7] Laughlin, J. L., Money, Credit, and Prices, Vol. 1, pp. 235-6, The University of Chicago Press. 1931.

the decline was probably due to its reduced use as money, and to the scarcity of gold. Gold would decline in value if it were no longer used as money, because the monetary stocks would be thrown on the industrial market and the market for about 56 per cent of the annual production would disappear.

Since 1894, the relative values of gold and silver have again been at a ratio a little more than twice as high as that which held for two centuries when both were generally used as money.

An exception to this more recent ratio occurred as a result of the discontinuance of the use of gold by many countries after 1916. By comparison with the general price level it is clear that this was due to a low value of gold because of low demand. With the return of the demand for gold, it again acquired its pre-war purchasing power for silver and for the average of all commodities.

For several centuries, bimetallism worked with considerable success. Its success would have been much greater had the ratios been the same in all countries. The reason why it was possible to make such a system operate was that the monetary demand was so much of the total demand. If the ratios were approximately right and if all countries used the same ratio, it would take a phenomenal increase in the supply of either one to throw it into exclusive use. If either one became relatively scarce so that it started to go out of use, it would at once throw so large a stock on the industrial market as to reduce its value and bring it back into monetary uses.

Bimetallism could be made to work if all countries agreed to it and adopted the same ratio. The ability to arrive at any such agreement and maintain it is very doubtful. It is unwise to try it because symmetallism would accomplish the desired result and would not require agreement of all nations.

If it is desired to remonetize silver, it would be much better to adopt symmetallism, which does not require international agreement and which would operate in a known way at all times.

Symmetallism.—Money made of a mixture of gold and silver called electrum was used by Greece and many other countries. It was sometimes a natural alloy and sometimes a definite mixture. The chief objection to it was that, with no satisfactory methods of preventing counterfeiting, the proportions could not be controlled.

Our present gold currency is not pure gold. We depend on law enforcement to prevent the circulation of coins with less gold. The same machinery would make electrum possible now.

In 1888, Marshall[8] proposed to the British Gold and Silver Commission the following plan:

"Ricardo suggested that we should use a paper currency resting on a basis, not of coin, but of stamped gold bars weighing 20 ounces each. . . . Within the country the paper would be a perfect medium of exchange, while for the payment of the balances of foreign trade stamped gold bars are better suited than coins. . . .

"I propose that currency should be exchangeable at the Mint or Issue Department, not for gold, but for gold and silver, at the rate of not £1 for 113 grains of gold, but £1 for 56½ grains of gold, together with, say, 20 times as many grains of silver. I would make up the gold and silver bars in gramme weights, so as to be useful for international trade. A gold bar of 100 grammes, together with a silver bar, say, 20 times as heavy, would be exchangeable at the Issue Department for an amount of the currency which would be calculated and fixed once for all when the scheme was introduced. (This number 20, or whatever it might be, would be fixed on arbitrarily once for all. If we wished the value of the currency to be regulated chiefly by gold we should have only a small bar of silver; if chiefly by silver we should have, perhaps, 50 or 100 times as heavy a bar of silver as that of gold. But if we wished the two metals to have about equal influence we should, taking account of the existing stocks of the two metals, probably choose our silver bar about 20 times as heavy as that of gold.)

"Anyone who wanted to buy or sell gold or silver alone in exchange for currency could get what he wanted by exchanging gold for silver, or silver for gold, at the market rate. Government fixing its own rates from day to day, so as to keep its reserves of the two metals in about the right proportion, might safely undertake this exchange itself, and then anyone could buy or sell either gold or silver for currency in one operation."

Such a proposal would have money based on the average value of two commodities rather than on the value of one commodity. When the two happened to be going in opposite directions, as they were in the eighties and nineties, the price level would be more stable than with a single commodity.

If symmetallism were adopted by only one important country, a ratio of 20 to 1 might be as good as any. If adopted by many coun-

[8] Marshall, A., Money Credit and Commerce, pp. 65-66, Macmillan, 1923. Official papers by Alfred Marshall. Answers to questions by the Royal Commission of Trade and Industry 1886, pp. 28-29, 1926.

tries, a ratio of perhaps 10 to 1 would be more logical because it is nearer the proportion in which they are produced. This ratio would have nothing to do with the value of money, which would be controlled by the total weight of gold and silver set by law. But, as Marshall states, any proportion could be used. It would be better to keep the bars in the Treasury, but coins could be made of the legal mixture.

If such a measure were adopted by a large country, it would raise the demand for silver and increase its value. This would tend to

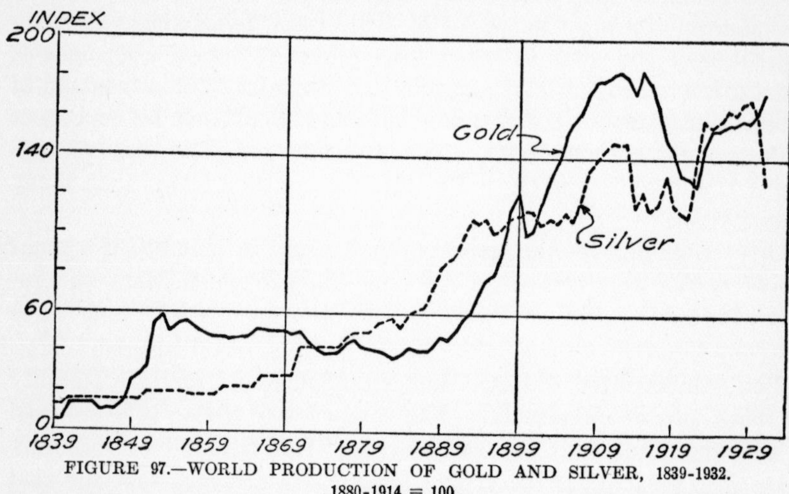

FIGURE 97.—WORLD PRODUCTION OF GOLD AND SILVER, 1839-1932. 1880-1914 = 100.

Silver production is much more uniform than the production of gold. Symmetallism would give a more stable measure of value than gold, but would not be entirely stable.

lower prices in silver-using countries. It would decrease the demand for gold and tend to lower its value, depending on how many countries adopted the system. The world stock and world production of gold and silver suggest that, if symmetallism were generally adopted, the increased use of silver and decreased demand for gold might bring the relative values approximately in the ratio that held for so many years when bimetallism was common.

If such a system were adopted in a gold-using country, it would make the foreign exchange situation more stable when trading with a silver-using country, but would increase variations when dealing with a gold-using country. The variations would not be anything like the violent ones that have existed most of the time since 1914, when many countries have been on a paper basis.

Such a system would make it easier for all countries to adopt the same standard. The effort of silver-using countries to change to gold places a pressure on the gold supply of all gold-using countries.

If such a monetary standard were adopted in the United States, the actual circulation would be paper dollars and minor coins just as at present. The difference would be that when one presented a dollar in currency for redemption, he would receive, perhaps, 11.61 grains of gold plus a certain weight of silver which would be specified in the law instead of 23.22 grains of gold as at present.

Symmetallism would always work because the money would be exchangeable for a given weight of gold plus a given weight of silver regardless of the value of either, just as money is now exchangeable for a given weight of gold regardless of its value. The advantage of symmetallism lies in the fact that currency would not be dependent on accidental discoveries of a single commodity. The disadvantage lies in the fact that only two commodities are used rather than many commodities.

Greater stability of the monetary unit would be obtained if a number of metals were treated in the same manner which Marshall proposed for gold and silver. Platinum and other metals with high value per pound, so that they could be stored cheaply, could be used.

The compensated dollar.—Symmetallism would increase stability by using two or more metals. The compensated dollar is a proposal to establish a scientific measure of value. This proposal has been developed in great detail by Irving Fisher.[9] He proposes that the gold dollar shall cease to be a constant weight of gold with a variable purchasing power, and shall become a variable weight of gold with a purchasing power as nearly constant as possible. This is sometimes called a rubber dollar by persons who do not understand it. The dollar has to be rubber as to either weight or value. It cannot have both its weight and its value fixed. This proposal lets the weight rather than the value vary. It is like substituting a fixed yard for measuring length instead of using the distance from the king's nose to the end of his thumb. Either the yard or the king had to vary.

With such a system, there would no longer be any coinage of gold. The government's gold supply would be kept in gold bars. The actual circulation would be the same as at present, i.e., paper dollars and small coins. All the currency would be exchangeable for gold on demand, as at present, but the amount of gold that a dollar would exchange for would vary with the price level, that is, the price of gold

[9] Fisher, I., Stabilizing the Dollar, 1920.

would be allowed to vary with its value just as the price of wheat varies with its value.

If prices rose 0.1 per cent in a week, the weight of gold purchasable by a dollar would be increased 0.1 per cent until any rise was corrected. If prices fell 0.1 per cent, the weight of the gold purchasable by a dollar would be decreased 0.1 per cent. There would be a small difference between the buying and selling price for gold. This is an all-commodity dollar rather than a one-commodity dollar. This would make the dollar have the same value at all times. It would be independent of business cycles.

Such an all-commodity dollar would do much to eliminate the nightmare of the unfavorable balance of trade. Nations have learned that a loss of the gold supply at best means deflation and, if it goes too far, means being forced off the gold standard. Therefore, they strive to foster exports and prevent imports, not because this is good trade policy, but to protect the money of the country.

In the nineties, Europe had large sums of money invested in America. The expectation was that payment would be made with goods, but gold became so scarce that goods brought little, and the maintenance of a favorable balance of trade became difficult. The gold supply of the nation was drained away. No nation cares to face such a situation twice. It wishes to have enough gold to meet all foreign calls.

During 1922 to 1929, vast foreign loans were made. The borrowers expected to pay with goods. The price collapse made it impossible to pay with goods. Runs began on the gold supplies of South America, then on England, and then on the United States. Even after a loss of a billion dollars and after having to pass legislation to prevent being forced off the gold basis, the United States had more than its pre-war share of the world gold supply. Further runs on the gold supplies of different countries are to be expected in the years to come.

Bounties, export debentures, McNary-Haugen bills, the Farm Board, and regulations to prevent a foreign student from working for his living, are only a few of the innumerable cumbersome and ineffectual means used to prevent prices from declining when gold rises in value.

A country could adopt a compensated dollar without waiting for international agreements of any kind. There is much to be said for an international currency, but there is also much to be said for currency that will not be distorted every time some country decides to dump gold or hoard it. With the compensated dollar, an inflow of gold would not cause inflation. It would make gold cheap, just as an inflow of coffee would make coffee cheap. An outflow of gold would raise the price of gold and make that country a good place in which to buy commodities. It would not cause a price collapse, unemployment, or bankruptcy.

Such a money would enable one to borrow with a definite knowledge of what repayment means. One could lend with greater certainty that he would be repaid. It would enable one to save for old age, or leave life insurance for a family with assurance that the sum would not shrink, and that it would not grow so unjustly large as to cause the bank or company to fail.

An objection raised to this proposal is: An all-commodity dollar would not completely eliminate business cycles. This is true, but they would be cycles and not precipices. Business cycles in periods when commodity prices return to the previous level at the close of the cycle have not been extremely serious. All the extremely violent cycles have occurred when prices were rising to a new level or declining to a new level. The latter are the ones that cause the great calamities.

During a business cycle, commodity prices fall so that bankruptcies occur. An all-commodity dollar would keep the value of the dollar stable and would, therefore, do much to check booms and depressions.

Another objection to this means of stabilization is that international exchange would be affected. This effect would be smaller than the uncertainties in the exchange which have always existed when a country on a gold basis is trading with some other country on a silver basis, and it would be trivial in comparison with the uncertainties between gold-using countries and countries that suspended gold payments from 1914 to 1932.

Another objection is that, during a war, this, as well as any other monetary system, might be overwhelmed by government borrowing. It could stand much of such borrowing.

Another objection to the plan is that there would be speculation in gold. Speculation in gold would be no more serious than speculation in wheat, silver or foreign exchange.

As discussed on pages 156 and 158, some index numbers of wholesale prices of commodities should be used in carrying out this plan. A limited number of basic commodities might be specified by the law, or an index like that prepared by the Bureau of Labor Statistics might be prescribed, or a commission might be set up for the continuous calculation of an index number.

Any kind of an index number would be far more stable than the value of a single commodity. From 1873 to 1896, the value of gold in England almost doubled (table 8). From 1896 to 1914, it declined nearly one-third. From 1914 to 1920, its value declined more than one-half. From 1920 to 1931, it more than doubled. When we are attempting to make some improvement over such a chaotic measure of value, differences in index numbers are trivial. For example, the index number of wholesale prices in England in 1880 was 107 (table 8, page 75) and in the United States an index for different commodities, prepared by a different method, was 100. In spite of influences of war, tariffs, and the like, the index numbers 48 years later were 145 for England and 141 for the United States.

An all-commodity dollar could be combined with symmetallism. It would merely mean that the weight of the two metals purchasable by a dollar would be reduced 0.1 per cent if prices fell 0.1 per cent, and raised if prices rose. Since symmetallism itself would increase stability, the amount of necessary price changes would be reduced. This combination would therefore be better than an all-commodity dollar redeemable in any one metal.

When any new proposal for human progress is made, there is always a tendency to compare the new proposal with some perfect ideal. Trivial difficulties are magnified. An ant hill in an untraveled country seems larger than a mountain that has been crossed. All that is necessary to prove for a new method is that it is the best that is feasible at the time and that it is enough better than the old to pay for the inconvenience of making the change. No human device is free from imperfections.

At the date of adoption of such a measure, consideration should be given to the price level at which outstanding debts were contracted, building and other permanent improvements constructed, and the level to which wages, freight rates, and the like, are most nearly adjusted.

Managed currency.—Keynes[10] proposes that the central bank keep gold reserves in bar form, but that there be no fixed ratios of reserves to note circulation. The central bank would change its buying and selling price for gold just as it regulates the discount rate. The intelligence necessary to operate one of these could operate the other. The bank would use both these methods to keep commodity prices stable. His plan is in some respects like the Fisher Plan, but action is made at the discretion of the central bank board. The successful operation of this plan necessitates that the board be free from

[10] Keynes, J. M., Monetary Reform, pp. 203-13, 1924.

political influence and uninfluenced by the desire for profits. Keynes believes that the Bank of England is capable of doing this. The main features of his proposal are as follows:

"Whilst it would not be advisable to postpone action until it was called for by an actual movement of prices, it would promote confidence and furnish an objective standard of value, if, an official index number having been compiled of such a character as to register the price of a standard composite commodity, the authorities were to adopt this composite commodity as their standard of value in the sense that they would employ all their resources to prevent a movement of its price by more than a certain percentage in either direction away from the normal. . . . Actual price movements must of course provide the most important datum; but the state of employment, the volume of production, the effective demand for credit as felt by the banks, the rate of interest on investments of various types, the volume of new issues, the flow of cash into circulation, the statistics of foreign trade and the level of the exchanges must all be taken into account. The main point is that the *objective* of the authorities, pursued with such means as are at their command, should be the stability of prices. . . . It is the great advantage of the gold standard that it overcomes the excessive sensitiveness of the exchanges to temporary influences. Our object must be to secure this advantage, if we can, without committing ourselves to follow big movements in the value of gold itself.

"I believe that we can go a long way in this direction if the Bank of England will take over the duty of regulating the price of gold, just as it already regulates the rate of discount. The Bank of England should have a buying and a selling price for gold, and this price might remain unchanged for considerable periods, just as the bank rate does. But it would not be fixed or 'pegged' once and for all, any more than the bank rate is fixed . . .

"If we agree that gold is not to be employed in the circulation, and that it is better to employ some other criterion than the ratio of gold reserves to note issue in deciding to raise or to lower the bank rate, it follows that the only employment for gold (nevertheless important) is as a store of value to be held as a war-chest against emergencies and as a means of rapidly correcting the influence of a temporarily adverse balance of international payments and thus maintaining a day-to-day stability of the sterling-dollar exchange . . . Therefore I make the proposal—which may seem, but should not be, shocking—of separating entirely the gold reserve from the note issue."

Paper currency.—At innumerable times, paper currency has been issued based solely on the government's credit. At times, such a currency has been maintained at a fairly stable level for a considerable period of time, showing that such a currency is possible.

In primitive society, the money must be worth its face value as metal. The gold-using countries now have paper currencies in part secured by gold and in part based on credit. This proposal would base all money on the government's credit.

The trials of such a currency have nearly always been made as a result of war when the nation's credit had already become so exhausted as to cause a breakdown in the gold standard and in the regular currency system. Under such circumstances, it has been very difficult to exercise the necessary discretion in order to maintain the stability of such a currency for a considerable length of time. When the gold standard fails completely, the paper standard is used, and if the country is not completely bankrupt, it has in many cases succeeded fairly well.

Proposals are often made that an irredeemable paper currency be established and that the supply of it be regulated by law, either by issuing a definite addition each year to keep pace with the growth of business or by varying the amount of it so as to keep an index number of wholesale prices stable. Such currency could be used in the more stable countries. The compensated dollar would be a less radical change, as it would be based on the traditional gold reserves. It would be more definite and less subject to political action, and would keep the buying power of the dollar fixed at all times.

The time may come when a paper money, the amount of which is controlled by law, will make a good permanent currency, but a currency redeemable in gold or gold and silver and definitely controlled by law is probably better adapted to the present state of economic knowledge and political stability.

Bank policy.—An important step in central bank policy was taken in 1844 when, after a long period of financial troubles, the principle of using the bank to aid in monetary problems developed. Keynes[11] describes this as follows:

"The efficacy of Bank-rate for the management of a managed money was a great discovery and also a most novel one—a few years earlier the Bank of England had not had the slightest understanding of any connection between bank-rate policy and the maintenance of the standard."

[11] Keynes, J. M., A Treatise on Money, Vol. 1, p. 17, 1930.

The Federal Reserve system is an attempt to use bank policy in managing credit, but there is no clear understanding of the relationship of bank policy to commodity prices, and there is no general acceptance of the principle that these banks should consider commodity prices. By means of the discount rate and the purchase and sale of securities, it is possible for such banks to do a little in stabilizing prices. The Federal Reserve law involves the questionable idea that the currency should be increased when business is active and curtailed when a depression comes. The idea that, when men are willing to give more notes, these notes should create new currency is a very risky theory. It tends to violent fluctuations rather than to stability.

The banks can control credit within the limits set by the requirement of maintaining gold payments. If they approach this limit, fear develops, and they must either contract credit or stop gold payments (page 107). Some persons contend that, since credit is a matter of confidence, there is no reason for limiting it. It would be as logical to say that there is no reason to limit bank reserves since the security of a bank is a matter of confidence. It is not merely a matter of confidence. Even if it were, credit would have to be kept within bounds, for when confidence is shaken, chaos results.

A move in the direction of a definite bank policy was attempted May 2, 1932, when the House passed the Goldsborough bill, by a vote of 289 to 59. House of Representatives Bill No. 10517 directed the Federal Reserve Board and the Federal Reserve Banks to take all available steps to raise the present deflated wholesale commodity level of prices as speedily as possible to the level existing before the present deflation.

The government can maintain its money as a fixed weight of gold or as a fixed value in terms of all commodities. It cannot do both. The original Goldsborough bill provided for this by directing that if necessary the price of gold be changed to maintain a stable value for the dollar. This original proposal was substantially the Keynes proposal.

Suspension of gold payments.—Any means of restoring prices will probably require suspension of gold payments while the plan is being discussed. By 1932, this had been done by all other important countries except those that had cut the weight of gold in their money.

The wild inflation in Germany is commonly believed to be an inevitable result of leaving the gold standard. The only cases of wild inflation have come after government bankruptcy. During the American and French Revolutions, both countries inflated until the money was "not worth a Continental." Similar inflation occurred during the German Revolution and their attempts to pay reparations. Russia is in a revolutionary period and has had violent inflation.

England suspended gold payments for 24 years in the Napoleonic War period. She also suspended gold payments from 1914 to 1925 and suspended in 1931. This makes a total of 36 out of 136 years off gold, but no case of wild inflation has occurred.

The United States has suspended gold payments 4 times, but even in the Civil War did not have wild inflation. Our average prices for the year 1864 were 193. Prices in England on a gold basis were 127. The worst inflation that has occurred since the Revolutionary War was on a gold basis in 1920, when prices averaged 226.

There is no serious danger of wild inflation except following revolution.

Legal changes in the weight of gold in the monetary unit.— There are innumerable cases in history of changing the weight of gold or silver in the monetary unit. In 1834, the weight of gold in the dollar was reduced by 6.26 per cent (page 87).

The pound sterling was originally one pound of silver with a purity of 37/40, which was known as sterling fineness. Although the name of the pound was retained, the weight was reduced from time to time until it stood at a little less than a third of a pound of silver at the time of the adoption of the gold standard. The name is still retained, but it is not a pound, not sterling, not silver. At the time this is written it is not gold, and it promises to be reduced in weight when it again becomes gold.

Before the World War, the French franc was 290.322 milligrams of pure gold; on June 25, 1928, it was reduced to 58.95 milligrams.[12] Public and private debts and all other monetary transactions could then be paid with a franc having a value similar to its value when most of these obligations were incurred.

Since France was still inflating her currency up to 1926 she avoided the depression of 1920 and most of the depression of 1929-30 because her price level was five times pre-war (figure 98).

The decline in 1931 caused a depression in France but nothing comparable to the situation in England and the United States. The only public or private debts that were troublesome were those that were contracted at a price level of over four times pre-war.

On Oct. 25, 1926, the Belgian currency was established on a

[12] Laughlin, J. L., Money, Credit, and Prices, Vol. 1, p. 179, 1931.

gold basis, with a new unit of currency,[13] the belga, with a content of 209.211 milligrams of fine gold and a fixed relationship to the Belgian paper franc of about 7 to 1. By this act, Belgium reduced the weight of gold in the franc from 290.322 milligrams of fine gold to 41.842 milligrams.

Before the war, the Italian lira was 290.322 milligrams of fine gold. On December 22, 1927, this was reduced to 79.1911 milligrams.[14] Public and private debts were therefore payable at approximately the price level at which they were incurred, and all services and charges were left in the same relationship which they held previous to stabilization.

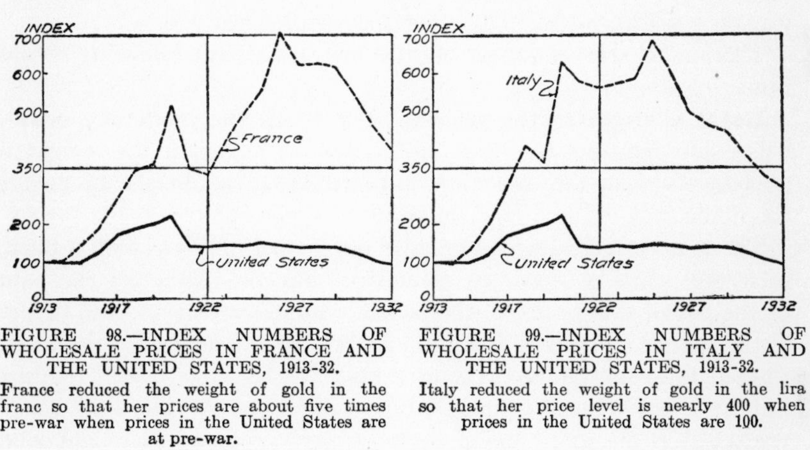

FIGURE 98.—INDEX NUMBERS OF WHOLESALE PRICES IN FRANCE AND THE UNITED STATES, 1913-32.
France reduced the weight of gold in the franc so that her prices are about five times pre-war when prices in the United States are at pre-war.

FIGURE 99.—INDEX NUMBERS OF WHOLESALE PRICES IN ITALY AND THE UNITED STATES, 1913-32.
Italy reduced the weight of gold in the lira so that her price level is nearly 400 when prices in the United States are 100.

Since Italy was inflating the currency up to 1927, she avoided the deflation of 1920. Prices fell in 1931 so that deflation was felt (figure 99).

Germany inflated her currency until it became almost worthless. On November 15, 1923, the Rentenmark was provided for. One trillion of the old paper marks was equal to one Rentenmark. These were replaced by the gold Reichmark in the autumn of 1924.

The inflation was extremely serious for the country, but the serious effects of deflation were avoided. Any debts that were incurred with the paper mark could be paid with the Rentenmark at the ratio of one trillion to one. There was no need to reduce the innumerable fixed prices, because stabilization at the fantastic level was nevertheless

[13] Federal Reserve Bulletin, Vol. 12, No. 11, p. 763, November 1926; No. 12, p. 842, December 1926.

[14] Federal Reserve Bulletin, Vol. 14, No. 1, p. 27, January 1928.

a continuance of the old price level. This was entirely different from deflation.

Germany felt the full effect of the deflation of 1929-31 because she had incurred a new indebtedness and fixed charges at the price levels of 1925-29.

In 1931-32, England and 31 other countries discontinued the gold standard. Presumably most of these countries will follow the example of France and Italy and reduce the weight of gold in their currencies when they return to a gold basis.

No country likes to revalue its money; but when prices have risen too high, an attempt to deflate causes such universal bankruptcy that creditors instead of profiting by being paid money with a higher value lose so much of the principal that it is to their interest as well as to the interest of debtors to revalue the currency. An attempt to deflate requires such unusual and drastic writing down of debts, wages, freight rates, telephone charges, fees, and every other economic charge as to cause unemployment, reduced national production, and national poverty. To attempt to meet such a situation, government loans, price control measures and other undesirable legislation is tried. Rather than undergo these calamities, it is much better to revalue the currency and allow business to proceed.

Prices in 1931 at the time when a large number of the countries gave up the effort to deflate are shown in table 28. At this time, prices in England had declined 65 per cent from the average of the 24 months

TABLE 28.—COMPARATIVE DECLINES IN WHOLESALE PRICES

	England: Statist-Sauerbeck index* 1910–14=100	France: Statistique Générale index† 1910–14=100	Italy: Riccardo Bachi index‡ 1913=100	Germany: Statistisches Reichsamt index‡ 1913=100	United States: Bureau of Labor all-commodity index 1910–14=100§
Highest 24 months	275	667	599	8,310,000,000,000¶	215
August 1931......	96	450	322	110	105
Points decline....	179	217	277	....	110
Per cent decline...	65	33	46	....	51
June 1932........	93	403	297	96	93
Per cent decline...	66	40	50	....	57

* The Statist, Vol. CXIV, No. 2812, p. 80, Jan. 16, 1932. The index numbers on the 11-year base 1867–77 were converted to the five years 1910–14 by multiplying by 1.2107.

† Annuaire Statistique for 1928, Vol. 44, p. 115, 1929. To convert from the 1901–10 base, multiply by 0.87260; from the July 1914 base by 0.9888; and from the 1913 base by 1.0096.

‡ Monthly Labor Review, United States Bureau of Labor Statistics, Vol. XIII, No. 6, p. 71, December 1921; Vol. 31, No. 6, p. 217, December 1930; and Vol. 33, No. 6, p. 238–9, December 1931.

§ Table 1, p. 10.

The highest 24 months were: England, February 1919–January 1921; France, November 1925–October 1927; Italy, January 1925–December 1926; United States, November 1918–October 1920; Germany, January 1922–December 1923.

¶ Table 2, p. 17.

with highest prices. This amount of price decline caused such prolonged unemployment, so many bankruptcies, and other disastrous conditions, that the process could not be continued. By doles and other means, national governments had attempted to tide over the situation, but such drastic deflation proved to be beyond the power of national finance to alleviate.

This leaves the United States with a price decline of 57 per cent as the most striking deflation for any large country that continued the effort to maintain its pre-war currency. In 10 to 20 years the full results of this effort will be apparent.

Revaluing the currency is a single drastic procedure to correct a single situation. It does not provide a continuing stability of money. France and Italy revalued their money in conformity with their price level when commodity prices in the gold-using countries were about 40 per cent above pre-war. This avoided any of the difficulty that the United States and England experienced in going from a price level of more than 200 to 140, but it did not avoid the difficulties that came with the decline in prices in 1931-32. If England and the other countries that left the gold basis in 1931 revalue their currencies so as to bring their prices back to the level of 1929, they will be in a better position than France, as they will avoid the continuance of the deflated prices of 1932.

Many obligations contain the "gold clause" calling for payment in gold dollars of present weight and fineness. This clause is most frequent in bonds of various units of government and corporations. It does not apply to most farm mortgages, life insurance, or ordinary business transactions.

According to the constitution, "Congress shall have power . . . to coin money, regulate the value thereof, and of foreign coin, and fix the standard of weights and measures." Article I, Section 8.

"No person shall . . . be deprived of life, liberty, or property, without due process of law. . . ." Amendment V.

"No state shall . . . pass any . . . law impairing the obligation of contracts. . . ." Article I, Section 10.

If it becomes necessary to change the dollar, there is little question of the power of Congress to invalidate such contracts. Many Supreme Court decisions have held that while states may not invalidate contracts, Congress can do so.

In any event, revaluation would allow payment of the many debts in dollars and would allow adjustment of the innumerable fixed charges that wreck business when prices fall, so that business would proceed and there would be money with which to pay debts, taxes, and wages. The gold clause is a trivial matter compared with the restoration of the opportunity to work. If deflation is continued, it is not a question of the kind of money in which debts will be paid but a question of what debts can be paid at all.

The question is often raised as to just what would happen if the price of gold were raised 50 per cent. Innumerable charges that have not declined would not rise, but would be relieved of the necessity of declining. Among these are public and private debts, freight rates, telephone charges, and the like. Total tax payments would increase because taxes could be paid. Therefore tax rates would be lowered.

Prices of cotton and wheat at export points would rise a little more than 50 per cent. The following illustrations are based on prices for December 1932. If wheat at New York rose from 64 to 96 cents, wheat in Nebraska would rise about 32 cents. There have been so many examples of just such a change that we can be sure of the effect on the Nebraska price. But this would more than double the Nebraska price. Corn at New York City would also increase about 50 per cent or about 21 cents per bushel. This would much more than double prices on Iowa farms.

The above changes would occur without any change in prices in foreign countries. The increased business which rising prices cause would result in still further price increases. These would be very decided increases for basic commodities.

Even with no improved prospects for business, prices of industrial stocks would increase about 50 per cent. Prices of such stocks in London and New York keep on the same basis in ounces of gold. On December 15, 1932, 1.6 ounces of gold were required to buy a share of United States steel stock in London, and 1.5 ounces were required in New York. On the same day, 0.73 ounces of gold were required to buy a share of Pennsylvania railway stock in London and 0.71 ounces in New York. Of course a rise in the price level would stimulate business and cause much more than a 50 per cent increase in security prices. A bale of cotton was worth 1.5 ounces of gold in New York and 1.8 ounces in England.

The value of lumber and other building materials in a house would at once rise by 50 per cent. This would stop bankrupt sales and before long would result in more building. Lumber far from market would rise in price by a much greater percentage. The prices of cement, brick, and metals would also advance.

In general, those prices which have not declined would be relieved of the necessity of declining and prices of basic commodities far from market would rise most. These effects are the same as a rise in prices brought about by any other cause.

There would be one major difference,—gold would also rise in price. Expectation of such a change would probably result in hoarding gold. It would, however, be much more profitable to hoard basic commodities such as lumber, cotton, corn, wheat, copper, and the like, at points far from market. It would also be more profitable to hoard common stocks than gold. With everything else at panic prices, gold would be one of the least profitable things to hold.

If such a change were made in the price of gold, it would probably be preceded by the suspension of gold payments as has been the case in most of the world, or would probably require the suspension of such payments while the subject was being discussed.

Legal compulsory adjustments of all prices.—The popular explanation of high prices has always been shortage of everything. When prices are low, the popular explanation is that there is a surplus of everything. When inflation occurs, the government always sets up food administrators, commissions, dictators, and dollar-a-year men to hold prices of this or that commodity down at the same time that the printing presses are running to make more money. With inflation, the favorite point of attack is food. When deflation occurs, the favorite points of attack are wages and taxes. The theory is that, if wages could be lowered so that costs would be lowered, business would be active, not recognizing that it was declining prices that killed business (page 265). The major difficulty is debts, and the major reason why debts become the difficulty is that buildings and commodities on which the debts are based have shrunk in price so much that the debtor's equity has been wiped out. The public fails to see that a further drop in prices, if it could be brought about by reducing wages, would wipe out more equities and cause still more bankruptcies. If during deflation reductions are to be made, the logical point of first attack would be to reduce all debts. Germany did this for East Prussia in 1931 when all debts were reduced 50 per cent.[15] It is not improbable that the total collections by all creditors would be greater than if they attempted to collect the whole sum.

To carry out the full logic of this method of procedure, everything for which money was paid would be reduced in price. Germany tried to carry out this plan in 1931 by reducing by law all freight rates, doctors' fees, rents, prices of commodities, wages, salaries, commissions, etc.[16] Most of the cuts were 10 per cent. Interest rates were re-

[15] New York Times, p. 8, Nov. 18, 1931.
[16] New York Times, Dec. 9, 1931.

duced much more. If very high, they were reduced 50 per cent. The law provided that, in foreclosure sales at auction, no bid of less than 70 per cent of the property value need be accepted.

Any attempt to correct a rise in the value of the commodity used as money must either deal with money or with every price transaction, if equity is to be restored.

In the United States, prices, wages, hours of labor and interest rates are often subject to law, but it is probably unconstitutional to scale down debts by law. In efforts to collect a dollar that is worth a third more than the one which was lent, the creditor often gets nothing. He frequently gets even less, for he may hold a home or farm and finally sell it for less than the carrying cost, so that he would have been better off had he canceled the debt and not dispossessed the owner. The process of reducing debts to the new value of gold destroys values and injures creditors as well as debtors.

Summary of stabilization plans.—Before anything is done to establish a more stable measure of value, there must be an understanding of the relationship of money to prices and the relationship of prices to national welfare. It is not to be expected that any perfect means can be devised; the problem is to provide the best measure of value possible. Anything that is not so bad as the present system is worthy of consideration. There are at least three types of procedure that are being seriously discussed, and many others that could be suggested.

1. The use of two or more metals, not as alternates, but as provided by Marshall's symmetallism. This is the practical method of accomplishing what the bimetallists desire.

2. The practical emergency measure seems to be the method which has already been followed by France, Italy, and other countries, and which promises to be followed by England and still more countries, of reducing the weight of metal in the monetary unit. This does not provide continuing stability in value but is a single drastic adjustment to meet a catastrophe resulting from declining prices. Before taking such a step, each of the countries suspended gold payments.

3. A scientific measure of value, and the ultimate ideal, is a dollar that has a constant buying power, not for one commodity but for all commodities at wholesale prices.

These proposals are not antagonistic. Any combination of them could be used.

The problem of trying to maintain a fixed price on gold, regardless of the accidents of discovery or the whims of foreign countries in demanding it or dumping it, grows worse generation after generation, as men become less self-sufficient. If this kind of price-fixing is not corrected, it is in danger of forcing some kind of a socialistic state that will attempt to regulate distribution by government action. When the medium of exchange fails to function, the organization of society that depends on this medium is attacked. The world will not tolerate starvation in the midst of plenty. It will attempt to find some means of exchanging goods. The scientific method is some form of an all-commodity, or many-commodity, dollar; but if something approaching this is not developed, there is danger that the cumbersome machinery of government, i.e., committee action, may be attempted.

BIBLIOGRAPHY

Arendtz, H. F., The Way Out of Depression. 1931.

Edie, L. D., Money, Bank Credit, and Prices. 1928.

Fisher, I., Stabilizing the Dollar. 1920.

Fisher, I., The Money Illusion. 1928.

Fisher, I., The Purchasing Power of Money. 1920.

Fisher, I., Booms and Depressions. 1932.

Fisher, W. C., The Tabular Standard in Massachusetts History. Quarterly Journal of Economics, Vol. XXVII, No. 3, pp. 417-451. May 1913.

Jevons, W. S., Money and the Mechanism of Exchange, p. 325. 1896.

Jordan, V., Some Aspects of National Stabilization. Bulletin of the Taylor Society, Vol. 16, No. 6, pp. 244-51. December 1931.

Jordan, V., Foster, W. T., and Person, H. S., Avoidance of Depression. Stabilization through fiscal policy; stabilization through money and credit; stabilization through regulation of investment. Bulletin of the Taylor Society, Vol. 17, No. 3, pp. 113-132. June 1932.

Keynes, J. M., Monetary Reform. 1924.

Keynes, J. M., A Treatise on Money, Vols. 1 and 2. 1930.

Lawrence, J. S., Stabilization of Prices. 1928.

Lloyd, E. M. H., Stabilisation. 1923.

Lowe, J., The Present State of England in Regard to Agriculture, Trade, and Finance. 1824.

Marshall, A., Remedies for Fluctuations of General Prices, Contemporary Review, Vol. LI, pp. 355-375. March 1887.

Marshall, A., Money, Credit, and Commerce, pp. 256-263. 1924.

McKenna, R., The Gold Standard and Monetary Management. The inescapable choice. Midland Bank Monthly Review, pp. 1-4. January-February 1932.

Newcomb, S., The Standard of Value, The North American Review, Vol. CXXIX, No. CCLXXIV, pp. 223-237. September 1879.

Newcomb, S., Principles of Political Economy, pp. 328, 346. 1885.

Porter, G. R., The Progress of the Nation, Section III, p. 235. 1838.

Robertson, D. H., Banking Policy and the Price Level. 1926.

Scrope, G. P., Principles of Political Economy, p. 406. 1833.

Taussig, F. W., The Plan for a Compensated Dollar. Quarterly Journal of Economics, Vol. XXVII, No. 3, pp. 401-16. May 1913.

Veeder, N., Cometallism: A plan for combining gold and silver in coinage, for uniting and blending their values in paper money and for establishing a composite Single Standard Dollar of account. 1885.

CHAPTER X

CAUSES OF INFLATION AND DEFLATION

What is inflation?—Inflation takes place when the circulating medium increases faster than trade. If money always changed in quantity exactly in proportion to the physical amount of business done, there would never be any inflation or deflation, and the general price level would remain approximately constant, although the prices of individual commodities would continue to fluctuate.

The value of money depends on supply and demand exactly as does the value of any other commodity. An increase in the circulating medium, relative to trade needs, results in depreciation in the monetary unit. The purchasing power of money is reduced.

Causes of inflation.—Depreciation may result from four causes:

1. Large issues of paper money.
2. Reducing the weight of metal in the monetary unit.
3. Reduced demand for the monetary metal.
4. Large additions in supplies of metal without any change in the unit.

The Continental currency of the Revolutionary War period, greenbacks of the Civil War period, and European paper during the World War are examples of inflation brought about by issuing large amounts of paper money. On each of these occasions, there was also inflation for countries that remained on a metal basis.

At innumerable times in history, either the weight or purity of the money has been reduced and inflation resulted.

The demonetization of silver reduced the demand for it to such a striking degree that its value declined. This resulted in inflation for countries that continued on a silver basis. In precisely the same way, the reduced demand for gold, because of the substitution of paper currencies during the World War, reduced the value of gold and caused inflation in countries that continued on a gold basis. The most serious case of inflation in the United States since the Revolutionary War was primarily due to the inflow of gold from countries that temporarily abandoned it.

During the World War, the large amount of gold that came from

Europe to the United States caused inflation although the world supply of gold did not increase rapidly. From 1914 to 1917, the monetary stocks of gold in the United States increased 70 per cent and prices rose 74 per cent. Monetary circulation and bank deposits per dollar of gold were unusually low; inflation occurred because of the low demand for gold.

Although the United States continued on the gold basis throughout the war period, the inflation was greater than that which occurred during the Civil War when the greenbacks were issued. The situation was more precarious than during the Civil War period because it was fairly certain that European countries would make desperate efforts to get the gold back, whereas greenback-inflation was controlled by American laws. Since the effects of inflation are entirely independent of the cause, the inflation of the World War period was worse than the inflation of the Civil War period.

In 1929, the world gold supplies were 152 when the pre-war amount is 100. Since production of other commodities when compared with pre-war was 140 and the price level 139, the world needed gold stocks of nearly double pre-war to prevent deflation ($1.39 \times 1.40 = 1.95$). The effort of each country to build up gold stocks caused the price collapse.

Gold and silver taken from America to Europe after the discovery of America resulted in inflation by large additions to the monetary stocks. The same thing occurred after the discovery of gold in the Klondike and in South Africa.

Most of the other striking cases of inflation in the last two centuries have been due to the new discoveries of gold or to the printing of paper money to finance wars. The latter is responsible for all the extremely violent cases.

Before the invention of paper money the common way to finance war was to contract large obligations and then reissue the metal coins with a smaller amount of precious metals. Paper money has even more possibilities than debasement. When one country stops bidding for gold, all other gold countries are affected.

Violent inflation has rarely been resorted to when other means could have been used. In an overwhelming crisis, a country can obtain credit by inflation when it cannot do so through taxation or the sale of bonds. The Revolutionary War was financed by printing paper currency. It is very doubtful if it could have been financed in any other way, because there was no strong central government. According to Gallatin, "The Continental money carried the United States through the most arduous and perilous stages of the war, and . . . it cannot be denied that it saved the country."[1]

Causes of deflation.—Deflation may occur from four causes:

1. Contraction of the amount of money in circulation.
2. Increasing the weight of metal in the monetary unit.
3. Increased demand for the monetary metal.
4. Failure of the supply of the monetary metal to increase as rapidly as trade needs.

After a country has issued sufficient paper money to result in suspension of gold payments, it is seriously impressed with the objections to inflation. The popular idea is that deflation is the remedy. The only remedy for inflation is stabilization at a somewhat reduced price level, in case the inflated price level has prevailed for only a short time. Any given amount of deflation is far more serious than the same amount of inflation. This truth is not generally recognized, and therefore inflation is often followed by an infinitely worse disease—deflation.

Before the days of paper currency, the weight of metal in the monetary unit was sometimes reduced so much as to cause a reaction to a higher weight.

Probably, history's most striking case of deflation brought about by increased demand for the monetary metal was the result of the frantic demand for gold which culminated in the Panic of 1929. In addition to the demand from all the European countries, an effort was made to place India on the gold basis. In 1928, France put Indo-China on a gold basis and sold its silver.[2] Siam also shifted from silver to gold.

The long period of declining prices from 1880 to 1896 was due to the failure to find gold. The deflation following the World War was also in part due to the same cause.

Inflation and deflation.—Deflation is so much more destructive than an equal amount of inflation that it never goes to the same extremes. With inflation, business is extremely active. Those who go in debt can pay their debts. Production is so profitable that there is a feverish demand for labor. Such a situation can continue almost indefinitely. For example, in Germany after the World War, inflation continued until a trillion paper marks were worth no more than one of the original marks. Germany did not deflate. She revalued the cur-

[1] Leavitt, S., Our Money Wars, p. 24, 1894.
[2] New York Times, July 3, 1932.

rency on the basis of a trillion to one—which is entirely different from deflation.

France inflated until prices in 1926 reached a point seven times pre-war. It was manifestly impossible to deflate, and the franc was re-valued on a basis of 5 to 1. Thus any debt contracted at a price level of 500 was not increased by deflation.

As a result of gold and currency inflation in the United States, prices reached a level of 244 in May 1920. The combination of this inflation and the economic results of the war was small in comparison with the difficulties of a deflation of about one-third from 1929 to 1932. With inflation, there was full employment and active business, and debtors could pay their debts. Creditors received less purchasing power than they anticipated, but the debts were paid. With deflation, production was checked, millions were unemployed, debtors were unable to pay, and many creditors failed to get anything.

There have been no other important cases of an attempt to deflate as much as England and the United States attempted from 1920 to 1931. From a peak of prices of 322 in April 1920, England continued to deflate until prices reached 96 in August 1931—a decline of 70 per cent. This effort resulted in continuous and serious unemployment, a general strike, the passage of innumerable laws for relief, and a protective tariff. The full effects of these will not be known for a generation. The hopeless task of deflation was discontinued when England abandoned the gold basis on September 21, 1931.

The next most serious deflation was that attempted by the United States, in which commodity prices declined from a peak of 244 in May 1920 to 93 in June 1932, or a decline of 62 per cent.

Probably no country could stand such a decline all at once. In 1920, the debt structure and many other economic relationships had not become adjusted to the price level, so that the decline was less serious. The second decline from a price level of 141 in August 1929 to 93 in June 1932, or a decline of 34 per cent, resulted in the innumerable catastrophes of the worst panic ever experienced in the history of the country.

Apparently no countries but the most conservative ones will tolerate such a decline in the price level; whereas a very large degree of inflation is possible.

Because of the recent cases of extreme inflation, and because this generation had no previous knowledge of deflation, it feared inflation more than it feared deflation. Still another reason for the greater fear of inflation is that in history it has often come as a result of some other catastrophe for which inflation is blamed. For example, in Germany after the war, reparations payments in gold were required. Germany had just been through a revolution and suppressed a counter-revolution. Much of her best agricultural land and many of her mines had been taken away. There was not food enough in the country to prevent starvation. Strangely enough, the world would not buy her bonds but would buy her paper marks. By printing them she was able to buy food. It would be interesting to know what the conditions in Germany would have been had she deflated under such circumstances.

Inflation is bad enough in itself, but one of the reasons for fearing inflation is that it is often followed by deflation.

It is possible to have inflation without deflation and deflation without inflation, and it is possible for inflation to precede deflation or for deflation to precede inflation. All these combinations have occurred in history.

The only just or desirable price level is the level to which society is most nearly adjusted.

BIBLIOGRAPHY

Kemmerer, E. W., High Prices and Deflation. 1920.

King, W. I., Why Has the Price Level Fallen? The Burroughs Clearing House, Vol. 16, No. 5, pp. 17-19, 28. February 1932.

Macrosty, H. W., Inflation and Deflation in the United States and the United Kingdom, 1919-23; Journal of the Royal Statistical Society, Vol. XC, Part 1, pp. 45-135. 1927.

Pigou, A. C., Inflation. Economic Journal, Vol. XXVII, No. 108, pp. 486-494. December 1917.

Stamp, J., The Financial Aftermath of War. 1932.

CHAPTER XI

PRICE CHAOS CAUSED BY INFLATION AND DEFLATION

There is no merit in any price level except the one that has prevailed. If the average of the level of all commodity prices should remain stable for twenty-five years, prices and wages would become fairly well adjusted to the price level regardless of what that level was. Any decline or rise in this level would throw prices out of adjustment.

Even twenty-five years is not long enough for a perfect price adjustment because orchards, bridges, buildings, tile drains, railroads, and the like last for many years and some bonds and mortgages run for more than twenty-five years.

When farmers and other persons were more self-sufficient, changes in the price level were less important, and a crude measure of value, such as a single commodity, was less serious. This depression has brought on a great deal of discussion of the desirability of subsistence farming. Subsistence farming has gone, never to return. The only way to reestablish it would be to have civilization break down completely. This is an age when innumerable things are necessary that were formerly undreamed of. Many of these things are done collectively. Children are educated at public expense. Canals, roads, parks, and bridges are maintained at public expense. All these things call for taxes, and no farmer can eat enough vegetables from his garden to pay the taxes. Even if the farmer discarded the automobile, bathroom, radio, and telephone, he would still need harness and wagons, mowing machines, and the like, which self-sufficient farmers cannot produce. To attempt to turn civilization back is like attempting to put a chicken back in the shell.

Every step in economic progress is based on division of labor which enables the nation to have a high output of goods, because of the efficiency resulting from specialization. The last previous case of serious deflation lasted for about a generation, ending in 1896. Phenomenal progress has been made since that time, but every step in progress makes the exchange system more important. It makes a decline in the price level much more serious.

The statement is often made that all prices should be adjusted at once when deflation occurs, and that then deflation would be all right. This is true, but ridiculous. If a broken leg would instantaneously heal, it might be as good as new—but it does not.

It is sometimes said that daylight-saving could be accomplished without changing the clocks, by having everyone set his mind instead of the clocks ahead on a certain day. This is far easier than changing the whole price level. To change the whole price level suddenly would require a change in the legal system. Instead of changing thousands of things, many of which cannot be changed for a generation, one thing can be changed which will keep the entire price level in adjustment—that is, change the measure of value so as to keep it stable.

When the value of money changes, it affects prices of certain things at certain points fairly quickly, but innumerable prices are unaffected for months or years. For example, if the value of money rises or falls by one-fourth, the retail price of food begins to respond fairly quickly. But the price of a meal in a hotel or restaurant may remain unchanged for a long time, and it is many years before the price drops as much as the value of the money has risen. This is not unreasonable, because rent must be paid, or, if the property is owned, interest and principal on mortgages must be paid, and these items and taxes are not reduced. The taxes may be for sewer, paving, bonds, and the like. Wages also respond slowly. The dishes and table cloth were purchased when prices were higher, and they may not be paid for.

The costs of living are thrown into chaotic relationships. When retail prices of food decline, they decline less than prices that farmers receive. Rents decline slowly. Doctors' fees decline very slowly—yet doctors do not profit by deflation, because of less business and inability to collect. Hospitals may raise their charges because gifts are smaller and occupancy declines. Universities often raise tuition because of reduced gifts and declining yields on investments.

Life insurance dues on old policies continue unchanged, but dividends are reduced and so the costs rise. The incomes of those who are insured fall, so that the payments require too large a portion of the income and policies are canceled.

Effects of declining prices on producers' and consumers' prices.—When prices rise, producers' prices rise faster than consumers' prices. For the year 1917, American-grown food sold at 56 per cent above pre-war retail prices. Farmers received 81 per cent above pre-war farm prices. With declining prices, this same food sold at retail in 1923 at 54 per cent above pre-war, but farmers received only 24 per cent above pre-war. In these two years retail prices were practically identical, but prices which farmers received fell from an index of 181 to 124. These relationships for other years are shown in figure 100. For the year 1931, retail prices of American-grown food averaged 135 when pre-war is 100. The cost of distribution averaged 178. The farmer received prices only 89 per cent of pre-war. The same relationship holds for other products. The index for 30 basic commodities for 1931 was 90, but the cost of living index averaged 151.

In June 1932, farmers who produced milk for the New York City market received about two cents a quart, or 88 per cent of pre-war

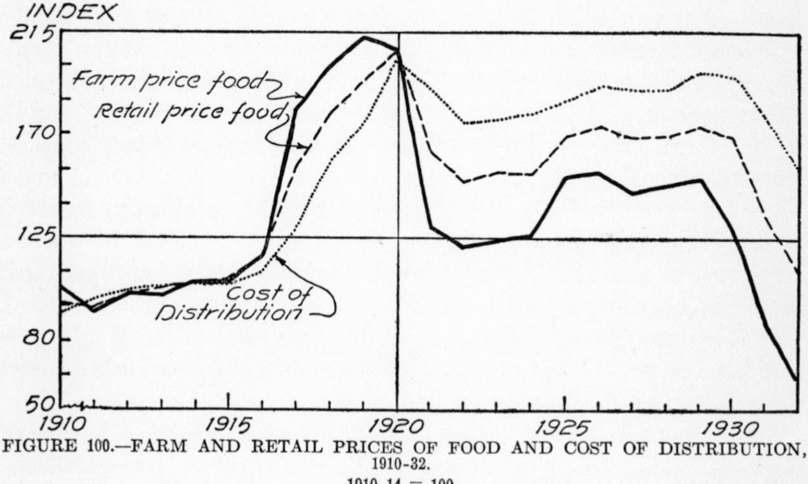

FIGURE 100.—FARM AND RETAIL PRICES OF FOOD AND COST OF DISTRIBUTION, 1910-32.

1910-14 = 100.

When prices rise, costs of distribution rise less rapidly and farm prices more rapidly than retail prices. When the prices decline, costs of distribution remain high and farm prices decline more than retail prices.

prices. Grade B milk in New York City retailed at 12 cents, or 33 per cent above pre-war. Had the farmers sent their milk to New York free and made a slight subscription in addition, retail prices in New York would have been at the pre-war level. If the value of gold should remain at the pre-war level, it would probably require a generation to get the farm and retail prices adjusted to their usual relationship. It takes much longer to make adjustments to deflation than to inflation.

Farmers sell at wholesale and buy at retail. In a period of declining prices there is a wide discrepancy between the prices at which they buy and those at which they sell. This discrepancy began in 1920, and will continue so long as prices decline. If prices rise above the cost of distribution, the situation would be reversed. If the general price level should remain stable, adjustment would ultimately occur, but this would require many years. How slowly the adjustment takes place is shown by the changes that occurred from 1921 to 1929. In that period, the general price level was fairly stable. For the year 1929, index numbers of retail prices of food were 174 and farmers received 151. Had prices remained stable another ten years, the readjustment probably would have been completed. For farmers who are not heavily in debt, this price discrepancy is the most serious single effect of declining prices.

Manufacturers have the problem of hiring labor which has a high cost of living to produce products at a low price. Farmers have the additional problem of buying at retail and selling at wholesale. Manufacturers buy at wholesale prices which are low and sell at wholesale prices which are also low, but the farmer buys at high prices and sells at low prices. This is the reason that farmers are so anxious to buy cooperatively at wholesale.

Cost of distribution.—Declining prices cause a standstill in business and bring on unemployment. This reduces the demand for practically everything. Cotton, steel, and similar industrial products are very seriously affected. The demand for food is less seriously affected.

The quantity of food which the ultimate consumer will take depends on the price which he has to pay. Since farm products are produced in advance of need, the retail price must be placed at such a figure as will lead consumers to take the product or else a part of it must be thrown away. This occurs when the price at which consumers will take all of the product is less than the cost of distribution.

Similarly, if prices are rising, the retail price has to rise to such a point as to make the supplies last throughout the year. For these reasons, the price structure is thrown into chaos by inflation or deflation. The index numbers of prices paid to farmers for food products are shown in table 29. The index numbers of prices which consumers paid for these same food products are shown in table 30. The index numbers of the cost of distributing these same foods are given in table 31. In June 1932, the retail price of American-grown food in cities averaged 109, considering pre-war as 100. The cost of distribution averaged 152. This left prices paid to farmers at only 61 per cent of pre-war. Since the cost of distribution is so much above pre-war, there would be nothing left for farmers if retail prices fell much below pre-war.

TABLE 29.—INDEX NUMBERS OF PRICES PAID TO FARMERS FOR FOOD IN THE UNITED STATES, 1910–1933*

1910-14=100

Year	Jan.	Feb.	Mar.	Apr.	May	June	July	Aug.	Sept.	Oct.	Nov.	Dec.	Average
1910	104	105	107	108	105	103	101	101	102	100	99	98	103
1911	99	94	91	88	87	87	90	93	92	92	94	95	92
1912	96	99	99	102	105	104	102	101	98	98	97	97	100
1913	95	97	99	100	99	101	102	100	100	103	104	105	100
1914	105	105	105	103	103	105	105	105	108	106	105	105	105
1915	107	111	109	107	112	112	106	104	101	101	103	102	106
1916	106	111	111	112	116	117	116	117	124	128	138	143	117
1917	142	152	165	173	200	202	191	192	187	191	191	190	181
1918	193	195	199	195	202	195	198	204	204	206	206	209	200
1919	211	205	201	211	230	230	229	227	209	199	203	206	213
1920	215	217	216	219	233	241	234	218	208	198	183	160	207
1921	155	146	139	130	124	120	121	128	124	122	120	119	130
1922	116	117	123	121	126	128	125	119	115	118	123	126	121
1923	125	123	124	124	128	128	124	120	124	123	122	121	124
1924	119	120	117	118	120	121	125	131	130	135	137	140	126
1925	148	146	150	148	151	154	157	158	150	149	159	159	152
1926	157	156	154	158	161	161	156	147	148	148	151	150	154
1927	145	145	142	143	146	149	148	145	146	147	147	145	145
1928	143	142	143	147	157	156	156	151	154	148	146	143	149
1929	141	146	150	149	152	154	158	159	156	153	151	147	151
1930	145	143	137	139	137	136	124	121	126	120	117	108	129
1931	104	97	99	100	96	91	89	88	84	80	83	74	89
1932	70	67	68	66	64	61	67	67	65	61	61	57	64
1933	54	51	53	58	70	72	84	80	76	74	75		

* Warren, G. F., and Pearson, F. A., Farm, Wholesale, and Retail Prices of Food in the United States, Farm Economics No. 42, p. 616, February 1927.

The commodities were weighted in the following manner: corn, 5; wheat, 16; rye, 1; oats, 1; potatoes, 4; chickens, 4; eggs, 9; milk, 10; butter, 11; veal calves, 2; beef cattle, 17; sheep, 1; lambs, 1; and hogs, 18. The prices paid to producers are those reported by the United States Department of Agriculture, except for milk, which is the net pool price of 3.7 per cent milk at Utica, New York.

TABLE 30.—INDEX NUMBERS OF RETAIL PRICES PAID BY CONSUMERS FOR FOOD IN THE UNITED STATES, 1910–1933*

1910-14=100

Year	Jan.	Feb.	Mar.	Apr.	May	June	July	Aug.	Sept.	Oct.	Nov.	Dec.	Average
1910	97	97	97	96	96	96	95	96	95	96	96	97	96
1911	96	95	94	93	93	94	96	95	94	94	95	96	94
1912	100	101	99	102	103	101	99	99	99	100	99	98	100
1913	100	101	104	104	103	103	103	103	104	104	104	103	103
1914	106	106	106	105	106	106	107	108	108	106	105	105	106
1915	108	108	107	108	109	108	106	105	104	106	105	106	107
1916	109	111	114	115	115	116	114	115	120	123	127	126	117
1917	132	142	144	157	165	165	158	160	164	165	162	163	156
1918	171	176	170	171	176	178	181	182	186	188	188	190	180
1919	192	184	190	197	200	196	200	199	193	191	193	196	194
1920	204	206	209	217	219	220	218	207	207	204	196	182	207
1921	182	171	171	167	159	156	159	165	161	158	154	152	163
1922	147	151	152	151	152	152	152	148	148	150	150	151	150
1923	153	152	153	153	152	151	153	152	155	155	153	151	154
1924	153	155	153	151	150	151	150	151	153	155	154	155	153
1925	163	164	168	168	168	168	172	172	170	171	173	171	169
1926	174	175	177	180	179	177	172	169	171	171	170	169	174
1927	171	171	172	172	172	172	167	165	166	168	166	165	169
1928	168	168	168	170	172	170	170	171	174	171	168	166	170
1929	169	173	175	175	177	176	178	178	177	175	171	169	174
1930	172	172	172	173	170	166	160	159	160	158	152	147	169
1931	146	143	145	144	140	135	135	134	133	131	124	119	135
1932	115	113	114	113	111	109	111	110	109	107	104	101	109
1933	100	97	99	98	103	105	111	113	113				

* Warren, G. F., and Pearson, F. A., Farm, Wholesale, and Retail Prices of Food in the United States, Farm Economics No. 42, p. 616, February 1927.

The commodities were weighted in the following manner: corn meal, 5; wheat flour, 5; bread, 13 (the farm prices include oats and rye; since retail prices for these are not included, the weight for oat meal was added to flour and the weight for rye flour was added to bread); potatoes, 4; hens, 4; eggs strictly fresh, 9; milk, fresh, New York City, 10; butter, 11; sirloin steak, 5; round steak, 4; rib roast, 4; chuck roast, 3; plate beef, 3; leg of lamb, 2; pork chops, 5; bacon, 4; ham, 5; and lard, 4. The retail prices, reported by the United States Bureau of Labor Statistics, are an average of prices prevailing in 51 cities in the United States, except the retail prices of milk, which are for New York City.

TABLE 31.—COST OF DISTRIBUTING FOOD IN THE UNITED STATES, 1910–33*
1910-14=100

Year	Jan.	Feb.	Mar.	Apr.	May	June	July	Aug.	Sept.	Oct.	Nov.	Dec.	Average
1910	91	92	83	83	84	88	91	94	90	97	99	111	92
1911	98	99	102	104	99	100	96	95	95	95	95	95	98
1912	102	104	103	101	102	102	105	100	100	104	100	94	102
1913	103	101	104	106	107	104	104	104	106	103	102	97	104
1914	107	105	108	107	105	105	105	108	106	101	101	107	105
1915	105	107	106	108	103	101	107	103	108	111	105	105	105
1916	110	105	108	110	109	110	108	110	116	115	113	109	110
1917	115	124	115	135	125	123	129	132	133	137	138	144	129
1918	148	156	156	149	152	158	161	160	162	170	167	178	159
1919	188	165	170	184	175	169	175	167	172	173	174	188	174
1920	192	191	198	214	199	197	202	205	208	207	210	206	202
1921	206	198	201	207	193	182	186	192	191	187	182	183	190
1922	183	181	179	179	170	168	174	175	176	178	170	172	175
1923	180	177	179	180	174	176	178	175	186	185	177	174	177
1924	183	187	190	191	174	173	178	175	186	182	169	180	180
1925	186	180	185	191	182	180	182	182	188	193	186	190	185
1926	195	193	197	200	190	188	190	191	197	196	183	185	192
1927	194	191	193	200	192	182	186	186	191	194	183	188	190
1928	193	193	192	196	186	183	189	189	196	196	191	198	190
1929	202	199	201	202	199	196	195	194	201	196	196	208	198
1930	210	211	206	209	199	191	191	193	196	197	190	201	196
1931	197	192	192	192	178	172	175	175	173	180	165	168	178
1932	167	161	161	161	154	152	148	151	154	154	143	147	153
1933	148	143	143	138	133	131	135	140	149	150			

* Warren, G. F., and Pearson, F. A., Cost of Distributing Food, Farm Economics No. 50, pp. 830–836. January 1928. The index was based on the cost of distributing the products from 10 major farm foods. The cost of distribution for each product was the difference between what the consumer paid for the products and the amount which the farmer received. The commodities were weighted in the following manner: beef, 21; pork, 18; milk, 10; butter, 11; hens, 4; eggs, 9; wheat, 5; wheat bread 13; corn meal, 5; and potatoes, 4. The retail prices reported by the United States Bureau of Labor Statistics are an average of the prices prevailing in 51 cities in the United States, except those of milk and eggs, which are for New York City. The farm prices, reported by the United States Department of Agriculture, are an average of the prices paid to producers in the United States, except the price of milk, which is the net pool price of 3.7 per cent milk at Utica, New York, and prices of butterfat, which are for southern Minnesota.

Wages and the cost of distribution.—Changes in the costs of distribution and in the earnings of New York factory workers are shown in figure 101. Wages are not the only item in the cost of distribution, but they make up so large an amount of the cost of distribution that the two curves are quite similar.

Price chaos in the channels of trade.—In May 1932, the wholesale price of hams in Chicago was 20 per cent below pre-war prices, but the retail price was 10 per cent above pre-war. Live fowls at wholesale in Chicago were below pre-war prices, but at retail they were 27 per cent above pre-war (table 32).

Chaos in the geography of prices.—From 1917 to 1919, prices of corn, oats, and wheat for Illinois, Iowa, and Nebraska averaged 224, pre-war being 100, and in three New England states, rose to only 209 (table 33).

In May 1932, the index numbers for the three western states had fallen to 52, but for the three New England states it had fallen to only 78.

TABLE 32.—PRICE CHAOS IN THE CHANNELS OF TRADE

	Price			Index numbers May 1913 = 100	
	May 1913	May 1917	May 1932	May 1917	May 1932
Hams, Chicago					
Retail price sliced ham, cents per pound	32.5	40.3	35.9	124	110
Wholesale price cured hams, cents per pound	16.9	26.6	13.6	157	80
Fowls, Chicago					
Retail price of hens, cents per pound	21.2	28.5	26.9	134	127
Wholesale price of live fowls, cents per pound	17.8	21.5	13.7	121	77
Flour, Buffalo					
Retail price of flour, cents per pound	3.0	8.8	3.1	293	103
Wholesale price of hard winter wheat flour, standard patents, dollars per barrel	5.53	15.26	4.83	276	87
Milk, New York City					
Retail price of milk, cents per quart	9.0	10.9	12.0	121	133
Wholesale price of milk, dollars per 100 pounds	1.18	2.18	1.10	185	93

Such discrepancies are inevitable when inflation and deflation occur. With inflation, prices rise the most at points far from market. With deflation, they fall most in such regions.

Inflation always places an artificial stimulus on production far from market. Deflation artificially depresses such regions. When inflation occurs, it is the food consumers in the industrial centers that demand a food administration. When deflation occurs, radical movements develop in the farm areas far from market. The population at the centers of trade has little realization of conditions far from market.

TABLE 33.—CHAOS IN THE GEOGRAPHY OF FARM PRICES

Region	Index numbers of the farm price of corn, oats, and wheat. 1910–14 = 100			
	December 1917–19	December 1920–22	December 1931	May 1932
Maine, Vermont, New Hampshire	209	138	78	78
New York, Pennsylvania, Ohio	210	121	65	60
Illinois, Iowa, Nebraska	224	107	62	52

TABLE 34.—INDEX NUMBERS OF PRICES PAID TO PRODUCERS OF FARM PRODUCTS*

Corresponding months 1910–14 = 100

Year	Vermont	New Jersey	Pennsylvania	Ohio	Michigan	Indiana	Illinois	Wisconsin	Missouri	Iowa	Maryland	Virginia	No. Carolina	Georgia	Alabama	Kentucky	Oklahoma	Texas	Minnesota	So. Dakota	No. Dakota	Utah	Oregon
1910		96	99	103	99	103	100	99	101	102	99	97		110	111	103	111	108	105		110	108	107
1911		99	94	89	93	88	89	91	88	87	95	98		103	102	94	94	98	97		102	93	97
1912		105	101	101	105	100	102	102	101	99	100	102		86	91	98	99	92	99		101	98	96
1913		99	100	105	101	103	102	104	106	104	101	102		98	101	102	106	100	97		89	100	98
1914	101	99	103	105	103	105	108	105	110	108	107	99		91	96	108	90	95	102		100	101	102
1915	100	93	102	106	104	102	105	101	108	103	106	96		80	85	99	107	93	103	95	121	108	106
1916	115	118	115	121	127	116	119	122	120	120	119	116		117	116	112	110	120	125	122	131	125	114
1917	156	174	170	182	186	176	185	174	178	181	172	174		184	175	159	213	177	186	190	202	179	168
1918	196	195	193	203	199	195	202	198	200	207	210	200		242	230	207	238	220	204	207	224	193	191
1919	215	211	206	218	215	205	214	215	208	219	216	228		238	230	211	259	222	217	225	238	202	198
1920	232	205	217	212	222	189	200	203	188	189	223	205	215	257	244	216	201	217	202	192	237	212	195
1921	160	142	140	132	137	111	115	128	114	104	148	151	118	105	109	167	124	105	114	100	123	112	119
1922	147	134	127	127	139	112	114	124	112	111	134	142	123	147	144	157	143	132	113	106	115	124	119
1923	168	162	138	134	143	110	119	137	112	115	144	148	146	202	189	158	172	167	116	109	109	139	119
1924	151	162	136	133	140	116	127	128	116	122	155	144	146	202	190	154	160	166	123	120	123	139	121
1925	167	179	154	159	158	143	148	144	143	147	166	153	147	170	166	159	164	156	145	149	153	154	147
1926	177	159	160	155	164	140	139	152	141	141	158	148	127	129	131	155	127	126	150	147	150	143	137
1927	177	155	153	147	156	130	136	154	137	140	158	145	126	128	132	140	156	129	143	137	137	142	132
1928	176	160	155	154	163	137	144	156	147	145	157	141	141	150	150	175	154	150	141	139	129	148	143
1929	180	170	151	151	165	140	144	155	147	147	163	150	142	143	146	184	149	145	147	143	128	150	146
1930	162	144	139	129	142	121	125	129	125	127	144	130	120	102	108	146	103	109	124	119	100	121	114
1931	121	114	103	91	100	84	86	90	87	86	115	88	86	67	72	87	63	70	84	81	65	92	78
1932	98	88	75	63	69	58	58	67	63	56	84	72	64	50	53	60	52	51	58	53	50	73	63
1932																							
Jan.	95	87	79	69	75	63	65	76	67	63	93	69	67	51	55	70	54	54	67	66	60	81	69
Feb.	95	85	77	64	71	59	61	71	63	57	91	70	65	52	54	62	52	54	63	63	60	79	65
Mar.	95	83	76	64	70	62	62	70	62	62	84	77	66	54	56	61	54	57	65	64	62	79	69
Apr.	97	81	77	64	68	58	60	66	62	60	86	79	62	49	53	60	51	52	62	62	58	80	66
May	104	90	76	61	65	53	55	62	58	53	82	80	59	45	50	56	48	47	59	52	54	78	65
June	101	90	76	59	65	52	53	60	56	49	94	81	58	40	46	54	42	42	54	47	44	73	60
July	102	94	78	63	70	61	61	65	67	63	82	69	60	44	49	56	47	47	63	57	44	72	61
Aug.	103	86	77	66	70	62	60	66	67	61	91	73	65	54	56	59	52	54	56	55	46	67	62
Sept.	99	99	75	65	69	60	59	69	67	57	84	75	68	57	62	58	55	58	53	54	46	67	63
Oct.	94	87	74	61	68	56	55	69	63	49	80	76	67	54	55	57	52	53	51	45	41	67	60
Nov.	94	80	71	61	67	55	55	69	61	49	79	74	64	51	53	58	50	51	53	44	41	68	57
Dec.	94	77	69	60	67	54	52	69	58	43	76	74	62	46	49	72	47	47	50	38	39	68	56

* Index numbers for Vermont were prepared by C. W. Gilbert, those for New Jersey by D. T. Pitt, those for Pennsylvania by F. P. Weaver, those for Ohio by J. I. Falconer, those for Michigan by O. Ulrey, those for Indiana by E. C. Young and O. A. Day, those for Illinois by O. A. Day, those for Wisconsin by W. H. Ebling, G. T. Gustafson and S. J. Gilbert, those for Missouri by D. R. G. Cowan and F. L. Thomsen, those for Iowa by K. Bjorka, those for Maryland by S. H. De Vault, those for Virginia by H. N. Young, those for North Carolina by F. Parker, those for Alabama by J. D. Pope, those for Kentucky by C. U. Jett and D. G. Card, those for Oklahoma by J. O. Ellsworth and P. H. Stephens, those for Minnesota by A. G. Black and W. C. Waite, those for South Dakota by R. E. Post, those for North Dakota by O. M. Fuller, those for Utah by W. P. Thomas.

Farm prices in various states.—In general, price inflation caused a greater rise in prices in the states far from market than in those near market that produced the same type of product. With deflation, prices in states near market generally fell less than in those far from market (table 34).

Price chaos between raw materials and the fabricated products.—From 1913 to 1917, the index of prices of steel scrap rose to 225 when pre-war is 100, but steel rails increased to only 143 (table 35). With deflation, the index numbers for May 1932 were: steel scrap, 61; pig iron, 96; steel rails, 154; and saws, 222. The manufacturers of iron and steel and their products stopped production, but scrap continued to be thrown on the market.

The comparison of hides and shoes is even more striking. In 1917,

TABLE 35.—PRICE CHAOS BETWEEN RAW MATERIALS AND MANUFACTURED PRODUCTS BROUGHT ABOUT BY FLUCTUATING PRICES

	Prices			Index numbers May 1913=100	
	May 1913	May 1917	May 1932	May 1917	May 1932
Iron and steel and their products					
Steel scrap, heavy melting composite price* at Pittsburgh, Chicago, and Philadelphia, dollars per gross ton	12.30	27.63	7.48	225	61
Pig iron, Bessemer, delivered Pittsburgh, dollars per gross ton	17.74	45.15	17.09	255	96
Steel rails, standard, open hearth, dollars per gross ton, mill	28.00	40.00	43.00	143	154
Saws, Disston crosscut, No. 2, 6-foot, Philadelphia, dollars each	1.78	2.76	3.95	155	222
Rubber and its products					
Cord tires, composite price, factory, dollars each	32.07†	33.95	4.46	106	14
Rubber, crude Para Island and plantation, smoked ribbed sheets, New York, cents per pound	78.0	72.5	3.2	93	4
Hides and their products					
Hides, packer, green heavy native steers, Chicago, cents per pound	16.6	31.5	4.3	190	26
Leather, chrome calf, B grade, Boston, cents per square foot	27.0	56.0	25.0	207	93
Shoes, men's black Goodyear welt, Blucher calf, factory, dollars per pair	3.10	4.75	5.75	153	185
Shoes, women's patent leather pump, McKay sewed, factory, dollars per pair	1.38†	2.75	3.00	199	217
Cotton and its products					
Cotton middling, New Orleans, cents per pound	12.0	20.0	5.6	167	47
Cotton yarn carded, white, northern cones 22/1 mill, cents per pound	24.5	42.3	16.2	173	66
Gingham, Amoskeog 27-inch mill, cents per yard	6.75	11.0	6.0	163	89
Wheat and its products					
Wheat, hard winter Kansas, cents per bushel	79	266	37	337	47
Flour, hard winter wheat flour, winter standard patents Buffalo, dollars per barrel	5.53	15.26	4.83	276	87
Hogs and their products					
Hogs, Iowa, dollars per hundred pounds	7.70	15.10	2.70	196	35
Hams, cured, Chicago, cents per pound	16.9	26.6	13.6	157	80

* Iron Age composite price.
† Year.

prices of hides increased 90 per cent but men's shoes increased only 53 per cent.

In 1932, hides were worth about one-fourth pre-war prices, but shoes were twice pre-war prices.

Similarly, in 1932, cotton at New Orleans was worth less than half pre-war; cotton yarns were two-thirds of pre-war; and gingham was approximately at pre-war prices.

In 1917, the farm price of wheat in Kansas was more than three times pre-war, but flour was only 176 per cent above pre-war.

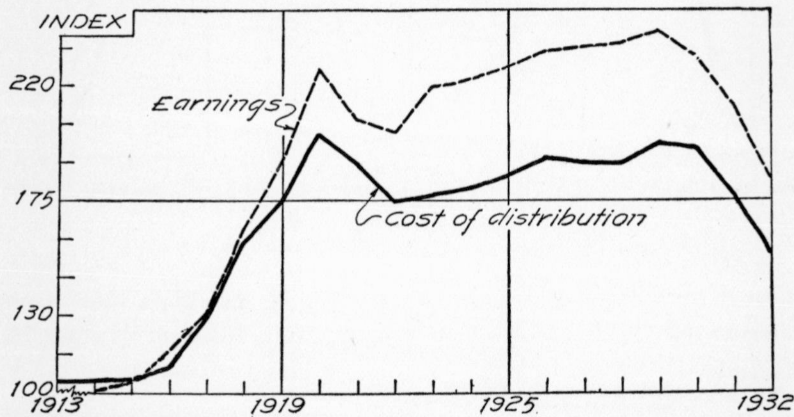

FIGURE 101.—INDEX NUMBERS OF THE COST OF DISTRIBUTION OF FOOD IN THE UNITED STATES, AND EARNINGS OF NEW YORK FACTORY WORKERS, 1913-32. Costs of distribution lag behind the earnings of factory workers.

In 1932, the Kansas price of wheat was about one-half of pre-war prices, but flour sold for nearly pre-war prices.

Deflation and the time required to complete an article.—The longer the period from the beginning to the completion of an article, the more serious are the effects of deflation. If the producer can sell his finished product in a few months after he has purchased the raw materials, he may succeed in spite of deflation. If the process of deflation requires one, two, or more years, as is true in agriculture, the results are exceedingly serious.

Horses must be fed for three years before they are of any use. They are a ten- to twelve-year investment. A dairy cow is not ready to produce until she is two years old. She is not in her prime until she is five or six years old. Dairying is an eight-year investment. It is no accident that farmers are more interested in the money question than are city persons. It is not because farmers are radical; they are, in fact, less radical than most other groups. It is because deflation places on them an intolerable burden. The farmers of England were so adversely

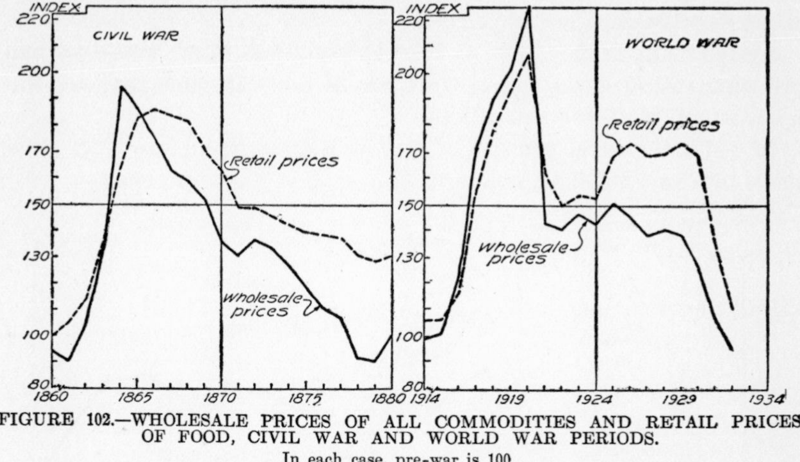

FIGURE 102.—WHOLESALE PRICES OF ALL COMMODITIES AND RETAIL PRICES OF FOOD, CIVIL WAR AND WORLD WAR PERIODS.

In each case, pre-war is 100.

In each case, retail prices of food lagged behind changes in wholesale prices.

affected by the deflation following the Napoleonic Wars that many inquiries were made into the state of agriculture. Again in the nineties,

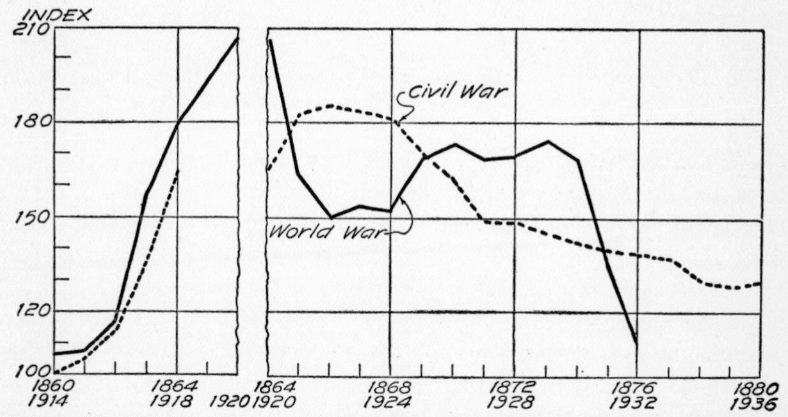

FIGURE 103.—RETAIL PRICES OF FOOD IN CITIES, CIVIL WAR AND WORLD WAR PERIODS.

In each case, pre-war is 100.

After the World War, prices fluctuated more violently than after the Civil War.

the unfortunate condition of English agriculture received the spiritual benefits of an investigation. Its physical state, however, was not improved until the value of money started to decline.

Retail prices of food—World War and Civil War periods.—When prices rise, retail prices rise less rapidly than wholesale prices, and prices paid to farmers are then high relative to retail prices (figures 102 and 103). In each case, wages change still more slowly, so that food is difficult to buy when prices are rising and easy to buy when prices are falling, except for persons who are unemployed.

TABLE 36.—RETAIL PRICES OF FOOD AND THE COST OF LIVING, CIVIL WAR AND WORLD WAR

Retail prices of food				Cost of living			
Year	Civil War* 1860 = 100	Year	World War† 1910–14 = 100	Year	Civil War‡ 1860 = 100	Year	World War§ 1910–14 = 100
1860	100	1914	106	1860	100	1914	104
1861	105	1915	107	1861	104	1915	102
1862	114	1916	117	1862	111	1916	112
1863	136	1917	156	1863	128	1917	131
1864	165	1918	180	1864	150	1918	160
1865	183	1919	194	1865	163	1919	182
1866	186	1920	207	1866	173	1920	212
1867	184	1921	163	1867	169	1921	180
1868	182	1922	150	1868	166	1922	168
1869	171	1923	154	1869	163	1923	172
1870	163	1924	153	1870	162	1924	170
1871	149	1925	169	1871	153	1925	175
1872	149	1926	174	1872	147	1926	176
1873	146	1927	169	1873	147	1927	173
1874	143	1928	170	1874	143	1928	171
1875	140	1929	174	1875	141	1929	172
1876	139	1930	169	1876	134	1930	167
1877	138	1931	135	1877	134	1931	151
1878	131	1932	109	1878	127	1932	138
1879	129			1879	128		
1880	131			1880	131		

* The index numbers of retail prices from 1860 to 1880 are based on the following commodities and weights: beans, 2; beef, fresh, 13; beef, canned, 3; veal, 3; butter, 11; cheese, 3; corn meal, 3; starch, 2; eggs, 9; rye flour, 2; wheat flour, 16; lard, 4; fresh pork, 5; preserved pork, 9; milk, 7; mutton, 4; and potatoes, 4. Based on relative retail prices as reported by Mitchell, W. C., Gold, Prices, and Wages under the Greenback Standard, University of California Publications in Economics, Vol. I, pp. 67–68, March 1908.

† Table 30, p. 187.

‡ The annual index numbers of the cost of living in eastern cities from 1860 to 1880 are those reported by Mitchell, W. C., Gold, Prices, and Wages under the Greenback Standard, University of California Publications in Economics, Vol. I, p. 89–90, March 1908.

§ Farm Economics No. 78, October 1932.

Cost of living, World War and Civil War periods.—During both periods, the cost of living rose less rapidly than wholesale prices, and declined less rapidly (figure 104). In 1917, all commodities were 72 per cent above pre-war, but the cost of living was only 31 per cent above. In 1931, all commodities were only 7 per cent above pre-war, but the cost of living was 51 per cent above, and 15 per cent higher than it was in 1917 (tables 1 and 36).

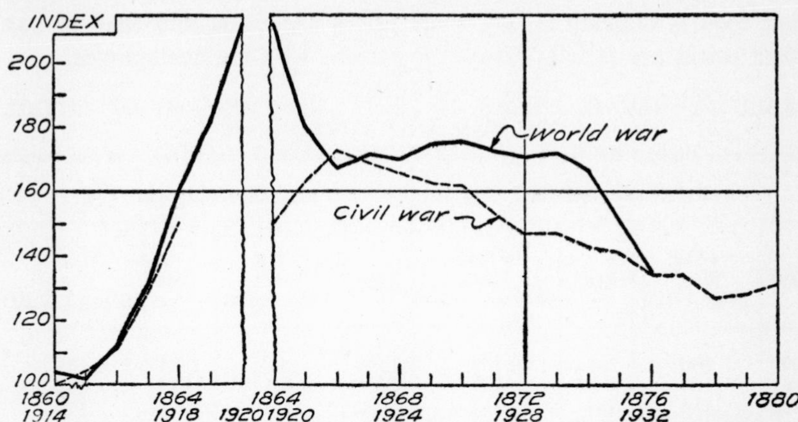

FIGURE 104.—COSTS OF LIVING, CIVIL WAR AND WORLD WAR PERIODS.
In each case, pre-war is 100.
There is much similarity in the two periods, but greater violence is shown in the World War period.

BIBLIOGRAPHY

POWERS, L. G., Modern Variations in the Purchasing Power of Gold. Minnesota Bureau of Labor Statistics, Fifth Biennial Report. 1896.

WARREN, G. F., and PEARSON, F. A., The Agricultural Situation. 1924.

The Agricultural Crisis and its Causes. Report of the Joint Commission of Agricultural Inquiry submitted by Mr. Sidney Anderson, 67th Congress, First Session Report No. 408, Part I. 1921.

CHAPTER XII

WAGES

LONG-TIME TRENDS IN THE PURCHASING POWER OF WAGES

Wages in the United States for one hundred and forty years.—Wages just before the World War were three times as high as they had been seventy years before (figure 105). Because prices rose very

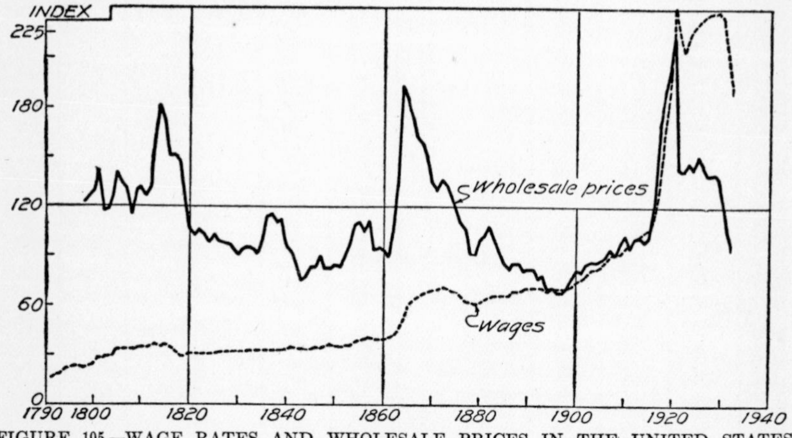

FIGURE 105.—WAGE RATES AND WHOLESALE PRICES IN THE UNITED STATES, 1790-1932.

From 1840 to 1914, wages trebled, but prices were about the same at the beginning as at the end of the period.

little, the purchasing power of wages was trebled. This meant that for each hour's work the laborer was able to obtain three times as much goods as he secured in 1840. This marvelous increase was made possible by the increased productiveness of labor which resulted from the use of machinery in industry and agriculture. During short periods of time, labor may receive more or less than it produces. Over longer periods, real wages can rise only as the production per man increases, and when production is increased, wages rise.

Purchasing power of wages in the United States.—If the index numbers of wages are divided by the index numbers of wholesale prices, the result is the purchasing power of wages, at wholesale prices. From 1840 to 1914, the purchasing power of wages increased at the

TABLE 37.—INDEX NUMBERS OF WAGES PER HOUR (EXCLUSIVE OF AGRICULTURE), WHOLESALE PRICES, AND PURCHASING POWER OF WAGES IN THE UNITED STATES, 1840–1932

1910–14 = 100

Year	Wages*	Wholesale prices†	Purchasing power	Year	Wages*	Wholesale prices†	Purchasing power	Year	Wages*	Whole sale prices†	Purchasing power
1840	34	95	36	1880	62	100	62	1920	240	226	106
1841	35	92	38	1881	64	103	62	1921	224	143	157
1842	34	82	41	1882	65	108	60	1922	214	141	152
1843	34	75	45	1883	66	101	65	1923	223	147	152
1844	33	77	43	1884	66	93	71	1924	229	143	161
1845	34	83	41	1885	66	85	78	1925	232	151	154
1846	35	83	42	1886	66	82	80	1926	235	146	161
1847	35	90	39	1887	69	85	81	1927	237	139	171
1848	36	82	44	1888	69	86	80	1928	238	141	169
1849	37	82	45	1889	70	81	86	1929	239	139	172
1850	36	84	43	1890	71	82	87	1930	235	126	187
1851	35	83	42	1891	71	82	87	1931	223	107	208
1852	36	89	40	1892	71	76	93	1932	191‡	95	201‡
1853	36	97	37	1893	71	78	91				
1854	38	108	35	1894	69	70	99				
1855	39	110	35	1895	70	71	99				
1856	40	105	38	1896	71	68	104				
1857	41	111	37	1897	71	68	104				
1858	40	93	43	1898	71	71	100				
1859	40	95	42	1899	72	77	94				
1860	40	93	43	1900	75	82	91				
1861	41	89	46	1901	76	81	94				
1862	42	104	40	1902	79	86	92				
1863	45	133	34	1903	82	87	94				
1864	51	193	26	1904	82	87	94				
1865	60	185	32	1905	84	88	95				
1866	63	174	36	1906	87	90	97				
1867	65	162	40	1907	91	95	96				
1868	67	158	42	1908	91	92	99				
1869	68	151	45	1909	92	99	93				
1870	69	135	51	1910	95	103	92				
1871	70	130	54	1911	98	95	103				
1872	71	136	52	1912	100	101	99				
1873	71	133	53	1913	103	102	101				
1874	69	126	55	1914	105	99	106				
1875	69	118	58	1915	106	101	105				
1876	66	110	60	1916	114	125	91				
1877	63	106	59	1917	131	172	76				
1878	62	91	68	1918	166	191	87				
1879	61	90	68	1919	189	202	94				

* Monthly Labor Review, Vol. 37, No. 3, p. 632, September 1933.
† Table 1, p. 10.
‡ Estimated.

compound rate of **1.71** per cent per year (figure 106). That is, if prices remained stationary, the normal rise in wages would be 1.71 per cent per year. It has been shown that the physical volume of production per capita increased at the rate of **1.73** per cent per year (figure 38, page 47). Over a long period of time, the buying power of wages increased at the same rate as the physical volume of production per capita. It is not surprising that the purchasing power of wages must keep pace with the production per capita.[1] In order to consume the

[1] The percentage of the population that is employed as reported by the Census seems to show no striking change. In the earlier period, less time was spent in

steadily increasing output of labor, a steadily rising buying power of wages is necessary. The great increase in production could not be consumed by a few persons even if they had unlimited buying power. They might use the increased efficiency in building pyramids if the laborers would keep working.

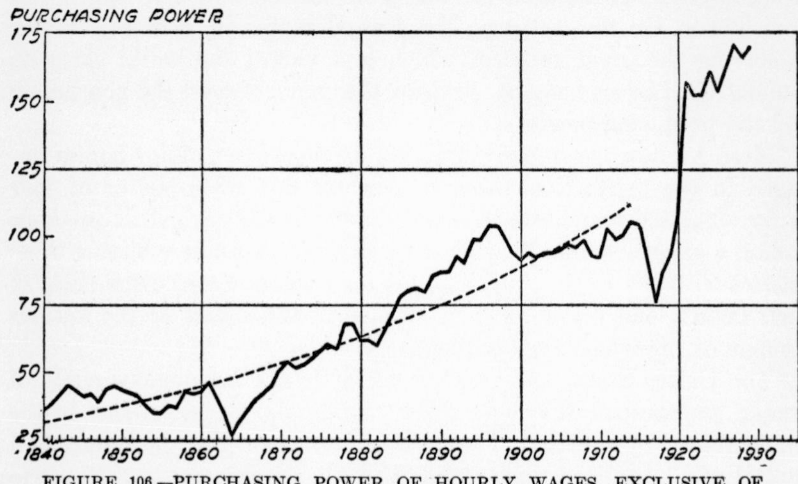

FIGURE 106.—PURCHASING POWER OF HOURLY WAGES, EXCLUSIVE OF AGRICULTURE, IN THE UNITED STATES, 1840-1929.
1910-14 = 100.

From 1840 to 1914, the purchasing power of wages, at wholesale commodity prices, increased at a compound rate of 1.71 per cent per year. This increased buying power is the same as the increased output per capita. Inflation or deflation causes maladjustments for a time.

The long-time trend in the purchasing power of wages is upward at about the same rate as the increase in efficiency, but the short-time trend is strikingly influenced by inflation and deflation (figure 106). When prices rise suddenly, wages rise less rapidly and the buying power is reduced. This was the case during the Civil War and World War periods. The reduction is less striking than figure 106 indicates, because there is full employment when prices are rising.

When deflation occurs, wages fall less rapidly than prices, and the

---

school but children constituted a higher proportion of the population. The hours of labor per year were probably more. Farm wages probably rose faster than other wages. The slave portion of the population doubtless received more goods after it was freed than before.

A steadily increasing percentage of the laborer's income is expended for education, entertainment, and the like. Also, a steadily increasing percentage of the population is engaged in these occupations. The physical volume of production per capita for those engaged in producing physical things is therefore higher than the rate of increase per capita for the nation. All these various factors seem to balance over a long period of time because the buying power of wages rises approximately as the output per worker increases.

nominal buying power is very high. Since unemployment is serious, the actual buying power may not be high.

Winston Churchill, formerly Chancellor of the Exchequer,[2] described conditions in the United States since 1928 as follows:

"I do not regard what happened in the United States in 1929 merely as an orgy of speculation, for which we are all now suffering a just punishment. On the contrary, the United States in 1928 was nearer to solving the great problem which had baffled the world since its foundation. She had nearly bridged the gap between the consuming and the producing power.

"Here we saw the breadwinners of twenty-five million homes engaged in the production either of food or raw materials or of four or five hundred standardized articles, by the most scientific methods and on a gigantic scale. We saw these same breadwinners buying these articles with the wages they received for making them, using them in their homes, and investing their surplus in the shares of the various companies for which they worked.

"The United States had reached nearer to the harmonious circle of human transactions than any other community has ever done in the whole history of mankind. They had almost reconciled the interests of capital and labor, and we saw the days when employers were eager to maintain a high level of wages so that their workmen could buy the things they made, and to shorten hours of labor so that their workmen should have time to use and enjoy these things. Labor was itself consciously interested in the efficiency of production, from which it felt itself a direct beneficiary. The United States had got its elbows on the ledge of the greatest advance that has ever been made in human economics. . . .

"The American people were forced off the ledge. They fell down to the bottom of the crag, where we all lie together in misfortune today; and where the first thing we have to do is not to kick one another.

"But the way to world prosperity has been shown and other attempts will be made to follow it."

Purchasing power of wages in England.—Wages and the purchasing power of wages in England are shown in table 38 and figures 107 and 108. From 1790 to 1914, the purchasing power of wages in England increased at the rate of 1.30 per cent per year (figure 108). The increase was irregular because of inflation and deflation.

[2] Churchill, W., Are We too Clever? Collier's, Vol. 90, No. 9, p. 48, August 27, 1932.

From 1850 to 1914, the average rate of increase in the purchasing power of wages in England was 1.52 per cent per year. This increase was again irregular owing to inflation and deflation. The rate of increase in purchasing power was less than the rate for the United States. It is probable that the production per capita rose less rapidly than in the United States.

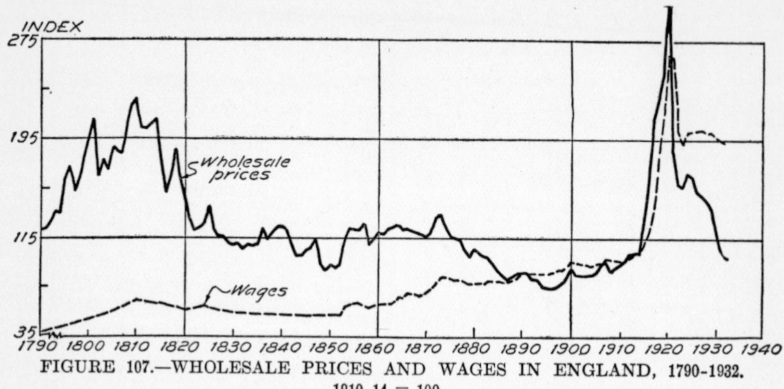

FIGURE 107.—WHOLESALE PRICES AND WAGES IN ENGLAND, 1790-1932. 1910-14 = 100.

Wages in England have risen relative to wholesale prices.

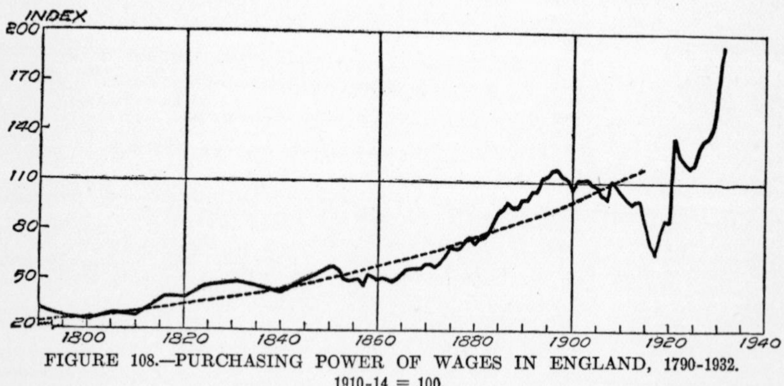

FIGURE 108.—PURCHASING POWER OF WAGES IN ENGLAND, 1790-1932. 1910-14 = 100.

For the 125-year period 1790 to 1914, the purchasing power of wages increased at the compound rate of 1.30 per cent per year. From 1850 to 1914, the rate was 1.52 per cent per year.

Purchasing power of wages in France.—Wages in France advanced more than two and one-half times in the past century. In spite of the fact that the cost of living also increased, the purchasing power of wages doubled. The purchasing power rose less rapidly than in the United States.

TABLE 38.—INDEX NUMBERS OF WAGES AND PURCHASING POWER OF WAGES IN ENGLAND, 1790–1932

1910–14 = 100

Year	Wages*	Purchasing power†	Year	Wages*	Purchasing power†	Year	Wages*	Purchasing power†	Year	Wages*	Purchasing power†
1790	38	31	1869	69	58	1899	92	112	1929	201	145
1795	43	27	1870	71	61	1900	96	105	1930	197	168
1800	49	25	1871	74	61	1901	95	112	1931	195	193
1805	55	29	1872	78	59	1902	94	112	1932	193	195
1810	64	28	1873	83	62	1903	94	112			
1816	61	40	1874	83	67	1904	93	109			
1820	57	39	1875	82	71	1905	94	108			
1824	59	46	1876	81	70	1906	95	102			
1831	54	49	1877	81	71	1907	98	101			
1840	53	43	1878	79	75	1908	98	111			
1845	52	50	1879	78	77	1909	97	108			
1850	53	57	1880	78	73	1910	97	103			
1851	53	58	1881	78	76	1911	97	100			
1852	53	56	1882	78	77	1912	100	97			
1853	59	51	1883	80	81	1913	103	100			
1854	61	50	1884	80	87	1914	103	100			
1855	62	51	1885	80	92	1915	111	85			
1856	62	51	1886	79	94	1916	121	73			
1857	60	47	1887	80	98	1917	142	67			
1858	59	54	1888	81	95	1918	183	79			
1859	60	53	1889	83	95	1919	219	88			
1860	61	51	1890	87	100	1920	263	87			
1861	61	52	1891	87	100	1921	262	139			
1862	62	51	1892	86	105	1922	202	127			
1863	62	50	1893	86	105	1923	192	123			
1864	66	52	1894	86	113	1924	201	120			
1865	67	55	1895	86	115	1925	202	122			
1866	70	57	1896	87	118	1926	202	132			
1867	70	58	1897	89	119	1927	203	137			
1868	69	58	1898	89	114	1928	201	139			

* 1790–1845, Wood, G. H., The Course of Wages between 1790 and 1860, The Economic Journal, Vol. IX, p. 591, December 1899. The index numbers on the 1840 base were converted to the 1910–14 base by multiplying by 0.527, using the years 1850, 1855, and 1860 as a basis for conversion.

1850–1899, Wood, G. H., Real Wages and the Standard of Comfort since 1850, Journal of the Royal Statistical Society, Vol. LXXII, Part I, p. 102, March 1909. The index numbers on the 1850 base were converted to the 1910–14 base by multiplying by 0.5337, using the years 1900–1902 as a basis for conversion.

1900–1919, Trend of Wages, Earnings and Food Prices in England Since 1920, Monthly Labor Review, United States Department of Labor, Vol. XIX, No. 6, p. 41, December 1924. The index numbers on the 1900 base were converted to the 1910–14 base by multiplying by 0.9643.

1920–1922, London and Cambridge Economic Service, Vol. 2, Number 1, p. 17, Jan. 23, 1924. The index numbers on the 1913 base were converted to the 1910–14 base by multiplying by 1.03.

1923, estimated from rate in Statistical Abstract of the United Kingdom 1927, No. 72, p. 97, 1929.

1924–1928, New Index of Weekly Wages, London and Cambridge Economic Service, Vol. 7, No. 1, p. 21, Jan. 23, 1929.

Bowley, A. L., A New Index Number of Wages, London and Cambridge Economic Service, Special Memorandum No. 28, p. 6, January 1929. The index numbers on the July 1914 base were multiplied by 1.03 to convert them to the 1910–14 base.

1929–1931, London and Cambridge Economic Service, Vol. 8, No. 7, p. 221, July 23, 1930; Vol. 9, No. 8, p. 263, Aug. 22, 1931; Vol. 10, No. 6, p. 187, June 23, 1932. The index numbers on the December 1924 base were converted to the 1910–14 base by multiplying by 2.0085.

† The purchasing power is found by dividing the index numbers of wages by the index numbers of wholesale prices in table 8, p. 75.

Wages in terms of wheat.—Wages in England for 300 years and the purchasing power of these wages in terms of wheat are shown in table 39 and figure 109. For the two centuries from 1600 to 1800, wages more than trebled, but the buying power of wages in terms of wheat was practically stationary. The primary reason for the increase in the price of wheat was the bringing in of the precious metals from the New World. The increase in efficiency was relatively small, and the buying power of wages increased very slowly.

From 1800 to 1914, commodity prices did not change strikingly, but the buying power of wages in wheat increased more than five times. The compound rate of increase in the buying power of wages was 1.61 per cent per year, or a little more than the increase in purchasing power of wages for all commodities in England, and a little less than the rate of increase of purchasing power of wages in the United States

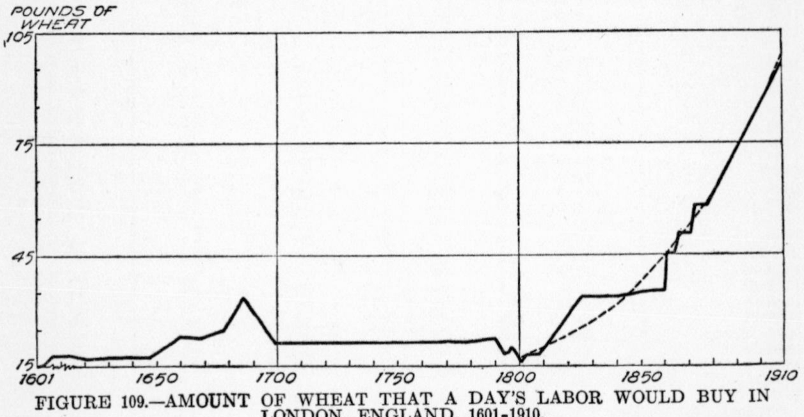

FIGURE 109.—AMOUNT OF WHEAT THAT A DAY'S LABOR WOULD BUY IN LONDON, ENGLAND, 1601-1910.

From 1600 to 1800 there was little increase in efficiency, and wages in terms of wheat were comparatively stable. Beginning about 1800, there was a rapid increase in the amount of wheat that a day's wages would buy. From 1800 to 1914, wheat wages increased at the compound rate of 1.61 per cent per year.

for 75 years before the war. This was a period of rapid increase in the physical volume of output per worker, and there was a corresponding increase in the purchasing power of wages.

EFFECT OF INFLATION AND DEFLATION ON WAGES

Wages in England during the Napoleonic War period.—When prices were rising, wages rose less rapidly (figure 110). After the war, prices declined one-half, but wage rates declined only 15 per cent. By leaving wages practically stationary as prices declined, the increase in efficiency brought wages into adjustment and wage rates again began to increase. If the buying power of wages had increased at the rate of 1.52 per cent per year (page 200), wages in 1850 would have been 83 per cent higher than prices. They were 81 per cent higher.

Wages in the United States during the Civil War period.—During the Civil War period, wages in the United States rose much

TABLE 39.—WAGES PER DAY IN LONDON EXPRESSED IN TERMS OF THE CURRENCY OF 1601 AND LATER*

Years	Wages of carpenters, masons, bricklayers, and joiners, in pence	Wages in pounds of wheat	Wages of laborers in pence	Wages in pounds of wheat	Average pounds of wheat for both classes of labor
1601	13.00	18	9.00	12	15.0
1603	14.00	19	9.00	12	15.5
1607	16.50	22	10.00	14	18.0
1612–13	19.50	22	12.00	14	18.0
1621	19.50	21	12.00	13	17.0
1639	23.00	21	15.00	14	17.5
1646–47	26.00	22	15.00	13	17.5
1660	27.00	28	17.00	18	23.0
1667–68	27.00	26	17.00	17	21.5
1677–78	30.00	29	21.00	20	24.5
1686	31.00	39	22.00	28	33.5
1699	30.00	25	20.00	17	21.0
1778	33.00	26	21.00	17	21.5
1788	36.00	27	22.00	17	22.0
1790	36.00	27	22.00	17	22.0
1794	40.00	23	22.00	13	18.0
1796	40.00	23	24.50	14	18.5
1797	42.00	24	27.00	16	20.0
1801	48.50	20	29.00	12	16.0
1803	58.50	24	29.00	12	18.0
1808	59.00	24	29.00	12	18.0
1826–41	60.00	42	36.00	25	33.5
1853–61	60.00	44	36.00	26	35.0
1861–65	70.00	55	42.50	34	44.5
1865–66	75.00	59	45.00	36	47.5
1866–72	80.00	63	47.50	38	50.5
1872–73	85.00	67	52.50	42	54.5
1873–78	90.00	71	57.50	45	58.0
1914	115.00	120	80.00	83	101.5

* Hardy, W., History of Wages, A Record of Seven Centuries, London Times, No. 42503, p. 16, Aug. 31, 1920. Also presented in Wages in the United States and Foreign Countries prepared by the Tariff Commission.

less rapidly than prices. Although prices started to decline in 1864, wages continued to rise until 1873. Prices declined one-half but wages fell only 15 per cent (figure 111).

Wages in the United States normally rose in purchasing power 1.71 per cent per year. From the five-year average before the Civil War to 1880, this would call for a rise of 47 per cent in wages compared with prices. Wages were 55 per cent above prices.

Wages in England during the World War period.—When prices rose, wages rose less rapidly. By 1917, prices had increased to 212 when pre-war is 100, but wages rose to only 142. By 1920, prices rose to 302; and wages to 263. Prices declined precipitously, but wages continued to rise (figure 112).

In 1929, wages were 201 and prices 139. Before the war, the purchasing power of wages in England was rising 1.52 per cent per year. At this rate, wages in 1929 should have been 28 per cent higher than prices. Since prices were 139, wages of 178 would have been expected

(1.28 × 1.39 = 1.78). Wages in England were 201. Since the cost of living was out of line with prices, these wages were approximately

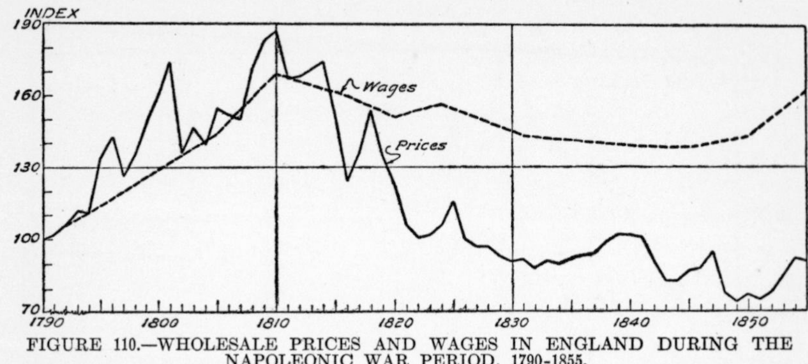

FIGURE 110.—WHOLESALE PRICES AND WAGES IN ENGLAND DURING THE NAPOLEONIC WAR PERIOD, 1790-1855.

1790 = 100.

From 1810 to 1831, prices declined nearly one-half, but wages declined only 15 per cent. Considering the average increase in efficiency, wages and prices were in adjustment in 1850.

normal, as far as the laborer was concerned, but were high for the employer who sold at wholesale prices.

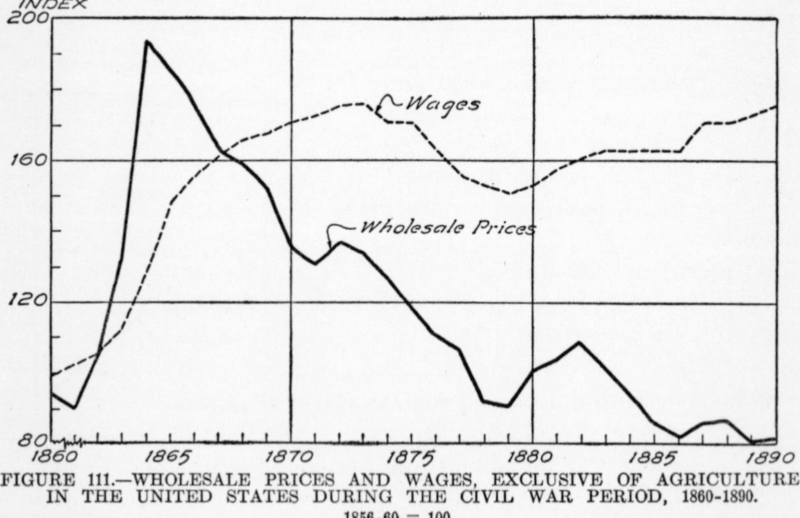

FIGURE 111.—WHOLESALE PRICES AND WAGES, EXCLUSIVE OF AGRICULTURE, IN THE UNITED STATES DURING THE CIVIL WAR PERIOD, 1860-1890.

1856-60 = 100.

Prices reached a peak in 1864 but wages continued to rise for 9 years. By 1879, prices were cut in half but wages had declined only 15 per cent. Considering the average increase in efficiency, wages and prices were approximately in adjustment by 1880.

Wages in the United States during the World War.—During the World War period, prices rose faster than wages. In 1917, prices were 172 when pre-war is 100, but wages had risen only to 131 (figure 113). By 1920, wages were becoming adjusted to prices. Prices then declined, and wages lagged. In 1929, prices were 139, and wages were

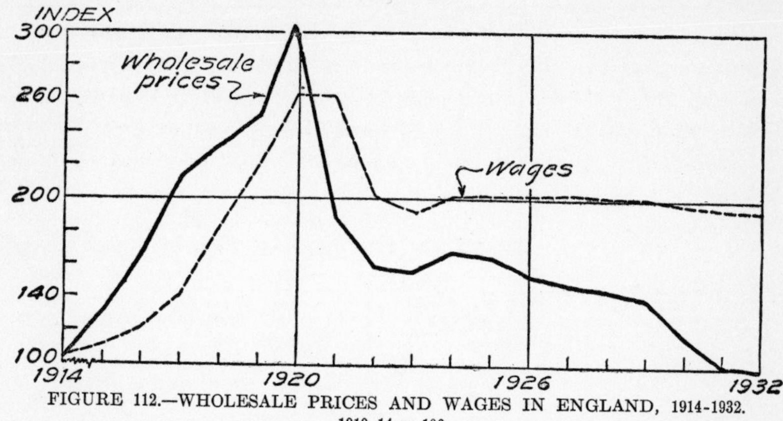

FIGURE 112.—WHOLESALE PRICES AND WAGES IN ENGLAND, 1914-1932. 1910-14 = 100.

During the rise in commodity prices from 1914 to 1920, wages lagged. Wages dropped somewhat during the drastic liquidation of 1921-22, but have remained comparatively stable since that time in spite of the continued decline in commodity prices.

239. In this 16.5-year period, the normal increase in the purchasing power of wages would have been 32 per cent. At prices of 139, this

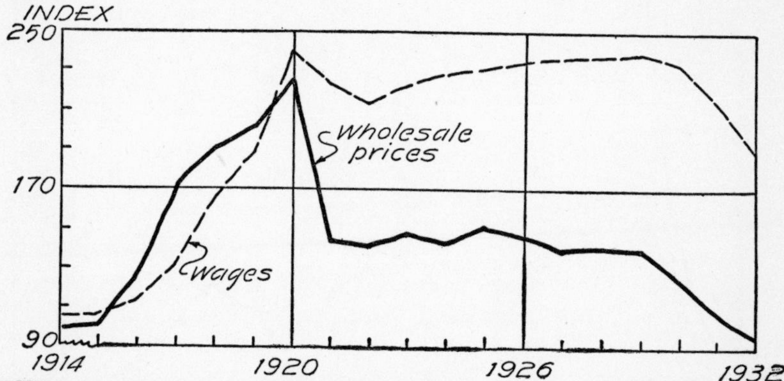

FIGURE 113.—WHOLESALE PRICES AND WAGES IN THE UNITED STATES DURING THE WORLD WAR PERIOD, 1914-32. 1910-14 = 100.

From 1914 to 1920, prices rose more rapidly than wages. Since 1920, wages have followed the normal procedure and remained high despite the decline in commodity prices. The figure for 1932 is estimated.

would have called for wages of 183 ($1.32 \times 1.39 = 1.83$). Deflation left the cost of living out of line with wholesale prices. The cost of living index was 172, so that wages of 227 would have been necessary for a normal buying power. The wage level was not seriously out of line with prices.

From 1929 to 1932, prices declined precipitously, and wages again lagged.

If the period of liquidation follows the Civil War time schedule, as it has done thus far, the worst of the immediate unemployment would be past by 1936. At that time, wages would be expected to have a buying power of 52 per cent above pre-war. If the cost of living should then be a third above pre-war, wages of twice pre-war would be expected.

TABLE 40.—INDEX NUMBERS OF WHOLESALE PRICES AND WAGES

Napoleonic War Period 1790 = 100			Civil War Period 1856–60 = 100			World War Period 1910–14 = 100				
	England			United States			England		United States	
Year	Wholesale prices*	Wages†	Year	Wholesale prices‡	Wages§	Year	Wholesale prices*	Wages¶	Wholesale prices‡	Wages§
1790	100	100	1860	94	99	1914	103	103	99	105
1795	134	114	1861	90	102	1915	131	111	101	106
1800	160	129	1862	105	105	1916	165	121	125	114
1805	155	144	1863	134	112	1917	212	142	172	131
1810	188	169	1864	194	128	1918	232	183	191	166
1816	125	160	1865	186	148	1919	249	219	202	189
1820	121	151	1866	175	156	1920	304	263	226	240
1824	106	156	1867	163	161	1921	188	262	143	224
1831	92	143	1868	159	166	1922	159	202	141	214
1840	102	139	1869	152	168	1923	156	192	147	223
1845	87	138	1870	136	171	1924	168	201	143	229
1850	77	139	1871	131	173	1925	165	202	151	232
1855	101	163	1872	137	176	1926	153	202	146	235
			1873	134	176	1927	148	203	139	237
			1874	127	171	1928	145	201	141	238
			1875	119	171	1929	139	201	139	239
			1876	111	163	1930	117	197	126	233
			1877	107	156	1931	101	195	107	214
			1878	92	153	1932	99	193	95	189
			1879	91	151					
			1880	101	153					

* Table 8.
† Wood, G. H., The Course of Wages between 1790 and 1860, The Economic Journal, Vol. IX, p. 591, December 1899.
‡ Table 1.
§ Table 37.
¶ Table 38.

The cost of living.—When prices rise, wholesale prices of commodities rise more rapidly than retail prices and therefore outrun the cost of living (figure 114). When prices fall, retail prices and the cost of living lag. The manufacturer is primarily interested in wholesale prices and wages. The laborer is primarily interested in wages and the cost of living. Since manufacturers' prices rise so rapidly, during inflation they could increase wages much more rapidly than the cost of living rises and yet make a good profit.

When deflation occurs, manufacturers' prices fall more rapidly than the cost of living of the laborer that produces the goods.

Wages and the cost of living.—In view of the fact that wages lag behind prices, the cost of living becomes an important question when prices are rising. During such periods, labor insists that wages must rise to keep pace with the advancing costs of living. Employers who gain from the lagging adjustment are loathe to increase wages.

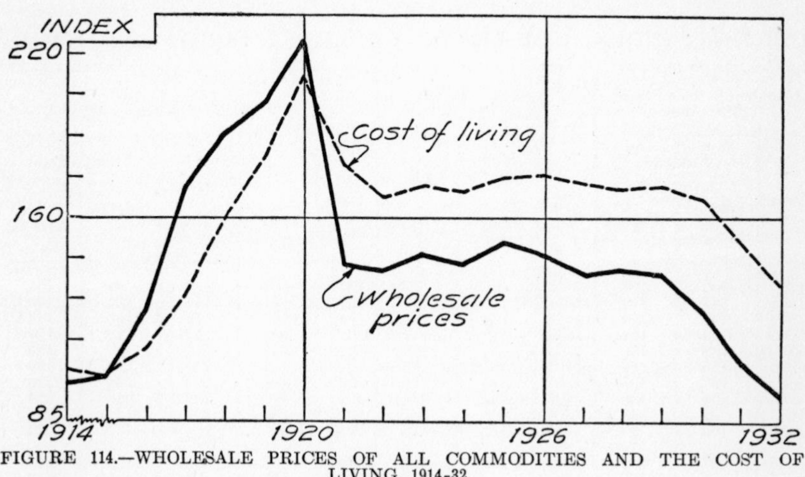

FIGURE 114.—WHOLESALE PRICES OF ALL COMMODITIES AND THE COST OF LIVING, 1914-32.
1910-14 = 100.
When prices rose, wholesale prices rose faster than the cost of living. When prices fell, wholesale prices fell more rapidly than the cost of living.

During the violent price fluctuations of the World War period, the cost of living was used by many nations as a method of settling wage disputes. During periods of falling prices, and particularly in 1921 and in 1932, employers insisted that wages must decline with the cost of living. Labor then resists the cost-of-living theory of wages. This theory is always wrong when comparison is made between two years that are far apart. Wages should rise about 1.7 per cent per year if the cost of living were stationary, in order that the population may be able to consume its increasing output. If wages and the cost of living are both held constant, and if there is an increasing product, it cannot be consumed. The employer who desires to have national efficiency increase, but wishes to leave laborers with a stable buying power, is asking the impossible.

Wages from the point of view of the employer and the employee.—Over a long period of time, wholesale prices and the cost of living follow a somewhat similar course. Inflation and deflation disturb this relationship. If inflation occurs, wages and the cost of living rise less rapidly than wholesale prices. If deflation occurs, wages and the cost of living fall less rapidly.

If the pre-war trend in wages had continued until 1929, and if prices had remained at 100, wages would normally have been 132 when the five years before the war is 100. This would have given them a purchasing power of 32 per cent above pre-war, which would have been the normal growth in purchasing power in the 16.5 years. But wholesale prices in 1929 were 139 when pre-war is 100. In order to have their normal buying power, wages should have been 183.

Owing to declining prices, wholesale prices were out of line with retail prices. In 1929, the laborer could not buy at a price level of 139. The cost of food at retail was 174; and the cost of living, 172. At an index of 172, wages of 227 were necessary to have a buying power of 32 per cent above pre-war ($1.72 \times 1.32 = 2.27$).

Other evidence of the fact that a wage level of more than double pre-war was a reasonable wage level in 1929 is indicated by the fact that industry was able to pay this wage level and be decidedly prosperous. Some wages were much more than double pre-war, but farm wages and some other wages were not double pre-war.

A collapse in the price structure throws consumers' prices out of line with producers' prices. The laborer is not concerned with wholesale prices when they are out of line with retail prices. If the price level would remain stable, wholesale prices would keep approximately in line with retail prices. In 1931, wholesale prices of all commodities averaged 107 when the five years before the war is called 100. The cost of living index averaged 151. If the buying power of wages had continued at the pre-war rate of increase, it would have been 137 in 1931. With wholesale prices at an index of 107, the manufacturer might have anticipated wages of 147 ($1.37 \times 1.07 = 1.47$). If manufacturers could have hired labor at this level and sold the product at 107, industry would have been prosperous, if not in debt, and production would have been at a high level. But in order that the laborers might consume the output that the manufacturers would have produced, they would have required a buying power of 137 with the cost of living at a level of 151. This required wages of 207 ($1.37 \times 1.51 = 2.07$) to buy the products of industry. This shows the impossible situation that inevitably develops when the price structure collapses. The manufacturer could not proceed with a wage level of 207 and a price level of 107, but the laborer could not consume the product unless he received these wages. The result was that both production and consumption stopped.

A visionary reply is sometimes made that all other prices should come down. To reduce all freight rates, all telephone charges, all taxes, all wages, all rents, all commissions, all debts, and all doctors', lawyers' and dentists' fees quickly could occur only in Alice in Wonderland. Long years of unemployment, bankruptcies, and distress, are the only means of bringing a collapsed price structure into balance. It could, of course, be brought into balance quickly if the old price level were restored. When unemployment has continued long enough, the great shortage of goods causes industry to start for a time. But a period of declining prices is, as a whole, a period of unemployment.

Such a situation also causes innumerable misunderstandings and violent controversies. The manufacturer who sells his product at an index of 107 feels that wages 50 per cent above pre-war should be a delight to the laborer. He cannot understand the situation. The laborer who should have wages of twice pre-war to consume the product at a price level of 151 is unable to understand why the manufacturer is so unreasonable. The "standstill" is due to a collapse in the price structure for which neither party is to blame. Here is a definite illustration of the old conundrum of "What would happen if an irresistible force should meet an immovable body?"

The situation is much worse for both parties than the above picture presents. The employer has many fixed charges such as debts, taxes, and the like. He also sees the value of his property melting away because a new property can be built at less cost.

The cost of living includes rents, but many laborers have followed the highly commended practice of buying their own homes. Declining rents are an injury to these persons. They mean that the home is shrinking in value. This shrinkage is often sufficient to wipe out the life-time savings of the thrifty worker.

Laborers, like other persons, have investments which have melted away. When the wage level is rising as rapidly as the national output per capita increases, the efficient worker receives promotion, whereas the inefficient may be kept at the old wage. With declining prices, both the efficient and the inefficient workers continue at the same level, or receive a horizontal cut. Such a situation often results in a greater loss through failure to win promotion than by any contemplated cut in wages.

Wages will not decline as much as prices.—One of the most common errors is to assume that, if prices return to pre-war, wages must return to pre-war to be in adjustment. This fails to take into account the buying power of wages as efficiency increases. To have wages and prices in adjustment at the pre-war level would require that all the labor-saving plans and inventions of nearly a generation be "uninvented." Fortunately no such calamity will occur. This would be as difficult a task as "unhatching" a chicken.

It must also be remembered that, since wages lag behind prices, maladjustment will always occur when prices are rising or falling. The greatest step that can be taken to avoid wage controversies is to adopt a stable measure of value.

EFFECT OF INFLATION AND DEFLATION ON DIFFERENT CLASSES OF WORKERS

Inflation and deflation cause maladjustments not only between wages and prices, but also among different classes of labor. When the price level is suddenly changed, the period of time required for adjustment is largely dependent on the time involved in the production of the articles or service in question. If the processes of production require only a short time, the supply of the article that was in the process of production is quickly exhausted. An additional supply is not forthcoming until the price is adjusted.

If the process of production requires a long time for completion, the supply that is in the process of making may be sufficient to last a

TABLE 41.—INDEX NUMBERS OF WAGES OF FIREMEN AND ENGINEERS AND WHOLESALE PRICES IN THE UNITED STATES

1856–60 = 100

Year	Wholesale prices*	Engineers†	Firemen†	General wages§
1860	94	96	90	99
1861	90	96	102	102
1862	105	96	102	105
1863	134	100	105	112
1864	194	101	105	128
1865	186	120	137	148
1866	175	125	137	156
1867	163	140	137	161
1868	159	138	137	166
1869	152	137	137	168

* Table 1, p. 10.

† Wholesale Prices, Wages, and Transportation, Report by Mr. Aldrich, from the Committee on Finance, 52nd Congress, 2d Session, Report 1394, Part I, p. 160, 1893.

§ Table 37, p. 197.

long time before the effect of changing production is apparent. For example, it takes several years to raise a horse. If prices are out of adjustment, there are three or four crops of colts to be disposed of before readjustment can be made.

Much the same relationships hold for human services. The occupation for which little or no training is necessary is quickly adjusted to a new price level. The pay in an occupation for which a long training is necessary is very slowly adjusted.

Wages of firemen and engineers during the Civil War period.—During the Civil War period all wages lagged behind prices. Wages

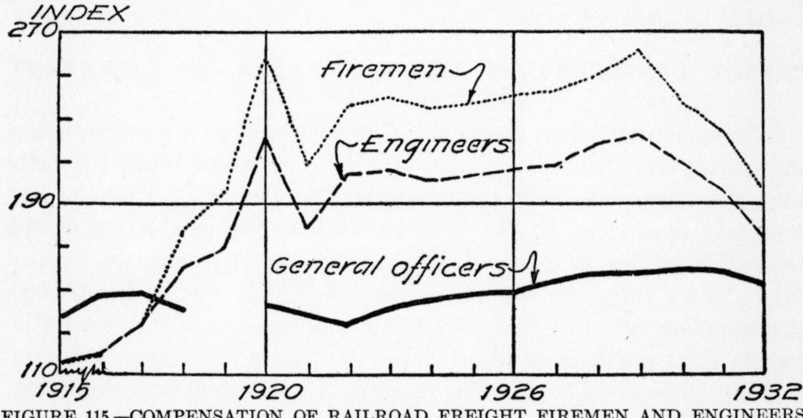

FIGURE 115.—COMPENSATION OF RAILROAD FREIGHT FIREMEN AND ENGINEERS AND GENERAL OFFICERS IN THE UNITED STATES, 1915-32.
1910-14 = 100.
The compensation of those requiring the least training, the firemen, has been relatively high; and of those requiring the most training, the engineers and general officers, has been relatively low.

of railroad firemen rose less promptly than general wages. Wages of engineers rose still more slowly (table 41). The same principle held for Canadian brakemen and conductors during the World War.

Wages of firemen and engineers and salaries of railway officers during the World War period.—In 1920, wages of freight firemen on railroads of the United States had increased to 160 per cent above the pre-war level. The pay of engineers had increased 122 per cent, and the salaries of general officers had increased only 43 per cent, above pre-war (figure 115).

Wages of government employees.—Ordinarily a government is much slower than private enterprises in making wage adjustments. Wages of government employees are very slow to go up and very slow to go down. The result is that some energetic men leave government work when prices are rising. This is likely to leave the government service with some inferior men who will cling tenaciously to their positions when prices decline.

The rapid rise in prices from 1897 to 1913 resulted in a slight increase in the salaries of government employees. Since prices rose more rapidly than salaries, the purchasing power of salaries was reduced. When prices rose rapidly during the World War, the purchasing power of salaries was strikingly reduced, being only half of what it was in the nineties (figure 116 and table 42). In some cases, individuals with

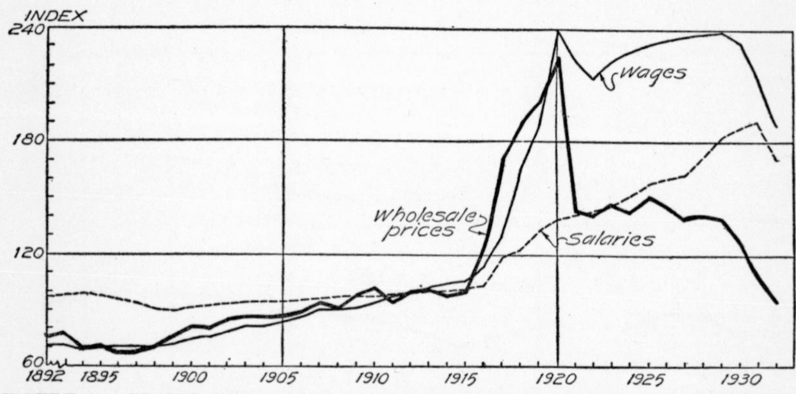

FIGURE 116.—PRICES AND WAGES COMPARED WITH SALARIES OF GOVERNMENT EMPLOYEES IN THE UNITED STATES, 1892-1932.
1910-14 = 100.
From 1915 to 1932, the salaries of government employees lagged behind the advance in the general wage level and in commodity prices.

poorer qualifications were employed so that the reduction in purchasing power was no greater than the reduction in service rendered.

The violent deflation of 1929-32 resulted in vigorous clamor for a reduction of wages of government employees. These were the visible evidence of taxes, but public debts were more serious. Since debts and other fixed charges represent such a large part of expenses of government, the reduction in wages does not bring the expected tax relief. If government workers had received the same increase in pay as industrial workers, the index of their salaries in 1929 would have been 239 instead of 183. A 20 per cent reduction from the 239 would have left them higher than they actually were before reduction.

In government service, deflation results in a leveling-down process because the persons with higher pay are generally cut most. Since wages and salaries always vary less than the variations in value of services,

TABLE 42.—SALARIES OF UNITED STATES GOVERNMENT EMPLOYEES IN WASHINGTON, D. C.

Year	Wholesale prices of all commodities* 1910–14 = 100	Average salaries†	Index number of salaries 1910–14 = 100	Purchasing power of salaries	Year	Wholesale prices of all commodities* 1910–14 = 100	Average salaries†	Index number of salaries 1910–14 = 100	Purchasing power of salaries
1892	76	$1096	97	128	1922	141	$1625	144	102
1893	78	1101	98	126	1923	147	1658	147	100
1894	70	1110	99	141	1924	143	1708	152	106
1895	71	1104	98	138	1925	151	1776	158	105
1896	68	1084	96	141	1926	146	1809	161	110
1897	68	1057	94	138	1927	139	1836	163	117
1898	71	1025	91	128	1928	141	1940	172	122
1899	77	1017	90	117	1929	139	2061	183	132
1900	82	1033	92	112	1930	126	2113	188	149
1901	81	1047	93	115	1931	107	2146	191	179
1902	86	1061	94	109	1932	95	1930‡	171‡	180‡
1903	87	1067	95	109					
1904	87	1066	95	109					
1905	88	1072	95	108					
1906	90	1084	96	107					
1907	95	1094	97	102					
1908	92	1102	98	107					
1909	99	1106	98	99					
1910	103	1108	98	95					
1911	95	1116	99	104					
1912	101	1128	100	99					
1913	102	1136	101	99					
1914	99	1140	101	102					
1915	101	1152	102	101					
1916	125	1174	104	83					
1917	172	1342	119	69					
1918	191	1381	123	64					
1919	202	1494	133	66					
1920	226	1570	139	62					
1921	143	1593	142	99					

* Table 1, p. 10.
† The data from 1913 to 1928 were taken from Closing Report of Wage and Personnel Survey, Personnel Classification Board, p. 221, 1931. Data from 1929 to 1931 were furnished through the courtesy of I. Baruch, Assistant Director of the Personnel Classification Board. The data are for the calendar year. From 1917 to 1924, bonuses are included.
‡ Estimated.

inflation and deflation cause an increased maladjustment between pay and the value of the services.

Wages and prices in Germany.—During the inflation in Germany, prices rose so high that they show the ultimate tendency to bring all workers to the same pay when money is unstable. When such a rapid change in the price level occurs, the unskilled workers may even receive more than the skilled. In 1921, the pay of high-salaried government officials was four times the pay in 1913, that of low-salaried officials eight times, skilled workers nine times and unskilled workers fourteen times (table 43). In 1913, the skilled workers received about two-thirds more than the unskilled workers, but in 1921 they received less than 10 per cent more.

The tendency is to raise the wages of the less highly skilled the most when prices rise. The most highly skilled suffer more than the less skilled. The attempt is to put everybody on a subsistence basis.

Moderate deflation generally lowers wages of unskilled labor most. But if the deflation is violent enough to have the government cut wages, the leveling-down process is followed by the public and by others. Wages of the most highly skilled are often cut by a higher percentage than the less skilled. This was the policy followed by the United States Government in 1932.

TABLE 43.—AVERAGE EARNINGS OF EMPLOYEES IN GERMANY*

Class of workers	Marks per year		Index number for 1921 1913 = 100
	1913	1921	
High salaried officials	6500	28,350	436
Medium salaried officials	3820	18,985	497
Low salaried officials	1640	13,325	812
Skilled workers	1613	14,976	928
Semi-skilled workers	1260	13,978	1109
Unskilled workers	992	13,728	1384

* Wages and Salaries of Manual Workers and Officials in the German Government Service, Monthly Labor Review, Vol. 13, No. 6, p. 100, December 1921.

Changes in wages in other countries.—In Switzerland, the percentage increase in wages was more than twice as great for the lowest-paid groups as for the highest.

In 1919, skilled workers in Copenhagen were receiving 125 per cent more wages than in 1914, unskilled workers 196 per cent more.[3]

In the iron and steel industry in the vicinity of Paris, wages increased 216 per cent for ordinary labor and 62 per cent for skilled labor.[4]

Salaries of teachers, Civil War period.—When prices began to rise rapidly owing to inflation of the Civil War period, it was three years before teachers' wages were affected. When prices had doubled, teachers' wages had risen less than one-fourth (figure 117). General wages rose more promptly but not so rapidly as prices. Teachers' salaries continued to rise after prices began to fall (table 44), and by 1870 the purchasing power was higher than before the war. After

[3] Wages and Hours of Labor in Denmark, Monthly Labor Review, Vol. 10, No. 5, p. 1182, May 1920.

[4] Wages in Various Occupations in Certain Foreign Countries, Monthly Labor Review, Vol. 12, No. 3, p. 585, March 1921.

TABLE 44.—TEACHERS' WAGES IN BARNSTABLE COUNTY, MASSACHUSETTS, GENERAL WAGES, AND WHOLESALE PRICES, 1860–1890

1856–60 = 100

Year	Wholesale prices of all commodities*	Male teachers†	Female teachers†	General wages§
1860	94	101	107	99
1861	90	102	101	102
1862	105	101	106	105
1863	134	103	100	112
1864	194	106	104	128
1865	186	124	116	148
1866	175	133	126	156
1867	163	139	132	161
1868	159	143	146	166
1869	152	158	149	168
1870	136	154	149	171
1871	131	155	153	173
1872	137	151	160	176
1873	134	169	174	176
1874	127	177	161	171
1875	119	172	180	171
1876	111	168	179	163
1877	107	163	173	156
1878	92	163	174	153
1879	91	162	163	151
1880	101	157	165	153
1881	104	149	168	158
1882	109	163	176	161
1883	102	153	180	163
1884	94	161	189	163
1885	86	158	184	163
1886	82	164	184	163
1887	86	170	186	171
1888	87	167	190	171
1889	81	177	193	173
1890	82	169	195	176

* Table 1, p. 10.

† Wholesale Prices, Wages and Transportation, Report by Mr. Aldrich for the Committee on Finance, 52nd Congress, 2d Session, Report 1394, Vol. I, pp. 174, 189, March 3, 1893.

§ Index Numbers of Wages per Hour, 1840–1929, Monthly Labor Review, Vol. 32, No. 2, p. 143, February 1931; and table 37, p. 197.

1870, prices continued to fall but teachers' wages rose slightly. By 1890, the purchasing power of wages of female teachers was 138 per cent above the five-year pre-war average. This was slightly greater than the advance in general wages, which increased 115 per cent in purchasing power.

Salaries of teachers, World War period.—In 1920, prices were 126 per cent above pre-war and wages of laborers 140 per cent; but

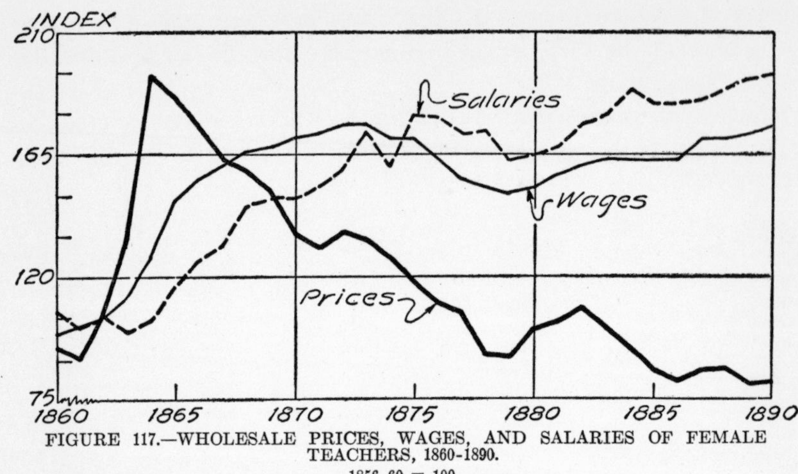

FIGURE 117.—WHOLESALE PRICES, WAGES, AND SALARIES OF FEMALE TEACHERS, 1860-1890.

1856-60 = 100.

Wages lagged behind prices when they were rising and when they were falling. Teachers' wages lagged more than general wages.

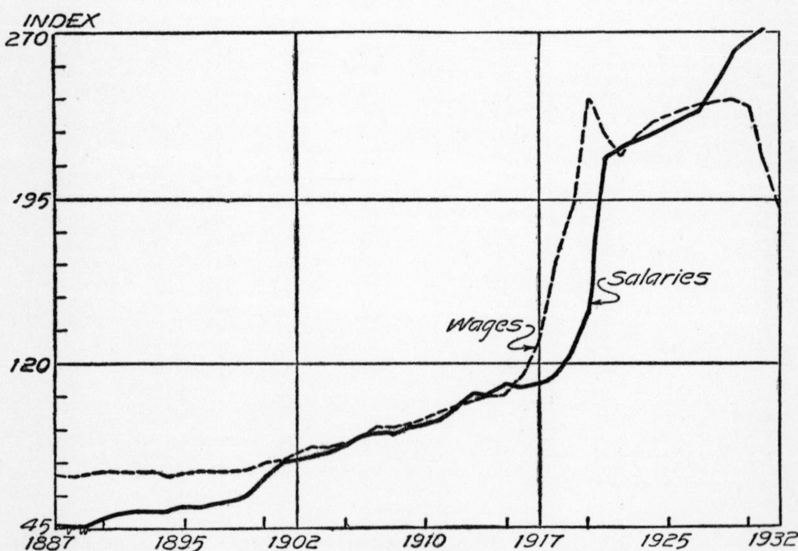

FIGURE 118.—INDEX NUMBERS OF SALARIES OF TEACHERS IN ALL PUBLIC SCHOOLS OF NEW YORK STATE AND HOURLY WAGES, EXCLUSIVE OF AGRICULTURE, 1887-1932.

1910-14 = 100.

Teachers' salaries followed the general wage level very closely.

From 1887 to 1914, teachers' salaries rose slightly compared with general wages. From 1916 to 1920, wages rose more rapidly than salaries.

salaries of teachers in cities of New York State were only 32 per cent above pre-war. In 1929, wages and salaries were in close adjustment (table 45 and figure 118).

Salaries of professors.—From the five-year pre-war average to 1918, prices rose 91 per cent. Wages rose 66 per cent, showing their

TABLE 45.—AVERAGE ANNUAL SALARIES OF MALE AND FEMALE TEACHERS IN ALL PUBLIC SCHOOLS IN NEW YORK STATE, 1887–1931*

Year	Annual salaries			Index numbers 1910–14 = 100		
	Cities	Towns	State	Cities	Towns	State
1910–14	$1160	$ 468	$ 887	100	100	100
1887	687	262	410	59	56	46
1888	703	268	420	61	57	47
1889	689	270	419	59	58	47
1890	694	285	437	60	61	49
1891	719	292	452	62	62	51
1892	740	298	467	64	64	53
1893	728	304	468	63	65	53
1894	708	306	465	61	65	53
1895	733	311	484	63	66	55
1896	725	309	487	62	66	55
1897	720	315	495	62	67	56
1898	743	315	517	64	67	58
1899	772	318	541	67	68	61
1900	879	322	605	76	69	68
1901	977	329	663	84	70	75
1902	982	337	680	85	72	77
1903	992	345	696	86	74	78
1904	1000	354	708	86	76	80
1905	1036	363	736	89	78	83
1906	1090	368	772	94	79	87
1907	1088	388	787	94	83	89
1908	1056	407	784	91	87	88
1909	1072	423	805	92	90	91
1910	1093	440	829	94	94	93
1911	1102	452	839	95	97	95
1912	1168	466	888	101	100	100
1913	1230	477	936	106	102	106
1914	1208	503	941	104	107	106
1915	1250	514	975	108	110	110
1916	1221	522	967	105	112	109
1917	1241	544	988	107	116	111
1918	1272	587	1023	110	125	115
1919	1355	657	1108	117	140	125
1920	1531	807	1279	132	172	144
1921	2324	1065	1892	200	228	213
1922	2359	1119	1938	203	239	218
1923	2372	1148	1960	204	245	221
1924	2388	1193	1991	206	255	224
1925	2401	1248	2021	207	267	228
1926	2413	1297	2046	208	277	231
1927	2446	1340	2086	211	286	235
1928	2587	1388	2194	223	297	247
1929	2748	1439	2314	237	307	261
1930†	2812	....	2372	242	....	267
1931†	2839	....	2408	245	....	271

* Twelfth Annual Report of the Department of Education, Vol. I, p. 202, 1916. Twenty-sixth Annual Report of the Education Department, Vol. 2, p. 31, 1930.

† 1930 and 1931 from letter, July 19, 1932, from Alice McCormack, State Education Department, Albany, N. Y.

usual lag (table 46). Salaries of professors rose 9 per cent.[5] By 1920, prices had risen 126 per cent and wages 140 per cent, but professors' salaries still lagged, having risen only 21 per cent. Prices declined and wages and salaries continued to increase. By 1929, prices were 39 per cent above pre-war, wages 139, and professors' salaries 62 (figure 119).

Tabulations by Arnett showed salary increases in 1920 of 24 per cent in the middle Atlantic states, and 34 per cent in the middle west. In 1927, the increases were 79 and 92 per cent (table 47). These are for smaller colleges and universities. When prices rise or fall, wages

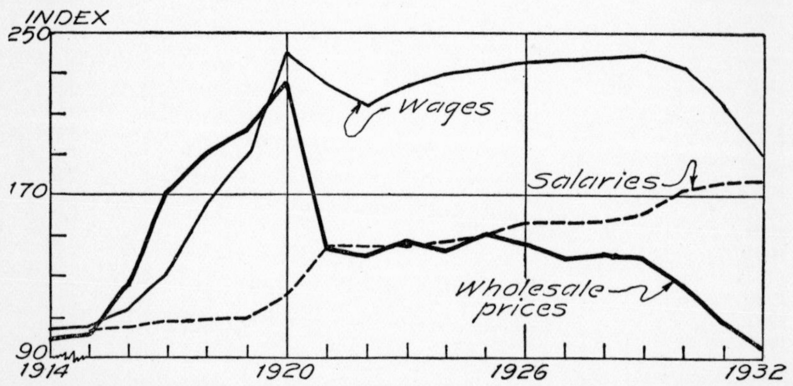

FIGURE 119.—WHOLESALE PRICES, WAGES, AND PROFESSORS' SALARIES, 1914-32. 1910-14 = 100.

All wages rose less rapidly than prices. Professors' salaries rose much less rapidly than wages. Although they did not fall so soon, they remained low relative to wages.

increase before salaries. Salaries of high school teachers rise before the salaries of college teachers, and these in turn rise before university professors' salaries.

The pay of teachers and others who require a long period of preparation responds very slowly to rising prices. The upward adjustment is made too slowly and results very seriously for those who are employed.

When prices are rising rapidly, the increases for beginners in the service are much greater than for those who have been in the work for many years. Conversely, when prices fall, beginners receive decreases before the pay of those who have been in the service has been affected.

If a small amount of deflation occurs, salaries are not reduced. If deflation is drastic, there is a tendency to cut the salaries of professors by a higher percentage than the pay of clerks and janitors. The ones

[5] Salaries for professors for the year 1918-19 are listed under the year 1919. These salaries were paid for about 3 months' work in 1918.

TABLE 46.—WHOLESALE PRICES, WAGES, AND SALARIES OF PROFESSORS

1910–14 = 100

Year	Wholesale prices*	Wages†	Salaries of university professors‡
1914	99	105	...
1915	101	106	103
1916	125	114	105
1917	172	131	108
1918	191	166	109
1919	202	189	110
1920	226	240	121
1921	143	224	145
1922	141	214	145
1923	147	223	145
1924	143	229	147
1925	151	232	151
1926	146	235	157
1927	139	237	157
1928	141	238	158
1929	139	239	162
1930	126	233§	173
1931	107	214§	177
1932	95	189§	178

* Table 1, p. 10.
† Table 37, p. 197.
‡ July 1910 to June 1915 = 100.
§ Estimated.

TABLE 47.—SALARIES OF PROFESSORS OF EDUCATIONAL INSTITUTIONS IN THE MIDDLE ATLANTIC AND MIDDLE WESTERN STATES, 1914–15 to 1926–27*

Period	Average annual salary		Index numbers	
	Middle Atlantic States	Middle Western States	Middle Atlantic States	Middle Western States
1914–15	2182	1543	100	100
1910–20	2708	2065	124	134
1926–27	3914	2960	179	192

* Arnett, T., Teachers Salaries in Certain Endowed Colleges and Universities in the United States, Publications of the General Education Board, Occasional Papers 7, pp. 23, 26, 1921; No. 8, pp. 49, 51, 1928. The salaries apply to "Grade B" institutions with 500 to 1000 students.

that have risen least are cut most. This is another illustration of the deadening effect of unstable money. In 1929, wages were 139 per cent above pre-war; teachers, 137 per cent; and professors, 62 per cent. Under normal conditions, the young man starts at a low salary and receives promotions if he shows ability. Under deflation, there is a tendency to stop all promotions and hence again tend to a dead level.

Farm and city wages.—Farm wages are influenced by prices of farm products and by city wages. In the United States as a whole, farm wages are more influenced by farm prices than by city wages. In New York state, wages of farm labor are usually more affected by city wages than by prices of farm products because of proximity to industrial centers. In periods of extremely severe unemployment, they follow farm prices (figures 120 and 121).

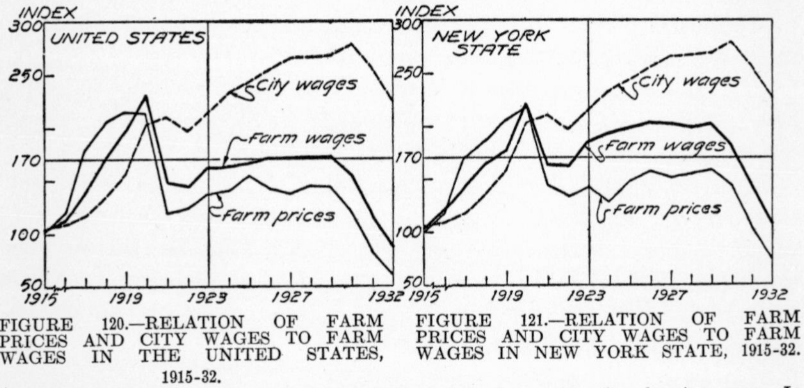

FIGURE 120.—RELATION OF FARM PRICES AND CITY WAGES TO FARM WAGES IN THE UNITED STATES, 1915-32.

FIGURE 121.—RELATION OF FARM PRICES AND CITY WAGES TO FARM WAGES IN NEW YORK STATE, 1915-32.

In the United States, farm wages are more influenced by farm prices than by city wages. In New York State, farm wages are more affected by city wages than by prices of farm products.

During the period of rapidly rising prices following 1914, farm wages advanced more rapidly than did union wage rates. Conversely, when prices fell in 1920 and in 1931, farm wages responded more quickly. In 1931, farm wages were but 17 per cent above the pre-war level whereas union wage rates were more than double pre-war. Farm wages were below pre-war in the states where the agricultural depression was most severe. The same differences occurred during the Civil War period.

Farm workers in the United States are not unionized as are city workers. During periods of rapidly changing prices, contracts between employers and labor unions tend to retard the changes in wage scales.

Wages are so inflexible that employers are very anxious that they shall not rise, knowing how difficult it is to get them down. Labor unions are equally adverse to reducing wages, knowing how hard it is to get them up.

In a period of severe deflation, it is easier for the manufacturer to stop production than to lower wages. Even if he lowered wages he could not sell the product. After men have been unemployed for a time, some of them drift into other industries at lower wages and others may return to their previous work at reduced pay. The same result is sometimes accomplished by giving part-time employment.

The majority of farmers have no regular hired help. Comparatively few have more than one hired man. In 1917, in eight counties in New York, 26 per cent of the farmers had one hired man, 5.0 per cent had two, and 2.5 per cent had three or more.[6]

The farmer works with the hired man and finds it difficult not to share his prosperity with him. Similarly, when the farmer is losing money, the hired man usually knows it and is more willing to accept lower wages than are factory employees who do not have enough direct contact with the industry to realize its financial condition.

Farm wages result from a large number of individual agreements that may be difficult to adjust, but are nevertheless much easier to adjust than are industrial wages. No great commotion occurs when the hired man leaves to work for a neighbor at higher pay. Nor is any great commotion made when some farmer finds he cannot continue to pay his hired man and hence allows him to leave or to work for his board.

Furthermore, when farming is prosperous, many hired men find it possible to start farming for themselves as tenants. The other hired men see the profits made by tenants and become dissatisfied unless their wages are raised. Farmers who are in poor health or are approaching the age of retirement retire more rapidly when prices are rising. All these factors tend to bring about a reasonably prompt adjustment of wages to advancing prices.

When prices fall, many persons who have bought farms on small payments lose their property and drop back into the hired man class. Many tenants also lose their property and again become hired men. This results in a reduction of wages.

With severe unemployment, some men work on farms for their board.

Effect of inflation and deflation on the movement to and from farms.—The movement to and from farms is always going on. Many persons leave farms every year and many return to farms every

[6] Census of Agricultural Resources of New York, p. 12, 1917.

year. Since farm families are larger than city families, and since farmers are steadily becoming more efficient, the net movement is always away from farms except in periods of extreme depression.

The movement is more influenced by prosperity in cities than by prosperity on farms. The movement to cities is very rapid during periods of prosperity. In a period of severe depression, the net movement may be to farms. Many persons return to live with their relatives or friends. Others move to the country to escape living expenses even though they find little work.

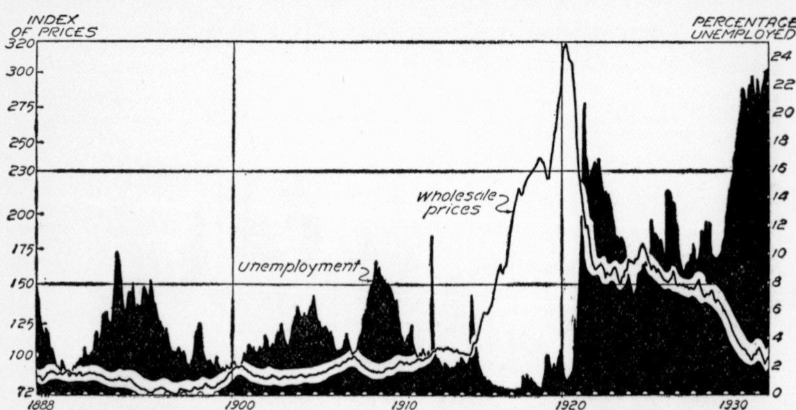

FIGURE 122.—WHOLESALE PRICES AND PERCENTAGE OF UNEMPLOYED[7] AMONG TRADE UNIONS AND INSURED WORKPEOPLE IN GREAT BRITAIN, 1888-1932. When prices are rising, unemployment declines. Conversely, falling prices result in an increase in the percentage of unemployed.

Effects of inflation and deflation on unemployment.—When prices are rising, producers generally make a profit on all purchases of materials. They also make a profit on labor because wages lag behind prices. This results in feverish desire to buy materials and employ labor. Unemployment is reduced to a minimum. In all countries unemployment is very low until deflation begins.

When deflation is taking place, the producer generally loses on his purchases and on his employment of labor because wages lag behind prices. Both the material and wages in his finished products

[7] From 1888 to 1926 inclusive, the percentage of unemployed is based on percentage unemployed at the end of each month among members of trade unions making returns, Nineteenth Abstract of Labour Statistics of the United Kingdom, p. 79, 1928. From 1926 to 1932 inclusive, the percentage of unemployed is based on percentage of unemployed at or near the end of the month among insured workpeople. The Ministry of Labour Gazette, Vol. 35, No. 1, p. 2, January 1927, gives both series for each month of the year 1926. There is very little difference in the two series. The new series was taken from various numbers of the Labour Gazette. Prices are given in table 8, p. 75.

must be disposed of in a lower market. Often the only way to avoid financial failure is to discharge workers. Unemployment began to increase rapidly in the United States in June 1920. In November, it began in Canada; in December, Sweden and Denmark were affected; and in the following March, unemployment began in England. In Germany, where inflation continued, there was very little unemployment. When unemployment in Denmark and Sweden affected a quarter of the workers, there was still practically no unemployment in Germany. These data show the striking effects of deflation.

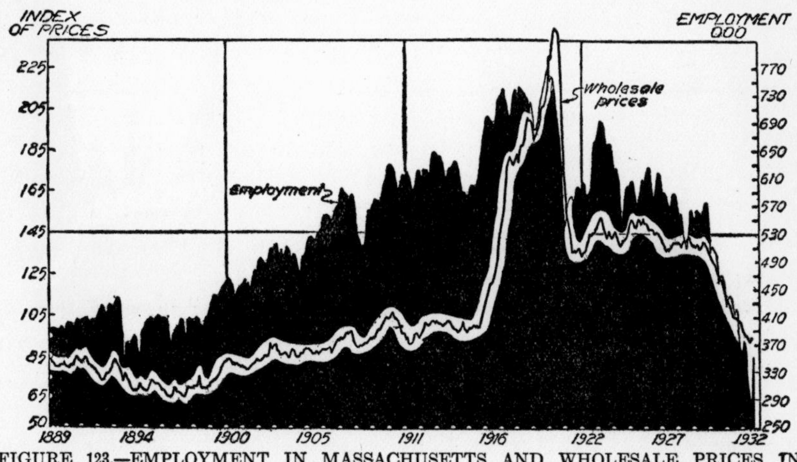

FIGURE 123.—EMPLOYMENT IN MASSACHUSETTS AND WHOLESALE PRICES IN THE UNITED STATES, 1889-1932.

Inflation caused a great increase in employment. The deflation of 1929 threw most of the workers out of employment.

The unemployment following the Panic of 1929 was the worst that has ever occurred.

The relationship of rising and falling prices to unemployment in Great Britain is shown in figure 122. Many persons discuss the unemployment in England in terms of a decadent nation. England is an industrial country and is therefore more affected by a wreck of the price structure than is any other country. Unemployment in England is a natural consequence of the amount of deflation which England attempted.

Employment in Massachusetts.—Fluctuations in the number of persons employed in Massachusetts were strikingly affected by the price level (figure 123). The number of people employed reached its highest point from 1916 to 1919. At no time since 1920 have so many persons been employed as in that period. In July 1932, the employment was about one-third as much as during the period of rising prices.

The short-time fluctuations in employment due to short-time changes in prices are also shown (figure 123). The changes are about simultaneous with changes in the price level.

Technological unemployment.—When new machines and new processes are developed, skill in old methods ceases to have its former value. The number of workers in a particular factory may be reduced. The adjustment is always difficult for older persons. The invention of the automobile reduced the value of the skill of the old carriage maker and blacksmith. If industry is proceeding in a normal way, all but the oldest workers can readily shift to other occupations. They must suffer some temporary personal inconvenience, but it is by this means that the progress of society as a whole takes place, and even those who are temporarily inconvenienced are much better off to spend their lives in such a society than in a stagnant one. The great difficulty comes not from this type of shifts but from falling prices which stop production of things that are needed.

Regional shifts in industry.—The worker in an active industrial center usually finds no great difficulty in making adjustment to new inventions. Occasionally all the industry of a region has to be discontinued, in which case houses cease to have a value. This sometimes occurs in small communities, but is a rare occurrence in a diversified industrial section. In such regions a new industry usually develops when an old one goes out.

Effect of inflation and deflation on wage-earners.—When inflation occurs, prices rise more rapidly than wages. "Real wages," that is, the purchasing power of wages, decline. If the inflation is gradual, for most workers the loss is more than compensated for by the full employment, ease of getting work, opportunities to choose the desired kind of work, and opportunities for promotion. Old men and other workers who are below standard can get work. All members of the family can work. If the worker owns his home, it rises in value. Savings accounts decline in buying power but are secure. If the laborer is in debt, he finds it easier to pay.

When deflation occurs, the cost of living declines more rapidly than wages decline, and real wages rise. This would appear to improve the laborer's position. But nothing is more serious for labor than a declining price level. It brings on unemployment—the worst nightmare of labor. The enthusiasm generated by the possibility of promotions is replaced by the fear of loss of position. Older persons and the poorer workers are thrown out of employment and may never again be taken back. The public objects to having all members of the family work. Since work is scarce, it is believed that no one family should have too much of it.

If the deflation is severe, banks may fail and the savings that were to provide for just such a situation are lost. Those who have bought homes or other property that is not fully paid for often lose their entire savings. If they have purchased shares in the company or any other stocks, the values shrink. If these have to be sold to get money to live on, the savings are largely lost. If the laborer succeeds in holding his position, he is likely to have to support children and other relatives who have lost their places.

The danger of unemployment is somewhat less for farm workers than for city workers; but when prices decline, farm wages in most parts of the United States decline more than the cost of living. These laborers, therefore, suffer by deflation.

Supply of and demand for labor.—A sudden change in the supply of workers affects wages. A striking case followed the "Black Death," a disease which swept over Europe in 1349. It probably took off one-third of the population of England and was equally severe in other countries. The King of England issued a proclamation that no higher than the customary wages should be paid, but the mandate could not be enforced.[8]

Wages in a new country are normally higher than in old countries. Farm wages in the western states have usually been higher than those in eastern states. Although labor is considered to be relatively mobile, it takes many years to equalize wages. Probably they will not be equalized until the ratio of population to used resources is equalized. Families in a new country are usually large. This is due to the prosperity of the worker and to the fact that children are an asset.

Wages in fertile districts are permanently higher than wages in districts that have poor soils. After a century of farming in New York State, wages in a township with fertile soils continue to be higher than wages in adjoining infertile townships. Wages in a township that has poor crops are lower in the following year than wages in a township that had a good season. For example, in 1921 four counties in northeastern New York had a severe drought. The next spring the reduction in wages was greater than the average reduction of the state.

[8] Rogers, J. E. T., Six Centuries of Work and Wages, Vol. I, p. 228, 1884.

Although the tendency is for wages to be equalized, a very large amount of economic friction has to be overcome. Very large differences may last for a time, and considerable differences may continue permanently.

There is a continual contest between labor and capital in regard to the supply of labor. The laborers attempt to raise the age at which employment can begin, increase the period of apprenticeship, and restrict immigration. The employers are usually looking for a supply of cheap labor and too frequently are willing to sacrifice the national welfare for a temporary gain. Therefore, frequently they obstruct the passage of laws which require more years of school attendance, and are sometimes willing to bring into the country any kind of labor regardless of its effects on national welfare.

The most striking instance in American history is the bringing into the south of negro slaves. This resulted in profits for a few individuals for a short time but also resulted in the Civil War. It placed a permanent handicap in the way of the southern white man who must make his start in life by manual labor. This great mistake is the dominating fact in southern civilization. It affects every human problem—the school, church, business, government, and the home.

The same mistake is still repeated in a less extreme degree when persons urge that what we need in immigrants is brawn regardless of brains or race. The literacy test and percentage limitation on immigration both help in selecting immigrants who by race and traditions will carry on American institutions. Of course, it is easy to find exceptions, but thinking people should form their judgment on the bases of all cases rather than on the basis of unusual cases.

When the World War broke out, the most vigorous portion of the population was removed from industry. A great demand for labor ensued. Women, children, and old persons who had not been actively engaged in industry entered the ranks of the wage workers. This in part supplied the shortage. In the more highly developed countries, the supply of labor from these sources was very great. In the more backward countries, where the production per person was normally low, the percentage of the population engaged in industry was so high in peace times that the reserves were low.

Strikes, unions, and prices.—When prices are rapidly rising, wages lag. Strikes are numerous and are usually successful. Labor unions grow rapidly, and the labor leader sleeps well. When prices are rapidly falling, wages again lag. Strikes are less numerous and are less likely to succeed. Labor unions have a struggle to hold their own.

In most of the countries the membership in labor unions doubled or trebled in seven years after inflation began. Usually the most rapid increase took place at the time when prices were rising most rapidly.

During inflation, the yearly number of recorded industrial disputes in the United States was three times as many as in 1930.

Attempts to increase prosperity by reducing production.—Whenever deflation occurs, there is difficulty in selling. This leads to the erroneous conclusion that there is too much of everything and that the unemployed and hungry people are a result of too great production. Pursuing this erroneous line of reasoning, it is proposed that the nation should find ways of preventing man from producing so much. This foolish philosophy takes many forms.

It is proposed that farmers stop producing commodities for sale and start a subsistence type of farming.

It is also proposed that the unemployed people be located on garden patches. A hundred "starvers" on five hundred acres of poor cheap land seems to be the common pattern. The assumption is that these people will produce all their living on five acres. Just what they would do for clothing, doctors' and dentists' bills, and the like is not stated. To locate a family on such a tract of land means that they will be perpetually unemployed, and could not possibly have a reasonable standard of living. Of course there are poultry farms, greenhouses, and vegetable farms of less than five acres. These provide work and income but require capital. They are not small enterprises.

One sound movement is rapidly taking place throughout the United States. It is a movement to live outside of a city but work in the city industries. This allows more elbow room and a chance to reduce living costs. It gives opportunity for profitable work outside of industrial hours and on holidays. Usually the best place for such a development is outside of a good-sized city with several diversified industries. For satisfactory development, it is necessary to have a road that is at all times passable and telephone and electric lines.

Another form of the attempt to reduce production is to propose that the hours of labor per week be reduced to eighteen or some other number. This is based on the assumption of productive capacity far beyond the facts.

Other forms of this same movement are to prevent wives from

working or to go back to hand labor in order to spend more time doing the same thing.

Ways of benefiting by increased efficiency.—There is no possibility of a sudden and enormous increase in the nation's output per capita (page 61). There can be a sudden decrease because of unemployment.

For seventy-five years before the war, the output per worker in the United States increased about 1.7 per cent per year (page 47). It is because of this increase that there are larger and better houses, improved roads, more hospitals, choicer foods, better clothes, and the like. If the output per worker were to be halved, it would be necessary to return to the living conditions that prevailed more than a generation ago.

Much of the increased efficiency will go for the production and consumption of more things per capita. There are innumerable things that are greatly desired and badly needed. There are millions of homes in the United States without electric light, power, bathrooms, running water, modern heating facilities, refrigerators, or telephones. Many homes are located on roads that are impassable for a considerable part of the year. Many city families lack adequate room, light, air, and play grounds. Many persons lack food and clothing. These are all things that are greatly desired and for which men are willing to work. Many persons prefer to have these things rather than to take more leisure.

We have scarcely begun to take care of teeth and health. Most persons would be willing to work additional time if they could be assured that this work would express itself in medical and hospital service at such times as these are needed.

Another way of profiting by the increased production is to spend more years in school. This shortens the years of work. This also becomes a means of maintaining the increased output per worker so that we may live better.

A sudden and violent decrease in hours of work per week, or per year, for the whole population is not possible, without drastic curtailment in the standard of living. American people are not anxious enough for more leisure to be willing to reduce the standard of living to obtain it. A primitive people might be willing to do so, but they would lack the education and efficiency that would make it possible.

For an indefinite number of years, the American people will continue to increase the use of commodities and services rather than take all the increased efficiency in leisure.

Studies in China and observation in other countries suggest that the hours of labor per year may be higher today than in primitive society.

If one must work a certain number of hours during his lifetime, most people prefer to delay the time of beginning work by attending school longer, and to work hard enough in middle life to be assured of some leisure in old age.

If a certain number of hours must be spent in work after leaving school and before old age, most persons prefer to group the leisure time so as to have a vacation period every year and a long vacation period occasionally.

If a certain number of hours must be spent in a given week and if this does not require extremely long days, people prefer to do the work in five days with the week-end free, rather than work a shorter time every day.

The more primitive and savage persons usually prefer to have all their pleasures immediately. They would take all their leisure at once.

There is no need to fear that we will become unemployed and starve because of increasing efficiency. We should fear a breakdown caused by a breakdown in the exchange system.

If the next generation continues to increase efficiency, it will use a larger quantity and higher quality of physical things per capita, will spend more time in school, will make better provision for sickness and old age, will take more vacations, and will do more traveling. No spectacular increase can occur in a single year, because no spectacular increase in efficiency can occur in a single year.

BIBLIOGRAPHY

Ashley, W. J., The Progress of the German Working Classes in the Last Quarter of a Century. 1904.

Berridge, W. A., Cycles of Unemployment in the United States, 1903-1922. Publication of the Pollak Foundation for Economic Research, No. 4. 1923.

Bowley, A. L., Changes in Average Wages (Nominal and Real) in the United Kingdom between 1860 and 1891, Journal of the Royal Statistical Society, Vol. LVIII, Part II, pp. 223-278. June 1895 and other numbers.

Bowley, A. L., Wages in the United Kingdom in the Nineteenth Century. 1900.

Bowley, A. L., Prices and Wages in the United Kingdom 1914-1920. 1921.

Brissenden, P. F., Earnings of Factory Workers, United States Department of Commerce, Bureau of Census Monograph X. 1929.

Douglas, P. H., Real Wages in the United States 1890-1926, Publication of the Pollak Foundation for Economic Research, No. 9. 1930.

Giffen, R., Recent Changes in Prices and Incomes Compared, Journal of the Royal Statistical Society, Vol. LI, Part IV, pp. 713-805. December 1888 and other numbers.

GIFFEN, R., Economic Inquiries and Studies, Vol. I, pp. 156-228. 1904.
HANSEN, A. H., Factors Affecting the Trend of Real Wages, American Economic Review, Vol. XV, No. 1, pp. 27-42. March 1925.
HANSEN, A. H., The Best Measure of Real Wages, American Economic Review, Vol. XVI, No. 1, Supplement pp. 5-16. March 1926.
HOBSON, J. A., Gold, Prices and Wages. 1913.
JEROME, H., Migration and Business Cycles, Publication of National Bureau of Economic Research, No. 9. 1926.
KING, W. I., Employment Hours and Earnings in Prosperity and Depression, National Bureau of Economic Research, No. 5. 1923.
MITCHELL, W. C., History of the Greenbacks, Decennial Publications, 2nd Ser. Vol. IX, pp. 280-351. 1903.
MITCHELL, W. C., Gold, Prices and Wages under the Greenback Standard, University of California Publications in Economics, Vol. I. March 27, 1908.
OGDEN, W. F., Measurement of the Cost of Living and Wages, The Annals of the American Academy of Political and Social Science, Vol. LXXXI, Whole Number 170, pp. 110-122. January 1919.
ROGERS, J. E. T., Six Centuries of Work and Wages. 1884.
RUBINOW, I. M., The Recent Trend of Real Wages, American Economic Review, Vol. IV, No. 4, pp. 793-817. December 1914.
WARREN, G. F., and PEARSON, F. A., Wages, Farm Economics No. 74, pp. 1671-1677. February 1932.
WOOD, G. H., Some Statistics Relating to Working Class Progress Since 1860, Journal of the Royal Statistical Society, Vol. LXII, Part IV, pp. 639-666. December 1899 and later numbers.
WRIGHT, C. D., Comparative Wages, Prices, and Cost of Living. 1889.
Final Report of the Industrial Commission, Vol. XIX, p. 722. 1902.
Wholesale Prices, Wages and Transportation, 52nd Congress, 2nd Sess., Senate Report 1394. 1893.

CHAPTER XIII

WEALTH AND DEBTS

National wealth.—National wealth expressed in dollars and the wealth divided by index numbers of prices of all commodities, with 1912 as 100, are shown in figure 124 and table 48. Wealth expressed in terms of dollars has followed an erratic course. It more than doubled from 1914 to 1920, but fell precipitously in the Panic of 1920. The rise and the fall were due to changes in prices. When expressed in 1912 dollars, the estimates of national wealth have followed a very consistent course. For 65 years before the war, wealth increased at a compound rate of 4.78 per cent per year,[1] or slightly faster than the growth in production (page 46).

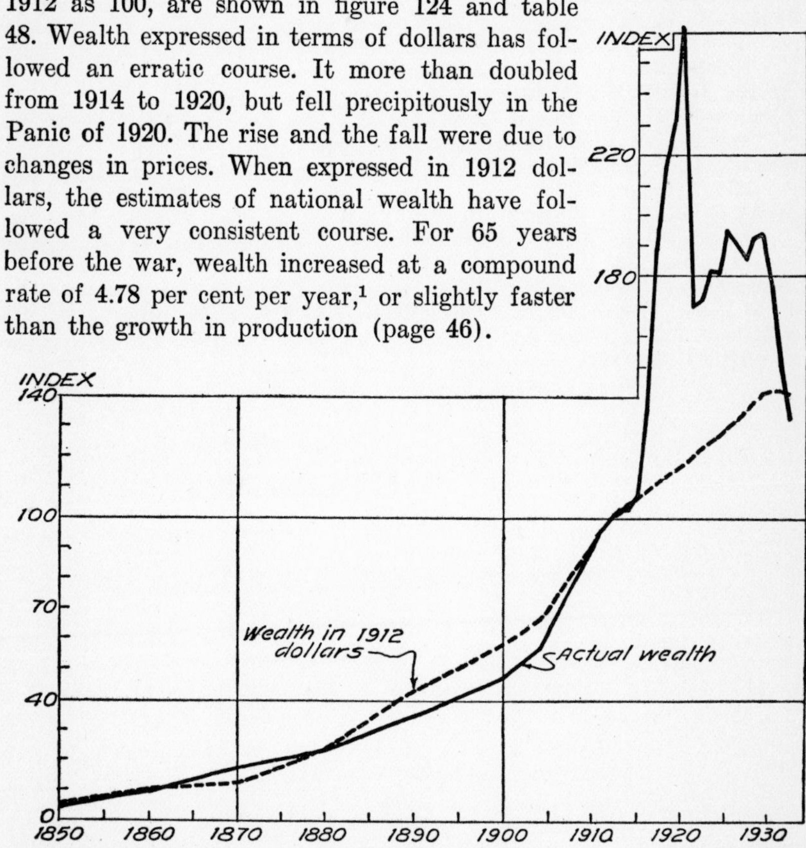

FIGURE 124.—INDEX NUMBERS OF NATIONAL WEALTH AND WEALTH EXPRESSED IN 1912 DOLLARS, 1850-1932.
1912 = 100.

National wealth rose spectacularly from 1915 to 1920, but the rise was due to the shrinkage in the value of money. The increase in wealth in terms of pre-war dollars has been slower than for 65 years before the war.

[1] $y = 5.5732\ (1.0478)^x$.

TABLE 48.—ESTIMATED NATIONAL WEALTH AND PHYSICAL VOLUME OF PRODUCTION*

Year	National wealth, millions	Index numbers of national wealth, 1912 = 100	Index numbers of wholesale prices† 1912 = 100	National wealth in 1912 dollars, millions	Index numbers of national wealth in 1912 dollars, 1912 = 100	Index numbers of the physical volume of production‡ 1912 = 100	National wealth per capita	National wealth per capita in 1912 dollars	Index numbers of national wealth per capita	Index numbers of national wealth per capita in 1912 dollars	Index numbers of physical volume of production per capita,‡ 1912 = 100
1850	$ 7,636‖	4.1	83	$ 9,200	4.9	8.9**	$ 328	$ 395	17	20	37**
1860	17,291‖	9.3	92	18,795	10.1	14.9**	549	597	28	31	46**
1870§	*25,739*‖	*13.8*	*116*	......	.....	17.7	*665*	....	*34*	...	43
1870¶	32,174‖	17.3	134	24,010	12.9	17.7	831	620	43	32	43
1880	43,642	23.4	99	44,083	23.7	29.9	868	876	45	45	57
1890	65,037	34.9	81	80,293	43.1	39.7	1031	1272	53	65	60
1900	88,517	47.5	81	109,280	58.7	62.0	1163	1436	60	73	78
1904	107,104	57.5	86	124,540	66.8	75.5	1297	1508	67	77	87
1912	186,300	100	100	186,300	100	100.0	1950	1950	100	100	100
1913	192,500	103	101	190,594	102	94.1	1994	1974	102	101	93
1914	192,000	103	98	195,918	105	98.1	1961	2001	101	103	95
1915	200,200	107	100	200,200	107	104.9	2015	2015	103	103	100
1916	251,200	135	124	202,581	109	103.9	2493	2010	128	103	98
1917	351,700	189	170	206,882	111	110.1	3442	2025	177	104	102
1918	400,500	215	189	211,905	114	109.8	3866	2046	198	105	101
1919	431,000	231	200	215,500	116	106.6	4104	2052	210	105	97
1920	488,700	262	224	218,170	117	117.0	4587	2048	235	105	105
1921	317,200	170	142	223,380	120	96.3	2932	2065	150	106	85
1922	320,800	172	140	229,143	123	109.6	2918	2084	150	107	95
1923	339,900	182	146	232,808	125	123.2	3048	2088	156	107	105
1924	337,900	181	142	237,958	127	120.4	2985	2102	153	108	101
1925	362,400	195	150	241,600	130	125.3	3155	2103	162	108	104
1926	356,500	191	145	245,862	132	131.1	3060	2110	157	108	107
1927	346,400	186	138	251,014	135	131.5	2931	2124	150	109	106
1928	360,100	193	140	257,214	138	136.0	3004	2146	154	110	108
1929	361,800	194	138	262,174	141	136.8	2977	2157	153	111	107
1930	329,700	177	125	263,760	142	122.9	2677	2142	137	110	95
1931	280,300	150	106	264,434	142	112.5	2259	2131	116	109	86
1932	247,300	133	94	263,085	141	97.0	1981	2107	102	108	74

* From 1850 to 1912, estimated national wealth, Wealth, Debt and Taxation, 1922, Bureau of Census, United States Department of Commerce, pp. 25–27, 1924. From 1912 to 1932, National Wealth and National Income, The Conference Board Bulletin, Vol. VII, No. 5, p. 34, May 20, 1933. National Industrial Conference Board. † The index numbers were converted from the 1910–14 base (table 1, p. 10) by multiplying by 0.990099.

‡ Table 5, p. 44. ** Production for the years 1849 and 1859. § Gold. ¶ Currency.

‖ The estimated national wealth for 1850 to 1870 is for taxable property only. The estimates for later years gave the total property as about 7 per cent more than the taxable. The estimates for taxable property were increased by 7 per cent to obtain the estimates here given.

The spectacular increase in wealth after 1915 was one of the reasons for the rise in the stock market. If commodity prices remain at pre-war values, national wealth will decline to the normal trend expressed in 1912 dollars, or to about 45 per cent above the national wealth of 1912. In 1929, debts were approximately three times the debts of 1912.

At the June 1932 level of commodity prices, the national wealth would be approximately 35 per cent above the wealth of 1912, but the debts would be over 3 times the 1912 debts.

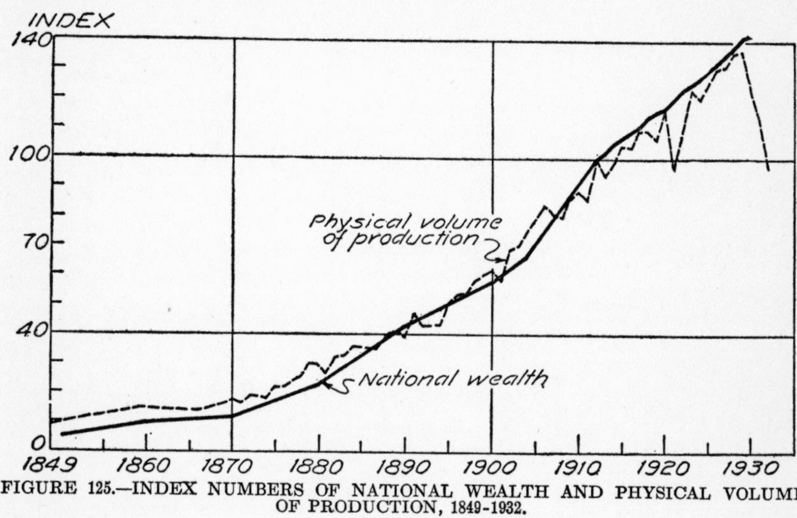

FIGURE 125.—INDEX NUMBERS OF NATIONAL WEALTH AND PHYSICAL VOLUME OF PRODUCTION, 1849-1932.

1912 = 100.

From 1849 to 1912, national wealth expressed in 1912 dollars has increased at the rate of 4.78 per cent per year, which is about the same as the rate of increase in production of basic commodities, which was 4.03 per cent per year.

This would make the national wealth in 1932 about $251 billion. The debts of 1932 are not known, but those of 1929 were $203 billion. In a panic period, all quotations obtained by any reporting agency tend to be higher than actual sales. Those who report are not inclined to regard distressed sales as indicative of the market. At the actual prices being received in June 1932, the debts were probably about equal to the wealth.

Production and national wealth.—The physical volume of production in the United States (table 5, page 44) and national wealth expressed in 1912 dollars (table 48) are shown in figure 125. Before the World War, the physical volume of production increased 4.03 per cent per year (table 5, page 44). The national wealth increased

4.78 per cent per year. The slightly more rapid growth in wealth than in production is due primarily to the low wealth figures before 1880, which are less dependable than the production series. Apparently the two series increase at practically the same rate, but it is possible that wealth may increase a trifle faster than production. Since the outbreak of the war, the national wealth measured in stable dollars has been increasing with production. If, for any reason, production does not proceed at its normal rate, it is to be expected that the rate of growth of national wealth will decline.

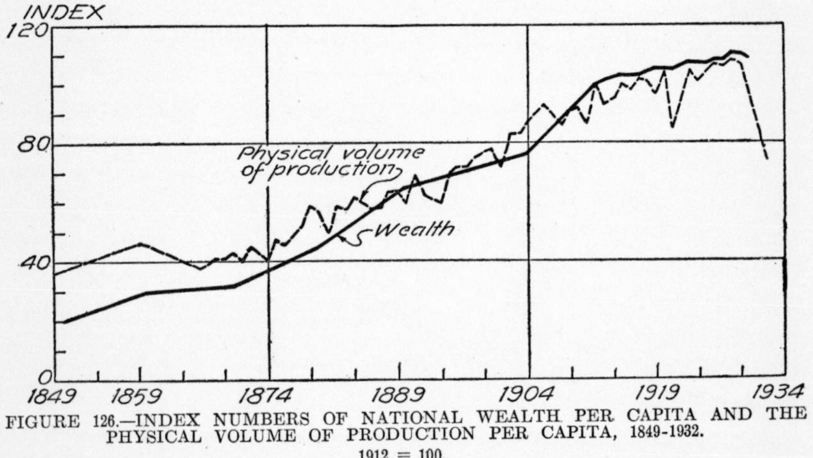

FIGURE 126.—INDEX NUMBERS OF NATIONAL WEALTH PER CAPITA AND THE PHYSICAL VOLUME OF PRODUCTION PER CAPITA, 1849-1932.
1912 = 100.

Before the war, production per capita increased at the rate of 1.73 per cent per year. National wealth expressed in 1912 dollars increased at about the same rate, 2.51 per cent per year.

These two curves are the result of three independent series of data: one on production; one on wealth; and one on the general price level; their close relationship is therefore significant.

National wealth and production per capita.—Before the war, the national wealth per capita, expressed in 1912 dollars, increased 2.51 per cent per year,[2] and the physical volume of production increased 1.73 per cent per year (table 5, page 44).

Since the outbreak of the war, production per capita has increased less rapidly than formerly, and the additions to wealth per capita have also increased less rapidly than normal, when expressed in 1912 dollars (figure 126).

The high profits and high wealth, when money was cheap, resulted in debts per capita that are excessive if they are to be paid with dol-

[2] $y = 21.256\ (1.0251)^x$.

lars of the 1932 value rather than the dollars which were borrowed. In 1912, the wealth per capita was $1959 (table 48). Public and private debts were $663 (table 50). At the June 1932 price level, the wealth was probably about $2000 per capita, although the panic would probably have prevented selling at this value. The total of public and private debts of 1929 was approximately $1672 per capita. They were reduced somewhat by 1932, but were so close to the wealth as to make many of them uncollectable, unless the price level rises. The many devices to protect creditors fail when deflation is so violent.

Debts adjusted to commodity prices.—With the progress of civilization, business is based more and more on credit. Innumerable individuals in their youth have little money. They borrow money to provide working facilities to produce commodities to sell.

Large numbers of persons are encouraged to buy homes, and gradually pay for them by paying a little more than rent. By careful occupancy, savings can be made by reducing depreciation. The owner also often saves by making minor repairs. The desire to get the home paid for stimulates savings on other expenses. This is usually considered to be a desirable method of procedure for young persons.

More and more services are being performed by school districts, municipalities, counties, and other public agencies. Improvements that will last a number of years are commonly financed by bond issues.

An increasing amount of business is done by corporations, which raise a considerable proportion of their money by selling bonds.

The farmer, storekeeper, and manufacturer commonly borrow from banks for short periods of time for financing the production and handling of commodities.

The major proportion of all this debt structure rests on commodities. If commodity prices rise, the debts are easy to pay. If commodity prices fall, they are difficult to pay. If the fall is small, creditors may profit at the expense of debtors. If a price collapse occurs, most debtors are unable to pay, and both creditors and debtors lose.

International loans are made not merely by governments, but by individuals. After the World War, war debts and reparation payments were called for. These can be paid by shipping goods, carrying ocean freight, entertaining tourists, and in some minor ways. The major method of making payment is by shipping goods, just as the primary method of canceling personal debts within a country is by goods. The farmer and the manufacturer sell commodities with which to pay their debts and with which to pay taxes to liquidate public debts. If commodities drop in value, the debts cannot be paid.

Debts, of course, are in adjustment to the price at the time at which the debts were incurred. If a railroad issues bonds to pay for steel rails or a new station, they are related to the cost of the improvement. If a family builds or buys a home, the debt is related to the cost. The storekeeper who borrows to finance the goods on his shelves borrows in proportion to prices. If commodity prices collapse, the entire credit structure collapses. If the debtors cannot pay, banks become insolvent; and if the matter goes far enough, life insurance companies are affected.

Debts and the Panic of 1929.—From 1912 to 1922, the estimated public and private debts in the United States more than doubled (table 50). By 1929, the total debt had more than trebled. Debts increased faster than the wealth of the country. This was due in part to the growth in public debts, resulting from the war, and in part to the increase in private debts. The major part of the increase in debts was due merely to rising prices. The rising prices made debts easy to pay, but the debt structure was too high even for the price structure.

The major cause of the high debt structure was the high level of commodity prices. The major reason for the high price level was the fact that most of the world ceased to use gold as money and made gold cheap.

It makes no difference why prices and debts rose; the fact is that the debts were a certain sum. If under such circumstances prices fall

TABLE 49.—ESTIMATED DEBTS IN UNITED STATES IN 1929*

Debt	Total debts, billions
National	$ 16
State, county and local	17
Corporation	76
Urban mortgages	37
Bank loans	42
Farm mortgages	9
Life insurance policy loans and premium notes	2
Retail installment paper	3
Pawnbrokers' and similar loans	1
	$203

* Warren, G. F., and Pearson, F. A., Effect of Declining Prices on Debts, Farm Economics No. 74, p. 1667, February 1932.

seriously, regardless of the cause, a large portion of the debts cannot be paid.

The total estimated wealth in the United States in 1929 was $362 billion (table 51). The estimated debts amounted to $203 billion, or 56 per cent of the wealth. In three years' time, commodity prices de-

TABLE 50.—ESTIMATED PUBLIC AND PRIVATE DEBTS IN THE UNITED STATES, 1912–32*

Year	Public debts, billions	Private debts, billions	Total debts, billions	Public debts per capita	Private debts per capita	Total debts per capita
1912	$ 5	$ 58	$ 63	$ 53	$ 610	$ 663
1922	31	105	136	282	956	1,238
1929	33	170	203	272	1,400	1,672
1932	38	137	175	304	1,098	1,402

* Hearings before the Committee on Banking and Currency, United States Senate, 72nd Congress, 1st Session on H. R. 11499 and S. 4429, p. 61, May 12, 1932.

TABLE 51.—RELATION OF WEALTH TO DEBTS

Year	Estimated wealth of the United States, billions	Estimated public and private debts, billions	Per cent indebtedness
1912	$186	$ 63	34
1922	321	136	42
1929	362	203	56
1932	247	175	71

clined one-third. This would call for a greater drop in the national wealth, because goods in fixed forms, such as buildings, drop more than movable commodities. The panic and severe unemployment reduced maintenance and new production so that the physical property deteriorated in intrinsic value. The lumber, iron, and steel rotted and rusted away faster than they were produced. To make matters still worse, the thousands of bankrupt properties made selling almost impossible. At the actual market prices in the spring of 1932, the property of the country was probably worth little more than the debts. Such a condition of universal bankruptcy was worse than anything that ever before occurred in the United States.

Popular opinion assumed that, "Prosperity is just around the corner," and that, if the confidence could be restored, prices would rise so that debts could be paid. On this theory, the government lent millions of dollars to banks and railroads. Such loans prevented failures but did not solve the debt question. The only ways to solve this are to have commodity prices rise, or continue the bankruptcy process.

The process of debt liquidation.—When prices fall, debtors and creditors anticipate that payment can be made if the time is extended. This might be true in a business cycle, but is more difficult if the trouble is a price collapse. Finally, creditors take over the property. They usually hold the property for a long time, hoping to avoid serious loss. Finally they reach a point where they are willing to sell the property for what it will bring in order to avoid taxes and operating deficits (page 270). Sometimes they would have been better off if they had given it to the previous owner.

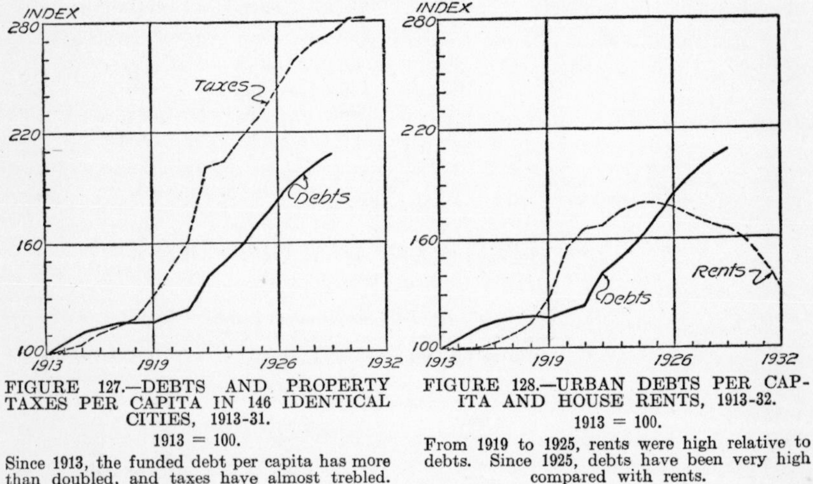

FIGURE 127.—DEBTS AND PROPERTY TAXES PER CAPITA IN 146 IDENTICAL CITIES, 1913-31.
1913 = 100.
Since 1913, the funded debt per capita has more than doubled, and taxes have almost trebled.

FIGURE 128.—URBAN DEBTS PER CAPITA AND HOUSE RENTS, 1913-32.
1913 = 100.
From 1919 to 1925, rents were high relative to debts. Since 1925, debts have been very high compared with rents.

In 1932, private debts were being reduced, largely by bankruptcy and to some extent by payments. The debt of the Federal government was rising rapidly. The Federal government lent large sums to banks, railroads, life insurance companies, and cities. Debts were being shifted from us individually to us collectively.

The business philosophy of the world is based on the pre-war increase in gold stocks faster than business grew. After each business decline, prices rose to a still higher level. If a business concern could only hold out until this rise occurred, it could usually pay. This is much less certain now that gold production is not keeping pace with the normal growth of business.

Urban debts and city taxes.—From 1913 to 1929, a reliable research agency reports that the net funded debt per capita of 146 identical cities doubled, and general property taxes per capita almost trebled (table 52 and figure 127).

Although rents declined 11 per cent from 1929 to 1931, the general property tax continued to increase. It is very difficult to reduce the budget because of debts and increased costs for charity. Many taxpayers are unable to pay, and so the tax burden grows heavier on those who can pay.

In New York City in 1931, interest and amortization of debts were one-third of the budget.[3] Many cities had a much higher debt service. The politician who promises to feed the unemployed and greatly

TABLE 52.—URBAN DEBTS AND PROPERTY TAXES PER CAPITA AND HOUSE RENTS, 1913–32

Year	Net funded debt per capita, 146 identical cities* 1913 = 100	General property taxes per capita, 146 identical cities* 1913 = 100	House rents, 8 large cities† 1914 = 100
1913	100	100	....
1914	....	....	100
1915	112	105	100
1916	115	111	103
1917	117	115	108
1918	117	119	114
1919	117	131	128
1920	....	....	155
1921	124	162	165
1922	141	201	167
1923	149	204	175
1924	159	217	179
1925	172	228	179
1926	185	244	177
1927	194	259	172
1928	202	268	168
1929	208	273	165
1930	....	281	159
1931	....	281	147
1932	....	....	126

* Data furnished through the courtesy of a large concern doing very reliable statistical research. The source for 1913–29 is Financial Statistics of Cities, United States Department of Commerce, Bureau of the Census. The figure for general property taxes for 1929 was adjusted for the exclusion of Chicago; the figures for 1930 and 1931 were estimated on the basis of data published by the Municipal Administration Service.

† Table 55, p. 267.

[3] New York Times, Oct. 23, 1932. Section 8, p. 1.

reduce taxes is promising the impossible. He may cut useful services but is not likely to reduce taxes.

As the legal tax limit is being approached in many of these cities, it is evident that they will have to seek revenue from sources that were formerly free from taxation.

House rents and city debts.—From 1913 to 1929, the net funded debt per capita of 146 identical cities doubled (table 52 and figure 128). In the same period, the index of house rents in 8 large cities rose 65 per cent. From 1913 to 1921, rents increased more rapidly than taxes, which, no doubt, stimulated building. Since that time, debts

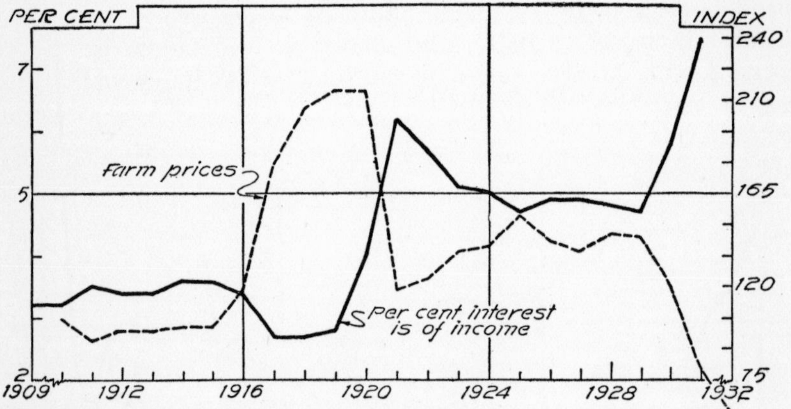

FIGURE 129.—FARM PRICES IN THE UNITED STATES AND THE PER CENT THAT INTEREST PAYMENTS ON FARM MORTGAGES ARE OF GROSS INCOME FROM FARM PRODUCTION, 1909-32.

When prices are high, the percentage of farm income taken by interest payments is small. When prices fall, the proportion of income transferred to the creditor rises very rapidly.

have risen more rapidly than rents, and this has made taxes very burdensome.

Farm prices and interest payments on farm mortgages.—The interest payments increased rather rapidly until 1920, and since that time have been comparatively stable.

Before the war, the annual interest payments on farm mortgages averaged a little above $225,000,000. In 1931, they were about twice this amount.

The gross income has also increased but has fluctuated very violently owing to weather and the value of gold. The gross income of American agriculture rose from a little over $6 billion before the war to almost $17 billion in 1919. In 1931, the income declined to less than $7 billion and in 1932 declined to $5 billion.

In 1909, the interest payments represented a little over 3 per cent of the gross farm income; by 1931, they represented 7.5 per cent of income. The percentage of farm income used for interest payments declines very slowly with rising prices but rises very sharply with falling prices (figure 129).

When prices rise, farmers retire at an earlier age; and there are more land sales at advancing prices, which result in an increase in the mortgage indebtedness. When prices fall, land sales stop, and it is impossible to reduce the old mortgages except through foreclosure or adjustment, which is a slow procedure.

Business failures.—From 1921 to 1932, there were 10,223 bank suspensions in the United States, or 33 per cent of the number of banks in 1921. Other banks avoided failure by merging with stronger banks. A multitude of failures would

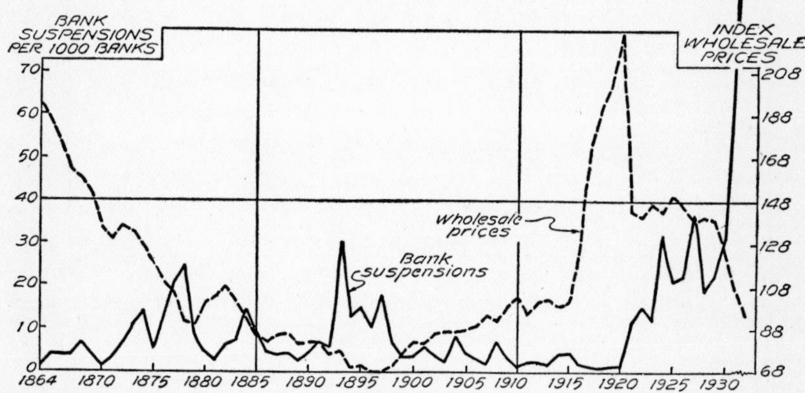

FIGURE 130.—NUMBER OF BANK SUSPENSIONS PER 1000 BANKS AND COMMODITY PRICES, 1864-1932.

Every drop in prices causes an increase in bank failures. The recent collapse of prices and increase in bank failures are the worst ever known.

have occurred in 1932 had it not been for government loans. Many others were kept open by obtaining agreements of depositors not to withdraw deposits. If deflation is checked, many of these may become solvent. If commodity prices do not rise it will be years before all the failures resulting from deflation will have occurred.

The relation of bank suspensions to changes in the price level is shown in figure 130. Every severe drop in commodity prices causes bank failures, but nothing like the catastrophes of the World War period has previously occurred.

Very few farmers who lose their property go through bankruptcy—

most of them make private settlement with their creditors, or lose the property through foreclosure. The number of farm bankruptcies is an indication of the date when liquidation was most severe. This was several years after the depression of 1920. It will probably be several years before the maximum number of failures due to the depression of 1929 is reached.

Nominal vs. real debts.—Considerable attention has been given to the difference between "nominal wages" and "real wages," that is, between money wages and the buying power of wages. Exactly the same distinction should be made between "nominal debts" and "real debts." A debt of $1000 contracted from 1921 to 1929 and paid in 1932 would have required the transfer of about 30 per cent more buying power to the lender than either the borrower or the lender anticipated. The real debt was increased 30 per cent because of the instability of the value of the money. It is sometimes said that the debt was unchanged because the weight of gold was unchanged. This is not the case. Gold is merely used as a medium of exchange. Usually neither party has any interest in gold. Both parties are interested in buying power.

Deflation places an artificial premium on savings and on delayed purchases, and an artificial repression is placed on business and on immediate purchases. False standards of business are established. The man who uses credit is penalized despite the fact that he may have used this credit in a very efficient manner. The Merchant of Venice was written about a period of deflation. Had it been a story of inflation, the profiteer instead of the money lender would probably have been the leading character.

Price level to which debts are adjusted.—When money is lent or loans paid, the transaction is in gold, but neither the borrower nor the lender is interested in gold. They are interested in buying power, usually in buying power for commodities. When gold doubles in value, the borrower has to return twice the commodities that he anticipated, besides paying interest, the value of which is also doubled. Justice calls for a return of the buying power which was borrowed. Creditors would profit by such an increase, but when the change is so drastic debtors are often overwhelmed and unable to pay anything.

Outstanding debts at any given time have been contracted at the various price levels of previous years. Since prices have never been stable, there is no price level that will establish justice between all debtors and creditors. A price level that will cause the least algebraic sum of injustice is the nearest to an honest price level.

In 1912, the total debts outstanding amounted to only 32 per cent of the debts of 1929. Had all these debts continued in existence, they would have represented less than a third of the total. It is evident that very few of the outstanding debts in 1929 were pre-war debts, and very few creditors were justly entitled to collect at a pre-war price level. Nearly all the debt of the Federal government was contracted during 1918 and 1919 at a time when prices were about double pre-war. Nearly all the striking increase in debts of states and cities came after 1921 when the price level was 40 to 50 per cent above pre-war. The price level was 40 to 50 per cent above pre-war for ten years, and for four preceding years it had been much higher.

The weighted average of the price level at the time the debts outstanding in 1929 were contracted was about 145. Since 1929, some debts have been paid and some new ones have been contracted. Others have been written off by bankruptcy, so that this average is reduced somewhat. New debts incurred in 1930 were at an average price level of 126; those in 1931, at a price level of 107. Debt payment has been slow, and the overwhelming amount of the outstanding debts was contracted at higher price levels. Probably the average indebtedness outstanding in 1932 was contracted at a price level between 135 and 140.

BIBLIOGRAPHY

Chase, S., The Case for Inflation, Harper's Magazine, Vol. 165, pp. 198-209. July 1932.

Cocker, W. H., Relief of Mortgagors in New Zealand. The Economic Record (Melbourne), Vol. VIII, No. 14, pp. 110-112. May 1932.

Edie, L. D., 1932's Legacy of Domestic Debts. American Bankers Association Journal, Vol. XXV, No. 2, pp. 19, 69-71. August 1932.

Hazlitt, H., Rubber Money and Iron Debts, The Nation, Vol. CXXXIII, No. 3468, pp. 691-3. Dec. 23, 1931.

Kemmerer, E. W., High Prices and Deflation. 1920.

Moulton, H. G., and Pasvolsky, L., War Debts and Prosperity. 1932.

Seligman, E. R. A., Currency Inflation and Public Debts. 1921.

Snyder, C., The Influence of the Interest Rate on the Business Cycle, American Economic Review, Vol. XV, No. 4, pp. 684-700. December 1925.

Stamp, J., The Financial Aftermath of War. 1932.

Warren, G. F., and Pearson, F. A., Effect of Declining Prices on Debts, Farm Economics No. 74, p. 1667. February 1932.

World Economic Survey, 1931-32. League of Nations II. Economic and Financial. 1932. II. A. 18, pp. 245-267. 1932.

the cost of such charity more than equals any possible savings made by reducing salaries and eliminating services. An appearance of saving is sometimes accomplished by going in debt.

In a period of depression, taxes do not yield the anticipated income; therefore new and heavier taxes have to be levied. For example, in January 1932, Congress had to face a situation where the income from federal taxes was not equal to the required interest, debt payments, soldiers' pensions, and other war costs. Had every function of the government been dropped, there would not have been enough revenue. Every function of government that was continued had to be paid for out of new revenue or else the government would run a deficit. The national debt increased, tax rates increased, and new taxes were levied.

In 1932, 29 per cent of the federal expenses were for interest and debts; 27 per cent for pensions and other veteran expenses; and 16 per cent for national defense. This left only 28 per cent for all functions of government other than war, past, present, and future.[1]

Farm taxes in various states.—Taxes in 1930 in most states were two to three times pre-war. Since prices of farm products in 1932 fell far below pre-war, taxes became a very serious burden.

Taxes and national income.—Before the war, taxes took 6 to 7 per cent of the national income. In 1919, they took 11 per cent. With the decline in income in 1921, taxes were 16 per cent of income. With the greater prosperity from 1923 to 1929, the percentage of the income taken by taxes was 10 to 11. War debts had to be paid, and roads and some other new services were provided. With normal business activity, the taxes in these years were not seriously burdensome. But when incomes declined in 1929 and public feeding became necessary, and new taxes had to be levied to make up for the low yields of old taxes, the tax problem became serious. In 1931, taxes probably took nearly a fifth of the national income.

Taxes and gross farm income.—Before the war, about 4 per cent of the gross farm income went for taxes. This dropped to a little more than 2 per cent in 1919 and ranged from 6 to 7 per cent before the Panic of 1929 (figure 133).

Relation of taxes to farm income.—On 3463 farms in New York state for the period 1913 to 1916, the receipts less business expenses, other than taxes, amounted to $1305 per farm.[2] Land taxes were $73,

[1] New York Herald-Tribune, Sunday, Aug. 14, 1932.

[2] Mereness, E. H., Taxes on Farm Real Estate in New York, A Report to the New York State Tax Commission for the Revision of the Tax Laws, p. 6, 1932.

or 5.6 per cent of the income. This left $1232 to reimburse the farmer for his year's labor, for the labor of his family, and for the use of a capital of $11,796. This was available for payment of interest, debts, and living expenses.

On 2985 farms in New York state for the period 1925-30, the receipts less business expenditures other than taxes amounted to $1720 per farm. Land taxes were $173, or 10 per cent of the income. There remained $1547 to reimburse the farmer for his year's labor, for the labor of his family, and for the use of a capital of $15,010, a part of which was borrowed. This was available for interest, debts, and living expenses.

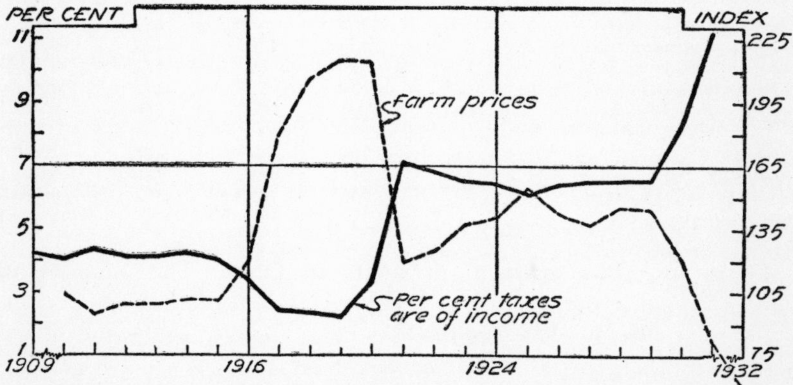

FIGURE 133.—FARM PRICES AND THE PERCENTAGE THAT TAXES ARE OF GROSS FARM INCOME IN THE UNITED STATES, 1909-32.

When farm prices are low, taxes represent a high proportion of gross farm income. When prices are high, taxes are easy to pay because they are a small proportion of gross income.

On a number of successful farms in New York state on which cost accounts were kept, the income available for the payment of the farmer's time, for interest, and taxes amounted to $1514 in 1914; of this amount, taxes were $111 or 7.3 per cent. In 1919, the income was $3394, of which taxes took only 4.6 per cent. In 1931, after paying business expenses there was left $59 to pay for his labor, to pay taxes of $281, and to pay interest on his capital. If there had been no taxes, income would have declined from $3394 to $59. The tax problem is primarily a problem of income. Merely reducing taxes does not solve it.

Amount of farm products required to pay taxes.—In 1914, 90 bushels of corn would have paid the taxes on an average Ohio farm of 91.6 acres. In 1932, it would have required 430 bushels, because taxes had risen and prices had fallen (table 53).

In 1914, it would have required 1333 pounds of hogs to pay the taxes on an Iowa farm of 156.8 acres. In 1932, it would have required 6076 pounds to pay the taxes.

TABLE 53.—AMOUNT OF FARM PRODUCE AT FEBRUARY FARM PRICES REQUIRED TO PAY TAXES ON AVERAGE FARMS

	Amount required			Index, 1914 = 100	
	1914	1930	1932 if taxes are same as in 1930	1930	1932
Ohio, bushels of corn	90	168	430	187	478
Indiana, dozens of eggs	370	453	1207	122	326
Illinois, bushels of corn	126	220	601	175	477
Minnesota, bushels of wheat	78	135	251	173	322
Iowa, pounds of hogs	1333	2004	6076	150	456
North Dakota, bushels of wheat	145	185	334	128	230
Oklahoma, pounds of cotton	440	571	1504	130	342
Texas, pounds of cotton	397	645	1623	162	409

Taxes in terms of farm products in Ohio.—The quantity of farm products required to pay taxes in Ohio increased about four times from 1880 to 1932 (figure 134). The increase was rapid in the period of falling prices which ended about 1896. When prices rose, taxes rose less rapidly and took a smaller quantity of farm products. This was strikingly true during the World War period. Prices rose so much more rapidly than taxes, that taxes took a smaller quantity of farm products than at any other time since 1881. With deflation, taxes rose and prices fell so that the quantity of farm products required to pay taxes more than doubled. In 1932, the quantity of farm products required to pay taxes was about three times as much as for the five years before the war.

In a period of declining prices, from 1880 to 1896, farm prices declined 2 per cent per year, but taxes declined little. In a period of rising prices from 1897 to 1913, farm prices rose more than 3 per cent per year. Taxes rose more slowly so that they took a declining proportion of farm products.

Farm taxes and rates of growth.—The American system of farm taxation is a capital levy. The common method is to have the farm, and often personal property, appraised, and to require that taxes paid be a certain percentage of this sum. This system gives no attention to income. It worked fairly satisfactorily when all the taxpayers held the same kind of property, because relative values of property were then related to income. It works very poorly when the same rate is levied on a grocery store, a young animal, an orchard, and growing timber. In some industries an investment of $100 brings quick returns, but an investment of $100 in calves usually brings no return for two years and calls for additional outlays.

To grow an apple orchard requires a considerable number of years of expense and consequently the orchard has a high investment value before any return occurs. The growth of timber is even slower. On the Cornell University farm woodlots, which contain trees of all ages, the annual growth was 1.8 per cent of the volume of timber on hand at the beginning of the year.

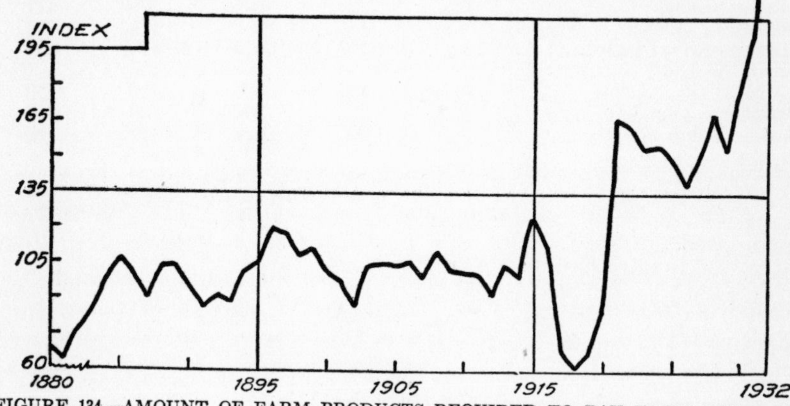

FIGURE 134.—AMOUNT OF FARM PRODUCTS REQUIRED TO PAY FARM TAXES IN OHIO, 1880-1932.
1910-14 = 100.
In 1918, a smaller quantity of farm products was required to pay taxes than in any previous year since 1881. In 1932, the amount was the highest in history.

Manifestly, a tax rate of 1.8 per cent would take all the new growth and leave nothing to pay for the care of the woodlot. Farms in this vicinity are often taxed as high a percentage as this. The only way for a farmer to make a profit out of such a situation is to sell the lumber and all the other salable material and then sell the stump lot, if he can find a buyer.

A century of taxes in New York.—Taxes on 6 New York state farms in 1825 averaged $2.97 per farm. A century later, they averaged $129.35, or increased 44 times (table 54).

On these farms, 3 bushels of wheat were required to pay taxes in 1825, but 104 bushels were required a century later. About 6 days of labor at current wages, in addition to some road work, were required to pay taxes in 1825. One hundred years later, 37 days' work at current wages was required.

The taxes were low in 1825, but the services also were low. A farmer had to mow his roadside and care for his road. If he made any considerable trip, he paid tolls on roads and bridges. Roads were impassable much of the time.

Only a few months of very inferior schooling were available at public expense. High school and college education were not provided for by taxation. There was no rural mail delivery or parcel post; no county agricultural agents; no free state or federal agricultural bulletins; no county or state health service; no hospital; no state troopers. The farmers supported their own cooperative protective associations for the chasing of horse thieves. The feeble-minded, mildly insane, and

TABLE 54.—AVERAGE TAXES ON 6 NEW YORK FARMS, 1825 and 1925*

	1825	1925
Average assessed value	$624	$4480
Average area, acres	128	117
Taxes per farm	$ 2.97	$ 129.35
Taxes per acre	$ 0.02	$ 1.11
Bushels of wheat required to pay taxes	3	104
Days' labor at farm wages required to pay taxes	6	37

* Genung, A. B., What 100 Years Have Done for Farm Taxes, Farm Economics No. 25, p. 285, June 1925.

paupers were taken care of mostly by relatives. The farmers paid little in taxes and received little in return.

There was comparatively little complaint of increased taxes until the price level collapsed and prevented normal earnings. The real difficulty is the collapse in earnings. Taxes are merely one of the forms in which this expresses itself. Inability to pay debts and high prices of purchased goods are other forms.

The progress of civilization requires a steady increase in the number of services performed at public expense. There can be no more than a temporary slowing up of this movement.

It involves no difficulty so long as the price level is stable, but a decline in prices reduces the ability to pay taxes without the possibility of a corresponding decrease in these costs.

Relation of rent and taxes in England.—In England, taxes are not levied on the value of the property but on the rent received or on the rental value.[3] A study of rent and taxes on about 23,000 acres of farm land shows that, in 1908, taxes were £2020, or 13.6 per cent of the rent, £14,801. In 1923, taxes took more than 50 per cent of the rent.

City property taxes and house rents.—From pre-war to 1931, the index numbers of general property taxes per capita rose from 100 to 281 (table 52, page 239). In the same period of time, house rents rose from 100 to 147 (figure 135). The proportion of the rent

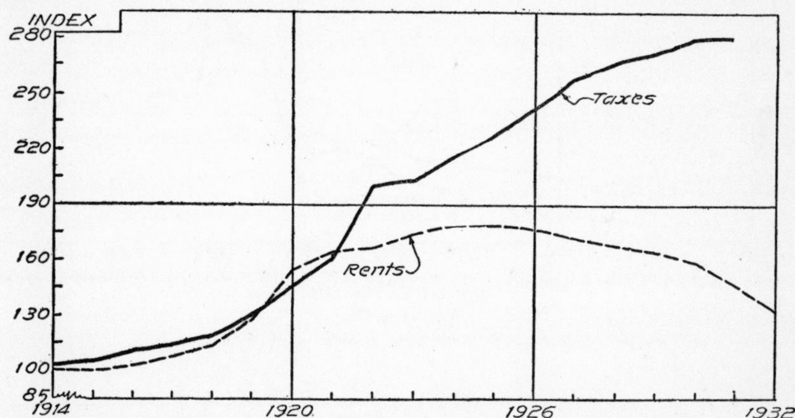

FIGURE 135.—GENERAL PROPERTY TAXES PER CAPITA IN 146 IDENTICAL CITIES AND HOUSE RENTS IN 8 LARGE CITIES, 1914-32.
Pre-war = 100.
Since 1921, general property taxes per capita have risen relative to rents.

taken by taxes increased rather gradually; by 1931 the proportion of rent going to taxes was almost double that of 1913.

Taxes on railroads.—Taxes on railroads as well as taxes on farms are made burdensome by deflation. Before the war, taxes were about 4 per cent of gross earnings. In 1931, they were 7 per cent. Both figures are the same as for farms (page 247).

Taxes in the Civil War and World War periods.—When pre-war is 100, the state and local taxes on real estate per capita in New York state in 1873 amounted to 266. These were reduced to an index of 214 in 1882, which was the lowest point reached (figure 137). In the World War period, total state and local taxes per capita reached an index of 257 in 1929.

[3] Orwin, C. S., and Kersey, H. W., Estate Accounts, pp. 40-42, 1926. The rental and taxes were read from charts.

The Civil War experience may give some indication of the results to be expected from the strenuous efforts to reduce taxes. Those who expect striking results should remember that the debts must be paid

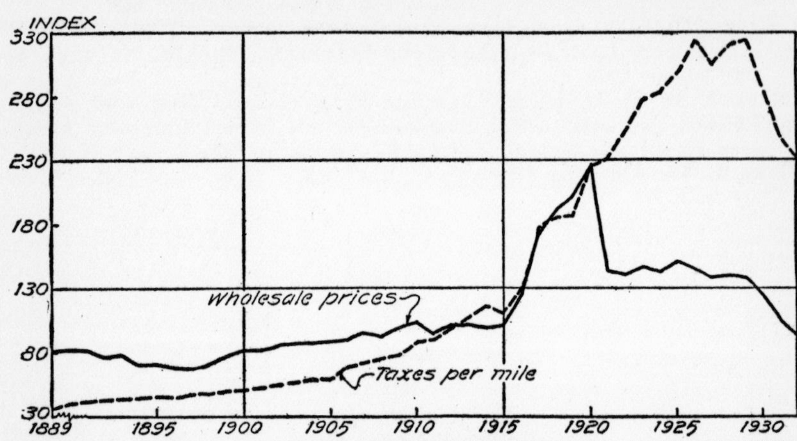

FIGURE 136.—INDEX NUMBERS OF WHOLESALE PRICES AND RAILROAD TAXES PER MILE, 1889-1932.

1910-14 = 100.

Railroad taxes per mile have risen relative to commodity prices.

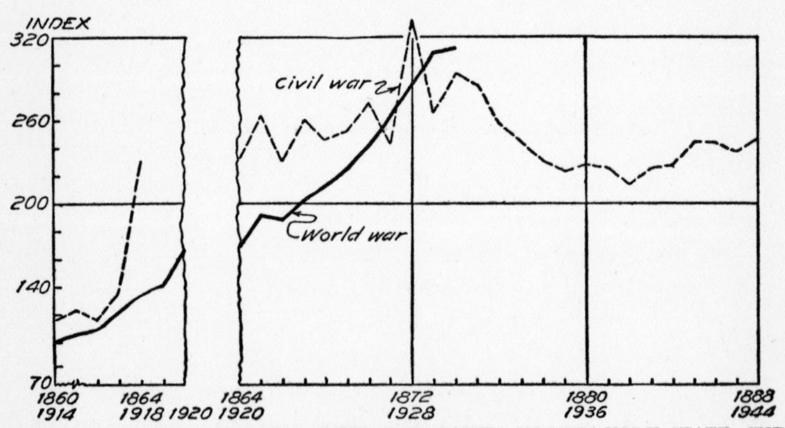

FIGURE 137.—STATE AND LOCAL TAXES PER CAPITA IN NEW YORK STATE, CIVIL WAR AND WORLD WAR PERIODS.

Pre-war = 100.

In both cases, the maximum taxes were reached about the time of the financial crash. Only a limited decline occurred after the Civil War.

and the poor must be fed. There is only one way to make taxes easy to pay, and that is to restore the price level so that the unemployed can find work and the taxpayer can have income.

BIBLIOGRAPHY

ALLIN, B. W., JACKSON, D., and WESTON, J. L., Farm Real Estate Taxes, 1913-1930, New England States. United States Department of Agriculture, Bureau of Agricultural Economics, Mimeograph Report. September 1932.

ENGLUND, E., Adjustments Necessary in Taxation in view of the possibility of a lower price level. Journal of Farm Economics, Vol. XIV, No. 1, pp. 94-106. January 1932.

KENDRICK, M. S., An Index Number of Farm Taxes in New York, and Its Relation to Various Other Economic Factors, Cornell University Agricultural Experiment Station, Bulletin 467. December 1926.

STAMP, J., The Financial Aftermath of War. 1932.

CHAPTER XV

PRICES OF FARM LANDS

What is a farm?—A farm includes buildings, fences, roads, tile drains, and water supply. It may include irrigation systems, leveling, stones picked, weeds eliminated, injurious animals such as prairie-dogs eliminated. It includes crops in many stages of production, orchards of varying ages, clover, timothy, and alfalfa fields, lands that are plowed but not yet planted. It includes roots of previous crops and farm manures previously applied. Some soils are so deficient in lime and other elements that they have to be heavily fertilized before they are ready to produce good crops and must be continually treated. The fields then carry varying amounts of residual applications. By these treatments, the various bacteria, earthworms, and other forms of life that are favorable for crops are maintained. The farm also includes its interest in schools, roads, and drainage and irrigation systems that have been paid for out of previous income just as the farmer's house has been paid for out of previous income.

No segregation of the various elements that make up the farms in the United States has ever been made. Farmers sell all these things as a unit. A farm is not land. It is a living thing—a biological manufacturing plant including many kinds of equipment, and numerous expenditures for maintaining the continuity of production. The Census Bureau obtains the value of the farm and the value of the buildings. No data have been obtained on the value of other improvements. The mistake has been made of subtracting the value of the buildings from the value of the farm and calling the remainder "land." This difference is commonly used as an indication of what the farm is worth independently of the labor and expenditures made by the farmer.

The error is very great. A growing wheat crop has required much labor, seed, and possibly fertilizer. The expenditures of starting the crop are in most regions from 10 to 30 per cent of the value of the land. A stand of growing clover or alfalfa has cost a large amount for labor and seed. A drainage system often amounts to 10 to 50 per cent of the value of the land. When wells, windmills, orchards and innumerable other things are included, it will be observed that what is called farm land includes an endless variety of things largely created by man. As science progresses, farms are less and less the creation of Providence, and more and more man-made.

How great these items are is illustrated by the real value of land that does not have them. In regions where farms sell at $100 per acre, a piece of land that lacks growing crops, fall plowing, grass seeding, fences, drains, water supply, buildings, often has no real value as a farm although it may have a sale price. One who buys such a piece of land and makes a farm of it and keeps a record of his expenditures will often find that he has spent more than $100 per acre and has in addition had to wait many years to establish a "going concern." Such a piece of land may have a value, however, if attached to a farm that is already in operation.

Competition for farm lands.—Farm land has a value to prospective operators. In some regions it has a value to landlords, and at some periods it has a value because of expected appreciation. In the middle west, the prices of corn and wheat lands were often the result of competition by persons who were interested for each of these reasons. In this region, the system of renting is so simple that land is looked upon as an investment by persons who do not care to farm. Until 1920, these lands had always advanced in price so that landlords were willing to look to an advance in price to supplement the low return from rents. The willingness of investors to purchase farms which they did not care to operate always provided a ready market for farm land. With declining prices investors disappeared, and the difficulties of selling were accentuated.

In the United States, the general tendency is for large land holdings to be broken up; only occasionally is there any effort to combine small holdings into large holdings. Land is a small investment. The competition for land by persons who expect to operate it, and in some regions the added competition by persons who look on land as a place to invest small savings, keeps the price of land too high to be attractive to wealthy persons. They cannot obtain the income that persons of moderate means obtain as a result of giving personal supervision to the operations.

Prices of good and poor farm land.—When profits in farming increase, a portion of the increase is reflected in land prices, but only a portion. The first effect is a rapid increase in wages. Later, a portion goes to land prices. When a farmer prospers, he shares his prosperity with the hired man, country doctor, school teacher, banker, and merchant, and he raises his own standard of living. Only a portion is left to raise land prices.

When prices rise, farm wages advance more rapidly than city wages; and when prices decline, fall more promptly. Over long periods of time, farm and city wages may be out of adjustment. During the 17 years from 1897 to 1913, prices of farm products advanced more rapidly than the general price level and farm wages rose more rapidly than city wages.

Adjoining townships are often very different in productiveness. After a century of farming, these differences are not fully reflected in land prices. A portion of the differences is borne by farm operators, hired men, school teachers, and doctors. The wages paid to equally good men are higher in the more productive districts. There is a tendency for hired men to be scarce in the poorer region, but those who are hired there receive lower wages than they could get in good regions. The land prices in the better districts are higher, but not enough higher to cover all the differences. The operator of a good farm also makes a higher labor income for himself.

The land prices in a poor township in New York averaged $38 per acre, and the labor income $275. In a good township in the same county, the land values were $70, and labor incomes $524. Tenants made more than twice as much in the good townships as in the adjoining poorer ones. The difference in price of land per acre was $32. The difference would have had to be $80 an acre to make the farmers' labor incomes equal.[1] If the hired men, school teachers, and others, had been paid equally, a much greater difference would have been left for land prices to absorb.

The same principle has been found to hold in successive years for many different regions. Such differences last permanently. If comparison is made between two regions settled by the same people but unequally good for farming, it is doubtful whether more than half of the inequalities are capitalized in land prices.

Seventy-five years ago, men were willing to work two days for a bushel of wheat. They could use very poor land. Before the World War, about two bushels of wheat were required to pay a day's wages. In 1923, it required about three bushels. Where it is possible to use machinery on large tracts, poor land may sometimes be worked with

[1] Warren, G. F., and Livermore, K. C., An Agricultural Survey, Townships of Ithaca, Dryden, Danby, and Lansing, Tompkins County, N. Y., Cornell University Agricultural Experiment Station Bulletin 295, pp. 399, 429, 434, 1911.

sufficient profit, so that this land has risen in price, but much rough land that was once farmed is now uncultivated.

Some of the costs of farm operations are interest, taxes, fertilizer, labor, fencing, machinery, and seeds. Changes in the relative costs of these items affect different classes of land differently. During the past fifty years, labor advanced more than the other factors. This resulted in a decline in prices of lands on which labor could not be used effectively, at the same time that better lands rose in price.

Marginal lands.—Land values are due in part to incomes derived from operation and in part to expected possibilities of sale. Farm lands are not held out of use when it would pay to operate them. Lands that cannot be profitably used still have a market value and pay taxes. The price of such land is based on the expectation that it may later be possible to sell it at a profit. A large part of the price of cheap land is based on the hope of a sale rather than on productivity. For this reason it is usually difficult to pay for lands that are near the margin by farming them. The case is similar to a useless horse. Nearly every horse has a trading value although he may be a detriment to the person who keeps him.

Some persons define marginal land in such a way as to include any lands that are not in use. A better definition would be land that would not be farmed if the operator had known the facts. Owing to mistakes in judgment and accidents of being stranded on such lands, a large amount of sub-marginal land is always in use. There is a constant movement of new settlers to regions that have such lands. They come in with some money and much optimism. They may operate such farms and then leave. Sometimes they do not leave until their funds are gone.

Often a farm composed in part of good land and in part of sub-marginal land is all operated, the income from the good land being sufficient to disguise the loss on the poor land.

In some of the eastern states a considerable amount of land is sub-marginal except for the unexhausted improvements. On such lands, improvements are rarely made, but so long as the present houses and barns stand, the farms are used. As the fences, houses, and barns deteriorate, the land ceases to be operated.

Since sub-marginal land has a sale value based on hope, taxes are paid on it although the land itself cannot pay them.

Land values following the Napoleonic War period.—When the prices of farm products rise, land values normally follow, but prices of land lag behind other prices and usually do not reflect the full increase.

As a result of financial inflation, the average value of land in fourteen counties in Pennsylvania rose from \$53 per acre in 1809 to \$111 after the War of 1812. Deflation reduced the prices to \$38 in 1819.[2] In the words of Gouge, "Farms rose in price from fifty to a hundred per cent, and sank again as rapidly as they had risen. Thousands were reduced to poverty and a few rose to wealth on the ruin of their neighbors."[3]

Rents secured from a farm in Norfolk, England, rose from £80 in 1712 to £200 before the Napoleonic Wars. After the Napoleonic Wars the currency was inflated and there were high tariffs on food. Rents

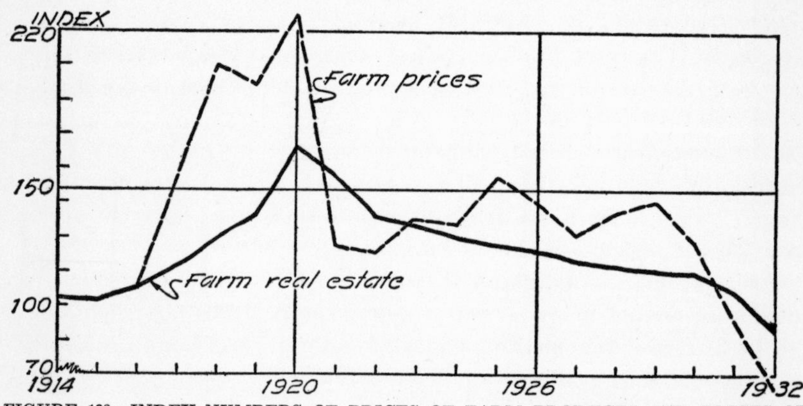

FIGURE 138.—INDEX NUMBERS OF PRICES OF FARM PRODUCTS AND PRICES OF FARM LAND IN THE UNITED STATES, 1914-32.

Pre-war = 100.

With rising commodity prices, land values rose. Conversely, with falling prices they fell. Land values move more slowly than farm prices, and do not fully reflect changes in profits.

rose to £700.[4] With deflation and final elimination of the tariff on food, rents declined, and one hundred years later this farm rented for £160.

Prices of farm land in the World War period.—From 1916 to 1920, prices paid to farmers rose very rapidly to more than double pre-war. Many economists, bankers, and business men believed such prices were to continue. Had they continued, they would have justified prices of farm land much higher than prevailed. The maximum price

[2] Gouge, W. M., A Short History of Paper Money and Banking, Chap. XIII, p. 35, 1835.

[3] Gouge, W. M., An Inquiry into the Principles of American Banking, Chap. VI, p. 14, 1833.

[4] Thompson, R. J., An Inquiry into the Rent of Agricultural Lands in England and Wales During the Nineteenth Century, Jour. Roy. Stat. Soc., Vol. LXX, Part IV, 1907.

of farm land was reached in 1920, when land prices averaged 70 per cent above pre-war. In 1921, prices of farm products fell almost to the pre-war level. During the high-price period, wages, taxes, freight rates, and prices of machinery and supplies rose. These declined very slowly. Had such conditions continued, farm buildings, fences, and land would have lost practically all their value. During the next seven years, prices of farm products were about 40 to 50 per cent above pre-war. Prices of farm land were gradually approaching the pre-war level when the Panic of 1929 occurred.

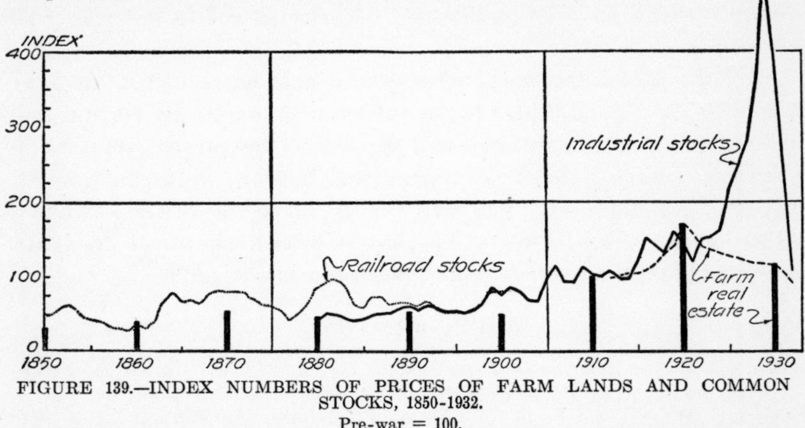

FIGURE 139.—INDEX NUMBERS OF PRICES OF FARM LANDS AND COMMON STOCKS, 1850-1932.

Pre-war = 100.

There is considerable similarity in prices except for the stock market boom of 1929.

Prices of land always lag a number of years behind profits in farming. When prices are rising, the conditions are better than the index numbers indicate because it is easy to sell property. When commodity prices are falling, conditions are worse than the figures indicate because quoted prices are above the market and it is very difficult to make sales.

Prices of farm lands and common stocks.—Prices of common stocks and the average value of farms per acre are shown in figure 139. There is considerable similarity except for the wild boom in the stock market after the World War. Farm land is more seriously depressed by falling prices because of the lag in distributing charges, which are city income (page 186).

Newspapers are edited by city-minded persons. They are quick to note the mote in the farmer's eye. There was endless criticism of farmers because the prices of farm land rose in 1920. These same newspapers noted nothing wrong with the stock market in 1928. In 1932, the stock market fell as low as farm land.

If prices paid to farmers continue below pre-war levels, farm land will fall far below pre-war, because costs cannot be reduced to pre-war.

Prospective prices of farm land.—Nominal prices of farm land in 1932 were higher than actual prices, because few sales could be made at the nominal prices. For example, farm land in Iowa was reported as worth 80 per cent of pre-war prices in the spring of 1932, but relatively few sales could be made at this figure. The average for the United States was reported at 89 per cent of pre-war. To sell a farm in 1932 as readily as it could have been sold before the war probably would have required that the price be cut to less than half of pre-war.

If all the gold-using world returns to a gold basis, and if the price of gold in the United States is not raised, it is practically certain that nominal prices of farm land will go below the present quotations. Ultimately, large numbers of farms will have to be taken over by creditors, and these creditors will finally place the prices at such a point that sales can be made. The lowest forced sale prices are likely to occur before the quoted figures reach the lowest point.

BIBLIOGRAPHY

Chambers, C. R., Relation of Land Income to Land Value. United States Department of Agriculture. Department Bulletin 1224. May 1924.

Thrun, F. M., A Local Farm Real Estate Price Index. Agricultural Experiment Station, Michigan, Technical Bulletin 96. March 1929.

Wiecking, E. H., and Stauber, B. R., The Farm Real Estate Situation, 1929-30. United States Department of Agriculture Circular 150. November 1930.

CHAPTER XVI

CITY REAL ESTATE

Deflation and rents.—Rents lag behind the movement of prices. From pre-war to 1920, prices in the United States more than doubled, but rents in eight large cities rose only 55 per cent and in smaller cities only 46 per cent. The deflation of 1920 caused a large amount

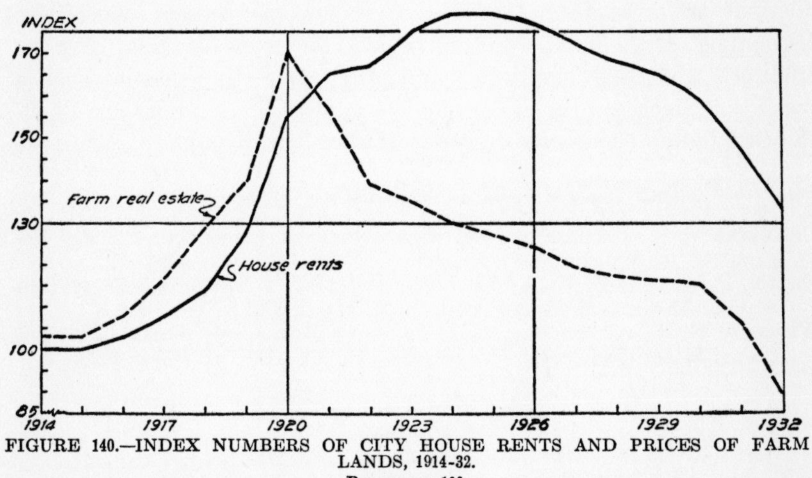

FIGURE 140.—INDEX NUMBERS OF CITY HOUSE RENTS AND PRICES OF FARM LANDS, 1914-32.

Pre-war = 100.

Farm lands reached a peak in 1920. Rents reached a peak 5 years later. Prices of city real estate reached a peak at a still later date. Cheap food helped to raise the city demand for homes.

of unemployment for a short time but was not prolonged because debts had not risen seriously.

Rents in eight large cities and prices of farm land are shown in figure 140. Prices of farm land reached their peak in 1920, but rents reached theirs in 1924 and 1925. When prices rise, wages rise less rapidly. Laborers, therefore, economize on houses, so that city real estate prices are depressed or do not rise so quickly as prices of farm land.

Prices of food and rents are shown in figure 141. After the depression of 1920, there was a shortage of houses due to reduced building during the war period. Farmers then received very little for food because distributing charges remained high. These charges remained as receipts to persons in cities. The net payment by cities for food is

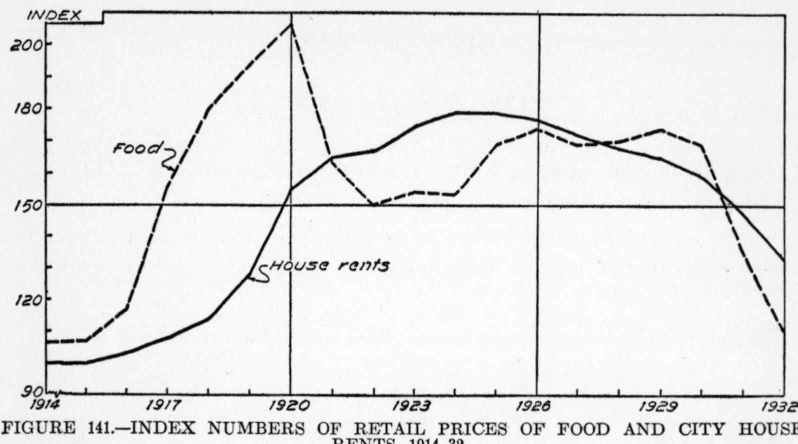

FIGURE 141.—INDEX NUMBERS OF RETAIL PRICES OF FOOD AND CITY HOUSE RENTS, 1914-32.

Pre-war = 100.

When prices rise, the prices of foods rise faster than wages, therefore rents rise slowly and building is checked. Deflation reduces the cost of food and rents rise.

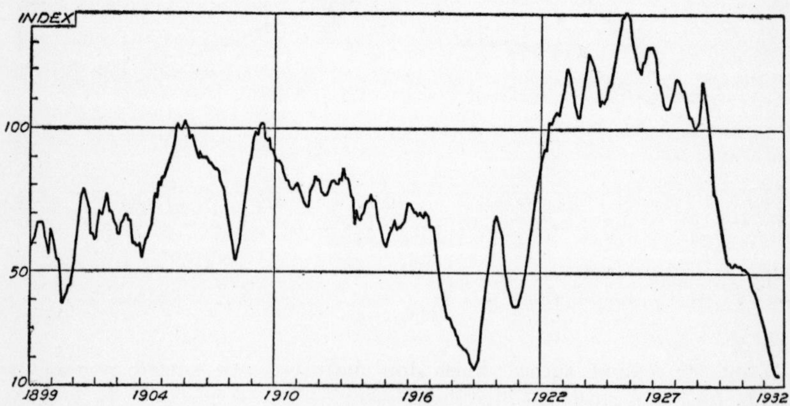

FIGURE 142.—MONTHLY VOLUME OF BUILDING CONSTRUCTION IN THE UNITED STATES, 1899-1932.

1926-30 = 100.

Before the war, building construction was increasing at the average rate of 3.40 per cent per year, about the same as the increase in total basic production. A peak of construction occurred about 1925.

what the farmer gets, not the retail price. After 1920, farmers were feeding the city population at abnormally low prices at a time when there was a shortage of houses. This resulted in a high demand for houses at a time when the supply was short.

The same situation developed following the Civil War. Prices reached a peak in 1864, but rents reached their peak in 1869 and continued high until 1873 (figure 144).

Volume of building.—A physical measure of the quantity of building in the United States, including residential and non-residential building, is shown in figure 142. Adjustments were made to eliminate changes in construction costs and seasonal variation so that the index number represents the physical amount of building.[1]

From 1899 to 1914, building increased at the average rate of 3.40 per cent per year.[2] Building construction is sensitive to business conditions and is extremely variable.

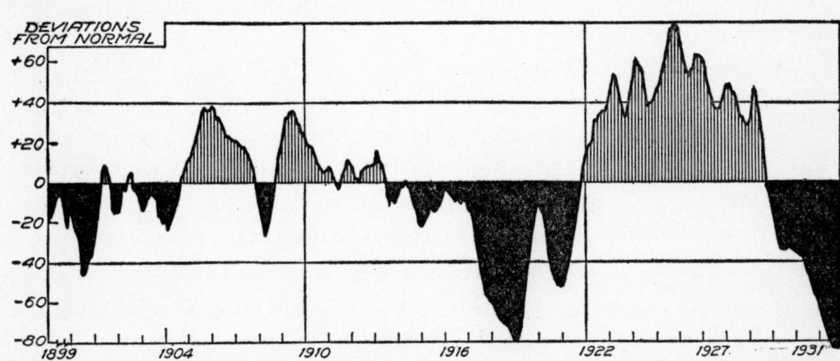

FIGURE 143.—INDEX NUMBERS OF THE VOLUME OF BUILDING PERMITS IN THE UNITED STATES COMPARED WITH NORMAL, 1899-1932.
1926-30 = 100.
The great deficit in building during the war period was made up and some over-building occurred from 1922 to 1929. Since then, this over-building has been offset by reduced building.

During the war, construction was very low, particularly in 1918. There was a serious shortage of buildings in 1919, and construction began but was temporarily interrupted by the Panic of 1920. Since little building had been done and since prices of building had not risen strikingly, the debt burden on buildings was low.[3]

[1] A reliable research agency, which does not care to be quoted, studied the records for various cities and obtained the daily average value of building permits. These were adjusted for changes in construction costs, corrected for seasonal variation, and expressed in terms of a six months' moving average, entered on the sixth month so as to reflect the relative amounts of construction in progress (figure 142).

The data were also expressed as deviations from a straight-line trend (figure 143).

The original data were divided by population to get the building construction per capita (figure 146).

[2] $y = 1.8676x + 55.00$.

[3] Warren, G. F., and Pearson, F. A., Farm Economics, pp. 80, 611, 1026, 1179, 1428, 1466, 1549, 1668; The Agricultural Situation, pp. 270-3, August 1924.

There was a similar situation when prices first dropped after the Civil War. In both cases, this was due to the fact that, when prices are rising rapidly, wages rise less rapidly and a higher proportion of the budget is expended for food; therefore, the demand for buildings is reduced. This was accentuated by taking many men away from homes to the army. When they returned, many of them married and desired homes at once.

Shortage of buildings, the relatively small indebtedness, and cheap food made a strong demand for construction after the depression of 1920.

Building was above normal from 1922 to 1928. The total building more than made up the deficit of the war period for cities, but farm construction was low.

A period of low construction began in 1929, and by 1932 the shortage probably made up for the surplus of the previous years. There was, however, a decided apparent surplus. This appearance of surplus will continue until employment is general. The population will then again use its normal housing facilities, the apparent surplus will suddenly disappear, and the real shortage will be evident. Six years after the Panic of 1873, this situation occurred. In 1873, there was an over-supply. Cessation of building turned this into a shortage, but there appeared to be a surplus until the bankrupt properties were largely disposed of.

Were it not for the heavy indebtedness incurred when prices were higher, active business would have developed in 1932. But little construction is probable until bankrupt properties are disposed of, which requires several years.

During a period when bankrupt properties are being liquidated, they will always be offered at less than the cost to build, regardless of what that cost may be. This prevents active building and causes unemployment. This, in turn, causes crowding, and results in vacant properties and "for rent" signs. Casual observation attributes this to over-production. If several more years are required for debt liquidation, there will be a shortage of buildings and another period of active construction will occur. If the general price level should then be approximately at pre-war, the intrinsic values of buildings after the liquidation is over will be approximately pre-war, but may be somewhat reduced because of public indebtedness.

During the period of liquidation, properties will be sold at much less than pre-war prices.

Effects of declining costs on apparent surplus of houses. If we were in an ideal state of economic equilibrium with no more houses than we needed, and no over- or under-production of anything else, and if the costs of building should decline 20 per cent, a panic would ensue and during the panic there would be the appearance of great over-building.

In a perfect situation there would be tenants who were thinking of buying or building, others who had bought homes on contract with payments all the way from a few dollars to a high percentage of the value of the property. There would be sales between relatives with little or no cash payment. Builders would have houses in all stages of construction and would have made sales with various down payments. Banks and lumber dealers would be financing these builders. Bankers and mortgage companies would have mortgages representing various percentages of the value of the property.

The next real customer is the man who is thinking of buying a home. If costs of building decline, he will see his neighbors who have made small payments lose their equities, and the properties anxiously seeking buyers. Such a warning discourages most prospective buyers. Builders, credit agencies, and home owners with small equities must sell. In such a situation, although costs of building decline only 20 per cent, it might be necessary to offer properties at twice this reduction. This in turn would wipe out the equities of still other persons and force more properties on the market. Most building would stop. This would throw men out of work. Since building is one of the great basic industries, all kinds of industrial establishments would have to discharge workmen. These unemployed people use less home room in such a period, and vacant properties would appear. The popular explanation would be over-production. This discussion began with the assumption of perfect equilibrium except that costs of new construction dropped.

If in such a period a way were found to reduce building costs still further, it would make the matter much worse, because properties would drop still further in value, persons with higher equities would be wiped out, and more properties would be thrown on the market. There is only one remedy for declining prices, that is, a restoration of prices.

A business depression that is caused by a drop in commodity prices requires a complete readjustment of equities before business can start again. Since the panic is a period of adjustment of equities, it is not cured by reducing costs, but by transferring property from one group of people to another. Anything that increases the drop in prices increases the trouble.

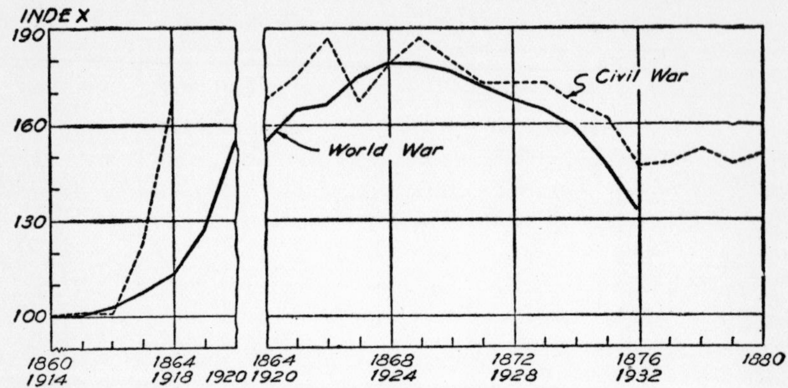

FIGURE 144.—RENTS IN FIVE LARGE CITIES IN THE CIVIL WAR PERIOD AND IN EIGHT LARGE CITIES IN THE WORLD WAR PERIOD.

In each case, pre-war is 100.

Thus far the experiences of the Civil War have been repeated.

After readjustments have been made, many properties will be in the hands of new owners who have acquired them at bargain prices, and can therefore operate very cheaply. This is one way of reducing costs.

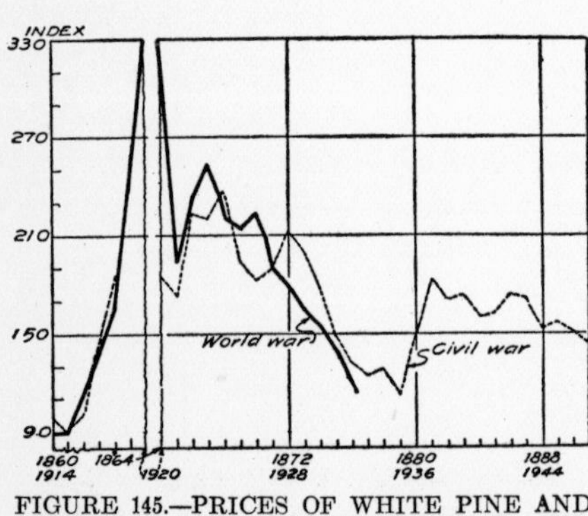

FIGURE 145.—PRICES OF WHITE PINE AND BRICK FOR THE CIVIL WAR PERIOD, AND OF YELLOW PINE AND BRICK FOR THE WORLD WAR PERIOD.

In each case, pre-war is 100.

The course of prices is similar in the two war periods but is more violent this time. If the similarity continues, prices will rise in 1936.

Rents, World War and Civil War periods.—In both war periods, rents rose less rapidly than prices but continued to rise several years after deflation began. The course of rents was much the same after each war, not because the wars were similar but because the amounts of inflation and deflation were similar (figure 144).

Prices of pine and brick.—The home owner's security is in the value of a home. If commodity prices fall so that the home can be built for 20 per cent less than he paid, his equity is gone unless he paid more than 20 per cent down. But when all the bankrupt properties are thrown on the market, buyers disappear as if by magic, and

TABLE 55.—RENTS IN LARGE AND SMALL CITIES IN THE UNITED STATES, 1860–80 AND 1914–32

Civil War*		World War†		
Year	Five large cities 1860 = 100	Year	Eight large cities 1914 = 100	Ten lesser cities 1914 = 100
1860	100	1914	100	100
1861	101	1915	100	97
1862	101	1916	103	95
1863	123	1917	108	94
1864	168	1918	114	111
1865	175	1919	128	128
1866	187			
1867	167	1920	155	146
1868	179	1921	165	151
1869	187	1922	167	149
		1923	175	149
1870	180	1924	179	147
1871	173	1925	179	146
1872	173	1926	177	145
1873	173	1927	172	140
1874	166	1928	168	133
1875	162	1929	165	130
1876	147			
1877	148	1930	159	125
1878	152	1931	147	118
1879	148	1932	126	103
1880	151			

* The rents for 5 large cities from 1860 to 1880 include Boston, Philadelphia, Cincinnati, Louisville, and St. Louis. Weeks, J. D., Report on the Average Retail Price of Necessaries of Life in the United States. Report on the Statistics of Wages in Manufacturing Industries, Tenth Census of the United States, Census Office, Department of the Interior, Vol. 20, pp. 104–107, 1886.

† Cost of Living, Monthly Labor Review, United States Bureau of Labor Statistics, Vol. 28, No. 2, p. 178, February 1929, and later numbers. The rents for 8 large cities from 1914–1928 include Baltimore, Boston, Buffalo, Chicago, Cleveland, Detroit, New York, and Philadelphia. The rents for 10 lesser cities include Houston, Jacksonville, Los Angeles, Mobile, Norfolk, Portland (Maine), Portland (Oregon), San Francisco and Oakland, Seattle, and Washington, D. C.

the multitude of sellers depress prices so that an owner who paid 50 per cent down may see his equity disappear. In such a time it is well to remember that well-constructed, well-located homes have a permanent value even if they are unsalable for a time.

The prices of white pine and brick in the Civil War period and of yellow pine and brick in the World War period are shown in figure 145.

City homes are much like agriculture in that they have a very slow turnover. Most industrial and mercantile operations have a relatively rapid turnover so that adjustment is completed before many years. Agriculture being a biological industry has a slow turnover, and homes last for many years.

After the Panic of 1873, building materials declined in price for six years. Apparently, building equities were then liquidated, for prices of building materials rose. If the readjustment requires the same period of time in this depression, home building would be expected to commence in 1936.

Cycles in building construction.—The volume of building construction per capita is shown in figure 146. Apparently there are cycles of about 20 years, with peaks at about 1905 and 1925. Apparently, low points would have come about 1915 and 1935 if there had been no war. This agrees with the period of liquidation following the Panic

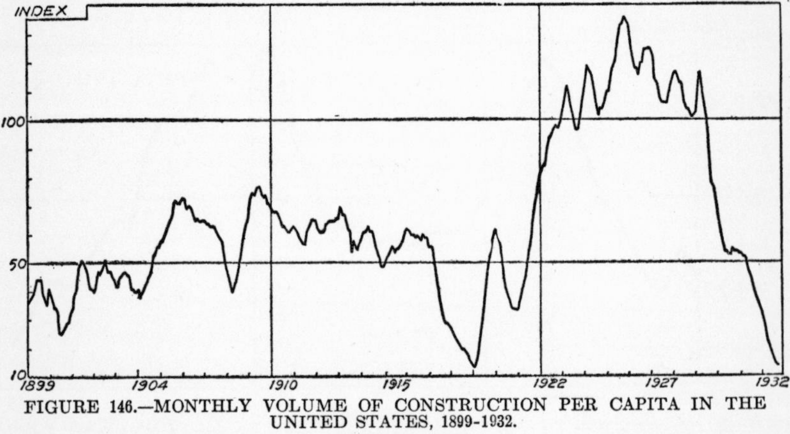

FIGURE 146.—MONTHLY VOLUME OF CONSTRUCTION PER CAPITA IN THE UNITED STATES, 1899-1932.
1926-30 = 100.
The war caused a great deficit in building. This deficit and cheap food caused a construction boom.

of 1873 in estimating that building may turn upward about 1936. Since fluctuations in world demand for gold have been the dominating price factor since 1915, violent changes in this demand may at any time offset all business cycles.

A study of real estate activity in San Francisco[4] from 1853 to 1930 indicates that there are very distinct cycles in the industry (figure 88). The first complete cycle of the ratio of deeds per year to the estimated population of San Francisco was about fifteen years; and the second was about twenty years.

[4] Maverick, L. A., Cycles in Real Estate Activity, The Journal of Land and Public Utility Economics, Vol. VIII, No. 2, p. 199, May 1932, and San Francisco Real Estate Circular, published by Thomas Magee and Sons, San Francisco. The data were transcribed through the courtesy of Dr. H. J. Stover of the University of California. Wenzlick, R., of The Real Estate Analysts, Inc., St. Louis, Missouri, has found similar cycles and has made a most thorough study of the causes of them.

It appears that the expansion of real estate activity takes place rapidly and the contraction is a relatively slow process. The three periods of expansion were about eight, seven, and six years, respectively. The periods of contraction were about fourteen, nine, and fourteen, respectively.

In England, there seems to be a building cycle about 20 years in length[5] with peaks in 1881 and 1901. The low points in building occurred in 1890 and 1912 (figure 147). An increase in building in the United States started a year before the outbreak of the war, but was stopped by the war, so that there was an unusual shortage at the

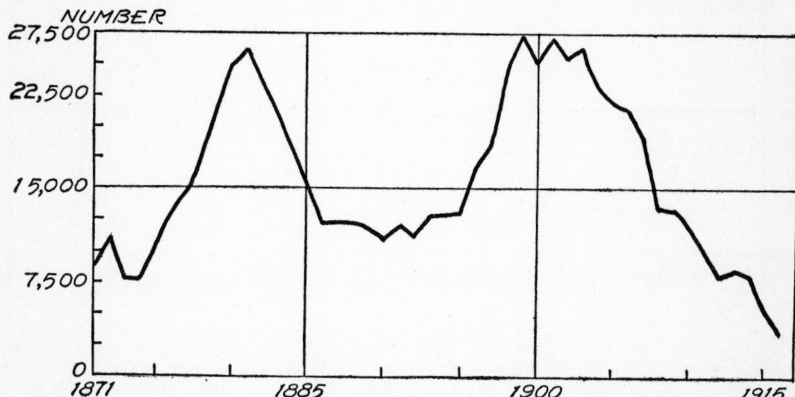

FIGURE 147.—NUMBER OF NEW HOUSES BUILT IN THE METROPOLITAN POLICE DISTRICT OF LONDON, ENGLAND, 1871-1916.
Apparently there is a building cycle about 20 years in length.

close of the war. In England and all over Europe, a great construction boom began soon after the World War, reaching a peak at about the same time as in the United States. There was general over-construction by 1925, but the low construction is eliminating this and a period of shortage is developing. In a few years, an upswing in construction will start unless interfered with by wars or monetary factors. As usual, the time of greatest pessimism will probably be just before building begins. There will then be discussions of the ability of the population to raise enough children to fill the houses. There is no definite limit for housing desires. A great increase in the amount of house room per capita is desired, and will be used whenever the population is fully employed.

[5] Spensley, J. C., Urban Housing Problems, Journal of the Royal Statistical Society, Vol. LXXXI, Part II, p. 170, March 1918.

The outlook for city real estate.—If commodity prices do not rise to the level at which the debts were contracted, city debts must be liquidated to the price level. This throws innumerable properties on the market at a time when there is unemployment and the resulting apparent surplus of houses. Taxes are high and many properties produce no income. This situation results in so much despondency and such an unfavorable market that many persons who have a real equity lose their properties. If the experience of the Civil War is repeated, this process will be sufficiently completed by about 1936 so that construction will begin. It is possible that government lending may delay this slightly, and it is also possible that variations in the world demand for gold or monetary legislation may change the results. It is certain that the price level must rise or the debts must be liquidated.

The process of mortgage liquidation is very slow. For several years, borrowers and lenders both hold on, expecting that prosperity is "just around the corner." At the present time, there is little market for office buildings, homes, hotels, and the like. If the process of deflation is continued, the properties must be foreclosed and taken over by the creditors. Unfortunately this drastic step does not clear up the situation. Most of the creditors do not want these properties, and they must pass into the hands of those who want them.

When the period of adjustment is over, well-located houses will be worth the new costs to build less depreciation and obsolescence. Many persons will profit by purchasing at panic prices.

BIBLIOGRAPHY

Clark, W. C., The Construction Industry in 1932. The Review of Economic Statistics, Vol. XIV, No. 2, pp. 74-79. May 15, 1932.

Holden, A. C., The Crisis in Real Estate. Harper's Magazine, Vol. 163, No. 978, pp. 671-679. November 1931.

Maverick, L. A., Cycles in Real Estate Activity. The Journal of Land and Public Utility Economics, Vol. 8, No. 2, pp. 191-199. May 1932.

Spensley, J. C., Urban Housing Problems. Journal of the Royal Statistical Society, Vol. LXXXI, Part II, pp. 161-210. March 1918.

Warren, G. F., and Pearson, F. A., Effect of Declining Prices on Home Owners. Farm Economics No. 74, p. 1668. February 1932.

CHAPTER XVII

STOCKS AND BONDS

What is interest?—In all cases where money is lent, some element of risk is involved, so that interest always includes at least some part that is payment for risk. This item is least in securities of a sound government, but there is some element of risk in these securities, as is evidenced by all history.

In all loans some expense is involved also in the process of making the loan and in collecting the interest and principal. For small loans this is often more than the pay for the use of the money. When loans are both small and risky, the combined payment for costs, risks, and pure interest is so large that what is called interest is very high. What the interest rate would be if neither risk nor expense were involved is not known.

There is no way of avoiding risk, but risks may be shifted to some extent. The devices of stocks and bonds for financing industry are a method of shifting risks. The stockholder guarantees the bond holder a fixed income. Some risk still remains. Persons who are willing to take a greater risk buy stocks.

In general, stocks pay a higher return than bonds but are much more irregular and the risk of total loss is greater. If bankruptcy occurs, the stockholder loses everything before the bond holder loses anything.

Effect of prices on interest rates.—One who lends money in a period of rising prices gets it back when it has a smaller buying power. He does not receive the "real income" which either he or the borrower anticipated. The borrower makes an unexpected profit from the rise in prices. If such a condition continues, lenders ask and borrowers are willing to pay a steadily rising interest rate, or prices of bonds with a fixed interest rate decline.

In a period of declining prices, the process is reversed. Lenders receive their money back when it is worth more. Borrowers have to sell a greater quantity of goods than they had anticipated in order to pay debts. If the period continues long enough for the public to become aware of the situation, interest rates decline because lenders would rather take a low rate of interest than invest in business, and because borrowers learn how difficult it is to operate a business profitably with declining prices. Safe investments become scarce.

The individual may not give thought to the prospective price levels; but, when prices continue to rise, society observes that borrowers prosper and there is a general movement to borrow. Mortgages are not considered seriously. With a falling price level, society observes that those who borrow are likely to lose. Debts are looked on with disfavor and mortgages with abhorrence.

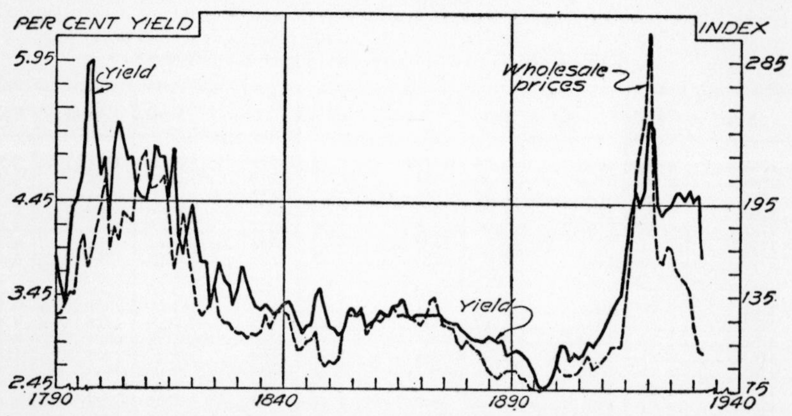

FIGURE 148.—WHOLESALE PRICES AND YIELD ON BRITISH CONSOLS, 1790-1932. For more than a century, the yield on consols followed the price level. With declining prices, the yields declined. Conversely, with rising prices, they rose. If commodity prices continue to decline and political conditions are stable, it is to be expected that less than 3 per cent will again be a good return.

For many years before the discovery of America, there was such a growing scarcity of gold and silver that going in debt was considered immoral. Those who took interest were looked down on. One of the points of debate in economic and religious thought was whether anything should be charged for the use of money.

From 1873 to 1896, to be termed a bond holder was a reproach.

Yield on British consols.—Consols bore interest at 3 per cent from 1751 to 1888. In 1889, the rate was changed to 2.75 per cent, and in 1903 it was reduced to 2.5 per cent. The actual interest rates earned on the consols at the current price at which they sold are given in table 56.

Since consols are long-time investments, the prices are somewhat stable so that the earned interest is less variable than the rate charged on short-time loans.

When interest rates are high, consols fall in price, so that the yield on consols purchased at this price is high.

The yield on the consols was high during the Napoleonic Wars (figure 148). After the wars, there was a gradual decline in yield amounting to more than 1 per cent. For over fifty years the yield was comparatively steady, but in general declined. A more rapid decline culminated in 1897 with a yield of 2.45 per cent. The period of rapidly rising prices then set in, and the yield increased almost 1 per cent before the World War. During the World War, the price of consols declined so much that the yield rose rapidly, and was even higher than during the Napoleonic Wars.

TABLE 56.—YIELD ON BRITISH CONSOLS*

Year	Yield	Year	Yield	Year	Yield	Year	Yield	Year	Yield
1753	2.86	1793	3.96	1833	3.42	1873	3.24	1913	3.39
1754	2.91	1794	4.40	1834	3.32	1874	3.24	1914	3.46
1755	3.14	1795	4.52	1835	3.29	1875	3.20	1915	3.82
1756	3.37	1796	4.80	1836	3.35	1876	3.16	1916	4.31
1757	3.39	1797	5.90	1837	3.30	1877	3.15	1917	4.58
1758	3.21	1798	5.94	1838	3.23	1878	3.15	1918	4.40
1759	3.59	1799	5.07	1839	3.28	1879	3.08	1919	4.62
1760	3.77	1800	4.71	1840	3.35	1880	3.05	1920	5.32
1761	3.90	1801	4.92	1841	3.38	1881	3.00	1921	5.21
1762	4.29	1802	4.23	1842	3.27	1882	2.99	1922	4.43
1763	3.37	1803	4.99	1843	3.17	1883	2.97	1923	4.31
1764	3.61	1804	5.30	1844	3.03	1884	2.97	1924	4.39
1765	3.41	1805	5.04	1845	3.12	1885	3.02	1925	4.43
1766	3.39	1806	4.87	1846	3.13	1886	2.98	1926	4.55
1767	3.37	1807	4.92	1847	3.44	1887	2.95	1927	4.56
1768	3.31	1808	4.55	1848	3.51	1888	2.97	1928	4.47
1769	3.47	1809	4.49	1849	3.24	1889	2.81	1929	4.60
1770	3.64	1810	4.47	1850	3.11	1890	2.85	1930	4.46
1771	3.55	1811	4.67	1851	3.09	1891	2.87	1931	4.53
1772	3.30	1812	5.08	1852	3.02	1892	2.84	**1932**	3.74
1773	3.47	1813	4.92	1853	3.07	1893	2.79		
1774	3.43	1814	4.92	1854	3.27	1894	2.72		
1775	3.39	1815	4.48	1855	3.31	1895	2.59		
1776	3.51	1816	5.02	1856	3.22	1896	2.48		
1777	3.85	1817	4.10	1857	3.27	1897	2.45		
1778	4.51	1818	3.87	1858	3.10	1898	2.48		
1779	4.88	1819	4.17	1859	3.15	1899	2.57		
1780	4.88	1820	4.42	1860	3.19	1900	2.76		
1781	5.22	1821	4.07	1861	3.28	1901	2.92		
1782	5.26	1822	3.79	1862	3.23	1902	2.91		
1783	4.76	1823	3.80	1863	3.24	1903	2.75		
1784	5.41	1824	3.30	1864	3.33	1904	2.83		
1785	4.76	1825	3.54	1865	3.35	1905	2.78		
1786	....	1826	3.79	1866	3.41	1906	2.83		
1787	4.08	1827	3.61	1867	3.23	1907	2.97		
1788	....	1828	3.54	1868	3.20	1908	2.90		
1789	3.92	1829	3.34	1869	3.23	1909	2.98		
1790	3.90	1830	3.49	1870	3.24	1910	3.08		
1791	3.58	1831	3.76	1871	3.23	1911	3.15		
1792	3.33	1832	3.58	1872	3.24	1912	3.28		

* Francis, J., History of the Bank of England, The Bankers' Magazine and Statistical Register, Vol. XVII, p. 418, 1862–63. The yield was obtained by dividing 3 by the average price. Silberling, N., British Financial Experience 1790–1830, The Review of Economic Statistics Preliminary Vol. 1, p. 289, October 1919. The Decline of Consols, Bradstreet's, Vol. 31, No. 1291, p. 194, March 28, 1903. Sauerbeck, A., Prices of the Precious Metals. Journal of Royal Statistical Society, Vol. XLIX, Part III, p. 648, September 1886. Paish, Sir George, Wholesale Prices in 1920. Journal of Royal Statistical Society, Vol. LXXXIV, Part III, p. 255, March 1921, and later numbers.

Relation of interest and prices in England.—When world gold stocks increase more rapidly than the total production of other things, interest rates rise. When stocks increase less rapidly, interest rates fall. The initiating cause is the surplus or deficiency in the gold supply. This causes commodity prices to rise or fall.

In general, when prices are rising, the rate of interest is high but not sufficiently high to compensate for the rise. When prices are falling, the rate of interest is usually low but not sufficiently low to compensate for the decline in prices.

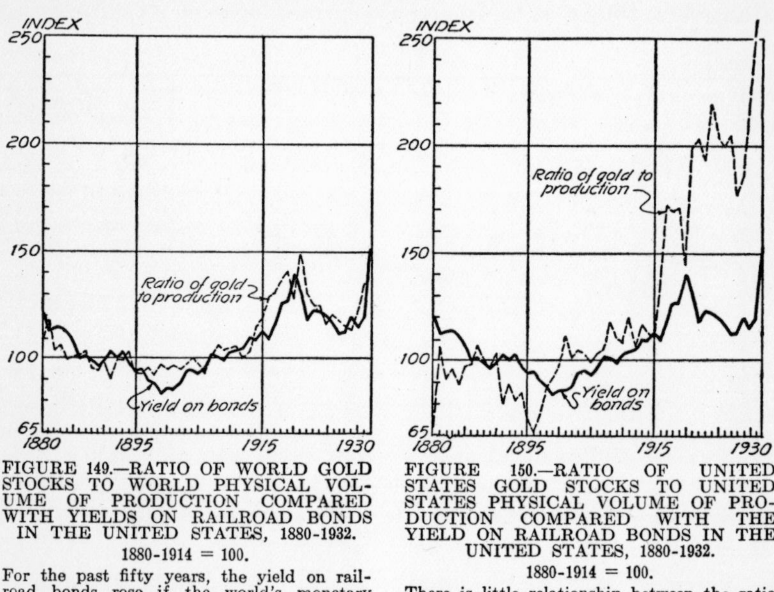

FIGURE 149.—RATIO OF WORLD GOLD STOCKS TO WORLD PHYSICAL VOLUME OF PRODUCTION COMPARED WITH YIELDS ON RAILROAD BONDS IN THE UNITED STATES, 1880-1932.

1880-1914 = 100.

For the past fifty years, the yield on railroad bonds rose if the world's monetary stocks of gold rose more rapidly than the production of other things and fell if gold increased less rapidly.

FIGURE 150.—RATIO OF UNITED STATES GOLD STOCKS TO UNITED STATES PHYSICAL VOLUME OF PRODUCTION COMPARED WITH THE YIELD ON RAILROAD BONDS IN THE UNITED STATES, 1880-1932.

1880-1914 = 100.

There is little relationship between the ratio of United States stocks of gold to United States physical volume of production and the yield on railroad bonds.

If the price level continued to rise or fall steadily and uniformly for many years, interest rates might come to such an adjustment as to compensate for the change in prices. No such period of change in price has continued long enough to determine whether or not a full adjustment would ever occur.

Ratio of world gold stocks to world basic production and yield on railroad bonds.—It has been shown (pages 76 to 82) that the ratio of the world's monetary stocks of gold to the production of other commodities controls the price of commodities, that is, controls the value of gold. This same ratio also influences interest rates, or the price of capital.

From 1880 to 1896, the ratio of world gold stocks to production of other commodities declined about one-fifth, and the yield on railroad bonds declined about one-fifth (figure 149). By 1914, the ratio of gold to production had risen more than one-fifth, and the yield on railroad bonds, almost one-fifth. The same principle holds for yields on British consols from 1880 to 1914. The relationship was not so close for earlier years.

Prices of bonds, Civil War and World War periods.—In the Civil War period, prices of bonds fell very low (figure 151). When deflation came, they rose to the pre-war level. They rose steadily through

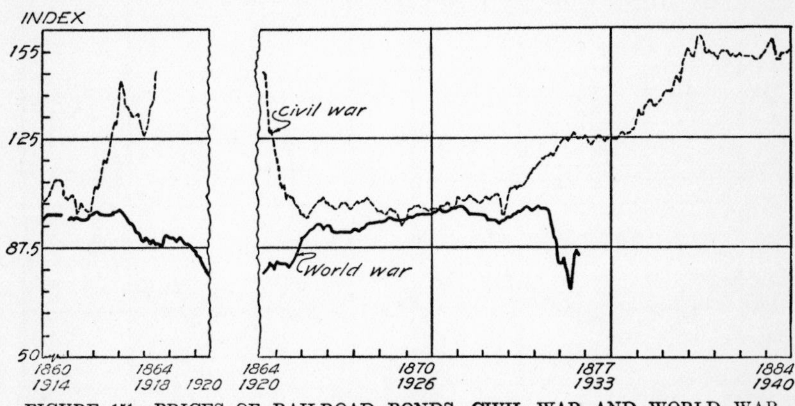

FIGURE 151.—PRICES OF RAILROAD BONDS, CIVIL WAR AND WORLD WAR PERIODS.
In each case, pre-war is 100.
Prices of bonds rose during the Panic of 1873. They began to rise during the Panic of 1929, but deflation was so drastic as to reduce the value of bonds as well as of stocks.

the Panic of 1873 and continued upward until 1899. Bond prices started to rise after the depression in 1929, but it was so severe that there was doubt of the ability to make payment, and a sudden collapse occurred. If deflation continues, prices of bonds that can be paid will be expected to rise steadily. Although bonds fell in price during the Panic of 1929, rates for call loans were extremely low. The public was looking for something safe regardless of income. In a less severe panic, as in the Panic of 1873, bonds were considered safe and rose in price.

Eleven years after deflation began in the Civil War period, the yield on high-grade railroad bonds was a little more than 5 per cent. The long period of declining prices in the nineties raised the prices of these bonds until the yield fell to 3.25 per cent. Rising commodity prices before the World War caused a decline in bond prices, and yields rose to 4 per cent. If the decline in commodity prices continues, it is to be expected that the price of high-class bonds will rise and reduce the yields materially. Ultimately, such a process brings lower interest rates to established industries, but the danger of loss of principal in a panic period is so great that very high interest rates are charged to farmers and business men at a time when call money brings very little.

In periods of prosperity, second-grade bonds can be paid. This causes them to rise in price more than the rise for first-class bonds. In periods of depression, there is doubt as to whether the second-class bonds can be paid and the prices fall precipitously.

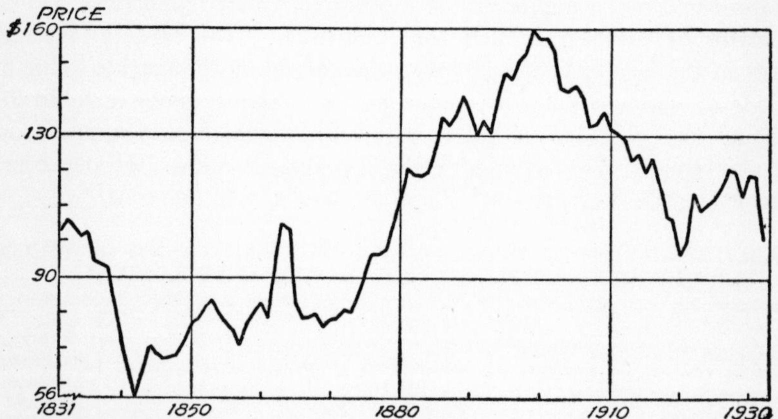

FIGURE 152.—PRICES OF HIGH-GRADE AMERICAN RAILROAD BONDS, 1831-1932. With falling commodity prices from 1870-1899, the prices of bonds doubled. With rising commodity prices ending in 1920, the price of bonds declined almost 40 per cent.

Yield on United States government sixes after the Civil War.—The rise in the price of 6 per cent government bonds was so great after the Civil War that the interest received on the market value fell rapidly. In 1876, the price was such that they yielded only 2.0 per cent. The profits made by persons who bought the bonds during the war were very large. If they continued to hold the bonds, they obtained a very high rate of interest on their cost at a time when interest rates were low. The declining prices placed a heavy burden on taxpayers. To be a bond holder became a reproach. During the World War, bonds were issued the income of which was exempt from taxation. It is probable that, as interest rates fall and the full burden of taxation is realized, to be a holder of tax-exempt securities will be a reproach.

It is unwise to issue long-term non-callable bonds at high rates of interest or to issue tax-exempt securities.

Interest rates in a new country.—When a country is new, it is very short of capital. Most of the settlers are young men who come without money. The competition for funds is very keen. Persons living in older regions are uncertain as to the reliability of the new country and fear to lend except at high rates. In 1860, savings banks in California paid as much as 15 per cent in dividends.[1]

Before the war, the physical volume of production in the United States was increasing at about 4 per cent per year, whereas world production increased at only about 3 per cent. Therefore the United States could pay a higher rate of interest than older countries.

Rates of interest in different countries.—The rates of interest paid on the face of bonds and the rates earned on the market value of bonds of various countries from 1901 to 1913 are given in table 57. The average yields are indicated by the last figures in the equations of secular trends. The average yields on consols were 2.94 per cent; French rentes, 3.12 per cent; Japanese bonds, 4.73 per cent.

TABLE 57.—RATES OF INTEREST AND SECULAR TREND OF YIELDS ON GOVERNMENT SECURITIES, 1901-13 INCLUSIVE*

Country	Rate of interest, per cent	Equation of secular trend	Yearly percentage increases on yield for 1907
Brazil, 1889	4	$y = -0.084x + 4.94$	−1.70
China, gold	4½	$y = -0.044x + 4.74$	−0.93
Japan, sterling	4	$y = -0.033x + 4.73$	−0.70
Argentina, 1886–87	5	$y = -0.030x + 4.93$	−0.61
Russia	4	$y = 0.028x + 4.43$	0.63
Austria, gold 1876	4	$y = 0.030x + 4.07$	0.74
France	3	$y = 0.025x + 3.12$	0.80
Cape of Good Hope	3	$y = 0.032x + 3.47$	0.92
New Zealand	3	$y = 0.042x + 3.41$	1.23
German bonds	3	$y = 0.047x + 3.54$	1.33
Canada stock	3	$y = 0.043x + 3.15$	1.37
Hungarian gold, 1881–92	4	$y = 0.068x + 4.24$	1.60
United States 1925	4	$y = 0.063x + 3.21$	1.96
United Kingdom consols	2½	$y = 0.058x + 2.94$	1.97
India stock	3	$y = 0.082x + 3.36$	2.44

* Based on material presented in Cost of Living, Report of the Board of Inquiry, Ottawa, Canada, Vol. II, pp. 707–716, 1915.

[1] Plehn, C. C., Taxation of Mortgages in California, Yale Review, Vol. 8, p. 52, May 1899.

In this period of world-wide rise in commodity prices, the yield on bonds increased in all but four of the countries listed. The price level, of course, is not the only factor influencing the yield on bonds. The financial stability of the country is important. The improvement in financial conditions in Brazil, China, Japan, and Argentina was sufficient to offset the effect of rising prices. The prices of the bonds of these countries rose during this period and consequently the yields fell. In the countries where the financial affairs were more firmly established before this period, the rate of increase in yield was very great, but was not sufficient fully to offset the rising prices.

Normal yields on bonds.—In a period of rising prices, debtors find it easy to pay debts, and creditors do not receive the "real income" which they anticipate. Therefore interest rates rise. With falling prices, the process is reversed. Since we have never had a considerable period when money was stable in value, it is difficult to know what the normal interest rate would be if prices were stable.

In the nineties, the yield on British consols was as low as 2.45 per cent (figure 148). The average for 21 years centered on 1896, so that it included 10 years of falling prices and 10 years of rising prices, was 2.77 per cent.

For the same 21 years, the average yields on United States bonds were 2.22 per cent.

The yield on French rentes averaged 3.16 per cent, and German bonds 3.46.

The yield on American railroad bonds for the 21 years centered on 1896 averaged 3.51.

The yield on American municipal bonds from 1900 to 1904 averaged 3.26 per cent. This was a period of rising prices, and these yields may be high.

If prices were stable, it is probable that high-grade government securities would yield between 2 and 3 per cent, or possibly less. This may be looked on as approximating a "pure interest rate," that is, the amount paid for money without risk. Anything above this may be looked on as payment for risk of failure to pay, risk of a rising price level, or expenses of making loans at retail.

It may be that this interest rate is related to the annual increase in physical volume of production in the world, which for many years before the war was 3.15 per cent. If one lender commanded all the commodities produced in the world in one year and received an interest rate of 3.15 per cent, he would command all the commodities produced in the following year. If he received more than this interest rate, he would command more than all the commodities produced in the world.

The national wealth appears to increase at about the same rate as the physical volume of production (page 234). Therefore, if one owned all the physical property in the world at the beginning of the year and drew a rate of interest equal to the increases in the physical volume of production, he would own all the property at the end of the year.

This rate is less than 3 per cent for old countries and more than 3 per cent for progressive new countries. If the price level were rising, a higher rate might be paid; if falling, a lower rate.

A similar result would be expected if the loans approached a half of the value of the property and were at a rate of 6 per cent.

In 1932, the public and private debts of the United States were probably close to the value of the property. Evidently, many of them cannot be paid unless the price level is restored.

The general custom in the United States is to restrict loans on farms, homes, and business properties, to about half the value. For some years the charge for interest has been about 6 per cent, which involves a payment of 3 per cent on the full value of the property. This custom may be related to the same set of fundamental facts. If the price level falls, such loans are unsafe. If the price level rises, larger loans can be made with safety.

If a penny had been placed at 2 per cent compound interest at the beginning of the Christian era, it would in the 1929 years have amounted to $389,000,000,000,000, or more than one thousand times the national wealth of the United States. Such figures indicate why it is impossible for vast fortunes to be perpetually maintained.

Thus far in the history of the world, laws have been largely in the interest of creditors. Following the War of 1812, Pennsylvania jails were filled with farmers and other debtors (page 334). Most of these laws were repealed after the Panic of 1837. Much progress has been made in the century, but the ways of the debtor are not easy ways, particularly in a period of declining prices.

The present attitude of the population of the world toward debts is based on a generation of rising prices. This attitude will change with falling prices.

Monetary chaos since 1914 has resulted in government and private borrowing in all countries in vast amounts at very high interest rates. Most of these debts could have been refunded at a lower interest rate had the price level remained at the level at which the debts were contracted. The rise in the value of gold made it necessary for a general writing off of debts except in countries where the price of gold was raised. Since international debts were payable in gold, these were generally written off.

In some countries, the government has arbitrarily reduced the rate of interest on government bonds. In some countries, private debts were reduced by law, but our Constitution prevents such adjustments.

By foreseeing the trend of industries, life insurance companies can shift to growing industries and growing regions and so obtain yields above the normal government bond rate. But yields of much more than 3 per cent are not to be expected with stable or slowly falling commodity prices.

After a considerable period of rising prices, the yield on British consols from 1910 to 1914 averaged 3.27 per cent. With prices rising violently, the yield in 1920 averaged 5.32 per cent. Since that time, yields have declined and may be expected to continue to decline so long as prices fall, unless disturbed by political unrest. The United States refunded war loans made to England at 3.5 per cent. This interest rate looked low at the time, but is a high rate if prices are to be stable or continue to fall.

Effect of rising and falling commodity prices on prices of stocks.—When prices are rising, the profits of industrial concerns are increased because prices advance while the commodity is being produced, and all costs lag. In periods of falling prices, profits are reduced, many concerns fail, and prices of stocks of those that continue rise more slowly than in periods of rising commodity prices. From 1897 to 1913, prices of industrial stocks rose an average of 3.1 per cent per year based on the middle year as 100. In the 17 years of falling prices ending with 1896, stock prices advanced only 1.3 per cent per year.

In both cases, the price advances are greater than the average investor would obtain because he would have invested in some stocks which looked good at the time but represented shares in companies that failed. These failures were more numerous with falling prices, so that the differences were greater than the figures indicate.

Prices of industrial stocks rose very slowly from 1880 to 1896. They rose more rapidly from 1897 to 1913 when prices were rising.

They rose with great rapidity from 1923 to 1929 (figure 153). The first part of the rise was a recovery from the depression of 1920. The period of striking increase in the demand for industrial products occurred partly because of the shortage of goods and partly because of cheap food. This reduced profits on farms but increased profits on city enterprises. Stocks of fertilizer companies rose very little. All these adjustments caused a rapid rise in prices of stocks. Prices rose so rapidly that a multitude of investors appeared who were primarily interested in the rise rather than the earnings. Stocks rose because they rose—just as Florida real estate rose because it rose regardless of its intrinsic value. In 1928 and particularly in 1929, a wild boom developed. When the crash came, nearly a third of the prices of stocks was lost almost instantaneously. Successive declines and rebounds carried prices down for nearly three years. In June 1932, the various index numbers declined below pre-war. Considerable recovery then occurred from the extremely low prices.

The course of prices of railroad stocks is shown in figure 154. Railroad stocks were high in the ten years before the World War. Temporarily they shared in the wild boom of 1929. In June 1932, they were worth less than one-tenth of the values prevailing in 1929 and less than one-seventh of the pre-war values. The loss of passenger business to the auto-

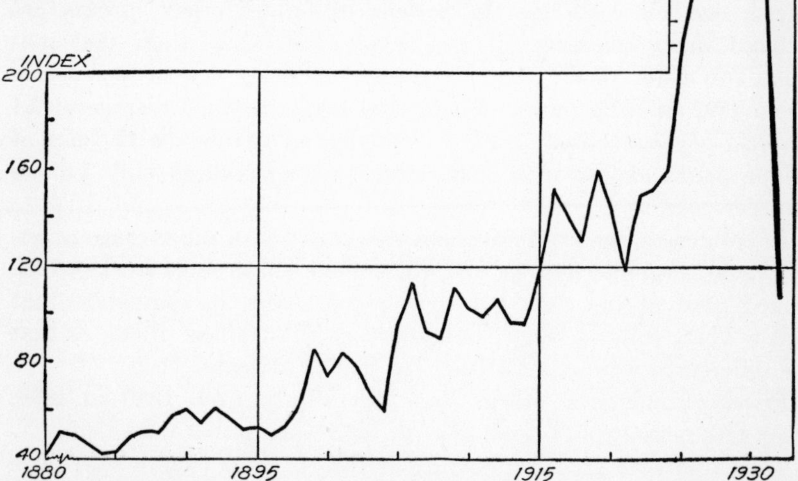

FIGURE 153.—INDEX NUMBERS OF PRICES OF INDUSTRIAL STOCKS, 1880-1932. 1910-14 = 100.

Over long periods of time, there is a tendency for stocks to rise. When commodity prices are falling, the rise is very slow. When prices are rising, the rise is rapid. The wild boom of 1929 carried industrial stocks to 5 times the pre-war level.

TABLE 58.—PRICES OF STOCKS AND BONDS

	Average 1910–14	Sept. 1929	Sept. 1931	June 1932	Sept. 1932	Nov. 1932
Industrial stocks						
Dow-Jones, 30 stocks, dollars per share*.......	62.5	364.9	118.8	46.9	72.6	62.2
New York Times, 25 stocks, dollars per share..	62.0	450.5	161.6	68.5	101.3	91.6
Dow-Jones & Standard Statistics, 351 stocks, index, 1926 = 100........................	43.1	216.1	75.8	33.5	55.8	45.4
Railroad stocks						
Dow-Jones, 20 stocks, dollars per share........	113.5	181.5	60.8	15.7	35.3	27.8
New York Times, 25 stocks, dollars per share..	85.9†	151.6	49.4	12.4	28.5	22.3
Standard Statistics, 33 stocks, index, 1926 = 100.	.....	168.1	56.1	14.1	34.5	25.5
New York Herald Tribune, 30 stocks, dollars per share............................	.....	156.7	49.2	14.9	32.6	25.1
Public utility						
Standard Statistics, 37 stocks, index, 1926 = 100.	.....	321.0	131.9	55.0	91.4	77.6
Agricultural machinery						
Standard Statistics, 4 stocks, index, 1926 = 100.	.....	444.8	94.0	40.7	84.1	62.0
Fertilizers						
Standard Statistics, 4 stocks, index, 1926 = 100.	.....	94.5	13.7	4.8	13.9	9.4
Preferred stocks						
Standard Statistics, 20 stocks, index, 1926 = 100.	109.9	126.8	121.2	83.6	101.8	97.4
Bonds						
New York Times, 40 bonds, dollars per share..	87.2	85.8	77.0	55.3	70.2	65.5
Standard Statistics, 60 bonds, index, 1926 = 100.	98.4	94.8	95.6	72.2	85.8	81.9

* The Dow-Jones index number is for 12 stocks prior to December 1914. From December 1914 to 1916, 20 stocks, and thereafter 30 stocks.

† The base period for all New York Times index numbers is 1911–14 = 100, except for bonds, which is 1913–14.

Standard Trade and Securities, Base Book, Standard Statistical Bulletin Vol. 63, No. 7, Section 3, pp. 66–137, January 1932, and Statistical Bulletin, Vol. 66, pp. 8, 27, 28, and 30, October 1932 and December 1932.

TABLE 59.—INDEX NUMBERS OF PRICES OF STOCKS AND BONDS

	Average 1910–14	Sept. 1929	Sept. 1931	June 1932	Sept. 1932	Nov. 1932
Industrial stocks						
Dow-Jones, 30 stocks*......................	100	584	190	75	116	100
New York Times, 25 stocks†................	100	727	261	110	163	148
Dow-Jones & Standard Statistics, 351 stocks...	100	501	176	78	129	105
Railroad stocks						
Dow-Jones, 20 stocks.......................	100	160	54	14	31	24
New York Times, 25 stocks†................	100	176	58	14	33	26
Preferred stocks						
Standard Statistics, 20 stocks................	100	115	110	76	93	89
Bonds						
New York Times, 40 bonds†.................	100	98	88	63	81	75
Standard Statistics, 60 bonds................	100	96	97	73	87	83

* The Dow-Jones index is for 12 stocks prior to December 1914; for 20 stocks December 1914 to 1916, and thereafter 30 stocks. Adjustment has been made so that figures are comparable.

† The base period for all New York Times index numbers is 1911–14 = 100, except for bonds, which is 1913–14.

mobile, and the maintenance of multitudes of branch lines which are obsolete now that trucks and automobiles are available, make the outlook for prices of railroad stocks less favorable than formerly.

If deflation continues and if the profitable main lines are to continue to carry the burden of obsolete branches, it is possible that some of the railroads will pass into the hands of the government. The first step in such a procedure is to lend government money to the railroads for refinancing and repairs.

Prices of common stocks during the Civil War and the World War periods.—Prices of railroad stocks in the Civil War period and industrial stocks in the World War period are shown in figure 155. The fluctuations of the World War period are somewhat similar to those of the Civil War period except that there was a wild boom in 1928-29 and the crash was much worse than that which occurred in the Panic of 1873. In both cases, the crash occurred nine years after the deflation began. A rebound from the depth of the depression occurred in 1932, one year sooner than the first reaction after the Panic of 1873. It is probable that the government loans to banks,

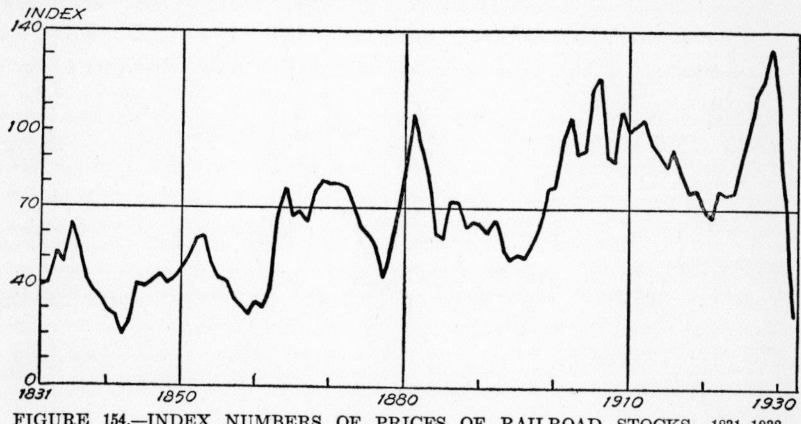

FIGURE 154.—INDEX NUMBERS OF PRICES OF RAILROAD STOCKS, 1831-1932. 1910-14 = 100.

There was a gradual rise in the price of railroad stocks up to about 1910. Railroad stocks in June 1932 were at the lowest level ever recorded, and were exactly the same as for March 1842.

railroads, and corporations may have caused the rebound one year sooner than otherwise would have occurred.

From the depth of the depression in the Civil War period, prices rose 50 per cent rather quickly. There was little further rise for about two years. A decided rise then occurred after real estate loans were liquidated so that construction could begin.

Since our prices were on a currency basis and gold was at a premium, the prices to English investors in the Civil War period were lower than the currency prices shown in figure 155.

By investing small sums of gold in our railroads, the English built up credits that required the transfer of large amounts of goods in later years.

If commodity prices do not rise so as to restore equities in city real estate, it is to be expected that profits of industrial concerns will generally remain low until the process of debt liquidation is completed (page 135).

Comparison of stocks and bonds.—Apparently in a period of stable prices a yield of from 2 to 3 per cent on the best government bonds is all that should be expected. High-grade municipal bonds might be expected to yield ½ per cent more, and good industrial bonds perhaps 1 per cent above government bonds.

Stocks are much more variable in earning power, and there is much more danger of loss of principal. They might be expected to yield a half more than government bonds.

As previously stated, these normal relationships cannot be determined because the price level is so unstable that it is constantly upsetting normal relationships. With rising com-

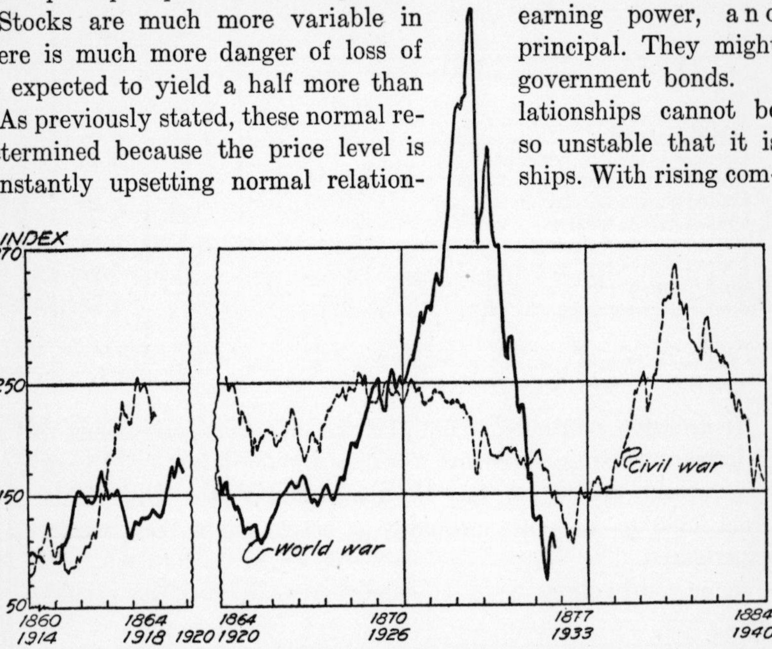

FIGURE 155.—PRICES OF RAILROAD STOCKS, CIVIL WAR PERIOD, AND PRICES OF INDUSTRIAL STOCKS, WORLD WAR PERIOD.

In each case, pre-war = 100.

The course of prices of common stocks was somewhat similar, except for the wild boom of 1928-29. In both cases, prices fell 9 years after deflation began, and some rebound occurred from the extremely low prices. In the Civil War period, no general recovery occurred until real estate was liquidated.

modity prices there is an active demand for money and the yield on all classes of securities increases. During a business panic or such a catastrophe as occurred in 1929, there is risk of the loss of principal, and prices of stocks and bonds decline. In a long period of declining prices, the safe securities rise in price so that the yields are reduced.

Failure to recognize the effects of falling prices on interest rates results in the issuance of long-term bonds before such a period. Usually it is wise business policy to have such bonds callable so that the high rate may not continue. Conversely, those who are investing before a period of falling prices should give more attention to the call date. This requires a forecast of the supply of and demand for gold, before making investments.

TABLE 60.—COMPARATIVE YIELDS ON SECURITIES

	1886 to 1906	1900 to 1904	1910 to 1914
Bonds			
British consols	2.77	2.83	3.27
French rentes*	3.16	3.02	....
German loans 3½ per cent*	3.46	3.49	....
United States government 4 per cent of 1907*	2.22	1.65	....
United States municipals	....	3.26	4.06
United States utilities	....	4.53	4.83
United States railroads	....	3.98	4.28
United States industrials	....	4.82	4.87
United States preferred stocks	....	....	6.38
United States common stocks	....	4.82	5.72

* Andrew, A. Piatt, Statistics for the United States, 1867–1909, National Monetary Commission, 61st Congress, 2d Session, Senate Document 570, p. 281, 1910.

If deflation continues, it is to be expected that good bonds will rise in price to such an extent as to cause a much lower yield than the present generation has been accustomed to. The yields from 1886 to 1906 are probably a better guide than recent experiences.

Some court rulings have indicated that public utilities should

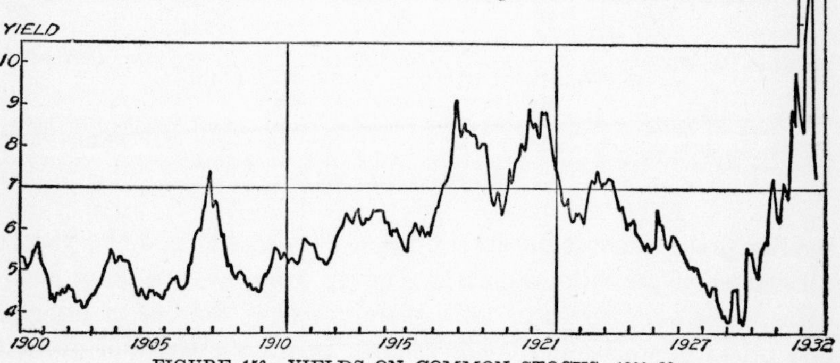

FIGURE 156.—YIELDS ON COMMON STOCKS, 1900-32.
In periods of depression, prices fall so low that the yields are high.

be entitled to earn 7 per cent on their total capital. This idea is the result of a generation of rising prices. This is much more than the usual investment in business can earn in a period of stable prices. A portion of the capital can usually be borrowed at 4 to 5 per cent. If a third of the capital is borrowed at 4.5 per cent (table 60), a yield of 7 per cent on the total capital would allow a yield of 8.25 per cent on the remaining capital.

Yields on common stocks.—The average yields on all dividend paying common stocks regularly traded on the New York Stock Exchange, as presented by The Cleveland Trust Co., are shown in table 61 and figure 156. From 1900 to 1914, the yields averaged 5.24 per cent. This is higher than would be expected in a period of stable prices. The yields averaged only 4.8 per cent for the first five years of the period. Prices of stocks in the summer of 1932 were extremely

TABLE 61.—YIELDS ON ALL DIVIDEND-PAYING COMMON STOCKS, 1900–1933*

Year	Jan.	Feb.	Mar.	Apr.	May	June	July	Aug.	Sept.	Oct.	Nov.	Dec.	Average
1900	5.32	5.32	5.31	5.01	5.14	5.21	5.47	5.44	5.58	5.68	5.29	5.07	5.32
1901	4.99	4.89	4.70	4.29	4.44	4.22	4.46	4.43	4.42	4.55	4.44	4.47	4.52
1902	4.64	4.54	4.53	4.25	4.24	4.27	4.27	4.11	4.12	4.18	4.30	4.37	4.32
1903	4.45	4.43	4.59	4.65	4.72	4.92	5.07	5.21	5.30	5.53	5.44	5.21	4.96
1904	5.21	5.35	5.35	5.23	5.25	5.25	5.12	4.97	4.83	4.63	4.45	4.42	5.00
1905	4.60	4.48	4.43	4.33	4.56	4.51	4.55	4.44	4.48	4.44	4.40	4.36	4.46
1906	4.54	4.56	4.69	4.75	4.83	4.79	4.91	4.65	4.58	4.60	4.66	4.70	4.69
1907	5.17	5.20	5.75	5.86	6.00	6.04	6.01	6.48	6.56	7.01	7.45	7.21	6.23
1908	6.53	6.71	6.58	6.15	5.86	5.90	5.45	5.15	5.17	5.10	4.88	4.81	5.69
1909	4.95	5.02	4.95	4.92	4.69	4.64	4.71	4.57	4.56	4.59	4.55	4.51	4.72
1910	4.80	4.97	4.89	5.03	5.17	5.33	5.61	5.54	5.47	5.30	5.34	5.47	5.24
1911	5.35	5.21	5.30	5.34	5.26	5.20	5.22	5.45	5.74	5.83	5.69	5.67	5.44
1912	5.64	5.64	5.50	5.33	5.31	5.28	5.29	5.19	5.18	5.27	5.36	5.53	5.38
1913	5.77	5.91	6.03	6.04	6.20	6.44	6.37	6.24	6.16	6.34	6.47	6.51	6.21
1914	6.23	6.12	6.16	6.30	6.27	6.30	6.49	6.49	6.48	6.48	6.47	6.47	6.35
1915	6.17	6.20	6.09	5.86	6.01	5.98	6.05	5.89	5.75	5.63	5.49	5.49	5.88
1916	5.87	5.95	5.99	6.18	6.05	5.87	6.10	6.02	5.85	5.98	5.89	6.07	5.98
1917	6.31	6.56	6.58	6.83	7.09	7.13	7.17	7.36	7.76	8.22	8.93	9.17	7.43
1918	8.59	8.25	8.44	8.61	8.38	8.40	8.31	8.30	8.33	8.04	7.97	8.04	8.31
1919	8.11	8.11	7.79	7.19	6.81	6.58	6.60	6.95	6.87	6.34	6.49	6.70	7.04
1920	6.94	7.48	7.15	7.22	7.65	7.73	7.78	8.11	7.97	7.92	8.32	8.96	7.77
1921	8.57	8.47	8.62	8.33	8.22	8.90	8.82	8.87	8.56	8.41	8.01	7.69	8.46
1922	7.55	7.27	7.08	6.70	6.61	6.63	6.80	6.47	6.22	6.24	6.44	6.36	6.70
1923	6.45	6.31	6.20	6.52	6.86	7.04	7.25	7.15	7.15	7.46	7.24	7.05	6.89
1924	7.16	7.15	7.27	7.24	7.25	7.11	6.79	6.56	6.51	6.61	6.31	6.05	6.83
1925	6.21	6.17	6.27	6.17	5.90	5.88	5.81	5.68	5.52	5.72	5.59	5.52	5.87
1926	5.58	5.61	6.56	6.17	6.16	5.92	5.68	5.56	5.63	5.88	5.89	5.79	5.83
1927	5.72	5.59	5.49	5.41	5.32	5.16	5.10	5.13	5.05	5.11	5.00	4.82	5.24
1928	4.68	4.75	4.64	4.49	4.41	4.64	4.64	4.48	4.18	4.08	3.88	3.91	4.40
1929	3.79	3.79	3.92	4.56	4.56	4.58	3.77	3.85	3.68	4.08	5.58	5.44	4.17
1930	5.45	5.14	5.01	4.82	5.12	5.58	5.64	5.72	5.67	6.54	6.89	7.26	5.74
1931	7.03	6.30	6.18	6.63	7.13	7.04	6.74	6.98	7.86	8.91	8.51	9.82	7.43
1932	9.48	8.75	8.32	10.72	11.37	11.96	14.88	8.26	7.30	7.98	7.96	8.14	9.59
1933	7.58	7.61	7.53	6.90	5.31	4.81	4.49	4.58	4.44				

* The index of stock yields compiled by The Cleveland Trust Company is based on monthly data for all the common stocks dealt in on the New York Stock Exchange that were traded with sufficient frequency to afford reasonably regular quotations, and that paid dividends for at least two successive years. The number of stocks included has shifted constantly from 1900 to the present time and has greatly increased in that period. The yields are ascertained by finding for each month the average of the aggregate of the high prices and of the low prices of all the stocks, and computing the relationship of this price figure to the sum of the regular dividends and "regular extras" paid during that quarter and so increased as to give the annual dividend equivalent.

low in proportion to yields, and yields were therefore high in proportion to usual expectations.

Comparative yields of stocks and bonds during prosperity and depression.—During the Panic of 1920, prices of stocks fell so low that, when business picked up, the yields were very high. The high yields caused prices to rise. The rise was so rapid that the profits from the rise were much greater than the yields from earnings. A speculative boom developed in which stocks sold on the basis of the recent rise rather than on the basis of recent earnings. When such a situation develops, it has left reality and can go on until something happens to check it. Since the value is based on the recent rise rather than on earnings, the rise must continue or trouble develops.

In 1929, prices of bonds of industrial concerns fell so that the yields were over 5 per cent. Stocks rose so high in price that the earnings were only about 3.25 per cent. Since this was a period of higher earnings than could be expected to continue, and since the yields were far below the yields on bonds, a readjustment had to occur.

CHAPTER XVIII

INVESTMENTS WHEN THE DOLLAR IS UNSTABLE

If one had left an estate with a guaranteed annual income of $100 per year in gold in the United States or in England in 1873, and if the guarantee had been fulfilled, by 1896 the beneficiary would have had a purchasing power of twice the anticipated amount. This was due to low gold production.

If a similar provision had been made in 1896, the buying power of the income by 1913 would have shrunk to two-thirds the anticipated amount. This was due to finding large amounts of gold. By 1920, the added fact of low demand for gold would have cut the buying power to less than one-third of the anticipated amount.

If the investment had been made in 1920, and if the agency paying the dividends had not gone bankrupt, the buying power would have increased almost two and one-half times by 1932. This was due to low demand for gold for money in other countries, followed by high demand.

The instability is much greater than the above figures indicate, particularly when prices decline. If prices rise, the buying power declines but the agency which agrees to make the payment is likely to remain solvent so that some income is secured. If prices decline too much, the buying power of the income would be greatly increased if obtained, but the agency that agreed to make it would likely be insolvent. The following are some classes of investments which can be combined so as to help in providing security against unstable money.

Life insurance is safer than most investments. The money is likely to be lost by the beneficiary unless it is paid in an annuity form. For protection of dependents, it is desirable to have some readily available cash in the event of death. The safest way is to have the balance of any life insurance in an annuity form which will run for a definite number of years until children are educated. For older dependents, the safest form is as a life annuity. If inflation occurs, the value of these will decline, but payment is certain. If violent deflation occurs, the value rises if paid, but payment may be stopped because of failure. Some additional security can be attained by having insurance in different companies.

Government bonds are usually the safest type of security, but there is no certainty that inflation will not reduce their value. Nor is there certainty that deflation may not require a reduction in the interest rate or in payments. In 1932, England reduced the rate of interest from 5 to 3½ per cent on about $10,000,000,000 of bonds.

The security of other bonds depends on the success of the concern issuing them. If prices rise, the bonds are likely to be paid, but the buying power will be less. If prices decline, many such bonds become worthless, because they cannot be paid.

In the United States, many bonds carry the so-called gold clause. This requires payment in gold dollars of the present weight and fineness. If prices rise, such payment is easy for the debtor. If prices fall, it is an attempt to make sure that no act of Congress will prevent the creditor from extracting from the borrower a purchasing power greater than that which either party anticipated. If deflation is too serious, the debtor is unable to pay. The effort to exact the last "pound of flesh" results in getting nothing. The gold clause is of doubtful value. If conditions get so bad that it has to be invoked, it will probably be impossible to collect.

There is a constant shift in industries. At one time, street railway bonds were considered to be "gilt-edged." For many years, railroad bonds were a favorite form of investment. Invention of the automobile changed the situation. Similar changes are always taking place. Bankers and others in the habit of making investments are usually conservative and sceptical of new inventions. They often delay too long in shifting.

Mortgages are much the same as bonds, but are less easily marketable. The security back of a mortgage on distant properties is usually difficult to determine. The buyer is sometimes more able to determine values of mortgages on nearby properties than he is to determine the value of bonds.

Savings banks are carefully supervised and are a good place to invest when prices are stable. If much deflation occurs, they may fail. In periods of violent deflation, when safety of principal rather than income becomes the major consideration, postal savings are the safest form of investment and keep the money in use, whereas hoarding of gold in a safety deposit box puts gold out of use.

Preferred stocks are intermediate in position between bonds and common stocks. A corporation must pay interest on its bonds if it can. Usually it must pay a fixed dividend on preferred stock before it pays anything on common stock. The value of any security is dependent on ability to pay.

Common stocks are even more violently affected by inflation and deflation than are preferred stocks. They are the highest-yielding form of investment when prices are rising, and the most dangerous form when deflation occurs. For 17 years before the war, commodity prices were rising at a compound rate of 2.3 per cent per year, or rose 46 per cent. As a result of this unstable value of gold, many persons came to look on common stocks as a very safe form of investment. But the situation is very different with a declining price level.

There is no way in which an individual can fully protect himself from the devastating effect of variations in the value of gold. Certain combinations of investments will help.

The safest investment is in education. This is the only investment that has any assurance of stability for a lifetime. For most persons, education of the children is a greater safeguard for their own protection in old age than any other investment they are likely to make.

The next safest investment is life insurance for dependents and an annuity policy for one's self.

If the family plans to live in one place, a farm or home is the next best investment. Until it is completely paid for, investments in stocks and bonds usually are not advisable.

The combination of a farm or home with life insurance and an annuity policy is some protection against inflation and deflation. If inflation occurs, all the investments are secure, but the buying power of the life insurance and annuity declines. The farm or home is likely to rise in price if well located. If deflation occurs, the buying power of the life insurance and annuity rises if the companies remain solvent. The farm or home falls in value, but is still of use unless the deflation is so severe as to make the taxes consume the value.

If a farm or home is not purchased, the life insurance and annuity policies should be larger. If money is available for additional investments, government bonds or mortgages are advisable. If still more is available, good common stocks are desirable. When in doubt, it is desirable to select several industries that have promising futures.

There is no such thing as a sound investment policy until one knows whether gold is to rise or fall in value. Much of the assurance in the minds of those who invested for themselves or for universities, hospitals, and the like, has faded away, since the generation of rising prices has turned to a period of falling prices. By the time investment ideas have been shifted to a deflation philosophy, inflation may occur. The first step in attempting to make sound investments is to estimate the probable value of gold during the lifetime of the investment.

When real estate is sold, it is a common practice for owners of real estate to have a mortgage on it and to sell it subject to the mortgage. The seller often forgets the property after the sale is made, but he is still liable on the mortgage. During the Panic of 1929, many persons who had their investments in what they considered to be good order, were bankrupt by mortgages on which they were liable.

If prices are rising, it may pay to go in debt, but if prices are falling the debts should be closely limited to earning power. It is not sufficient that they be related to the present value of the property.

If there is to be a period of stable or declining prices, life insurance companies and other investing agencies should give especial attention to the dates of maturity of the bonds which they buy. If they can purchase long-time, non-callable bonds, they can help hold up their earnings because equally good bonds will probably cost materially more later.

Since profits in business will be more difficult to make, care will need to be exercised to avoid making loans on farms, homes, or business concerns that are near the margin. Before the war, a loan of 50 per cent on a home or farm was fairly safe for both the borrower and lender. With falling prices, loans of even 25 per cent have proved dangerous. For some years to come, loans on homes of half the cost to build at the time the loan is made are likely to be more risky than before the war.

BIBLIOGRAPHY

Fisher, I., Purchasing Power of Money. 1920.

Fisher, I., and others, How to Invest When Prices Are Rising. 1912.

Huebner, S. S., The Investment Objectives of Life Insurance, The Annals of the American Academy of Political and Social Science, Vol. 161, pp. 14-19. May 1932.

Keynes, J. M., Monetary Reform, pp. 7-21, 1924.

King, W. I., Circulating Credit: Its Nature and Relation to Public Welfare. American Economic Review, Vol. X, No. 4, p. 746. December 1920.

Smith, E. L., Common Stocks as Long Term Investments. 1924.

Van Strum, K. S., Investing in Purchasing Power. 1925.

Winkler, M., The Foreign Bond Bubble. American Mercury, Vol. 25, No. 100, pp. 480-485. April 1932.

CHAPTER XIX

OTHER EFFECTS OF INFLATION AND DEFLATION

INFLATION

Effects of inflation on war industries.—Many as are the injurious effects of inflation, it has some beneficial effects. Theoretically, it would be better to finance wars by taxation so that the endless series of social injustices that result from inflation and deflation would be avoided. But inflation is the line of least resistance.

With the outbreak of war, many of the most able-bodied men must be withdrawn from various walks of life. At the same time many new industries must be started. If this is to be done, many persons not previously employed must enter industrial work and many other persons must change their occupations. All this might be brought about by universal conscription of capital and labor. If conscription is not used, wage rates must be the basis on which individuals will choose their occupations. If no inflation were to take place, shifts in occupation would necessitate drastic reduction in wages in many industries. This is always a slow and painful process. But if money is increased, wages may be strikingly increased in some war industries and left nominally at the pre-war basis in the non-essential industries. Although this reduces the real wages in the latter industries, such changes are accepted with the minimum of complaint. The high wages in the war industries result in a stampede from the non-essential industries and from idleness. All wages lag behind inflation at first, so that although nominal or money wages are rising, real wages fall. This results in enforced economy. The non-essential industries are automatically curbed.

The cutting down of pensions, incomes from interest, and the like, even though they have painful results in individual cases, result as a whole in forcing older persons, retired persons, and others with fixed incomes to supplement them by performing some remunerative work. It would be exceedingly difficult to devise another means that would so quickly bring out latent labor and so quickly shift labor from peace-time to war-time industries. In Massachusetts in 1919, in spite of the number of workers who had gone to war, the number of employed was about 20 per cent above the pre-war number. Were it not for the deflation which is likely to follow, these effects of moderate inflation in a war period might be viewed with complacency.

Business expansion.—While inflation is taking place, prices rise rapidly. With prices rising more rapidly than is anticipated, it is practically impossible to fail. The more rashly one goes into debt, the more certain he is to profit. This creates an optimism which, if it occurred in times of peace, would expand production. Marginal lands and marginal mines would be brought into use. Many inefficient producers would be drawn in.

Although all this would result in expansion in production, it also establishes false business standards. Men cease to use reasonable business caution. They borrow unduly and become scornful of minor details of thrift. Production regardless of cost becomes the standard. Speculation in goods is encouraged.

During the war period, many workers are taken out of their ordinary pursuits. Inflation tends to speed up the work of those who are left at home, so that the reduced production is less than would otherwise occur.

Effect on non-war industries.—Industries not directly contributing to the war, particularly long-time industries, are curtailed. Since wages do not rise so rapidly as prices, real wages fall. One of the first items on which to economize is rent. Families move to smaller houses or take in roomers. The withdrawal of a large number of men to sleep in tents or temporary shelters reduces the demand for permanent buildings. Building is checked. The persons engaged in these occupations find their places in war industries.

Effect of inflation on public utilities.—Now that charges for public services are regulated by commissions, they respond very slowly to economic changes. The abnormal condition must exist for a long time before the commission acts. Usually public pressure prevents action, until the service fails to meet the public need. In the meantime the demand for increased wages, because of the high cost of living, results in wage advances. The materials purchased advance rapidly. This results in curtailment of all expansion and neglect of repairs and upkeep. During the World War, wage increases were made to railroad employees long before freight rates were raised. A large advance in freight rates was made in 1920, after the panic had begun. During the period of inflation, freight rates were held down and some goods were shipped that should not have moved. This increased the artificial boom. The 40 per cent increase in freight rates after the panic had started similarly resulted in an artificial repression in business. As an example, before rates were raised, hay was shipped from far western states to eastern states because freight rates were out of adjustment with general prices. This resulted in a hay boom in states as far west as Montana. When prices began to fall, the great increase in freight rates ruined many producers. Travel on passenger trains was artificially stimulated when rates were held down and was repressed when rates were raised after deflation had begun. In general, street-car fares

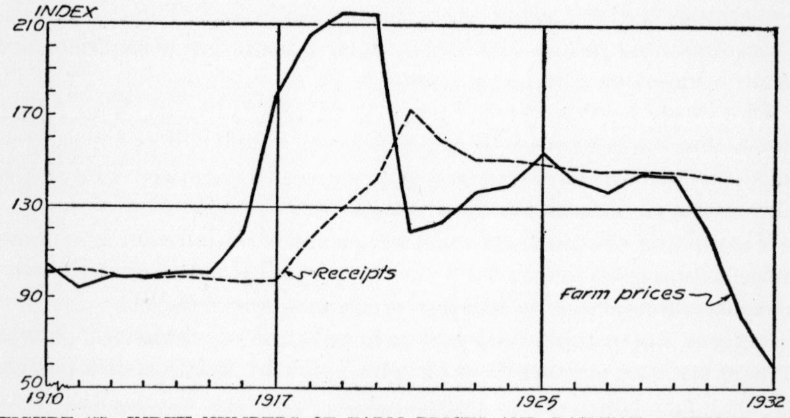

FIGURE 157.—INDEX NUMBERS OF FARM PRICES AND RAILWAY REVENUE PER TON-MILE, 1910-32.
1910-14 = 100.
Freight rates were held down when farm prices were rising, and were raised when prices fell in 1920 and 1931.

were held low when men were fully employed and were raised at about the time when the panic and unemployment occurred.

The results of such a situation caused a serious impairment of the physical and the financial condition of public utilities.

Other effects of inflation.—Inflation causes reckless buying. Many persons purchase far in advance of their needs for fear that prices will rise, and the violence of price fluctuations is thereby increased. Persons engaged in professions and high-salaried positions do not receive increases promptly, but persons who ordinarily receive little pay obtain large increases. As a whole, the latter class is more numerous and is less inclined to save. This results in rapid and indiscriminate buying. The silk shirt has its day. Persons who have saved money and who depend on interest and rents find their buying power reduced.

Great numbers of "new rich" appear. As a whole, this latter class is less thrifty. This again results in rapid spending.

Wages lag when prices are rising. At first thought, this would appear injurious to workers, but moderate inflation creates good times for workmen. There is a feverish demand for labor. Everyone can find work. It is very easy for the efficient to get promotions. Even though the buying power of wage rates declines, the buying power of most individual workers rises. Labor unions flourish. It is easy to show the benefits of organization when every strike is successful.

Farmers see the profit that middlemen make as prices rise while goods are passing through the channels of trade. They, therefore, become interested in forming cooperative associations. These are sometimes organized just in time to buy their property at peak prices and begin business on a falling market.

Fire losses decrease because property is rising in value. With falling prices, fire losses increase, because property values fall and unscrupulous persons burn their own property to get the insurance. Fire risk is also increased because repairs are neglected.

The mining of gold is retarded because general inflation is synonymous with a reduction in the value of gold. This means that the purchasing power of gold in terms of goods has been reduced.

Persons whose sole investments are in bonds or mortgages, or who live on pensions or other fixed incomes, suffer by inflation. If a portion of their investments is in homes and stocks, their net position may not be injured.

If inflation goes to great extremes, as it did in Germany, it has devastating effects. If it goes no farther than in the United States and England, the injuries resulting from it are small in comparison with an equal amount of deflation. Whether or not deflation occurs after inflation depends on the laws which a country chooses to pass. It is very common practice to deflate if possible.

These are but a few of the innumerable effects of inflation. Every human act is affected.

DEFLATION

Marvelous progress in the past century has been due to the division of labor. By specialization, each person produces so much of something that everyone can have more of everything. But specialization means that most of one's wants are supplied by purchases. Innumerable transactions are necessary. The battery that keeps this machine running is the medium of exchange—money. When money is stable in value, the machine works well. When inflation occurs, the machine runs wild. When deflation occurs, it stalls. The popular explanation during inflation is that there is a shortage of goods. The popular explanation of deflation is over-production, and the fantastic remedy of trying to find ways of becoming less efficient is proposed.

Deflation stops business.—Inflation results in unusual business activity. Deflation stops business. When prices are falling, every consumer and dealer soon learns that he could have done better on every purchase if he had delayed buying. This results in indefinitely putting off some purchases and in delaying buying of articles that cannot be indefinitely postponed. This results in low stocks in the homes and in the stores. It ultimately provides conditions for expansion of business, but much of the demand is permanently lost. Since everyone who produces anything or handles any commodity finds that it shrivels in his possession, and if sold often results in bad debts, business stops. Storekeepers discharge their clerks and manufacturers close their plants.

The unemployed people wear their old clothes and use less house room. Cotton stocks pile up, and the public attributes the increase to over-production. When prosperity returns, there is an active demand for clothing, but if the depression has been long, there is not a demand for the full amount that would have been used. Therefore some time is necessary to get rid of the accumulated stocks of cotton. Similarly, if an automobile has been run one more year than it normally would be before being scrapped, that much demand has been permanently lost. The increased sales after the depression is over will be less than the total sales had there been no panic.

Buying in quantity, which is normally a sound business practice, is discouraged because the savings in freights, handling, and the like are less than the losses due to declining prices. In general, those who follow good business practices are penalized, and those who are slow to spend and who purchase from hand to mouth suffer the least.

Prices of regulated services.—Under present conditions in the United States, the rates for a considerable number of public services, such as telephones, telegraphs, freight, express, street cars, city water, and the like, furnished by private corporations, are fixed by commissions. The number of this type of services is steadily increasing. They are usually under the jurisdiction of public-service commissions. The laws recognize that these corporations should have a reasonable return on their investments. The small volume of business reduces the return, so that often the charges are raised when the general price level is falling. This type of price fixing is exactly the opposite of a normal economic trend. The price of these services rises very slowly and declines very slowly.

For example, in 1917 the average price paid to farmers for farm products had risen to 180 when pre-war equals 100, but freight rates on fifty agricultural commodities were only 1 per cent above pre-war.[1] The major rise in freight rates came in August 1920 after the agricultural depression had begun. Prices of farm products in 1921 averaged 19 per cent above pre-war and freight rates on farm products averaged 77 per cent above pre-war (figure 157).

An increase in freight rates was again granted in 1931, two years after the beginning of the worst panic in history. An increase in fares of commuters to New York City was being considered in 1932, after nearly three years of depression, when millions were unemployed.

Under our present system, charges of this sort are likely to be low when they should be high, and high when they should be low. This is just another of the innumerable developments of modern civilization that work when prices are stable but that make unstable money intolerable.

Date of birth.—The financial success of an individual is due in part to his own ability and in part to the time when he was born. The young man who started farming after the Civil War and who showed the most energy and courage usually suffered the most. Prices declined so rapidly that it was difficult to maintain the capital, to say nothing of making a profit. From 1897 to 1913, prices of farm products rose rapidly. The young man who started farming early in this period and who went heavily in debt was successful. The uninformed point with pride to the initiative and success of this individual, as compared with his father, when in reality the only extra credit that is due to him is in the choice of the time to be born.

"Buy British."—With the collapse of commodity prices and the consequent difficulty of balancing the budget, the British have abandoned their policy of free trade for the protective tariff. In a further endeavor to curtail imports and improve the economic status of their producers, they have inaugurated a widespread advertising campaign to "buy British."

"Buy native."—When prices decline, the tendency of economic isolation is not only the policy of nations, but appears in many forms in various states and communities within each country. The Consti-

[1] Yearbook of Agriculture, 1922, United States Department of Agriculture, p. 1011, 1923.

tution of the United States forbids the enactment of tariff laws within the country, but does not restrict the state legislatures in applying the same principle in the form of taxation or disease control.

Kansas passed a law that certain public institutions must buy materials from persons or firms within the state whenever the price is equal to that submitted by others. North Dakota, Minnesota, Missouri, and Oklahoma passed legislation of a similar nature. In Wyoming, a premium not to exceed 5 per cent may be paid by municipalities or state institutes for Wyoming articles that compete with those of other states. Colorado passed a similar law.

Many states passed laws or regulations ostensibly regulating the importation of diseased seeds, plants, or animals but really designed to protect home industries.

Many counties and states also began to object to the employment of persons who were not residents.

Going primitive.—Before money was invented, the common method of exchanging goods was by barter. When the monetary systems break down, there is reversion to barter. Recently there have appeared curious testimonials to the low prices, tariffs, quota systems, and the like, that have interfered with the normal course of trade. Farmers barter their products for products and services which they need. This country and Brazil exchanged wheat for coffee. The London Chamber of Commerce proposes that the governments or Central Banks of 35 countries set up clearing houses for the exchange of goods, by barter units or barter bonds.

Deflation and gold mining.—Declining prices result in rising purchasing power of gold. This stimulates the search for gold. When eggs are five cents a dozen, hogs three cents a pound, and wheat thirty cents a bushel, a small amount of gold buys a relatively large amount of other things. It is therefore obvious that a large number of individuals and many organizations will prospect.

Deflation and wealth.—Whenever prices change, production is affected. Slowly falling prices curtail production somewhat. Rapidly falling prices curtail production quickly and drastically. Anything that curtails production reduces wealth and well-being. We cannot have the extra things which we desire if we reduce production.

One of the great problems of the world has been and always will be the keeping of the ownership of wealth in the hands of those who are justly entitled to it.

Falling prices not only reduce wealth but also produce sweeping transfers in its ownership. Deflation takes property from the hands of those who are justly entitled to it and transfers it to those who are not justly entitled to it. The action is so insidious that most persons feel the injustice without knowing the real cause.

Attacks on government.—In order to function, an economic society that is based on the private ownership of property must have a reliable medium of exchange. When the medium of exchange rises in value, the chaos that results leads persons to challenge this economic order. The thing that has broken down is not "capitalism," which is another name for private enterprise, but merely the medium of exchange. Capitalism is no more to blame for this than it is to blame for the failure of a bridge to carry a certain load. One of the necessary tools of society has failed. The remedy is to supply a tool that will work. The only tool that will work is a measure of value that will keep the average price of commodities stable. There are many ways in which such a measure can be provided, whenever the science involved is understood, just as there are many ways of strengthening the bridge when the sciences involved are understood. If we change from a society based on private enterprise to a communistic one, it should be done on the basis of the relative merits of these two systems and not because we have failed to invent a reliable measure of value.

When serious deflation occurs, the party in power is usually voted out or revolution comes. As a result of the deflation in 1929, most of the political parties that were in power were thrown out and in many countries revolutions occurred. Probably we have not yet seen the last of these. Popular demand is generally for a dictator. The assumption is that democratic government is a failure. Since neither the dictator nor the democratic government knows the cause or the remedy, the shift to a dictator is merely a backward step in civilization, which has portentous implications for the future.

A civilization based on private enterprise is a very effective but delicate machine. Money is the battery that keeps it going. If this tool functions badly, the thing to change is the tool and not the form of government.

Some effects of inflation and deflation.—When inflation goes to the extremes that it did in Germany, bonds, life insurance, endowments become worthless. There are no examples of extreme cases of deflation in history, as these would bring utter chaos.

A comparison of the effects of doubling the price level and then restoring it are given on page 300.

Doubling the price level by Inflation	Halving the price level by Deflation
1. Commodity prices double.	1. Commodities fall 50 per cent.
2. Commodity prices overshoot the 200 mark but return to it.	2. Prices decline below the 100 mark but return to it.
3. Debts are easy to pay.	3. Debts are difficult of payment.
4. Bond holders and other creditors lose, but even poor debts are collectible.	4. Creditors gain if they can collect, but often lose everything.
5. Life insurance earnings rise.	5. Life insurance earnings fall.
6. The buying power of the income of universities declines but new funds are available.	6. Universities suffer because income is reduced and new funds do not appear.
7. Buying on credit is popular and is commended.	7. All debts are abhorrent.
8. Taxes are easy to pay.	8. Taxes are difficult to pay.
9. Public services expand.	9. Taxpayers' leagues are formed but accomplish little.
10. Tramps disappear.	10. Many self-respecting persons are fed at public expense.
11. "New rich" appear.	11. "New poor" appear.
12. Labor union membership rises.	12. Labor union membership falls.
13. Wages lag but there is work for everyone.	13. Wages lag but jobs disappear.
14. Promotions to higher class of labor are easy to obtain.	14. Promotions are slow. Demotions are common.
15. Farmers prosper.	15. Farm depression is long and severe.
16. The standard of living of the southern mule improves.	16. The mule's standard of living is reduced.
17. Building of city residences is checked.	17. Building in cities is overdone and then stopped.
18. Fire insurance losses are small.	18. Fire insurance losses are large.
19. Goods are hoarded.	19. Cash is hoarded.
20. The laundry business increases.	20. Sales of washing machines increase.
21. Doctors' fees lag, but business increases and debts can be collected.	21. Doctors' fees lag, but business decreases and many debts are uncollectible.
22. Hospital fees lag, but hospitals are filled and gifts are large.	22. Hospital fees lag, but hospitals are not filled and gifts decline so that higher fees are needed.
23. Suicides decrease.	23. Suicides increase.
24. Stealing decreases.	24. Stealing increases.
25. Interest rates rise.	25. Interest rates decline on safe papers.
26. The size of life and fire insurance policies increases.	26. The size of life and fire insurance policies decreases.

Nobody profits by deflation.—It is popularly assumed that creditors gain what the debtors lose by deflation. The fallacy of this is well illustrated by the following example of a house which was sold at foreclosure sale in Rochester, New York, in 1932. The house had once sold for $14,000 cash. In a subsequent sale, the owner paid $6500 cash, giving a first mortgage for $5000 and a second mortgage for $2500. Having lost his position, the owner was unable to make payments, and the first-mortgage holder bid in the property because no one else bid. He acquired the property for the first mortgage but had to pay delinquent taxes and foreclosure costs and lost an interest payment. The property cost him about $6000. He leased the property back to the previous owner for enough to pay taxes and maintenance charges. The home owner lost $6500—which was all that he had. The second-mortgage holder lost all that he had in the property, and since he had many second mortgages he found that he had suddenly changed from a comparatively wealthy man to a poor man. The first-mortgage holder acquired a property that he did not want and which did not yield any net income, and which he would be glad to sell for considerably less than the mortgage. Nobody gained.

In a period of severe deflation, the only man who could gain would be the man who hid his gold in a safe-deposit box or who continually speculated on the negative side by always selling things which he did not have, but not selling enough to be caught in one of the minor rises.

Most of the stories about misers were written about periods of deflation when "misering" was a good business.

In a long period of moderate price declines, a lender who confines himself to very safe loans would profit. In the deflation of 1873, first-class bonds continued to rise; but in the deflation of 1929, the deflation was so drastic that bonds declined in price and many became valueless.

It is also commonly said that laborers profit by deflation because wages lag, but promotion is slow, jobs are insecure, and unemployment is frequent. Deflation is the greatest nightmare of labor, because it results in unemployment and lack of promotion.

Even if some one theoretical group did profit, few individuals would profit, because very few individuals have only one class of interest. A workman who owns a home and a life insurance policy, and has a job, is a capitalist, laborer, and real estate owner. Deflation endangers his job, reduces the value of his home, and cuts his life insurance dividends, and if it goes far enough the company may fail.

When a rise in prices occurs after deflation, those who have previously acquired bankrupt properties profit.

BIBLIOGRAPHY

Adams, L. P., Agricultural Depression and Farm Relief in England, 1813-1852. 1932.

Coyle, E. S., A Review of Recent Bank Failures. The Review of Economic Statistics, Vol. XIV, No. 1, pp. 38-41. Feb. 15, 1932.

Hansen, A. H., The Effect of Price Fluctuations on Agriculture. Journal of Political Economy, Vol. XXXIII, No. 2, pp. 196-216. April 1925.

JEVONS, W. S., A Serious Fall in the Value of Gold Ascertained and Its Social Effects Set Forth. 1863.

KEYNES, J. M., Monetary Reform. 1924.

MARSHALL, A., Official Papers, pp. 9-16, 90-98. 1926.

WARREN, G. F., and PEARSON, F. A., Effects of Declining Prices. Farm Economics No. 74, pp. 1665-1671. February 1932.

WARREN, G. F., and PEARSON, F. A., The Agricultural Situation. 1924.

WICKENS, D. L., Farm-Mortgage Credit. United States Department of Agriculture, Technical Bulletin 288. February 1932.

Committee on Finance and Industry. Report presented to Parliament by the financial secretary to the Treasury by command of His Majesty, June 1931. C md. 3897. 1931.

CHAPTER XX

PRICE-SUPPORTING MEASURES[1]

The world-wide attempt to maintain a fixed price for gold resulted in a collapse of commodity prices. This inevitably brought about government action throughout the world for the purpose of raising and maintaining prices of farm products.

These price-supporting measures took a variety of forms. For example, the United Kingdom and Netherlands, which are importing countries, resorted to the tariff to raise the price of the home-produced products. In Canada and Australia, wheat bonus measures were tried. A great variety of restrictions may be imposed on imports, such as the tariff, import quotas, government licensing, import monopolies, milling and mixing regulations, sanitary restrictions, requirement of a minimum percentage of home-grown produce, and the like.

The most important type of price-supporting measures is the tariff. A second type of legislation is aid to branches of agriculture which are on an export basis. The regulations may take the form of an artificial restriction of exports or an artificial stimulation of exports. The international sugar agreement limits the exports of the surplus sugar-producing countries.

The Egyptian government has placed restrictions on the cotton acreage, thereby indirectly affecting exports, and for several years Brazil has restricted coffee exports.

This type of price legislation which restricts exports represents an attempt to raise the world price level for particular commodities. Attempts to stimulate exports have been more common. The plans to stimulate exports have for their purpose the disposal of surpluses on foreign markets at whatever they will bring, while the rest of the crop is sold on the domestic market at a higher price. Such plans make use of export premiums or bounties, equalization fees, or export deben-

[1] The authors wish to acknowledge the assistance of Mr. A. R. Gans, who very kindly prepared this abstract from Edminster, L. R., Schaben, L. J., and Lynsky, M., Agricultural Price-Supporting Measures in Foreign Countries, Bureau of Agricultural Economics, Mimeographed report F. S. 56, July 1932.

tures. Some of the Danubian countries, South Africa, Southern Rhodesia, and Australia have used such plans.

A third type of measure is that of production bounties or other aids given directly to the producer. Such measures are either for the purpose of stimulating exports or reducing imports, depending on whether the country is already on an import or export basis for the commodity affected. The Australian and Canadian wheat bounties fell in this group. Other examples are the British and Netherlands subsidies of the sugar-beet industry, the French production premium on flax, and the Belgian subsidies for cultivation of new land.

Summaries of important price-maintenance measures in some of the leading agricultural countries follow:

Argentina.—Since agricultural production in Argentina is predominantly on an export basis, governmental action designed to affect agricultural prices has been aimed largely at reducing production and marketing costs rather than directly at price maintenance. Recently, however, measures more definitely related to price maintenance have been enacted. Four times during 1931, new tariff laws were enacted which either increased existing rates or increased the number of dutiable products. In October 1931, an ad valorem tax of 10 per cent, effective for one year, was levied on all imports. This tax was in addition to those already existing. Moreover, seasonal embargoes and sanitary restrictions were placed on some products, and an anti-dumping law was passed. Restriction of sugar production was also undertaken for the 1931-32 crop.

Australia.—All imports are assessed a primage duty of 10 per cent ad valorem plus a sales tax of 6 per cent; many products have additional duties. Sugar marketing is a government monopoly, and imports are prohibited except in case of shortage. The entire cotton crop is also marketed through a governmental agency. Both the state and federal governments support cooperative marketing organizations, some of which are compulsory and others voluntary pools. The Patterson Plan for marketing butter is an important example of the latter type of pool. Under this plan, the cooperative and private creameries are under the control of a Stabilization Committee. To this committee, the creameries pay a levy of a few cents a pound (3.5 cents in 1932), and this money is used to pay a bounty on the butter exported. From 1926 to date (1932), this bounty has varied from 5 to 9 cents per pound. The price of domestic butter is kept above a parity with foreign markets by means of a tariff which amounted to 14 cents per pound in 1932.

Cash bounties have been paid on the production of wheat, cotton, and flax. The bounty on wheat, for the 1931-32 crop only, was 9 cents per bushel. The bounty on cotton was 3 cents per pound through 1932. At first, the bounty on flax was 15 per cent of the selling price received by the producer, but after two years this was to be reduced to 10 per cent and after four years to 7.5 per cent, after which it is to expire.

Brazil.—The valorization of coffee is probably one of the most familiar examples of governmental support of prices. With about two-thirds of the world's supply produced there, Brazil enjoyed a position approaching a monopoly, and valorization operations were generally profitable from the time they were started in 1905. Plantings had been increasing rapidly, however, and with nearly a year's supply on hand the price dropped from 16 cents a pound in September to 11.5 cents in November 1929. Further increases in stocks and declines in prices during 1930 resulted in the government's purchase of large amounts of coffee which were later destroyed. To curb further increases in production, a tax of 6.5 cents per tree was placed on new plantings, and also a tax of 1.8 cents per pound on all coffee exported.

Brazil maintains high tariffs on agricultural products and an embargo on wheat flour. The government has also established a cacao institute to promote standardization of export grades of cacao and to lower costs of marketing.

Canada.—Until recently most of the governmental aid to Canadian agriculture had been in the form of measures to promote lower production and marketing costs. During recent years, however, more direct support has appeared in the form of the bounty of 5 cents per bushel for the 1931 wheat crop, and in further restrictions on the importation of agricultural products, as well as in an anti-dumping law. Since 1929, the Dominion Government also has assumed the financial responsibility of the three voluntary wheat pools in Saskatchewan, Alberta, and Manitoba.

France.—Import restrictions long have been important price-influencing measures in France. These measures include tariffs, milling and mixing restrictions, import quotas, import licenses, sanitary restrictions, production premiums, and direct price fixing. Most of the products imported from the United States pay maximum tariff rates, but two important ones, cotton and tobacco, are admitted free. During the last two or three years, tariff rates on foodstuffs, especially cereals, have been increased sharply. In July 1931, the rate on refined sugar was $6.04 per 100 pounds, and on wheat $1.71 cents per bushel. In November 1931, a special ad valorem tax was placed on all products coming from countries with depreciated exchange. Since November 1929, France also has had milling restrictions to control the proportion of foreign wheat used in milling. The proportion of foreign wheat permitted in flour has ranged from 3 to 50 per cent. In order to avoid evasion of these requirements, wheat imported for uses other than human consumption had to be colored.

Definite import quotas also have been fixed for many products, particularly livestock, poultry, and dairy products, and vegetables. To avoid the rush of imports at the beginning of each quota period, importers were required to obtain licenses which were issued from time to time in proportion to imports during the preceding year. Sanitary restrictions prohibit the importation of fruit from any country where San José scale exists, unless accompanied by certificates of inspection.

Germany.—Since 1925, Germany has had a high tariff on all important agricultural products. Tariff rates were increased steadily from that time until 1930, when the Federal government was given powers to change the tariffs on rye, wheat, barley, and peas as the domestic prices of these products changed. In March 1931, this decree was extended to include all agricultural products. From January to October 1930, the import duty on wheat was increased from 48.6 to 162.1 cents per bushel.

Since 1929, Germany also has had milling quotas to regulate the percentage of foreign wheat used in flour-making. This percentage has varied from 3 to 60 per cent. In addition, mixing regulations for various agricultural products have been imposed. For example, the proportion of alcohol made from specified materials was fixed, and also the proportion of alcohol used with motor fuels.

An import certificate system also has been used, which is essentially an export debenture system. The principle involved is that certificates obtained by exportation of certain products may be used to obtain free importation of other products.

New Zealand.—The agriculture of this country is predominantly on an export basis, hence the government aid to agriculture has been directed largely toward stimulating exports. Export control boards have been established for the principal products, namely meat, dairy products, fruit, and honey. The primary object of these boards is to obtain better prices for New Zealand products through standardization and improvement in quality of products, development of markets, and orderly shipping. The Dairy Produce Control Board did have absolute control of exportation of dairy products for a time but now operates largely as a grading and shipping agency. The Fruit Control Board guarantees minimum prices for exported apples which meet prescribed standards. Anti-dumping legislation has been in effect in New Zealand for more than a decade.

South Africa.—In South Africa, the important price-supporting measures are tariffs, import restrictions, and export quotas and subsidies. During recent years, tariffs have been revised upward sharply. In March 1930, the duty on wheat was increased from 32 to 39 cents per bushel; that on wheat flour from $1.95 to $3.04 per 100 pounds; and that on sugar from $1.95 to $3.04 per 100 pounds. In October 1931, an additional duty of 5 per cent ad valorem was placed on practically all imports, and in March 1932 a new customs surtax of 7.5 per cent was levied on all goods except those used predominantly for agricultural purposes. In November 1931, an exchange dumping duty provided for protection from dumping by countries with depreciated exchange.

Since March 1930, restrictions on wheat importations have been in effect to maintain the domestic price above a world market level. To the same end, provision also has been made for the compulsory exportation of a specified proportion of the corn crop. This amounts to dumping abroad in order to maintain domestic prices. In May 1932, a similar law was enacted for tobacco exports. In addition, an act of Nov. 30, 1931, authorized one-year export subsidies for many agricultural products. The funds for payment of these subsidies were obtained by a special 5 per cent ad valorem tax on practically all imports.

United Kingdom.—Since October 1931, a general policy of protection has been adopted. The first tariff measure authorized duties as high as 100 per cent on certain luxury or "non-essential" fruits, vegetables, and floricultural products. The list included cherries, currants, gooseberries, hot-house grapes, plums, strawberries, asparagus, green peas, broccoli, cauliflower, carrots, salad chicory, cucumbers, lettuce, mushrooms, new potatoes, tomatoes, turnips, cut flowers, flowers attached to bulbs, foliage bulbs, and rose trees. All these products were admitted free from Empire countries.

A general tariff act of March 1932 imposed a 10 per cent ad valorem duty on imports from outside the Empire which were not already subject to duty. However, many important agricultural products, such as wheat, corn, meats, live animals, raw cotton, wool, and hides were exempted. In April, the general 10 per cent tariff on most classes of manufactured goods was raised to rates of 15 to 33 1/3 per cent.

Since 1925, a production bounty has been paid to the domestic beet sugar industry. Under this bounty, the number of sugar beet growers increased from 4,039 in 1924 to 40,415 in 1930, and the acreage from 22,637 to 348,920.

In May 1932, an act to fix the price of British wheat was put into effect. This act, which is more or less unique in many respects, guarantees producers a price of 10 shillings per hundredweight (about $1.30 per bushel at par) and obligates millers and importers to make payments into a special fund for maintaining this price. No tariff is imposed on wheat, and no milling restrictions are placed on the use of foreign wheat. The amount of wheat eligible for the fixed price is determined at the beginning of each crop year.

In addition to these measures of direct aid to agriculture, the British Agricultural Marketing Act, passed in 1931, has for its purpose the improvement of methods of marketing, surplus control, collection of statistical data, research, and education in cooperative marketing.

Cuba.—Prior to the adoption of the International Sugar Agreement, or Chadbourne Plan, in 1931, Cuba had attempted to influence the price of sugar by restricting the grinding season and the size of the crop. The first attempt was made in 1925. In 1927, a central selling agency was established to market that part of the crop not allocated to the United States. Difficulties were encountered as a result of the world-wide collapse in commodity prices in 1930, and the central selling agency was discontinued.

In May 1931, the International Sugar Agreement was entered into by Cuba, Java, Germany, Czechoslovakia, Poland, Hungary, and Belgium. These seven countries produce about 40 per cent of the world's sugar, and about 90 per cent of that exported. The agreement provided for gradual elimination of excess stocks through annual disposal of specified amounts each year, restriction of production, and limitation of exports by each country. Provisions were made for increasing the export quotas as prices made sustained advances. The excess stocks of each country were fixed and also the rate of disposal of these stocks.

Although total production in the seven countries was reduced 23 per cent from 1930-31 to 1931-32, raw sugar prices declined to the lowest level in 38 years. In 1932, the original agreement was modified to provide for further restriction of exports.

Although governmental measures designed to influence agricultural prices in Cuba have dealt primarily with sugar, import duties on other products have been increased markedly in the last two years to encourage greater diversification of agriculture. In addition, the use of a minimum of 10 per cent of Yucca flour in bread and other bakery products has been made obligatory, and a minimum price to farmers for milk has been fixed.

Estonia, Latvia, and Lithuania.—The price-supporting measures of these three small countries are of interest because of their far-reaching nature. Aside from tariffs, export bounties, import licenses, and government monopolies, particularly the latter, have been used extensively. In Estonia and Latvia, the governments exercise complete monopoly control over the grain trade, as to fixation of domestic prices and as to imports. For the 1931-32 wheat crop, Estonia fixed the price at 0.18 to 0.22 kroon per kilogram (equivalent to $1.31 to $1.60 per bushel at par exchange). In Latvia, the prices set for the 1932-33 wheat and rye crops were equivalent to $1.42 and $1.06 per bushel, respectively. The Lithuanian government also has attempted to support grain prices by purchases at fixed prices.

All three countries have an export bounty on hogs and bacon, and Latvia also has bounties on butter and on flax. These three countries and Finland have concluded a series of treaties with each other which facilitate commerce.

English Colonies.—Another notable example of governmental price-supporting activity is the Stevenson Plan to control the marketing of rubber from the two British Colonies, Ceylon and Malaya. The drastic decline in the price of rubber during 1920, from about 50 cents to 15 cents per pound, was the principal reason for adoption of the plan. It was in operation from November 1922 to November 1928. In brief, the method of operation was to limit the export of each rubber holding to a certain percentage of its production for the year ending in October 1920. Provision was made for changes in the export quota as the market price varied above and below certain levels.

The trend of rubber prices was upward for 4 years after the plan was put in operation, but in 1928 prices were practically the same as in 1922. While the plan was in operation, rubber production increased rapidly in the Dutch East Indies where restrictive measures were not in use. As is usually true when price-supporting measures do not control directly a very large proportion of the total production, the Stevenson Plan appears to have held the proverbial umbrella over producing areas not operating under the plan.

Danubian countries.—The attempt of Bulgaria, Hungary, Rumania, and Yugoslavia to obtain preferential tariffs in European grain markets played an important part in several international conferences during 1930 and 1931. Bulgaria has negotiated no treaties with preferential clauses as a result of these conferences. Hungary has negotiated or concluded treaties with Austria, France, Germany, and Italy for trade preferences. Rumania has treaties with Austria, France, and Germany. Yugoslavia has commercial treaties with Czechoslovakia, Austria, and Rumania.

The four Danubian countries have a cooperative agreement among themselves, whereby each is kept informed daily of sales prices by others in order that prices may be maintained at the same level in all four countries.

The world is demonstrating once more the difficulty of holding up the price of this or that commodity when the rising value of the monetary unit pulls the whole price level down.

BIBLIOGRAPHY

Ball, W., Price Fixing in New Zealand. 1932.

Edminster, L. R., Schaben, L. J., and Lynsky, M., Agricultural Price-Supporting Measures in Foreign Countries. United States Department of Agriculture, Bureau of Agricultural Economics, Mimeographed report F. S. 56.

Lawrence, J. S., Stabilization of Prices. 1928.

Seligman, E. R. A., Economics of Farm Relief. 1929.

Spillman, W. J., Balancing the Farm Output. 1927.

Wallace, H. C., Our Debt and Duty to the Farmer. 1925.

Warren, G. F., and Pearson, F. A., The Agricultural Situation. 1924.

Warren, G. F., and Wehrwein, G. S., Which Does Agriculture Need—Readjustment or Legislation? Journal of Farm Economics, Vol. 10, No. 1. January, 1928.

Whittlesey, C. R., Governmental Control of Crude Rubber. 1931.

CHAPTER XXI

EFFECTS OF THE DISCOVERY OF AMERICA ON PRICES

Prices of wheat for twenty-five centuries.—Landrin and Roswag collected prices of wheat from 600 B.C. to the nineteenth century. The amount of silver that could be purchased with a bushel of wheat is shown in table 62 and figure 158. The salient features of the data are the relative stability of prices for 2000 years from the time of Alexander the Great to the discovery of America and the rapid increase thereafter. The greater part of the change is due to the depreciation of silver rather than to appreciation in wheat. Silver, which was the common money, became cheap in terms of nearly all other things. In the words of the layman, everything rose in price.

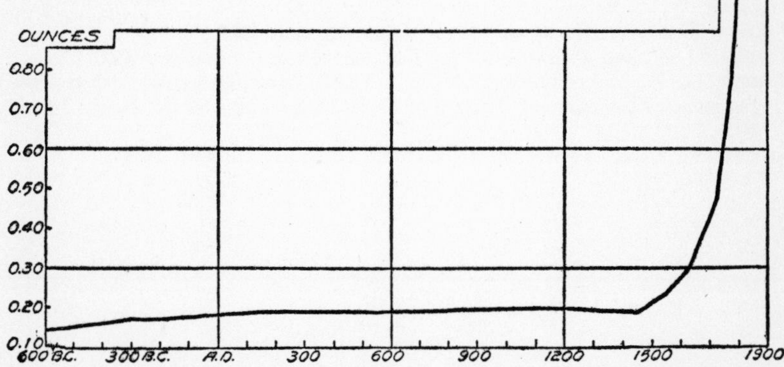

FIGURE 158.—PRICES OF WHEAT IN SILVER FOR 2500 YEARS.
The price of wheat was comparatively stable until great quantities of silver came from America. Prices then rose, not because of the supply of wheat or the demand for it but because money became abundant.

During the thirteenth, fourteenth, and fifteenth centuries, there was a shortage of precious metals throughout Europe. The expansion of industry and agriculture inevitably resulted in declining prices. The declining prices made it difficult to collect taxes, balance budgets, and relieve the poor and unemployed. In order to overcome this situation,

TABLE 62.—PRICE OF WHEAT FOR 2500 YEARS*

Period	Pounds of wheat for an ounce of silver	Ounces of silver that could be purchased with a bushel of wheat
600 B.C.	430	0.14
300 B.C.	360	0.17
200 B.C.	346	0.17
50 B.C.	330	0.18
A.D. 50–300	324	0.19
A.D. 301–500	320	0.19
A.D. 501–800	314	0.19
A.D. 801–1400	307	0.20
A.D. 1401–1500	314	0.19
A.D. 1501–1600	250	0.24
A.D. 1601–1650	200	0.30
A.D. 1651–1700	154	0.39
A.D. 1701–1750	124	0.48
A.D. 1751–1800	75	0.80
A.D. 1801–1850	37	1.62
A.D. 1851–1880	34	1.76

* Mulhall, M. G., The Dictionary of Statistics, p. 468, 1909.

debasement of the currency was widespread. The debasement was sporadic, temporarily relieving the government and other debtors from the injustice of falling prices. The low production and high value of silver and gold stimulated the various voyages among which were those of Columbus.[1]

According to most students, there was a marked rise of commodity prices at the end of the fourteenth century, which was due to the great advance following the Black Death. The plague reduced the production of commodities so that there was more money in proportion to business. In the century before the discovery of America, the trend in commodity prices was distinctly downward. Feavearyear[2] shows that prices dropped from one-third to one-half during this century.

Price of wheat in England.—Over long periods of time, the price of wheat gives an accurate measure of the trend of commodity prices.[3]

[1] Haring, C. H., American Gold and Silver Production in the First Half of the Sixteenth Century, Quarterly Journal of Economics, Vol. 29, pp. 433-474, May 1915.

[2] Feavearyear, A. E., The Pound Sterling, pp. 40, 64. 1931.

[3] Locke, writing in the latter part of the seventeenth century, suggested that wheat was a good measure of value. He stated that for "this part of the world, wheat being the constant and most general food, not altering with the fashion, not growing by chance; but as the farmers sow more, or less of it, which they endeavour to proportion, as near as can be guessed, to the consumption. . . . Wheat, therefore, in this part of the world . . . is the fittest measure to judge the altered value of things, in any long tract of time: and therefore, wheat here,

For 135 years, the price of wheat in the United States has followed very closely the general price level (figure 12, page 28). Compilations of wheat prices in England indicate that, from 1259 to about 1500, the price of wheat varied from 9 to 31 cents per bushel (figure 159). With the huge imports of silver following the discovery of the New World, wheat prices began to rise. From the decade 1500-09 to the decade 1640-49, wheat rose from an average of 17 cents to 133 cents per bushel. About this time the new imports of gold and

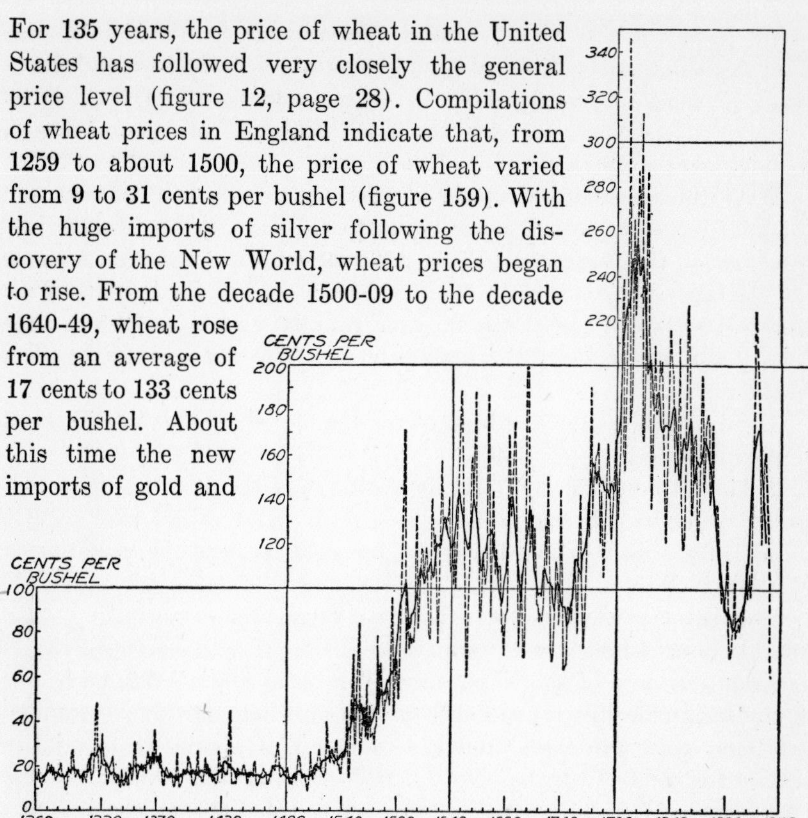

FIGURE 159.—WHEAT PRICES IN ENGLAND,[4] 1259-1932.
Wheat prices were stable during the three centuries from 1250 to 1550. They rose about 4 times in the century after the precious metals came from the New World.

rice in Turkey, &c. is the fittest thing . . . designed to be constantly the same for all future ages. But money is the best measure of the altered value of things in a few years." Locke, J., The Works of John Locke, Vol. 5, p. 47, Eleventh Edition, 1812.

[4] In equivalent of cents per bushel, based on the present weight and fineness of sterling and silver prior to 1377; gold and silver until 1816; and gold thereafter.

Murray, N. C., Wheat Prices in England. Clement, Curtis, and Company, Chicago, Ill. Feb. 4, 1931.

This material is also available in the Yearbook 1922, United States Department of Agriculture, p. 605, 1923.

The original material was reported in the following:

1259-1771. Rogers, J. E. T., A History of Agriculture, Vol. I, pp. 226-234, 1866; Vol. IV, pp. 282-290, 1882; Vol. V, pp. 268-274, 1887; and Vol. VII, Pt. II, 1902.

1772-1869. Agricultural Returns for Great Britain 1898, Board of Agriculture (C.-9304), pp. 121-123, 1899.

1870-1920. Agricultural Statistics, England and Wales, 1920. Ministry of Agriculture and Fisheries, Vol. LV, Part III, p. 123. 1921.

1921-1930. Agricultural Statistics 1930. Ministry of Agriculture and Fisheries, Vol. LXV, Part II, p. 147. 1931.

silver from the New World declined, the advance in wheat prices was retarded, and prices declined somewhat (tables 24 and 64 and figure 162). During the decade 1740-49, wheat sold at an average of 92 cents per bushel, which was about 31 per cent less than prices a hundred years previous.

With the increasing supplies of precious metals from Brazil and Mexico, prices of wheat again began to rise, and by the decade just previous to the Napoleonic Wars, 1780-89, wheat sold for an average of 140 cents, or prices had advanced 52 per cent in forty years. With the Napoleonic Wars, prices mounted rapidly, and from 1805 to 1814 sold for an average of 253 cents per bushel. This rise was due to three factors:

1. Silver production had been increasing and about this time reached a peak (table 24, page 139).

2. Gold production had been increasing, and the peak of production was past (table 15, page 97).

3. There was a reduced demand for gold, as was the case during the World War.

The higher prices for this period have often been erroneously attributed to poor harvests or to tariffs.[5]

From the close of the Napoleonic Wars until about 1895, there was a continuous decline in prices which was only temporarily interrupted by poor crops, the Irish famine, Crimean War, discovery of gold in California and Australia, our Civil War, and the like. From the Napoleonic Wars to the end of the nineteenth century, the ten-year average price of wheat declined from 253 to 87 cents.

The experiences of most of the present generation are limited to the twentieth century. With the discovery of gold in South Africa and the cyanide process, gold production increased very rapidly and wheat prices almost doubled from 1896 to 1914.

Although the prices were pegged and are expressed in gold, wheat sold for 183 cents in 1920.

[5] The Corn Laws were revised in 1773. This provided a duty of 16*s* per quarter on wheat when the price was at or below 48*s*: above this price there was only a nominal duty of 6*d*. The farmers protested as the tariff was not effective, since the price was normally above the base price, 48*s* per quarter. The Act of 1791 raised the base price and imposed a heavy duty on all wheat imported at a lower price. Preferential treatment was also granted British colonies. With the ever-rising prices, the Act afforded little protection to the farmer; and another act was passed raising the base price to 63*s*. This law was also a dead letter until prices collapsed in 1814 and 1815. Prices fluctuated violently during this period because of unstable money. Adams, L. P., Agricultural Depression and Farm Relief in England, 1813-1815, pp. 17-26, 1932.

From 1920 to 1932, the price of wheat declined from 183 to 60 cents per bushel. In a little more than a decade, the price of wheat declined 67 per cent, which was approximately the same as occurred in the 90 years following the Napoleonic Wars (66 per cent).

Beginning with 1926 and ending in 1932, the price of wheat has declined continuously for six years. Only once before in the 674 years, shown in figure 159, has the price of wheat continued in the same direction for six successive years. Only four times during this long period did the price of wheat decline five years in succession; seven other times the price advanced five years in succession; and ten times the price declined four years in succession.

As was shown on pages 49 and 131, and figures 42, 43, and 88, there appears to be a 20-year cycle in the production of wheat. A study of the 10-year moving average of wheat prices, shown in figure 159, indicates that in the 674-year period there were about 32 periods of high prices, averaging about 21 years apart.

Prices in England and France after the downfall of Rome.—With the abandonment of Great Britain the Romans took the precious metals with them and prices fell very low. During this time "living money" became legal. If a man owed a debt and could not pay it in coin, he could supply the deficiency in slaves, horses, cows, or sheep at rates that were fixed by law. The level to which prices fell during the reign of Ethelred, about 997, is indicated by the following converted into American dollars:

Price of a man or a slave	$13.69	Cow	$1.50
Horse	8.56	Hog	0.46
Mare or colt	5.70	Sheep	0.28
Mule	3.43	Goat	0.09
Ox	1.71		

The level to which prices fell in France is shown by the maximum prices fixed by Charlemagne in 794. Following the bad harvests an edict was issued to protect the consumers. The price of wheat flour was fixed at the equivalent of 6 American cents for 24 pounds.[6]

According to Hume, "Falling prices, and misery and destruction are inseparable companions. The disasters of the dark ages were caused by decreasing money and falling prices. With the increase in money, labor and industry gain new life."

Debasement of the English pound sterling.—The Saxon, or "tower," pound was in common use at the time of the Norman Con-

[6] Jacob, W., An Historical Inquiry into the Production and Consumption of the Precious Metals, Vol. I, pp. 315, 319, 1831.

quest. This pound contained 5,400 grains troy weight. The pound sterling was an actual pound in weight of silver with a percentage of purity of 92.5. Various kings reduced the weight of the coin, and others debased it by reducing the percentage of silver (table 63). The weight was reduced many times before changes in the composition were made. The most rapid reduction came after a long period of declining prices (figures 160 and 161).

Debasement in France.—From 780 to 1740, the amount of silver in the livre Tournois was reduced from 430 grams of pure silver to 4.5.[7] It is interesting to note that the debasement was influenced by the supplies of precious metals and the consequent trend in commodity prices.

The greatest debasement of the currency occurred prior to the importation of precious metals from the New World. From 780 to 1507, the grams of pure silver in the livre Tournois fell from 430 to 20. During the period of generally rising prices from 1500 to 1600 the livre varied from 20.4 to 11.1. With the decline of gold and silver imports from the New World, the amount of silver in the livre fell from 11.1 to 2.5 grams.

TABLE 63.—HISTORY OF THE ENGLISH POUND STERLING*

Ruler	Year	Weight of the coin, grains troy	Per cent of silver	Weight of pure silver, grains troy	Index number
Conquest	1066	5400	92.5	4995	291
Edward I	1300	5333	92.5	4933	287
Edward III	1344	4872	92.5	4507	262
Edward III	1346	4800	92.5	4440	258
Edward III	1353	4320	92.5	3996	232
Henry IV	1412	3600	92.5	3330	194
Edward IV	1464	2880	92.5	2664	155
Henry VIII	1527	2560	92.5	2368	138
Henry VIII	1543	2400	83.3	1999	116
Henry VIII	1545	2400	50.0	1200	70
Henry VIII	1546	2400	33.3	799	46
Edward VI	1549	1600	50.0	800	46
Edward VI	1551	1600	25.0	400	23
Edward VI	1552	1920	92.1	1768	103
Mary	1553	1920	91.7	1761	102
Elizabeth	1560	1920	92.5	1776	103
Elizabeth	1601	1858	92.5	1719	100

* McCulloch, J. R., Tracts on Money, p. 444, 1856.

[7] Usher, A. P., The General Course of Wheat Prices in France: 1350-1788, The Review of Economic Statistics, Vol. XII, No. 4, p. 167, November 1930.

As one looks back at the debasement of the livre, it is easy to be very critical of the management of the debasement. It is probable that at times the debasement arose from the selfish interests of the rulers to relieve themselves of intolerable debt burdens arising from selfish wars or falling prices or both. At other times, debasement may have been undertaken with altruistic motives, to relieve the subjects of the inevitable economic difficulties that arise from a shortage of money and declining prices.

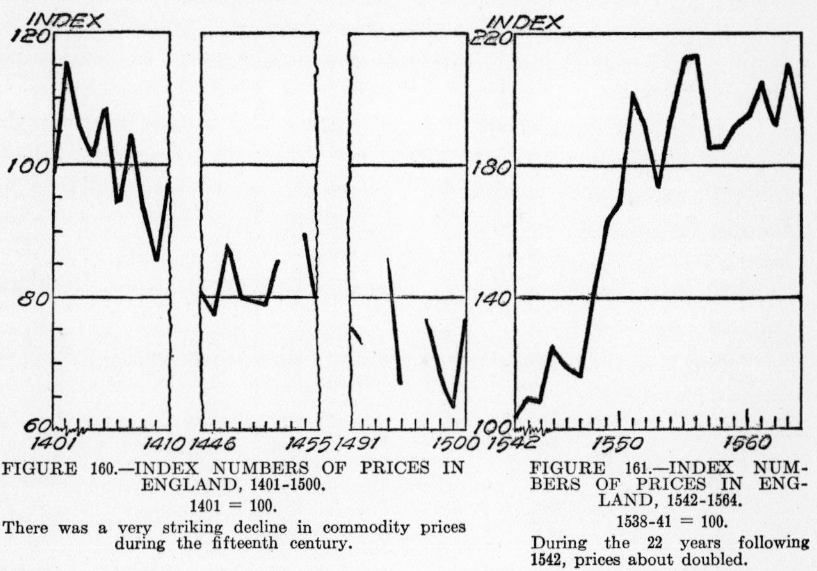

FIGURE 160.—INDEX NUMBERS OF PRICES IN ENGLAND, 1401-1500.
1401 = 100.
There was a very striking decline in commodity prices during the fifteenth century.

FIGURE 161.—INDEX NUMBERS OF PRICES IN ENGLAND, 1542-1564.
1538-41 = 100.
During the 22 years following 1542, prices about doubled.

It is probable that most of those who managed the debasement did not realize the sweeping changes that they produced. Despite the disparagement of their acts, they did from time to time relieve the people of the burden of declining prices. The most unfortunate thing is that the methods used in debasement were not more scientific. During the 727 years prior to the large imports of gold from the New World, the amount of silver in the livre fell from 230 to 20.4 grams. If the supply of silver had risen as rapidly as the production of other things, prices would have risen eleven times. This rise in prices would have been at the rate of two-thirds of 1 per cent per year, which is about one-third as fast as the rise from 1897 to 1914. The unfortunate thing was that at certain times changes were made very rapidly. For instance, from 1295 to 1303 the weight was reduced from 64.6 to 21.3 grams, in 1305 was increased to 73.9, and in 1309 decreased to 64.6.

Discovery of precious metals in America.—The influx of precious metals from America precipitated one of the greatest price revolutions on a specie basis of which we have a record, except the one caused by the World War. After a thorough study of original records in Spain, Hamilton[8] reports that 16,632,648 kilograms of pure silver and 181,235 kilograms of pure gold were registered as received from the New World from 1503 to 1660. In addition, there was considerable smuggled metal

TABLE 64.—AVERAGE YEARLY IMPORTS OF AMERICAN GOLD AND SILVER INTO SPAIN, 1503–1660

Five-year period	Imports in silver maravedis*			Per cent of silver†
	Public	Private	Total	
1503–1505	14,582,495	No records	....	....
1506–1510	19,246,848	No records	....	....
1511–1515	28,191,145	No records	....	....
1516–1520	23,419,572	No records	....	....
1521–1525	3,163,717	No records	....	2.9
1526–1530	24,486,329	No records	....	
1531–1535	38,912,475	No records	....	89.6
1536–1540	121,579,635	232,830,652	354,410,287	
1541–1545	68,200,956	377,659,472	445,860,428	87.7
1546–1550	143,340,441	352,443,547	495,783,988	
1551–1555	326,565,593	561,332,224	887,897,817	87.7
1556–1560	141,164,609	578,745,262	719,909,871	
1561–1565	163,757,969	844,920,233	1,008,678,102	98.8
1566–1570	340,626,866	932,082,539	1,272,709,405	
1571–1575	296,879,446	774,715,381	1,071,594,827	99.2
1576–1580	598,471,066	954,203,622	1,552,674,689	
1581–1585	679,554,365	1,964,160,726	2,643,715,091	99.4
1586–1590	723,889,112	1,421,047,635	2,144,936,746	
1591–1595	902,101,378	2,264,536,250	3,166,637,628	99.3
1596–1600	987,688,615	2,110,876,441	3,098,565,056	
1601–1605	586,789,679	1,609,509,844	2,196,299,523	99.5
1606–1610	769,471,096	2,056,997,538	2,826,468,634	
1611–1615	649,162,963	1,558,367,904	2,207,530,867	99.6
1616–1620	391,300,935	2,318,820,468	2,710,121,403	
1621–1625	440,204,052	1,990,757,020	2,430,961,072	99.8
1626–1630	415,692,062	1,830,215,310	2,245,907,373	
1631–1635	426,044,219	1,113,932,634	1,539,976,853	99.9
1636–1640	422,217,252	1,046,096,931	1,468,314,183	
1641–1645	417,929,569	820,812,648	1,238,742,217	99.8
1646–1650	149,860,132	909,489,115	1,059,349,247	
1651–1655	201,499,037	454,940,011	656,439,048	99.9
1656–1660	54,587,172	247,913,248	302,500,420	

* Hamilton, E. J., American Treasure and Andalusian Prices, 1503–1660, Journal of Economic and Business History, Vol. I, No. 1, p. 6, November 1928.
† Hamilton, E. J., Imports of American Gold and Silver into Spain, 1503–1660, The Quarterly Journal of Economics, Vol. XLIII, No. 3, pp. 464–468, May 1929.

[8] Hamilton, E. J., Imports of American Gold and Silver into Spain, 1503-1660, Quarterly Journal of Economics, Vol. XLIII, No. 3, pp. 436, 468, May 1929.

that has been estimated from 10 to 50 per cent of that registered. Hamilton thinks the smuggled metal was much nearer 10 than 50 per cent.

The movement of prices in Spain.—The upheaval of prices in Europe in the sixteenth and seventeenth centuries has been the subject of considerable comment by many writers, but Hamilton was the first student to make a thorough study of prices in Spain.[9]

TABLE 65.—INDEX NUMBERS OF PRICES OF 24 COMMODITIES IN ANDALUSIA, SPAIN, 1503–1660*

1573–81 = 100

Year	Index number	Year	Index number	Year	Index number
1503	25	1565	81	1613	108
1505	28	1567	87	1615	104
1507	37	1569	80	1617	115
1511	25	1572	96	1619	107
1513	25	1573	90	1621	124
1515	32	1575	102	1626	114
1517	29	1577	90	1628	112
1519	34	1579	105	1637	145
1530	48	1581	109	1639	111
1532	43	1585	99	1642	106
1537	45	1588	97	1644	93
1539	50	1589	110	1645	101
1542	54	1591	112	1647	116
1548	63	1593	117	1648	106
1549	57	1595	109	1651	129
1552	67	1597	141	1653	142
1553	72	1599	125	1655	100
1555	68	1601	111	1657	121
1557	89	1603	118	1658	98
1559	70	1605	132	1660	119
1561	80	1609	112		
1563	85	1611	108		

* Hamilton, E. J., Wages and Subsistence on Spanish Treasure Ships, 1503–1660, The Journal of Political Economy, Vol. XXXVII, No. 4, p. 447, August 1929.

[9] Rogers, J. E. T., A History of Agriculture and Prices in England, Vols. III-VI, 1882-87. d'Avenel, V., Histoire économique de la propriétés, des salaires, des denrées, et de tous prix en général, Vols. 1-7. 1894-1926. Wiebe, G., Zur Geschichte der Preisrevolution des XVI. und XVII. Jahrhunderts 1895. Shuckburgh-Evelyn, Sir George, An Account of Some Endeavours to Ascertain a Standard of Weight and Measure, Philosophical Transactions of the Royal Society of London, Part I, No. VIII, pp. 175-177, 1798. Hamilton, E. J., American Treasure and Andalusian Prices, 1503-1660, Journal of Economic and Business History, Vol. 1, No. 1, pp. 1-35, November 1928; American Treasure and the Rise of Capitalism (1500-1700), Economica, pp. 338-357, November 1929; Imports of Gold and Silver into Spain, 1503-1660, Quarterly Journal of Economics, Vol. 43, No. 3, pp. 436-472, May 1929; Wages and Subsistence on Spanish Treasure Ships, 1503-1660, The Journal of Political Economy, Vol. 37, No. 4, pp. 430-450, August 1929.

The silver was taken to Spain, which naturally first felt the full impact of the price upheaval which occurred throughout Europe, during the sixteenth century.

Prices rose from an index of 25 in 1503 to 141 in 1597 (table 65 and figure 162). In a little less than a century, commodity prices rose almost five times at a remarkably uniform compound rate of 1.9 per cent per year. This rise was less than that which occurred in the United States from 1897 to 1914, but it continued for nearly a century.

From 1597 to 1660, the general level of Spanish commodity prices did not advance further. They moved sidewise for a half century and fluctuated very violently. From 1597 to 1615, prices declined 26 per cent; from 1615 to 1637, rose 39 per cent; from 1637 to 1644, fell 36 per cent; from 1644 to 1653, rose 53 per cent; and from 1653 to 1658, declined 31 per cent.[10]

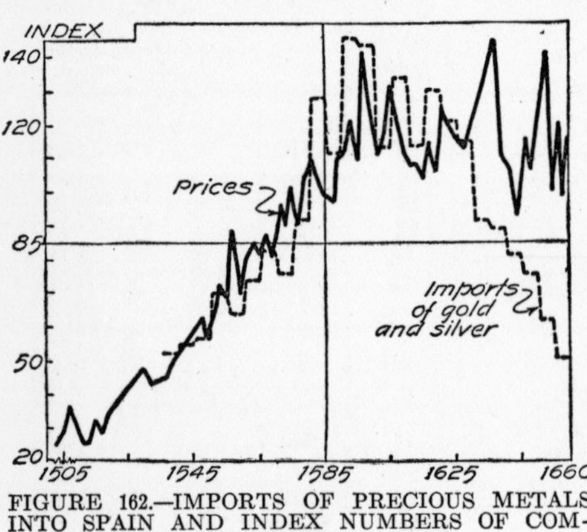

FIGURE 162.—IMPORTS OF PRECIOUS METALS INTO SPAIN AND INDEX NUMBERS OF COMMODITY PRICES, 1503-1660.

From 1503 to 1570, prices rose rapidly with the increasing imports.

The imports of gold and silver declined. The fact that prices did not decline more may be accounted for in part by the fact that the stocks resulting from previous shipments were on hand, also there was a debasement of the currency beginning about 1626, and over half of the prices after 1645 to 1666 were credit prices to be paid in silver at each return of the fleet.

The trend of prices in France.—The trend of French prices was quite similar to that in Spain. According to d'Avenel,[11] prices in France turned upward about 1498-1515, and reached a peak about the time of the change in Spanish prices (figure 163). However, according to d'Avenel, French prices rose only two to two and one-half times, whereas the Spanish prices rose about four to five times.

The movement of wheat prices in France as shown by Usher[12]

[10] Klein, J., The Mesta, p. 291, 1920, reports that there was a wholesale debasement of the currency in 1652.

[11] d'Avenel, V. G., Histoire économique de la propriété, des salaires, des denrées et de tous les prix en général, Vol. 1, p. 15, 1894.

[12] Usher, A. P., The General Course of Wheat Prices in France: 1350-1788, The Review of Economic Statistics, Vol. XII, No. 4, p. 162, November 1930.

indicates that wheat prices followed very closely the rising prices in Spain. Apparently, wheat prices rose about four times from 1500 to 1600.

Price changes in these various countries were not so rapid as in Spain, as some time was required for the precious metals to diffuse themselves. Probably French prices were influenced more promptly than prices in most other European countries.

The trend of prices in England.—The huge imports of precious metals into Spain soon affected the trend of commodity prices in England. During the hundred years from 1500 to 1600, Shuckburgh-Evelyn reports that commodity prices doubled

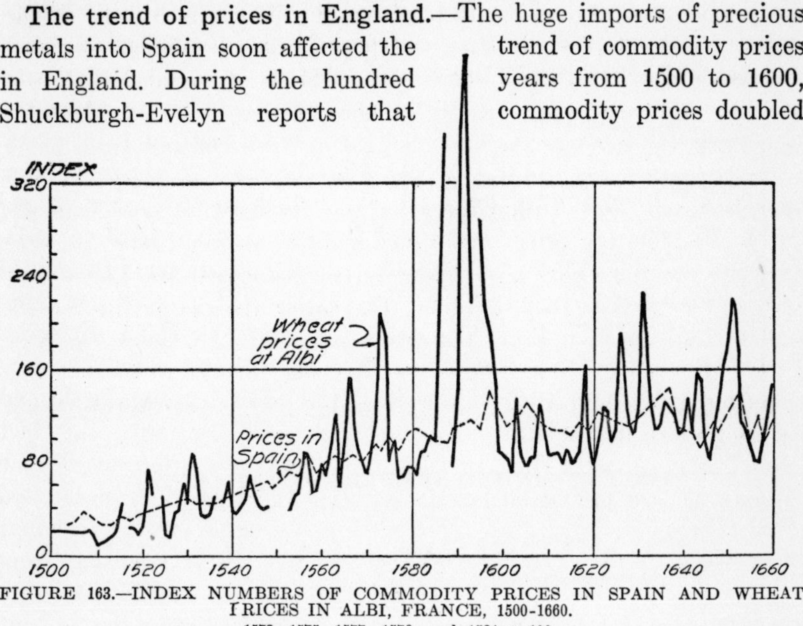

FIGURE 163.—INDEX NUMBERS OF COMMODITY PRICES IN SPAIN AND WHEAT PRICES IN ALBI, FRANCE, 1500-1660.
1573, 1575, 1577, 1579, and 1581 = 100.
Wheat prices in France followed very closely the changes in general prices in Spain.

as compared with a rise of four to five times in Spain. The Beveridge[13] study of wheat prices at Exeter indicates that wheat prices rose about four times. In both France and England, wheat rose as promptly as the average of all prices in Spain, but the general level of commodity prices rose less rapidly in England and France than in Spain.

The extent of the advance in prices in England was recognized by Benjamin Franklin,[14] who at 23 years of age wrote: "As those metals have grown much more plentiful in Europe since the discovery of

[13] Beveridge, W. H., A Statistical Crime of the Seventeenth Century, Journal of Economic and Business History, Vol. 1, No. 4, p. 531, August 1929.

[14] Franklin, B., A Modest Inquiry into the Nature and Necessity of a Paper Currency, 1729, cited from Sparks, J., The Works of Benjamin Franklin, Vol. 2, p. 266, 1836.

America, so they have sunk in value exceedingly; for to instance in England, formerly one penny of silver was worth a day's labor, but now it is hardly worth the sixth part of a day's labor. . . ."

Prices in Spanish America.—Apparently prices of commodities in the New World were at first very high. Precious metals were abundant, and other things very scarce. The treasury fleets brought over commodities and carried back precious metals. In the earlier part of the period the traders obtained provisions in Spain for the whole voyage. Towards the close of the period many commodities were cheaper in the New World than in the Old. It is recorded that beef could be purchased more cheaply in America than in Spain. Meat for the return voyages was therefore bought in American ports.

The situation was similar to the contrast between prices in San Francisco and New York City after the discovery of gold in California. In 1850, the prices of 16 commodities at San Francisco were 2.5 times the New York City prices for the same articles. The widest margin occurred in 1852, 3 times. Thereafter the margin decreased, and by 1855 the San Francisco prices were only 1.8 times the New York City prices. These differences were due in part to the expense of getting goods shipped to California and in part to the risk of having the gold stolen in transit.

TABLE 66.—INDEX NUMBERS OF THE PRICES OF 16 COMMODITIES AT SAN FRANCISCO, 1850–1855*

New York Prices = 100

Year	San Francisco index
1850	254
1851	282
1852	328
1853	237
1854	181
1855	177

* The 16 commodities were mess beef, mess pork, hams, lard, butter, cheese, flour, corn meal, rice, coffee, sugar, molasses, coal, candles, soap, and sperm oil. California Prices and Media of Exchange in the Days of the Gold Rush, Monthly Review of the Mercantile Trust Company of California, Vol. XII, No. 8, p. 176, August 1923. Report of the Secretary of the Treasury, 38th Congress, 1st Session, Senate Executive Document, pp. 334–45, 1863.

Effect of imports of precious metals.—The first effects of the imports of gold and silver were very pronounced. Prices rose; business was stimulated. These imports of precious metals and rising prices contributed to Spain's "golden age of literature and arts." Cervantes's writing at the time shows the effect of the American gold and silver on the life of the Spanish people. These imports financed the exploration and colonization of America. Magellan's memorable journey which demonstrated that the world was round was a result of these imports.

The long period of declining prices before the discovery of America resulted in low interest rates. These continued for a time, but the long period of rising prices resulted in high interest rates.

Repeated efforts were made to control prices of grain and other products by legal enactment.

The new silver made Spain a rich country. She increased her imports from other countries and established a standard of living far higher than the amount of manufacturing and industry could support. Large numbers of persons turned from industry and agriculture to the search for precious metals.

With the erratic prices after the imports of gold and silver declined, the advance in prices stopped, and poor relief became high.[15]

Rising prices and fixed rents.—Rising prices had much to do with the emancipation of the tenant farmers in England. The land was owned by the church and large land owners. Under the manorial system, when rents and the amounts and kinds of services were agreed upon they remained fixed, or changed very slowly. The titled class read the past, not the future, and did not forecast the rising prices. With stationary rents and rising prices, the landlord was in distress. The churches and especially the monasteries were affected, since they were large land owners. Land became a commercial asset, a commodity that was bought and sold—unheard of during the feudal age. Wages and prices rose, and the farmers and business men prospered. The church and nobility suffered.[16]

Writing of the effects of the new supplies of gold and silver, Winston Churchill,[17] former Chancellor of the British Exchequer, made the following statement:

"It is said that we had forgotten grim laws of supply and demand, as if these laws were absolute, constant, limiting factors forever beyond the reach of human control. There is no limit to human demand, and there is no limit to the power of mankind to meet that demand. For

[15] Klein, J., The Mesta, p. 289, 1920.

[16] Thompson, J. W., An Economic and Social History of the Middle Ages, p. 800, 1928.

[17] Churchill, W., Are We Too Clever? Collier's, Vol. 90, No. 9, pp. 48-49, Aug. 27, 1932.

hundreds of years, in the Middle Ages, the laws of supply and demand were stationary. Everything worked, year after year, at a uniformly low level, and all the populations lived miserably. Then, on a sudden, wages began to rise, enterprise began to quicken, all kinds of new articles and utensils appeared in the cottages or dwellings of the working people. All kinds of new luxuries and comforts opened to the rich and the middle classes. The laws of supply and demand suddenly began to work on a much larger and expanding scale.

"What had happened? A few small ships had come back from across the Atlantic Ocean full of gold and silver, and a gradual, subtle process of inflation had set in. It could not have been the trade of the New World which had refreshed the Old. These poor little ships could only bring spoonfuls of merchandise, and every voyage took over half a year. What they brought was the precious metals which altered, in the sense of expanding, the standards of value throughout the world, and made in those generations expansions in the good living of the human race which have never since been lost."

BIBLIOGRAPHY

d'Avenel, V., Histoire économique de la propriété des salaires, des denrées, et de tous prix en général, Vol. 1-7, 1894-1926.

Beveridge, W. H., A Statistical Crime of the Seventeenth Century, Journal of Economic and Business History, Vol. I, No. 4, pp. 501-533. August 1929.

Feavearyear, A. E., The Pound Sterling, pp. 40, 64. 1931.

Hamilton, E. J., American Treasure and Andalusian Prices, 1503-1660. The Journal of Economic and Business History, Vol. 1, No. 1, pp. 1-35. November 1928.

Hamilton, E. J., Imports of American Gold and Silver into Spain, 1503-1660, The Quarterly Journal of Economics, Vol. XLIII, No. 3, pp. 436-472. May 1929.

Hamilton, E. J., Wages and Subsistence on Spanish Treasure Ships, 1503-1660, The Journal of Political Economy, Vol. XXXVII, No. 4, pp. 430-50. August 1929.

Hamilton, E. J., American Treasure and the Rise of Capitalism (1500-1700), Economica, No. 27, pp. 338-357. November 1929.

Hamilton, E. J., Monetary Inflation in Castile, 1598-1660, Economic History, Vol. II, No. 6, pp. 177-212. January 1931.

Haring, C. H., American Gold and Silver Production in the First Half of the Sixteenth Century, Quarterly Journal of Economics, Vol. XXIX, No. 3, pp. 433-479. May 1915.

Haring, C. H., Trade and Navigation Between Spain and the Indies in the Time of the Hapsburgs. Harvard Economic Studies, Vol. XIX.

Jacob, W., An Historical Inquiry into the Production and Consumption of the Precious Metals. 1831.

Klein, J., The Mesta. A study in Spanish Economic History, 1273-1836. 1920.

Leslie, T. E. C., The Distribution and Value of the Precious Metals in the Sixteenth and Nineteenth Centuries. Macmillans' Magazine, Vol. X, pp. 301-319, August 1864; Essays in Political and Moral Philosophy, p. 264, 1879.

MERRIMAN, R. B., The Rise of the Spanish Empire in the Old and New World, Vol. III. 1925.

ROGERS, J. E. T., A History of Agriculture and Prices in England, 1882-87.

SHUCKBURGH-EVELYN, SIR GEORGE, An Account of Some Endeavours to Ascertain a Standard of Weight and Measure, Philosophical Transactions of the Royal Society of London, Part 1, pp. 175-76. 1798.

THOMPSON, J. W., An Economic and Social History of the Middle Ages (300-1300). 1928.

USHER, A. P., The General Course of Wheat Prices in France: 1350-1788, The Review of Economic Statistics, Vol. XII, No. 4, pp. 159-169. November 1930.

USHER, A. P., Prices of Wheat and Commodity Price Indexes for England, 1259-1930, The Review of Economic Statistics, Vol. XIII, No. 3, pp. 103-113. August 1931.

VAN HOUTTE, H., Documents pour servir a l'histoire des prix de 1381 à 1794, Commission Royale d'Histoire Bruxelles. 1902.

WIEBE, G., Zur Geschichte der Preisrevolution des XVI. und XVII. Jahrhunderts. 1895.

CHAPTER XXII

THE HISTORY OF PRICES IN THE UNITED STATES

The fluctuations in prices are so difficult to follow that it is almost impossible for the human mind to grasp their significance while they are taking place. It is frequently difficult to explain the changes even after they have occurred. These fluctuations cause more unhappiness, suffering, and misery than any other economic phenomena with which we deal.

If changes in prices are slow and gradual, adjustments are made with less friction. Violent changes, such as occurred from 1914 to 1932, cause so many injustices that man is arrayed against man, class against class, and nation against nation.

Prices at New York City and Philadelphia, 1720-75.—In 1720, prices at New York City were about 50 per cent of pre-war prices (table 1, page 10). The lowest level was probably reached in the forties, when prices were as low as 42 per cent of 1910-14 prices. This was coincident with a period of very low prices in England.

From about 1750 to the Revolutionary War, there was a steady advance in commodity prices. The course of prices at Philadelphia was very similar to that at New York City.

In Pennsylvania there was a shortage of money. This also led to demands for more currency. In the period from 1715-16 to 1721-22, the sheriff's docket doubled,[1] indicating increasing insolvencies due to growing shortage of money.

Such conditions culminated in the emission of paper money regardless of the fact that it was opposed by the English government and certain elements of the colonial population. In some instances, the colonial governors sympathized with the colonies and recommended plans to alleviate the difficulties.

Benjamin Franklin was one of the early advocates of the issues of paper money in Pennsylvania, and later the chief defender of the

[1] Warren, G. F., and Pearson, F. A., Prices of Commodities at Philadelphia, 1720-75, Farm Economics, No. 73, pp. 1631-2, November 1931. Macfarlane, C. W., Pennsylvania Paper Currency, Annals of the American Academy of Political and Social Science, Vol. 8, p. 51, 1896.

colonial paper money at London. Recognizing the need for money in Pennsylvania, Franklin wrote an article on paper money which he stated "was well received by the common people in general; but the rich men disliked it . . . and, they happened to have no writers among them that were able to answer it. . . ."[2]

Some of the colonies issued so much money that it depreciated. The question of the right to issue paper currencies led to extended controversies between the colonies and England. Apparently Pennsylvania issued its money in moderation. Prices rose as indicated in figure 164.

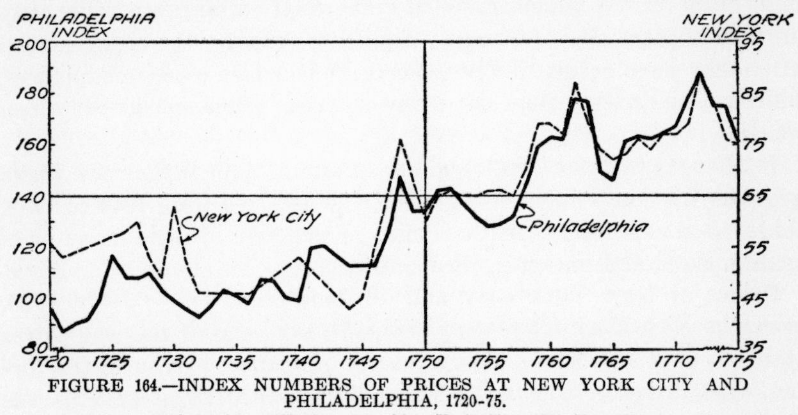

FIGURE 164.—INDEX NUMBERS OF PRICES AT NEW YORK CITY AND PHILADELPHIA, 1720-75.

Philadelphia, 1720-29 = 100. New York City, 1910-14 = 100.

Prices increased about 70 per cent in the 50 years preceding the Revolutionary War.

The rise was only about the same as the decline in the value of silver. There was constant friction between the colonies and England over the question of paper money. In 1764 a law was passed in Parliament forbidding all the colonies to issue paper money.

Franklin considered the increase in population and increase in business as evidence of the need of more money and stated that, "a dollar thereby coming to be rated at eight shillings in paper money of New York, and 7 s 6 d in paper of Pennsylvania, it has continued uniformly at those rates in both provinces now nearly forty years, without any variation upon new emissions; though in Pennsylvania the paper currency has at times increased from £15,000 the first sum, to £600,000 or near it. Nor has any alteration been occasioned by the paper money, in the price of necessaries of life, when compared with silver."[3]

[2] Franklin, B., comments on a pamphlet, A Modest Inquiry into the Nature and Necessity of a Paper Currency, which was printed anonymously but later acknowledged. Sparks, J., The Works of Benjamin Franklin, Vol. 2, p. 254, 1836.

[3] Franklin, B., Remarks and Facts Relative to the American Paper Money, 1764, cited from Sparks, J., The Works of Benjamin Franklin, Vol. 2, p. 351, 1836.

Adam Smith also commented as follows: "Pennsylvania was always more moderate in its emissions of paper money than any other of our Colonies. Its paper currency, accordingly, is said never to have sunk below the value of gold and silver which was current in the colony before the first emission of its paper money."[4]

Proud's History of Pennsylvania confirms the statement that this currency was kept close to par with gold and silver.[5]

Comparison of prices at Philadelphia and in England as calculated by Shuckburgh-Evelyn indicates that the general trend was very similar. This is a striking illustration of a "managed" currency that worked well for fifty years.

Prices during the Revolutionary War.—During the Revolutionary War, prices rose very high owing to the printing of paper money—the continental notes—and today we have the old expression: "not worth a continental." Commodity prices in terms of hard money reached 232 in 1779-80 when 1910-14 = 100 (table 1, page 10).

The first continental paper money was printed May 10, 1775. With subsequent emissions, the rate of exchange for hard money at Philadelphia rose very rapidly until May 31, 1781, when a dollar of hard money exchanged for $400 to $1000 currency.[6] "Thus *fell, ended,* and *died,* the Continental Currency, aged 6 *years* . . . without one groan or struggle."[6] By the Act of Aug. 4, 1790, the continental bills were funded at 1 cent on the dollar. As the currency depreciated, prices of commodities rose by leaps and bounds. In the words of Pelatiah Webster, the currency "corrupted the choicest interests of our country *more*, and done *more* injustice, than even the arms and artifices of our enemies."[7] It resulted in "the most pernicious shift of property . . . and the many thousands of fortunes . . . were ruined by it. . . ."[8]

Despite this rather pessimistic interpretation, Gallatin[9] tells us, "The Continental money carried the United States through the most arduous and perilous stages of the war, and . . . it cannot be denied that it saved the country."

Paper money was the only available means of financing the war.

[4] Smith, A., Wealth of Nations, Book 2, Chap. 2, p. 292.

[5] Gouge, W. M., A Short History of Paper Money and Banking in the United States, Part II, p. 9, 1833.

[6] Webster, P., Political Essays, p. 175, 1791; Remarks on the Resolution of Council, May 9, 1781.

[7] Webster, P., Political Essays, p. 51, 1791; A Third Essay on Free Trade and Finance, Jan. 8, 1780.

[8] Webster, P., Political Essays, p. 94, 1791; A Fourth Essay on Free Trade and Finance, Feb. 10, 1780.

[9] Leavitt, S., Our Money Wars, p. 24, 1894.

Depression following the Revolutionary War.—After the Revolutionary War, we find experiences similar to those after the Civil War and the World War. Immediately upon the declaration of peace, extravagance and luxury prevailed among all classes throughout the states. State and continental paper money was plentiful. The English merchants who were anxious to sell goods and had accumulated stocks during the war extended credits to facilitate sales. The foreign goods found a ready market, as the people had been deprived of them for almost ten years. They purchased the goods with little thought of how to pay for them. The apparent prosperity, however, did not last long, as the English creditors called for payment. The distress was widespread. Goods were offered for sale but would not bring fair prices because of the scarcity of money. Land that was sold for debts brought practically nothing. Prudent men did not consider it safe to lend money at the rates then prevailing, 25 to 30 per cent. Everywhere the papers were filled with notices of insolvencies. In one county of Maryland, the populace forced the suspension of all civil suits and in another the people would not allow anyone to bid on land offered at sheriff sales.[10] In Rhode Island, a paper money party was formed. In Massachusetts, the discontent was expressed by Shay's Rebellion, which was a farmers' revolt against deflation. Farmers had borrowed money at high prices with an inflated paper currency, and it was impossible for them to meet their obligations after prices dropped. Although the rebellion was put down, the state recognized the injustice and legalized a moratorium for debtors.[11]

The First Bank of the United States.—The first United States bank was established in 1792. In speaking of Hamilton, Webster described the results as follows: "He was made Secretary of the Treasury; and how he fulfilled the duties, at such a time, the whole nation received with delight, and the whole world saw with admiration. He smote the rock of natural resources, and abundant streams of revenue gushed forth. He touched the dead corpse of public credit, and it sprang to its feet."[12] He might have added that prices rose rapidly. The highest prices of this period occurred from 1797 to 1801. Just prior to this time, the United States was not a large exporter, but with the Napoleonic Wars there was a strong demand for goods and much of the carrying trade fell into our hands. The country was highly pros-

[10] Behrens, K. L., Paper Money in Maryland, Johns Hopkins University Studies in Historical and Political Science, Series 41, No. 1, pp. 78-9, 1923.

[11] Sumner, W. G., A History of American Currency, pp. 50-54, 1874.

[12] Kinley, D., The Independent Treasury of the United States, p. 3, 1893.

perous. On account of the various embargoes and other war measures, prices were very erratic. In 1801-02, prices declined from 148 to 111. Domestic goods, as well as imported goods, declined. At this time, Great Britain and the rest of Europe were at peace, crops were good, agricultural prices declined, shipping was depressed.

France and Great Britain resumed hostilities, and American products were in demand. From 1803 to 1806, prices rose from 113 to 137. American merchants and carriers of freight prospered until Jefferson laid the embargo on all ships in American ports.[13]

In 1806, England issued a proclamation blockading all the ports from southern France to northern Germany. Napoleon retaliated with the Berlin decree which declared the British Isles in a state of blockade. These and various other measures made it difficult for us to reach European markets, and prices in the United States were erratic and declined. In 1807, the United States passed the Embargo Act, forbidding American vessels to depart for any foreign port or foreign vessels to load in American ports. This act was disastrous to American trade, and prices fell from an index of 137 to 112. A few years later, a less restrictive measure, the Non-intercourse Act, was substituted, and prices rose.

Agricultural discontent in the Mississippi Valley.—During the period, 1802 to 1805, wholesale prices at the seaboard rose about 31 per cent. Although index numbers are not available, the literature of the time indicates that prices rose much more in the Mississippi Valley. Settlers crowded to the frontier in unprecedented numbers. From 1800 to 1805, the population of Cincinnati increased 28 per cent.[14]

From 1805 to 1808, prices at New York City declined 23 per cent. The decline at points along the Ohio River was no doubt much greater. Immigration into Ohio virtually ceased, and those who had previously purchased land found it impossible to meet their obligations. The Ohio legislature petitioned Congress for relief. Stay-laws and relief to debtors were common in Kentucky, Tennessee, and the Mississippi territory.

Low prices for home-produced goods and high prices for imported goods focused attention on proposals to stimulate local manufacturers, and to force changes in the commercial regulations of the Old World.

[13] Smith, W. B., Wholesale Commodity Prices in the United States, 1795-1824, The Review of Economic Statistics, Vol. 9, No. 4, p. 176, October 1927.

[14] Taylor, G. R., Agrarian Discontent in the Mississippi Valley Preceding the War of 1812, Journal of Political Economy, Vol. XXXIX, No. 4, pp. 473-505, August 1931.

It was the farm bloc, western representatives in Congress, that advocated and supported a policy of commercial coercion which resulted in the Embargo[15] Act of December 1807.

The events of the next two years continued to inflame western hatred against the Old World and especially against Great Britain. The insurgent leaders have since been called the "War Hawks of 1812." In July 1809, news reached the west of the extension of the British Continental Blockade and of the new duties to be levied on cotton. In western Tennessee and the Mississippi territory, cotton was almost the only cash crop, and in the autumn of 1811, a petition was presented to Congress to permit the farmers to defer payments on public lands because of low prices and the "severe pressure of the times."

The predominance of the war spirit is indicated by the following quotation from an oration at Frankfort, Kentucky, in July 1811: "Embargoes, non-intercourse and negotiations are but illy calculated to secure our rights . . . let us now try old Roman policy and maintain them with the sword."

The agricultural situation was aggravated by declining prices of farm products. It was further intensified by the low purchasing power of farm prices which was the inevitable result of rapidly declining farm prices and relatively stable prices of other products. Based on wholesale prices at New York City, the purchasing power of farm products fell 18 per cent from September 1810 to July 1812. If prices changed so spectacularly at New York City, it is impossible to visualize the magnitude of the price fluctuations that must have occurred on the frontier.[16]

The frontiersman was also confronted with more or less fixed costs, such as wages, cost of negroes, expenses for river transportation, stable federal land prices, interest payments, and rising taxes, which were relatively inflexible. There is no question but that there was a real

[15] According to Galpin, W. F., The American Grain Trade under the Embargo of 1808, Journal of Economic and Business History, Vol. II, No. 1, pp. 72-75, November 1929, the Embargo Act forbade clearance of any ship for a foreign port except under presidential license. Prices declined in the United States. With flour selling at $30 to $40 in the West Indies, there were many evasions. There was an English order allowing ships from the United States to enter and clear all British ports without papers of any kind.

[16] Taylor, G. R., Prices in the Mississippi Valley Preceding the War of 1812, Journal of Economic and Business History, Vol. III, No. 1, p. 153, November 1930, indicates that from 1808 to 1811 there was an increasing spread between prices at Boston and New Orleans, the market for Ohio and Mississippi Valley produce.

basis for discontent and that the fundamental cause was the instability of prices.

War of 1812.—The charter of the first United States bank expired in 1811, and was not renewed because of the opposition of the state banks. The bank was dissolved and $7,000,000 of the bank's $10,000,000 capital was remitted to British investors.[17] In 1811, there were 88 state banks and in 1813 there were 208. During 1813-14, Pennsylvania alone chartered 41 banks.[18]

The War of 1812 was financed largely by loans. The state banks purchased the United States notes and issued their own paper money payable on demand. The bank note circulation increased from $45,000,000 in 1812 to $100,000,000 in 1817,[19] which is almost the same percentage increase as occurred in bank deposits in the World War; and prices rose from an index of 126 to 182.

Specie payment was suspended except in New England. The war was not popular in New England, since it interfered with their shipping. New England banks refused to lend to the government. The financing of the War of 1812 fell heavily on the banks of the Middle Atlantic states. The Treasury levied against the resources of the Middle Atlantic banks to obtain funds. For this reason, specie moved from the Middle Atlantic states to New England (table 67). The south could not export cotton because of blockade by the British Navy, and shipped gold and silver to New England to pay for merchandise in much the same way as gold moved to the United States during the World War. The specie movement reached a peak in 1814 and then specie moved out of New England.

The experience of Massachusetts was similar to that of the United States during the World War. Silver and gold moved to New England and caused price inflation without suspending specie payment. The flow of gold and silver to Boston was sufficient to cause prices to rise as rapidly as in Philadelphia, Baltimore, and New York. The rise continued in the other markets as the paper currency depreciated (table 68). After the war, silver and gold returned to other states and deflation occurred in New England. New England therefore had sudden inflation and sudden deflation without suspending specie payments, just as the United States had in the World War period. The decline occurred in Boston previous to the decline in the other markets. This

[17] Gallatin, A., Considerations on the Currency and Banking Systems in the United States, p. 44, 1831.

[18] Hickernell, W. F., Financial and Business Forecasting, Vol. 1, p. 143, 1928.

[19] Dewey, D. R., Financial History of the United States, 8th ed., p. 144, 1920.

again repeats the similarity to the situation of the United States and Europe during the deflation after the World War.

TABLE 67.—SPECIE HELD IN MASSACHUSETTS BANKS*

Year	Specie
1811	$1,709,000
1812	3,915,000
1813	6,171,000
1814	7,326,000
1815	3,915,000
1816	1,270,000

* Sumner, W. G., History of the American Currency, p. 67, 1874.

In 1815, the United States 6 per cent bonds were selling at about 80 compared with 103 before the war.[20] The drop in these bonds had an immediate effect upon the value of bank notes issued by the New York City, Philadelphia, and Baltimore banks, and in turn on prices. From 1811 to 1815 the circulation per capita[21] rose 83 per cent (table 14, page 92). Wholesale prices at Philadelphia rose 52 per cent; at Baltimore, 68 per cent; and at New York City, 68 per cent.

In 1815, the banks of Pennsylvania increased their loans, and business was active and prices were high,[22] despite the fact that prices declined in Boston. During 1815-16, commodity prices at New York City, Philadelphia, and Baltimore were high compared with commodity prices at Boston.[23] The divergence of prices at New York, Philadelphia, and Baltimore was due to the "over-issue" of bank notes. The banks were not required to redeem the notes in hard money.

During 1816, money was scarce and some of the banks reduced their loans and discounts with the intention of resuming specie payment. Commodity prices at all points declined rapidly. Domestic producers complained of unemployment, importers protested that they had to sell goods far below cost. For the Senate of the State of Pennsylvania, Raguet[24] made a thorough study of the crisis, and reports that lands and houses sold for less than half, a third, or one-fourth of their former value. There was a general scarcity of money throughout the

[20] Seybert, A., Statistical Annals of the United States of America, p. 749, 1818.

[21] Hepburn, A. B., History of Coinage and Currency in the United States and the Perennial Contest for Sound Money, pp. 75 and 120, 1903.

[22] Sumner, W. G., A History of American Currency, p. 68, 1874.

[23] Smith, W. B., Wholesale Commodity Prices in the United States, 1795-1824, The Review of Economic Statistics, Vol. IX, No. 4, pp. 174, 178, 182, October 1927.

[24] Raguet, C., Banking, pp. 291-2, 1840. Cited from Smith, W. B., Wholesale Prices in the United States, 1795-1824, The Review of Economic Statistics, Vol. IX, No. 4, p. 179, October 1927.

country. Little was to be had, and that at exorbitant rates. Prisons overflowed with debtors. The experiences were like the deflation of 1929 except that the debtors are now deprived of their property only. They are not now deprived of their liberty.

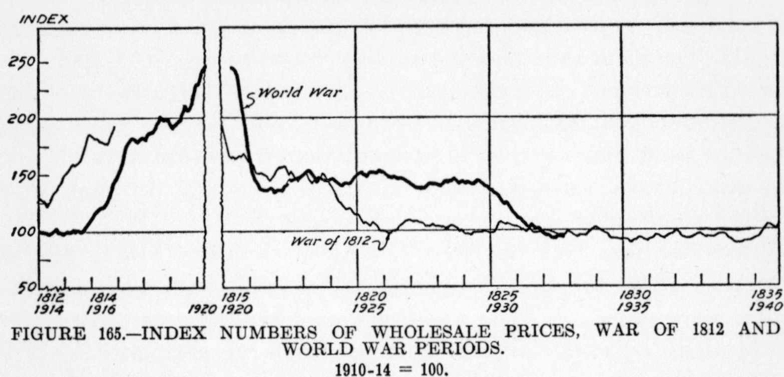

FIGURE 165.—INDEX NUMBERS OF WHOLESALE PRICES, WAR OF 1812 AND WORLD WAR PERIODS.
1910-14 = 100.

During and following the War of 1812, prices rose and fell as they did during the World War except that the fluctuations were less violent (figure 165).

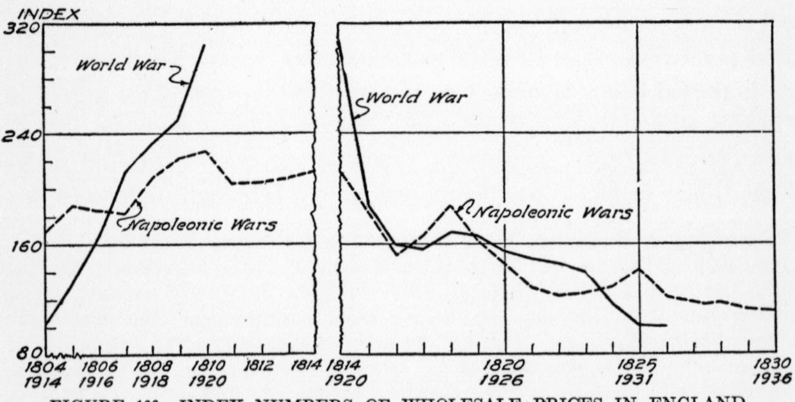

FIGURE 166.—INDEX NUMBERS OF WHOLESALE PRICES IN ENGLAND, NAPOLEONIC WAR AND WORLD WAR PERIODS.
Pre-war = 100.
The fluctuations in prices were quite similar following the two wars, but were much more violent following the World War than following the Napoleonic War.

The same situation prevailed in England. Prices rose during and collapsed after the Napoleonic Wars. The fluctuations during and following the World War were similar but much more violent (figure 166).

The Second Bank of the United States.—The chaos which inevitably followed declining prices recalled the valuable services rendered by the First Bank of the United States, and political antagonism melted away.

The Second Bank of the United States was formed in 1816 and in the next two years expanded rapidly. Specie payment was resumed in 1817. The bank expanded too rapidly,[25] became alarmed, and contracted its currency. This precipitated the crisis of 1818. The currency was reduced from $8,300,000 in 1818 to $3,600,000 two years later. Thus the bank contracted its note circulation 57 per cent in two years. The state banks contracted their circulation only 32 per cent. This is a sad commentary on central bank policy.

Prices dropped from an index of 151 in October 1818 to 100 in December 1820. According to Gouge, "The Bank was saved and the people were ruined."[26] After another war, a century later, prices declined almost exactly the same amount. From the prosperity of 1929 to December 1931, prices fell from about 150 to exactly 100. In this case the people were again ruined, but not all the banks were saved.

A man in West Virginia who formerly purchased a year's subscription to Niles Register with a barrel of flour stopped his subscription because four barrels were required. Wheat sold as low as 20 cents a bushel in Kentucky. It is also recorded that at Pittsburgh, flour was $1.00 per barrel; boards, $2.00 per thousand; sheep, $1.00 per head; but imported goods remained at the old price level.[27] This agrees in principle with the agricultural panic 100 years later, when, as is well known to all farmers, agricultural products were very cheap but prices of the things farmers bought dropped slowly. The only difference was

[25] According to Hickernell, W. F., Financial and Business Forecasting, Vol. I, p. 151, 1928, and Gouge, W. M., A Short History of Paper Money and Banking in the United States, Part II, p. 87, 1833, the bank was nearly wrecked during the first year of its existence. A politician was made president; the state banks in Philadelphia, Baltimore, Norfolk, and other centers refused to resume specie payment unless the bank assisted them; large losses occurred in Ohio, Tennessee, Kentucky, and elsewhere as they used the money obtained from the bank to buy land, build new banks, and speculate; the manager of the Baltimore branch of the United States Bank lost $1,400,000 of the bank's capital speculating in the bank's stock; and in calling for the $35,000,000 capital, the bank obtained only $2,000,000 in cash, $21,000,000 in government bonds, and the remaining $12,000,000 consisted of promissory notes of the original stockholders, who had borrowed to buy the bank stock.

[26] Gouge, W. M., A Short History of Paper Money and Banking in the United States, Part II, p. 110, 1833.

[27] Sumner, W. G., History of American Currency, p. 82, 1874.

that in 1820 the manufactured goods were imported, whereas in 1929 they were made largely in the United States.

The results of this wild inflation and deflation and mismanagement of the central bank are evidenced in the agriculture of the time. In Lancaster County, Pennsylvania, land rose from $85 to $275 and then dropped to $65. In Cumberland County, land rose from $50 to $175 per acre and then dropped to $35.[28]

The deflation policy of this period had its greatest effect on the farmers of the south and middle west. The settlement of the west, as measured by land sales, almost stopped.

Prosperity continued in the western country until the middle of 1818. Huntington[29] calls it "The Golden Age of the Western Country," and in the words of Gouge, "Silver could hardly have been more plentiful at Jerusalem in the days of Solomon than paper money was in Ohio, Kentucky, and the adjoining regions."[30] Large quantities of goods were brought into the country, and with the collapse, the specie moved east to pay for these goods. Prices fell and the paper currencies depreciated.

One writer comments on the decline in prices at Steubenville, Ohio, where at a marshal's sale an elegant sideboard gig and a very valuable horse sold for $4, and concludes with the comment that a man with a little money could make a fortune attending marshal's and sheriff's sales.[31]

In March 1822, Dayton prices were: Flour $2.50 per barrel; whiskey 12½ cents per gallon; wheat 20 cents, rye 25 cents, and corn 12 cents per bushel; fresh beef 1 to 3 cents per pound; butter 5 to 8 cents per pound; eggs 3 to 5 cents per dozen; and chickens 50 to 75 cents per dozen.[32]

The "Era of Good Feeling."—After this panic, the Second Bank of the United States was on a sound basis and for a decade was fully established in the confidence of the people. The circulation per capita increased slightly, but was remarkably stable during the period. Prices declined slightly, but were relatively stable for a decade at

[28] Gouge, W. M., A Short History of Paper Money and Banking in the United States, Part II, p. 122, 1833.

[29] Huntington, C. C., A History of Banking and Currency in Ohio before the Civil War, Ohio Archaeological and Historical Publications, Vol. 24, p. 285, 1915.

[30] Gouge's Journal of Banking, p. 320, March 30, 1842.

[31] Western Herald and Steubenville Gazette, Aug. 19, 1820, cited from Huntington, C. C., A History of Banking and Currency in Ohio before the Civil War, Ohio Archaeological and Historical Publications, Vol. 24, p. 298, 1915.

[32] Ohio Archaeological and Historical Publications, Vol. 24, p. 298, 1915.

about the 1910 to 1914 level. Land sales increased at a rather uniform rate with no indication of rampant speculation as occurred in 1818, 1836, and 1854. There was increasing but not excessive expenditure for canals, railroads, and other internal improvements. The Erie and other canals were built during this period. Money had a relatively stable purchasing power, and people were happy and contented. This period was called the "Era of Good Feeling." All financial writers comment on the soundness of the United States bank policy of the period as contrasted with the mismanagement that occurred in England. Had this bank continued, the financial history of United States in the succeeding century might have been quite different.

Panic of 1834.—Andrew Jackson was raised in Tennessee and had seen the struggle of the farmers developing a new country under very adverse conditions. He felt that the Bank of the United States should help the farmers as it had helped the business men. He insisted that the bank should lend to agriculture as well as to trade. What he really wanted was a Federal Land Bank System. The bank had been so successful that it was not expedient to attack the financial policies, so he attacked the social policies.

Jackson was a persistent enemy of the Second Bank of the United States. He ordered that the public funds be deposited in certain specified state banks known as "Jackson's pets." This unsettled the money market so that the bank contracted its loans and currency from $66 to $52 millions.

At this time, the country was on a bimetallic basis, but silver was the common coin. By the coinage act of June 24, 1834, the ratio was changed from 15:1 to 16:1, and the gold coins were reduced from 247.5 grains of fine gold to 232 grains.[33] Thus the gold coins were debased 6.26 per cent. This act definitely shifted the United States to a gold currency. After 1840, American silver dollars were seldom seen, because they were worth more than gold.

"Wild-cat" banking.—It was well known that the charter of the Second Bank of the United States would not be renewed. Its expiration in 1836 resulted in the establishment of many state banks. From 1834 to 1837, the money in circulation increased 50 per cent, and prices rose from an index of 88 to 129. These index numbers are based on prices at New York City, where wild banking was not prevalent.

Although the expansion of the currency and the rise in prices were quite general throughout the country, they were by no means uni-

[33] Laughlin, J. L., Money, Credit, and Prices, Vol. 1, p. 236, 1931.

form. The expansion was greatest in the southern and western states, and least in the New England states.

In many states, uncontrolled banking was substituted for conservative banking. Banks were located in the depths of the forest and were known as "wild-cat banks." "Apropos to the plan of establishing banks at inaccessible places is the incident related by a gentleman of this city, who, in wild-cat days, was travelling through the woods of Shiawassee county. The country was very new, with only here and there a log cabin in the woods, surrounded by a little clearing. The road had never been worked, and was principally indicated by 'blazed' trees. Toward night of an early June day he came upon a fork in the road, and was uncertain which track to take. He had not gone far upon the one which he had chosen before he became satisfied that it was only a wood road—that is, it had been used for hauling out wood or lumber. . . . He had not proceeded far, when in a little clearing before him there loomed up a large frame structure, across the front of which was the conspicuous sign, 'Bank of Shiawassee.' It was one of the wild-cats quartered in the native haunts of that animal, the depths of the forest."[34]

Expansion of the thirties.—This was a period of rapid expansion. In the preceding quarter of a century the finances of the country were on a sound basis.

By 1835, the public debt of the United States was paid off and the state debts were not excessive. The credit of the country was in an enviable position. The cheap money and idle funds of Europe eagerly sought investments in our railroad, municipal, and state bonds. It was a period of interior improvements and expansion of business, agriculture, waterways, turnpikes, and railroads.

Grain was high priced on the Atlantic seaboard, and some was imported from Europe. It was unfortunate that grain should have been imported from Europe when the middle western states could produce much more than was needed and prices were ridiculously low.[35] It took little imagination to prove that transportation was necessary. Borrow money and build canals, as they would pay for themselves, was the popular cry. The Erie Canal had been producing a million dollars in revenue. New York State was in the midst of vast internal development.

Massachusetts issued state bonds to finance railroads to bring Massachusetts in touch with western commerce.

[34] Report of the Pioneer Society of the State of Michigan, Vol. V, p. 217, 1884.
[35] Harlow, A. F., Old Towpaths, p. 109, 1926.

In 1835-36, the Indiana Legislature authorized the construction of more than 1200 miles of canals and two long railroads. Illinois planned no less than nine railroads and 1300 miles of canals criss-crossing the state, and the improvement of five rivers. Michigan was the most enthusiastic. With 100,000 persons, the state bonded itself for three railroads and several canals.

The demands for internal improvements resulted in a great increase in state debts. Two-thirds of all the debts authorized during the nineteen years from 1820 to 1838 were authorized in the three-and-one-half-year period, 1835 to 1838. One-third of these funds was spent on canals, one-third on banks, and one-fourth on railroads. Rising prices, expansion of credit, and transportation resulted in speculation in land.

The speculative spirit is indicated by the valuation of real property in New York City, which rose 50 per cent in five years. Land on Long Island brought $1000 per acre. Rumors of diminishing lumber supplies in Maine resulted in purchases of timber land at $15 to $50 per acre, that formerly sold for only $5 to $10 per acre. Emigrants poured into the middle west; money was plentiful. Land was purchased from the government at $12 per acre and plotted in town lots which sold for $20 per lot. Chicago was the center of a land craze. Salesmen went back to New York and Boston to sell lots in imaginary cities. In Chicago, which had a population of 4000, water front lots sold for $7000.

Mushroom towns sprang up everywhere. In Michigan, eastern capitalists laid out a town with 124 blocks, on which fifteen dwellings, a mill, and a lighthouse were built. In addition, a $30,000 hotel was erected. In the crash of 1837, the hotel and some of the lots were sold for less than the cost of the glass and paint, and the rest of the land was bought for its hemlock bark.[36] Recently, similar experiences were recorded in Florida.

In the thirties, speculation took the form of farm lands and city real estate. Ninety years later, speculation was centered on Florida land, city real estate, and the stock market.

Panic of 1837.—Reckless expenditures for farm land, city lots, cotton, grain, slaves, railroads, canals, and public improvements culminated in the Panic of 1837. The panic was hastened by the so-called "specie circular," on July 11, 1836, which ordered the federal agents to accept only hard money in payment for farm land. During the sec-

[36] Fuller, G. N., Economic and Social Beginnings of Michigan, University of Michigan Historical Series No. 1, pp. 439, 440, 1916.

ond quarter of 1836, the sales of public land by the United States aggregated $8,423,000, the largest recorded. Two years later, the quarterly receipts were $524,000.[37] The check placed on land sales by the specie circular[38] interfered with the operations of banks throughout the country. Money was transferred like dead freight instead of lubricating the business of the country. There was a scramble for liquidity; the loans and discounts of the state banks declined very rapidly. From February to May 1837, wholesale prices at New York City declined 15 per cent; and the Panic of 1837 was on. On May 10, 1837, the New York banks suspended specie payment and the decline in commodity prices stopped; by July it had risen 3 per cent.

On July 15, 1837, American gold coins at New York City commanded a premium of 9 to 10 per cent, and Spanish dollars 11 to 12 per cent.[39] The difficulties involved in the transfer of funds are indicated by the discounts at New York City for sight bills from various cities. On July 15, 1837, sight bills on New Orleans were at an 11 to 12 per cent discount.[40] On April 14, 1838, bills on Nashville, Tennessee, were at a 20 to 25 per cent discount; Mobile, Alabama, 17 to 20 per cent; Michigan, 10 to 13 per cent; and Baltimore, 5½ to 5¾ per cent.

The pressure for liquidity is indicated by the great increase in specie held by New York banks from June 1837 to May 1838. In the same period there was a decrease in the bank notes in circulation and the bills discounted. In June 1837, there were $3.09 of bank notes per dollar of specie, and in 1838, $0.48.

From 1836 to 1843, the total circulation per capita declined from $15.06 to $7.87,[41] and commodity prices at New York City declined from an index of 129 in February 1837 to 73 in March 1843. Circulation per capita declined 48 per cent and commodity prices 43 per cent. The declines in prices in the central west were much more severe. Index numbers of wholesale prices at Cincinnati, Ohio, declined 66 per cent. There was a shortage of money, particularly of small coins. Corporations of the city of Philadelphia issued, in violation of law, small notes or tickets, of denominations less than $5, payable at a

[37] Cole, A. H., Cyclical and Sectional Variations in the Sales of Public Lands, 1816-60, The Review of Economic Statistics, Vol. IX, No. 1, p. 51, January 1927.

[38] The opposition to the specie circular was so great that Congress passed a bill to annul it but had no opportunity to pass it over the President's veto, March 3, 1837.

[39] Financial Register of the United States, Vol. 1, No. 4, p. 60, Aug. 16, 1837.

[40] Financial Register of the United States, Vol. 1, No. 22, p. 351, April 25, 1838.

[41] Hepburn, A. B., History of Coinage and Currency in the United States and the Perennial Contest for Sound Money, pp. 120, 154, 1903.

distant day, bearing interest at 1 or 2 per cent. The legislature of New Jersey passed an act authorizing the banks to issue notes of a less denomination than $5.[42] Connecticut passed a bill to repeal the laws imposing restrictions upon the circulation of small bills.[43]

The panic came somewhat later in the central west. By 1839, however, farm prices declined and money was scarce. Much of the indebtedness in Illinois to eastern merchants was liquidated in produce. Notes were drawn payable in corn, horses, or other farm products. Interest rates ranged from 10 to 50 per cent. Wisconsin was flooded with spurious paper money. By 1841 it is estimated that one-third of the banks of Ohio had failed and riots occurred. Wisconsin, Tennessee, Kentucky, Indiana, and Michigan had similar experiences.[44]

In Kentucky, the legislature recognized the impossibility of farmers' paying their obligations and "stay-laws" were passed giving debtors two years to pay.[45]

"In Hinds county, Mississippi, more than a thousand suits have been brought. The citizens in self-defence petitioned the governor to convene the legislature for the purpose of passing a relief or replevin law. He not having done so, they have called upon the sheriff to resign just before the April term commences, threatening vengeance against any one who will accept the office *pro tempore*."[46] The price of a slave, which was a good barometer of southern conditions, declined from $1300 to about $700.[47] Cotton fell from 19.1 cents per pound to 10.1 cents at New Orleans. "Speculation has been making poor men rich and rich men princes. . . . A revulsion has taken place. Mississippi is ruined. Her rich men are poor, and her poor men beggars. . . . Lands . . . that once commanded from thirty to fifty dollars per acre may now be bought for three or five dollars."

The common complaint was that the farmers placed too much reliance on a single crop and bought everything else. This is not an unfamiliar note.

[42] On the Circulation of Small Notes or Tickets, The Financial Register of the United States, Vol. 1, No. 17, p. 272, February 1838.

[43] The Financial Register of the United States, Vol. II, No. 2, p. 31, July 11, 1838.

[44] McGrane, R. C., The Panic of 1837, pp. 12, 32, 33, 34, 127, 130, 1924.

[45] Hickernell, W. F., Financial and Business Forecasting, p. 158, 1928.

[46] The Winding Up of General Jackson's "Humble Efforts to Restore the Constitutional Currency," The Financial Register of the United States, Vol. 1, No. 9, p. 130, Oct. 25, 1837.

[47] Phillips, U. B., American Negro Slavery, D. Appleton & Company, p. 372, 1918.

Disparity in prices during the Panic of 1837.—The deflation produced its usual effects, which are now so apparent. Prices of food at interior points fell much more than at large centers.

Comparisons of index numbers of prices of farm products at Cincinnati, Ohio, and New York City indicate that, at the peak, prices at Cincinnati had advanced 94 per cent and at New York City only 55 per cent. With the contraction, prices at Cincinnati fell 66 per cent and at New York City only 50 per cent.[48]

The low level and declining prices accentuated the margin between prices in producing and consuming centers. The margins between prices of farm products at New York City and Cincinnati were very large. On July 15, 1842, the Cincinnati price of wheat was only 43 per cent of the New York City price. Articles that farmers bought were very high at Cincinnati compared with prices at New York City. The price of mackerel was 38 per cent higher at Cincinnati than at New York City.

The collapse of public credit.—The credit of a nation is an extremely fickle thing. From 1834 to 1838, the United States imported over $28,000,000 more goods than it exported. For the five years, 1839 to 1843, imports and exports practically balanced. The nation, not being able to borrow, paid for all the imports with exports instead of credit. Foreign investors lost $35,000,000 on the Bank of the United States.

Because of declining prices and reduced government income from the sales of public lands and other sources, the income of the government declined from $50,826,000 in 1836 to $16,860,000 in 1841, and an annual federal deficit was a common occurrence.[49]

By 1839, the European market for United States securities was destroyed, and there was little addition to the volume of state debts. Many states omitted interest payments, which increased the debts. Johnston championed the recommendation that the national government assume the state debts. His report gives us the first official information on the total amount of state debts, which in 1843 was $207,894,613.35.[50] This provided a favorable opportunity for the protectionists, and the Tariff Act of 1842 was passed.

[48] The index numbers of December 1 prices at Cincinnati are based on prices of wheat, flour, corn, whiskey, hogs, mess pork, and lard, as reported by Huntington, C. C., Banking and Currency in Ohio before the Civil War, Ohio Archeological and Historical Quarterly, Vol. 24, p. 519, 1915.

[49] Dewey, D. R., Financial History of the United States, pp. 237-9, 1922.

[50] Report of William Cost Johnston of Maryland, House of Representatives, 27th Congress, 3rd Session, Report 296, pp. 120-1, March 2, 1843.

All the states were in difficulty. Michigan repudiated her debts. Indiana compromised with her creditors, forcing them to take less than was due. Illinois stopped all improvements, raised taxes, and protected the state's credit. Pennsylvania bonds fell below par, and in 1840 the state defaulted on the payment of interest.[51]

Maryland was involved in extensive internal improvements involving the Chesapeake and Ohio Canal Company and the Baltimore and Ohio Railroad. In 1842, state script was down to 43 cents on the dollar.

By 1842, New York 6 per cent bonds sold at 83; Ohio, 53; Arkansas, 30; Indiana, 16; and Illinois, 15.

The Mississippi state legislature in 1842 took the attitude that the governor and not the state had approved the sale of the bonds, and that to repudiate them was a righteous defense of liberty. Naturally, American credit was at a very low ebb. We are frequently reminded of these debts by the English. It might be good policy to pay these repudiated debts with a part of the sum that England owes the United States.

The collapse of real estate, trade, and security prices.—The effect of contraction and declining prices on the value of real estate is shown in the striking declines in assessed value of property at New York City. In 1836 the assessed value of real estate per capita was $859; in 1842, $513.

It is probable that with falling prices, reduced incomes, and rising taxes, the actual sale prices of the properties dropped much more.

When prices decline rapidly, the volume of trade slackens. This is clearly shown by the 15 per cent decline in the volume of trade per capita from 1836 to 1843. Trade receded for more than six years, but was quickly stimulated by the slowly rising prices that followed.[52]

When commodity prices decline, profits melt away and prices of stocks decline more than commodity prices. The deadening influence of declining commodity prices on business is shown by the decline in prices of railroad stocks which fell in seven years, from 122 to 30.[53]

[51] Harlow, A. F., Old Towpaths, pp. 107-116, 1926.

[52] The index of volume of trade is based on boats passing locks, tolls collected, freight carried on canals, freight and passengers carried on railroads, post office receipts, auction duties in New York, river steamboats at New Orleans, imports of woolen cloth produced in Massachusetts, and corporations chartered in New York and New Jersey. Cole, A. H., Statistical Background of the Crisis Period, 1837-42, The Review of Economic Statistics, Vol. X, No. 4, pp. 184-5, November 1928.

[53] Cole, A. H., and Frickey, E., The Course of Stock Prices, 1825-66, The Review of Economic Statistics, Vol. X, No. 3, p. 129, August 1928.

In the same period, the prices of railroad bonds fell 50 per cent.

This was one of the worst periods of deflation that the country has ever experienced. Prices and public and private debts had become adjusted to a high price level and were over-expanded at that level. With the break in commodity prices, the number of dollars in the debt remained fixed but the value of the dollars rose so that general bankruptcy occurred. When the full history of the Panic of 1929 is written, the picture will be worse.

The late forties.—From 1845 to 1850, there was about the normal increase in circulation per capita and bank loans per dollar of specie were remarkably stable. The country had no central bank, but the "bank policy," if there was such, was handled to the best interests of the country. Commodity prices were fairly stable (table 1, page 10).

The Walker Tariff Act of 1846, which lowered metal duties, was accompanied by a striking decline in the index numbers of prices of metals and metal products. From 1846 to 1852, metals fell 25 per cent and farm products rose 33 per cent. Rising farm prices and falling metal prices resulted in a rapid expansion of construction. This was reflected in prices paid for railroad stocks,[54] which rose 67 per cent from January 1846 to December 1852.

The disastrous rains in Europe in 1845, accompanied by the Irish famine,[55] and the reduction in import duties by the repeal of the Corn Laws, caused an advance of 67 per cent in farm prices. In the words of Morley, it "rained away the Corn Laws."

There was a remarkable increase in our exports of breadstuffs, which rose from $7,445,000 in 1845 to $53,262,000 in 1847.[56] There was a general advance in prices of farm products, and the large exports at high prices resulted in an inflow of money.

In the agricultural states of the west and south, the enthusiasm for a tariff based on the home-market argument had perceptibly cooled, and with stable prices, increasing land sales, advancing trade, and increasing revenue from customs, the protectionists lost their argument of tariff for revenue. In 1846, the Walker tariff resulted in a striking

[54] Cole, A. H., and Frickey, E., The Course of Stock Prices, 1825-66, The Review of Economic Statistics, Vol. X, No. 3, p. 129, August 1928.

[55] Cole, A. H., Wholesale Prices in the United States, 1843-62, The Review of Economic Statistics, Vol. 11, No. 1, p. 35, February 1929.

[56] Bullock, C. J., Williams, J. H., and Tucker, R. S., The Balance of Trade of the United States, The Review of Economic Statistics, Vol. 1, No. 3, p. 220, July 1919.

reduction in rates. Indeed, this was said to be the beginning of a period of free trade, but it was in reality one of moderate protection.[57]

This was one of the golden eras in American history. Early writers and travelers who were usually from the better-educated and leisure classes of Europe did not always understand but always commented on the passion for work, the ingenuity in mechanical inventions, the resourcefulness of business,[58] and the prosperity of the country.

The expansion of the fifties.—In 1848, gold was discovered in California. In 1849, $8,000,000 was produced, and in 1850, $33,000,000; in 1856, production reached the maximum, $70,000,000. From 1851 to 1857, commodity prices rose 34 per cent. This was a period of great prosperity in the United States. Immigrants arrived in increasing numbers. Europeans were eager to lend funds to American industries, and there were large foreign borrowings.

The lure of gold stimulated the westward movement. By July 1850, 9720 wagons and 42,000 persons registered at Fort Laramie.[59] Before 1849, there were no railroads west of the Mississippi River, and in 1850 Congress adopted the policy of making land grants to assist in the promotion of railroad construction in the west.

Our large production and exports of gold and of farm products, a return of confidence on the part of foreign investors in the stability of the country, reduction of import duties resulting in large imports, and rising prices of commodities, railroad stocks, and bonds were a constant temptation for the expansion of credit and domestic business.

Compared with 1842, the price of railroad stocks at New York City had doubled by 1848-49 and trebled by 1852-53. From 1842 to 1853, the price of railroad bonds rose more than 50 per cent.[60]

No doubt the expansion was accelerated by the liberal policy of grants of public lands. It is estimated that from 1850 to 1856 more than 20,000,000 acres of public land were granted as subsidies for new lines in the west and south. From 1850 to 1857, the miles of railroad in operation increased from 9021 to 24,503.[61] A considerable part of this increase was in anticipation of the actual needs of the country.

The development of transportation was an important problem in

[57] Taussig, F. W., The Tariff History of the United States, pp. 115, 123-4, 1923.

[58] Recent Economic Changes in the United States, National Bureau of Economic Research, Vol. 1, p. 7, 1929.

[59] Hickernell, W. F., Financial and Business Forecasting, Vol. 1, p. 243, 1928.

[60] Ayres, L. P., Business Activity and Four Price Series, The Cleveland Trust Company, March 1932.

[61] Dunbar, C. F., Economic Essays, p. 272, 1904, Statistical Abstract of the United States, 1912, No. 35, Department of Commerce and Labor, p. 783, 1913.

and their New York agent defaulted.[66] Failure among the country banks of the west followed rapidly, and the scramble for liquidation was on. Loans were contracted, bank notes came in for redemption, and the banks accumulated specie. From 1857 to 1858, the circulation of state banks declined 28 per cent.[67] As a result, business firms of high standing gave way and heightened the panic. This accentuated the wild race for liquidity. No corporation seemed strong enough to resist the pressure for enforced liquidation. The notes of the Reading Railroad went to protest; the Erie suspended payment; the Illinois Central made an assignment of its property for the benefit of creditors; and the Michigan Central asked for an extension of time.[68] Just before the suspension of specie payment, "Business had been reduced to complete paralysis."[68] On September 24, the banks suspended specie payment and gold dollars commanded a premium at New York. After the suspension, the process of liquidation continued. The heavy discount on western bank notes in New York City drove them back home. After the race was over, Dunbar comments that "Specie was heaped up beyond all precedent in the banking history of New York."[69] Land sales declined 84 per cent; mortgages on real estate in Ohio fell from $38,000,000 in 1857 to $25,000,000 in 1858; the number of incoming immigrants declined about 50 per cent; there were almost 5000 failures in 1857; thirty-seven banks failed in the state of Maine alone; merchandise was a drug on the market; wholesale prices of all commodities declined 21 per cent; wholesale prices of farm food fell 33 per cent; the fall in security prices was still greater; railroad stocks fell 48 per cent; railroad bonds declined 20 per cent;[70] and state bonds fell 10 per cent.[71] The quotations for the United States 6 per cent bonds were maintained by the purchase of about $4,000,000 by the United States Treasury.[71] The worst effect was on the laboring classes. Unemployment was widespread. The boot and shoe and the textile industries of New England and the iron trade of Pennsylvania were especially hard hit.

Fluctuating commodity prices had the usual effects on the federal

[66] Lightner, O. C., The History of Business Depressions, pp. 142, 147, 1922.

[67] Hepburn, A. B., History of Coinage and Currency in the United States and the Perennial Contest for Sound Money, p. 174, 1903.

[68] Dunbar, C. F., Economic Essays, pp. 282-4, 1904.

[69] Dunbar, C. F., Economic Essays, p. 286, 1904.

[70] Ayres, L. P., Business Activity and Four Price Series, The Cleveland Trust Company, March 1932.

[71] Dunbar, C. F., Economic Essays, pp. 281, 285, 1904.

budget. With the rising commodity prices of the early fifties, there was a continual surplus; and with the collapse of commodity prices, the usual deficit.[72]

Civil War period.—As is usual in war periods, prices dropped when the Civil War broke out. The index numbers (table 1, page 10) show no decided rise in prices until the latter part of 1862. A very rapid rise then began and continued until the summer of 1865. In the closing days of 1861, specie payment was suspended by the government. In February 1862, Congress passed a bill authorizing the issue of $150,000,000 in legal tender United States notes. In July 1862 another 150 million issue was authorized, followed by another 150 million in 1863. The popularity of this method of financing the war is shown by the fact that the bill passed the House the day it was presented and the Senate the following day by a vote of 38 to 2. Of the $450,000,000 of these notes authorized, $431,000,000 were outstanding in June 1864. At first the greenbacks could be converted into bonds, the interest of which was payable in gold. The right to convert was discontinued in 1863.

The monetary circulation rose from $335,000,000 in 1862 to $715,000,000 in 1865. Prices rose from 83 to 225. This was the beginning of the greenbacks, which played such an important rôle in the political and price history following the Civil War. The increasing amounts of currency were accompanied by advancing prices and a depreciation in the value of the greenbacks. In July 1864 it took $2.58 in greenbacks to buy one gold dollar, or a greenback was worth 39 cents in gold (table 69). The price of greenbacks fluctuated with the fortunes of war but usually depreciated in advance of the rises in commodity prices. After the war, expanding business and declining prices played such an important rôle that paper currency was the paramount question. Late in 1865, with but six dissenting votes, the House of Representatives passed a resolution approving the contraction of the currency as early as possible in order to resume specie payment. Apparently the people were not so unanimously agreed as the legislators at Washington. They soon had their ears to the ground, however, and the greenbacks were the center of controversy for the next 15 years. Various methods were proposed. One group suggested a speedy return to specie payment. According to the New York Tribune, "The way to resume was to resume." Eastern bankers advised the accumulation of gold to raise the value of greenbacks to a gold standard. David A. Wells suggested the "cremation process."

[72] Dewey, D. R., Financial History of the United States, p. 269, 1922.

This involved drawing in a few greenbacks each week and destroying them. Another suggestion was to redeem them in gold at, say, 90 per cent of the face value. Still others advocated a do-nothing policy and suggested that resumption would take place by "growing up to specie payment."

There was another important group which was destined to develop into a powerful institution. This group was opposed to contraction and advocated expansion of the currency. This group grew by leaps and bounds and in a few years was consolidated into the Greenback party.[73]

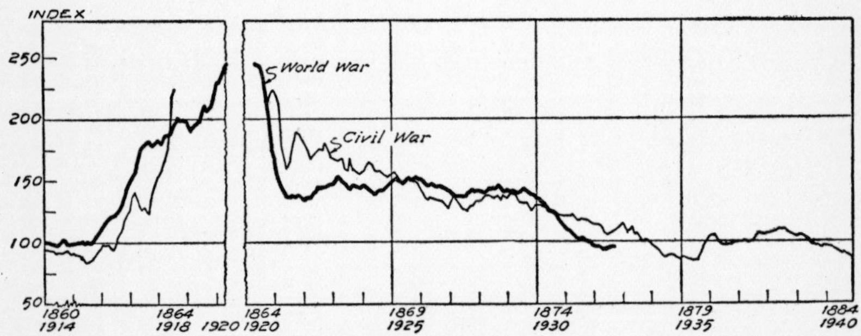

FIGURE 168.—INDEX NUMBERS OF WHOLESALE PRICES IN THE CIVIL WAR AND WORLD WAR PERIODS.

1910-14 = 100.

The price declines following the World War were similar to the declines following the Civil War, but were more violent.

By the Funding Act of 1866, a slight contraction of the currency resulted,[74] but the discontent of the farmers in the west where the farms were heavily mortgaged made it increasingly difficult to continue the contraction, and in 1868 Congress passed measures condemning contraction and suspending further contraction.

Declining prices after the Civil War.—From September 1864, prices declined from an index of 225 to 174 two years later. This was quite similar to the collapse in 1920-21 but less severe.

A large volume of bonds was sold to finance the Civil War. The interest on some of the bond issues was payable in gold; for others, no mention was made of the method of interest payment. At first, the

[73] Dewey, D. R., Financial History of the United States, pp. 336-8, 1922.

[74] During the two years of contraction, $44,000,000 in greenbacks was withdrawn from circulation. Dewey, D. R., Financial History of the United States, pp. 343-4, 1922.

TABLE 69.—GOLD VALUE OF CURRENCY IN THE UNITED STATES, 1814–78*

Year	Jan.	Feb.	Mar.	Apr.	May	June	July	Aug.	Sept.	Oct.	Nov.	Dec.	Yearly average
	¢	¢	¢	¢	¢	¢	¢	¢	¢	¢	¢	¢	¢
1814	.....	.....	.....	.....	.....	.....	.....	.....	90.0	90.0	89.0	89.0	....
1815	85.0	98.0	95.0	94.5	95.0	88.5	86.0	87.5	87.0	84.0	87.5	87.5	89.6
1816	87.5	91.0	87.5	90.0	87.5	87.5	94.0	95.0	97.0	98.0	98.3	97.8	92.6
1817	97.5	97.5	.....	.....	.....	.....	.....	.....	.....	.....	.....	.....	....
1837	100.0	100.0	100.0	100.0	95.1	91.1	91.7	92.0	92.9	94.9	94.6	95.7	95.7
1838	96.1	96.8	98.3	98.9	99.5	99.9	99.9	99.9	99.9	99.9	99.8	99.7	99.0
1839	99.7	99.7	99.7	99.7	99.7	99.7	99.7	99.7	99.7	99.7	99.7	99.7	99.7
1840	99.7	99.7	99.7	99.7	99.7	99.7	99.7	99.7	99.7	99.7	99.7	99.7	99.7
1841	99.7	99.7	99.7	99.7	99.7	99.7	99.7	99.8	100.0	100.0	100.0	100.0	99.8
1842	100.0	100.0	100.0	100.0	100.0	100.0	100.0	100.0	100.0	99.9	99.7	99.9	100.0
1843	99.9	100.0	100.0	99.9	99.9	99.9	99.9	99.9	99.9	99.8	99.8	100.0	99.9
1862	97.6	96.6	98.2	98.5	96.8	93.9	86.6	87.3	84.4	77.8	76.3	75.6	88.3
1863	68.9	62.3	64.7	66.0	67.2	69.2	76.6	79.5	74.5	67.7	67.6	66.2	68.9
1864	64.3	63.1	61.4	57.9	56.7	47.5	38.7	39.4	44.9	48.3	42.8	44.0	49.2
1865	46.3	48.7	57.5	67.3	73.7	71.4	70.4	69.7	69.5	68.7	68.0	68.4	63.6
1866	71.4	72.3	76.6	78.6	75.9	67.2	66.0	67.2	68.7	67.4	69.5	73.2	71.0
1867	74.3	72.8	74.1	73.7	73.0	72.7	71.7	71.0	69.7	69.7	71.6	74.2	72.4
1868	72.2	70.7	71.7	72.1	71.6	71.4	70.1	68.7	69.6	72.9	74.4	74.0	71.6
1869	73.7	74.4	76.2	75.2	71.8	72.4	73.5	74.5	73.1	76.8	79.2	82.3	75.2
1870	82.4	83.7	88.8	88.4	87.2	88.6	85.6	84.8	87.1	88.7	89.8	90.3	87.0
1871	90.3	89.7	90.1	90.4	89.7	89.0	89.0	89.0	87.3	88.3	89.9	91.5	89.5
1872	91.7	90.7	90.8	90.0	88.0	87.8	87.5	87.4	88.1	88.3	88.6	89.1	89.0
1873	88.7	87.6	86.6	84.9	85.0	85.8	86.4	86.7	88.7	91.8	92.1	90.9	87.9
1874	89.7	89.1	89.2	88.2	89.0	90.0	91.0	91.2	91.2	91.0	90.2	89.6	89.9
1875	88.9	87.3	86.6	87.1	86.3	85.4	87.2	88.1	86.4	85.9	87.2	87.8	87.0
1876	88.6	88.2	87.5	88.5	88.8	88.9	89.4	89.9	90.9	91.2	91.7	92.6	89.8
1877	94.0	94.8	95.4	94.2	93.5	94.9	94.9	95.2	96.8	97.3	97.3	97.3	95.4
1878	97.9	98.0	98.8	99.4	99.3	99.2	99.5	99.5	99.6	99.5	99.8	99.9	99.2

* The gold value of currency from 1814 to 1817 was taken from Gallatin, A., Considerations on the Currency and Banking Systems of the United States, p. 106, 1831.

From 1837 to 1843, Warren, G. F., Pearson, F. A., and Stoker, H. M., Wholesale Prices for 213 Years, 1720 to 1932, Cornell University Agricultural Experiment Station, Memoir 142, table 30, November 1932.

From 1862 to 1878, Mitchell, W. C., Gold, Prices, and Wages under the Greenback Standard, University of California Publications in Economics, Vol. 1, pp. 5–13, March 27, 1908.

Gold payments were suspended on Sept. 28, 1857. Premiums on gold may have occurred at this time.

discussions centered around the principle of justice to the bond holder and the credit position of the government. Although this was the position of the government, the sentiment in the middle west was quite different. The greenbacks of the farmer, laborer, merchant, and soldier were good enough for the bond holder. It was contended that the bond holder should accept the "lawful money"—which meant greenbacks. This was known as the "Ohio idea."[75]

It was a period of very rapid expansion in railroads, industry, and agriculture, which was very similar to although not so great as that which occurred from 1924 to 1929.

[75] The Democratic and the Republican party championed it. Grant, the Republican candidate, was elected and declared that the national honor must be protected, and that every dollar of government indebtedness should be paid in gold.

The effect of post-war economic changes is well put by McCulloch, Secretary of the Treasury in 1865:[76] "Steamboats are crowded with passengers, and hotels with guests; that cities are full to overflowing, and rents and the prices of necessaries of life as well as luxuries, are daily advancing. . . ."

In 1866, prices were high; labor scarce; speculation rampant; there was a housing shortage; interest rates were high; business was good; foreign trade was active; and there was a large physical volume of production. In fact, the conditions were more or less similar to those prevailing after the World War (figure 168).

In 1872, prices in the United States were close to the level of prices in England. From then on, most of the decline was due to the world-wide shortage of gold. From 1872 to 1878, prices in England declined 20 per cent, and in the United States 26 per cent (tables 8 and 9). This striking decline curtailed imports and stimulated exports.

Before 1873, there was a rapid expansion of railroads and homes. The country borrowed more than $1,500,000,000 in Europe, for which there was an annual interest charge of about $80,000,000.[77] In the fall of 1873, about crop-moving time, when credit tightened, a severe panic swept over the country, which was the beginning of a long period of financial and industrial depression. In 1873 an inflation measure was introduced which passed both houses, but which was quickly vetoed by Grant.[78]

The change in our foreign trade situation was very sudden. Imports decreased and exports increased. In 1873, the United States imported $120,000,000 more merchandise than it exported. In 1874, the exports exceeded the imports by $9,000,000.

Commodity prices declined from 139 in April 1873 to 85 in June 1879. Although prices of all commodities declined 39 per cent, the most striking changes were in prices of metals and textiles, both of which declined approximately 50 per cent. Prices of railroad stocks fell approximately the same amount; prices of railroad bonds rose about 20 per cent; interest rates declined; the number of immigrants arriving declined 70 per cent; the consumption of malt liquors per capita declined 9 per cent; the tonnage of American vessels con-

[76] McCulloch, H., Report of the United States Special Commissioner of Revenue, 1869, cited from Persons, W. M., Tuttle, P. M., and Frickey, E., Business and Financial Conditions Following the Civil War in the United States, The Review of Economic Statistics, Vol. 2, Supplement p. 6, 1920.

[77] Dewey, D. R., Financial History of the United States, p. 371, 1922.

[78] Hepburn, A. B., The History of Currency in the United States, p. 273, 1924.

structed fell 59 per cent; and production of pig iron declined 27 per cent.

From 1866 to 1873, the income of the federal government exceeded the expenses. In 1874, the income declined, expenses rose, and a deficit ensued.

"The Crime of 1873."—Since silver had been under-valued at the mint, little silver circulated. The Act of 1873 codified the mint laws and declared the gold dollar of 23.22 grains of pure gold to be the unit of value. At the time, no comment was made on omission of the standard silver dollar, probably because at that time silver was too valuable to circulate. With the subsequent scarcity and rising values of gold and consequent falling commodity prices, there was a persistent attempt to show that the act was the result of a conspiracy on the part of eastern bankers and others to demonetize silver without the general knowledge of the public. This was labeled the "Crime of 1873."

National banking system.—The national banking system was started by the Act of March 3, 1865, which levied a tax of 10 per cent on notes of any state banks issued after July 1, 1866. The state banks that wished to enjoy circulation privileges were forced to reorganize under federal charters. The national bank notes were limited to $300,000,000[79] and were secured to 90 per cent of their value by United States bonds. This naturally influenced the price of the bonds required for security, which apparently was not foreseen. Nor was it foreseen that the amount of the national bank notes in circulation would rise or fall with the price of bonds, nor that the currency would decline as the bonds were paid. The circulation of the national banks increased to $341,000,000 in 1873. Thereafter, there was usually less rather than more of these in circulation.[80] As the government bonds were paid off, the price of the bonds rose, decreasing the profit obtained from note issues. Although several attempts were made to remedy the ridiculous situation, the hatred was so intense that nothing was done.

With the rising value of gold, a powerful faction developed which demanded money in the form of silver. In 1877, the House of Representatives passed a bill which permitted free and unlimited coin-

[79] This was increased to $354,000,000 by the funding act of July 12, 1870.

[80] The amount of national bank notes in circulation stood at $341,000,000 in 1873; fell to $301,000,000 in 1877; rose to $352,000,000 in 1882; and fell to $162,000,000 in 1891. Statistical Abstract of the United States, 1912, No. 35, p. 740, United States Department of Commerce and Labor, 1913.

age of silver. The vote, 163 to 34, probably expressed the desires of the people. The bill was changed in the Senate under the leadership of Allison. Silver was made full legal tender. The treasury was authorized to buy not less than $2,000,000 and not more than $4,000,000 of silver bullion per month and coin silver dollars. The Bland-Allison Act of 1878 was passed over the veto of President Hayes.[81]

The silver issue.—The declining commodity prices and the continuation of the distress arising from the Panic of 1873 led to the conviction that relief depended on additional currency. Grant vetoed a measure to increase the Treasury notes. The ardor of those who attempted to relieve the situation, however, was not dampened.

The greenback movement gave way to agitation for the unlimited coinage of silver, and the crusade for the free coinage of silver monopolized the attention of Congress.

The adoption of the gold standard and the demonetization of silver in Germany in 1871, the limitation of coinage of silver by countries of the Latin Union in 1874, and the large increase in silver production in the United States resulted in a decline in the value of silver, at a time when gold production was declining and gold was rapidly increasing in value.

Resumption of specie payment.—The opposition to the resumption of specie payment came from the agricultural states of the south and west. Resumption was decreed by the Act of 1875. Western representatives demanded the repeal of the act; several bills were introduced but none passed. During the campaign of 1876, the inflationist group broke away from the two parties and formed the Greenback party, which polled 81,740 votes in 1876, and more than 1,000,000 in 1878. Prices began to rise, and it polled 308,578 in 1880, but only 175,370 in 1884.[82] After a great deal of controversy, the resumption of specie payment began in 1879. The inflationist group lost this contest, but they stopped once and for all further contraction of the greenbacks.

Expansion of the eighties.—From 1872 to 1878 the amount of money in circulation per capita fell from $20.43 to $17.23 (table 14, page 92). By 1883 the amount had risen to $22.91.[83] Wholesale prices rose from 85 in June 1879 to 111 in June 1882.

The crops were unusually good in 1879 and 1880. In 1879, the num-

[81] Dewey, D. R., Financial History of the United States, pp. 406-7, 1922.
[82] Dewey, D. R., Financial History of the United States, p. 381, 1922.
[83] The increase was due primarily to the increase in the number of silver certificates.

ber of pounds per capita of the six major starch crops was the largest of which we have a record.[84] The large food exports caused gold to flow into the country. Circulating medium was in demand, particularly in the west, and according to Taussig, for the three years 1881, 1882, and 1883, the silver currency was absorbed by the public as fast as the dollars were coined at the mint.[85] With the rising prices and surplus revenue, attention was diverted from the currency question long enough to pass the Tariff Act of 1883.

Foreign capital flowed in and railroad building began. The greatest mileage of new track ever laid in a ten-year period was laid in 1880-89. Railroad expansion on an extensive scale took place in Russia, Australia, Argentina, and Canada. Large amounts of credit were extended, and the London money market was so disturbed that the Bank of England borrowed $15,000,000 from the Bank of France.

From 1880 to 1890, the federal revenue exceeded the expenses, and the national debt was reduced rapidly.[86]

The Panic of 1893.—By the Sherman Act of 1890, Congress authorized the issue of an indefinite amount of legal tender notes in order to purchase silver bullion. As the notes were redeemed in gold or silver, the government was required to keep greenbacks, Treasury notes, and silver at a par with gold. One of the worst droughts that the United States ever had occurred in 1890. Instead of paying the interest on our debts with wheat and food products, we exported gold. Our financial condition shook the confidence of Europe, hastened the outflow of gold, and contributed to the Panic of 1893. The government ceased to purchase silver; the price fell from 82 to 67 cents in three days, and 573 banks closed their doors.

By 1894, 182 railroads, representing about one-fourth of the railroad capital, went into the hands of receivers.[87] Pig-iron production declined 27 per cent, commercial failures increased from $114,000,000 to $347,000,000, unemployment was widespread, and organized relief was undertaken. Strikes and riots were numerous. The Homestead strike in Pittsburgh and the Pullman strike in Chicago were out-

[84] Warren, G. F., Prices of Farm Products in the United States, United States Department of Agriculture Bulletin 999, p. 6, Aug. 26, 1921.

[85] Taussig, F. W., Silver Situation in the United States, p. 24, Second Edition, 1893. Courtesy G. P. Putnam's Sons, Publishers, New York and London.

[86] The public indebtedness was reduced from $1,996,000,000 in 1879 to $891,000,000 in 1890, Dewey, D. R., Financial History of the United States, p. 431, 1922.

[87] Daggett, S., Railroad Reorganizations, p. 21, 1908.

standing examples. Coxey's army of unemployed marched to Washington.

The usual effect of declining prices and depression on the federal budget followed. In 1890, there was a surplus of $105,000,000; in 1894, a deficit of $70,000,000.[88]

The free silver campaign.—The deflation from 1864 to 1896 placed a heavy burden on debtors and caused numerous periods of unemployment. A portion of this decline was due to contraction of the currency in order to return to the gold basis. This was completed in 1879. At the same time, world gold production failed to keep pace with business. During the decade from 1880 to 1889, less gold was produced than in any decade of the thirty previous years. Wholesale prices in England fell from 134 in 1873 to 74 in 1896. In the same period, prices in the United States fell from 133 to 68. The fundamental cause was not generally understood. There was confusion of war deflation, bank policy, and demonetization of silver. After years of trouble, the resulting injustices of a steadily rising value of money found expression in the political campaign of 1896. Bryan proposed as a remedy for the situation that there should be free and unlimited coinage of silver at the ratio of 16 to 1. A very bitter campaign was fought. The long years of search for gold were just beginning to be rewarded. World gold production nearly doubled from 1893 to 1896. As this was added to the monetary stocks, prices began to advance.

A period of prosperity.—The discoveries of gold in Australia, Cripple Creek, and the Klondike, and the expansion of production in South Africa by the invention of the cyanide process which enabled gold producers to work poorer ores and rework the refuse that had accumulated in previous years, made gold more plentiful. Prices rose rapidly.

During this period we had a continual excess of exports. These large exports were due to the large cumulative debt owed by debtors in the United States to European investors. Previous to this time, we had paid our interest in the form of wheat, food, cotton, and other raw materials. This period marks the end of the great expansion in our agricultural exports and the beginning of a rapid increase in manufactured goods. Up to this time, no one had disputed the right of Europe to produce most of the world's manufactured goods. In 1892, manufactures represented only 18 per cent of our exports, but by 1900 they were 35 per cent. This rapid expansion resulted in considerable agitation in Europe against the so-called "American invasion."

[88] Dewey, D. R., Financial History of the United States, p. 448, 1922.

Food prices rose, and "the high cost of living" became a very serious problem. Agriculture was prosperous. Farm mortgages were easy to pay.

The World War period.—The World War produced greater changes in the economic and financial structure of the world than any other event for which we have record.

Exports from Europe declined and they had to pay for their imports by returning stocks and bonds, by shipping gold, and by borrowing from American investors. This, of course, resulted in a rise in commodity prices in America.

The foreign investors sold about two billion dollars of American securities. The United States accumulated a billion dollars of gold. Private loans floated in the United States amounted to more than two billion dollars. Suddenly the United States changed from the world's greatest borrower to the world's greatest lender.

After the United States entered the war, we lent a few paltry billions to the allied governments—over which we are now quarreling and may continue to quarrel for a generation.

The net result was that prices rose to an index of 201 in September 1918 when pre-war is 100.

Post-war inflation.—From April 21 to May 10, 1919, the Victory Loan was floated. Ninety per cent of the bonds were sold on credit. This resulted in the post-war inflation, and prices rose to an index of 244 in May 1920.

Most of the rise in prices from 1914 to 1920 was due to the release of gold by a large part of the world. These countries not only stopped using gold but also stopped bidding for it. If half of the monetary gold in the world were at any given time released for use in the other half of the world, prices would be expected to double. A portion of the inflation in 1920 was due to other factors, but most of it was due to the release of gold by other countries (page 114).

When the secondary boom came, the optimism that it developed led to the popular conclusion that prices would never again drop materially. Wild buying began in all kinds of business. Goods were purchased far in advance of needs, often with the idea that, by contracting from several sources much more than was wanted, deliveries of the desired amount would be made. During the period of rapid rise in prices, many orders were left unfilled for one excuse or another, sometimes because of the impossibility of filling them and sometimes because sales could be made elsewhere at the new and higher prices.

Consumers were even worse hoarders. They bought wildly of all classes of goods. The higher prices went, the more they wanted to buy. When sugar went to 30 cents a pound at retail, the demand could not be met. When sales were limited to a pound a day, standing orders were left for a pound every day. Others traded at more than one store so as to acquire the privilege of buying more, before the prices went higher.

The food ministries and other buying agencies of the various governments were even greater hoarders than private families. It was two years before the government hoards were fully unloaded.

The sure way to make money was to buy or produce to sell on a later market. The universal desire to buy and to produce on credit led to great credit expansion. Sales were so profitable that the standing of creditors was not closely scrutinized. Large sales were also made to individuals in foreign countries on credit.

The general belief was that prices would remain high for many years. It was argued by many that comparisons with other wars were not valid, because with the Federal Reserve System, panics could not occur, not realizing that it is the highly developed machinery that makes panics possible. Others argued that laborers, having had good wages, would never again consent to work for low wages, hence prices would not drop, not realizing that the price the produce can be sold for, and not the laborer's likes, determine whether he can be employed. Farmers contended that they could not go back to pre-war prices, that their costs of production were high and they must sell at high prices. Similarly, the manufacturers of fertilizers and farm machinery contended that their costs had not dropped, hence their prices would have to remain at the high levels. When prices began to decline they sent out numerous briefs showing how impossible it was for them to cut prices. All these false premises were confounded as prices fell. It often became impossible to sell at any price, much less at the price that the producer chose.

Newspaper agitation and public clamor were constantly insisting on a reduction of prices. The general belief seemed to be that if prices could be brought down everyone would be much better off. The extent of the concern about high prices is indicated by the fact that on May 17, 1920, the United States Senate adopted a resolution requiring the Federal Reserve Board to "advise the Senate what steps it proposed to take or recommend to the member banks of the Federal Reserve System to meet the existing inflation of currency and credits and the consequent high prices."[89] The continued agitation had a strong psychological influence on consumers, producers, borrowers, and lenders.

The Panic of 1920.—In May 1920, wholesale prices were 244 when 1910-14 is 100. The drop in prices began in June, increased rapidly, continued for thirteen months, then remained about stationary for six months. The real recovery did not start until February 1922.

The severe character of the panic is shown by the drops in prices in successive months. The number of points decline in the index of prices for each month was as follows:

Month	Points	Month	Points
June	1	January	9
July	1	February	14
August	6	March	3
September	9	April	6
October	16	May	3
November	16	June	5
December	19	July	0

Prices dropped one point in June 1920. The drop increased in rapidity until prices dropped 19 points in the month of December. The total drop in a year was from 244 to 141. No such drop in prices had occurred in the United States since the Revolutionary War.

The total decline was 42 per cent in a year, or nearly 3.5 per cent a month. Manufacturing stopped, unemployment was serious, failures were numerous.

Prices of basic commodities respond more promptly and more violently than prices of all kinds of commodities. The extent of the panic is better shown by the basic commodity index. Prices of basic commodities dropped from 260 to 115 in 15 months. The number of points of drop in each month beginning with June 1920 was as follows:

Month	Points	Month	Points
June	7	December	25
July	8	January	8
August	3	February	11
September	9	March	7
October	20	April	9
November	30		

Those industries like agriculture that could not liquidate promptly were most injured. Conservative corporations with long records for dividend payments passed their dividends, and many were compelled to reorganize.

The failure to buy was popularly called the "Buyers' Strike." There were many reasons for failure to buy, the primary one being

[89] Credit, Report of Joint Commission of Agricultural Inquiry, House of Representatives, 67th Congress, 1st Session, Report 408, Part II, p. 86, 1922.

the belief that prices would be lower tomorrow. The fact that large hoards were on hand made delay in purchases possible. Unemployment and the inability to sell made it impossible to buy. During this decline the farm price of cotton fell from 38 cents in May 1920 to 9.4 cents a year later. Corn fell from $1.86 in July 1920 to 41 cents in November 1921. Sheep dropped from $10.66 in April 1920 to $3.84 in November 1921. Potatoes fell from $4.21 a bushel in June 1920 to 67 cents in June 1921.

The panic is sometimes said to have been world-wide, but those countries that did not deflate their currency in 1920 continued to have a business boom, full employment, and all the other phenomena which accompany inflation.

Price stability, 1922-29.—Very little railroad construction or home building had been carried on from 1914 to 1920. The amount of long-time debts to be liquidated was moderate, except the national debt and farm debt.

The city part of the Panic of 1920 was therefore short and was followed by reconstruction. For eight years there was a period of relative price stability, considering the chaotic condition of world finance. During this period, there was some over-building, and debts, wages, and taxes generally became adjusted to a price level about 50 per cent above pre-war. Tax returns were high, and public services were increased.

Maelstrom of 1929.—Most of the countries of the world began to attempt the reestablishment of the gold standard. Complete reestablishment is not made at a single step but by a succession of acts. France revalued the franc and established its gold basis in 1928. India attempted to establish a gold basis. Other countries returned to the gold standard with more than their pre-war demand because population and business had increased and large reserves were desired. Gold production had been decreasing. Long before gold was fully reestablished the crash came with a world-wide panic to get gold. This succeeded a period of large expenditures for public and private building at a time when public and private debts were high.

In August 1929, began one of the greatest peace-time declines in prices of which the world has a record. The index of prices fell from 141 in August 1929 to 93 in June 1932.

Economic changes, drastic in character, occurred with such rapidity that it was difficult for the human mind to foresee them or even grasp the significance of the changes after they occurred. The more important were: the precipitous decline in commodity prices, followed by the suspension of payments on reparations, war debts, and other international debts; the suspension of specie payment by most countries of the world; the drastic drop in the pound sterling and other exchanges; unprecedented exports of gold; hoarding of currency; advance in discount rates; the $500,000,000 national credit corporation; bank and business failures; the Interstate Commerce Commission's decision on freight rates; financial embarrassments of many municipalities, states, and railroads; huge federal deficit in the United States; the sweeping conservative victory and the protective tariff in England; repayments by the Bank of England; Snowden's plan for "voluntary conversion" of the ten-billion-dollar 5 per cent war loan to a lower rate; von Hindenburg's decree for a suspension of legal executions by creditors in East Prussia and a 50 per cent scale down in debts; the Reconstruction Finance Corporation; the campaign against hoarding; the proposals to increase the efficiency of the Federal Reserve System; the Glass-Steagall bill; suspension of foreclosures; lenient examination of banks; and violent fluctuations in prices of stocks and bonds.

There have been few, if any, periods in the world's history when so many disastrous events were recorded in so short a time.

The world has never experienced, in times of peace, such a prodigious destruction and transfer of wealth in so short a time. Most measures of industrial activity were about 40 to 60 per cent below normal. During the depression of 1921, Ayres' index of American industrial activity fell to 27 per cent below normal. The Panics of 1837 and 1893 were the only ones, prior to 1921, that carried business as much as 20 per cent below normal. In short, the business of the United States was at a level never before reached in the annals of American business. Honest men could not get work; creditors could not collect their debts; and "for rent" signs appeared everywhere. Changes came so quickly and values were being swept away so rapidly that fearless and honest men became so bewildered that they knew not how to act. They were like a gassed and wounded regiment in No Man's Land. After the deluge is over, we can look back and see some of our mistakes. However, in the midst of the depression, the farmers, the bankers, the business men, the unemployed, and not the least, the President of the United States, groped for light in order that, in the rapidly changing panorama, they might act promptly and wisely.

The suspension of the gold standard, 1933.—As the depression continued, foreclosure sales were in many places forcibly stopped by the citizens. In other cases, the neighbors appeared and bid only a few cents for a horse, cow, or a farm. By general understanding, no one was to bid more. Property thus purchased was turned back to the previous owner. The city mortgage situation was on the verge of collapse. The legal processes of debt collection were rapidly breaking down. A number of states passed laws prohibiting foreclosures and tax sales. So many taxpayers were unable to pay that even those who could pay often stopped payment. Many cities were unable to pay their debts.

Bank failures were most numerous in regions far from market, primarily because the percentage drop in prices was highest there. Many individuals withdrew their deposits. Large corporations withdrew deposits from outlying states and cities, and concentrated them in larger and still larger cities. Deposits in the New York banks grew rapidly. Superficial observers took this as a mark of confidence in the New York banks. It was, in fact, an indication of fright, and placed these banks in a position of danger, when the next step of shifting from deposits to hoarded gold and currency came. A general run on banks developed. Finally individuals and corporations began to withdraw gold. Bank holidays were declared in state after state. Finally, on March 3, all banks were closed by state orders.

On March 6, the President ordered all banks and security and commodity exchanges to remain closed, and prohibited the withdrawal of gold. On March 13, the Federal Reserve banks opened, and on the following day other banks began a gradual opening. Withdrawals of currency were limited, and no gold was allowed to be withdrawn. Foreign exchange operations were placed under control.

On March 12, the Treasury Department ordered the banks to turn in to the Federal Reserve system all gold and gold certificates. On April 5, the President ordered individuals to turn in all gold certificates and all gold in excess of $100.

During this time, the dollar was kept at par in foreign exchange by allowing transactions by permit. This kept the price level on a gold basis practically as completely as if the free gold standard had been kept in effect. Some buying developed in expectation that suspension would take place.

On April 19, the gold standard was definitely suspended. Exports of gold were prohibited. Immediately, the dollar fell below par in foreign countries. Prices of commodities and securities promptly rose in the United States. During this period, gold for industrial uses was sold on permit at the legal price of $20.67 per ounce, and gold produced by gold mines was required to be turned in to the government at this price.

On May 26, the President asked for the invalidation of the so-called "gold clause." This law was passed by the House with a vote of 283 to 57, and by the Senate by a vote of 48 to 20, and was signed by the President on June 5. The request for the invalidation of the gold clause was taken as a clear indication that the dollar would not again be brought to par. Therefore, this request brought an immediate response in prices of commodities and securities.

A century and a half of monetary chaos.—This century and a half of chaotic history of prices, which meant prosperity or ruined the lifetime opportunities of innumerable individuals, was not due to acts of Providence. It was due to lack of knowledge of economic principles, or failure to apply the little knowledge that there was. The common assumption at any given date has always been that the conditions were world-wide and inevitable either as a punishment for present sins or because of some benign force working for our good. The price history of no two countries is alike. In each country the price history is a result of legislative acts and accidental discoveries of or failure to discover the particular metal which legislative acts designate as money.

Our political acts are based largely on experience. These price disturbances are not often repeated in the same direction in one generation. It frequently happens that the generation which is to act on a situation has derived all its experiences from the opposite set of conditions. If such price chaos is to be avoided in the future, the scientific principles that govern prices must be discovered, made common knowledge, and applied. The world's monetary history is as chaotic as was its medical practice before bacteria were known—and for the same reason—lack of knowledge.

BIBLIOGRAPHY

Bolles, A. S., The Financial History of the United States, 1861-1885. 1886.

Cole, A. H., Cyclical and Sectional Variations in the Sale of Public Lands, 1816-60. The Review of Economic Statistics, Vol. IX, No. 1, pp. 41-53. January 1927.

Cole, A. H., Wholesale Commodity Prices in the United States, 1843-62. The Review of Economic Statistics, Vol. XI, No. 1, pp. 26-37. February 1929.

Cole, A. H., Statistical Background of the Crisis of 1857. The Review of Economic Statistics, Vol. XII, No. 4, pp. 170-180. November 1930.

Dewey, D. R., Financial History of the United States. 1922.

Dieterlen, P., La depression des prix après 1873 et en 1930, Revue d'Économie Politique, 44e Année, No. 6, pp. 1519-1568. Novembre-Decembre 1930.

GALLATIN, A., Considerations on the Currency and Banking Systems of the United States, p. 44. 1831.

GOUGE, W. M., A Short History of Paper Money and Banking in the United States. 1833.

HEPBURN, A. B., History of Coinage and Currency in the United States and the Perennial Contest for Sound Money. 1903.

HICKERNELL, W. F., Financial and Business Forecasting, Vol. 1. 1928.

HUNTINGTON, C. C., A History of Banking and Currency in Ohio Before the Civil War, Ohio Archaeological and Historical Publications, Vol. XXIV, pp. 235-526. 1915.

McGRANE, R. C., The Panic of 1837. 1924.

MITCHELL, W. C., A History of the Greenbacks, The University of Chicago, Decennial Publications, Second Series, Vol. IX. 1903.

MITCHELL, W. C., Business Cycles, University of California. 1913.

MITCHELL, W. C., Gold, Prices, and Wages under the Greenback Standard, University of California Publications in Economics, Vol. 1. March 1908.

NOYES, A. D., Thirty Years of American Finance. 1898.

PERSONS, W. M., TUTTLE, P. M., and FRICKEY, E., Business and Financial Conditions Following the Civil War in the United States. The Review of Economic Statistics, Vol. 2, Supplement, pp. 1-55. July 1920.

PHILLIPS, H., JR., Historical Sketches of the Paper Currency of the American Colonies Prior to the Adoption of the Federal Constitution, Vols. 1 and 2. 1865.

PRATT, J. W., Expansionists of 1812. 1925.

PRATT, J. W., Western Aims in the War of 1812. Mississippi Valley Historical Review, Vol. XII, No. 1, pp. 36-50, June 1925.

SCOTT, W. A., Repudiation of State Debts. 1893.

SMITH, W. B., Wholesale Commodity Prices in the United States, 1795-1824. The Review of Economic Statistics, Vol. 9, No. 4, pp. 171-83. October 1927.

SUMNER, W. G., A History of American Currency. 1874.

TAUSSIG, F. W., The Silver Situation in the United States. 1893.

TAYLOR, G. R., Agrarian Discontent in the Mississippi Valley Preceding the War of 1812, The Journal of Political Economy, Vol. XXXIX, No. 4, pp. 471-505. August 1931.

TAYLOR, G. R., Prices in the Mississippi Valley Preceding the War of 1812, Journal of Economic and Business History, Vol. III, No. 1, pp. 148-163. November 1930.

UPTON, J. K., Money in Politics. 1884.

WEBSTER, P., Political Essays. 1791.

WILDMAN, M. S., Money Inflation in the United States. 1905.

Reports of the Pioneer Society of the State of Michigan.

Recent Economic Changes in the United States, National Bureau of Economic Research 13, Vol. I. 1929.

Stabilization of Commodity Prices. Hearings Before the Subcommittee of the Committee on Banking and Currency, House of Representatives, 72nd Congress, 1st Session on House of Representatives 10517, Part I, p. 247. 1932.

CHAPTER XXIII

THE PRICE OUTLOOK

The price outlook is the resultant of a combination of four unknowns: (1) supply of commodities; (2) demand for commodities; (3) supply of gold; (4) demand for gold. At the present time, consideration must also be given to the probability of a monetary change.

The outlook for an individual commodity is determined by the general price outlook resulting from the above factors modified by the supply of and demand for the particular product, making seven factors to consider.

Supply of all commodities.—The normal steady increase of about 3.15 per cent per year in the world production of all commodities was interfered with by the war. Had this rate of increase held, the production in 1929 would have been 173, whereas it was only 140 (table 6).

It is too soon to be sure what the new base will be. It will certainly not be so high as it would have been had there been no war. Instead of the spectacular increase in efficiency which popular superstition accepts, there has undoubtedly been a permanent lowering of the base on which increased production rises. It is too soon to know just what the new normal base will be, but an index of about 135 for 1929 or about 147 for 1932 is not improbable.

The rate of increase before the war was 3.15 per cent per year. It is possible that scarcity of gold and continuous unemployment may reduce this rate.

The probability of any successful attempt to reduce production by governmental or private action is extremely remote. The severe unemployment is resulting in a shortage of goods that will tend to raise prices temporarily.

As a long-time outlook, production is very stable and probably will not be the cause of either inflation or deflation of prices (page 49).

Demand for all commodities.—There is no such thing as a prolonged cessation in the demand for commodities. When money suddenly rises in value, demand for commodities is temporarily checked, but this comes about through the money factor. Total world demand for commodities as an initiating cause of prices is of small importance except during fluctuations in business cycles. Temporarily it is of great importance for some individual commodities, particularly for shoes, clothing, and housing. There are violent fluctuations in the demand for these. But it does not seem probable that this will be a source of inflation or deflation.

Supply of gold.—The world monetary supply of gold in 1932, with world production at the new normal of about 50 per cent above pre-war, would be about sufficient to support pre-war prices with all the former gold-using world on a gold basis, provided the pre-war rate of efficiency in the use of gold had continued, but inefficiency is to be expected.

It seems practically certain that world gold production will be too low to sustain any price level which is established. That is, if all the gold-using world returns to gold and if a country revalues its currency to bring prices into adjustment with the present gold supply, prices would be expected to decline. In a country that does not revalue its currency, it is to be expected that prices will have to become adjusted to the gold supply by the type of violent adjustment that has been occurring and that after they are adjusted they will continue to decline gradually. If such an adjustment were made, the present rate of gold production would call for a decline in commodity prices of about 1 per cent per year (page 106).

Demand for gold.—The use of gold in industry normally increases at about the same rate as the production of all commodities, about 3 per cent per year. There is no indication of any fundamental change in the demand for gold in industry (page 100).

For 75 years before the war, world monetary stocks of gold had to increase at the same rate as the production of all commodities in order to maintain a stable price level. There is no indication of any improvement in this relationship. During the period of low demand for gold, from 1915 to 1928, prices were out of line with the gold supply, but prices in England and the United States in 1931 and 1932 were lower than the pre-war relationship would call for.

During the 75 years before the war, gold was gradually being adopted by various countries—a process that promises to continue. Russia, India, and a number of other countries desire gold supplies in order that they may establish gold standards.

After years of world monetary chaos, instead of a given weight of gold supporting its normal price level, the expectation is that it will be a number of years before the price level will be as high as normal compared with the gold supply, if all the world is back on a gold basis.

Fantastic trade barriers, vast international public and private debts, great monetary losses, all make it desirable for each country to hold high gold reserves so as to be ready for an international run on the gold supply such as occurred from 1929 to 1932.

It is not to be expected that prices will follow the supply of gold so closely as before the war, because of violent fluctuations in the demand for gold. This will cause striking temporary irregularities.

The individual commodity.—It is comparatively easy to make business adjustments that are required by changes in the supply of or demand for an individual commodity. Most of the difficulties that are attributed to these factors are initiated by movements in the whole price structure rather than by changes in the value of the individual commodity.

There is no reason for supposing that the prices of such important basic commodities as cotton, wheat, or corn have permanently changed either their relationships to each other or to all commodities (pages 27, 28, 31).

The hog, beef, and horse cycles will be expected to continue (figure 88, page 130). The prices of these will be expected to fluctuate about the general level of prices.

The prices of many basic commodities are out of line with the average for all commodities and with the gold supply. Some recovery in such prices is inevitable.

The price outlook if gold is demonetized by England.—If an important country such as England should demonetize gold, the permanent reduction in demand would lower the value of gold and raise prices in countries that continued on a gold basis. Although such a procedure is possible, it is more probable that these countries will work towards some kind of a gold standard so that the demand for gold will continue. Countries that have suspended the gold standard have placed themselves in a favorable position for obtaining gold and gold credits because it makes it easy for them to sell and difficult to sell to them.

In 1931, England and 31 other countries had suspended the gold standard. This caused some reduction in the demand for gold so that prices rose somewhat. There is no way of foretelling how far this may go. It might cause a considerable rise in commodity prices, but the more prices rise, the more certainly these countries will return to the gold standard because it will appear easy to them. Therefore, the more prices rise, the more certain they are to fall again in gold-using countries.

If gold were demonetized, the effects would be the same as the reduced demand for gold during the World War period. For half a generation, most of the nations of the world stopped using gold and stopped bidding for it. It moved to the few countries in which it was freely purchased. The low demand made gold cheap or made prices high.

The attempt to return to the gold standard caused a frantic demand for gold and the collapse in commodity prices.

The value of gold is determined by world supply and world demand —not merely by location of the supply.

The price outlook if deflation is completed.—If all the former gold-using countries return to the gold basis and if the United States continues to maintain its present monetary standard, it is to be expected that commodity prices will average below pre-war for the next ten years.

Price fluctuations may be expected to be violent. The present low production of commodities may be expected to cause a material rise in commodity prices as soon as the debts on city real estate are liquidated to such an extent as to allow construction to proceed. This will require several years (page 266).

If deflation is completed, the following are some of the innumerable adjustments yet to be made.

At the new price levels, public and private debts are nearly equal to the national wealth. These debts will have to be reduced. The only plan thus far proposed for reducing them is bankruptcy and private adjustment. This will probably require three or four years for the major adjustment and a generation to complete the process. While the more serious part of this is taking place, bankrupt homes, farms, and other properties will always be for sale at less than new costs of construction, regardless of how low these costs may fall. Therefore little building of any kind is to be expected. Consequently most of the basic industries will operate at low capacity and severe unemployment will be continuous. Business cycles in such a period will be suppressed cycles (page 137).

The vigorous efforts to reduce taxes will do well if they succeed in making the cuts equal to the new taxes necessary to feed the unemployed. Some shifting from real estate to other forms of taxation may occur.

Public debts will increase, and some of the government units will find it impossible to meet their obligations.

Adjusting a price level down requires much more time than adjusting it up. It is not difficult to adjust public and private debts to a higher price level, but it is very difficult to reduce them. To adjust debts up merely requires that the usual purchases be made at the new price level with the usual percentage of credit transactions. To adjust debts down means the slow process of bankruptcy. Bankruptcy acts like a house of cards—each bankruptcy starts another.

Bank deposits will decline because of the reduced amount of business, the lower prices at which the business is done, and the tendency to use cash rather than checks. This latter movement is encouraged by fear of banks, lack of banks, lower interest payments on deposits, charges for checks, taxes on checks, and high postage rates. Many more bank failures will occur.

Because of severe unemployment, some individuals are working for extremely low wages, but it is not to be expected that the general wage level will decline to the price level. The long-time tendency is for wages to rise as the output per worker increases. Whenever the debts are liquidated so that business can proceed, wages will be far above pre-war (page 198).

Interest rates will be much below pre-war for safe securities, but a large part of the business will be on such a precarious basis that, for some years, rates for agriculture and industry may be high. Interest payments on bank deposits will be decidedly reduced. Life insurance rates will probably rise. The average size of policies will be reduced.

The size of fire insurance policies will be reduced, losses will be increased, and rates probably will be raised.

Innumerable prices which have not declined will fall. Some of these are freight rates, telephone charges, price of newspapers, doctors' fees, dentists' fees, and telegraph charges.

Large numbers of corporations will disappear by bankruptcy or by combination to avoid bankruptcy.

Wholesale writing down of the capital of industrial plants, farms, and city real estate will continue. This process is far from complete.

Costs of distribution will gradually decline so that prices paid to farmers will again come into adjustment with the prices which they pay. Much of this can be done in a few years. Probably it can be completed in a generation.

Some basic commodity prices have fallen too low even for the conditions and will rise.

Innumerable measures will be tried in attempts to hold up prices of this or that thing. Tariffs, bounties, farm boards, domestic allotments, restrictions on trade between states under sanitary and other guises, pools, gentlemen's agreements, and many others will continue to be tried and will continue to result in disillusion and disappointment. Maintaining the present price of gold means bringing the whole debt and price structure down. To attempt to hold each individual thing up and yet bring the whole down is like sinking a ship but attempting to hold up each rivet and door knob in it.

It is not improbable that the high value of gold will result in discoveries of it, so that a later generation will have inflation (page 97).

The general attitude of the public seems to be to prefer to write everything down in terms of gold rather than raise the price of gold. The strain on public credit to feed unemployed and the social confusion from such general bankruptcies may make it impossible to complete the process. No such violent deflation has yet been carried through by any modern nation.

If the process is carried through, a new generation can be prosperous—except as foolish laws remain to plague it. Any price level is satisfactory after business is adjusted to it.

Attempts to restore the price level by means of credit.—A gradual decrease in the amount of monetary circulation per dollar of gold and a gradual increase in the bank credit per dollar of gold in the United States have been taking place since 1880. There is no indication that the Federal Reserve system has speeded up this normal growth of circulation plus credit per dollar of gold (page 107).

Some persons believe that the Federal Reserve system is to blame for the decline in prices and that there is gold enough to maintain pre-deflation prices if credit were properly managed. The evidence indicates that a rise in the value of gold was inevitable with the return of the world-wide demand for it. Credit management might have prevented a part of the stock market boom. No evidence has been found that credit management could have prevented a decline in commodity prices, or that the 1929 commodity prices can be restored by credit management and still maintain the present price of gold.

By the management of credit, it is possible to throw commodity prices out of line with gold by a limited amount. There is no indication that any permanent change in this relationship can be accomplished in this way. Over-expansion of credit brings on a reaction, and so does over-contraction of credit. The policy of the federal government in 1932 was based on the theory that prices could be raised by credit. The Reconstruction Finance Corporation lent money to many agencies in the expectation that credit expansion by the Reconstruction Finance Corporation and the Federal Reserve banks would raise prices, restore equities back of securities, and start business activity. The policy did check contraction, but only a rise in the price structure can stop bankruptcies and start employment. It is not possible to expand credit sufficiently to do this and still maintain the present price of gold.

Currency expansion.—It is very easy to raise the price level by an expansion of the currency, but any expansion that is sufficient to restore the prices of commodities to the debt level would make it impossible to continue to redeem each of the paper dollars with 23.22 grains of gold. There is no way of printing paper money that will make it possible materially to change the relative values of gold and commodities.

Remonetization of silver.—By adopting bimetallism or symmetallism, it is possible to set any price level that is desired. Symmetallism would tend to keep prices more stable in the future than the continuance of the gold standard (page 160).

Revaluation.—By reducing the weight of gold in the dollar, any desired price level can be established. The future course of prices would then depend on future supplies of and demand for gold. France reduced the weight of gold in the franc to one-fifth of the pre-war amount. Prices in France are therefore about five times as high as in the United States when compared with pre-war (page 171).

The compensated dollar.—Two proposals have been advanced to provide for a permanently stable measure of value. One of these proposes a managed currency to be controlled by central banks in such a way as to keep the average of commodity prices stable. To operate such a system requires willingness and intelligence in the bank management, and freedom from influence by politics or desire for profits. The other proposal is a currency governed by law which provides that the amount of gold for which a dollar is redeemed shall vary with the index number of prices of all commodities. If such a dollar were adopted, any desired price level could be set and thereafter could be maintained at a substantially stable level (page 163).

Price outlook if the price level is restored.—The effect of rising prices is the same regardless of the cause. If for any reason the price level is restored, it does not mean that all prices will rise equally. Many prices have not declined, or have declined little. Restoring the price level would relieve them of the necessity of declining. The major ones are debts and taxes. If commodity prices were raised, buying would begin, because rising prices cause buying. Jobs would be available. Houses would be in demand. The debts and taxes on the houses and farms could be paid, and the debts would not have to be cut by bankruptcy.

The former amount of life insurance would be desired.

Many charges, such as freight rates, doctors' fees, telephone rates, and the like, are already adjusted to the price level that would be established. They would not rise, but would be relieved from falling.

Costs of distribution would rise very little. Therefore prices paid to farmers and other producers would rise much more than retail prices. This would bring farm prices into adjustment with other prices. It is sometimes said that two steps are necessary: first, restore the price level; and second, restore the relationship of farm prices to other prices. If the first step is taken, the second follows automatically (page 186).

Prices of basic commodities, such as copper, corn, wheat, and cotton, would rise very decidedly because they are so far below the price level that would be restored.

The declines in values of homes and farms would be stopped.

In general, the prices that have not yet declined would be relieved from declining, and those that have declined would be restored.

Short-time price outlook.—The price level must be raised to the debt level or the debt level lowered to the price level. Unless the price of gold is raised, the process of bankruptcy and deflation has been only temporarily arrested. There can be no general employment until it is largely completed. This is not a matter of psychology or confidence. It is a grim reality that, at present values of gold and commodities, many of the debts are more than the properties are worth.

The most important immediate factors to watch are the demand for gold and the rate of liquidation of debts. When debts are liquidated so that building can begin, there will be a period of active business. Probably the most serious part of this liquidation can be completed in about three to four years and will be followed by a period of active business and a decided rise in prices such as occurred from 1880 to 1882. But the process of liquidation will not even then be completed. Some liquidation will continue for a generation.

The setting for business recovery is a shortage of automobiles, clothing, food, and buildings, with no bankrupt supply on the market. In 1932 there was a shortage of clothing and shoes. This caused a little business activity. But there was an unparalleled supply of bankrupt homes and farms on the market. By the time these bankrupt properties have passed through the hands of the creditors to new owners, there will be a shortage of clothing, automobiles, and homes. This will form the basis for a decided business-cycle type of temporary recovery.

Although it is possible that reduced world demand for gold may raise prices, or that a monetary change will be made, the safe policy for any farmer or business concern is to plan for prices below pre-war but to be on the alert for violent price fluctuations which are certain, for possible changes in the demand for gold, or for a monetary change.

Long-time outlook.—If all the world returns to a gold basis, commodity prices in any country that maintains its pre-war currency may be expected to average somewhat less than pre-war, and to decline until large new discoveries of gold are made. In any event, extremely violent price fluctuations are to be expected as drastic efforts are made by each country to get more than its pre-war share of the gold supply, and as erratic price relationships are readjusted.

A tremendous search for gold always develops when the commodity price level falls precipitously. After 30 years of falling prices in the first half of the past century, large amounts of gold were found. This caused prices to rise 51 per cent in England from 1849 to 1873. The long period of falling prices from 1873 to 1896 carried prices in England down 45 per cent, and was followed in the nineties by the discovery of gold. This caused English prices to rise 39 per cent from 1896 to 1912 (table 8). The present price decline is causing an intense search for gold. Since discoveries are fortuitous, there is no way of knowing when these efforts will be rewarded. It is, of course, possible that some new chemical process will make it possible to extract gold that is not now available. In no previous case have the discoveries been sufficient to affect prices suddenly. It is first necessary to increase production to stop the price decrease. From 1845 to 1914, prices lagged about 13 years behind gold production, because prices are controlled by total stocks and not by one year's output (figure 80, page 104).

There is, of course, a possibility that the United States will make a monetary change that will restore prices.

CHAPTER XXIV

PRICES FOLLOWING THE SUSPENSION OF THE GOLD STANDARD IN THE UNITED STATES

The price outlook for a country that maintains its pre-war currency.—From 1914 to 1928, world monetary stocks of gold increased 38 per cent; and world physical volume of production also increased 38 per cent. Pre-war prices were therefore to be expected. But in England prices were 45 per cent above the five-year pre-war average; and in the United States, 41 per cent above.

With the return of demand for gold, the presumption would be that prices would return to pre-war, but such a violent drop in prices would inevitably cause hoarding and other inefficiency in the use of gold. Prices below pre-war were therefore to be expected (pages 74 to 125).

France returned to the gold standard on June 25, 1928, and the gold panic was soon on. Prices in all gold-standard countries continued to decline. In 1932, they fell below the pre-war level in every country that attempted to maintain its pre-war currency. In the United States, they reached an index of 87 in February 1933. In the Netherlands, the index is primarily composed of basic commodities, and this index agreed closely with the index for basic commodities in the United States, which fell to 66 in February (table 70).

TABLE 70.—GOLD AND PRICES

World monetary stocks of gold, 1914	388,000,000 oz.
World monetary stocks of gold, 1928	537,000,000 oz.
Percentage increase in stocks of gold	38
Percentage increase in world physical volume of production of basic commodities	38
Commodity prices to be expected in a country using pre-war currency when all the world returns to gold basis	Pre-war
Prices for 1928, when 1910–14 = 100	
England	145
United States	141
Prices for February 1933, when pre-war = 100	
United States, all commodities	87
Switzerland	90
Germany	91
United States, basic commodities	66
Netherlands	74

Gold production in 1932 was the highest on record; but even at this rate of mining, production was not sufficient to maintain pre-war prices, with normal business. If a country were adjusted to pre-war prices, gold production would call for a decline in commodity prices of about one per cent per year. It is therefore to be expected that, in any country that maintains its pre-war currency, prices for the next ten years will average below pre-war (page 103).

If gold currencies are generally reestablished on a revalued base, some decline in prices is to be expected after readjustment has occurred.

Price outlook for countries that have suspended the gold standard.—When a country has an irredeemable paper currency, it can have any price level that it desires. Prices are then dependent on currency and credit, and the expectation of the level at which revaluation will occur. In no case has a country suspended gold payments without having the gold value of its currency decline. When the value of gold was rapidly rising, the currencies in a number of countries off the gold standard depreciated at about the same rate as gold prices were declining, so that prices were stable. Countries like South Africa and the United States, which left the gold standard after the rise in the value of gold was completed, experienced an immediate advance in prices.

Thus far, practically all the countries that have not had revolutions have followed an extremely conservative course. England has not reduced the value of her currency sufficiently to restore the price level to the debt level, nor to restore an equilibrium between different classes of prices. England stopped deflation without reflation. Reflation is needed. There seems to be very little danger of inflation except in countries that follow such a conservative course as to cause a violent reaction. Apparently there is more danger of revaluation at too high a level than at too low a level. In April, the United States began an attempt to restore the price level.

Business conditions in various countries.—From 1929 to 1932, prices in Italy and the United States followed practically the same course. Freight-car loadings in the two countries declined at almost an identical rate (figures 169 and 170).

The United States and Germany both attempted to maintain pre-war currencies, and prices in the two countries followed an almost identical downward course. Freight-car loadings declined at the same rate in both countries (figures 171 and 172).

It is worth noting that the United States had large supplies of gold and that Germany had little, yet her price level was as fully con-

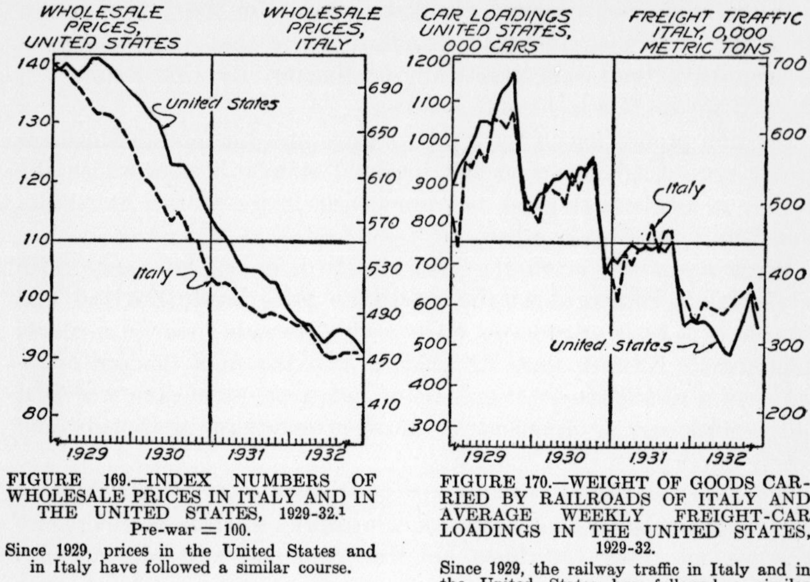

FIGURE 169.—INDEX NUMBERS OF WHOLESALE PRICES IN ITALY AND IN THE UNITED STATES, 1929-32.[1] Pre-war = 100.

Since 1929, prices in the United States and in Italy have followed a similar course.

FIGURE 170.—WEIGHT OF GOODS CARRIED BY RAILROADS OF ITALY AND AVERAGE WEEKLY FREIGHT-CAR LOADINGS IN THE UNITED STATES, 1929-32.

Since 1929, the railway traffic in Italy and in the United States has followed a similar course.

trolled by gold as were prices in the United States. It is world supply and world demand for gold that determine its value, and not the location of the supply.

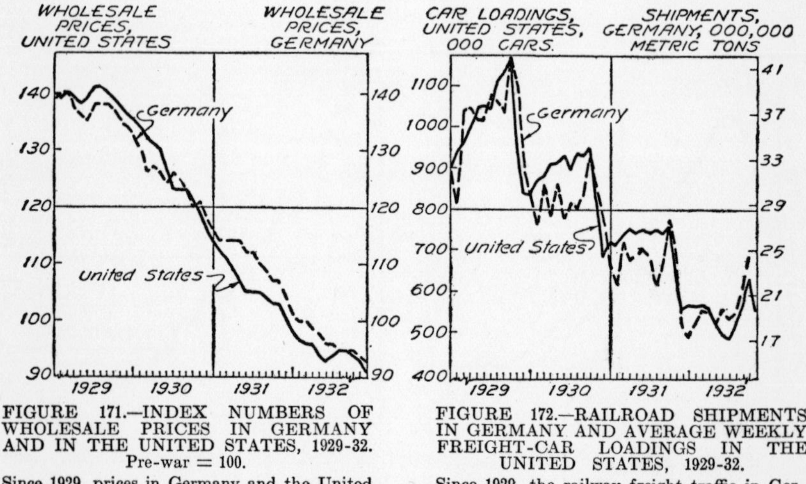

FIGURE 171.—INDEX NUMBERS OF WHOLESALE PRICES IN GERMANY AND IN THE UNITED STATES, 1929-32. Pre-war = 100.

Since 1929, prices in Germany and the United States have followed a similar course.

FIGURE 172.—RAILROAD SHIPMENTS IN GERMANY AND AVERAGE WEEKLY FREIGHT-CAR LOADINGS IN THE UNITED STATES, 1929-32.

Since 1929, the railway freight traffic in Germany and the United States has followed similar courses.

[1] The sources of the data used in the preparation of figures 169 to 180 are reported in Warren, G. F., and Pearson, F. A., Farm Economics No. 79, p. 1830, February 1933; and No. 80, p. 1882, May 1933.

Prices in Sweden declined about with prices in the United States until she suspended the gold standard. Since that time, prices in Sweden have been held practically stationary. By this means, she stopped the decline in her car loadings.

Pig-iron production in the United States and England declined together until England suspended the gold standard, after which the decline in England stopped, but production in the United States declined by more than one-half.

When a country is off the gold standard, it can have any price level that it desires. Australia raised its price level; England and Sweden kept their price levels fairly stable. Canada followed a course intermediate between those of England and the gold-standard countries. As a result, the total volume of industrial production was held fairly stationary in England; it declined one-third in Canada and nearly one-half in the United States.

When prices decline, the weaker companies may be bankrupt so that their stocks become worthless. The stocks of stronger companies may become almost worthless, but the bonds may still have a value. If the decline in prices is moderate, stocks decline and bonds rise. In a collapse such as we have had recently, not only the stocks but also the bonds are undermined.

In the Panic of 1873, commodity prices declined enough to break the stock market but only temporarily affected the bond market. Thereafter, bonds rose in price until 1896.

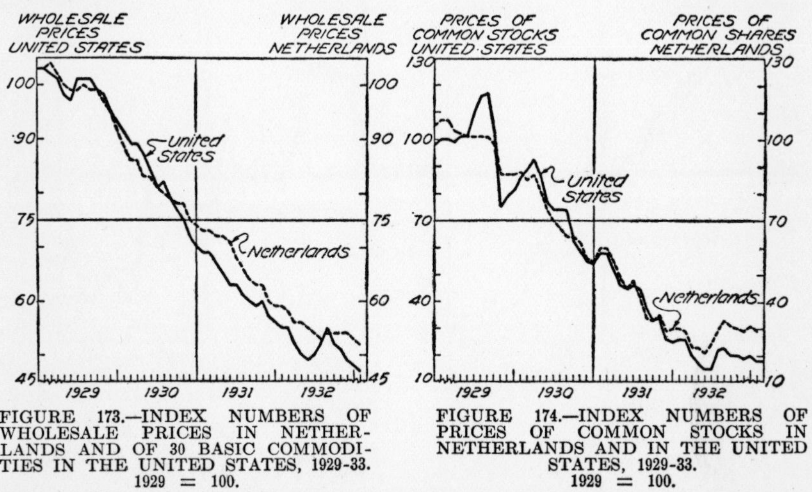

FIGURE 173.—INDEX NUMBERS OF WHOLESALE PRICES IN NETHERLANDS AND OF 30 BASIC COMMODITIES IN THE UNITED STATES, 1929-33. 1929 = 100.

FIGURE 174.—INDEX NUMBERS OF PRICES OF COMMON STOCKS IN NETHERLANDS AND IN THE UNITED STATES, 1929-33. 1929 = 100.

During this period, the United States and Netherlands maintained their pre-war fixed prices for gold. Prices of commodities in the two countries followed a very similar course. This collapse in commodity prices resulted in a similar collapse in security prices in the two countries.

Conversely, by reducing the gold value of the dollar, the weaker stocks and bonds rise most.

The index of commodity prices for the Netherlands is primarily a

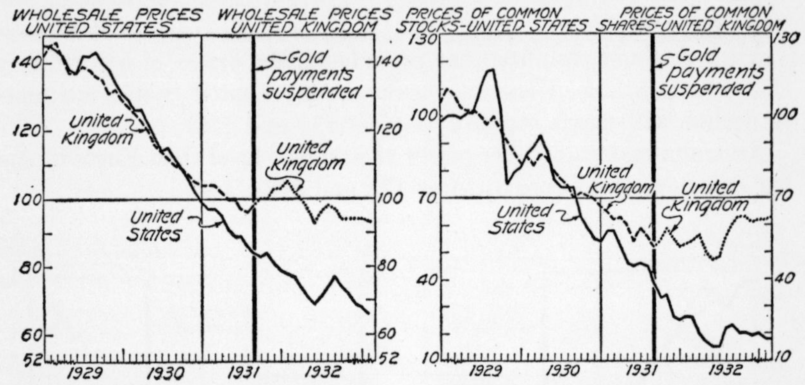

FIGURE 175.—INDEX NUMBERS OF WHOLESALE PRICES IN THE UNITED KINGDOM AND 30 BASIC COMMODITIES IN THE UNITED STATES, 1929-33. 1910-14 = 100.

Prices followed a similar course in the two countries until England left the gold basis on September 21, 1931. Since then, prices in the United Kingdom have been comparatively stable, but prices in the United States have continued to decline.

FIGURE 176.—INDEX NUMBERS OF PRICES OF COMMON SHARES IN THE UNITED KINGDOM AND OF COMMON STOCKS IN THE UNITED STATES, 1929-33. 1929 = 100.

Prices of common stocks followed a somewhat similar course in the two countries until England suspended gold payments September 21, 1931. In March 1933, prices of common shares in England were 22 per cent higher than in September 1931; in the United States, 52 per cent lower.

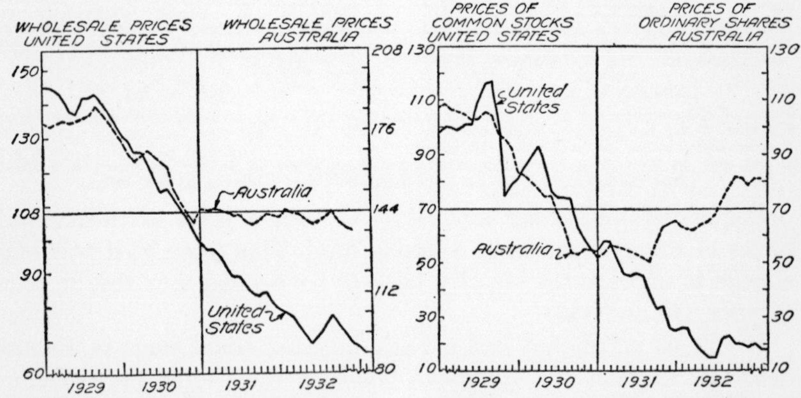

FIGURE 177.—INDEX NUMBERS OF WHOLESALE PRICES IN AUSTRALIA AND INDEX NUMBERS OF 30 BASIC COMMODITIES IN THE UNITED STATES, 1929-33.

Pre-war = 100.

Since Australia reduced the gold value of the pound, commodity prices in Australia have been comparatively stable. In the same period, prices in the United States have declined 22 per cent.

FIGURE 178.—INDEX NUMBERS OF PRICES OF ORDINARY SHARES IN AUSTRALIA AND COMMON STOCKS IN THE UNITED STATES, 1929-33.

Post-war = 100.

The prices of common stocks in the two countries followed a downward course until Australia began to manage her currency. Since that time, prices of common stocks in Australia have risen 55 per cent, and in the United States declined 63 per cent.

basic index. These prices followed practically the same downward course as prices of basic commodities in the United States. Prices of common stocks in the two countries followed the same course (figures 173 and 174). The same comparison holds for Belgium and the United States.

After England stabilized her price level, the prices of her ordinary shares were stable. Common stocks in the United States continued to decline with great rapidity (figures 175 and 176).

Australia maintained her prices at a higher level than England, and her common stocks rose (figures 177 and 178).

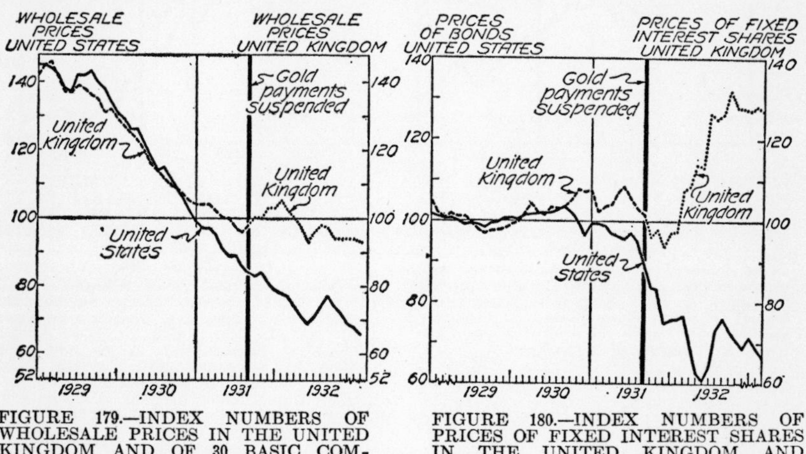

FIGURE 179.—INDEX NUMBERS OF WHOLESALE PRICES IN THE UNITED KINGDOM AND OF 30 BASIC COMMODITIES IN THE UNITED STATES, 1929-33.
1910-14 = 100.

FIGURE 180.—INDEX NUMBERS OF PRICES OF FIXED INTEREST SHARES IN THE UNITED KINGDOM AND BONDS IN THE UNITED STATES, 1929-33.
1929 = 100.

Prices of commodities and bonds followed a similar course in the two countries until the United Kingdom suspended gold payments September 21, 1931. After that time, commodity prices were comparatively stable in the United Kingdom and prices of fixed interest shares in London rose 25 per cent. In the United States, commodity prices continued to decline and prices of bonds in New York City fell 25 per cent from September 1931 to March 1933.

England stabilized her price level at such a point as to maintain prices of common stocks at a stable level. This price level was high enough to improve the security back of bonds, and they rose in price (figures 179 and 180).

It will be noted that had a bank invested equal sums in English bonds in England and American bonds in the United States before England suspended gold payments, the value of the bonds at the time our banks closed would have been twice as great in England as in the United States. Bank failures in the United States are commonly attributed to differences in the banking system. The condition of our banks would have been very different had the United States stopped deflation at the time England stopped.

Prices in the United States since suspension of the gold standard.—On March 6, the gold standard was suspended internally, but the dollar was kept at par in foreign exchange, redemonstrating just

TABLE 71.—PRICES IN NEW YORK CITY, 1933

Product	February 28	April 17	April 20	June 3	Per cent change		
					February 28 to April 17	April 17 to April 20	April 17 to June 3
Gold, per ounce	$20.67	$20.67	$23.20	$24.53	0	12	19
Wheat, per bushel	0.678	0.844	0.908	0.958	24	8	14
Corn, per bushel	0.390	0.481	0.513	0.569	23	7	18
Oats, per bushel	0.268	0.325	0.348	0.350	21	7	8
Lard, per pound	0.042	0.048	0.055	0.069	14	15	44
Coffee, per pound	0.081	0.078	0.075	0.078	−4	−4	0
Sugar, per pound	0.029	0.031	0.033	0.033	7	6	6
Cocoa	3.200	3.490	3.900	4.540	9	12	30
Cottonseed oil	3.500	3.900	4.300	5.250	11	10	35
Cotton, per pound	0.061	0.067	0.075	0.091	10	12	36
Silk, per pound	1.175	1.300	1.550	1.750	11	19	35
Print cloths, per yard	0.030	0.035	0.038	0.055	17	9	57
Hides, per pound	0.045	0.060	0.070	0.120	33	17	100
Rubber, per pound	0.028	0.036	0.040	0.064	29	11	78
Copper, per pound	0.050	0.054	0.060	0.080	8	11	48
Tin, per pound	0.233	0.255	0.295	0.413	9	16	62
Zinc, per pound	0.027	0.032	0.038	0.044	19	19	38
Silver, per ounce	0.265	0.286	0.355	0.355	8	24	24
17 basic commodities, 1910–14 = 100	66.3	76.1	84.9	104.5	15	12	37

what Germany had demonstrated—that so long as the dollar is kept at par in the foreign exchanges of countries on the gold standard, the price level is definitely controlled by gold.

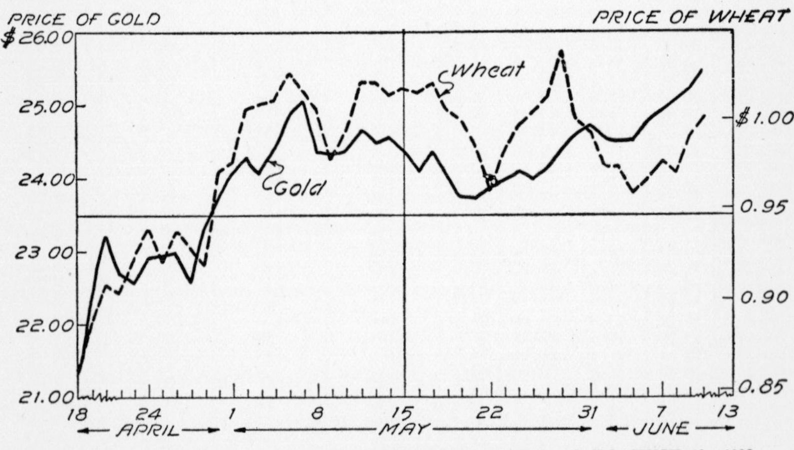

FIGURE 181.—PRICES OF WHEAT AND GOLD, APRIL 18 TO JUNE 10, 1933. Almost all the rise in the price of wheat after April 18 was due to the suspension of the gold standard and the consequent shrinkage in the dollar.

On April 19, the United States gave up the attempt to maintain the gold standard, and commodity prices rose immediately. In fact, prices rose in advance of the act because of anticipation of it.

After the gold standard was suspended, there was no free market for gold in the United States, but in England there was a market for

TABLE 72.—GOLD VALUE OF THE DOLLAR AND PRICES IN THE UNITED STATES

Date	Grains gold in dollar	Per cent depreciation in dollar	Price of an ounce of gold	Per cent above par	Prices of 17 basic commodities, April 17, 1933 = 100	Prices of 25 industrial stocks, April 17, 1933 = 100	Prices of No. 2 red wheat N. Y., cents per bushel	Prices of upland middling cotton N. Y., cents per pound
Par......	23.22	0	$20.67	0	100	100	....	....
April 18..	22.58	2.8	21.26	2.9	101	102	86.1	6.85
April 19..	21.51	7.4	22.32	8.0	106	108	88.6	7.25
April 20..	20.69	10.9	23.20	12.2	112	115	90.8	7.45
April 21..	21.16	8.9	22.68	9.7	112	111	90.3	7.50
April 22..	21.27	8.4	22.57	9.2	112	115	92.3	7.60
April 24..	20.94	9.8	22.92	10.9	115	117	93.9	7.65
April 25..	20.90	10.0	22.97	11.1	114	115	92.0	7.60
April 26..	20.88	10.1	22.99	11.2	115	115	93.8	7.60
April 27..	21.27	8.4	22.57	9.2	115	114	92.8	7.60
April 28..	20.61	11.2	23.29	12.7	114	116	91.8	7.50
April 29..	20.24	12.8	23.71	14.7	117	123	97.0	7.90
May 1..	19.94	14.1	24.07	16.4	121	125	97.5	8.25
May 2..	19.77	14.9	24.28	17.5	122	125	100.5	8.25
May 3..	19.94	14.1	24.07	16.4	122	125	100.8	8.30
May 4..	19.67	15.3	24.40	18.0	123	128	101.0	8.30
May 5..	19.32	16.8	24.84	20.2	124	129	102.4	8.55
May 6..	19.18	17.4	25.03	21.1	125	125	101.5	8.60
May 8..	19.71	15.1	24.35	17.8	124	124	100.4	8.40
May 9..	19.75	14.9	24.30	17.6	124	125	97.6	8.35
May 10..	19.70	15.2	24.36	17.9	125	130	99.1	8.65
May 11..	19.47	16.1	24.65	19.3	128	134	102.0	8.95
May 12..	19.61	15.5	24.48	18.4	129	133	101.9	8.95
May 13..	19.55	15.8	24.55	18.8	129	131	101.3	8.85
May 15..	19.68	15.2	24.39	18.0	128	129	101.6	8.70
May 16..	19.93	14.2	24.08	16.5	127	132	101.4	8.65
May 17..	19.70	15.2	24.37	17.9	129	134	101.9	8.75
May 18..	19.98	14.0	24.03	16.3	128	134	100.4	8.60
May 19..	20.22	12.9	23.74	14.9	127	132	99.8	8.50
May 20..	20.23	12.9	23.73	14.8	126	129	98.4	8.25
May 22..	20.09	13.5	23.89	15.6	126	129	95.9	8.40
May 23..	20.02	13.8	23.98	16.0	127	134	98.0	8.60
May 24..	19.92	14.2	24.10	16.6	130	137	99.6	8.70
May 25..	20.01	13.8	23.99	16.1	130	136	100.3	8.55
May 26..	19.89	14.3	24.13	16.7	132	142	101.1	9.00
May 27..	19.67	15.3	24.40	18.0	135	148	103.6	9.15
May 29..	19.52	15.9	24.59	19.0	135	147	100.0	9.20
May 31..	19.42	16.4	24.72	19.6	138	144	99.1	9.35
June 1..	19.57	15.7	24.53	18.7	137	146	97.3	9.25
June 2..	19.59	15.6	24.50	18.5	138	152	97.3	9.25
June 3..	19.57	15.7	24.53	18.7	137	147	95.8	9.10
June 5..	.....	....	.....	....	138	151	96.8	9.30
June 6..	19.37	16.6	24.78	19.9	139	150	96.6	9.15
June 7..	19.26	17.1	24.92	20.6	140	150	97.6	9.25
June 8..	19.16	17.5	25.05	21.2	141	151	96.9	9.10
June 9..	19.06	17.9	25.19	21.9	143	153	98.9	9.25
June 10..	18.85	18.8	25.46	23.2	145	153	100.1	9.35
June 12..	18.79	19.1	25.54	23.6	144	158	99.8	9.45
June 13..	19.17	17.4	25.04	21.1	145	154	99.1	9.40
June 14..	19.15	17.5	25.06	21.2	142	151	97.9	9.35
June 15..	19.54	15.8	24.56	18.8	141	144	96.6	8.95
June 16..	19.30	16.9	24.87	20.3	139	144	91.9	9.25
June 17..	19.28	17.0	24.89	20.4	139	145	91.6	9.05
June 19..	18.94	18.4	25.34	22.6	142	154	93.3	9.35
June 20..	18.89	18.6	25.41	22.9	142	152	92.1	9.25
June 21..	18.80	19.0	25.53	23.5	143	153	94.4	9.40

both gold and dollars. For example, on April 20, the quotation for gold was 120.5 shillings per ounce, and a pound was worth $3.85. An ounce of gold was, therefore, worth 6.025 English pounds or $23.20. Since at par an ounce was worth $20.67, the price of gold in dollars had risen 12 per cent by reason of the suspension of the gold standard (table 72).

Anticipation of final suspension of the gold standard caused prices to rise even before the standard was actually suspended. In the case of wheat, the poor condition of the crop was a further cause of a rise in price. Prices in New York City rose 24 per cent from February 28 to April 17 (table 71). Thereafter, nearly all the advance in wheat prices was due to a shrinkage in the value of the dollar. Practically every time the dollar changed, wheat followed (table 72 and figure 181).

Cotton advanced 10 per cent from February 28 to April 17 (table 71). On the suspension of the gold standard, it advanced 12 per cent in three days, which was the same as the advance in the price of gold. For nearly four years the buying of clothing was below normal. Improved business conditions increased the demand for cotton for clothing and for industrial uses. From April 17 to June 3, cotton rose 36 per cent, whereas the price of gold rose only 19 per cent (table 71 and figure 182).

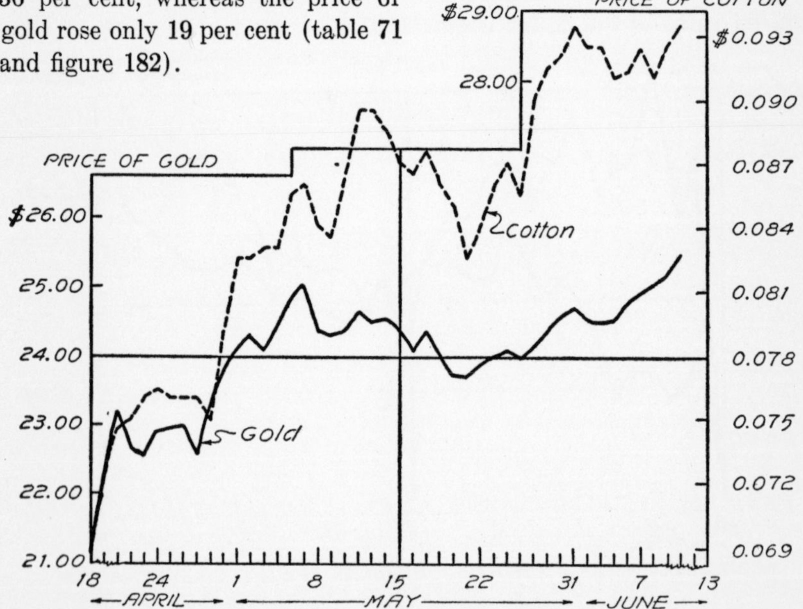

FIGURE 182.—PRICES OF COTTON AND GOLD, APRIL 18 TO JUNE 10, 1933. Improved business conditions caused such an increase in the demand for cotton as to raise its prices more than gold rose in price.

Improved business causes some improved demand for wheat, but a remarkable improvement in the demand for cotton. If the price level is restored so as to cause normal business activity, it would not be surprising if the apparent surplus of cotton would quickly disappear. An inventory of cotton to determine the surplus should include the shirts and sheets as well as the bales. The shortage of cotton products in homes and factories during 1933 was probably the greatest that had ever occurred. These apparent surpluses will be quickly transferred to the dresser drawers, closets, and backs of the people when the world goes back to work.

From April 17 to June 3, the prices of eight non-food products advanced 53 per cent compared with 19 per cent for nine food products.

Prices of such commodities as oats, sugar, and coffee changed very little from April 17 to June 3 (table 71).

Hides are even more strikingly influenced by business. Prices advanced 100 per cent from April 17 to June 3.

Speculation as to the possibility of remonetization of silver caused a boom in the price of silver when the gold standard was suspended. This subsided and the exchange values of gold and silver were practically restored, so that the price of silver was accounted for by the reduced value of the dollar (figure 183).

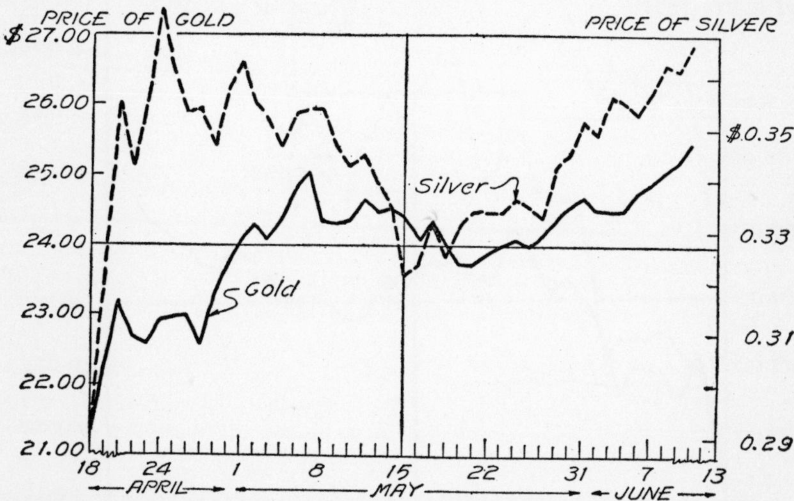

FIGURE 183.—PRICES OF SILVER AND GOLD, APRIL 18 TO JUNE 10, 1933. Silver first rose in the expectation of remonetization, but later followed the price of gold.

From April 17 to 20, the price of gold rose 12 per cent, and prices of 17 basic commodities also rose 12 per cent. By May 6, the price of gold was 21 per cent above par, and prices of 17 basic commodities had risen 25 per cent. The dollar then strengthened, and the advance in basic commodities was checked (table 72 and figure 184). On May 26, the President called on Congress to invalidate the gold clause. This was a clear indication that the dollar would not again return to par, and commodity prices rose. From May 26 to June 10, the price of gold rose from $24.13 to $25.46 per fine ounce and the index of the prices of 17 basic commodities rose from 132 to 145. The percentage increase in the price of gold was 5.5; in the prices of basic commodities, 9.8.

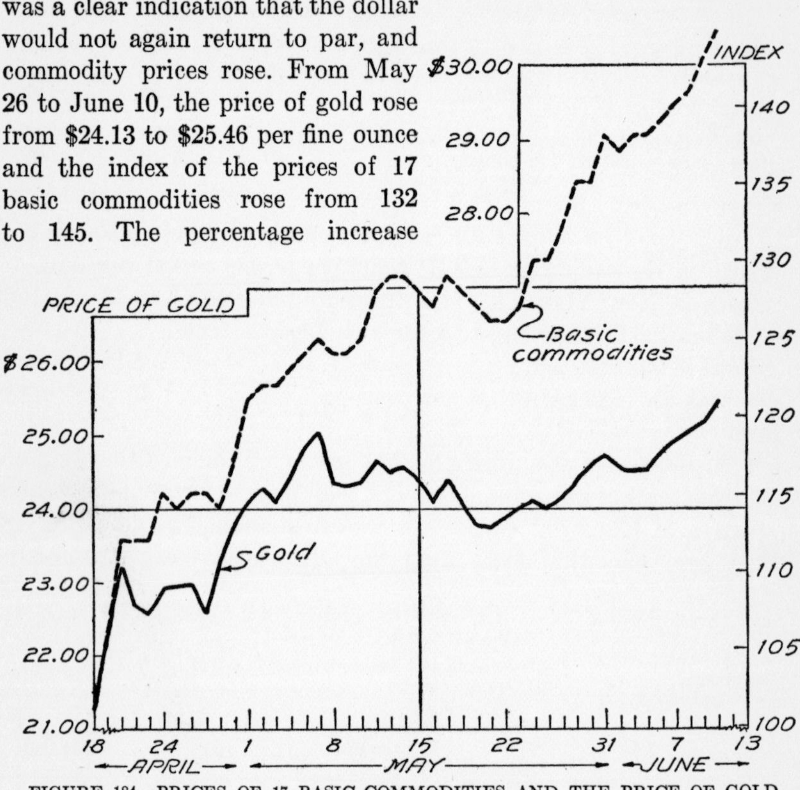

FIGURE 184.—PRICES OF 17 BASIC COMMODITIES AND THE PRICE OF GOLD, APRIL 18 TO JUNE 10, 1933.
Prices of basic commodities rose more than the advance in the price of gold.

The increase in the price of gold from April 17, when the United States departed from the gold standard, to June 10 was 23.2 per cent; in the prices of basic commodities, 45 per cent.

Prices of 17 basic commodities would be expected to rise more than the price of gold because they were extremely low.

The method by which farm prices are brought into adjustment with wholesale prices is shown in table 73. From February 15 to May

TABLE 73.—WHOLESALE PRICES AND FARM PRICES, 1933

	February 15	May 15	Percentage rise
Wheat			
Wholesale price at New York City, per bushel	$0.68	$1.02	50
Kansas farm price, per bushel	0.28	0.59	111
Corn			
Wholesale price at New York City, per bushel	0.40	0.61	53
Nebraska farm price, per bushel	0.12	0.30	150
Live hogs			
Wholesale price Chicago, per 100 pounds	3.75	5.05	35
Iowa farm price, per 100 pounds	2.80	4.10	46

15, wheat in New York City rose 34 cents per bushel or 50 per cent. Wheat on Kansas farms rose 31 cents per bushel or 111 per cent.

Corn in New York City rose 21 cents per bushel or 53 per cent; on Nebraska farms, it rose 18 cents or 150 per cent.

Hogs in Chicago and on Iowa farms rose $1.30 per hundred pounds; this was an increase of 35 per cent in Chicago and 46 per cent in Iowa.

This illustrates the principle that prices of commodities at points far from market rise relatively more than prices at consuming centers.

Prices of industrial stocks are shown in table 72 and figure 185. They rose somewhat more than the advance in basic commodities.

TABLE 74.—CHANGES IN PRICES OF STOCKS IN VARIOUS COUNTRIES*

Last Saturday of December 1927 = 100

City	February 25, 1933	May 27, 1933	Per cent advance
Amsterdam	28.5	33.3	17
Berlin	28.5	31.7	11
Brussels	29.2	31.6	8
London	55.2	60.3	9
Paris	58.9	65.2	11
Prague	52.9	56.9	8
Stockholm	8.9	11.3	27
Vienna	36.3	35.7	−2
Zurich	41.0	48.3	18
Average	37.7	41.6	10
New York	28.7	54.6	90

* New York Times, June 4, 1933.

Basic commodities and stocks are very sensitive to changes in the value of the dollar. Whenever the dollar strengthens, prices weaken.

Index numbers of prices of stocks in various countries are shown in table 74. Such index numbers contain varying percentages of high-grade stocks, which influences the violence of fluctuations, but the movements are so striking as to establish the reliability of the conclusion. Prices of stocks in most countries rose moderately from February 25 to May 27, but in the United States they almost doubled.

At par, the dollar contains 23.22 grains of gold. After the suspension of the gold standard, it was possible to purchase a dollar in England with about 20 grains of gold.

The gold certificates were called in, and the gold clause invalidated, both for present and future obligations. These acts were

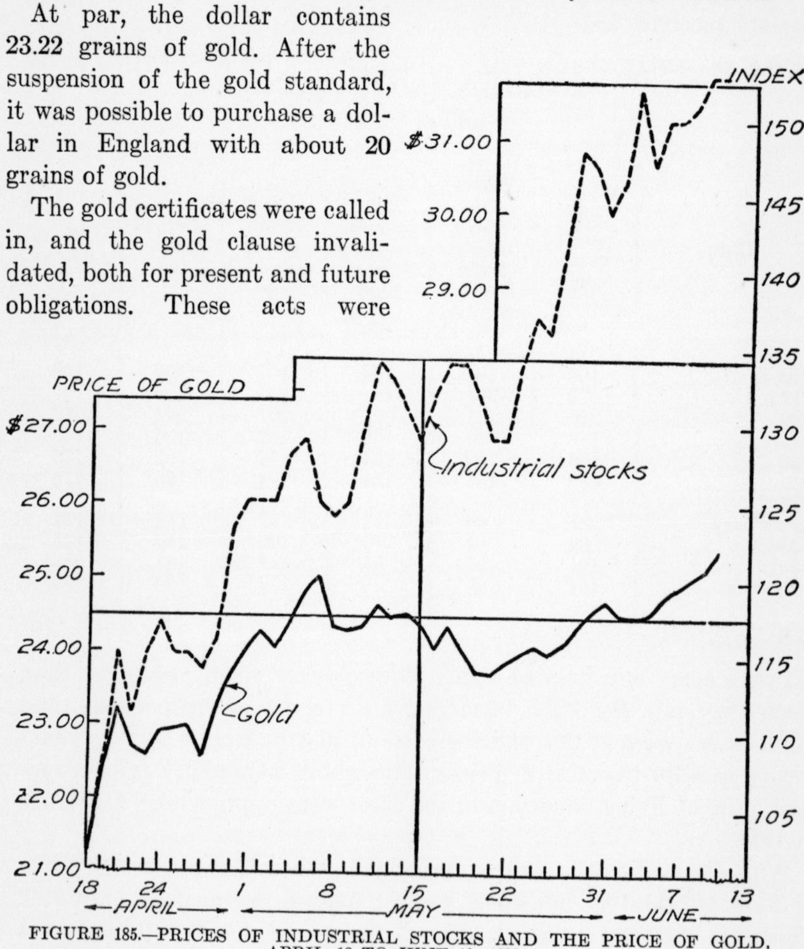

FIGURE 185.—PRICES OF INDUSTRIAL STOCKS AND THE PRICE OF GOLD, APRIL 18 TO JUNE 10, 1933.
Prices of industrial stocks rose more rapidly than the rise in the price for gold.

merely a recognition of the fact that the process of deflation could not be completed.

Maladjustment in the price structure resulting from inflation and deflation.—When prices rise, basic commodities rise most, and wholesale prices of finished products rise more than retail prices. All these rise more than the costs of living and costs of distribution.

From pre-war to 1917, prices of 30 basic commodities rose from an index of 100 to 201 (table 75). Average prices of all commodities advanced to only 172. Prices of food at retail were 156, but because the slowly adjusting costs of distribution had reached only 129, farmers received 181.

TABLE 75.—CHANGES IN THE PRICE STRUCTURE RESULTING FROM INFLATION AND DEFLATION

1910–14 = 100

Date	Wholesale prices of all commodities	Wholesale prices of 30 basic commodities	United States farm price of food	United States retail prices of food	Costs of distribution	Costs of living
1910–14	100	100	100	100	100	100
1917	172	201	181	156	129	131
1920	226	231	207	207	202	212
1921	143	126	130	163	190	180
1926	146	146	154	174	192	176
1929	139	141	151	174	198	172
1933						
February	87	66	51	97	143	124
May	92	81	70	103	133	124
July	101	97	84	111	135	131*
October	104	95	74	112*	150	135*

* Preliminary.

Prices come into balance much more quickly when prices rise than when they fall. By 1920, farm prices of food had reached 207, and retail prices were at 207 because costs of distribution were then practically in adjustment with prices. The whole commodity price structure, cost of living, wages, and the like, were approaching a balance in 1920.

With the collapse in prices during the following year, retail prices of food fell to 163, but costs of distribution declined to only 190. Therefore, farmers received 130. Although food was retailing at a higher price than in 1917, the index of prices paid to farmers for this same food dropped from 181 to 130.

In 1920, basic commodities were slightly higher than all commodities. In 1921, basic commodities fell to an index of 126, whereas all commodities fell to only 143.

In 1929, basic commodities, all commodities, and prices paid to farmers were approximately in adjustment, but costs of distribution were so high that retail prices and the cost of living were high, relative to farm prices. Prices paid to farmers can be brought into line with retail prices in a few years if the price level doubles, but it would probably require at least 25 years to bring about adjustment if the price level is cut in half, because costs of distribution can be raised in a few years, but it requires a long time to reduce them if once raised.

From 1929 to February 1933, prices of all commodities fell from an index of 139 to 87, but 30 basic commodities fell from 141 to 66. They followed the universal law that, with declining prices, basic commodities decline more than all commodities.

Prices of food at retail declined from 174 to 97, but prices paid to farmers for this same food declined from 151 to 51, because the index of the cost of distribution was still 143.

From February to May, prices of 30 basic commodities rose from 66 to about 80. All commodities rose from an index of 87 to about 92. Reflation quickly reestablished the normal relationship between prices of basic commodities and all commodities. So long as the dollar declines in value, the index numbers of prices of basic commodities will be expected to be as high as or higher than the index for all commodities.

Prices paid to farmers for food products rose from an index of 51 to 70, or rose 37 per cent.

To bring farm prices in adjustment with retail prices would require that wholesale prices rise to about the 1926 level, because in February 1933, costs of distribution were in adjustment with wholesale prices in 1926. If wholesale prices rise to that level, there will be comparatively small changes in the cost of distribution.

The above discussion indicates the type of maladjustment in the price structure brought about by changes in the value of money. It is extremely difficult to make price adjustments downward. The attempt to carry out the amount of deflation that the rise in the value of gold called for has failed in practically every country. The alternative is to reduce the value of money by such an amount as to bring the price and debt structure into equilibrium at the previous price level, or bring wholesale prices of all commodities to about the 1926 level. This is 2 per cent below the 15-year average ending with 1932. Even at that level, public and private debts will be a fairly heavy burden for some years to come.

Many persons who are unfamiliar with the laws of prices have argued that to reduce the value of money would raise all prices equally and therefore would do no good. These few elementary laws of prices show the fallacy of this argument.

Prices when 1926 = 100.—The authors have at all times used 1910-14 as 100 because they have anticipated a return of gold to its pre-war value or higher (page 117). When any given price level has prevailed for a considerable period of time, business becomes adjusted to it. Business adjusts promptly and with comparative ease to a doubling of the price level, but slowly and with great distress to cutting the price level 50 per cent. If 100 is used to represent the price level to which business is adjusted, a pre-war base is incorrect. The Bureau of Labor Statistics publishes its index with the year 1926 as 100.

Wholesale prices of all commodities in the United States are as follows, when 1926 = 100:

Year 1926	100
Average 15 years, 1918–32 inclusive	102
March 1933	60
May 1933	63

The authors have made estimates which indicate that the weighted average level of prices at the time when the present outstanding debts were contracted was nearly equal to the 1926 level. Delinquent taxes are piling up. These are generally at a level far above 1926 prices. Many debtors are also behind in their interest payments.

Some persons have purchased outstanding securities recently. Often they have purchased below par. If the price level is raised sufficiently, they will receive more dollars than they paid because the debtor will be able to pay. If they purchased at par, their interests will be in establishing conditions that will enable the debtor to pay. For example, if a mortgage on a home was given when the price level stood at 100, it is no advantage to the present holder of the mortgage to attempt to collect more than can be collected. The creditor's interests are best served by giving attention to the debtor's situation.

More important than any abstract equity for the creditor is a price level that will enable debtors to pay. It is probable that the total collections to be made by all creditors would be higher in purchasing power if made at the price level of 1926 than if made at a lower price level. Of course, the higher the price level, the fewer the complete failures.

More important than any theoretical abstraction of equity is the problem of getting men back to work. To do this, the price level must rise high enough to restore equities in city homes and farms, because if this is not done the process of bankruptcy must be continued. So long as there are vast numbers of bankrupt homes and farms on the market, there will be little building. The heavy industries will be in distress. There will be serious unemployment. A number of years will be required to complete these adjustments. After the debts are reduced, business could again be prosperous. The only other way to get men back to work is to raise the price level.

Another problem of declining prices is the slowness of adjustment in costs of distribution. When 1910-14 is 100, prices of all commodities in 1926 were 146. In February 1933, costs of distribution were 143. Since a rise in prices would have a little effect on the costs of distribution, prices would have to be restored to a point a little above the 1926 level to bring retail prices and the costs of distribution into adjustment, or it would take a price level a little above 1926 to bring prices of things that farmers buy into adjustment with prices of things that farmers sell. If prices rise to the 15-year average, farm prices will at once come nearer into adjustment with retail prices than they have been at any time since 1920.

If prices remain at any given level, the costs of distribution will come into adjustment in time; but judging by the rate of adjustment for the 10 years following 1920, it will require about a generation to complete the adjustment to present commodity prices. The lag in distribution costs is particularly serious for farmers. Other manufacturers buy at wholesale prices which are low and sell at wholesale prices which are also low. For both business and personal requirements, farmers buy at retail prices which remain high and sell at wholesale prices which are low.

What will happen if the gold value of the dollar is reduced enough to restore an equilibrium in the price structure?—Wholesale prices of all commodities would gradually rise to the average level that prevailed at the time public and private debts were contracted, and the level to which taxes, costs of distribution, and other slow-moving charges are adjusted. This would require that wholesale prices be restored to approximately the 1926 level. Costs of distribution would then be more nearly in adjustment with wholesale prices than they were in 1926, because they would rise less than they have declined. They were out of adjustment in 1926. Prices of basic commodities would for a time be higher than prices of all commodities, but would later come into adjustment automatically.

Index numbers of prices of food at retail would rise a little higher than prices paid to farmers, because, even at the wholesale price level of 1926, costs of distribution would be rather high. The only thing that could change this would be a shortage of food relative to other commodities, which would make farm prices high relative to retail prices. Such a shortage is a possibility. Much of the apparent surplus is due to low consumption because of unemployment in the countries that have not reflated.

The cost of living would be somewhat lower than in 1926 because costs of distribution would be lower than they were in that year and because rents would not rise to the 1926 level. The index numbers of the cost of living would be somewhat higher than the index numbers of wholesale prices, but not so much higher as they were in 1926.

The long-time trend of wages in the United States is to rise in purchasing power at the rate of 1.71 per cent per year. This is practically the same as the normal increase in output of commodities per capita. The buying power of wages is thrown out of line by either inflation or deflation. A restoration of the price level would avoid the long years of unemployment that are an inevitable accompaniment of deflation (pages 196 and 208).

If the pre-war trend of wages had continued to 1934 and if wholesale prices had remained at the 1910-14 level, or 100, wages would have been expected to be 144, which is the normal increase in purchasing power in 21.5 years.

If wholesale prices return to the 1926 level (146 when 1910-14 equals 100), wages would be expected to be 210.

In 1926, city wages were 235; farm wages, 171; wages of government employees, 161; and college professors, 157. In the Spring of 1933, wages were in utter chaos. Many persons were working on farms and elsewhere for less than pre-war wages. Some workers were receiving almost as high wages as they received in 1929. A restoration of the commodity price level would gradually bring approximate equilibrium in wage rates for different kinds of work.

If wholesale prices of all commodities are restored to the 1926 level and the cost-of-living index is somewhat higher than the all-commodity index but somewhat lower than it was in 1929, as is to be expected, it is probable that the general level of all wages will return approximately to the 1926 level. Wages paid to farm labor were relatively low in 1926. They would probably rise above the 1926 level. Wages in the construction industry were relatively high in 1926 and might not return to that level. All the above discussion is based on a restoration of the price level so as to stop deflation without causing inflation. If instead of reflation the deflation process is resumed, the

INDEX

C

D

E

T

Y